TERRORISM: POLITICAL VIOLENCE AND SECURITY OF NATIONS

TERRORISM : POLITICAL VIOLENCE AND SECURITY OF NATIONS

. GLOBAL SURVEY OF SOCIO-ECONOMIC, POLITICA AND LEGAL ASPECTS OF NATIONAL, REGIONAL, AND INTERNATIONAL TERRORISM

By

Attar Chand

GYAN

ISBN : 978-81-212-0199-5

Published, 2018

Published by

Gyan Publishing House
5, Ansari Road
Daryaganj, New Delhi-110002
Phone: 011-47034999, 9811692060
www.gyanbooks.com
E-mail: books@gyanbooks.com

Printed at: G. Print Process, Delhi.

FOREWORDS

JOINT EFFORTS TO FIGHT TERRORISM

Certain big powers do not like India talking of non-alignment, South Africa or disarmament because their own balance of power will be affected. That is why they have been making relentless efforts to divide the Indian people.

People's power is the greatest power and unity is the need of the hour.

India is determined to move forward in the world community with its independent foreign policy, secularism and democratic principles, and without being pressurised by any neo-colonial power.

Terrorism has to be fought politically with the help of the people. It will take a while, but we will get rid of terrorism.

There can be no place for terrorism in a democracy. The Indian Republic built on the principle that differences are always capable of being resolved through political dialogue. Anti-regional elements are unhappy that the problem of Punjab is being solved in this way. They seem to be out to create trouble at the time of election.

RAJIV GANDHI
Prime Minister of India
New Delhi

TERRORISM—NO BASE AMONG THE PEOPLE

There is no question of handing over Punjab to the army as the democratically elected Government is getting all help from the Centre to meet the situation.

The Centre is as worried about the situation as the Punjab Chief Minister is. What has happened at Ludhiana is most unfortunate and condemnable. The Centre has extended all support to the Punjab Government and we will continue to do so in future. Terrorism has to be fought at every level by the people of Punjab.

The people of Punjab want peace and prosperity and terrorists do not have any base among the people.

The problem of terrorism has to be dealt with very firmly. The aim of terrorists is to undermine the concept of secularism and mutual co-existence.

ARUN NEHRU
Member of Parliament
Formerly Union Minister of State
for Internal Security
New Delhi

MEDIA AND TERRORISM

The only solution to terrorism could come by accepting one rule in society i. e. on no account, whatsoever, would violence be tolerated. The Press must come out strongly in condemning individual violence, Media should not directly or indirectly justify or glorify the acts of violence as, in his opinion, terrorism was growing merely because the terrorists who wanted recognition were being backed, eulogised and called martyrs in a small quarter, society at large must condemn it.

VASANT SATHE
Union Minister of Energy
New Delhi

DOWRY AS TERRORISM

The dowry system in India originated as *stree dhan*—a daughter's share of family wealth given her at the time of marriage. But in recent years the practice has often degenerated into horrific cases of "bride-burning" where young brides who have failed to bring sufficient material goods into a marriage are burnt to death by a husband or his family. Although the dowry system has been illegal since 1961, laws have been largely ineffective. Recent amendments have tightened anti-dowry laws but women's rights groups want stricter implementation.

The Dowry Prohibition Act was passed in 1961. However, the implementation was not effective. In 1984, another amendment was made by Parliament which made the provisions of the law more stringent. It expanded the definition of dowry to include dowry demands before, during and after marriage. The amendment requires the bride and bridegroom to maintain a list of presents received by them at the time of marriage. Voluntary organisations working for the welfare of women have been authorised to lodge complaints regarding dowry offences with the courts of law. The amended act was made effective on Oct 2, 1985.

The ultimate penalty for murder is death by hanging. Such a verdict is awarded only when the case is proved beyond all doubts and where circumstances justify it...You are referring to the Rajasthan High Court's award of public hanging in two bride-burning cases, which was reversed by the Supreme Court. The High court Judges believed that hanging in a public place with adequate publicity would be a deterrent to future bride-burning. They failed to realise that there is already sufficient publicity in the press but this has hardly acted as a deterrent. What hanging cannot achieve, public hanging hardly can.

One is complementary to the other. The great social reformers of the 19th and 20th centuries had striven hard for the abolition (of dowry). However, our society, because of its tradition and greed, has not fulfilled this cherished desire. Modernisation, urbanisation and industrialisation have fostered the growth of the dowry system, requiring strong legal deterrents.

It is not correct to say that the dowry cells have proved ineffective. Considering the magnitude of the problem, they have been able to render valuable service to dowry victims within the purview of the Dowry Prohibition Act and its rules. The special cell within the Delhi Police which deals with dowry cases has been further strengthened. The police have also been given guidelines by magistrates for recording the dying declarations of dowry victims.

MARGARET ALVA
Minister of State for Youth Affairs
and Women's Welfare
New Delhi

TERRORISM : A BIG CONSPIRACY

There is a big conspiracy behind such activities (killings in Punjab) and we must tackle the terrorist menace unitedly in the interest of the country.

Terrorism is a problem of the entire nation and not confined to any one State or region.

BAL RAM JAKHAR
Speaker, Lok Sabha
New Delhi

DOWRY–THE CONTINUING EVIL

We must strive to change the social atmosphere which permits the perpetuation of this evil practice. Society is becoming pervaded by the culture of easy money--people wanting to become rich overnight. Even families of modest means demand dowry in the form of scooters and other electronic gadgets which are regarded as status symbols. These demands continue for months after marriage.

The tragic situation is the result of an ancient society being suddenly presented with the opportunities and prospects of the modern age ; a society in transition, with the joint family system trying to come to terms with the growth of material instincts and comforts, which is the natural corollary of economic development. This pressure on the traditional family structure leads to an imbalance in the mental outlook of the members within the family. A false sense of superiority develops in the husband to the detriment of the new entrant in the family. Marriage is seen not as a partnership of equals but as a favour bestowed on the girl for which she is supposed to remain ever grateful.

The role of the modern woman is difficult. In olden days our women were only entrusted with the responsibilities of maintaining family harmony and bringing up children. Their world was devoid of the attractions of power and fame—the glamour world which men jealously preserved for themselves. But today the Indian women performs her duty as a mother and also stands shoulder to shoulder with men to contribute to the progress of our country. Her role today is challenging. Unfortunately this consciousness of the woman's dual responsibility and her rightful claim to a place of dignity and equality with men is not matched by a corresponding awareness in us that gives due recognition to the change in the role of the woman. This culminates in tensions which the traditional family is unable to cope with. In many cases such tensions and maladjustments could be resolved but for the intervention of the in-laws, who live in an old world with clearly defined parameters.

MADHAVRAO SCINDIA
State Minister of Railways,
New Delhi

TACKLING TERRORISM

Prime Minister Mr. Rajiv Gandhi understands and realises our difficulties. Though the law, and order situation is improving, there are still stray incidents which show that there are some people who want to create conditions of instability.

Those people, mainly youths must be brought back to the national mainstream and that has to be done jointly by the Centre and the State.

Terrorism is a problem. We shall try to reduce this problem and gradually we will try to eradicate this problem. Because we will go to the roots.

Like I have been saying, there were parties, there were groups and there were people who encouraged them. If we go to the roots and eradicate the cause then terrorism is likely to be eradicated in the course of time.

SURJIT SINGH BARNALA
Chief Minister of Punjab
Chandigarh

IMPERIALISM AND TERRORISM

The world is facing the danger of a nuclear catastrophe because of the nuclear arms drive engaged in by the Reagan administration in USA and his preparations for "star wars."

But this policy is also met with strong resistance from peace forces all over the world including USA. Even some of the NATO countries are opposed to Reagan's star wars programme. On the other hand the peace policies of the Soviet Union are receiving massive support throughout the world.

It is a matter of happiness that India stands for peace, stability and friendship with the Soviet Union and other socialist countries.

USA and other imperialist countries are creating tension and instability around India. Here I would like to mention the supply of sophisticated arms to Pakistan, massacre of Tamilians in Srilanka, support to terrorists by external forces to create violence and chaos within the country.

The terrorists want to start communal clashes, both in Punjab and outside. They think that such communal clashes will result in an exodus of Hindus from Punjab and inflow of Sikhs from other states into the state. Such transfer of population will result in the creation of *Khalistan*.

C. RAJESWARA RAO
General Secretary,
Communist Party of India,
New Delhi

TERRORISM AND INTELLIGENCE AGENCIES

While the object of the Terrorist and Disruptive Activities (Prevention) Act 1985 is laudable as it seeks to create confidence in the society, the way in which Government has thought of implementing the same, is shocking to say the least. It is more the failure of the intelligence agency and the law enforcement machinery that is to blame and not the lack of any power under the present laws which has prevented the Government from taking any effective measures against the terrorists. It is only to divert the attention of the people from those failures that this legislation has been brought forward.

The wide powers assumed by Government under this legislation are liable of being misused to curb legitimate political activity. Authority given to the police to keep a suspect under remand for 90 days (in case of murder) and 60 days in other cases without furnishing a charge-sheet for a year, is wholly uncalled for. This provision is meant to cover up inefficiency of the police to trace the culprits and will enable it to keep under arrest any person on mere suspicion, and thus encroaches upon the civil liberties of the people.

It is too much of an interference in judicial proceedings on the part of Government to transfer cases, though it be with the concurrence of Chief Justice. The power of such transfers could have been invested in the judiciary itself. The provision of direct appeal to the Supreme Court is wholly unnecessary. Public interest would not suffer if normal procedure was followed.

CHARAN SINGH
Late President,
Lok Dal, New Delhi

CHALLENGE OF TERRORISM

Where is that leadership which could transmit to *Hindus* and *Sikhs* the old sense of amity and friendship, the old mutual confidence and security ? When the late Sant Bhindranwale was being promoted and encouraged, it was known that he did not stand for friendship and security. Recently, his father Joginder Singh has been flexing his muscles against the leadership of Sant Longowal and strangely his most trusted aide is Inderjit Singh Khalsa alias Sekhon. This gentleman had reportedly filed a sworn affidavit in the Punjab High Court that he had always been a loyal worker of the Congress (I). If then, the authorship of this new move on the chessboard of the politics of the Punjab is being ascribed to the old hands, there need-be no surprise.

SURENDRA MOHAN
Janata Party
New Delhi

TERRORISM AND LEGISLATION

The harmful feature of the Terrorist and Disruptive Activities Prevention Bill, 1985 is that the definition of "disruptive activity" is so wide as to include a mere expression of opinion, not accompanied by any violence or incitement to violence. Any Sikh who says that he agrees with the *Anand Saheb Resolution*, any Muslim who says that there should be a plebicite in Jammu & Kashmir, and Naga or Mizo or Manipuri who says that the people of his State should have the right of self-determination, guilty of "disruptive activity" and can be punished by a sentence which may extend to imprisonment for a term of three years.

Those who drafted this legislation have failed to realise that the unity and integrity of India can be maintained only by the spontaneous sense of loyalty and cooperation of the people of different regions of the country and not be recourse to oppression and coersion. Such draconian laws are counter-productive, because they drive secessionist movements underground, where they thrive on the dissatisfaction of the local population.

V.M. TARKUNDE
President
Citizens for Democracy and
Adviser People's Union For
Civil Liberties, New Delhi

VICTIMS OF TERRORISM

Turkey has suffered the worst form of terrorism in the world, some thirty diplomats having become victims of terrorist attack outside the country and 5,000 people killed within the country. Turkey will support any international action to contain and combat terrorist activities.

TURGUT OZAL
Prime Minister
The Republic of Turkey

TERRORISM & NEO-COLONIALISM

Terrorism is as much the brain-child of neo-colonialism as of dictatorial regimes that provide them protective covers (even training facilities). Such manipulations aim at undermining the democratic institutions while terrorists themselves are not inhibited by any ideological or policy constraints.

Firmly set on the democratic course, Indian polity is an anathema to several powers that can impose their hegemony only through creation of economic dependencies and regimes run by pliable individuals. India has evolved into a socially cohesive, economically self-reliant and politically dependent national entity. Its present-day urges to take gigantic strides into the realm of science and technology are an index of this vibrant self-confidence. The secular and socialist idea provides it with philosophic projections of political and socio-economic import.

In this context, the situation has to be tackled with rationally braved and bold initiatives. There is a need to go about with serious-minded devotion to be able to fulfil the social and political obligations irrespective of the threats and antics of .the hit-and-run gun-runners.

The persistence of violent activity has to be faced with perseverance and patience without giving in to the threats—much less being cowed down by them. Terrorism is as much a subject to be tackled by the law-keeping machinery as it calls for effective political action to counter it. The hydra has its inherent weaknesses that are also its major disadvantages, these hinge round its isolation from the mainstream, lack of popular support and total inability for organised action. Therein lies the chance to frighten it out of existence.

ANSER KIDWAI
Editor
National Herald
New Delhi

WAR AGAINST TERRORISM

The *Spectator* of London commenting on the hijacking of the Egypt air plane, in which 60 lives were lost, had four lines which I found singularly applicable to our own situation. "Tyrannicide (killing of tyrants) has long been recognised as a justified and even a moral act. Terroricide (killing of terrorists) can be too. If there is any just war in the world today, it is the war against terrorism". Translated into plain Hindustani : if there is any just *dharamyuddha* (sacred war) in India, it is the *yudh* (war) against *atankavaad* (terrorism).

I can understand the public apathy towards the menace ; no one is willing to stick their neck out in what they regard as solely a police situation. As long as this *aseen kee laina* (how does it concern us) attitude persists, we will never be able to combat these criminals. Nor will the police. One outcome of the attempt on the life of the high priest, Giani Sahib Singh, while at prayer in the Harmandir on Guru Nanak's birthday and the slaying of his bodyguard bearing the name of the founder—Guru, Nanak Singh, is the sense of revulsion it has created in the minds of the Sikh masses. What then is keeping the high priests of the five *takhts* from proclaiming that men who wield guns against innocent people are criminals and must be ostracised? Are they scared of guns being turned against them? Such pusillanimity does not become representatives of a community which rightly prides itself on its courage.

KUSHWANT SINGH
Writer & Journalist
New Delhi

TERRORISM : THREAT TO PEACE AND HARMONY

We are all concerned about the present growing threat to peace and harmony in our society. It is a fact of history that in face of social tensions, the young men and women in our universities and other educational institutions have often taken the lead in showing the path of mutual amity.

The entire university must thus pledge itself to work actively to defeat those whose aim today is to victimise innocent people and disrupt our social harmony through inhuman and barbaric actions.

PROFESSOR MOONIS RAZA
—Vice-Chancellor
University of Delhi
—Formerly Visiting Professor
Cornell University
—Founder Chairman
Centre for the Study of
Regional Development
—Rector, Jawaharlal Nehru
University
—Member, Advisory Committee, U.N. Centre for
Regional Development,
Nagoya, Japan

TERRORISM AND MASS POLITICAL MISMANAGEMENT

By now after 38 years of freedom, I would have thought we were equipped to deal with Sikh terrorism. After all, we have been playing this role from the earliest years of our freedom, and again t terrorism in many forms. There are the continuing tribal insurgencies in the North-East ; the killings of the so-called Marxist-Leninist Naxalites whicb when stamped out at some point, the political gangesterism of the Hindi speaking "heartland", and the mixed up liberationist culture of the Tamils against Sri Lankan oppression.

Terrorism is always the weapon of a "hard core", tribal, Naxal, Sikh or Tamil. It cannot be equated with a community even though tacit support is offered. What is special about "the Indian" situation is that every type of terrorism is sought to be met by official terrorism. We children of colonialism know no other way. The operations of the police, military and paramilitary are punctuated by brutal and insanely cruel acts. There is also an overall lack of any political perspective and this invariably assists the building and expansion of the terrorist base.

The effort to mobilise the people against terrorism on the solid argument that armed confrontations destroy the democratic process, is also nullified by the general public adherence to soft and convenient options. All that is seen in the North-East are the "atrocities" of the military. The Naxal killings are after all against "blood-sucking" landlords. The Tamil "tigers" have no alternative in the face of "genocidal attacks" in Sri Lanka. And the criminalised terrorists in Punjab are dressed up in some mythical role and not condemned for what they are. We live at various levels of so-called "commitment".

There are other layers of contradiction too. Some condemn Sikh terrorism and urge the toughest of repression, but their attitude to Naxal killings is very different. Liberation passions are welcome where the Tamils are concerned but not when sections of the Sikhs and the tribes of the North-East start losing their balance. As for the Kashmiris, the less said the better, for they must naturally be Pakistani agents. This mess of contradictions disolves the quality of consistency on which firm commitments are based. Some are lost in anti-government phobias. Others intoxicate themselves on euphorias.

In this confused and chaotic situation, we cannot expect anything but a demoralised and vitiated police force, officered by subservient persons who can be shunted here and there on the flimsiest pretext. The many policing systems, under a variety of high-sounding names, are replicas of the main force. Whether it is the lumpenised Border Security Force or the Central Reserve Police, or the new supposedly elite

National Guards, there is little change except an increase in fire-power or mobility. And when the hard-pressed military is brought into salvage situations, the entire para-military structure begins to vibrate and crumble.

Terrorism cannot be fought with terrorism. We have to uncover and understand the causes of terrorism. Basically, it is the result of massive political mismanagement. Policies have to be devised to re-establish confidence among those who are resorting to the gun.

ROMESH THAPAR
Journalist
New Delhi

ANATOMY OF TERRORISM

We are witnessing in contemporary India, three types of terrorism : Insurgency in the North-East, ideological or class oriented terrorism of a sporadic nature in some parts of the country and secessionist variety linked to religion in Punjab. Of these, the last one has assumed menacing proportions owing to a lack of political will and initial failures. At present, it appears to have become well nigh impossible to isolate the groupscule which initially consisted of a few religious fanatics surrounded by other psychotic or criminal elements. To what extent are the Akalis on the same wavelength as the extremists led by the late Sant Bhindranwale, or, as assumed by some, merely captive to the extremists, is anybody's guess. On the other hand, there is a grave risk of an incipient civil war if the policy of drift continues. At this stage, even questions like entry into the Golden Temple (Amritsar) have become irrelevant.

In countering terrorist violence of the nature and complexity as in Punjab today, we must consider two important factors. The first is the immediate temptation to adopt totalitarian strategies as terrorism, however destructive, has little chance of success in an authoritarian state. But if we believe in the principles of a liberal democracy, can we fall into the same error as the terrorists who have no dearth of arguments to justify their means and ends. Indiscriminate repression is not only incompatible with the liberal values which we are trying to protect, but it is likely to make a rapproachement extremely difficult if not impossible.

S. VENUGOPAL RAO
—Formerly, I.G.P., C.B.I.,
—Professor, Emeritus Police
Training Institute, A.P.

VIOLENCE CANNOT CURB VIOLENCE

Civil rights organisations are only concerned with preventing the State from becoming authoritarian, from committing violence against citizens and demanding the right that the State conform to laws which it seeks to enforce against its citizens. This entire repression has been beyond the boundaries of law. So we say that this illegal terrorism by the State has no place in a democratic set-up, and that State violence is as much punishable as private violence. Our fight is against any discrimination in favour of State violence which is a danger to democracy.

If I want to raise my voice against private violence, there can be no end to it. It's a job that must be dealt with properly by the law. The State cannot resort to violence to curb violence. You have no right to commit a crime to detect a crime.

K.G. KANNABIRAN
—Advocate
Supreme Court of India,
—President
Andhra Pradesh Civil Liberties Committee

TERRORISM—A MINOR ABERRATION

To be secure is always good. Why should we upset the people. You see if someone throws a bomb it will definitely upset the homogeneity and the peace. Just suppose, there is some violence now and the elections are postponed. Then, again when the elections are held, someone else throws a bomb. So you will say, postpone the elections again. Is that how countries are run ?

Terrorism is not a real threat, it is a minor aberration. It is an aberration which disturbs the peace and amity among the people. How can just a few challenge the nation ? The public, the people of India are sick of it. The press can help by not reporting the activities of the terrorists—let them stew in their own juices.

GEN. R.S. SPARROW
President
Punjab Pradesh Congress Committee (I)
Chandigarh

PEACE THROUGH GOODWILL AND TOLERANCE

As a Buddhist monk I appeal to everyone to let their goodwill and humanity dictate their actions. There is the need for solving the Punjab problem through discussion. I am convinced that only through goodwill and tolerance all concerned can prevent the already bad situation from deteriorating further.

DALAI LAMA

FACE OF TERRORISM

I assure the Government and the people of India that the British Political will and the full resources of British law are, and will continue to be, rigorously devoted to stamping out terrorism. The existing British law is strong enough to deal with terrorism. The Government of Britain will try to modify the existing laws through amendment in British Parliament to make it more harsh.

Mr. Timothy Renton, a Minister in the British Foreign Office, will be designated to sit with the Indian counterparts to explore how the extradition treaty could be worked out. We are trying to strengthen the braces that already exist between India and Britain.

I was with British Prime Minister Margaret Thatcher when the bombs went up in the hotel room. I know the face of terrorism from close quarter and believe me, we are doing everything we can.

SIR GEOFFREY HOWE
Secretary of State for Foreign
Affairs & Commonwealth Affairs
The United Kingdom

COMBATING STATE TERRORISM

Prime Minister, Mr. Rajiv Gandhi's call to all political parties to unite to fight terrorism in Punjab should make every Indian ponder over what is happening—in that state—the land of brave soldiers of freedom, secularism and democracy, whose sacrifices in the freedom struggle had inspired men and women in the entire sub-continent.

Today, a handful of terrorists, hand in glove with some foreign powers are out to destroy the integrity and unity of our Indian nation. There is no short-cut to contain the menace of terrorism. Merely agitating for the resignation of the Barnala government in this hour of crisis does not solve the problem. In fact an allout support to it is the need of the hour. The Barnala Government is an elected Government, and is true democrats it should be our bounden duty to extend the hand of cooperation to the Government in combating this menacc. "It is in this context that the presidium of the All-India Freedom Fighters' Organisation (AIFFO), headed by Mr. Sheel Bhadra Yajee. Prof. N.G Ranga and Baba Prithvi Singh Azad and a host of heros of the freedom struggle, particularly from the northern belt, can play a positive role in meeting the challenge of terrorism.

"It is good that the Nagpur Session of the All-India Freedom Fighters Conference, has been called off. Let the leaders of AIFFO convene the meeting of the presidium of the organisation not only to take stock of the situation but consider the formation of 'shanti senas' in every nook and corner of Punjab to act as watchdogs and thus help the Central and State Governments in combating terrorism.

V.H. DESAI
President, Freedom Fighters'
Forum, Hyderabad

PREVENTING TERRORISM

Terrorism is of public interest but I wouldn't say that it was of major day-to-day importance.

If you compare, to put it crudely, the number of people who are killed or injured in terrorist activities as opposed to the victims of drug crime, it is much less.

Also we have an article in our constitution which forbids us from dealing with political, racial, religious and military crimes.

However, if you have a terrorist incident like the shootings at Rome and Vienna airports or the bomb planted at Bologne railway station in Italy, where 90 people were killed, it would be ridiculous to say that, because they are politically motivated we cannot deal with them.

Aircraft and boat hijackings, assassinations and bomb attempts all fall within our ambit. It is easier to say what we do not deal with—people's political opinions, religious beliefs and military deserters.

The budget is limited (18 million Swiss Francs) but I do hope to introduce new measures to prevent terrorism. At the moment everything possible is done to prevent armed hijackers getting on board planes. There are extensive security checks at airports but still people manage to get through our controls. We want to stop this.

It's clear that we also need as much information as we can gather on the hijackers themselves because then we can work out how negotiations might take place.

Terrorists are often thought of as fanatics but they plan their actions just as carefully as bank robbers choose their target, prepare their attack and escape. I don't believe that terrorism is a delicate issue. It is just another crime and I think we should be realistic about it.

RAY KENDALL
Chief of Interpol

TERRORISM AND PEACE

Terrorists are trying to defeat Middle East peace efforts and should be prevented by Europe from achieving their goals.

As free men of Europe, we will not permit terrorism—together with those who support and arm it behind the scenes—to succeed in its project of defeating the prospects of peace. Europe will have to back Middle East negotiations with all its might.

We will strive for the realisation of conditions which will make it possible for Israel to live in peace and harmony with its Arab neighbours. And we will strive to prevent terrorism from shattering this dream.

GIOVANNI SPADOLINI
Defence Minister of Italy
Rome

PORNO-VIOLENCE AND RAPE CRIMES

There is empirical evidence suggesting that there are links between lesser sex crimes, as well as rape, and the consumption of pornography. In the U.S. there is a very well-done study of all 50 States that found that the States with higher circulations of what they called the "sex magazines", i. e. Penthouse, Playboy, Oui, had the higher rape rates, and those with the lowest circulations had the lowest rates. The correlation was 0.64. The correlation between a person's height and weight is only 0.8.

Psychologists haven't agreed on how the consumption of sex-explicit materials leads to sex-related crimes. But several models have been constructed to explain the link. One is that the sex-explicit material especially porno-violence, the depiction of rape or sadistic acts in pornographic literature, will dis-inhibit the reader of any social constraints that may restrain a person from doing the undesirable sex-related crimes. The second one is called the "social learning theory" We model ourselves after the people in the movies or magazines in their raping or in their sex-deviant behaviour. The third possibility is what we call the "rape myth"—the myth that women enjoy being raped.

There is still a fourth one ; that the depiction of rape in pornographic literature and movies will give the general public a feeling that we are not so concerned with so-related crimes. So the values and the morals of the society will change and this will lead indirectly to an increase in the rape rate.

Some people are talking about women inducing men to engage in the act of rape. Rape is a very fuzzy concept. Recently in the media there was a case recorded that a woman was raped many times by a Chinese herbal doctor. In fact they had been co-habiting for years. We don't know how to define rape and therefore we don't know what is meant by the woman inducing or causing a person to rape.

DR. C. HARRY HUI
Lecturer in Psychology,
Univ. of Hongkong

RAPE : A VERY VIOLENT SEXUAL ATTACK

Recent trends show a higher incidence of gang rape and various sexual aberrations are becoming the norm. Pornographic video tapes are passed around illicitly. I am told that they have increasingly novel ways of depicting various deviations of sexual behaviour. Some may even start off with a rape scene, implying that the victim enjoys it after a while. This is a mistaken belief : rape is a very violent sexual attack, and no woman enjoys it. But I believe these films have influenced the behaviour pattern of men, more so in the urban areas. It's difficult to say that pornography effects the actual number of rapes, as there is no comprehensive analysis.

It was totally unfounded and unwarranted (but) it reflects the general attitude of many men and even some women in Malaysia. Police statistics say that only 4% of the rapes here were "provoked" by the victim, and the provocation was merely walking or dressing in a way that society defines as attractive. There were even isolated incidents of women who were completely covered wearing traditional Muslim clothes and veils and who were raped. Rape victims range from three years old to 52 years old.

RITA REDDY
Vice-President
Malaysia's Association of Women Lawyers

MIND OF A TERRORIST

Interpreting the mental profile of a terrorist from the Jungian viewpoint, any individual or any person who has taken to terroristic acts of violence has failed to keep a lid on the darker thoughts and experiences of his personal unconscious and thus the repressed evil thoughts sneak into his conscious psyche. These repressed thoughts and experiences which are not contained at the conscious level, contaminate the rational aspect of the mind and a person, who has failed to differentiate in him "the good you and the bad you", takes to vandalism or terroristic acts.

If the conscious level of the mind has been built socially and morally on a firm footing through family upbringing, exposure to healthy moral, religious and legal education in that case an individual's conscious level works as bulwark against the darker part of the mind. That is why that all our Sikh youth have not been contaminated by the terroristic virus, despite that everyone has the darker level in one's mental psyche.

Failure of family and social institutions in building a strong moral and legal sensor (Freudian-Super-Edgo) among our youth due to rigid or permissive family norms, poor under-the-ceiling culture, involved social and political climate, breed a class of youngsters who are predisposed to violence, vandalism and terroristic acts. Such youngsters, who fail to derive warmth, affection and belongingness from family fall an easy prey in the hands of proclaimed gangsters and anti-social cliques. The precipitating factors like communal hatred, unemployment, alienation and a host of socially unhealthy factors work as explosives and thus trigger off the venom of those socially sick youngsters.

An organised effort to contain the terrorist activities could be possible if the social institutions in general, and Sikhs intelligentia and Sikh leadership in particular would claim back the derailed youngsters by persuasion and re-education.

DR. M. L. LIDHOO
Reader in Psychology
Department of Education,
Kashmir University, Srinagar

DANGEROUS DIFFERENCES

Khalistani terrorism in Punjab is potentially more dangerous than the Naxalite insurgency we had in Calcutta and West Bengal in 1969-71 (one deliberately terms it Khalistani terror and not Sikh for the vast majority of this community is patriotic and their culture is not cowardly and terroristic). The Naxalites borrowed their ideology originally from the Maoist doctrines and the far-eastern kind of insurgency. When, however, they shifted themselves to Calcutta and the industrial suburbs they adopted the organisational structure of the far-west (mainly Brazil and Uruguay). But while borrowing the elitist methods of the Tupamaro and Carlos Marighella they did not change their weaponry, suitable only for mass insurgency. (In communist thinking arms and ideology are often connected : Marshal Tukachevsky was liquidated for recommending and adopting Liddell Hart's concept of tanks and tri-dimensional battle). In Calcutta we usually encountered pipeguns and knives. Sophisticated weapons were a rarity, though we came across a time bomb in Metro cinema in 1970 and a body trap in Nandia later. In contrast, the Khalistanis have highly sophisticated fire-arms and infernal devices like transistor bombs, a trend which will manifest itself increasingly in other forms.

The centre of Khalistani activism is more likely to be Delhi than Amritsar. Here, the task of the police force is clear. The terrorists have to be isolated from the people, and put down very quickly. Time is of essence ; and isolation of a must. The police may have to take severe physical punishments, but any over-reaction against the Sikh community will be fatal. And the lack of speed will only help the Khalistanis underground to spread ; for some Sikhs who can be faulted for being "macho" (often lauded by some of their own intellectuals) may be attracted by some armed activism.

RANJIT GUPTA
Police Services
Calcutta, West Bengal

ZIONIST TERRORISM

The Israeli bombing of the PLO headquarters in Tunis on October 1, 1985 has once again proved that Israel is the worst enemy of all the principles and values, which are cornerstones and necessary for maintaining international relation. If the world remains silent over such Zionist terrorism, it is feared the peace an international level would be in danger. They deserve punishment for this serious offence.

The organised terrorism of Israeli rulers has clearly proved the contradiction in their saying and deeds. The United States of America, which often complains of being victim of terrorism, itself encourages the Israeli terrorism and helps the Zionist rulers in achieving what they want.

It is now not a secret that the Israeli jets, which raided the PLO headquarters in Tunis, stopped for refuelling on the Mediterranean where the U.S. Sixth Fleet is stationed.

In the light of this fact, it can be said that America was not only aware of the raid in advance, but it cooperated with them in their notorious act. It is not a matter of surprise. Everybody knows that

Israel never takes a step without taking approval from American rulers.

Allah (God) saved Mr. Yasser Arafat (PLO Chairman), who was the main target in the raid. All the justice-loving people of the world must be happy that Abu Ammar is safe. All the justice loving governments of the world, particularly the Muslim rulers, should take notice of this fresh terrorism and forge unity in their rank, and files forgetting all the differences at this critical juncture.

The Freedom of Palestine and taking back of Harme-Awwal are not only problems of the Arab countries, it is worrisome problem for the entire Islamic world. The Muslim rulers must sit at a common platform to think seriously over it.

May Allah give long life to the PLO Chief, Mr. Yasser Arafat. Indian Muslims are with him and are waiting for the day when Harm-e-Awwal would be taken back. May that day come soon, *Ameen* !

MAULANA ABUL LAIS ISLAHI NADVI AMEER
Jamaat-e-Islami Hind, Delhi

CESSPOOL OF BLOOD

Not only the Government but even God is losing credibility in India. The entire society should do penace for the atrocities committed against innocent people. What crime did these children commit.

The such terrible things should have happened in the Capital (Delhi) of the country meant that the nation is sick.

Parliament should have understood their problems and solved them by now.

The killings and the failure of the administration to bring to book those responsible for the crime will remain a terrible blot on the nation's face.

The widows and their children should try and stand on their own feet instead of depending on the Government. You should forget the past and build a united democratic India where everyone is equal.

There is danger of involving the army in the country's political issues.

If the Government cannot control the situation in Kashmir, Punjab even after such a big mandate and has to call in the army every time, then where is democracy.

The country is now bartering human beings. The spirit of nationalism is being drowned in a cesspool of blood.

BABA MURLIDHAR DEVIDAS AMTE
Social Worker
People United for Serving Humanity
—Leader : Knit India Movement
—Magsaysay Award Winner

IMPERIALISM : QUEST FOR DOMINATION

The might of imperialism is declining but not its quest for domination. But I am confident that "win we will". History and time are on our side. World socialism today is strong enough to stand by national liberation movements in our regions and elsewhere.

The three centres of world capitalism, US, Europe and Japan, are afflicted with several internal contradictions. The US today is not that strong and it is not in position to have everything going its way. The recent collapse of dictatorships in Latin America, one after the other, is proof enough of what I am saying. These dictatorships were being proposed up by imperialism and they have fallen like nine pins. I have spelled out this phenomenon in great detail in my book, "The Caribbean whose Backyard" ? I am conscious that our struggle is long and hard but history is proving us right and that is what lends strength and confidence to our struggle.

Events in Jamaica, Bolivia, Peru, Argentina and Brazil have recently shown that imperialism is on the decline though not its craving for domination. The United States tried to make Jamaica a showpiece of capitalism but within just five years everything there lies in ruins. The dictatorships in other Latin American countries have also been collapsing. Nicaragua has exposed the myth of imperialism's invincibility. But we have to guard against providing opportunity to US to foment bloodshed as it has been desperately trying to do in El-Salvador. It is with this danger in view, that we are striving for patriotic unity not only within our own country but in the entire region.

My socialist ideology draws inspirations from Lenin just as my political approach is inspired by Gandhi and Nehru.

DR. CHEDDI JAGAN
Former Prime Minister of Guyana

TERRORISM—THE HIJACKINGS

We are in transition. When the Sikhs and other Indians get more involved in British politics, its affairs and fight elections to the councils and integrate into the British society, their focus would shift from India to Britain. This would help in the improvement of the situation.

The non-aligned, the western and the eastern blocs shall have to come to an agreement like not allowing a hijacked plane to land or expedite extradition proceedings.

The world airlines could come to an agreement. A tighter code devised and police cooperation intensified, more in the field of finding evidence. This would do a great deal in checking hijackings.

(MRS) SHIRLEY WILLIAMS
Founder-Leader
The Social Democratic Party of Britain,

AIR TERRORISM AND DETECTIVE DEVICES

The 1990s will see almost no terrorism in the air because of the development of nearly infallible detection devices for personal and baggage checks ; that on many flights—particularly the 700-100 seater Jumbos on point to point operation, mobile immigration and customs officials will clear the passengers in flight so that they do not clutter up the terminal buildings.

Twentieth century has seen its last fuel crisis—in fact, any fuel crisis occurring now will be a crisis in reverse, i.e., sharply declining prices in real terms ; and lastly operation of international services will continue to remain, for the industry as a whole, a business with low profitability. This will result in some smaller carriers folding up and will also result in more stringent bilaterals with a high price having to be paid for carriage of fifth freedom traffic.

C.L. SHARMA
Deputy Managing Director
Air India

FIGHT AGAINST INTERNATIONAL TERRORISM

The perpetrators of terrorist acts carry or proclaim various ideological and political lebels—there are major and minor categories of terrorism—methods and scale of terrorist activity differ from incident to incident—but all terrorism retains as a common denominator its totalitarian and anti-human character. It seeks to destroy the fabric of society, to disrupt the equilibrium of peaceful commerce. It strikes down the innocent bystander. It denies the individual. It has murderous contempt for the very basis of human freedom.

Since the roots and motivations of terrorism appear to be so diverse and often irrational, we are far from hoping for any success in its prevention. I know that some argue persuasively that the demonstrated futility of political terrorism ultimately militates against the success and even survival of terrorism as an instrument of international political pressure. I am naturally anxious to see this view vindicated. Certainly there is evidence that terrorism is essentially ineffective in bending political will to what are, most frequently, poorly articulated political objectives. But that does not give us hope that terrorism will cease to be an instrument for international mischief and destabilization. In the absence of any known cure of prevention, I must urge drastic surgery as the only reasonable course—and by that I mean determined action, firmness under the duress of blackmail, and swift and effective retribution.

In a world of nation-states, state terror, confined to national boundaries, enjoys the protection of sovereignty and claims immunity from external interference. Lest we blunt our own devotion to individual freedom, we must not close our eyes to the existence of terror in any form anywhere in the world, for such tolerance makes us vulnerable to the cancer of international terrorism by weakening our confidence and our resolve. Specifically, we cannot rely on much aid and comfort from non-democratic States in protecting our institutions and our way of life—the threat of terrorism is to freedom and not to totalitarianism. Progress in regional cooperation has been minimal. Much more remains to be done. Above all, as free men, we must assiduously cultivate the habit of fierce and merciless resentment towards all those who disrupt public tranquillity ; this habit will make us safe and keep us free.

GEORGE BUSH
—Member, The Republican Party
—A Career Diplomat
—Director, CIA, 1976-77
—Chief U.S. Liaison Officer in Peking, 1974-75.
—U.S. Ambassador to the UN, 1971-72
—Chairman, the Republican National Committee.

TERRORISM CALLS FOR A NEW APPROACH

Since time immemorial, violence has been the other side of the growth of human civilization. It manifests itself in its most fierce form in the context of State, which was ostensibly created for providing law and order and for ensuring peace for the mankind. But the lust for territorial expansion and aspirations of the rulers to become supreme, *chakravartin*, ruler of this planet have subjected the human civilization to a perpetual state of *Mahabharata*, the epic world war fought in our part of the world thousands of years ago. The civilization has suffered from not less than 14,000 wars with ever-increasing human loss. A climax was reached when 85 million died and 90 million were wounded during the Second World War (1939-1945). Dropping of the nuclear bomb on Hiroshima and Nagasaki brought an end to the war but numbed the entire mankind. Immediately after this tragic end, the "managers of war" ritually called for a lasting peace and created a supranational organization, namely the United Nations, for eliminating the scourge of wars from the earth. But it was to be a chimera so long as the psyche of the managers of statecraft remained unchanged. Therefore, the humanity remains subjected to an un-ending war in one part of the world or the other, since the creation of the UN, to win the race for supremacy of the world. The false advance towards peace is reflected in the growth of nuclear weapons which have the capability of causing total destruction many times over. At the close of the last world war there was almost no nuclear weapon, whereas at present a stockpile of 50,000 thermonuclear weapons, which are hundred times more deadlier, exists on our planet. The nations are being helplessly dragged to a global nuclear war and humanity is being kept in a state of perpetual fear with war clouds hovering on the horizon.

In recent years, "terrorism" by going wild has, however, generated more shock waves for the humanity. Every morning the press reports gruesome acts committed by "terrorists". Without giving thought to the consequences of this mass projection, the media network widely covers the "terrorist" news and helps in escalating "terrorism" both in its intensity and territorial limits. Every living person is being dragged into the grip of the "fear zone" of "terrorism". In the present day world, it is considered in political terms the worst destabilizing and destructive force. Before it the all too terrifying horror of the nuclear holocast has paled into insignificance.

What is terrorism ? Various theories have been propounded, from time to time, to define the concept in terms of the rising tide of world-wide "terrorist" activities. However, so far there is no commonly accepted theory on "terrorism". According to the *UN Ad Hoc Committee on International Terrorism* "murder", assassination, sabotage and subversion ; the destruction of public records, the spreading of rumours, the closing of churches, the sequestration of property, the breakdown of criminal law enforcement, the prostitution of courts, the narcosis of the press—all these, as they contribute to a common end, constitute terror". However, dissenting from the majority opinion, the French representative on this Committee opined that "any heinous act of barbarism committee in the territory of a third state by a foreigner against a person possessing a nationality other than that of the offender for the purpose of exerting pressure in a conflict not strictly internal in nature would be an act of terrorism". A legal luminary of the United States, Eduardo Jimenez Arechaga defined "terrorism" as nothing but a crime committed "with the deliberate intention of causing panic, disorder and terror within an organized society, in order to destroy social discipline, paralyze the forces of reaction of a society, and increase the misery and suffering of the community".

There can be no denial that the violent actions for personal ends cannot be considered more than "criminal" acts. Any unlawful act committed by an individual or a group of individuals seeking self-aggrandisement would be a crime, not only against an individual, community or State but also against humanity. However, this does not explain the "terrorist" phenomenon. Conventionally, "terrorism" had been linked directly with political activity of an individual or a group of individuals who intended to change the political system or the wielders of political power in a State. Their motives might emanate from a broad spectrum of factors ranging from social, economic, political or even religious considerations.

Guerrilla activities, which are termed as "terrorist" acts, have, however, many dimensions. Though Michael Jenkins, the internationally renowned expert on terrorism, has tried to underrate the force of the revolutionaries' thesis by stating that the activists resort to violence "to gain attention and to create fear and alarm, which in turn will cause people to exaggerate the strength of the terrorists and the importance of their cause", but as we look at the march of subject nations towards freedom in the twentieth century, we find the weak subject people have been compelled to resort to guerrilla warfare to throw out the mighty oppressive imperial yoke. Explaining their activities during the struggle for the freedom of India, the revolutionary martyr Bhagat Singh said that "Terrorism is a phase, a necessarily inevitable phase, in the process of revolution. Terrorism is not the complete revolution and the revolution is not complete without terrorism . . . terrorism shatters the spell of superiority of the (imperial) ruling class and raises the status of the subject race in the eyes of the world because it is the most convincing proof of a nation's hunger for freedom."

N.P. Thornton, therefore, considers "terrorism" as a political phenomenon. He defines that "the use of terror is a symbolic act designed to influence political behaviour by extra-normal means, entailing the use or threat of violence." Agreeing with this, William Laugh believes that "Terrorism is political, goal-oriented, involving the use or threat of extraordinary violence, performed for psychological than instrumental". B. McClure who has studied "terrorism" in detail, points out that "it is another form of dissent or protest. The range of actions begins with legal and accepted forms of dissent, such as individual oral protests, petition or grievances, and peaceful demonstrations ; moves to illegal but often tolerated behaviour such as coercive demonstrations, violent demonstrations, seizure of property and vandalism, and finally escalates to illegal and unacceptable behaviour such as, sabotage, personal assault, bombing, kidnapping, and assassination". While this was also a political, over the years, this strategy itself degenerated into unscrupulous acts. While the guerrilla activities were branded as "terrorist" acts, the imperial powers themselves resorted to "terrorist" acts to overawe the people against joining the struggle for the freedom of their countries. Authors like G. Pontara brought their activities within its premises by defining that "A terrorist act is any action carried out as a part of a method of political struggle, aimed at influencing, or conquering or *defending the State power*, implying the use of extreme violence against innocent non-combatant persons". This brought an ever-increasing wave of "terrorist" activities in the subject countries and the imperial countries and their allies.

Some analysts like Prof. Metin Tamikoe have tried to explain this dimension in terms of cold war politics. Tamikoe equates the cold war struggle with political and has identified three means for its resolution : (a) peaceful, (b) limited use of force, and (c) open warfare. "When one of the parties in a conflict without exhausting all peaceful means of resolution, engages in violent acts, directed not against his opponent but against a third innocent party, such acts of violence must be considered illegal in any legal system". He adds that this type of "violence (is) directed not against opponents to accede to the demands of terrorists". He thus defines "terrorism" as "an illegal act of violence", and holds that the Bolshevik revolutionary struggle for world domination encourages such "illegal" acts of violence. He further explains that "The Bolshevism of Lenin and his cohorts was only one of many conspiratorial revolutionary movements inspired by Bakunin and Nechayev (the anarchist writers) which grew up among the Russian intelligentsia ; however, it succeeded where others failed. Today the Soviet grand children of the Bolsheviks have influenced the formation of anarchist, terrorist movements in the rest of the world, but also indirectly have managed the operations of individual terrorists. In addition, they have precipitated, abetted, and aided insurgency movements in colonial territories and supported the wars of national liberation". "The principal strategy of the Soviets," he further adds, "is the destruction of their opponents from within by way of infiltration, subversion, terrorism, and *internal war which obviates thermonuclear confrontation*. Their strategy is to bring the whole world under the control of the Soviet Union, a dream that justjfies *any means short of the use of nuclear weapons*".

But the premises of the foregoing analysis preclude the causes and the aims of those committing the terrorist acts. What are the reasons that terrorism is more widespread in the developing countries than in the developed ones ? Of course, the developed countries are also its victims. According to a Rand Study, two out of every three terrorist acts of international importance involved the United States directly or indirectly. But the cause of almost all these terrorist acts did not originate in the United States. Excepting Great Britain, the cause of these acts generally originated in the developing countries. Secondly, almost all these terrorist acts affected developing countries opposed to or supported by the US Administration. Thus there is a linkage between the developing and developed countries rocked by terrorism.

If we call spade a spade, we would find that the political violence aggravated only after the imperial (as also the authoritarian) regimes resorted to "terrorist" strategy to deny their people legitimate rights. Apartheid regime in South Africa, for example, is not only perpetrating violence against the indigenous black population, but also adopted "terrorist" strategy against the neighbouring independent black States. The developed countries extended support to such regimes thus denying the political and economic independence to a larger part of the population of the developing countries. Thus, Tamikoe's theory holds good more in the context of the strategy adopted by the ex-imperial interests and their allies vis-a-vis beneficiaries to perpetuate their domination on the developing countries and deny them gains of their political freedom.

Despite a variance in the countries affected by "terrorism", we find a common approach and common result insofar as the "terrorists" activities are concerned. Terrorism adversely affects the State and aggravates political destabilization. Political destabilization further accentuates the violent approach amongst the pressure groups. In this way, the States get in the grip of a vicious circle of terrorism.

Thus terrorism cannot redress the grievances. Rather it proves in the end counter-productive. Terrorist activity would give birth to more and intensified terrorist acts. The mad race of the rulers to be *chakravartin* would develop terrorist activities parallel to the war between the nations and between the various pressure groups within a nation. The on-going US Libya confrontation amply justifies our observation.

It calls for a new approach. The actors in the power structure need pondering over the problem from a different angle than resorting to confrontation. Confrontation would certainly lead to more confrontations. This situation would help "terrorism" trample the humanity and we might be thrown back to the primitive stage where State would wither away. The ensuing anarchy shall cause total destruction of different nature without a nuclear holocaust.

Mr. Attar Chand has brought forth a good deal of literature on "terrorism" in the present book. One can safely hope that it will help provoke thinkers to re-define "terrorism" and suggest means for its resolution before it is too late.

Dr. DHARAMPAL
Secretary
Indian Society for Afro-Asian Studies (ISAAS)
New Delhi

STATE TERRORISM

State terrorism has become a hot subject these days, although terrorism as a tool of the foreign policy of many States has been used and practised since ancient times ; only their methods and techniques have varied from time to time. States have practised or resorted to various forms of terrorism—political, economic, military and psychological—to attain their foreign policy objectives. However, never before has State terrorism been practised in such a blatant form as it is being done today. What is specially disturbing today is that even legitimate political activity of people for their emancipation from the yoke of colonialism, racism and Zionism is described as a "terrorist" activity. For instance, the armed struggle led by SWAPO, ANC, Polisario Front and PLO are dubbed as terrorist activities and the parties themselves are branded as terrorist organizations and not as liberation movements. Surprisingly, this is done by states which had attained their own independence through violent means such as the United States. Another disturbing trend today is that some states have assumed the role of international policemen and have taken upon their shoulders the responsibility of crushing the so-called terrorist activity of other states. However, their real motive is as clear as day : it is to remove leaders who refuse to be in their camp. This growing tendency on the part of the western powers has put the sovereignty and territorial integrity of weaker and smaller states in serious jeopardy.

Another disturbing trend in modern times is that big powers, while accusing others of practising State terrorism, themselves indulge in open "terrorist" activity with the aim of overthrowing legitimate Governments of sovereign States which are of leftist nature. This is done by openly assisting the dissident groups in such a State with finance and military hardware. The open financial and military aid being provided by the United States to UNITA and FNLA to enable them to overthrow the legitimate government of Angola led by MPLA is a case in point. Another case in point is that of Israel which is encouraged by the western powers to commit terrorist acts against practically all the neighbouring States. Now, if these trends continue to gain momentum, the time does not seem to be far off when the independence of all militarily weak states would be at the mercy of big powers. It is necessary, therefore, to raise a powerful voice against forces which, in the guise of combating terrorism, are actually trying to remove leaders who are following progressive policies and who refuse to adopt an anti-Soviet posture in their foreign policy.

Those who are today leading the crusade against state terrorism ought to realize that they are themselves responsible for forcing people to take to arms in pursuance of their legitimate political objectives.

If SWAPO, for instance, is resorting to armed struggle, it is not its fault since the doors to the peaceful settlement of the problem of Namibia's independence have been blocked by them. SWAPO is willing to order cease-fire tomorrow provided, steps are immediately taken for the implementation of resolution 435 (1978) which, *inter alia*, contains the United Nations' plan for peaceful advent of independence in Namibia. Unfortunately, all conceivable efforts have been, and are being, made to thwart the peaceful settlement of the problem. The same is the case with ANC. The terrible violence let loose upon Africans by a minority racist regime, backed by the same self-styled crusaders against terrorism, and their refusal to pull down the structure of *apartheid* has forced the ANC to persist with, and escalate, its armed struggle. Similarly, the denial of right to self-determination to the Palestinian people gives rise to lot of militant activity by PLO and several of its splinter groups which are dubbed as "terrorist". The most unfortunate thing is that first the western powers do all that lies in their power to prevent peaceful settlement of problems and, when the liberation movements are compelled to resort to violent struggle, they are branded as "terrorist" organizations. If all these activities which are wrongly dubbed as "terrorist" activities are sought to be ended, it is necessary that political solutions must be found for all those problems whose continued existence gives rise to violence. Naked aggressions would certainly not bring them to a stop ; in fact, they would increase such activities.

It is unfortunate that no serious effort has so far been made to cope with the terrorist menace. It is true that the whole world stood up as one man to condemn and denounce United States' aggression against Libya —and rightly so—but it is doubtful if this unity and solidarity displayed by an overwhelming majority of nations of the world would be enough to deter the big powers from misusing their military might against weaker states in future. The chances are bleak because the United States has already warned Libya that it would strike at it again. The United States Government is looking for excuses for attacking Syria and Iran also. The meeting of the Coordinating Bureau of the Non-Aligned Movement, held in New Delhi in April 1986, failed to come to the grip of the problem. Apart from condemning the United States' aggression against Libya, one of the problems to which the aforesaid NAM meeting should have addressed itself to was the definition of "terrorism". This was necessary because as yet no agreed definition of "terrorism" exists with the result that different states interpret "terrorism" in accordance with their national interests and their foreign policy goals. Therefore, it would be in fitness of things if the forthcoming NAM Summit at Harare (Zimbabwe) sets up a committee to define "terrorism". A carefully worded definition of "terrorism" would have to rule out a variety of activities that are wrongly branded today as "terrorist". The definition should be comprehensive enough to make it clear as to which acts of a state or an organization would be deemed to be "terrorist", and which would not be regarded as "terrorist". For instance, any armed struggle which aims at destroying the shackles of colonialism and racism should be declared to be legitimate political activity and not a terrorist activity. Similarly, if people of a state struggle for the restoration of democratic rights in their country, their struggle should be upheld as morally, legally and politically just.

In the interest of promoting and strengthening world peace it would be necessary to declare certain acts of states as blatantly "terrorist". For instance, any effort by a state to remove the ruler of another state or to destabilize his regime, whether it is of leftist or rightist orientation, should be proclaimed as a terrorist act. Secondly, any attack by one state upon another should also be deemed to be a terrorist act if it is not preceded by a formal declaration of war, and states committing such aggressive acts should be made liable to pay full damages caused to life and property in the state victim of aggression. Thirdly, deployment of forces by any state near the borders of another state in an intimidating manner should also be branded as a terrorist act because the intention of any deployment of forces in excess of its normal defense requirement is to terrorize the other state. Fourthly, the holding of military and/or naval exercises at the door-step of another state should be deemed to be a terrorist act because in this case also the objective is to terrorize the state near whose territory such exercises are held. Fifthly, the sending of assassination squads with the object to killing the Heads of State and Government and high officials of another state should also be branded as a "terrorist" act. Sixthly, it should be deemed to be a terrorist act if any State train the citizens of another State on its territory in the use of arms with a view to causing civil disorder in that country or promoting secessionism in that state. A declaration on terrorism should embody all these principles. If NAM Summit is unable to make such a declaration, the International Commission of Jurists can be called upon to make such a declaration. Even the U. N. General Assembly can issue such a declaration. Who issues such a declaration is not very important ; what is important is that a declaration on terrorism should be formulated and proclaimed with the widest possible support.

Apart from defining "terrorism" and clearly identifying acts of terrorism, it is also necessary that there should be an independent International Commission on Terrorism which should monitor and investigate all complaints of terrorism. The Commission should collect all evidence in this connection and then it should publish all that evidence along with its findings so that everybody is able to know whether or not the charge of practising terrorism made against a particular State is baseless. Often a State accuses another state of committing terrorism claiming that it has sufficient evidence to support its allegation but it refuses to publish that evidence in "national interest". The publication of evidence is necessary to eliminate the possibility of any state making a false charge of practising terrorism against a state. Publication of evidence would also deter states from committing aggression against another state on the pretext that its action is in consequence of the terrorism practiced by that State. Even if the charge of "terrorism" against any state is proved, no state should be permitted to commit aggression against that state. The international community should exert its moral pressure against that State and persuade it to desist such activities in the future. This would definitely be a better way of curbing state terrorism and, at the same time, ensuring world peace. Let no State be permitted to counter an alleged case of terrorism by a state by committing a bigger or more heinous form of terrorism in the form of naked aggression against it. Let no State which commits aggression against any state for the ostensible reason of punishing it for practising terrorism be allowed to escape without paying full compensation to that State for the damage caused to life or property on its territory.

In view of the importance of the subject in present times, a book on "terrorism" by Mr. Attar Chand is most welcome. Mr. Attar Chand deserves our heartiest congratulations for taking great pains to bring out this book on terrorism which, I am confident would be widely read all over the country as well as abroad. The book offers abundant material for all research scholars, journalists and others interested in reading the complex subject of terrorism.

Dr. S.C. SAXENA
Delhi University

DAMAGE TO NATIONAL FIGHT

We are very interested in combating terrorism since every terrorist act is attributed to the Palestinian Liberation Organisation (PLO) an attitude causing serious damage to our national fight.

ABU IYAD
Member, The Central Committee
of Fatah, The Palestinian
Liberation Organization

APARTHEID TERRORISM

Apartheid is an insult to humanity and should be condemned by all. It is the right of the people of Africa to rise against the oppressive situation and put up a heroic fight which should be recognised by all.

Words and propaganda are not going to free the people of South Africa, it is only the struggle by the people which will ultimately give freedom.

The recent brutal aerial raids on the three frontline African states by the Pretoria regime is a clear pointer to the international community that unless it is quelled neither the salvation of the people of South Africa nor the achievement of the regional peace and stability is feasible.

AMRE M. MOUSSA
Former Ambassador of the Arab
Republic of Egypt

DEATH AND DESTRUCTION

The new unprovoked aggression committed by the South African regime against three sovereign African States is an attempt to deter the struggle of the national movements and is proof of that the apartheid regime only believes in the law of force.

The brutal aggression, aimed at the capitals of the three African states (viz. Zambia, Zimbabwe, Botswana) also had, amongst its targets, a refugees camp sponsored by the U. N. The excuse given for this brutal attack was resistance to "terrorism" which has become a fashion nowadays since hidden behind it is the real terrorism, the terrorism committed official by states in order to liquidate any legitimate struggle for self-determination and freedom.

The time has come for the international community to realize the extent to which the Pretorian regime flouts international law—quite like the Zionist regime in Tel Aviv so that it has allowed itself to spread death and destruction on the soil of its neighbours.

The time has also come for the international community to put an end to such continuous defiance from the country which has hoisted the flag of apartheid, and to impose the required sanctions against it. Such sanctions should not be confined to verbal condemnation only which has no value whatsoever.

The Arab States continue to consider the cause of freedom in South Africa as an Arab cause and express their complete solidarity with these brotherly States, and reiterates the acute need for everyone to work together to end this aggressive policy of apartheid to impose sanctions upon it. We must give our full support to the African movements and to the frontline States.

His Excellency CHEDLI KLIBI
Secretary General
The League of Arab States
Tunis

TERRORISM AND SECURITY OF GULF STATES

Terrorist actions in any one of the Gulf States will be regarded by all of them as an attack on all of us.

The six Gulf Co-operation Council (GOC) States are already co-operating in security matters and this is now likely to be further strengthened.

SHEIKH KHALIFA
BIN SULMAN AL-KHALIFA
Prime Minister of Bahrain

HARD-CORE TERRORISM

Canada over the course of its history has been basically a non-violent country. We have not had very many problems of hard-core terrorism. Canada has been known to be a quiet country. I think we must see the situation against this background. At the same time, let me assure you that as far as the Canadian authorities are concerned the drive against terrorist activities has been a top priority for us.

We give the highest priority to combating potential terrorist activity. We are hundred and fifty percent against terrorism. As our Deputy Prime Minister said the other day, we will not allow our country to become a killing ground. I am afraid that like all other countries we too are afflicted by the modern phenomenon of terrorism. We have no intention to import extremism from other countries.

WILLIAM WARDEN
High Commissioner of
Canada (1983-1986)
New Delhi

ABBREVIATIONS USED

— Alexander, Yonah, *et. al. eds. Terrorism : Theory and practice* Boulder, Westview, 1979. Pp. 280 =TTP

— Alexander, Yonah and Kenneth A. Myers, *eds. Terrorism in Europe.* London, Croom Helm, 1982. Pp. 216 = TIE

— Carlton, David and Carlo Schaerf ed. *International terrorism and world security.* London, Croom Helm, 1975. Pp. 332 = ITWS

— Evans, Alona E. and John F. Murphy *ed. Legal aspects of international terrorism.* Toronto, Lexington Books, 1978. Pp. 690 = LAIT

— Freedman, Lawrence and Yonah Alexander, *eds. Perspectives on terrorism.* Delhi, Hindustan Publishing House, 1985. Pp. 254 = POT

— *International terrorism and the drug connection.* Ankara University, 1984. Pp. 294 =ITDC

— Livingston, Marius, H. *ed. International terrorism in the contemporary world,* London, Greenwood Press, 1978. Pp. 522 = ITCW

— Mommsen, W. J and J. Osterhammel, *ed. Imperialism and after* London, Allen & Unwin, 1986. Pp. 368 =IAA.

— Netanyahu, Benjamin, *ed. International terrorism : Challenge and response.* London, Transanction Books, 1981. Pp. 383. = ITCR

— Niezing, John, *ed. Urban guerilla.* Rotterdam University Press, 1974. Pp. 149 = UG

— O'Neill, Bard E. *et. al. eds. Insurgency in the modern world.* Boulder, Westview Press, 1980. Pp. 291, = IMW

— Saksena, N. S. *Terrorism : History and facets in the World and in India.* New Delhi, Abhinav, 1985. Pp. 323 = THF

— Shaw, J. *et. al. eds. Ten years of terrorism.* New York, 1979. Pp. 192 = TYT

— *Who are the terrorists ? : Aspects of Zionist and Israeli terrorism.* Beirut, Institute for Palestine Studies, 1972. Pp. 74 = WTAZIT

January	Jan
February	Feb
March	Mar
April	Apr
May	May
June	Jun
July	Jul
August	Aug
September	Sep
October	Oct
November	Nov
December	Dec
Book Review	BR
Doctoral Dissertation	DD
No Date	n. d.
Autumn	Aut
Summer	Sum
Winter	Win

INTRODUCTION : UNDERSTANDING TERRORISM

We can define terrorism as the deliberate, systematic murder, maiming and menacing of the innocent to inspire fear in order to gain political ends.

The name terrorism has been to a new form of crime, a new departure in politics, a new danger to freedom. (See Stephen Segaller, *Invisible armies*. London, 1986).

The weapon of terrorism is as old as society and the law enacted from time to time to combat and check it could not contain it as has been possible in the cases of murder, robbery, theft, adultery, etc. As distinct from other crimes it particularly retards development, progress and peace of a nation. The weapon of terrorism has been used by militant individuals, groups and nations against their rivals and enemies as a punitive measure either with a view to take revenge or to force the victim to negotiate on demand or demand which terrorists consider to be legitimate and just. Despite universal condemnation of terrorism by all goverments and nations, most of them seems to be not free from it. In other words, it has become a part of the political process for achievement and promotion of certain goals and interests. It is no more a secret that the breeding ground of terrorism and terrorist activities is the United States of America, the countries of Western Europe and the Middle East. Bombing of a number of places in Libya by US recently is but the latest proof of this fact.[1]

Terrorism as an issue has moved to the forefront of the international stage. Airliners are today flying half empty, air-terminals have become veritable arsenals and an air journey an enormous hassle. The international tourism industry is facing a bleak future. The security-related expenditure to protect important personages and installations has skyrocketed. Access of common people to their representatives and government leaders has tended to be restricted. Life today is not what it was in the Fifties and Sixties. The factor underlying all this is terrorism. There are two categories of terrorism—one which is plain criminal and the other political—and both are on the increases. Abductions of persons for ransom (the kidnapping of Ms. Jennifer Guinness in Ireland for a ransom demand of over £ 2 millions is an example) and threatening to poison certain products (injection of cyanide in Tylenol capsules or tampering with Contac capsules, both of which recently happened in the U.S.) to extract large sums of money, belong to the first category. Holding hostages, placing explosives in cars, department stores, aircraft, killing people as part of evoking political terror, hijacking of various other passenger vehicles and assassination of major political personalities fall into the second category. Modern industrial society has an extremely fragile infrastructure which is easy to disrupt and the modern communication media can ensure that such disruptions produce the maximum terror effect on the witness population and target group. Just a few telephone calls to media agencies that a particular popular consumer item or medicine has been contaminated in an advanced industrialised nation, and the information is flashed around the country in minutes and the product has to be taken off the shelves. Similarly the hijacking of a bus, ship, train or aircraft makes news the globe within minutes and creates panic among the target group, which is what the terrorist aims at.[2]

Since the time of terrorists' attack on sportsmen at Munich, the issue of International Terrorism has been discussed in the United Nations a number of times. Representatives of 93 nations referred to International Terrorism in the general debate at the Twenty-seventh Session of the UN General Assembly (November 2, 1972). The discussion on the subject revealed two schools of thought on the subject. One school of thought blamed the national liberation struggles as the source of terrorism and questioned their legitimacy whereas the second school of thought propounded that violence occurs only where reaction and imperialism shore up a regime of oppression, exploitation and repression. Advocates of the second school of thought while attaching great importance to the cooperation of nations in the struggle for prevention of International terrorist acts and suppression, prosecution and punishment of persons guilty of having committed such acts, upheld the people's inalienable right to self-determination, freedom and independence. This proposition is consistent with Paragraph 4 of Article 2 of the UN Charter which provided that all UN members "shall refrain in their international relations from the threat or use of force against the territorial integrity or political independence of any state, or in any other manner inconsistent with the purposes of the United Nations." International Law in any way does not include national liberation movements within the corpus delicit of terrorism. Prior to this the issue of terrorism has been discussed as early as 1926 (from July 26 to 29) at the first International Congress of Penal Law at Brussels, although the term "terrorism" was not used until 1929 at the Third International Conference which was held at Brussels. The fifth and sixth International Conference held at Madrid 1934 and Copenhagen 1935, also discussed the issue of terrorism and adopted a document which described terrorism as "outrages endangering the community or creating a state of terror'' which can produce tension in international relations and create a particular danger to peace.[3]

The world has witnessed terrori in various forms. Kidnapping and killing of diplomats and other nationals, assassination of leading personalities, that is, head of states, etc., siege of embassies, forcible overthrow of popular governments, bombings, sabotage and hijackings. For the first six offences besides UN national laws of respective nations are there to take care of as for the last one, air-hijacking, there are three conventions.

Firstly, the Convention on Offences and Certain Other Acts Committed on board Aircraft signed at Tokyo on September 14, 1963. This convention came into force on December 4, 1969 : it was ratified or acceded to by sixty nations, including, Hungary, Poland and Yugoslavia.

Secondly, the Convention for the Suppression of Unlawful Seizure of Aircraft signed at Hague on December 16, 1970. This Convention came into force on October 14, 1971 ; this has been ratified as accepted to by 39 nations, including eight socialist countries, as of January 1977.

Thirdly, the Convention for the Suppression of unlawful Acts against the Safety of Civil Aviation signed at Montreal on September 23, 1971. This convention came into force on January 26, 1973.

The Tokyo Convention only provides for the return of the hijacked aircraft, while the Hague Convention acknowledges the need for measures rooted in local and international law against the illegal seizure of aircraft ; the Montreal Convention condemns all acts of violence against civilian aircraft and urges all states to take strict measures to prevent them and to ensure the prosecution of the perpetrators. The "air-piracy" and "air-banditry" are also the terms used to describe the air-hijacking. These Conventions if strongly adhered to by all the states can be helpful in checking the aero-crime and punishing the crime-doers only to a certain extent since the provisions for extraditions in the Hague and Montreal Conventions have been made subject to conditions which provide an excuse for not extraditing the hijackers.

Since first hijacking in 1930 (seizure of Fokker F-7 aircraft by Peruvian revolutionaries), the hijacking has become a menace which not only restricts free passage but also results in loss of national property and innocent lives if the hijacked aircraft is blown up. Between 1930 and 1981 there were over 600 recorded hijacking incidents. The year 1985 witnessed seizure of Kuwaiti Air bus in Dubai wherein two Americans were murdered in the sky, while the Trans-World Airlines flight in Athens was taken over and four dozens Americans were held as hostages out of which one was killed. On June 23, 1985, Air India's Jumbo Jet 'Kanishka' plunged into the Atlantic Ocean, as a result of sabotage by the Sikh terrorists. The aircraft carried 329 persons, including 86 children which included not only Indians but also Canadians and Britishers. The terrorist activities have grown on an unprecedented scale despite the UN General Assembly Resolution 2625 (Twenty-fifth Session) of October 24, 1970 which lays down that every state has the duty to refrain from organising, instigating, assisting or participating in terrorist acts on the territory of another state or acquiescing in organised activities within its territory directed towards the commission of such acts.

India has been a centre for terrorist activities for quite some time. Terrorist activities are being carried out with a view to destabilise India. It has taken serious turn after the Army action in Golden Temple following which Indira Gandhi, Prime Minister of India was assassinated on October 31, 1984.

International terrorists also succeeded in removing from the world scene yet another crusader of peace, Olof Palme, Prime Minister of Sweden on February 28, 1986. On May 5, 1986 the world's seven major industrial nations USA, Britain, West Germany, France, Canada, Itlay and Japan following a meeting held at Tokyo announced severe measures including an arms embargo against Libya or any country which aided and abetted terrorist activities. The seven countries while calling on other nations to join them in fighting terrorism "relentlessly and without compromise" agreed that they would refuse "to export arms to states which sponsor or support terrorism."[4]

The position of the United States and USSR in fighting the terrorism is distinctive. The United States and its allies believe in terrorism. Existence of several mercenary schools in USA for training terrorists is a proof of this fact. Whereas USSR and other socialist countries, as also India and other non-aligned countries believe in fighting terrorism. Prime Minister Rajiv Gandhi has been trying to persuade the Governments of UK, Canada and USA to sign agreements for adopting anti-terrorist measures. USSR and other Socialist countries have extended their unambiguous support to the proposal for anti-terrorist measures.

In fact, the fight against the evils of terrorism has been incorporated by USSR in its Article 4 of the Criminal Responsibility for offences against the States as far back as December 25, 1958. In the same way, Article 109 of the Criminal Code and the Criminal Procedure Code of the German Democratic Republic ; Articles 106 and 107 of the Criminal Code and the Criminal Procedure Code of the People's Rupublic of Bulgaria; Articles 219, 220, 221, 222 and 224 of the Criminal Code of the Socialist Republic of Romania ; Article 64 of the Criminal Code of the Mongolean People's Republic ; Articles 283, 284 and 285 of the Criminal Code and the Criminal Code of the Polish People's Republic ; Article 221 of the Penal Code of Argentina ; the 1956 Decree 3135 of Columbia ; and Article 38 of the Act No. 59—29 of February 27, 1959 of Madagascar,—all these ensure State action against terrorism.

The US Government, too, has been compelled to set up a Cabinet Committee to combat terrorism which is chaired by the Secretary of State, to coordinate such activities as "intelligence relating to international terrorism, improved precautionary measures by police agencies, increased screening at airports to prevent hijackings, consideration of new legislation, and increased contingency planning."

The top statesman of the Western world have all condemned terrorism in strong words as a menace to peace, progress, civilisation and stability. But it is a open secret that political terrorism is flourishing because it enjoys partronage of the big powers. Behind all terrorist activity there is the hand of some imperialist power which not only supplies money and weapons to the terrorists but also trains them for such operations.

Recently, it has been revealed that there exist schools in certain parts of the world which regularly impart training for terrorist activities. One such training school has been found to be located at Alabama State of the United States of America. It was in this school that Sikh extremists received training for murdering the Indian Prime Minister Rajiv Gandhi when on his US tour. The government of the USA reportedly, has full knowledge about the existence of this school. And it is not the only school imparting training of terrorist ; Guerillas activities like murder sabotage, arson etc. Hundreds of such schools are, allegedly, being run in other American States ; to name only a few of them ; New York, Ilinois, New Mexico, Indiana etc.

Thus, it is, to say the least, a very shameful affair. It is really painful to find that a country which is considered to be the home of democracy and on whose land the headquarters of the UN are situated is giving protection and encouragement to training schools of terrorism. The entire world is shocked at this said revelation.

Sponsors of United Nations resolutions against hijacking, terrorism and hostage-taking are trying to find ways to strengthen the measures, spurred on by strong personal interest from Secretary-General Javier Perez de Cuellar.[5]

The Secretary-General has repeatedly deplored the suffering and loss of life caused by political terrorists. He was goaded into his strongest condemnation yet by the recent Trans World Airlines (TWA) hostage crisis and by an outbreak of lethal bombings.

Just hours after his arrival at Narita International Airport for an official visit to Japan, an explosion there killed two baggage-handlers unloading luggage from a Canadian Jumbo Jet. And 55 minutes later, on the other side of the world, an Air-India Boeing 747 was blown out of the skies of Ireland, killing all 329 persons aboard.

Both explosions were widely attributed to terror bombs.

Javier Perez de Cuellar recalled that the General Assembly already has adopted a convention against the taking of hostages. However, he added :

"I think that all mechanisms can be improved : and perhaps in the light of this latest very sad experience (the TWA hostage-taking), the members of the General Assembly will reconsider the question and improve the mechanism."

While he did not say so specifically, it is safe to infer that his suggestion for strengthening measures against hostage-taking applies equally to the Assembly's hijacking and anti-terrorism resolutions.

The U.N.'s consideration of terrorism began in 1972 when Secretary-General Kurt Waldheim asked the Assembly to put the issue on its agenda. Waldheim's proposal came in the wake of an outbreak of violence aimed at national leaders, diplomats, airline passengers and other innocent civilians. The Assembly set up a 35-member committee to study the problem.

But it was not until 1976 that the Assembly formally expressed concern over mounting terrorism. Even then, the resolution was adopted only after it had been stripped of any meaning by exempting from the definition of terrorism the guerrilla activities of "liberation movements".

The argument, put forward most forcefully by the Afro-Arab bloc boiled down to the axiom : "One person's terrorist is another person's hero". (A decade later, that sophism was adopted by U.S. President Ronald Reagan when he hailed Central America's anti-Sandinista terrorist as "freedom fighters.").

The UN Assembly on December 9, 1985, took what its President, Jaime de Pinies, hailed as a "historic" step when it unequivocally condemned "all acts, methods and practices" of terrorism and proposed measures to fight the escalating international threat.

In a resolution adopted by consensus, the Assembly condemned as "criminal" terrorism "wherever and by whomever committed, including those which jeopardise friendly relations among States and their security."

Secretary-General Javier Perez de Cuellar, called the Assembly's decision "a truly important achievement of this 40th session."

"It reflects a major move, in the widest possible scale, to deal with a problem having universal implications," he said.

Assembly President, De Pinies said : "At a time when the world-wide escalation of acts of terrorism in all its forms endanger or take innocent human lives. It is particularly gratifying that during this 40th anniversary of the United Nations, all members have found it possible to agree on how to deal with an issue on such importance for the international community."

The Assembly, among other things, called on States to take appropriate measures at the national level and to co-operate with each other to eliminate international terrorism.

It also urged States to contribute to the elimination of the "underlying causes of international terrorism" and requested the international maritime organisation to study the problem of terrorism aboard or against ships.

Nor is the Hyde Park Corner principle uniformly applied. One nears nothing in Britain, for instance, of the Puerto Rican liberation movement, or of Basque nationalists in the USA. Armenian independence terrorists are universally shunned. Whitehall was quick to pull up the Hongkong administration when, through carelessness or sheer ignorance, it endorsed a passport issued by a harmlessly eccentric Australian who styles himself Prince Leonard of Hutt River ; Malcolm Fraser's Government in Canberra City displayed similar alacrity in preventing Serbo-Croats from hoisting their national flag. Rarely to governments allow political refugees freedom of action without a political motive. Thus, Pakistan used to lavish marks of distinction on the family of the Nawab of Junagadh, the Egyptians nursed ex-Kind Idris of Libya as a possible reserve card against Colonel Gaddafi, and after Ian Smith's UDI in Rhodesia, Harold Wilson (as he then was) chose to countenance the presence in London of the rebel regime's envoy. It might have been a different matter if the IRA Provos were to declare a republic in the six countries of Ulster and try to set up an embassy in London. For that matter, Ottawa might think again if New Delhi were to recognize Canadian Indians who, historically, enjoy direct treaty relations with the British Crown, as a sovereign nation. National self-interest is no respecter of the laws of courtesy or hospitality. The deposed Shah of Iran's desperate shuttling amply demonstrated that none of the liberal democracies of the West allows compassion, gratitude or any other human consideration to impinge on hard-headed political calculation.[6]

But Khalistani activists seem free to move in and out of Britain, Canada and the USA, to lead demonstrations, disseminate sedition, assault Indian diplomats and damage Indian property. They are interviewed for radio and the Press and allowed to preen before television cameras. The resultant physical damage may not have been extensive until last weekend—if the crash was the handiwork of saboteurs, that is—but constant exposure in the media and an uninterrupted propaganda campaign have served a purpose that could be even more destructive in the long term than the loss of a Boeing and the killing of 329 innocent people. Tragically, that disaster may succeed in inducing a more serious view of Khalistani terrorism.

It is a matter of relief that the British Government has assured India that it would counter the threat posed by Sikh terrorists with "will and determination". The discussions between the Indian Foreign Secretary and his British counterpart, Sir Geoffrey Howe, also covered the growing international menace of terrorism and on ways to face this new challenge. That the Government of India thought it necessary to rush to London for talks on this issue underlined the priority New Delhi accorded to it and it is in tune with the world-wide concern over terrorism.

Terrorism has no place in a civilised society, but the fact that it has been increasing deserves to be studied in depth so as to identify the causes and sources of this menace. There is now little doubt that some countries have begun exploiting terrorism for global political purposes and for creating uncertainties in countries which are not pliable. For one reason or the other, Britain, the U.S.A. and Canada have chosen to turn a blind eye to complaints by India against the sanctuary they had been providing to certain elements from India in their countries. What is more, the disclosure that training schools exist in the US for preparing terrorists for such heinous crimes as assassinations, blowing up bridges and vital installations has shocked the world.

The U.S. too joined the world opinion in condemning terrorism and Secretary of State, George Shultz's address at East-West centre in Honolulu in July 1985 highlighted this eloquently. But U.S. Justice Department's stand that mercenary schools had liberty to operate had hardly brought glory to the concept of freedom in that country.

The only way to face this threat appears to be an intiative by the United Nations. The UN may call an international conference or take up the subject at the next General Assembly session and commit its members not to abet terrorism in any manner, covertly or overtly, or even in the name of any principle. Unless this is done, terrorism may assume much wider and more dangerous dimensions, particularly, when they are on the look-out for nuclear devices to further their ends.

India and Pakistan on December 21, 1986 agreed to formulate new ground rules covering illegal border crossing as Islamabad committed itself for the first time not to provide any support to terrorist activities against India in Punjab and elsewhere.

A joint Press note issued at the conclusion of Indian Home Secretary, C.G. Somiah's three-day visit to Pakistan reaffirmed the two country's commitment to the Simla Agreement and seek solution of the problems discussed on the basi- of good faith and mutual trust.

In India, the Central Government is in touch with the United States and Canada about various aspects of terrorist activity directed against our country.

Security agencies in the United States and Canada are on the look out for several terrorists who have escaped from India and are wanted by Government of India.

A special task force comprising best of men and officers from the para-military forces and Punjab police has been formed to combat the ever-increasing menace of terrorism in Punjab.

The decision to this effect was taken up at a high-level New Delhi on December 17, 1986.

In view of the changed climate even after persistent appeals for peace in the State, the task force now would swoop on the major headquarters of Khalistan Liberation Front and Khalistan Commando Force which had already been identified in the districts of Ferozepur, Amritsar among other places.

According to the Punjab governor, S.S. Ray, the state government was fully determined to crush terrorism and was doing everything possible to achieve this objective.[7]

Throughout history, instances of low-technology violence by the weak against the powerful have been a fact of life. In defiance of common sense, the press and politicians are increasingly playing into the hands of those desperate people who use violence to attract attention to their causes.

Virtually all "terrorist" acts violate criminal statutes. If those involved were treated as common criminals, politically motivated violence would lose much of its allure. Few people, no matter how bitter, enjoy being viewed as common criminals, but the label "international terrorist" can be worn as a badge of honour.

Those who "give in to terrorism" are those who permit terrorism to shake them and the world exalting every violent pinprick and fleabite, making each such act a focus of world attention or the excuse for unleashing the high-technology violence of the powerful against the weak, can only encourage such acts.

Compared to car accidents and wars, "international terrorism" takes a small toll. In the current climate of escalation, the need for mature perspective and restraint on the part of those who influence opinion and control missiles has rarely been greater.

In the sixties and early seventies airliner hijacking came into prominence as a means of attracting attention to political causes. Air piracy was an almost daily occurrence. Most commonly, U.S. airliners were diverted to Havana and, in Europe and West Asia commercial planes were commandered by factions of the Palestine Liberation Organisation. But when the airlines' home countries—almost all of them either West European or American—called for U.N. action, they were shouted down by Third World delegations insistent on the right of freedom fighters to use any weapon at hand to shake off oppression and colonialism.

More direct forms of "terrorism were carried out in that period" by the liberation movement. In the early seventies thousands of civilians were killed before guerrilla warfare waged by black Africans succeeded in forcing independence out of Ian Smith's white-dominated Rhodesian regime, itself seen by many as a government which ruled by terror.

The strategies offered a combat terrorism, especially hijacking and kidnapping, run along the following lines : Refusal to give any guarantee for their major demand. Satisfying their minor demands thus lowering the chances of aggression.

— Creation of conflict amongst themselves by manipulating their varying depth of involvement.
— It is possible to suggest, without jeopardising lives, that the achievement of their objectives is an impossibility then an avenue of escape may be offered in exchange for the hostages.
— It has been noticed that when a delay occurs in the negotiations, the hostages develop a common bond with the hijackers due to prolonged isolations. This situation called the Stockholm Syndrome can be successfully utilised.

These strategies and strict safety regulations are the only ways to combat terrorism. Even these can fail against a determined terrorist. Moreover there is no way of dealing with the genesis of the problem i.e. inequalities in the distribution of power. In its broadest dimensions, terrorism symbolizes outrage and frustration against this, which will exist forever.[8]

The fight against international terrorism would receive a boost if governments would co-operate more closely in arrest, prosecution or extradition of terrorists, Bhaichand Patel, Director of United Nations Information Centre stated in New Delhi.[9]

Speaking at a symposium organized by the Indian Federation of United Nations Associations at the India International Centre, New Delhi, Patel said that international terrorism could spring from misery, frustration, grievance and despair. One must try to alleviate and rectify those wrongs. As long as injustices prevail, such acts would continue.

At the same time, one must distinguish international terrorism from legitimate national liberation struggles and acts of resistance against the aggressor in occupied territories. To draw a parallel between those phenomena and international terrorism would be an affront to peoples struggling for the implementation of principles upheld by the United Nations.

"While people who were denied their fundamental right and freedoms must be assisted in regaining their rights, the use of force against innocent people is not an appropriate means for achieving this end. Aggression and occupation can be resisted without terrorism. The freedom to use inhuman means to achieve humanism must be repudiated. Loss of innocent civilian lives must always be condemned, regardless of the perpetrator, regardless of the goals".

The World over, soldiers, scribes, scholars and sleuths have tried for decades to fathom the complex chemistry of an extremists' mind. Yet no one has been able to say just what turns a perfectly normal young man into a terrorist or guerrilla, readily willing to sacrifice his life for a usually unattainable cause he does not know much about.

Terrorist attacks, including airplane hijackings, bombings and assassinations will increase by the end of the century, but a terrorist nuclear attack is not likely.

Increased resistance to terrorists may prompt terrorist groups to change tactics or become more violent.

Despite fears by some that terrorists will eventually use nuclear, chemical or biological weapons, I do not believe it likely.

A 1984 gallup poll of 1,346 people, who held key positions in U.S. Government, science and business, found that their greatest fear was of a "nuclear accident involving terrorists."

I believe the possibility of terrorists obtaining nuclear weapons has been greatly exaggerated in any event, the explosion of a nuclear weapon, or killing of large numbers of people with chemical or biological weapons, will not serve the purposes of most terrorist groups.

Terrorists want people watching their attacks so that they can achieve their political goals, but that large-scale killings will not advance a political agenda.

Certainly, in the face of a nuclear threat, the rules that now limit police authorities in most democracies would change.

They fear unleasing Government crackdowns that their groups might not survive.

In the year 2000 there can be increased bloodshed and casualties as the 21st century approaches.

If terrorism persists, and I expect it will, a new generation of terrorists will have taken the field.

Other factors also make an increase in terrorism likely.

Terrorists who have been in the field for many years have been brutalised by the long struggle killing becomes easier.

The composition of some terrorist groups has changed as the faint-hearted who have no stomach for indiscriminate killing, drop out or are shoved aside by more ruthless elements.

Terrorist may feel compelled to escalate their violence in order to keep public attention or to recover coercive power lost as Governments have become more resistant to their demands.

The Middle East, Gulf Region, South Asia and the Pacific will remain noted of terrorist activity because of the religious aspect of its conflicts.

A champion of civil liberties in the United States, Dr. Spock. once made a sweeping comment that "wherever there is terrorism, give full credit for it to the government of that country." In the present tension-filled political situation in the world, that verdict is not quite fair. National frontiers today provide no problem for international terrorists. Assassinations are done by remote control now. One country's efficiency in intelligence services alone cannot prevent such murders. The British police had once proclaimed that they had one of the best systems against such violence—an ancient weapon of creating public opinion. It is patent to everyone that weapon never discouraged the Irish Republican Army form silencing quite a few top men in the United Kingdom. The French and the Germans depend mostly on their famed ruthless efficiency. But then men of Dr. Spock's organisation are the first to kick up an uproar over such actions. Besides, De Gaulle of France had faced at least 18 assassination attempts in six years despite all such sophisticated efficiency. But then the very word terrorism has its origin in the French Revolution.

The only way then to tackle this problem of global malaise is by global strategy. The United Nations has been debating the point for quite some time, Despite some agreements on basic points, the talks got bogged down because of differences in approach by the nations on the ways to curb it, it is said. But the root cause of the UN failure was not the varied views on the methods to be adopted. The very definition of terrorism caused the rumpus. Terrorism is not confined to a few disgruntled groups like the PLO, the IRA or the Red Army of Japan. It has been the weapon of established Governments to undermine other establishments, considered unfriendly by them. What the United States is doing in Nicaragua and even El-Salvador and elsewhere is nothing but terrorism. So is the white minority régime in South Africa and Namibia or China in Kampuchea or Israel in the Arab countries. And if all these nations sit together and plan a strategy to contain global terrorism it can be termed only a cruel joke.

Terrorism is a fact and it remains a global scourge. It must be fought by the world community. But it cannot be fought by some countries assuming that they alone can define who terrorists are and what action, from the stand point of their own narrow interests, should be taken against them. Nor can those countries expect any longer to be taken seriously as leaders in the anti-terrorism campaign when it is discovered that they have been supping with the devil they have themselves publicly and repeatedly stood against.

Terrorism is a cancer that spreads. If it is not stopped it spreads through the body politic and it destroys democracies. It is not a marginal threat to democratic societies. It undermines the faith of people in the Government and in the rule of law. It is a precursor of anarchism, and anarchism is the precursor to totalitarianism.

1. B.K. Pal. Terrorism and Law. *Mainstream*, 17 May 1986 ; pp. 29-30.
2. K. Subrahmanyam. In a State of War. *Frontline* (Madras) 17 May 1986 ; p. 41.
3. B.K. Pal. *op. cit.*
4. *Ibid.*
5. Ted Morello. Terrorism and the U.N. *Tribune* 1 August 1985 ; 4.
6. Sunanda K. Dutta-Ray. Battle against terror. *Statesman* (New Delhi) 28 June 1985 ; p. 6.
7. *Times of India* (New Delhi) 22 Dec 1986.
8. Arun Rao. Cult of terrorism. *Nagpur Times* 9 January 1985 ; p. 7.
9. *UN Weekly Newsletter* (New Delhi) 37 (19) 7 June 1986 : p. 3.

CONTENTS

TERRORISM : MOTIVES AND MEANS

Terrorism is often described as mindless violence, senseless violence or irrational violence. If we put aside the actions of a few authentic lunatics, terrorism is seldom mindless or irrational. There is a theory of terrorism, and it often works. To understand the theory, it must first be understood that terrorism is a means to an end, not an end in itself. In other words, terrorism has objectives, although those who carry out acts of terrorism may be so dedicated to violent action that even they sometimes seem to miss this point.

Unless we try to think like terrorists, we are also liable to miss the point, for the objectives of terrorism are often obscured by the fact that specific terrorist attacks may appear to be random, directed against targets whose death or destruction does not appear directly to benefit the terrorist's cause. It is hard for us to understand how the killings of Olympic athletes in Munich or the hijacking of a Lufthansa airliner in Rome will ease the plight of Palestinians in the Middle East, or how blowing up an office in Manhattan will help topple a head of the State in Latin America. But the objectives of terrorism are not those of conventional combat. Terrorists do not try to take and hold ground or physically destroy their opponents' forces. Terrorists usually lack that kind of power, or having it, are constrained from applying it. We must be able to see beyond the apparent meaninglessness, sometimes even the tragic absurdity, of a single terrorist act to determine the objectives and the logic of terrorism.

While terrorists may kill by our standards sometimes wantonly, and while they may threaten a lot of people, the objective of terrorism is not mass murder. Terrorists want a lot of people watching and a lot of people listening, and not a lot of people dead. A credible threat, a demonstration of the capacity to strike, may be from the terrorists' point of view often preferable to actually carrying out the threatened deed, which may explain why, apart from the technical difficulties involved, terrorists have not done some of the terribly damaging and terrifying things they could do.

Chemical toxins and biological weapons have occasionally appeared in the schemes of political extremists, criminals and lunatics. An unconfirmed news-paper report claimed in 1970 that an undercover agent tipped off U.S. officials that members of the Weather Underground (at that time still called the Weathermen) were trying to steal germs from the bacteriological warfare center at Fort Detrick, Maryland, to contaminate a city water supply. In 1972, two boys, one a biology student, were arrested for plotting to use typhoid bacteria to poison the water supply of the city of Chicago. They claimed to be organizers of RISE, a group dedicated to creating a new master race. The two had recruited six or seven members who were to be inoculated against the disease, but two of the recruits panicked and tipped off the police. (The scheme would not have worked anyway, as routine treatment of the water with chlorine would have destroyed the bacteria). In 1973, a biologist in Germany threatened to infect water supplied with bacilli of anthrax and botulinum unless he was paid $ 8.5 million. According to another report, police searching one of the hideouts of the Symbionese Liberation Army in San Francisco found technical military manuals on germ warfare. The same group's use of cyanide bullets would seem to indicate fascination with exotic instruments of death. The socalled Alphabet Bomber of Los Angeles reportedly was in the process of making nerve gas when he was apprehended by police. Fifty-three canisters of mustard gas, which was used extensively in World War I, were stolen from a ammunition bunker in West Germany in 1975. West German authorities received threats that unless the government granted immunity to all political prisoners, the gas would be used against the population of Stuttgart, where the leaders of the Baader-Meinhof gang were about to go on trial. It is not known whether this threat was authored by the same people who took the gas. Some but not all of the canisters were later found.

In a bizarre extortion scheme, executives in various cities of the United States were mailed "tick letters" in 1976. The envelope contained ticks that, according to the accompanying letter, were deliberately infected with a "dangerous disease." Some of the ticks were smashed by postal cancelling machines ; some died of natural causes awaiting delivery. There had been earlier reports of a "germ letter" written on paper impregnated with deadly bacteria that would infect the recipient. In February 1976, police in Vienna and Berlin arrested members of a gang involved in the manufacture of nerve gas. A quantity of the toxin was seized. According to various reports, the gang was attempting to sell the gas to bank robbers or terrorists. The gang's motives were apparently purely economic. Later in 1976, U.S. postal authorities examined a suspicious small package. It was found to contain a small charge designed to explode a vial of nerve gas when the package was opened. According to press accounts, an Arab terrorist group was suspected.

Except for the tick letters, which achieved no success, none of these extortion plots was ever carried out. No one is known to have died as a result of chemical or biological warfare by terrorists. Nevertheless, the incidents provide evidence that extremists and extortionists certainly have considered using chemical and biological weapons.

The terrorists might somehow acquire nuclear weapons either by stealing them, or fabricating them by using stolen nuclear material, has become a topic of increasing public attention and concern. Even a relatively crude improvised nuclear explosive device, if successfully detonated, would have the destructive force of several hundred tons of conventional high explosives. This would exceed by a thousand times the largest explosive devices ever used by terrorists. Certain highly toxic nuclear materials also could theoretically be used against a target population in the same way that terrorists might employ chemical or biological agents.

There has been considerable debate about the difficulty (or ease) with which terrorists might acquire nuclear material of weapons grade, design, and fabricate a nuclear explosive device, or acquire and effectively disperse radio-active material. The assumption merits discussion that terrorists would see utility in causing casualties of the magnitude that nuclear weapons would product or would perceive some other peculiar advantage in going nuclear.

Nuclear material of weapons grade—highly enriched uranium and plutonium—has been available for several decades in weapons programmes and in the fuels used for nuclear-powered naval vessels and some research reactors. Nuclear power reactors use uranium of a much lower level of enrichment than would be required for a nuclear explosive device. Plutonium is a by-product of nuclear fuel burning and, when separated from the other reactor waste products, could be recycled as fuel for reactors or used to make weapons. Because of the rapid expansion of a civilian nuclear power industry throughout the world, plutonium production is rapidly increasing. A standard reactor produces

200 kilograms of plutonium annually. The current annual production of plutonium is approximately 20,000 kilograms. By 1987 the estimated annual production of plutonium worldwide may increase to around 90,000 kilograms (plus or minus 20 per cent owing to uncertainties), and by the end of the century annual production may reach 1 million kilograms. Currently plutonium is not being commercially separated from the other products in spent fuel rods in the United States, where the economics and the dangers of recycling plutonium for reactor fuel are topics of considerable debate. Reprocessing is currently being done in the United Kingdom, France, Belgium, Japan, and on a small scale, India. By the early 1980s, Sweden, West Germany, Italy, Spain, Yugoslavia, Canada, Brazil, Argentina and Taiwan may also have reprocessing capabilities.

The special roles and functions of governmental agencies, including the military, in countering and the controlling nuclear terrorism vary from country to country. The role of each agency is dependent on the laws of the particular nation, in most cases a direct result of the initial laws that established and controlled the nuclear program in that country. In some nations, the military has sole responsibility for all nuclear activities, as in Brazil ; in others, the military is secondary to the civilian sector, as in India. As a generalization, the nuclear program in all democratic countries is under the direct control of the national Government, with the commercial nuclear industry under the auspices of the civilian sector of the Government and the nuclear weapons program under the military. Thus, in discussing the role of non-military agencies, the United States resembles to a greater or lesser degree other nations with nuclear program. One Chief difference should be noted: in the United States the civilian nuclear industry makes the weapons for the military and military responsibility for them begins only with delivery. The Energy Research and Development Administration (ERDA) is charged with this responsibility and has several facilities that support military programs. Minor differences between the civilian-military division of authority and responsibility are to be noted among the nations with both military and commercial programs, with civilian agencies playing a greater role within the United States than elsewhere. By far, the United States has the largest number of civilian agencies with some nuclear-related function and responsibility.

Under the Atomic Energy Act of 1954, as amended, and the Energy Re-organization Act of 1974, the Federal Government has been given authority and responsibility to respond to nuclear incidents, either accidental or intentional. The law stresses that the response should be in coordination with State and local Governments, but clearly delineates the Federal Government as having full authority. Four departments and agencies have primary responsibility for planning and responding to nuclear terrorism : Nuclear Regulatory Commission (NRC), Federal Bureau of Investigation (FBI), ERDI and Department of Defence (DOD).

These menacing improvements in weaponry and organization have been brought about by the international availability of terrorist support, supply and training services and made possible, of course, by the relative freedom with which the terrorists can operate across the Northern Ireland border within the Irish Republic. As a result, the terrorists have unquestionably strengthened their military position in relation to the Security Forces. In this theatre, at least, barbarism is winning ground from civilization. And it is winning ground precisely because it can turn to an international infrastructure. Terrorism is not a purely national phenomenon, which can be conquered at a national level. It is an international offensive—an open and declared war against civilization itself—which can only be defeated by an international alliance of the civilized powers.

When I say that terrorism is war against civilization, I may be met by the objection that terrorists are often idealists pursuing worthy ultimate aims—national or regional independence and so forth. I do not accept this argument. I cannot agree that a terrorist can ever be an idealist, or that the objects sought can ever justify terrorism. The impact of terrorism, not merely on individual nations, but on humanity as a whole, is intrinsically evil, necessarily evil and wholly evil, and it is so for a number of demonstrable reasons.

Terrorism is the deliberate and cold-blooded exaltation of violence over other forms of public activity. The modern terrorist does not employ violence as a necessary evil, but as a desirable form of activity. There is a definite intellectual background to the present wave of terrorism.

There appears to be a continuing phenomenon with inadequate analytical tools. There is no consensus and no common language ; in fact, it may be that the very word terror is a hindrance in the investigation of violence. That investigation has been hampered by the emotive quality of those violent deeds, and a focus solely on violent deeds removed from context—the analysis of a technique—is a limited venture. One murder is much like another. Giving them numbers often is of little help ; those who inform us that out of thirty-two recent cases of kidnapping eleven ended fatally can tell us nothing of the twenty-two. Using these violent deeds as a fulcrum, however, there is much that can be done and often much that is of more than academic interest. Still, there are far more questions than answers. Who are these people ? What are their motives ? Are there valid generalizations to be made about the mind of the assassin, the profile of a sane bomber ? If the subjects remain elusive, should investigation be postponed ? How great is the threat to society ? Does the past, even the immediate past, reveal patterns of violence ? How does a democratic society respond ? How have representative Governments reacted recently and to what effect ? And for those in positions of responsibility, how best to cope ? No one has yet fashioned compelling or definitive conclusions.

Where does this take us ? The primary purpose of Government in whatever form is to provide security for its citizens. If Governments cannot protect their citizens, as terrorists seem to be demonstrating, will Governments as we know them become obsolete ? The historical growth of national Governments in the first place depended in part on national leadership, often a monarch, being able to monopolise the means of organised violence. If the military-power relationship are altered drastically in favour of small groups that obey no Government, will we enter an era of international warlordism in which the people of the world and their Governments are subjected to the extortion demands of many small groups ? Or, in the face of growing terrorism and the threat of worldwide anarchy, will Governments fall to the temptation of repression and use their still comparatively superior technical resources to become increasingly authoritarian ? Or will Governments put aside their political differences on this issue and delegate some of their jealously guarded sovereignty to an international force capable of dealing with international terrorists ? Or, will governments simply accept new concepts of warefare as redefined by terrorists, adopt their tactics to wage war against another nation, and take direct military action against enemy terrorists wherever they are ?

1. Abrahamian, M.A. : Forces *versus* terrorism. *International Herald Tribune* 6 Jan 1986 ; 4.

2. Alexander, Yonab *et al. eds.* : *Control of terrorism. International Documents.* New York, Crane, Russak, 1979.

3. Allemann, Fritz Rene : Terrorism : Definitional aspects. *Terrorism* 3 (3-4) 1980 ; 185-90.

4. Alper, Benedict S and Jerry F. Boren : *Crime* : *International agenda.* Lexington Books, 1972.

5. Anand, V.K. : Why terrorism is polemical ? *Caravan* (New Delhi) Jan (First) 1986 ; 30-32.

6. Andics, Hellmut : *Rule of Terror.* New York, 1969.

7. Ariel, Dan : *Explosion* ! Tel Aviv, Olive Books, 1972.

8. Armies of the night. *Asiaweek* 4 May 1986.

9. Attar Chand : SDI, Terrorism and NAM. *National Herald* 28 Feb 1986 ; 5.

10. Atwater, James : Time to get tough with terrorists : An interview with Brian Crozier. *Reader's Digest* Apr 1973 ; 89-93.

11. Awada, Ayman : Terrorism or resistance. *International Herald Tribune* 27 Feb 1986 ; 6.

12. Bailey, Clinton : Terrorism : The tribal disregard for human life. *International Herald Tribune* 2 Jul 1985 ; 4.

13. Bailey, Martin : Terrorism spreads. *Tribune* 15 Jul 1985 ; 4.

14. Baldwin, Oliver : *Questing beast.* London, 1932.

15. Barrett, David : Threat of terrorism in a broader concept. In *ITCR* ; 122-27.

This brings me to the second aspect of terrorism which is also inherently at odds with social democracy and that is, of course, violence. Violence not only begets immediate and, in the case of terrorists, indiscriminate cruelty, it also fosters the most undesirable and reactionary attitudes in society.

Such was the case almost a decade ago when Canada abruptly underwent a set of terrorist kidnappings. The attitude of the Government of the time was a reference point in modern Canadian history. Members of the New Democratic Party argued that the police had the powers under the criminal code to capture the terrorists. Despite this argument, the government proclaimed the War Measures Act. The police were able to arrest without charge and civil liberties were suspended right across the country. Eventually, discovery of the two groups involved occurred, but it should be noted it occurred through normal police work and it was not the result of any capricious arrests or searches carried out under the authority of the War Measures Act. Five years later, the Conservative Leader of the Opposition, Mr. Robert Stanfield, joined the growing number of Canadians who in sober reflection realized that the proclamation of the War Measures Act, in response to the 1970 terrorism, was wrong.

In mentioning the above example of Canadian political experience, I want to note the full dimension of the threat posed by terrorism to democratic societies. On the one hand, I see the real terror of those who take the law into their own hands. I see the justification for the full weight of the law failing on these individuals who flaunt the authority of the State for their own terrorist ends. On the other hand, Governments must make sure that the cure is never worse than the disease. The scar on Canada's record of civil liberties which occurred ten years ago is a classic illustration of, how the State, in an attempt to combat terrorism, overstepped its boundaries and actually threatened its own citizens. Democratic Governments cannot legitimately establish consent by the use of force.

Finally, it follows from this point of view that it is misleading to talk of terrorism as a "threat to civilization"—except in the sense that all violence, including war and state violence, is incompatible with a truly social and civilized condition. It is incorrect to equate the continuing existence of particular States, which may be democratic in name only, with the survival of a society.

The noted historian, Hannah Arendt. has pointed out a connection between terrorist violence and protest against tbe anonymous character of modern society. She was attempting to explain whatever it is—a tension of industrialization perhaps that seems to be the inevitable result of man purchasing his goods and services rather than producing them himself. I suspect this terrorism is more widespread than the public manifestations that the media report. It includes, for example, those members of society who "self destruct". Like other forms of terrorism it has its innocent victims, in this case, the battered spouses and children of those whose anger and frustration with the meaninglessness of their lives spill over into domestic conflict.

16. Bassiouni, M. Cherif : Criminological policy. In *LAIT*; 523-34.

Treaties, customary practice, and the national laws of States establish the bases for international cooperation in the prevention and suppression of criminality. The maxim commonly referred to in this context is aut dedere, aut judicare. The duty of States to cooperate is restricted to the submission of the alleged offender to extradition or prosecution. Consequently, that duty is an extension of the State's criminological policy of prevention and control of violence because a State's failure to carry out such a duty can only frustrate the effectiveness of any domestic crime control scheme. The effectiveness of the international duty to prosecute becomes a significant factor in assessing the effectiveness of the domestic preventive and enforcement scheme. It should be observed, however, that the principal impediment to this international duty of extradition is the "political-offense exception."

Not all acts of violence, even those that inspire "terror" or those that are committed against an internationally protected target or person or other innocent persons, are done with a view to achieving a power outcome. Indeed, such acts may be committed as a "last resort," by reason of "necessity," or "self-defence". These cases arise whenever the actor's fundamental human rights to personal freedom and safety, or those of such other persons whom he feels morally obligated to protect are the object of serious and repeated repression that by "reasonable standards" can be averted only through the commission of such a violation. Such a person is an ideologically motivated offender who could easily satisfy the definition of a "terrorist". Thus persons who commit acts of violence against others only as a means of safeguarding themselves or others for humanitarian or political reasons violate positive law, but they may have a claim to a defence of "necessity" or to a mitigation of punishment. This is the classic reason that states advance for the preservation of the political-offense exception in extradition, i.e., in order that States may provide persons who fall into this category of offender with humanitarian or political asylum. Thus States refuse to limit their prerogative of denying extradition whenever they deem that the political or humanitarian "necessity" was overriding in the actor's motivation for committing the criminal act.

It is essentially in recognition of this consideration, which is both humanitarian and political, that the duty to extradite in international criminal law is an alternative to the duty to prosecute. However, the trial of an ideologically motivated offender by a sympathizing tribunal could result in exonerating the accused or imposing a slight sentence or a conditi onal sentence. In these cases the trial and the criminal sanction are not int nded to be a deterrent to such a person or otheis but merely to be a fo mality designed to appease another State or world public opinion. As suc , it is designed, at best, to justify the denial of extradition and to provide the state in which the violation took place and whose request for extradition has been denied with some face-saving device.

All States presently exclude the category of political offender from the scope of their criminological policy and some States expand the definition beyond that description. Clearly, the problem is one of definition : What constitutes a "political offense" and under what conditions a person can claim a defence of "necessity" that would result in the denial of extradition, or in the case of a trial, exonerate him from criminal responsibility, or be considered a factor in the mitigation of punishment ? In the absence of an absolute duty to extradite or prosecute, and in the absence of a clear policy on the defence of "necessity" in exoneration of responsibility, or in the mitigation of punishment, the effectiveness of any national criminological policy is bound to be diminished. In fact, the reduction of the effectiveness of a domestic control scheme will usually be commensurate with the opportunities for freedom of movement from that State to others. It must be concluded, therefore, that the weaknesses of any domestic scheme for the control of violence are compounded by the opportunity of evading that scheme altogether by resorting to safe havens or to countries from which the likelihood of extradition is remote or where the prospects of a trial and serious punishment are limited.

Thus to the endemic problems of the ineffectiveness of the criminal sanction in the domestic process of the prevention and control of violence, we must add those of any international control scheme. The combination of both further weakens the policy of prevention and control of any legal system and may extend to other types and categories of criminal violation. Indeed, the destruction of the credibility of the criminal sanction is pervasive and all-encompassing, and the consequences that derive from the ineffectiveness of the criminal sanction in the control of "terror-violence" are likely to affect other aspects of the criminal control of social deviance.

17. Bassioumi, M. Cerif ed : *International terrorism and political crimes*. Springfield, Illinois, 1975.

18. Begin, Menachem : Freedom fighters and terrorists. In *ITCR*; 39-46.

What is the difference between a fight for freedom or liberation on the one hand and terrorism on the other ? For the answer to this question, one should apply two criteria : the aim and the methods.

Fights for liberation have taken place throughout the centuries from ancient times to our own days. There are historians who maintain that the most justified fight in the annals of mankind was that of Spartacus. That revolt took place in ancient Rome and ended when Crassus crushed it by raising a sea of crosses on which the rebels were slowly extinguished. It was justified because it was a fight not merely for political independence, but also for physical liberation in the literal sense of the world, a fight for breaking the shackles of the slaves and gladiators.

There is, however, a third kind of fight—a fight for physical survival. That was the fight we, the Jews, conducted :

> "I kept this letter for many years but, unfortunately", so writes Dr. Crawford, "after the death of my wife in 1970 and my own severe illness in 1971, I sold my house and went into a flat. And because of limited space I unwisely threw away a lot of my accumulated papers and correspondence. So the letter is no longer available. And Brigadier Sheridan has long since died. I hope these facts will be of some help to you.
>
> Many of my friends knew the story at the time. But few have survived. My sister-in-law will remember it clearly, as she was freindly with the Brigadier. She lived with us at that time. If you think it worthwhile I could contact her". Lord Janner finished his speech saying, "I did ask him to contact her and she worte a letter confirming what Dr. Crawford said."

Ladies and gentlemen, from my teacher Jabotinsky I learned the famous slogan of Thomas Masaryk, "Truth prevails and must win."

Since 1946 the debate went on. And now you have this letter proving that the officers got the warning. Unfortunately, tragically, they didn't heed it. But we gave that warning for half an hour because this is the difference between a fighter for freedom and a terrorist. A terrorist kills civilians. Fighter for freedom saves lives and fights on at the risk of his own life until liberty wins the day.

19. Bell, J. Bowyer : Revolutionary organisations : Special cases and imperfect models, In *ITWS*; 78-92.

The temptation in the academic analysis of revolutionary organisations for many at least is to construct elegant cross-national models generalisations for all seasons and most campaigns. In a sense, this tendency is little different from that of guerrilla analysis where the rebels assume that the rules of revolution and the laws of all national liberation struggles are universally applicable; what worked for Mao in China or Castro in Cuba should so work in Quebec or South Africa. The academician need only fear learned dissent with the prospect of fashioning a new and more elegant model, while the guerrilla, on the other hand, may have to pay a higher price for his conviction about the universality of revolutionary forms. In any case, a certain circumspection might be wise in proposing generalisations of all-inclusive schemata, and stages of development. In point of fact, there appear to be a whole spectrum of revolutionary organisations, employing various strategies and tactical mixes selected for varying reasons. These movements are limited or emboldened by varying traditions, differing cultural heritages, and special historical conditions.

Certainly these revolutionary organisations, like any set of organisations—parliaments, formal armies, trade unions—share certain common characteristics. After all, the overriding purpose in ever revolutionary case is to seize power by violent means. Nevertheless, each has been shaped by very special conditions. Few are classical models even when the leadership strives to copy an ideal and admired model—for example, Guevara constructing his foco a la Castro in the Bolivian bush. It might thus be a worthwhile exercise to examine in some detail three revolutionary movements—there are of course, no terrorist organisations which is the nomenclature of threatend authority. Each is a very special case. All however, do share common characteristics.

The struggle for an Irish Ireland, free and Gaelic, at times to observers seems to have continued for centuries : arisen at some distant point in the Celtic twillight. Certainly, the present guerrilla campaign in Northern Ireland traces its origin to the Republican ideals of Wolfe Tone and the Rising of 1798. In one form or another since that time, Irish Republicans have been engaged in fashioning strategies of physical force to break the connection with England that Tone called the never-failing source of all Ireland's ills, and again as Tone advocated, unite Catholic, Protestant, and Dissenter in the common name of Irishman. And with one notable exception they have largely been frustrated by the Power of Britain, by their own incompetence, by bad luck or perhaps at times by Celtic malice.

Despite French aid, the Rising of 1798 failed and began the long litany of Irish debacles. In 1803 a hapless plot aborted, in 1848 the Young Irishmen did no better. Later in the century, the Irish Republican Brotherhood and the Fenian assassins proved no more effective. Officials were assassinated, bombs detonated but the Republic came no closer. By the end of the century, the Irish rebels had tried most revolutionary means, even an invasion of Canada from American soil, a most elegant example of transnational revolution. Simultaneous with the plots and plans of the men of physical force, others, at times in isolation, at times in a conscious mix, had been applying other strategies : parliamentary agitation; boycotts; intimidation and extortion; monster meetings; and civil disobedience. And by the end of the century, much had been won—the land question largely solved, the Catholic Church recognised, the habits of parliamentary democracy instilled and the opportunities offered by the British Empire available to all. There seemed no place in the new Ireland for the old, pure Republicans, the assassins and bombers of the past, who still clung to the dream of an ideal Republic.

In 1916 a small band of hard-core Republicans, directed by the Irish Republican Brotherhood, hopeful of German aid, and supported by the tiny Irish Citizen's Army—a militia created by the Labour leader James Connolly—rose in revolt. This Easter Rising of 1916, limited almost entirely to Dublin as a result of bad luck, the collapse of the German connection, and poor planning, was regarded by most Irishmen of the time as a mad act of mad men, a futile gesture, that razed the centre of the city for no good purpose. On their way to prison, the Irish Volunteers—the Irish Republican Army (IRA)—were hooted by the crowds. Yet the swift British repression—the immediate execution of the leaders of the Rising—transformed Irish opinion and created a base of popular support that would permit a less spectacular but more effective revolt within two years. Between 1918 and 1921, the reorganised IRA waged what was to become the archetypal national liberation struggle. There were assassins in the cities, guerrilla columns in the hills.

20. Bell, J. Bowyer : Terror : An overview. In *ITCW*; 36-43.

Those who want to create a composite statistical account of the revolutionary, for instance, an IRAS volunteer, can marshall the record of the captured, the failed or foiled, but not of the covert activists. And those who want not to count but to talk must recognize that the specimens they see in the zoo are not those of the wild. Finally, there has been a tendency to shape generalizations about selected terrorists across cultural boundaries, assuming that Arabs and Germans and Irish if they perform certain acts then share certain characteristics. In some cases this may be true—youth and dedication and daring—but not very revealing; however, to find meaningful links, for example, between a middle-aged Belfast bookie, a medical graduate of the American University in Beirut, a retired Greek colonel, and a Latin American priest, is a task not lightly to be undertaken and not likely to be productive given the available data.

Another difficulty with the analysis of terrorism is that for many it has proven difficult to be disinterested. In fact, a number have begun at the end, with prescription, rather than at the beginning. At present those concerned, whatever their politics and tools of analysis, mostly clump about two general postures. At one extreme are those who feel that most terrorists are warped, their politics pathological and consequently unamenable to accommodation. Since their demands are essentially non-negotiable—what did Oswald want that could be given?—the appropriate response is placed on coercion, protection and punishment. Order is to be defended by stringent law, cunning safeguards and expanded security forces. Some sketch out as well a great conspiracy, seated in Havana or Moscow, to manipulate these rebels without a cause for a very real Communist cause. This threat, too, must be met by appropriate force, a swift and measured defence of Western society. Those who would sympathize with the mythical Guevara are dupes or innocents. Others less interested in international conspiracies or the pathology of the rebel mind insist, too, that swift, effective coercive force, is essential to protect democratic society. Ineffectual or uncertain Governments in Italy after World War I, in Germany during the depression, in Uruguay more recently, failed to keep their houses in order and democracy died. Tough-minded professors insist on the death penalty, on no deals with hostage-holders, on no talks with terrorists.

At the other pole are those who concentrate on the reasoned demands of the revolutionaries, who believe that in many cases accommodations or at least a dialogue is possible. They stress the reasons behind the massacres, the roots of violence, and the remedies to case real frustration. They put less stress on maintaining order by coercive law and more on the necessity for justice. Where law is stressed the focus is on international aggreements and compacts, on United Nations resolutions, on consensus building, on the end of sanctuary rather than on punishment. While there thus tends to be a left-right, liberal-conservative dimension to the two poles, this is not always the case. What is the case ? What does remain true is that the posture of the investigator quite often determines the result of his or her analysis.

Consequently, there has at times been more interest in accumulating sympathetic "evidence" or defining the nature of terrorism, so as to buttress long-held positions, than in value-free investigation. Those who oppose nuclear power are criticized for wishful thinking when they fashion doomladen terrorist scenarios and defend themselves by stressing the inadequacy of present safeguards. The hypothetical "terrorist" is dragged back and forth in this argument, first bogie and then strawman. All the special pleading makes it remarkably difficult for the responsible to sift out some useful reality. Even the predictions of future prospects vary immensely.

With all of this, there have been certain comforting developments. Much more useful information is available concerning the pathological end of the terrorist spectrum. A variety of techniques and tactics is evolving in preventive profiles, in hostage-bargaining, in various safeguards. More important, an increasingly informed debate is under way on various aspects of such violence : the appropriate response of the press and media, the scope and effectiveness of legal remedies, the actuality of the revolutionary threat to open societies. Yet there clearly continues to be a need for sophisticated interest in various quarters in discovering more rigorous answers, more effective approaches, a greater consensus.

21. Bell, J. Bowyer : Terrorism : Some observations. *Terrorism* 3 (3-4) 1980; 201-2.

22. Bell, J. Bowyer : *Time for terror*. New York, Basic Books, 1978.

23. Beloff, Max : Terrorism and the people. In *TYT*; 109-27.

24. Betts, Richard K and S.P. Huntington. : Dead dictators and rioting mobs : Does the demise of authoritarian rulers lead to political instability? *International Security* 10(3) Win 1985-86; 112-46.

25. Bion, W.R. : *Experience in groups*. London, 1961.

26. Birendranath, Dewan : Holy war against terrorists. *Madhya Pradesh Chronicle* 2 Feb 1986; 4.

27. Bite, Vita : *International terrorism*. Washington, Library of Congress. Congressional Research Service, 31 Oct 1975.

28. Blum, Yehuda Z. : State response to see acts of terrorism. *German Year book of International Law* 19, 1976; 223-37.

29. Blumenfeld, Eric : "No" to terrorism in any guise. In *ITCR*; 318-24.

30. Bouthoul, Gaston : Definitions of terror. In *ITWS*; 50-59.

All manifestations of conflict, inflexible demands, and ideological hatreds between rival groups, have a tendency to culminate in forms of collective violence. In general, such violence, which is intermittent, is produced by two basic motives. The first arises from the love of power, shown in what Machiavelli called 'wars of domination'. Each hostile group, brought into conflict with the other, tries by force to impose its will on the other, or to subject it to its own physical supremacy. The second basic set of motives for violent action falls under the general category of genocide which may be either the physical destruction of the adversary or that annihilation of his social identity which has become known as 'ethnocide'.

As far as collective psychology is concerned, the result of such conflicts is to make fear predominate over every other one of the weaker adversary's other sentiments : he will then resign himself to submitting to the will of his conqueror from fear of still greater evils.

Terror, culminating in the threat of death, is the ultima ratio of every socio-political and hiterarchical organisation. Terror sanctions that authority whose ultimate expression is : 'obey or you will die'. The conception of territory, so vital amongst animals as among the most primitive of tribes, is founded upon the same underlying threat. By definition, a frontier is a line which must not be crossed, unless authorised, without danger to life. Actual examples are the Berlin Wall and other contemporary frontiers marked by minefields, barbed wire, and defended by armed guards.

The first feeling of the newly born is one of the fear which is the basis of every hierarchy and manifestation of force, the function of this hierarchy being ambivalent. On the one hand, it has a protective function against threats from without and from within : this is its role of reassurance. On the other hand, the authority it wields is founded on penalties and punishments. These two aspects of hierarchy are contradictory and complementary; both act on the instinct of self-preservation which they reassure and disturb at the same time.

Terror underlines every armed conflict and every manifestation of violence. Invariably the aim is to subdue or paralyse the enemy by fear.

It s not, however, in man's nature to confuse terrorism and war. The battles of Cannae and Zama, of Austerlitz and Waterloo, were not acts of terrorism nor were the battles of Lepanto or Trafalgar acts of piracy. Terrorism differs equally from the brief, violent actions which are intended to seize power by surprise, such a conspiracies, palace revolutions, coups d'etat and putsches. These seek to surprise, but not to terrorise systematically.

Neither is guerrilla warfare necessarily terrorist action, but rather a way of conducting hostilities in certain circumstances. It is, in the last analysis, a particular form of military tactic characterised by the dispersals of forces, mobility, sudden strikes and what we today call commando action. Guerrilla tactics consist of refusing to be committed to large scale engagements. Often it is delaying strategy, awaiting propitious political and military circumstances. These were the methods of the famous Fabius Cunctator in the Second Punic War.

All these forms of violence have one common trait, namely that they are confrontations, on a small or large scale, and seen as such by both sides. Each side recognises the other as its enemy and declares this openly In this formal, almost gentlemanly, warfare, violence is practised between uniformed and recognisable combatants but does not involve enemy civilians. The last war to conform to these conventions was that of 1914. Since then, the new techniques of war, aerial bombardment of towns and later, the permanent targeting of nuclear weapons on great centres of population, seems superficially to resemble terrorism. Nonetheless, a distinction from some forms of terrorism remains in that targets are invariably the cities of the enemy.

Characteristics of Terrorism

Certain specific qualities of terrorism thus begin to appear. They are :

(i) Its clandestine nature : terrorist actions are the work of small and very secret groups. Even whilst collaborating, they are often ignorant of each other's identity for fear of treason and betrayal.

(ii) Terrorist action is not a battle : terrorists do not restrict themselves to attacks upon an overt enemy, but also strike at the innocent in order to create fear and insecurity. Today the availability of explosives permits murder and destruction at all times and in all places; booby-trapped vehicles, time-bombs, letter-bombs, plastic bombs and so on.

(iii) Terrorism attempts to act in secrecy : the anonymous, unidentifiable threat creates huge anxiety and the terrorist tries to spread fear by contagion, to immobilise and subjugate those living under this threat. At the same time, secrecy and anonymity stren then the terrorist's pride in his impunity, producing a paranoic emotion of infinite power. He feels himself the possessor of supreme authority, the right to give life or death, the symbol of absolute power. There are, however, ambivalent tendencies in the psychology of the terrorist. Although at one and the same time, he feels himself to be judge and martyr, added to this is a sporting factor : it seems at times as though he is involved in an exciting and dangerous game. In the chase, he feels himself to be not only the hunted but also the powerful hunter. Included also in this game with death—the death of others as well as his own—is a kind of necrophilia, which is akin to that of the sect of Thugs, the worshippers of the Gooddess Kali. The deaths of nearly a million victims during the nineteenth century have been attributed to this cult.

(iv) Extreme terrorism exhibits two other traits : the first is psychological : it is a tendency towards obsession, single-minded fanaticism, the logic of paranoia taken to its ultimate. The greatest atrocities are ennobled in the eyes of their perpetrators by an ideological justification which overrides the suffering of the victims and the mourning of the bereaved. Such acts are for the perpetrator an emotional release and, at the same time, a thrilling expression of his personality. The second trait may often be the manitestation of an Adlerian compensation complex, created by deeply resented frustrations and humiliations.

(v) Terrorism is much influenced by intellectual and doctrinal fashions. In examining its motivations, one discovers the changing ranks of ideological values. One after another, ideological trends unless a series of terrorist outrages whose justification is based, according to current thinking, on patrotism, nationalism, racism, cultural intolerance, religious fanaticism and political dogma. At the same time, it often presents itself as a form of propaganda action, aiming to promote a certain doctrine or set of demands, using the modern techniques of publicity. Thus Basque terrorists, Irish extremists and other contemporary movements justify outrages in order to draw attention to their cause.

(vi) There is also noticeable in terrorism an element of imitation in the techniques employed. For example, there were the many assassination attempts on heads of State during the nineteenth century, outrages by single terrorists at point blank ranges. Then came the fashion for bombs flung at processions. Today, after aircraft hijacking, there is a tendency to turn to massacres of crowds, such as that of Fiumicino (with forty-six dead), or at the Tower of London, or the murder of hostages at Maalot. A spectacular action, especially if the perpetrators escape with impunity, will in general inspire a series of imitators.

(vii) Among terrorists there is the power of suggestion : there are for example, solitary men who are controlled by and idee fixe. This is often the case with regicides such as Ravaillac and Damien, or assassins such as those of King Umberto or President Kennedy.

When terrorism involves groups, romanticism pedominates, its variety reflecting the character of the struggle, hatred or fervour, a territorial demand or love of a cause. Such romanticism and the idee fixe are sustained by constant repetition, propaganda and autotics. That of the Grand Master of the Sect of Assassins (also known as 'the Old Man of the Mountain) is one. In the eleventh century, he succeeded in creating a body of trained men, the 'faithful', ready to carry out, even at the risk of their own lives, the crimes he commanded them to commit. Some of them, cultured and distinguished, were successful in gaining entry to princely courts, living there for years, until the day when they would murder their host or one of his ministers to serve the policy of their Grand Master. It is related that when caught and tortured, before dying, they would denounce as their accomplices the leading men of the court who were opponents of the Sect. By means of these tactics, 'the Old Man of the Mountain' was able to dominate by terror the sovereigns of all the Near East and to impose his policies upon them. This enormous power has been attributed to the fact that he not only indoctrinated the 'faithful', but added to this the use of hashish, which has given rise to the word assassin, to give them a glimpse to paradise.

Certain recent crimes committed by those under the influence of drugs have shown how they favour the forms of suggestion mentioned above. The 'family directed by Charles Manson is a notable case : the addicts, under the influence of the 'Master' murdered a film star and six of her guests in California.

A power of suggestion just as effective is found among some of the most notable figures to have used terrorism, such as Hitler and other dictators of the twentieth century. Having flourished in Europe, this type of leader is now to be found in other continents, reviving the ancient traditions of despotism.

31. Breaking the chain of terror. *International Herald Tribune* 6 Jan 1986 ; 4.

32. Brosio, Manlio : Fighting terror within the international frame work. In *ITCR* ; 313-17.

33. Bryers, Gisele : Terrorism : Let's be fair. *International Herald Tribune* 20 May 1986 ; 7.

34. Buckley, William F. : Dance of the terrorists. *National Review* 26, 1974.

35. Bukovsky, Vladimir : Course of complicity. In *ITCR* ; 350—58.

36. Buruham, James : Notes on terrorism. *National Review* 24, 13 Oct 1972.

37. Camus, Albert : *Neither victims nor executioners.* Chicago, World Without War, 1968.

38. Caradon, Lord : International law and international terrorism. In *TYT* ; 147-69.

39. Chakravarty, Nickhil : What does terrorism mean ? *Times of India* Sunday Review 4 May 1986 ; IV.

40. Chakravarti, Robi : What's terrorism ? It depends ? *Amrita Bazar Patrika* 30 Apr 1986 ; 6.

41. Chalfont, Lord : Overcoming the climate of appeasement. In *ITCR* ; 79-89.

42. Chandulal, Sadajiwatlal : Rooting out terrorism. *Tribune* 24 Sep 1985 ; 4.

43. Charles, K.J. : Terrorism : An instrument of oppression. *Patriot* 11 Jun 1986 ; 4.

Terrorism is a common-place of the contemporary world scene. Apart from the Middle East and Sri Lanka, we hear of "fraction of the Red Army" in West Germany and of the "Japanese Red Army".

Terrorist activities lead to much loss of innocent lives and therefore deserve to be condemned. But that should neither prevent us from appreciating the noble causes that have often inspired ; these movements nor blind us to the frequently far more barbaric acts of violence of established Governments to which terrorism is often the response of oppressed groups. The Governments of Israel, South Africa and Sri Lanka have persistently refused to recognise the legitimate aspirations of oppressed peoples in territories under their jurisdiction. Terrorism is often the last desperate resort of persecuted groups who found every door of democratic representation slammed shut on their faces.

44. Choudhuri, S.R. : Torture as state policy. *Deccan Chronicle* 8 Oct 1985 ; 6.

45. Clifford, W. : Terrorism and overkill. *Terrorism* 5 (3) 1981 ; 281—286.

46. Cline, Ray S. : Strategic framework. In *ITCR* ; 90—100.

It is high time for the scholars and statesmen, who live in nations that have some right to call themselves free, to come to grips with the brute fact of the widespread adoption of calculated terrorism as a preferred instrument of policy by a finite, known number of modern states. The truth is that the use of physical and psychological force, involving intimidation, political coercion, assassination, and the wanton destruction of property, has become part of the arsenal of geopolitics and will be an important ingredient of international conflict in the 1980's. Terrorism is one of the weapons with which States organized on the principle that political power grows from the barrel of a gun attack on their enemies. Open societies built on the moral imperative of preserving the political and economic freedoms of individuals citizens are the main target.

Time is not on our side ! Terrorism is a part of a larger war ! We, the open societies, are the target ! It is later than we think ! In terms of geopolitical conflict we are approaching what may well come to be known as the fateful eighties.

The inhumanity of man to man since time immemorial and, especially, in recent years, the flood of TV images of brutality and suffering into our very living rooms, have tended to deaden our sensitivities to the home truth that terrorism today is more than an intrinsic, inescapable consequence of the flawed character of mankind—that it is instead a form of low intensity warfare.

Terrorism is intended by those who finance it, arm it and ideologically inspire it, to weaken and ultimately dissolve the fabric of civilized behaviour in open and pluralistic societies. Open and pluralistic societies, by my definition, are those in which Government provides guarantees for minorities to live with mutual respect for cultural and ethnic differences and wherein, by one political process or another, the making of important decisions reflects the views of an informed electorate. Let us make no mistake about it. These open societies for all their superior qualities of life are in a minority—only 20 per cent—in the world and they are under attack. One of the most insidious forms of attacks is the calculated use of terrorism by some States to undermine social order in others—and the others are ours ! I mean not only our host country, Israel, which lives daily under terrorist threats, but also the United Kingdom, Italy, Germany, and the United States. If the Conference brings this fact to the forefront of political consciousness, it will succeed.

47. Clutterbuck, Richard : *Living with terrorism*. London, Feb 1975.

48. Clutterbuck, Richard : Terrorism. In *TYT*; 56-75.

49. Coleman, Diane : Handling a touchy situation. *Emergency Product News* 8 (1) 1976; 36.

50. Colhando, Ken : Countering terrorism. *Hindustan Times* 23 Oct 1985; 9.

51. Copeland, Miles : Strategy of terrorism. *International Herald Tribune* 17 Jun 1986; 9.

52. Council of Europe : Legal Affairs : ECCP document (Working Paper). *Recent international measures of international terrorism*. June 1977 (unpublished).

53. Crayton, John W. : Terrorism and the psychology of the self. In *POT* ; 33-44.

54. Crenshaw, Martha. ed. *Terrorism, legitimacy and power*. Wesleyan University Press, 1983. p. 228.

55. Crosby, John : *Affair of strangers*. New York, Stein & Day, 1975.

56. Cross, James Eliot : *Conflict in the shadows*. New York, Doubleday, 1963,

57. Crozier, Brian : *Rebels : A study of post-war insurrections*. London, 1960.

58. Curbing terrorism. *Hindustan Times*. 26 Mar 1986 ; 9.

Despite some differences between India and the United States the two countries share a common view on the need to exterminate terrorism After some hesitation and prevarication on dealing with 'Khalistani' Sikhs resident in the US, the American Government seems to have finally been convinced that they are out to destablise India by funding and carrying out terrorist activities both in India and abroad. The FBI's arrest of Gurpartab Singh Birk, and his subsequent trial in New York on a charge of plotting to assassinate Prime Minister Rajiv Gandhi during a visit to the States, is an earnest of the US Administration's intent to deal firmly with such people. The Birk case must have also helped unveil the ugly face of the Khalistan movement.

One of the factors that was encouraging these extremists was their feeling that they could get asylum abroad. India was finding it difficult to get them extradition treaty because of the many loopholes in it. Thus the US Attorney-General's disclosure is that a group of lawyers of the two countries is to be constituted to plug these loopholes is to be welcomed. Edwin Meese III also told newsmen in Delhi that the US had already changed the regulations to prevent foreign nationals or potential terrorists from getting training in 'terrorist' schools. It would also investigate persons suspected of involvement in such activities and simultaneously tighten the laws to check the entry of suspected terrorists.

Thus it seems that India's long campaign to get foreign countries, especially the US, Canada and Britain, to take action against such bad elements is at last starting to bear fruit. It is hoped that the British Foreign Secretary, Sir Geoffrey Howe, will be as accommodating during his scheduled visit to India. High on the agenda is discussion on a draft extradition treaty that India wants to have with Britain and the measures needed to curb the virtual reign of terror by Sikh extremists in Britain against moderate Sikhs and other resident Indians.

59. Current trends in terrorism. *Terrorism* 7 (1) 1984; 81-85.

60. Davies, Donald M.: Terrorism : Motives and means. *Foreign Service Journal* Sep 1962 ; 19-21.

61. Davies, James C. ed. : *Men revolt and why*. New York, Free Press, 1971.

62. Davis, Lillian : Tolerance of ambiquity in international bargaining. In *ITWS*; 314-24.

63. Demaris, Ovid : *Brothers in blood* : *the international terrorist network.* New York 1977.

64. Dinstein, Yoram : Comments on the Fourth Interim Report of the ILA Committee on International Terrorism (1982). *Terrorism* 7 (2) 1984; 163-68.

65. *Disorders and terrorism* : *Report of the task force on disorders and terrorism.* Washington, National Advisory Committee on Criminal Justice Standards and Goals, 1976. See also *Terrorism* 2 (1-2) 1979; 139-47.

66. Dowling, Joseph A. : Prolegomina to a psychohistorical study of terrorism. In *ITCW*; 223-30.

To a definition of terrorism it seems highly desirable that some agreement be established as to what is meant by the term. It appears to include practically any type of violence involving some interference with the general functioning of society. It does not seem to include giant fights, muggings, and other such violent personal acts. For my purposes I intend to dismiss individual seizures of aeroplanes and other such non-political actions, even including ritualistic murder, although an analysis of these very well might be revealing in terms of psychobiographies and as revelations of societal disintegration. My concern will be with terror as both a political philosophy and a mode of political action. Or as Roland Gaucher put it, "Terrorism is—or seeks to be a—strategy". Thus, before developing a psychohistorical framework some historical comment is necessary.

Terrorism developed within the anarchist element of the nineteenth century revolutionary movement. The first great disciple of "propaganda by the deed" was the Russian Michael Bakunin, although it is entirely possible that the core of the terrorist argument was supplied by his strange and sinister young friend Nechaev. Together these men produced a most fascinating revolutionary document—The Revolutionary Catechism—from the publication of which, in 1869, historians date the emergence of philosophically based terrorism. Bakunin's famous comment, "Let us put our trust in the eternally creative source of life. The urge to destroy is also a creative urge", could in fact serve as the leitmotif of this discussion. Through Bakunin's personality and involvement in the revolutionary strugles of his time, the idea of terror as a political weapon passed into the revolutionary mentality of Europe and has been gradually developed and refined in other parts of the world. It is not my intention to try to encompass all of these movements but to start with Bakunin in order to establish a typology. Obviously a good deal of Bakunin's thought is tied to the romanticism of his era. The glorification of brigands as the only true revolutionaries, the posing as the man who has "no emotions...one science that of destruction", freed from all bourgeois sentimentality, all makes the romantic's belief in his power to re-create the world. In Faust, Goethe revealed both the romantic desire to re-create order and his emphasis on the deed.

One could argue that the turmoil in traditional patterns of European society which reached catastrophic levels with the French Revolution and the Napoleonic Wars forced men to seek personal and social shelter from their existential dilemma in movements ranging from de Maistre's reactionary Catholicism, through liberal nationalist revolts, to calls for the complete destruction, in Bakunin's words, of "this effect social world which has become impotent and sterile...We must first purify our atmosphere and transform completely the milieu in which we live; for it corrupts our instincts and our wills and contracts our heart and intelligence. The social question takes the form primarily of the overthrow of society" Bakunin resisted Marx and communism as "the negation of liberty and I can conceive of nothing human without liberty. This libertarian rejection of Marxism and the continued glorification of the heroic deed of terror lingered on in Italy and particularly Spain where the Spanish Civil War gave sad testament to this fatal split on the Left.

Anarchism and terrorism tended to fade away in northwest Europe after the failure of the Paris Commune, but in Italy and Spain endemic agrarian distress, reinforced by the impact of the new industrial processes on an old artisan class, carried on the belief in insurrection and acts of terrorism. That this connection with "romanticism" continued is testified to by E.J. Hobsbawm who recounts his attempt to get in touch with the anarchists in the 1950s : "when I tried to make contact...I was given a rendezvous at a cafe in Montmartre, by the Place Blanche, and somehow this reminder of a long-lost era of bohemians, rebels and avant-garde seemed only too characteristic.

To the anarchist as terrorist the act itself was to bring society down by actions which destroyed symbols of the oppressive state. This belief in propaganda by the deed not only provided for the removal of an oppressive individual or institution, but would, it was hoped, begin the unraveling of society. Here, and later in George Sorel, there is a contempt for the intellectual, for the organized, and for the elite. Bakunin and Sorel both believed that the proletariat would be educated in violence not in lectures and speeches and that violence itself was purifying. That this strikes many as irrational is of course exactly the point.

Terrorism is not simply the act of a demented few, but represents a deeper endemic impulse against repression in its most fundamental sense. Terrorism increases among political activists, as well as among psychopaths in direct ratio to control and rationalization in modern technetronic society and the seeming failure of other paths of revolutionary activity (that is, the failure of "socialism" in the Soviet Union). To the New Left of recent memory the hero was the urban guerrilla with such violence-glorifying slogans as "in order to get rid of the gun it is necessary to take up the gun". To which Andrew Kopkind added that morality came from the muzzle of gun.

67. Dugard, John : International terrorism : Problems of definitions. *International Affairs* (U.K.) 50 (1) Jan 1974; 67-81.

68. Dugard, John : International terrorism and the just war. *Stanford Journal of International Studies* 12, Apr 1977 ; 21-38.

69. Dugard, John : Toward the definition of international terrorism *Proceedings, American Society of International Law* 67, 1973.

70. Eggers, William : Terrorism : The slaughter of innocents. *California, Sage*, 1971.

71. Ellivtt, John. D. and L.D. Gibson : Contemporary Terrorism. Gaitherburg, MD : *International Association of Chiefs of Police*, 1978.

72. Billiott, John. D : Primers on terrorism. *Military Review* Oct 1976.

73. Ending global murder. *Times of India* 7 Jan 1986; 8.

74. Ending terrorism depends on people. *Mid-Day* (Bombay) 24 Aug 1985 ; 6.

75. Esson, D.M.R : Secret Weapon-terrorism. *Army Quarterly* 78, 1959; 167-80.

76. Evans, Alona E. : Apprehension and prosecution of offenders : Some current problems. In *LAIT* ; 493-522.

The apprehension and prosecution of offenders is the one means of control of international terrorism that has the advantages of being easily comprehended and apparently relatively uncomplicated. In fact, the injunction to "extradite or submit to prosecution" persons accused of international terrorist acts is appearing in an increasing number of multilateral and bilateral treaties. The question is whether this injunction is balanced by consideration of the realities of the situation that it comprehends or whether it is simply a convenient rule of thumb for treaty draftsmen. Before this rule becomes a maxim for treaty texts concerning matters of international criminal law relative to international terrorists, it would be well to make sure that the injunction is meaningful from a practical point of view. That is, whether in contemplating the apprehension of offenders, "extradition" is the term that is wanted or whether the concern is for "lawful return", and whether, in supplying an alternative to apprehension, "submit to prosecution" is recognized as being a concept that is open to widely varying interpretations reflecting particularist moral principles, legal precepts, political practices, and other considerations. If the scope and limits of these expressions are not appreciated, the results, in practical terms, may make for unnecessarily strained relations among States, while within States having a strong emphasis on individual rights and guarantees, there will be a fomentation of litigation as apprehended offenders object to alleged infringements of these rights and guarantees.

In international practice, the apprehension of offenders comprehends formal and informal processes as well as illegal methods of return. Extradition may be denominated as the only "formal" or "legal" method of apprehension. The extradition process, which is spelled out in treaties, statutes, or codes of criminal procedure, operates within a framework of customary rules regarding such matters as double criminality, specifically, provisional detention, evidentiary requirements, third-party requests, prescription, expenses, as well as various kinds of exemptions, e.g., nationals of the requested State or political offenders.

What are the alternatives to extradition ? Where there is concern for legal niceties, "informal" methods of return i.e., by exclusion or expulsion (deportation) — furnish the most convenient procedures, due allowance being made for the particularities of national immigration laws and the strictures of the Convention and Protocol on the Status of Refugees. That deportation is an administrative process, essentially civil in nature, that has not been designed as a surrogate for extradition, which is a criminal process, is an argument that does not outweight its convenience in practice.

Classifying extradition and deportation as "lawful" methods of apprehension and recognizing that lawfulness of apprehension is a matter of concern in countries such as the United States where the accused may challenge the circumstances of his return as a defence to prosecution, the only other method of apprehension is unalwful, i.e., resort to kidnaping, violence, or "voluntary" return that has been induced by threats of force, blackmail, and similar acts. Depending on the level of the criminal justice systems in the deporting State and the State of destination, these methods are hardly viable alternatives and their negative impact on relations between the States concerned may be of greater international significance than the affirmative impact of bringing an accused to trial.

An examination of 86 instances of efforts to apprehend international terrorists—including persons accused of such offenses as aircraft hijacking; sabotage of aircraft, attacks on urban airline office, attacks on air terminals, on prisons—indicates that deportation rather than extradition has been commonly used to acquire custody of such offenders. This is not to suggest, however that extradition is in desuetude. Between January 1, 1961 and June 30, 1977, 20 States requested the extradition of 87 persons from 21 states. Requests for 6 persons were granted. Requestes for the extradition of 75 other persons were denied ; it should be added, however, that more than half of these offenders were subsequently submitted to prosecution in the requested State. Extradition is not generally in desuetude, but with regard to international terrorist offences it is certainly not an effective means of rendition.

Between January 1, 1961, and June 30, 1977, 145 persons wanted for the commission of international terrorist acts, and many of them wanted on other criminal charges as well, were deported by 28 States to 25 destinations. The grounds for deportation can only be surmised for the most part ; certainly many of the deportations simply amounted to ridding the territorial state of an undesirable alien. In one instance, deportation was ordered as part of a terrorist extortion scheme. Even allowing for the scanty data base, deportation is clearly preferred to extradition as the method for apprehending international terrorists. It may be asked why deportation in preferred and why the method of rendition should be a matter of any interest as long as rendition is achieved.

77. Evans, E. : *Calling a truce to terror.* Westpot, Greenwood Press, 1979.

78. Execution of Minors. *Times of India.* 17 Jan 1986 ; 8.

Execution of minors has been a controversial subject in the U.S. for quite some time and now lawyers for an inmate in the state of Louisiana have petitioned the U.S. Supreme Court to decide constitutionality of death sentences for crimes committed before the age of 18. At present in America, the question is left to the States—30 of which permit execution of minors. Out of these, 16 have no minimum age for the death penalty while 14 others have set limits under 18. At 10 years, the State of Indina has set the lowest age limit for death penalty. According to Newsweek, 33 inmates convicted of murders committed before they attained legal adulthood now face capital punishment in the State of South Carolina. James Terry Roach is scheduled to die by electrocution this week for crimes he committed at the age of 17. In 1977, along with two friends he had brutally raped and murdered two young women. One of his two friends has already been executed and the other saved himself by turning State's evidence. Supporters of Roach say that he may be mildly retarded and may be suffering from a degenerative brain disorder. However, his request for clemency was turned down by the Governor of South Carolina. According to the Newsweek report, the Roach case is not the first experience of the State of South Carolina with executions of minors. In 1944, a 14 year old named George Stiney died in the State's electric chair. "The adult-size-straps barely held him in place ; during the execution the mask slipped off to reveal a weeping boy. "This kind of barbarism is reminiscent of the rule of Joseph Stalin in the USSR when the death penalty was prescribed for juvenile delinquents for even relatively petty crimes. Today, even countries as unforgiving as Libya and South Africa do not permit execution of minors. While the Western world was united in its criticism of Stalin, nearly fifty years later the U.S. which lays claims to being the champion of the "free" world has not been able to get rid of its barbaric laws which permit juvenile criminals to be sent to the electric chair.

79. Fattah, E.A. : Some reflections on the victimology of terrorism. *Terrorism* 3 (1-2) 1979 ; 81-108.

80. Fearsey, Robert A. : Introduction to international terrorism. In *ITCW* ; 25-35.

81. Ferracuti, Franco : Theories of terrorism. In *ITDC* ; 225-40.

82. Fener, Lewis S. : Conflict of generations, New York, Basic Books, 1969.

83. Fighting terrorism. *Patriot* 5 Aug 1985 ; 4.

84. Finer, S.E. : Stand on terrorism. *New Society* 22 Jan 1976.

85. Foley, Gerry : Terrorism out of control ? *International Viewpiont*. 21 Apr 1986 ; 28.

86. Fraser, Hugh : Tyranny of Terrorism. In *ITCR* ; 23-32.

For the human race, neither terrorism nor tyranny are noveltires. Indeed, of the hundred and fifty or so states represented at the United Nations, less than thirty can properly claim to have free and fully democratic institutions. Terrorism and the politics of violence have been growing, even if they are not on the same scale as at the end of the Roman Empire or at the collapse of that of the Incas in South America, or at the time of the religious wars in Europe or at that of the wars of wandering in South and Central Africa in the 1840s.

But project Ulster's 1,700 deaths by political violence over seven years from Northern Ireland to larger countries like Great Britain and the U.S.A. and you get the terrifying figures of 60,000 and 233,000 human beings slaughtered.

In the past, terrorism against tyranny and the doctrine of legitimate tyrannicide has been, and indeed still is, a morally approved instrument of betterment. But what I call "modern terrorism"—that is, the random destruction of innocent civilians—falls into a different category. In the political spectrum of the politics of violence, it stands at an intermediate stage somewhere between the violence of the politically motivated mob and the internationally directed "guerrilla" movement. Morally, it can only be totally condemned. Practically, its effect is to destroy the law itself—the only thing which stands between humanity and a state of permanent terror.

To refer to the tyranny of terrorism is a precise and exact description. The terrorist slaying civilians makes the tyrant's claim that he is above the law and by his random action endeavors to place the civilian outside the protection of the law. His object is essentially the object of political theatre ; however meaningless or brutal an act, it is to impress the public on the one hand and encourage on the other the State itself to move to tyrannical systems of oppression. Terrorism's continuance blights the whole democratic process. Terrorism, if it becomes an accepted disease, can rot the moral fabric of societies, until—as when an endemic cattle plague suddenly becomes mortiferous—there are set in motion cures as dangerous and tyrannical as terrorism's own murderous intentions. The direct or indirect destruction of the rule of law and its replacement by the tyranny either of the individual or of the

State is the only rational and connecting purpose or effect in the endless current catalogue of seemingly mindless and anarchic acts of terrorist brutality.

It is my fear that for a variety of reasons the threat of terrorism to individuals and to institutions, far from diminishing or petering out in failure, as waves of terrorism have done in the past, is on the contrary likely to grow. And both by accident and by design its worst impact will be on the democratic and liberal, fully-developed and largely Western countries. These are the States that are the most communications conscious and the most communications-prone ; the most glued to their television sets ; the richest for plundering ; the most humane, compassionate and tolerant ; the most materialist and yet the least conscious of on what a knife-edge hangs civilization and their own properity. They are also the least prepared, because like Babbit they believe "it can't happen here".

The peoples of these States are coming to believe that neither clear moral nor physical authority is necessary for the maintenance of freedom ; that freedom needs no defence because it has fully flourished for a few scores of years. I will not go on—far better to re-read Solzhenitsyn's lecture to the West.

But to look to the future ; made febrile by the new revolution of falling rather than rising expectations, social frictions—especially amongst the educated and easily-frustrated—are likely to grow, and with them extreme right to extreme left (or simply dotty) manifestations, despairing of the speed either of democratic change or Marxist victories. In the era of what could be prolonged recession, the spectrum of the politics of violence—which necessarily includes terrorism—is likely to expand, and workers as well as bourgeois and intellectuals become involved.

Hitherto, the aiding and abetting and full exploitation of terrorist situations, either by international terrorist organizations or by hostile authoritarian powers, has been sporadic and—except in such massacres as those at Lod and Fiumicino airports—indirect and limited to money, arms, and occasionally to training. The pot has been stirred, but the kitchen has not been commandeered. But now some new and ominous trends are emerging.

Such recent phenomena as the P.L.O's involvement in the Shah's overthrow, East German terror training camps in South Yemen and Zambia, and the stepping up of Libyan activities seem to indicate the potential of the concerted use of terror—both as a military and a political instrument—from which Israel already suffers.

New and more precise weapons are coming into service; new targets, such as government and military computer centers and oil or nuclear installations, and the causing and spreading of panic at moments of increasing international tension or even of red alert (terrorist Sixth Columns in effect), are no longer threats which are remote or easily discounted.

87. Freedman, Lawrence Zelic and Yorab Alexander, *eds.* : Perspectives on terrorism. Delaware, Scholarly Resources, 1983. p. 254.

88. Freedman, Lawrence Zelic : Terrorism : Problem of the polistaraxic. In *POT* ; 3-12.

89. Fried, Risto : Questions on terrorism. *Terrorism* 3 (3-4) 1980 ; 219-29.

90. Friedlander, Robert A. : Coping with terrorism : What is to be done ? In *TTP* ; 230-46.

91. Friedlander, Robert, A. : Origins of international terrorism. In *Terrorism* : Interdisciplinary perspectives. New York, John Jay Press, 1977.

92. Friedlander, Robert A. : Terrorism. *Barrister* 2, Sum 1975.

93. Friedlander, Robert A. : *Terrorism 2 Vols.* New York, Oceana Publications, 1979.

94. Friedlander, Robert A. : Terrorism and political violence : Do the ends justify the means ? In *ITCW* ; 316-24. *International Studies Notes* 2, Sum 1976.

The wanton and willful taking of life, the purposeful commission of serious bodily harm, and the intentional infliction of severe mental distress by force or by threat of force are phrases that are legal terms of art (lawyers' words) describing actions and activities designated as common crimes by every civilized society on this earth. The victims of these purposive and, I think, indefensible acts are persons whose selection as victims, whether randomized or calculated, was due solely to their waiting in a hotel lobby, sitting in an outdoor cafe, standing on a street corner, flying on an aeroplane, riding on a train or representing corporate interests in a country other than their own.

"No cause," argues French author Albert Camus, "justifies the death of the innocent," and terrorism is the slaughter of the innocent. No matter how we want to look at it, terrorism is a moral problem in addition to being a criminal act. As newspaper columnist, Father Andrew Greely has written : "Either terror is moral for everyone or it is moral for no one." To save oneself by killing another is destructive not only of law legal, systems but of civilized society itself. Our Anglo-American common law system is based upon the worth, the sanctity of one human life, and this conforms to the basic human rights principles which have come to be accepted in public international law since the end of World War II. The admonition of legal philosopher Edmund Cahn still rings true : "Whoever kills one kills mankind."

Traditional Anglo-American criminal law permits what are called "excusing conditions"—or, to use once again lawyers' terminology, mistake, necessity, provocation, duress and insanity—to excuse or to mitigate what other-wise would be criminal acts. However, neither duress nor necessity may operate as an excuse for the taking of human life. The civil law system of Europe and Latin America permits the defence to be raised of a "political crime" and, thereby, it may prevent extradition of a wanted felon. The Third World, in national politics and in the international arena, has given a large measure of support to perpetrators of political crimes. Their attitude is that the end justifies the means. As a result, the continuing public debate over the nature of international terrorism has unleashed a cacophony of national self-interest in the council of nations. Political terrorism has become largely a matter of global perspective. The fundamental issue is whether the primary focus should be upon the causes of violence or upon the acts of violence.

According to Eric Suy, Deputy Undersecretary General of the United Nations and its general counsel, "(t) the cause of terrorism is not a legal question." And the cure, he suggests, will not be found in international treaties or conventions, but by States acting alone, bilaterally or multilaterally. In fact, Suy is highly skeptical as to "the efficiency of international treaties." One of my critics likewise suggests that the answer to terrorism cannot be found in the law, but may be discovered in the hearts or the souls (if they have them) of the terrorizers themselves. Again, I must vigorously dissent, for reasons which I shall now discuss.

For more than a decade the spectre of international terrorism has been identified with the spread of ideological violence and the fragmentation or dismantling of existing sociopolitical structures. According to Frantz Fanon, the ideological godfather of the Algerian independence, movement : "National liberation, national renaissance, the restoration of nationhood to the people...is always a violent phenomenon." Thus, terror has become a political weapon to be used wherever and whenever a dissident group is unable to achieve its basic objectives by any legitimized means.

The term itself originated during the French Revolution and the Jacobin Reign of Terror. At first it was identified with State action. Later, it was applied to individual or group violence. Contemporary legal scholars and prevailing international legal standards divide terrorism into two major components : (1) individual or group terrorist activities and (2) National or governmental repression. The United States has been primarily concerned with the former category, as reflected in its Draft Convention for the Prevention and Punishment of Acts of International Terrorism submitted to the U.N. General Assembly during September 1972. The Third World nations have emphasized the latter view, particularly in the debates of the assembly's *ad hoc* Committee on International Terrorism which concentrated on the "repressive and terrorist acts by colonial, racist and alien regimes........."

Surprisingly, a legal definition of terrorism has yet to be formulated, and the lack of specificity about the nature of the subject continues to plague the international community. The Algerian analysis submitted to the Committee was actually a description of the United States role in South Vietnam, while Professor Tran-Tam, formerly of the University of Minh Duc in Saigon, in his contribution to a significant study of international criminal law, defined political terrorism and the activities of the Vietcong.

Terrorism in microcosm is a struggle for power, and its purpose is totallly destructive. The quintessence of the terrorist process, according to Professor E.V. Walter, centers on three factors : the source of violence, the victim, and the audience. The necessary concomitant of terrorism is fear and the ultimate objective is coercion.

95. Friedman, Thomas. L. : Sources of terrorism. *Times of India* 8 May 1986 ; 6. *International Herald Tribune* 29 Apr 1986 ; 6.

96. Fromhin, David : Strategy for terrorism. *Foreign Affairs* 53 (4) Jul 1975 ; 683-98.

97. Galor, Noemi : *International cooperation to suppress terrorism.* London, Croom-Helms 1985. p. 390.

98. Galtunng, Johan : Structural theory of aggression. *Journal of Peace Research* 1, 1964 ; 95-119.

99. Gandhi, Rajmohan : Blood, tears and a truth. *Indian Express* 25 Feb 1986 ; 6.

100. Gandhi, Rajmohan : Terrorism discouraged ? *Indian Express* 22 Apr 1986 ; 6.

101. Garrigan, Timothy B and George A. Lopez : *Terrorism: A problem of political violence.* Columbas 1978.

102. Gasset, Jose Ortega : Barbarism of specialisation In. *Revolt of the masses.* London, George Allen & Unwin, 1951 ; 78-82.

103. Gasset, Jose Ortega : *Revolt of the masses.* London, George Allen & Unwin, 1951. p. 141.

104. Gaucher, R. : *Terrorists.* London, 1968.

105. Geraghty, Tony : Ten years of terrorism. In *TYT*; 170-87.

106. Ghosh, T.C. : Tactics to tackle terrorism. *Caravan* (New Delhi) Jan (First) 1986; 28-29.

Giap, Vo Naguyen : *Banner of people's war, the party's military live.* London, Pall Mall Press, 1970. p. 118.

108. Gilbert, Geoffrey S. : Terrorism and the political offence exemption reappraised. *International and Comparative Law Quarterly* 34(4) Oct 1985; 695-723. -

109. Gilboa, Eytan : Use of simulation in combating terrorism. *Terrorism* 5(3) 1981; 265-79.

110. Global menace. *Pioneer* 13 Jan 1985; 6.

111. Global terrorism. *Northern India Patrika* 9 Jan 1986; 4.

112. Goldberg, Yona : *Haganah or terror.* New York, Hechalvtz, 1947.

113. Goleman, Daniel : Making of a terrorist could begin in childhood. *International Herald Tribune* 12 Sep 1986; 4.

114. Golob-Nisk, Mirjana : New aspects of international terrorism. *Review of International Affairs* 26 (598) 1975; 26-28.

115. Green, L.C. : Aspects of terrorism. *Terrorism* 5(4) 1982; 373-400.

116. Grey, Lord : Political problems of terrorism and society. In *TYT*; 39-55.

117. Gude, E.W. : Dealing with worldwide terror. *Society* 10, Jan 1973

118. Gurr, Ted Robert : Some characteristics of political terrorism in the 1960s. In *POT*; 23-50.

The revolutionary dimensions of political terrorism also prove to have been a good deal less significant than common belief would have it. In fact, political terrorists are readily distinguishable from revolutionary and secessionist movements in a number of respects. They are much smaller in number than were the armies and cadres of, say, the Algerian or Angolan nationalists or the National Liberation Front in South Vietnam or the secessionists of the Southern Sudan or Northern Iraq or even Fidel Castro's guerrilla bands in 1958. Not only did they lack the manpower, most of them also lacked the broadly based class alliances and support that are characteristic of most revolutionary movements. Most striking of all, less than one-fourth of them had explicit revolutionary objectives.

Even if it is argued that many terrorist movements have had covert revolutionary aims, they have been singularly unsuccessful in achieving them. Only a handful of the 335 episodes and campaigns reviewed here appear to have had any lasting effects on national political systems at any time between 1961 and 1977. Terrorism by Algerian Muslims in France during the Algerian War may have contributed to the war weariness that led to a negotiated settlement. On the other side of the Mediterranean, terrorism by the OAS in Algeria certainly did not keep Algeria French, but made it all the more imperative for the colons to leave after independence. Terrorism in Northern Rhodesia, now Zambia, shortly before independence was a factional fight between nationalist parties jockeying for power and did not measurably affect the timetable for independence. In Latin America, the activities of Peronist terrorists helped to pave the way for the return of Peron in 1972, the consequences of which were so antirevolutionary that they stimulated still more terrorism. In Uruguay the Tupamaros pushed what had been a relatively open, democratic government into dictatorial repression in 1973, a condition whose theoretically revolutionary consequences in the long-run will have to be weighed against the present certainty of the elimination of both the revolutionaries and political freedom. In Brazil a decade of urban guerrilla activity has not shaken the military government's grip on power, nor has it had any visible effect on Brazil's econom'c boom.

Only in European countries can one find instances in this period of favourable political changes that might be attributed to terrorist activity. In the Alto Adige region of northern Italy, the German-speaking population gained a greater measure of autonomy in late 1960s after a period of terrorist activity. A terriorist campaign in Quebec in the 1960s coincided with a federal policy of devolution that markedly increased the autonomy of all the provinces. But in both these cases there was intensive political activity and pressure of a more conventional sort in the same direction, and to attribute to the terrorists the principal role in the outcome is romantic. In Northern Ireland, though, it is evident that the IRA can claim some of the credit for the British Government's decision to suspend the Storemont Parliament and assume direct rule. Whether that will prove to have been a gain in the long run is another matter, but at least it was a change in a political situation that had been frozen for 50 years.

The upshot of this quick sketch is that in perhaps a half dozen instances in the last 15 years, in the 87 countries being considered, terrorism has been associated with structural changes that might conceivably be said to advance the cause advocated by the terrorists. Some of these changes have been reformist, some reactionary, none revolutionary. On the basis of the record to date, the revolutionary potential of political terrorism is vastly overrated. Where it has had any impact at all, other powerfull political forces were pushing in the same direction.

Despite the lack of revolutionary success, the political use of terrorism flourishes, particularly in the more prosperious democracies. Terrorist campaigns are not so common, nor as enduring, in the new nations, and they are quite uncommon in authoritarian nations, both Left and Right. The evidence is not consistent with the view that political terrorism is a specific response to repressive government. In some cases, like South Africa and Spain, it is a response to repression, but where it thrives is in the kinds of political systems that have a track record of accommodating diverse political views and demands. No doubt that is one explanation for the commonality and persistence of political terrorism in Western and Latin democracies, terrorists can act with more impunity in quasi-open societies than in police States.

The next question is why some people chose terrorist tactics rather than the more conventional methods of political participation and protest. The militants' most likely answer is that conventional tactics don't work. What the militants are less likely to acknowledge is that they did not, or thought they could not, muster enough popular support to play effective electoral or pressure-group politics. Political terrorism in democratic societies, and in some others as well, is principally the tactic of groups that represent the interests and demands of small minorities. Revolutionaries in Western countries have adopted terroristic tactics because they are revolutionaries in societies where the great majority of the population finds the *status quo* tolerable.

119. Gurr, Ted Robert : *Why men rebel.* Princeton, 1970.

120. Hacker, Frederick J.: *Crusaders, Criminals and crazies : Terror and terrorism in our times.* New York, Norton, 1977.

121. Hacker, Frederick J. : Dialectic interrelationships of personal and political factors in terrorism. In *POT*; 19-20.

122. Hacker, Frederick J. : Terror and terrorism. *Terrorism* 4, 1980.

123. Hailbronner, Kay : International terrorism and the laws of war. *German Yearbook of International Law* 25, 1982; 169-98.

124. Hanny, William A. : International terrorism; the need for a fresh perspective. *International Lawyer* 268; 1974.

125. Hardman, J.B.S.: Terrorism. In *Encyclopaedia of the sociol sciences Vol. 14.* New York, Macmillan, 1937; 575-79.

126. Harris, F. Gentry : Hypothetical facets of ingredients of terrorism. *Terrorism* 3 (3-4) 1980; 239-44.

127. Hayden, T. : *Rebellion and repression.* New York, World Publ. Cy. 1969.

128. Hebbar, M.N. : Terrorism is top topic. *Free Press Journal* (Bombay) 5 Feb 1986; 4.

International terrorism has continued to remain in the news against the background of President Reagan's insistence that the European allies join him in economic sanctions against Libya. The allies have been noticeably cool towards the idea and the Federal Republic too has in effect rejected it although Bonn has couched its response in euphemisms. Its message is that economic sanctions have seldom, if ever, worked in creating political effects and that Libya was no exception either.

The arrival of John Whitehead, U.S. Deputy Secretary of State, in

Bonn and discussions with Foreign Minister Hans-Dietrich Genscher have not produced any perceptible results except insofar as both countries were in agreement on the condemnation of any fight against international terrorism as well as on the need for extremely close international co-operation in the law-enforcement sector.

While Whitehead briefed Bonn officials on the peaceful measures taken by the U.S. Government to convince the Libyan Government of the need to desist from lending any further support to international terrorism, the German Government described in detail measures taken by it in the recent past and gave its assurance that it would carefully examine the ideas and suggestions the former presented. Whitehead did not quite conceal his disappointment over the German stance.

It was significant that a Libyan delegation also arrived in Bonn at about the same time and held talks with the Ministry of Foreign Affairs. It is understood that the delegation delivered a message from the Libyan Foreign Minister Treiki regarding Libya's position on the regional situation, terrorism and the American boycott measures. Minister of State Juergen Moellemann, who met the delegation, referred to German and European Community efforts to help arrive at a settlement of the Middle East conflict, which was seen as basic to the question of solving the terrorism issue in the region.

Complementing the picture has been the arrival here of Simon Peres, the Israeli Prime Minister, whose first visit to Bonn was also centred on talks with Chancellor Kohl on the Middle East problem and the issue of international terrorism. His programme here also included a visit to the former concentration camp site Bergen-Belsen. Understandably, his arrival was greeted, in addition, by demonstrators protesting his visit. The talks have not produced headlines.

Nevertheless, Israel has officially expressed itself beholden to the Bonn Government for its unstinted advocacy of establishing diplomatic relations between Spain and Israel, a cause that has now turned into reality a couple of weeks ago. Bonn played an important part in the realisation of this development through its good offices with the Spanish Government, in connection with Spain's accession to the European Community.

129. Henry, Ernet : *Stop terrorism.* Moscow, Novosti, 1982. p. 201.

130. Herman, Edward : *Real-terror new-work.* Boston, Southend Press, 1982.

131. Hobsbawm, Eric, J. : *Bandits*. London, 1969.

132. Hobsbawn, Eric J. : *Primitive rebels*. Manchester University, 1972.

133. Holt, Simma : *Terror in the name of God*. Toronto, McClelland & Stewart, 1964.

134. Holton, Gerald : Reflections on modern terrorism. *Terrorism* 1(3-4) 1978.

135. Homer, Frederic D. : *Guns and garlic : Myths and realities of organised crime*. West Lafayette, Pardue University Press, 1974.

136. Horchem, Hans Josef : Pre-empting terror. In *ITCR*; 307-12.

137. How nations support terrorism. *Statesman* 16 Apr 1986; 10.

138. Howe, Irving : Return of terror. *Dissent* 22 (3) Sum 1975; 227-37.

139 Howe, Irving : Ultimate price of random terror. *Skeptic* (2) Jan-Feb 1976.

140. Hyams, Edward. H. : *Terrorist and Terrorism*. London, Dent, 1975.

141. Iceberg of terrorism : *Link* 30 Jun 1985; 32.

142. Inbar, Michael and Clarice Stall *eds* : *Simulation and gaining in social science*. New York, Free Press, 1972.

143. International Law Association, Paris Conference (1984) : Committee on International Terrorism. Committee Report. *Terrorism* 7 (2) 1984; 199-211.

144. International terrorism : *Nagpur Times* 28 Jun 1985; 4.

145. International terrorism. *Deccan Chronicle* 31 Jul 1985; 6.

146. Isidore (Dr). : International terrorism. *Daily* (Bombay) 28 Jan 1986; 9.

There are many modern international terrorist groups operating with ramifications in many parts of the world. These militant terrorists, it is reliably known, are aided and abetted by powerful individuals, Government agencies, and even heads of States.

Coming nearer home, terrorist activities in Punjab are motivated by political conspiracy aimed at the overthrow of the Government duly elected by the people and to create an independent State, which goes against the canons of the Constitution. In this context, it is indeed heartening to note that the present Akali Dal Government has at last awakened to the magnitude of the problem.

The need of the hour is for all right-thinking individuals at the national as well as international levels, to wake up to this menace and take effective measures, sanctions if need be, to combat the evil of terrorism. Just as South Africa has been segregated for its policy of colour bar, so also all nations that aid and abet terrorism and terrorist activities must come in for very severe castigation.

147. It is international terrorism : USSR. *Hindustan Times* 26 Mar 1986; 16.

Libyan strongman Muammar Gaddafi on March 25, 1986 declared his country's determination to "continue resisting valiantly the US aggression."

Col. Gaddafi was reaching to a White House statement expressing US determination to continue its naval exercises near the Libyan coast.

Col. Gaddafi told Libyan news agency JANA that his country was "defending not only itself but the whole of the Arab world and its future."

Soviet media described United States actions against Libya as "undisguised aggression and act of international terrorism".

Moscow Radio is putting out news flashes every half an hour.

According to the Radio, Tripoli Broadcasting Station suddenly interrupted its programme announcing the US air attack.

An urgent press conference has been convened in Moscow on March 25 by the Soviet Foreign Ministry in which the Soviet stand is likely to be discussed.

Syria and other Arab countries have strongly condemned American provocations leading to March 24 clashes between the Libyan and US forces.

Speaking at the Arab League ministerial meeting in Tunis on March 24, just before the news of the clashes came in, Arab League Secretary General Chadli Klibi sharply criticised the American air and naval manoeuvres.

Prime Minister Hussein Musavi of Iran expressed "full support" for Libya in its confrontation with the United States.

"The US aggression against the Gulf of Sidra is a flagrant violation against the territorial integrity of an Islamic country," Mr. Musavi was quoted as saying by the official Islamic Republic news agency.

Italian Premier Bettino Craxi called a meeting of his Cabinet to discuss the US Navy confrontation with Libyan forces.

148. Ivianski, Zeev : Chapter in the history of individual terror : Andrey Zhelyabov. In *POT*; 85-98.

149. Ivianski, Zeev : Provocation at the Center : A study in history of counter-terror. *Terrorism* 4 (3-4) 1980; 53-88.

150. Jackson, Henry M. : Terrorism as a weapon in intimation politics. In *ITCR*; 33-38.

The idea that one person's "terrorist" is another's "freedom fighter" cannot be sanctioned. Freedom fighters or revolutionaries don't blow up buses containing non-combatants ; terrorist murderers do. Freedom fighters don't set out to capture and slaughter school children; terrorist murderers do. Freedom fighters don't assassinate innocent businessmen, or hijack and hold hostage innocent men, women, and children; terrorist murderers do. It is a disgrace that democracies would allow the treasured word "freedom" to be associated with the acts of terrorists.

When PLO terrorists toss a bomb into a marketplace, or murder a holy man, or shoot rockets randomly at a village, each and every democracy in the world should stand up to condemn those radical Arab states and the others who train, arm, finance, harbor, and encourage them.

When an act of terrorism occurs and the odds are there, it will occur in one of the free countries, democracies should unite in sponsoring resolutions in the United Nations condemning the act. Where we have evidence of support for the terrorists by some other states, this support should be censured in the strongest terms. If the Socialist countries their allies, and the radical Arab and Third World States want to vote against such resolutions let them.

Let's educate the whole world as to who opposes and who tolerates international terrorism.

I am convinced that this will make a difference ; I am convinced, for instance, that the exposure of East European support for European terrorism has contributed to the lessening of this support and to the signs of some cooperation to combat terrorism between these countries and the nations of Western Europe.

151. Janke, Peter : Response to terrorism. In *TYT* ; 22-38.

152. Jay, Martin : Politics of terror. *Partisan Review* 28(1) 1972 ; 95-103.

153. Jenkins, Brian M. : International terrorism : A new mode of conflict. In *ITWS* ; 13-49.

Terrorism appears to have increased markedly in the past few years. Political and criminal extremists in various parts of the world have attacked passengers in airline terminals and railway stations; planted bombs in Government buildings, the offices of multination corporations, pubs and theatres ; hijacked airliners and ships, even ferryboats in Singapore; held hundreds of passengers hostage; seized embassies; and kidnapped Government officials, diplomats and business executives. We read of new incidents almost daily. Terrorists may strike citizens of another country while they are living overseas, in transit from one country to another, or at home in their own country. Terrorism has become a new element in international relations.

When we talk about terrorism, what exactly are we talking about ? The word has no precise or widely accepted definition. One noted lawyer has defined terrorism as acts which in themselves may be classic forms of crime—murder, arson, the use of explosives—but which differ from classic criminal acts in that they are executed 'with the deliberate intention of causing panic, disorder and terror within an organised society, in order to destroy social discipline, paralyse the forces of reaction of a society, and increase the misery and suffering of the community'. Two scholars in the United States have provided a somewhat broader definition of terrorism :

> 'murder, assassination, sabotage and subversion, the destruction of public records, the spreading of rumour, the closing of churches, the sequestration of property, the breakdown of criminal law enforcement, the prostitution of the courts, the narcotise of the press—all these, as they contribute to a common end, constitute terror.'

Without attempting to define terrorism in a way that will satisfy all lawyers and scholars, we may for the moment satisfy ourselves with the following description : the threat of violence, individual acts of violence, or a campaign of violence designed primarily to instil fear—to terrorise people may be called terrorism. Terrorism is violence for effect, not only, and sometimes not at all, for the effect on the actual victims of the terrorists. In fact, the victim may be totally unrelated to the terrorist's cause. Terrorism is violence aimed at the people watching. Fear is the intended effect, not the by-product of terrorism. That, at least, distinguishes terrorist tactics from mugging and other common forms of violent crime that may terrify but are not terrorism.

Terrorists may include revolutionaries and other political extremists, criminals professing political aims, and a few authentic lunatics. Terrorists may operate alone or may be members of a large and well-organised group. Terrorists may even be Government agents. Their cause may have extreme goals, such as the destruction of all Government—in itself not a new idea—or their cause may be one that is comparatively reasonable and understandable—self-rule for a particular ethnic group. Or their motive may be purely personal—money or revenge. The ambition of terrorists may be limited and local to overthrow of a particular regime—or that may be global—a simultaneous worldwide revolution.

The problem of defining terrorism is compounded by the fact that terrorism has recently become a fade word which is used promiscuously and is often applied to a variety of acts of violence which are not strictly terrorism by definition. It is generally a pejorative. Some Governments are prone to label as terrorism all violent acts committed by their political opponents, while anti-government extremists frequently claim to be the victims of Government terror. What is called terrorism thus seems to depend on point of view. Use of the term implies a moral judgment, and if one party can successfully attach the label 'terrorist' to its opponent, then it has indirectly persuaded others to adopt its moral viewpoint. Terrorism is what the bad guys do.

The term 'terrorism' is also an attention-getting word and therefore tends to be used, especially in the news media, to heighten the drama surrounding any act of violence. What we have, in sum, is the sloppy use of a word that is rather imprecisely defined to begin with. Terrorism may properly refer to a specific set of actions the primary intent of which is to produce fear and alarm for a variety of purposes, which we shall discuss. But terrorism in general usage frequently is also applied to similar acts of violence—all ransom kidnappings, all hijackings, thrill killings which are not intended by their perpetrators to be primarily terror producing. Once a group carries out a terrorist act, it acquires the label 'terrorist', a label that tends to stick, and from that point on, everything this group does, whether intended to produce terror or not, is also henceforth called terrorism. If it robs a bank or steals arms from an arsenal, are not necessarily acts of terrorism but common urban guerrilla tactics, these too are described as terrorism. Eventually all similar acts by other gangs or groups also come to be called terrorism. At some point in this expanding use of the term, terrorism can mean just what those who use the term (not the terrorists) want it to mean almost any violent act by any opponent.

154. Jenkins, Brian : International terrorism : A balance sheet. *Survival* 17 Jul-Aug 1975 ; 158-64.

155. Jenkins, Brian, *ed.* : *Terrorism and personal production*. Stoneham, Ma. Butterworth, 1985 p. 450.

156. Jenkins, Brian : Terrorist mindset and terrorist decision making : Two areas of ignorance. *Rand Corporation Paper* : p-6340. Jun 1979, *Terrorism* 3 (3-4) 1980 ; 245-50.

157. Johnson, Chalmers : List of hypotheses and assumptions. *Terrorism* 3 (3-4) 1980; 251-55.

158. Johnson, Chalmers : Perspectives on terrorism. In *Terrorism reader*. Ed. by W. Laqueur. New York, 1978 ; 267-85.

159. Johnson, Paul : Age of terror. *New Statesman* 88, 1974.

160. Johnson, Paul : Seven deadly sins of terrorism. In *ITCR* ; 12-22.

Before describing what I believe to be the correct approach to the problem of terrorism, let me indicate what I am certain is the wrong one. The wrong approach is to see terrorism as one of many symptoms of a deep-seated malice in our society, part of a pattern of violence which includes juvenile delinquency, rising crime rates, student riots, vandalism and football hooliganism, which is blamed on the shadow of the H-bomb, Eastern materialism, TV and cinema violence, rising divorce rates, inadequate welfare services and poverty, and which usually ends in the meaningless and defeatist conclusion that society itself is to blame and—to quote the caricature psychiatrist, 'We are all guilty'.

Such a loose, illogical and unscientific line of thought will get us nowhere. The truth is, international terrorism is not part of a generalized problem. It is a specific and identifiable problem on its own ; and because it can be isolated from the context which breeds it is a remediable problem. That is the first thing we must get clear.

When I say it is remediable, do not for one moment think I underestimate the size and danger of the terrorist phenomenon. On the contrary, I take the view that it is almost impossible to exaggerate the threat which terrorism holds for our civilization. It is a threat which is in many respects more serious than the risk of nuclear war, or the population explosion, or global pollution, or the exhaustion of the earth's resources. I believe these dangers to our civilization can be, have been, or are being contained. I believe the threat of terrorism is not being contained—that it is, on the contrary increasing steadily. I believe that one central reason why it is such a formidable threat is that very few people in the civilized world Governments and Parliaments, TV and newspapers, and the public generally take terrorism seriously enough.

161. Karacan, Ismet : Terrorism : concepts and constructs. In *ITDC*; 203-24.

162. Katsh, Abraham I. : Terror, holocaust and the will to live. In *ITCW* ; 430-35.

In the nineteenth century, Victor Hugo wrote, "War will be dead, the scaffold will be dead, hatred will be dead, frontiers will be dead, royalty will be dead, dogmas will be dead, man will begin to live." But here we are in the twentieth century. War is not dead, nor is the scaffold. Dogmas are not dead, and man trained by generations in science and education, is shockingly applying the results to the perfection of weapons of death. As man's capacity for destruction has become almost unlimited, the need becomes even greater to rekindle his awareness of a higher purpose in human destiny.

Our own generation has witnessed the unthinkable horror of the holocaust and the systematic extermination of six million Jews-men, women and children. Indeed Israel Zangwill was right when he said, "The people of Christ have become the Christ of the people."

> "The whole nation is sinking in a sea of horror and cruelty.......I do not know whether anyone else is recording the daily events. The conditions of life which surround us are not conducive to such literary labors...Anyone who keeps such a record endangers his life, but this doesn't alarm me. I sense within me the magnitude of this hour and my responsibility to it. I have an inner awareness that I am fulfilling a national obligation...My words are not rewritten, momentary reflexes shape them. Perhaps their value lies in this......My record will serve as source material for the future historian.

The Holocaust visited on the Jews was different from all earlier massacres in Jewish history because of its conscious and explicit planning, its systematic execution, and the absence of any emotional element in the remorselessly applied decision to exterminate everyone—everyone to ensure that no one might escape or survive. There was no chance for survival.

The terror inflicted on all Hitler's victims, and his total disregard of the commandment, "Thou shalt not kill"—nor take life without proper trial, nor kill the defenceless, not harm the innocent—was in this case so violent and unprecedent that it is difficult to grasp how even an insane or halfsane fanatic would find it in himself not only to conceive such a plan, but to decree that "Thou shalt kill" millions and an entire nation without evoking the immediate horrified reaction from the world : "Why, you must be out of your mind !"

How, we wonder, did Hitler obtain the consent and cooperation of his closest associates, the compliance of the mass of executioners and the resigned acceptance of the very many who did not care or who were unwilling to get into trouble ? They all knew fully, partially or dimly, what was going on and chose not to rebel or to ask questions.

A vast literature has been written on the Holocaust, but unfortunately, most of the world even in our own time shies away from reading it. Death is always tragic, but when death by murder is multiplied by six million in five years (counting only the Jewish victims) the deed becomes so enormous, so inconceivable that a new term had to be coined for it : genocide.

In a symposium on the Holocaust conducted in 1975 by the Joseph and Sally Handleman Communications Center of Dropsie University in Philadelphia, John Cardinal Krol of Philadelphia and Professor Roy A. Eckardt of Lehigh University took opposing views. Cardinal Krol saw the Holocaust as logical consequence of modern rationalism, which undermined the Judeo-Christian philosophy of life. Beginning with Descartes, who set up the human mind as the only source of truth, going on to Spinoza, Kant, Hegel, Wagner and Nietzsche, the cardinal saw a continuous process of degeneration which culminated in Hitler's conviction that morality is "a Jewish invention". The Nazi movement offered a "substitute religion" akin to that of the Bolsheviks and equally as destructive. He pointed out to theses three as the essence of Judaism—the One God, human dignity and freedom. Hitlerism resulted from an attack on these basic principles in our society.

Professor Eckardt, on the other hand, asserted that the ultimate root of anti-Semitism can be understood only as the remnants of the medieval heritage. He cited the long and sad litany of Christian mythology, which created the image of the Jew as a mystical enemy, an image that lent plausibility to Nazi propaganda. Luther continued and aggravated the demonic image of the Jew, transferring the medieval myth to modern Protestants.

163. Kaufman, Irving R. : Cruel murders, not freedom fighters. *International Herald Tribune*. 25 Aug 1986; 4.

Terrorism is a world coined by society to deplore a particular kind of political violence that lies wholly outside accepted conventions of warfare. The term is most frequently used to describe revolutionary violence, but established Governments are certainly no strangers to the systematic terrorizing of entire populations.

The aim is to destroy the morale of a nation; the method is the random murder of innocent people. Randomness is the distinctive trait. Harm must come by chance to unremarkable men and women, whether Americans or Britons or Jews, simply because of their nationality, religion or political affiliation. They must feel themselves fatally exposed and demand that their Governments should negotiate for their safety.

Since medieval times' philosophers have recognized the distinction between *jus ad bellum*, the justice of war, and *jus in bello*, justice in war, Terrorism is more a civilian strategy than what we commonly call war, but the distinction remains meaningful in this area as well. The moral reality of war is divided into two logically independent parts. We make judgments about the broader issues of aggression and self-defence ; but, employing a separate calculus, we make judgments about the observance or violation of the customary and positive rules of engagement.

164. Keegan, George J. : Preferred route. In *ITCR*; 338-42.

165. Kemp, Jack : Unseen hand. In *ITCR* ; 187-95.

166. Kerstetter, Wayne A. : Practical problems of law enforcement. In *LAIT*; 535-52.

In most countries, law enforcement and national security agencies are organized to respond to the traditional dichotomy between internal criminal activity and activity against the security of the State and its interests abroad. International and transnational terrorist activity, because it crosses national borders and has political overtones but uses traditional criminal activity, cuts across these estab'ished organizational lines. Thus the responsibility for responding to terrorism is often diffused. In the United States, for example, the FBI has a responsibility for law enforcement activity with regard to internal terrorist activity. At the same time, the Cabinet Committee to Combat Terrorism and the Working Group on Terrorism are centered in the State Department because terrorist acts often involve the interests and lives of U.S. citizens in foreign countries. Jurisdictional problems of this kind arise both here and in other countries.

One significant improvement would be the further definition of the relationships between members of the Cabinet Committee to Combat Terrorism and the Working Group on Terrorism. In particular, a clear assignment of authority to direct and coordinate the efforts of federal agencies in responding to a crisis situation is an urgent necessity.

The consistent and universal theme of the police agencies contacted during the research was the need for more and better information about the individuals and groups involved in terrorist activities. On the international level, an exchange of information is occurring among countries through a variety of channels, including the development of *ad hoc* groups in Western Europe; the Kilowatt System, a teletype information—sharing system—and the informal utilization of relationships developed in the course of NATO and Interpol activities. This exchange, particularly as it relates to Interpol, has not been under the official auspices of that organization. But police officials who have developed international contacts in other contexts have been able to use those contacts for this purpose.

Spurred by the failure of efforts to deal with the problem through the United Nations, the countries of Western Europe have begun approaching the problem on a regional basis. A limited group of these nations has been meeting and exchanging information as an *ad hoc* committee on a regular basis. Both strategic and tactical information have been included; however, accounts vary as to the scope of the interest in this *ad hoc* group and of its effectiveness. Precise information has been unobtainable.

In the United States, the *ad hoc* approach has been formalized around a Cabinet Committee on Terrorism chaired by the Secretary of State and supported by a working group composed of representatives from 23 federal agencies involved with the problem. This working group meets regularly and exchanges general or strategic information about trends and developments in terrorism. The group does not exchange tactical information about specific individuals and groups.

However, it does serve as a useful forum in which individuals representing the various agencies have an opportunity to meet and work together. This opportunity is important to the development of the trust and respect crucial to the exchange of information between the enforcement officials. The necessity of this personal underpinning to the organizational relationships is universally recognized at all levels of law enforcement both here and abroad. Without it, the necessary exchange of information may succeed despite obstacles. The working group served as a good first step.

Until recently there has been no attempt in the United States to collect and collate information on terrorist activity from various sources and to provide for the systematic analysis and dissemination of that information. This centralization is necessary given the large number of agencies involved in the working group and the need to bring together numerous items of information from many sources into a meaningful whole in order to develop useful intelligence about terrorist activities.

167. Khapton, R. : Answer to terrorism. *Hindustan Times* 17 Oct 1985; 9.

168. Kittrie, Nicholas N. : New look at political offences and terrorism. In *ITCW*; 354-75.

In recent years the international community has witnessed a growing number of unorthodox political activists and movements whose tactical arsenal has ranged from civil disobedience to coups d'etat, from tyrannicide to guerrilla war and terrorism. Their proclaimed goals have included self-determination and human rights, but unorthodox activism need not be confused with exclusively liberal and human pursuits. Both recent and earlier history has demonstrated that reactionary and oppressive goals may also be served by resort to extra legal or violent means.

Political activists have attracted an inordinate degree of public attention. More inches of newsprint have been devoted the past year in America and in many other countries to the adventures and trials of Patricia Hearst, Lynette "Squeeky" Fromme, and Sarah Moore than to any other topic in the field of criminal justice. What was uniquely common to all three was not merely their gender but the political character of their crimes. As one adds to these domestic headliners the coverage of such transnational violence as the South Moluccan train hijackers in Holland, the kidnapping of the OPEC oil ministers in Vienna, and the increasing worldwide speculations regarding the mysterious Carlos, it is apparent that political crime and terrorism, are this decade's favourite cops-and-robbers stories.

It is not the sheer number of those killed, injured, or otherwise affected by political crime and terrorism which accounts for the widespread public attention given this phenomenon. In the four worst yearsof domestic turmoil in America (1965-68), a grand total of 214 were killed and 9,000 were injured as a result of terrorism, protests and ghetto riots. But this compares with a national total of 12,000 murders and 250,000 aggravated assaults annually. During the height of the aircraft hijacking epidemic (1968-72), the number of persons who lost their lives or were injured in all domestic and international flights did not exceed 200. In the same period, the number of internationally protected persons subjected to attack, kidnapping, or threat of violence did not exceed forty-six, with sixteen meeting eventual death. The most recent statement issued by FBI Director, Clarence Kelley, pointing out to the growing threat posed by terrorist activities, lists eleven victims killed and seventy-two injured through bombings and other violence in America during 1975. Worldwide, it is estimated that in 1975 at least fifty people lost their lives and more than 150 were taken hostage in seventeen major acts of international terrorism. Thus, it is apparent that political crime and terrorism account for a mere fraction of all domestic and international crime. There are more people murdered annually in intrafamily strife or killed in automobile accidents in America alone than are killed as a result of political and terrorist activities worldwide.

What then underlies the significance of the public's as well as the media's preoccupation with terrorism and other forms of political crime? Others have commented on the political offender's denial of the very legality of the challenged system of justice and the terrorist's resort to "violence for effect", viewing a grip of panic as his ultimate goal.

Some additional observations need to be made regarding the functions of political violence in modern western societies. In the first place, political offences—frequently reflected in highly colourful deeds and offenders—are antidotes to public apathy and boredom. They appeal to the news consumer's prurient interest in the unexpected, the unpredictable, and the adventurous. There were times when motiveless psychopathic mass-killers had the major claim to public attention. At other times, the media spot-lighted organized crime and its "godfatherly" management system. There are growing indications that white-collar crime and business criminality—ranging from corporate disregard for safety and ethics to the practices of multinational corporations—might gain more attention in the future. But the current stage belongs to two major classes of political crime, posed like the obverse faces of the Roman god Janus.

On one side are the crimes perpetrated by those holding the reins of political power. These official or quasi-official offences range from such relatively "mild" abuses of justice as Watergate and election law frauds (what Kirchheimer terms "political justice") to such atrocities as the "reigns of terror" employed in postrevolutionary France, the Soviet Union and Nazi Germany. On the other side are the crimes undertaken by those who view themselves as being out of power : those politically, economically, racially, ethnically or otherwise subjected to discrimination. This second group of offences likewise ranges from mild displays of protest and civil disobedience (at times described as "political offences") to a full arsenal of violent tactics against authority and established institutions, sometimes labelled as a "siege of terror".

169. Knauss, Petter R. and D.A. Strickland : Political disintegration and latent terror. In *POT*; 77-118.

What is the exact distinction between terrorism and politics ? Our working hypothesis is that there is no such distinction, and that ordinary politics is suffused with latent and residual terror.

In search of evidence for the existence of a disjunction between normal politics and terror, we shall be looking at examples of chaotic interregnum, open cities and deadly stalemates. Here the question is: How well grounded in reality is the fear of social and political collapse ? We shall also refer to certain theories of social contract and anarchism in order to see how the conventional view of terrorism relates to systematic political theory. And finally, we shall examine some relevant cases, most extensively the Algerian situation, in which both authors shared as Fulbright professors at Oran and Algiers, respectively, in 1975-76.

That there is, from any angle, a paradox about the locus of terror which is illustrated by some statements by a leading authority on outlawry (Hobsbawm, 1969). He was able to speak of bandits as filling a void in publ c order (when they are not creating one), of being engaged in mere jurisdictional struggles with the police, and of becoming legitimate leaders. (Pancho Villa, for example, was eventually made a general in the Mexican Army).

Far (said Hobsbawm) from fleeing these bandits in panic, the peasant typically treats them with politeness and respect. "What else could he be expected to do ?" And the fear of marauding outlaws comes to resemble in its empirical manifestations (as distinct from official rhetoric) the everyday fear of the State, or what we shall call latent terror.

It is a part of the folklore of terrorism that it intends to, or does, or both intend to and odes, paralyze society (Moore, 1954, p. 176; Eckstein, 1964; Thronton, 1964, pp. 77-79; Walter, 1969, pp. 14, 26-27; Hutchinson, 1972, p. 388). To employ the frequent and familiar metaphon it unravels the social fabric. A French functionary lamented during the onset of the Algerian liberation struggle, for example, that the growing polarization would bring with it a "total collapse of economic life and social structure" (Soustelle, 1956, pp. 123-24). This fear of social breakdown is rarely if ever expressed as a specific fear of Governmental or regime decay although implicit in its appeal is the belief that Government is some sort of barrier between terrorists and the social chaos that they allegedly wish to bring about. More deeply hidden is apt to be an assumption that Government itself could not possibly be a source of terror (except, of course, foreign Governments that are perceived to be the enemies of our own regime and that are almost by definition themselves regimes of terror). Hegel, himself no friend of terrorism, had commented in relation to the destructiveness of liberation movements that "The victorious faction only is called the Government...."

Because the literature commonly insinuates that the outcome of terrorism is or would be the collapse of social relations, it is worth asking, in advance of any examination of the political aspects of this phenomenon, what it would be like to live through pure terror and whether social structurers, like some physical structures, are such as to be capable of collapsing in on themselves.

It is instructive that the sociologists have shied away from this spector of a total collapse of social life. The International Encyclopaedia of the Social Sciences (1968) offers no analysis of social disorganization. Leading text books tend to contain indices with entries such as : "Social dysfunction (see function)." They tend also to psychologize the concept by referring the reader to "anxiety" and "anomie" or to ideologize it by referring to "patholo gy", "crime," or "deviance" (see Bloch, 1956). This is quite odd, inasmuch as (1) from any macrosociological standpoint "crime" and "anxiety" are compatible with a reasonably stable social organization, and social breakdown must therefore entail something more than variable rates of divorce and alienation, and (2) the same discipline has often demonstrated the potential of conflict and extreme environments for heightening social cohesion (Coser, 1956 ; Shils and Janowitz, 1948).

One may even accept the difficult hypothesis that society has a sacred center (Shils, 1975) and profane periphery, without knowing what genuine social disorganization would look like. The reason is that the "center," like the "structure" in which it is embedded, is well nigh impossible to specify. Insofar as it is imagined to be static, it is part of a *status quo* ideology (Lefebvre, 1971) and bears no resemblance at all to real-life societies (though it is to the old social statics [that the metaphor of a structure, undermined and crumbling because of subversion, seems to refer).

But more to the point : Insofar as social collapse is conceived of as a quality of change, it is necessary to specify how it differs from other sorts of social change. Here we begin to approach the political dimension, because the aim of terrorist activity is often supposed to be (and is, very explicity, with the anarchist) the paralysis and destruction of the State, in the name of social order. But the immediate difficulty is that when sociologists used to write about social change from "Darwinist" and progressive standpoints (Ross, 1901 ; Cooley, 1918, 1922), they supposed some degree of "organic degeneration" to be a desirable process, or, as with the later Freudo-Marxists, they thought repression in the service of the existing social structure to be, on balance, a bad thing.

170. Knutson, Jeanne N. : Terrorists' dilemma : some implicit rules of the game. *Terrorism* 4 (1-4) 1980 ; 195-222.

171. Koeppel, Barbara : Waging wars in the dark is fast becoming a habit. *International Herald Tribune* 29 Apr 1986 ; 8.

172. Koestler, Arthur : *Thieves in the night,* London, Macmillan, 1946.

173. Kos-Rabcewicz—Zabklowski : Essential features of an international criminal court. In *ITCW* ; 333-40.

Cases referred by the international commission of inquiry to the international criminal court are tried in public. All parties, that is, the public prosecutor, the attorneys for victims-complainants and the attorneys for defendants, have the right to submit evidence and to question witnesses. Also the court, upon its own initiative, may summon witnesses and order other evidence.

The simplest solution would be to provide for detention of the suspect prior to and during the trial in a prison of the State where the international commission of inquiry and the international criminal court have their main offices. A special agreement with this state would assure the extranational control of such a suspect. It seems that the initial arrest of the suspect would require the cooperation of a national court and police. National authorities would act on behalf of the international commission of inquiry and or/of the international criminal court. Should the defendant be released prior to the trial the necessary surveillance, if any, would have to be provided by the organs of the same State.

Sentences of the international criminal court could be enforced by the State of its main office. There may be a problem with the execution of the capital punishment as this would require that the State in question recognized such type of punishment.

The decisions on parole and temporary leaves should be made by the international criminal court. The parolee could be transferred to the State of his citizenship or perhaps even to his permanent residence, provided the latter State accepts it.

While detention in national prison is an economically easy solution, in certain cases, for example, international terrorists, pressure may be made on the State in which the prison is situated in order to obtain the release of such terrorists against hostages, and so forth. An international prison could perhaps be a better solution as it would be known that there is no chance that the international criminal court controlling such a prison would yield to blackmail.

While the main purpose of an international criminal court would be to act as a court of the first instance (trial court), it could also hear appeals in certain matters such as : (1) appeals from final decisions of national courts in cases of international crimes ; (2) appeals from the decisions of national courts on the qualification as political of a given international crime ; (3) appeals from final decisions of national courts of asylum and deportation ; and (4) appeals from final decisions of national courts in extradition matter.

The international criminal court also deal with international conflicts of jurisdiction between national courts of two or more States.

International participation in cases of international crimes tried before national courts might constitute an intermediate solution between an exclusively national trial on one side and an exclusively international trial on the other.

It is suggested that an international attorney for prosecution and—or international attorney for defence could act in a subsidiary but in independent manner before national courts. Such an international participation could be envisaged in addition to a national prosecutor and attorney for defence. The international attorneys would *inter alia* strive to submit all pertinent evidence.

National police, prosecutors, investigating magistrates and judges may help the international criminal court significantly in fulfilling requests of this court for implementation of its various orders in their respective States.

174. Kranthamner, Charles : On fighting terror by degrees-Ph. Ds. *International Herald Tribune* 1-2 Nov 1986 ; 5.

175. Krauthammer, Charles : Terrorism deserves an answer. *International Herald Tribune* 22-23 Jun 1985 ; 4.

176. Krishnan, J.R. : Politics of terrorism. *Amrita Bazar Patrika* 5 May 1986 ; 6.

177. Kumar, S.R. : Terrorists' bluff. *Searchlight* (Patna) 6 May 1986 ; 4.

178. Kupperman, Robert and Darrell Trent : *Terrorism : Threat, reality, response.* Stanford, Hoover Institution Press, 1979.

179. Kutner, Luis : Constructive notice, a proposal to end international terrorism. *New York Law Forum* 19, 1973.

180. Kutner, Luis : Philosophical perspective on rebellion. In *International terrorism and political crimes.* Ed. by M. Cerif Bassiouni-Springfield, 1975.

181. Lampert, D.E. *et. al.* : Is there an international system ? *International Studies Quarterly* 22 (2) Mar 1978.

182. Laqueur, Walter : Anatomy of terrorism. In *TYT* 7-21.

183. Laqueur, Walter : Can terrorism succeed ? *Skeptic* (2) Jan-Feb 1976.

184. Laqueur, Walter : Futility of terrorism. *Hasper's* 252 (1510) Mar 1976.

185. League of Nations. *Proceedings of the International Conference on the repression of terrorism.* Series of League of Nations Publications. Vol. 3, 1938.

186. Leaute, Jacque : Terrorism. Action and reaction. In *ITDC* ; 289-93.

187. Leber, Jeffrey R. : International terrorism : criminal or political ? *Towson State Journal of International Affairs* 7 (2) ; 1973.

188. Leites, Nathan : Understanding the next act. *Terrorism* 3 (1-2) 1979 ; 1-46.

189. Lessing, Doris : Dial "T" for terror. *Free Press Journal, Sunday Press* (Bombay) 13 Oct 1985 ; IV.

190. Lewis, Flora : Terrorism : Frist let's define it. *International Herald Tribune* 31 Mar 1986 ; 4.

Everybody is talking about terrorism, but not everybody means the same thing. For some time, readers have been writing to ask : "What about aid to the Nicaraguan "contras' ?" What about Angola's Savimbi ?" "What about the Israelis in southern Lebonan ?" "What about Afghanistan", both sides ?

There are many forms of violence in the world. I consider all of them deplorable, whether a car bomb in Beirut, a plane or ship hijacking, an enforced psychiatric treatment in the Social Countries, blowing up a Nicaraguan village, the Iran-Iraq War.

But different systems of violence require different defences and countermeasures. A major reason for the feeble international response on dealing with terrorism is the failure to reach a specific definition of what it meant. If the term is blurred to mean political violence from opponents, while violence against opponents constitutes "wars of liberation" or "freedom fighting," then there will never be an effective cooperation front against terrorists.

But it should be possible to be clearer, and so to avoid the distasteful alibis for condoning random murder of uninvolved civilians for political reasons. The issue is not whether war, civil war, assassination or shooting up tourists at an airport is more or less disgusting. It is what can be done about these excuses for blind killing.

Terrorism is a specific form of political violence and requires a specific response, but that cannot be organized without a specific definition. Obviously international cooperation is necessary. There is evidence, enough that terrorist groups with quite different causes do cooperate—Libyan, Irish, Iranian, German, Palestinian and so on—and cannot be foiled by any nation alone.

Cooperation of authorities to prevent terrorism, however, has stumbled on disagreement about just what is involved. There has been a tendency to approach the problem in terms of what is considered a just or an unjust cause. This becomes an insuperable obstacle, dragging officials who profess to be the toughest opponents of terrorists into the quagmire. When Secretary of State, George Shultz advocates "moderate use of force" to capture suspects anywhere in the world to bring them to trial in the United States, he is suggesting that America go into the kidnapping business to get even with kidnappers.

Any useful definition of terrorism is necessarily arbitrary, making a distinction on the basis not of how heinous the crime or wanton the violence but of how it is organized. To call one act warfare, another revolution or counter - revolution and another terrorism can not establish an order of justification but an order of how to organize a response.

Its categories could be established more clearly, there would be a much better chance that Governments could agree at least on trying to suppress one mindless plague.

An appropriate definition for terrorism might be the use of force against parties who are not involved in a conflict, who do not even engage themselves or know that they are entering a danger zone, in order to make a political statement. Practically all use of force is intended to frighten and intimidate. The question is how directly or indirectly it is applied. Certainly, it is not how admirable or repellant the cause is.

The importance of arriving at such a nonpolemical definition is that it could bring a big advance toward the kind of international action that might be more effective. However much they may plan and indulge in violent acts, most Governments oppose the uncontrolled use of force for special purposes. Here is a ground for a general approach against terrorists.

This may seem cynical in a world that risks much more destructive violence from the organized forces of Government, but the facts of a balance of power and political relations impose a restraint that does not now exist on violence without avowed state responsibility.

There have been hints that the Russians, and may be even the Syrians, who have been targets of domestic terrorism from Arab enemies, would not be averse to cutting off the international opportunities for gangs whom they may once have aided but who have become self-propelled. Defining terrorism is the first step to organizing an international defence.

191. Lewis, Flora : Time for a convention against terrorism. *International Herald Tribune* 25 Jun 1985 ; 8.

192. Lewis, Flora : Time for terrorism's victims to organize. *International Herald Tribune* 4-5 Jan 1986; 4.

193. Lidhoo, M.L. : Profile of a terrorist. *Hindustan Times* 8 Jun 1985 ; 9.

194. Livingston, Narins H. *ed.* : *International terrorism in the contemporary world.* London, Greenwood Press, 1978. pp. 522.

195. Lodge, Juliet *ed.* : *Terrorism : A challenge to the state.* New York, 1981.

196. Lorenz, Konard : *On aggression.* London, Methuen, 1966.

197. Lucas, Colin R. : *Structure of the terror.* Oxford University Press, 1973.

198. Lyakhov, Ye : Whom does terrorism serve ? *New wave* 6 Oct 1985 ; 9, 11.

199. Maini, Darshan Singh : Dialect of terrorism I & II. *Tribune* 3 & 4 Dec 1986 ; 4.

Any examination of the nature of terrorism finally brings us to the nuclear question of the terrorist personality. What, we may ask, are the conditions and factors that create such a personality ? How does such a personality evolve and reach a point of no return ? How does it emerge as a pure machine of destruction, insensitiv to the objective reality around and unresponsive to the poetry of pity and compassion ? How may such a personality be recovered and restored to moral health, if ever ? There are no complete or final answers and whichever thesis we may tend to use springs a leak somewhere. While not ignoring the economic and ideological aspects of the problem, terrorism is primarily a question of psychopathology.

200. Malhotra, Inder : Terror, crime and state. *Times of India* 29 Aug 1985 ; 6.

201. Mallison, W.T. and S.V. : Concept of the public purpose terror in international law, doctrines and sanctions to reduce the destruction of human and material values. *Harvard Law Journal* 18, 1973.

202. Mallison, W. Thomas and Sally V. Mallison : Control of state terror through the application of the international humanitarian law of armed conflict. In *ITCW* ; 325-32.

The Civilians' Convention, as has been shown, is directed primarily at the protection of civilians in territory under the occupation of an enemy state. Civilians in unoccupied territories have, nevertheless, been exposed to great danger and destruction by the military operations of enemy states. In both Southeast Asia and Southwest Asia (also known as the Middle East) the Principal method of state terror against such civilians has been massive aerial bombardment. It should also be mentioned that the so called free fire zones involve the probability of the infliction of terror, in the form of death and destruction, upon any civilians who have the misfortune to live in the zone or indeed are merely passing through it.

The Third Session cf the Diplomatic Conference on the Reaffirmation and Development of International Humanitarian Law Applicable in Armed Conflicts met in Geneva from April 21 to June 11, 1976. The purpose of this conference was not to supercede, but to supplement the four existing Geneva Conventions for the Protection of War Victims. With this objective in view, the conference is working on two draft additional protocols which it is hoped will produce agreed upon texts at the end of this year's session. Protocol I deals with international conflicts and Protocol II deals with internal conflicts.

Some of the most significant articles of Protocol I concern the protection of civilians in international conflict situations. Draft Article 46, already agreed upon in committee, codifies the customary law doctrine that the civilian population as such, as well as individual civilians, may not be made the object of direct military attack. In a significant provision it specifies that : "Acts or threats of violence which have the primary object of spreading terror among the civilian population are prohibited." The article also prohibits indiscriminate attacks which are "of a nature to strike military objectives and civilians or civilian objects without distinction." The article further specifies that a bombardment which treats as a single military objective a number of clearly separated and distinct military objectives located in a city, town, village, or other area containing a concentration of civilians is indiscriminate and consequently prohibited.

If this article is adopted by the diplomatic conference and thereafter ratified by the states represented at Geneva (which are substantially the same as the membership of the United Nations) the result will be a specific prohibition upon area bombardment which, if it is enforced, will provide significant protection for civilians which they do not now have. The development of precision guided missiles, including so called smart bombs, makes it possible for the states possessing sophisticated weaponry to support this draft article without reducing military efficiency. The Third World states require no persuasion in order to support the article.

Draft Article 50 which has also been adopted in committee, concerns precautions which must be taken in conducting an attack. This article codifies the customary international law rule of proportionality by providing that those who plan or decide upon an attack shall :

> refrain from deciding to launch any attack which may be expected to cause incidental loss of civilian life......which would be excessive in relation to the concrete and direct military advantage anticipated.

203. Mark, Robert : Kidnapping, terrorism and the media in Britain. In *TYT*; 76-86.

204. May, W.F : Terrorism as strategy and ecstasy. *Social Research* 41, Sum 1974 ; 277-98.

205. Menace of terrorism. *National Herald* 22 Jul 1985 ; 7.

206. Merari, Ariel : Problems related to the symbtomatic treatment of terrorism. *Terrorism* 3 (3-4) 1980 ; 279-83.

207. Mickolus, Edward F. : *Codebook ITERATE* (International Terrorism : Attributes of Terrorist Events). Ann Arbor, Univ. of Michigan, 1976.

208. Mickolus, Edward F. : *Terrorism : International perspectives.* New York, 1978.

209. Mickolus, Edward F. : Transnational terrorism. In *POT*; 147-90.

Definitions of terrorism vary tremendously, both among Governments and among individual researchers. Incidents considered terrorist's by South Africa are merely the legitimate acts of freedom strugglers in the eyes of many Third World nations. Indeed, it has become so hard to satisfy all the governments of the world that in the United Nations one does not officially discuss "International Terrorism" but rather Item 92 : "Measures to Prevent International Terrorism which Endangers or Takes Innocent Human Lives or Jeopardizes Fundamental Freedoms, and Study of the Underlying Causes of Those Forms of

Terrorism and Acts of Violence Which Lie in Misery, Frustration, Grievance and Despair, and Which Cause Some People to Sacrifice Human Lives, Including Their Own, in an Attempt to Effect Radical Changes." Such a view borders on accepting the motivations of the terrorists and is also difficult to operationalize. For purposes of the present discussion, we can consider our research to be concerned with the use, or threat of use, of anxiety-inducing extranormal violence for political purposes by any individual or group, whether acting for, or in opposition to, established governmental authority, when such action is intended to influence the attitudes and when behaviour of a target group wider than the immediate victims and when, through the nationality or foreign ties of its perpetrators, its location, the nature of its institutional or human victims, or the mechanics of its resolution its ramifications transcend national boundaries. We can further isolate transnational terrorism from other forms of violence by making the following distinctions: International terrorism is such action (as described above) when carried out by individuals or groups controlled by a sovereign State. Examples would include attacks in Europe against Palestinian liberation groups by Israeli intelligence agents, the anti-Basque campaign recently launched in the south of France by the Spanish police, and so on. Transnational terrorism is such action when carried out by basically autonomous non-state actors, whether or not they enjoy some degree of support from symphathetic States. Examples include the kidnappings of U.S. Business executives overseas, the hijacking of international flights, and the machine-gun attacks on international airports by members of the Popular Front for the Liberation of Palestine (PFLP). Domestic terrorism is a behaviour that has the aforementioned characteristics of extranormal violence but does not involve nationals of more than one State. It is the domestic parallel to transnational terrorism in that it is carried on by basically autonomous non-state actors but only affects citizens of one State. The bombings in New York City by the Weather Underground, attacks by the Irish Republican Army and Ulster Defence Association upon the civilian population in Northern Ireland, and attempted assassinations of Governmental leaders by nationals of that state are examples. State terrorism includes terrorist actions conducted by a national government within the borders of that state and is the domestic parallel of international terrorism. Examples include genocide in Nazi Germany, the programmes in the Ukraine, and incidents of torture in police states. Schematically, we can locate transnational terrorism as being one cell of political terrorism as shown in Table I. Other types of non-political terrorism, such a criminal

TABLE 1

Types of Political Terrorism

		Direct involvement of nationals of more than one State.	
		Yes	No
Government controlled or directed	Yes	International	State
	No	Transnational	Domestic

terrorism in which the sole object is personal gain, are beyond the scope of the present inquiry.

Transnational terrorism has often been described as violence for effect. It differs from military concepts of war as a strategy in that it does not attempt to hold a specific piece of territory by dint of military engagement, rather, it attempts to give, the impression that the terrorist group is able to strike with impunity ; that the small, numerically weak band of terrorists should be considered a credible threat and that Governmental authorities cannot guarantee security to members of the society under its protection. Hence, although wars, be they civil wars, colonial wars, international wars, irredentist battles for a territory, and so on, may lead to great fear in non-combatant populations, their primary objective is the securing of populations and territory tactically as well as strategically.

210. Mickolus, Edward F. : *Transnational terrorism : A chronology of events, 1968-79.* Greenwood, 1980.

211. Mickolus, Edward : Trends in international terrorism. In *ITCW* ; 44-76.

In the last decade the world has seen the rise of a new type of actor on the global stage : the transnational terrorist. Groups of them have engaged in numerous types of acts to gain headlines and increase public awareness of their causes, willing to engage in the assassination of Government leaders, sabotage of critical facilities, bombing of embassies and foreign corporations, assaults on military installations, skyjackings, kidnappings of diplomats and business men, and the takeover of embassies and holding of their staffs for ransom. How great is this problem ? Is it worsening ? Are there any trends we can discover ? Can any nation consider itself safe from such attacks ? Are certain nations being singled out ? What groups are engaged in such activity ?

What is it they want ? Why do they resort to these methods ? And, finally, what does the future hold in store for the world ?

Definitions of terrorism vary tremendously, both among governments and among individual researchers. Incidents considered terrorist by South Africa are merely the legitimate acts of freedom strugglers in the eyes of many Third World nations. Indeed, it has become so difficult to satisfy all the governments of the world that in the United Nations one does not officially discuss "international terrorism" but rather Item 92 : "Measures to Prevent International Terrorism which Endangers or Takes Innocent Human Lives or Jeopardizes Fundamental Freedoms, and Study of the Underlying Causes of those Forms of Terrorism and Acts of Violence which Lie in Misery, Frustration, Grievance and Despair, and which Cause Some People to Sacrifice Human Lives, including Their Own, in an Attempt to Effect Radical Change." Such a view borders on accepting the motivations of the terrorists, and is also difficult to translate into action. For purposes of the present discussion, we can consider our research to be concerned with :

> The use, or threat of use, of anxiety-inducing extranormal violence for political purposes by an individual or group, whether acting for or in opposition to established Governmental authority, when such action is intended to influence the attitudes and behaviour of a target group wider than the immediate victims and when, through the nationality or foreign ties of its perpetrators, its location, the nature of its institutional or human victims, or the mechanics of its resolution, its ramifications of transcend national boundaries.

We can further isolate transnational terrorism from other forms of violence by making the following distinctions : International terrorism such action (as described above) when carried out by individuals or groups controlled by a sovereign State. Examples include attacks in Europe against Palestinian liberation groups by Israeli intelligence agents and the anti-Basque campaign recently launched in the south of France by the Spanish police. Transnational terrorism is such action when carried out by basically autonomous non-state actors, whether or not they enjoy some degree of support from sympathetic States. Examples include the kidnappings of United States businessmen overseas, the hijacking of international flights, and the machine gun attack on international airports by members of the Popular Front for the Liberation of Palestine. Domestic terrorism is that behaviour which has the aforementioned characteristics of extranormal violence, but does not involve nationals of more than one state. It is the domestic parallel to transnational terrorism in that it is carried on by basically autonomous non-state actors, but only affects citizens of one state. The bombings in New York City by the Weather Underground, attacks by the Irish Republican Army and Ulster Defence Association upon the civilian population in Northern Ireland, and attempted assassinations of governmental leaders by nationals of that state are examples. State terrorism includes terrorist actions conducted by a national government within the borders of that state, and is the domestic parallel of international terrorism. Examples include genocide in Nazi Germany, the pogroms in the Ukranine, and tortures in police states.

212. Milbank, David L. : *International and transnational terrorism : Diagnosis and prognosis.* Washington, CIA, April 1976.

213. Milte, Kerry : Terrorism and international order. *Australian and New Zealand Journal of Criminology* 101, 8, Jun 1975.

214. Monti, Daniel J. : Relation between terrorism and domestic civil disorders. *Terrorism* 4 (1-4) 1980; 123-42.

215. Moss, Robert : Terrorist state. In *ITCR*; 128-34.

216. Mossner : Barbary powers in international law. *In Grotian society papers, 1972.* Ed. by Alexandrowicz. The Hague, 1972.

217. Mullen, Robert : Mass destruction and terrorism. *Journal of International Affairs* 32 (1) Spr-Sum 1978; 63-89.

218. Murphy, John F. : Comments on the Fourth Interim Report of the ILA Committee on International Terrorism (1982). *Terrorism* 7 (2) 1984; 193-98.

219. Murphy, John F. : State self-help and problems of public international law. In *LAIT*: 553-74.

The salient facts of the Israeli raid at the Entebbe Airport in Uganda may be briefly summarized as follows. On June 27, 1976, four terrorists, members of the Popular Front for the Liberation of Palestine (PLO), took control of an Air France jet shortly after it had taken off from the Athens airport. The hijackers first flew their hostages to Benghazi, Libya, for refueling, and then to Entebbe Airport in Uganda, where they were held for six days in an unused passenger terminal. Israeli discussions with President Idi Amin of Uganada, as well as intelligence reports and other sources of information, indicated quite conclusively that not only was President Amin making efforts to free the hostages and apprehend the hijackers but was actively involved in suPPort of hijacking operation.

There was substantial objectives evidence that the Uganda government was actively supporting the hijacking operation. To cite only a few examples, when the aircraft landed in Entebbe six Palestinians, members of one or more divisions of the PLO, joined the hijackers. Ugandan soldiers assisted the hijackers in their surveillance of the hostages. Shortly after landing at Fntebbe, the hijiackers demanded that 53 prisoners be released (40 incarcerated in Israel, the other 13 elsewhere). President Amin informed the hostages that the hijackers had no grudge against them, but "only against the fascist Israeli government—and if the latter does not agree to the guerrillas' demands, it does not care about the fate of its citizens." The day after the plane arrived in Uganda, all Israelis were segregated in another part of the airport. On June 30, 47 non-Israeli women and children were released and allowed to go to Paris. On July 1, 100 French hostages were released and allowed to leave the country. The 96 Israelis remained at Entebbe under the guard of the hijackers, who were relieved from time to time by Ugandan armed forces.

As all the available evidence began to point ineluctably to the futility of attempts to resolve the problem diplomatically, the Israeli Government decided to go ahead with a military raid on Entebbe in an effort to rescue the Israeli hostages. Accordingly, on July 3, under cover of darkness, three planeloads of Israeli commandos made a surprise landing at the Entebbe Airfield and within less than an hour were airborne with the remaining Israeli hostages. In the course of the raid, 1 Israeli soldier, 3 hostages, 20 Ugandan soldiers, and apparently all of the hijackers were killed. An uncertain number of other persons were wounded. Ten Ugandan aircrafts were destroyed, and considerable damage was done to various parts of the airfield. One Israeli woman, who had been taken to a Ugandan hospital earlier in the week, had to be left behind. Never heard from again, she apparently was murdered by Ugandan soldiers in retaliation for the raid. After stopping in Nairobi to refuel and to carry out emergency surgery on the wounded—at least the tacit consent of the Kenya government to do so had been secured in advance—the hostages arrived back in Israel Sunday morning, exactly a week after their take off from Lod Airport aboard Air France Flight 139.

Five days after the raid on Entebbe, the Organization of African Unity submitted a complaint to the United Nations Security Council regarding "an act of aggression" by Israel against Uganda. Not surprisingly, their version of the facts regarding the raid at Entebbe differed sharply from those just set forth. The Foreign Minister of Uganda, Juma Oris Abdalla, and the representative of Mauritania'

Moulaye El Hassen, speaking on behalf of the African Group, argued that the Israeli raid constituted aggression under article 2 (4) of the U.N. Charter in that it had violated the territorial sovereignty and political independence of a member of the United Nations. According to their version of the facts, not only was the government of Uganda innocent of any collusion with the hijackers, but it was making every effort, in cooperation with other governments and the Secretary-General, to obtain the freedom of the hostages. Further, they contended that these efforts were leading to a peaceful resolution of the problem when Israel decided "to take the law into its own hands." Accordingly, they argued, the council should adopt a draft resolution, introduced by Benin, Libya, and Tanzania, that would have had the council condemn Israel's flagrant violation of Uganda's sovereignty and territorial integrity and demand that Israel meet the just claims of Uganda for full compensation for the damage and destruction inflicted on Uganda.

In response, the Israeli ambassador to the United Nations, Chaim Herzog, sharply disputed Uganda's version of the facts, repeatedly stressing evidence of Uganda's version of the facts, repeatedly stressing evidence of Uganda's collaboration with the hijackers and of the imminent danger to the Israeli hostages. On the basis of this version of the events, Herzog turned to a defence of the raid at Entebbe under principles of international law.

220. Namboodiri, P.K.S. : Terrorism and intervention. *Mainstream* 6 Jul 1985; 5, 32.

Terrorism hit the headlines all over the world recently. It was probably the single major preoccupation of world leaders in many capitals and the subject-matter of emergency meetings of international organisations and investigating agencies. A series of tragic events—the Kanishka tragedy, the Tokyo airport explosion, American hostages aboard the hijacked TWA plane in Beirut, explosions in Kathmandu, etc.—held the world breathless focussing on this new form of rampant violence.

Among the many uses of force to achieve political aims where do we fix terrorism? War is considered a continuation of politics by other means and it is the only legitimate form of mass violence. Insurgency or guerrilla warfare is of recent origin. It is resorted to when the opponent's power is over-whelming and the aim is not to win a war but to demoralise and harass him to the point of making political concessions. Terrorism is quite different. It began as a phenomenon among individual and group desperadoes who were either out right mercenaries or were motivated by egoistic and revolutionary self-image. Groups like Baader-Meinhof in West Germany, Red Brigade in Italy, Red Army factions of Japan and the Symbionese Liberation Army of the United States and individuals like the dreaded Carlos are examples. Nor do the better organised and politically motivated groups like IRA or the Basque separatists in Spain have been able to successfully carry through their tactics a political solution to their demands.

There is yet another form of terroristic violence which is the state-sponsored operations against its own population and also against other countries and populations. Political terrorism is, thus, defined as the use or threat of use of violence by an individual or a group, "whether acting for or in opposition to established authority", when such action is designed to create extreme anxiety and/or fear-inducing effect in a target group larger than the immediate victims with the purpose of coercing that group into acceding to the political demands of the perpetrators.

221. Natanyahu, Benjamin : Through common resolve, terror can be defeated. *International Herald Tribune* 17 May 1985; 4.

222. National resolve against terrorism. *New Age* 13 Apr 1986; 1.

223. Neale, William D. : Oldest weapon in the arsenal : Terror. *Army* Aug 1973; 10-13.

224. Netanya, Benjamin *ed.* : *International terrorism : Challenge and response,* London, Transaction Books, 1981; p. 383.

225. Netayanu, Benjamin *ed.* : Terrorism : How the West can win *International Herald Tribune* 10-11 May 1986; 14.

226. No fixed rules on terror. *International Herald Tribune* 27 Nov. 1985; 6.

227. No heroism in terrorism. *Deccan Chronicle* 7 Oct 1985; 6.

228. No way to end terrorism. *Egyptian Gazette* 16 Apr 1986; 4.

229. Oakley, Robert B. : Terrorism—overview and developments. *Department of State Bulletin* Nov 1985.

230. O'Ballance, Edgar : Terrorism : the new growth form of warfare. In *ITCW*; 415-22.

One of the first distinct evidences of international terrorism became apparent when in May 1974 three members of the Japanese Red Army, landing at Lod Airport in Israel, suddenly killed twenty-four people including Puerto Rican, pilgrims and injured other seventy-nine. This caused the fedayeen to claim for it had international support, but it was really the beginning of a process of penetration of that movement and others by international terrorists. The process began to coagulate, and in the past two years or so, a number of small terrorist networks of an international character have been unearthed. A culmination was the attack in December, 1974, ostensibly an Arab one, on the OPEC HQ. in Vienna, when people were killed and hostages taken, including eleven oil ministers. This was led by Carlos Martines, a South American, known as "The Jackal," who had no direct interest in the Palestine problem, declaring at the time that he was simply "working for world revolution."

No longer could there be any doubt that international terrorists were penetrating existing terrorist organizations in an attempt to gain control of them. With minuscule costs, as compared with those of even the smallest military campaign or modern sophisticated weapons, terrorism can be thought of both as "poor man's warfare" and as the weapon of the conventionally weak, capable of being used against strong adversaries by repressed or colonial people and other suffering restraints or injustices. The terrorist can strike almost anywhere at any time against any installation or unsuspecting victim, and in his violence, men, women, and children are expendable. Terrorism, against which there seems as yet to be no sure or positive defence, may eventually reach such a scale as to force governments to change their policies and adopt others alien to them.

Certain conditions must prevail, and terrorists need determination, dedication, political motive, money, weapons, support and, above all, a safe sanctuary. Few countries are prepared willingly to provide such a safe refuge for any and every terrorist, the exceptions being some Arab ones, but many do so selectively. Terrorism seems to thrive best in open democratic states, in the developed countries, where it is aided by the media. The terrorists especially need the media to gain publicity so as to transmit fear and apprehension. Under repressive regimes, where there is a controlled press, deprived of this advantage, they are far less successful. All terrorists are not "kamikaze"—conditioned, and the majority, estimated to be some 80 per cent, of terrorist acts are explosions, designed to make a political impact and create fear, while at the same time ensuring maximum security for the perpetrators.

There are many instances of terrorists taking hostages, usually to try to obtain the release of imprisoned comrades. This is especially true when a demand for a plane to fly them out to a "sanctuary" country has all too often been hastily met, owing to the government's high regard for human life. In kidnapping and hostage situations, the terrorists want something, apart from public impact, and if they have to kill their victims their effort is self-defeating; therefore, if hostages are not killed in the first moments of the incident they have a good chance of survival, and a study of some 300 cases showed that only 4 per cent were killed.

When it comes to bargaining for the life of a hostage, a conflict arises between the safety of the individual and the basic principles of justice and resisting blackmail. Attitudes tend to vary; some governments capitulate immediately, as has happened, while that of the United States is one of, no negotiation with terrorists, but with modifying variations that allow discussions and individuals in certain circumstances to intercede privately. Britain seems to be leading the way in evolving a policy of playing for time, of making a siege a long drawn-out test of nerves which have had several successes. A much harder policy is adopted by Israel, where response is swift and deadly, and where the principle of upholding the law seems to override the importance of the individual.

231. Obrien, Conor Cruise : Realities of terrorism. *Tribune* 28 Mar 1984 ; 4.

232. Ochberg, Frank M. List of hypotheses and assumptions on the phenomenon of terrorism. *Terrorism* 3 (3-4) 1980; 289-91.

233. Ohri, B. : TerrirusnL—The secret weapon. *Caravan* (New Delhi) Jan (First) 1985; 19-21.

234. O'loughlin, John : World-power competition and local conflicts in the Third World. In *World in crisis* ? Ed. by R.J. Johnston and P.J. Taylor Oxford, Basil Blackwell 1986; 231-68.

235. Panacea for terrorism. *Industrial Times* (Bombay) 14 Apr 1986; 2.

236. Panda, Rajaram ; Terrorism a worldwide menace. *Newstime* 18 Aug 1985; 8.

237. Parashar, S.L. : International terrorism. *Madhya Pradesh* Chronicle 22 Feb 1986; 4.

American (Super Power) feel helpless in the face of international terrorism and wants the government to do more to fight it, but are unsure that military action would help according to a poll. Fifty two per cent of the 1981 adults in a New York Times CBS news poll believed there is nothing individuals can do to protect themselves from terrorists and 57 per cent of the respondent said they were so concerned about the dangers of terrorism that they did not want friends to travel abroad.

Only 38 per cent said that US was doing enough to protect Americans and 55 per cent thought more could be done, the poll said.

What is Terror ? "Terror is a weapon as real as a gun and sometimes more deadly. For it can mill not only the body, but also the spirit of those lives it touches with fear." So begins "Terror in Vietnam" by Jay Mallin, a new book that pointed style systematically analysies the Vietcong's use of violence, Author Mallin added—"It is a highly developed, highly refined political weapon."

"Tactics of Terror could never have been employed more ruthlessly any where than in Vietnam which Mallin rightly defines as violence inflicted by armed men on helpless civilians. Whether it be mining of roads, machinegunning of busses, kidnapping villagers, burning homes, or torture and murder, the Vietcong employ brutality with purpose" to destroy the moral of the vietnamese citizens and discredit the Government. Any opportunity will do. When typhoon rains caused massive flooding in 1964 the Vietcong fired repeatedly at evacuation helicopters carrying civilians.

They will cut off the arms of the Chief's 12 years old daughter in order to frighten the neighbouring peasants into silence, about their whereabouts. Mallin, the author says they throw grenade into a crowded bar or toss a plastic bomb into a teeming market place. The purpose is to erode confidence in the Government's ability to provide protection and to try to discourage, business activity, cause investment capital to flee, and in general to undermine the economy.

They have varied strategies of terror. In the country side they will behead a village chief whereas in urban area banks or busy bus stands or Railway stations are the victims to create confusion and sheer disorder. They just kill for killing sake. Causing fear is the motive and more often than not, persons in authority preferably policemen are the main casualities.

Few countries are free from this new danger and India also is having her full share. The pattern is the same in the whole world.

238. Parry, Albert : Right-wing terror. In *Terrorism*. New York, 1976; 488-508.

239. Parry, Albert : *Terrorism : From Robespierre to Arafat*. New York, Vanguard Press, 1976.

240. Paul, Leslie : *Age of terror*. London, Faber, 1950.

241. Paust, Jordan J. Federal jurisdiction over extra territorial acts of terrorism and no immunity for foreign violators of international law under the FSIA and the Act of State Doctrine. *Virginia Journal of International Law*, Winter 1983.

242. Paust, Jordan J. : Private measures of sanction. In *LAIT* : 575-630.

This does not mean that there is little or no "law" in this area, but rather that law is not some static, printed set of words on a piece of paper but a dynamic process of human interaction reflecting both what people think and what people do. This balanced emphasis on people's attitudes and behaviour is realistic in that it mirrors the shared legal expectations of the community and the actual practices of states, private institutions, value groups, individuals, and other participants in the international legal process. A sanction decision will then be more authoritative and probably more efficatious than one that relies solely on either what people think or do, or on some aspect of these two components of law (such as past court practice, past state practice, or past elite expectation documented in a U.N. General Assembly resolution).

The McDougal-Lasswell value categories (enlightenment, respect. rectitude, wealth, well-being, skill, and power) are used here to facilitate a policy-oriented consideration of the decisions, conditions, and problems of private self-help sanction strategies. Past and possible future self-help responses will be related to the values generally affected by the self-help strategy and to the five decisional tasks identified by McDougal and Lasswell. These five decisional tasks are:

(1) the identification and clarification of the legal policies at stake in a given situation; (2) a description of relevant past trends in decision, if any; (3) an analysis of factors that affected those decisions; (4) a projection of future trends and 5) a recommendation of a continuation or change in policy, institutions, and procedures (policy alternatives). This inquiry will be prefaced by an attempt to identify relevant

problems, claims and policies. Thus the framework proceeds from an introductory overview into more specific problem areas.

One final point about the need for a definition : It is not the purpose here to provide an in-depth analysis of the definitional criteria, but a working definition seems necessary to avoid the confusion or ambiguity too often found in the General Assembly or in the literature. An objective definition of international terrorism is required to avoid politically loaded confusion because even though words will not dictate decisions, the impossibility of absolute definitional precision does not necessarily render complete confusion desirable. Furthermore, an objective definition, one that describes terrorism as a process, can be an extremely useful guide for decision-markers confronted with policy, claims, context and other questions involving legal competence and jurisdiction. The U.N. Secretary-General's report on international terrorism reflects the need for an objective definition in its attempt to articulate certain basic definitional components. The 1937 Convention on Terrorism and the efforts of subsequent scholars have identified other components of the process of terrorism.

In this chapter a descriptive definition of terrorism (i.e., one that also describes the terroristic process) will be used. "Terrorism" involves the international use of violence by the precipitator(s) against an instrumental target in order to communicate to a primary target a threat of future violence. The object is to use intense fear or anxiety to coerce the primary target into certain behaviour or to mould its attitudes in connection with a demanded power (political) outcome. It should be noted that in a specific-context the instrumental and primary targets could well be the same person or group. Also, terror can be caused by an unintended act, but the community does not seem to perceive such activity as terrorism, nor does it seek to regulate terror caused by conduct that does not include intense coercion or acts and threats of violence.

The key to this definition's utility is that it is primarily descriptive. It does not provide an answer to the separate question : Whether terrorism used in a given situation is permissible or impermissible. This approach, is not conclusion-oriented and does not dictate any particular decision about legality or permissibility. Further, this approach does not define away certain types of terrorism as if they do not exist, and it does not advance any particular political preference or seek prior acceptance of an ideological excuse for terror. Thus such a definition can provide a useful basis for politco-legal inquiry into what specific forms terrorism should be expressly prescribed by new international conventions or domestic criminal legislation.

243. Paust, Jordan J. : Responses to terrorism : A prologue to decisions concerning private measures of sanction. *Stanford Journal of International Studies* 12, Spr 1977; 79-130.

244. Paust, Jordan J. : Survey of possible legal responses to international terrorism. *Georgia Journal of International and Comparative Law* 431, 1975.

245. Paust, Jordan J. : Terrorism and "terrorism-specific" statu *Terrorism* 7 (2) 1984; 233-39.

246. Peres, Shimon. Threat and the response. In *ITCR*; 8-11.

The second part of 20th century has seen national and ethnic conflicts expressed in two different strategies : The Strategy which stems from the existence of nuclear arms and the strategy which is based upon the outburst of repeated terror. Strangely, the more deadly weapons, the less dangerous they are. I believe that negotiations on disarmament are an example of an effort aimed at having moral responsibility to overcome the forces of technology. It is the symmetry between the results of using those arms and not using them which has brought their possessors to a strategic understanding that we hope will continue.

Terror is an expression of virulence and extremism based upon a hope that the weaker side, the victim, will eventually give into its lack of logic and restraint. You cannot bring an end to terror around a negotiating table, because the motive of terror is to exact surrender by terrorizing the other side. You can negotiate with groups who have embarked upon the path of terror only after their leaders are totally convinced that terror itself will bear no fruit. In the case of sophisticated arms, negotiations may precede their usage ; in the case of terror, only when it ceases can negotiations proceed.

Terror, aside from affecting its victims, engenders a refusal to negotiate within its own ranks. Rifles in the hands of many without the rule of majority and without legitimacy create a permanent dialogue of fire. There is no room for moderation as long as the first to shoot can lead the group. I would not be surprised to learn that the number of victims within the terrorist groups exceeds the number of victims outside the terrorist groups. Terrorists live under the impression that their way of fighting is strategy and not just tactics. It becomes a way of life for them, an illusion which must be destroyed.

I believe that in fighting terrorism we have to follow several basic rules :

—There should never be a surrender to terrorism.

—We must have an elaborate intelligence system apparatus, a well-organized early warning system and properly trained people. Only these can nullify the terrorist advantage of surprise and indiscriminate attack.

—We must fight terrorists not only in the operational field but also on the psychological one. The tendency of terrorist groups to be deck themselves with such titles as "The Red Army" or "The Liberation Organization" should not beguile us or our often bewitched media. Those groups do not carry any message to the working class nor any message of liberation to their own people. They base their strength upon the promise of murder and it is murder which eventually replaces all promises. Terrorist groups should be described in their true colours—groups which are impatient with democracy, which are undisciplined, corrupted in their attitude to life and unable to free themselves from the domination of murder and hatred.

—Terror has become international and must be fought internationally. The terrorists consider most free nations and peoples as their enemies; countermeasures must therefore be internationally coordinated. The earlier this is done, the better will be the anti-terror operation. Since terror is carried out in the dark and clandestinely, it cannot be met squarely in the open field; its tactic of surprise must be met by a well-prepared strategy of surprise on the part of the international community.

Yetremembering Yoni, it is courage that counts. We do not lack courageous people. They are entitled to live in a world where courageous and responsible policies will ensure fulfilment of their potential. It is with this aim before us that we have met today to cherish a memorable individual and contribute to a better future. If we succeed, it may be as significant as the negotiations on arms limitations could be in our era. The Jonathan Institute will make it its business to contribute to this important effort : To enable a world of many opinions and different desires to conduct a dialogue without the murder and death of the innocent.

247. Plaff, William : Terrorism : There is another way to deal with it. *International Herald Tribune* 13-14 Sep 1986 ; 4.

The democracies have thus far tried two ways to deal with terrorism ; appeasement and intimidation. Neither has worked. Is there a third way, which might work? There is, but it is unrewarding for politicians and unexciting both to press and public.

Intimidation has been U.S. and Israeli policy. The atrocious events in Karachi and Istambul recently provided further demonstration, if any were needed, that bombing Libyans, Lebanese and Palestinians has proven worthless as a method for deterring terrorism. It incites it. It is also morally objectionable, because it kills and mutiliates people who have nothing to do with terrorism.

Why, then, do people go on doing it ? It is action. It both gratifies and rationalizes the normal human impulse to take revenge. While neither intelligent, useful, nor moral as policy, it thus continues.

Appeasement is a second false solution. This one is seductive because, in the short-term, it can get results. The French Government right now is considering whether to free the leader of a terrorist group, George Ibrahim Abdullah, who has been accused of playing a role in the murders of a U.S. military attache in France in 1982, Lieutenant Colonel Charles Ray and of an Israeli diplomat. The motive for releasing him would be to stop a series of bombings in Paris.

248. Pipes, Richard : Roots of involvement. In *ITCR*; 58-63.

The philosophical origin of modern terrorism may be found in the Catechism of the Revolutionary by the Russian Nechayev, who over a hundred years ago spelled out exactly what the function and morality of a terrorist should be. It is generally believed that Russian terrorism failed, that the terrorists did not achieve their purpose, and that in 1917 power was seized by a group—the Bolsheviks—who were hostile to terrorism. The more I study the history of the Russian Revolution, the more skeptical I become about this commonplace assumption.

The roots of Soviet terrorism, indeed of modern terrorism, date back to 1879. This year, therefore, marks the hundredth anniversary of the establishment of terrorism it is an organized political movement. It marks the founding of that organization which that it is the source of all modern terrorist groups, whether they be named the Tupamaros, the Baader-Meinhof group, the Weathermen, the Red Brigade or the PLO. I refer to the establishment in 1879 of a Congress in the small Russian town of Lipetsk of an organization known as Narodnaya Volya or the People's Will.

This small organization initially had hardly more than thirty members. Early in its existence it passed a death sentence on the then reigning Czar, Alexander II (known as the Czar Liberator because in 1861 he freed the Russian serfs). After a succession of failures, on March 1, 1881, it finally succeeded in murdering the Czar.

Why do I take the year of 1879 of which we are today "mourning" the first centenary, and maintain that it represents something really new in history ? Surely we have had innumerable political murders in the past. But those murders were of individual political leaders. The new development lies in the following distinction : the murder of political figures in the past had been carried out by individuals against individuals, by those who felt that a particular man in power represented or embodied political or social evil. These political assassins were not organized, they had no program and they had no vision beyond the assassination of those individuals who in their minds embodied this evil.

The People's Will organization was the first to consider the enemy to be the whole system, and by system against I emphasize it meant not only autocracy, but also capitalism, religion, law and everything else which kept the body politic intact. They had no particular hostility towards Alexander II personally; some of them indeed admired him for liberating the serfs. But he was regarded as an essential part of an inherently evil system, and had to be destroyed.

This was an innovation. I think there was nothing like it before in history, but there has been a great deal like it since.

After the assassination of Alexander II there was a revulsion against terrorism, and for about 20 years there was a hiatus when the movement lay dormant. It was revived in 1902, and was active for the next 5 years until it was finally broken by Prime Minister Stolypin. Thousands were killed, many of them innocent bystanders. I do not subscribe to the distinction by some that modern terrorism differs from previous terrorism in that it takes no account of civilians and innocent bystanders. That is not the case. Several anti-czar revolutionary groups very happily killed anybody who came in their way.

249. Pictograw : Anatomy of international terrorism. *US News and World Report* (Washington) 6 June 1980.

250. Pime, Georgia : Terrorism and so forth. *International Herald Tribune* 19 May 1986; 7.

251. Plastic terrorism. *Times of India* 29 Dec 1986; 8.

Science and technology are often said to be "amoral" in themselves, and take on good or evil roles, depending on which purpose man puts them to. This is now further evident in the manner in which terrorist activity has now become sophisticated, and arms and explosion material made from plastic material, are employed, to escape detection. The somewhat frequent use of plastic-based weapons has become a new challenge to manufacturers of hi-tech detection equipment, according to Mr. Rodney Wallis, security chief of the International Air-Transport Association, IATA. The sophisticated terrorist these days is aided and abetted by plastic weapons and plastic explosion materials which can be moulded both of which can escape detection by conventional detectors.

New techniques to detect such weapons and explosives are on the way, but might take some time. Mechanical suffers to identify nitrogen content in the explosives are ready—but a well-trained dog still performs better, X-ray equipment to detect low-density objects has been found useful as also "chemiluminiscence" where computers aid in thermal neutron activation and can detect plastic bombs. It is odd that new weapons technology should help the international terrorist to hoodwink airlines and airport security, but experts seem confident that the police would soon be one or two steps ahead of the modern terrorist, with his new-fangled plastic armoury.

252. Possony, Stefan T. : Kaleidoscopic views on terrorism. *Terrorism* 4 (1-4) 1980; 89-122.

253. Possony, Stefan T. and L.F. Bouchney : *International terrorism : The communist connection.* Washington, 1978.

254. Possony, Stefan T. : Terrorism : A global concern. *Defence Foreign Affairs Digest* Jan 1973; 4-5.

255. Post, Jerrold M. : Notes on a psychodynamic theory of terrorist behaviour. *Terrorism* 7 (3) 1984; 241-56.

256. Prairie fire. *Skeptic* (2) Jan-Feb 1976.

257. Prakash, Bharat : How terrorism can be curbed. *New Age* 4 May 1986; 6.

258. Puri, Rackshat : Meeting terrorism. *Hindustan Times* 2 Jul 1985; 9.

259. Quainton, Anthony C.E. : Terrorism : Policy, action and reaction. In *POT*; 169-76.

260. *Questions relating to international terrorism.* New York, United Nations, 1972.

261. Radovanovic, Ljubomir : Problem of international terrorism. *Review of International Affairs* 23, Oct 1972 ; 5-20.

262. Rai Singh : Rising trend of terrorism. *National Herald* 30 Dec 1984.

263. Rai Singh : Terrorism : Whose tool and for what ? *Caravan* (*New Delhi*) Jan (First) 1986; 22-24.

264. Raj, S.G. : Terrorism : The pitiless struggle. *Caravan* (New Delhi) Jan (First) 1986 ; 25-27.

265. Random retaliation promotes terrorism. *Egyptian Gazette* 8 Apr 1986 ; 2.

266. Rao, Arun : Cult of terrorism. *Nagpur Times* 9 Jan 1985 ; 7.

267. Rappoprt, David C. and Yonah Alexander ed. *Rationalization of terrorism.* Maryland, 1981.

268. Redefining terrorism : *Blitz* 14 Jun 1976 ; 2.

A wave of terror has been unleashed against Indians across Western Europe and North America, on the soil of those very nations screaming loudest "terrorism". To this day, the Federal Republic of Germany, yet to shake off the shock of the Berlin disco bombing, allows a "Khalistan Consulate" to operate on its territory.

To top it all, it is these very governments that are funding the blood-thirsty military junta in Pakistan, in the name of aiding Afghan "freedom fighters", to dislodge the Kabul government. Most of this aid is, in fact, converted into weapons like the F-16s which will inevitably be used against this nation, if history is any guide. To some extent, India has herself to blame for having borne all these outrages with so extreme a degree of tolerance.

National survival now dictates that Delhi should go on the offensive, pinning its enemies to the wall of world public opinion. For a start, a white paper detailing the activities of the governments in sponsoring, supporting and legitimising terrorism against India should be published and made available to the world. It would have the dual benefit of shaking their arrogance, while knocking the bottom of the canard, that it is Third World leaders who support terrorism.

269. Reisman, W.M. : Private armies in a global war system, prologue to decision. *Virginia Journal of International Law* 14, 1973.

270. Reston, James : No country is secure in an age of fanatics. *International Herald Tribune* 14 Oct 1985 ; 4.

271. Rise seen in terrorism, hijackings by 2000. *China Daily* 4 Dec 1985 ; 4.

272. Rosen, Steven J. and Robert Frank : *Measures against international terrorism*. In *ITWS*; 60-68.

What is shocking about international terrorism as a method of warfare is not the amount of bloodshed, which by any account is minimal compared to more conventional methods of armed struggle, but the character of the victims. The law and custom of conventional war permits almost unrestricted violence against the active armed forces of a hostile target state, but at the same time extends the maximum possible protection and exemption to innocent non-combatants, civilians, and neutrals of third states. In the terrorist mode of action, on the other hand, it is exactly these exempted and innocent parties who are the main target of action. The immediate victim may have no organic connection to the political policy of the target state, and may indeed not even be a citizen of that state nor have any influence over its policy, but if his victimisation might by some process of reasoning contribute to the weakening of that state or to the strengthening of the revolutionary movement, the action is considered legitimate. According to critics, this lack of proximity between the victim and the policy under attack thus puts terrorism on a different moral plane as a method of violent political behaviour.

States not parties to a dispute may be expected to object to the all-encompassing scope of the terrorists' field of battle, and at the minimum they will feel a responsibility for protecting the lives of their nationals at home and abroad. In principle, they may insist on a differentiation between creditable ends and unacceptable means—a distinction that is already well-established in the law of warfare, for example in the prohibition of germ warfare. The question, then, is what can the international community do to protect innocent civilians from random victimisation if international terrorists continue to claim an unrestricted global arena as a legitimate theatre of combat ?

273. Rosenbaum, H. Jon and Peter C. Steberg *eds. Vigilant politics*. University of Pannsylvania Press, 1976. p. 292.

274. Rothstein, Andrew : Terrorism : some plain words. *Labour Monthly* Sep 1973 ; 413-17.

275. Rozakis, Christos L. : Terrorism and the internationally protected persons in light of ILC's draft articles. *International and Comparative Law Quarterly* 23 (1) Jan 1971 ; 32-72.

276. Rubin, Alfred P. : Current legal approaches to international terrorism. *Terrorism* 7 (2) 1984 ; 147-62.

277. Rubin, Alfred P. International terrorism and international law In *TTP* ; 1979.

278. RUSI. : *Ten years of terrorism.* London, 1979.

279. Russell, Charles A. *et. al.* Out-inventing the terrorist. In *TTP* ; 3-44.

280. Russell, Charles A. and Bowman H. Miller : Profile of a terrorist. In *POT* ; 45-60.

281. Ryter, Stephen L. : Terror : A psychological weapon. *Review* May-Jun 1966 ; 145-50.

282. Sabetta, Anne R. : Transnational terror : Causes and implications for response. *Stanford Journal of International Studies* 12, Apr 1977 ; 157-64.

283. Saksena, N.S. : Assassination as a part of political terrorism, In *THF* ; 39-40.

284. Saksena, N.S : Growing roots of terrorism. *Hindustan Times* 14 Dec 1979 ; 9.

285. Saksena, N.S. : State terrorism against enemy states. In *THF* ; 49-50.

286. Saksena, N.S. : Supply of weapons to terrorists. In *THF* ; 217-25.

287. Saksena, N.S. : Terrorism : Present measures inadequate. *Times of India* 13 May 1985 ; 8.

288. Saksena, N.S. : Upsurge in international terrorism from 1968. In *THF* ; 53-54.

289. Saksena, N.S. : Why terrorism is so rampant ? *Times of India* 5 May 1981.

290. Sardeshpande, D.S. : Tackling terrorism. *Hindu* (Madras) 23 Aug 1986 ; 8.

291. Sawhney, R.G. : International terrorism : A one-sided debate. *Times of India* 16 May 1986 ; 8.

292. Schelling, Thomas C. : Phenomenon of terrorism. *Terrorism* 3(3-4) 1980 ; 303-4.

293. Schrastetter, Rudolf : Theses on terrorism. *Terrorism* 3(3-4) 1980 ; 305-9.

294. Schultz, Richard : Conceptualizing political terrorism A : typology. *Journal of International Affairs* Spr-Sum 1978 ; 7-16.

295. Scott, Andrew M. : *Revolution in statecraft : Intervention in the age of interdependence.* Durham, Duke Press Policy Studies, 1982.

296. Segaller, Stephen : *Invisible armies : Terrorism into the 1990s.* London, 1986. p. 311.

297. Sen, Sankar : Challenge of the terrorists. *Hindustan Times* 10 Jun 1935 ; 9. *Amrita Bazar Patrika* 4 Jul 1985 ; 6.

298. Severe steps against terrorism announced. (at the Toky summit) *Newstime* (Hyderabad) 6 May 1986 ; 1.

299. Shaper, J. : Terrorism has no morality. *International Herald Tribune* 17 Nov 1986 ; 5.

300. Sharma, Madan Lal : Patronising international terrorism. In *Terrorism : American style*. New Delhi, 1982 ; 79-99.

301. Sharon, Ariel : Terrorism : For alliance against these murderers. *International Herald Tribune* 1 Oct 1986 ; 4.

302. Shaw, Jennifer *et. al. eds.* : *Terrorism : Collected Views.* London. 1979.

303. Sirala, Martti : Some theses on terrorism. *Terrorism* 3(3-4) 1980 ; 311-27.

304. Silverstein, Martin E. : Hypotheses on terrorism. *Terrorism* 3(3-4) 1980 ; 329-33.

305. Simpson, Howard R. : Terror. *U.S. Naval Institute Proceedings.* 96, Apr 1970 ; 64-80.

306. Singh, S.P. : Crime and terrorism. *Indian Express* 28 Mar 1986 ; 6.

307. Sloan, Stephen : Simulating terrorism : From operational techniques to questions of policy. *International Studies Notes* 5(4) Win 1978 ; 3-8.

308. Sloan, Stephen : *Simulating terrorism.* Oklahoma University Press, 1981.

309. Smith, W.H. : International terrorism : A political analysis. *The Year Book of World Affairs* 31, 1977 (London).

310. Solan, Stephen and Richard Kearney : Analysis of a simulated terrorist incident. *Police Chief* Jun 1977 ; 57-59.

311. Sovetov, A. "Peace built on strength"—A doctrine of international terrorism. *International Affairs* (Moscow) (2) Feb 1984 ; 52-62.

312. Stohl, Michall. Myths and realities of political terrorism. In *POT* ; 1-22.

Political terrorism, while not a recent addition to the catalogue of humankind's problems, has achieved a position of notoriety rivaled by few contemporary global crises. Media fascination and the undeniable fact that terrorism provides a riveting spectacle, coupled with the honest concern of governments and their populations, have catapulated terrorism into a priority area for study. The burgeoning journalistic and scholarly literature that has resulted from this increased awareness has unfortunately not been accompanied by a commensurate increase in the understanding of the phenomenon.

The collection of essays illuminates the process of political terrorism. The authors, as students of terrorism, do not have the capability to eliminate the causes of terrorism, nor even the symptoms. However, it is hoped that the analytic and historical examinations of the processes of political terrorism presented here will help to eliminate the problem of delusion as humankind confronts terrorism in the future.

We begin the process of reducing the possibility of delusion by examining in this introductory essay eight pervasive myths regarding contemporary political terrorism. Next, we briefly explore some persistent realities of the purposes and processes of terrorism and conclude with an overview of the chapters of this volume. The eight myths discussed below are the following :

1. Political terrorism is the exclusive province of antigovernmental forces.

2. The purpose of political terrorism is the production of chaos.
3. Political terrorism is the province of madmen.
4. Terrorism is criminal, not political, activity.
5. All insurgent violence is political terrorism.
6. Governments always oppose non-governmental terrorism.
7. Terrorism is exclusively a problem relating to internal political conditions.
8. Political terrorism is a strategy of futility.

A note of caution and explanation prior to the discussion of these myths is appropriate here. Although each of the myths presented is widely accepted, it is doubtful that the set of myths as a whole is accepted by any individual. The discussion of the myths provides a vehicle to introduce the reader to the complexities of terrorism.

Perhaps the most important place to begin our survey of the myths of contemporary terrorism is with the myth that terrorism is the exclusive province of insurgents, dissidents or antigovernmental forces. Although scholars and diplomats continue to debate the precise definition of the term "terrorism", a quite typical approach to the meaning of the term may be found in the statement of William Hannay (1974, p. 268) that

> recent contemporary usage tends to restrict its (terrorism) meaning to either random or extortionate violence, aimed ultimately at the target state of a guerilla, resistance or liberation movement but which strikes at unarmed civilians, diplomats or non combatants. (See also Butler, 1976 ; Feary, 1976 ; Laqueur, 1976 ; Mallin, 1971, among many others).

The particular irony of this myth is that the first usage of the term "terror" developed in response to the systematic employment of violence and the guillotine by the Jacobin and Thermidorian regimes in France.

> Etymologists claim that the English terms terrorism, terrorist terrorise did not come into use until the equivalent French words terrorisms, terrorists, terroriser had developed in the revolutionary period 1793 and 1798. (Wilkinson, 1975, p. 9 ; see also Lefebvre, 1964, pp. 6-11).

The singular exception to this myth that is proposed by most liberal Western authors is the recognition that non-democratic, totalitarian, fascist, or communist states practise terrorism or are able to remain in power only because of their utilization of terrorist practices. The implicit conclusion of these writers is that terrorism is not something that is practised by the governments of liberal Western democracies. However, it has become clear that in the past 15 years, a number of U.S. governmental agencies and employees have engaged in actions against internal dissidents, which Western liberal authors would have labelled as terrorism if these actions had occurred in the Soviet Union or Spain. (See Blackstock, 1976; Halperin *et al.*, 1976; Wise, 1976 for an analysis of these activities).

Yet the myth persists. Its persistence in the scholarly literature is all the more peculiar in that the finest analytical work on the nature of terrorism has been conducted by scholars who were primarily interested in the use of terrorism by governments. I refer here to the outstanding contributions of Arendt (1966), Moore (1966), Walter (1969), and Dallin and Breslauer (1970). In an interesting speculative work on the problem of ruling new nations, Howard Wriggins (1969) in a style reminiscent of Machiavelli, entitles one of this chapters "Intimidate the Opponent and the Wavering Ally" and proceeds to examine different techniques which rulers have employed in retaining their powers. The important point to be considered before leaving this myth is that the Reign of Terror, which characterized the Jacobin period in France, was not an isolated phenomenon. There have been, are, and most likely will continue to be regimes that are dependent upon or employ terror as a basic component of their rule.

313. Storling, Claire. *Terror network.* New York, 1981.

314. Storr, Anthony. Sadism and paranoia. In *ITCW*; 231-39.

Many psychopaths show a failure of socialization, in that they have never formed ties of mutual regard with others, and thus live in a world which they assume to be indifferent or hostile. The development of conscience, that is, of an internal regulator of behaviour, appears to depend much more on the wish to preserve love than on the fear of punishment. Since many psychopaths come from homes in which there has been little love and a good deal of physical punishment, it is hardly surprising that they have not developed a normal conscience. A child cannot respond to the withdrawal of something which he has never had, it is understandable that those who have never felt themselves loved or approved of are not affected by disapproval. Although many psychopaths show both a lack of control of hostility and also an abnormal amount of hostility toward their fellows, much of the cruelty which they exhibit appears to be casual rather than deliberate. Thus, they may injure someone whom they are robbing or sexually assualting because they do not identify with their victim or care what he or she feels, which is obviously a different matter from the deliberate exercise of cruelty. In Holland, criminologists have experimented with confronting violent criminals with their victims. In some instances, this has brought home to the criminal for the first time that his victim is a person like himself, with the consequence that he has wished to make reparation.

It is possible that we may be able to understand the psychopath's lack of control over immediate impulse in physiological terms. Psychopaths are emotionally isolated even if not physically so; and, in other species isolation appears to produce heightened reactivity to dangerous stimuli, shown by a faster mobilization and a release of systematic norepinephrine. Human beings who, for one reason or another, have not learned to mix with their fellows in early childhood, often show inappropriate aggressive responses, sometimes overreacting because they perceive threat where none exists, sometimes underreacting because they have never learned to "stand up for themselves". In rodents, it has been shown that isolation produces a lower level of tonic aggressive arousal combined with the heightened reactivity to dangerous stimuli already mentioned; it would be worth investigating whether a similar physiological state of affairs occurs in human beings who have been isolated.

Since psychopaths constitute a small proportion of human beings, we cannot explain the human tendency toward cruelty by blaming it upon them alone, though the study of psychopaths may go some way towards, cruelty is the human tendency towards obedience. The experiments of Stanley Milgram are so well-known that I need hardly refer to them. They are summarized in his recently published book, 'Obedience to Authority'. To his surprise, around two-thirds of normal people would deliver what they believed to be extremely painful, possibly near-lethal, electric shocks to subject whom they thought was engaged in an experiment on the nature of learning because they were urged to do so by the experimenter. The excuse that they were only obeying authority is the one most frequently offered by those arraigned for torture or other forms of institutionalized cruelty, from Eichmann down. Obedience is clearly adaptive in human society as in many animal societies. A stable dominance hiearchy promotes pace within a society, markes possible organized resistance or organized escape if danger threatens, and allows for instant decision making by dominant individual. It is impossible to imagine a human society functioning at all adequately without a built-in tendency to obey.

However, obedience involving acts of violence and cruelty does not explain the cruelty of those who give the orders. At present, throughout the world, the use of torture appears to be increasing. There are two main uses. First is the obvious one of extracting information. Second is its use for the control of political dissent by creating an atmosphere of terror. It is an interesting and unexplained paradox that, while there is today a general consensus that torture is totally inadmissable, it is more widely employed than ever before. I do not believe that the tendency towards obedience entirely explains the compliance in cruelty of those who carry out cruel orders. It is certainly a powerful factor in military situations such as the Vietnam massacres or the recent execution of mercenaries. But orders to shoot women and children or one's comrades-in-arms are often backed up, in wartime, by the explicit or implicit threat that refusal might bring about one's own execution. Moreover, it is possible to imagine orders which would be resisted more strongly than orders to kill or torture. If an officer ordered his men to eat faces for breakfast, it may be supposed that few would obey, even if threatened with dire penalties.

The third factor conducive to cruelty is distance, whether this be measured in physical or psyhological terms. If human fights were confined to fisticuffs, there would not only be fewer deaths, but fewer instance of cruelty. A man who is a few hundred feet above his victims in an airplane will drop napalm upon them without a qualm. He would be less likely to produce a similar effect by pouring petrol over a child and igniting it if he was close enough to do so. Most terrorist acts, like the planting of bombs, result in harm not witnessed by the terrorist ; it is significant that the best way of saving lives of hostages held by terrorists is to allow time for a relationship to develop—that is, for psychological "distance" to diminish. Lorenz has argued that human beings possess inhibitory mechanisms against injuring their own kids which are not well-developed and which are easily overcome because they are not armed by nature with dangerous weapons like tusks or claws. Natural selection has not allowed for the invention of weapons which kill at a distance.

315. Subrahmanyam, K. : In a state of war. *Frontline* (Madras) 17-30 May 1986; 41-47.

316. Subrahmanyam, K. : Terrorism : To the forefront of the stage. *Strategic Analysis* (New Delhi) Jun 1986; 237-48.

Terrorism as an issue have moved to the forefront of the international stage. Airliners are today flying half empty, air terminals have become veritable arsenals and an air journey an enormous hassle. The international tourism industry is facing a bleak future. The security related expenditure to protect important personages and installations has skyrocketed. Access of common people to their representatives and government leaders has become restricted. Life today is not what it was in the fifties and sixties—the underlying factor being terrorism.

There are two categories of terrorism—one which is plain criminal and the other political and both are on the increase. Abduction of persons for ransom (kidnapping of Jennifer Guinness in Ireland for a ransom demand of over 2 million is an example) and threats to poison certain products (injection of cyanide in tylenol capsules or tampering with Contac capsules recently, both of which happened in the US) to extract large sums of money belong to the first category. Holding hostages, placing explosives in cars, departmental stores and aircrafts, killing people as part of evoking political terror, hijacking of various passenger vehicles, assassination of major political personalities etc. fall into the second category.

317. Sulzberger, C.L. : Deadline for more terror, *New York Times* 9 Apr 1977; 9.

318. Summaries of terrorist incidents by groups. *Terrorism* 7 (1) 1984; 97-117,

319. Summit (Tokyo) steps to curb terrorism. *Times of India* 6 May 1986; 16.

320. Sundar Rajan, K.R. : Politics of terrorism. *Amrita Bazar Patrika*. 7 May 1986; 6.

321. Sundberg, Jacob W.F. : Comments on the Fourth Interim Report of the Committee on International Terrorism. *Terrorism* 7(2) 1984 ; 185-92.

322. Sundberg, Jacob W.F. : Some points of interest and how to go about them. *Terrorism* 3 (3-4) 1980; 335-39.

323. Suspected terrorist incident—1982 *Terrorism* 7 (1) 1984 ; 117.

324. Tamkoc, Metin : *International Civil War*. Ankara METU Publication, 1968.

325. Targ, Harry R. : Social structure and revolutionary terrorism : A preliminary investigation. In *POT* ; 119-46.

For purposes of examining the central theme of this chapter, we shall survey studies on political violence and terrorism and examine data on terrorism, particularly assassinations. Because of the difficulty of gathering accurate data cross-culturally the following information serves as a preliminary test of the themes described and not a final confirmation.

This is particularly true because of the lack of data available concerning most of the variables included in the model.

For purposes of preliminary investigation, we may begin by examining the analysis of the linkages between multiple variables and political violence reported in Kirkham, Levy, and Crotty (1969). Particular attention is given by these authors to two data sets on political assassination gatherd by research groups headed by Carl Leiden and Ivo Feierabend.

Kirkham and his co-workers construct an index of the level of development to examine the hypothesis that violence and terrorism are causally linked to national economic development. Eight indicators of development were used : GNP per capita, literacy level, radios and newspapers per 1000 population, rate of urbanization, caloric intake per person per day, number of persons per physician, and the percentage of the population with telephones. Three sets of nations were discerned from the index : traditional, transitional, and modern. It was found that roughly half the traditional societies were unstable (much violence), two-thirds of the transitional societies were unstable, and one-third of the modern societies were unstable (Argentina, Belgium, East Germany, France, United States, and USSR). In reference to political assassinations particularly, only five of twenty-four modern nations had a high frequency of assassinations (more than two in 20 years). These nations were Argentina (nine), Czechoslovakia (five), France (fourteen), Israel (three), and the United States (sixteen). Sixteen of twenty-three traditional nations had high levels of assassinations and twenty-three of thirty-seven transitional societies had a high frequency of assassinations.

Kirkham and his co-workers conclude that "there is a definite relationship between level of development and incidence of political violence, including assassination. Developed countries tend to experience lower levels of political unrest and assassination than do less developed countries" (Kirkham, Levy, and Crotty, 1969, pp. 137-39). The United States and France are seen as "notable exceptions".

The authors further examine assassination data based on a five-nation typology found in the World Handbook of Political and Social Indicators. "Traditional primitive" societies have a low assassination rate, "traditional" societies a high rate, "transitional" societies have a lower rate than the traditional but nations with a high assassination rate in this category dwarf those with a lower assassination rate by two to one. Half of the "industrial revolutionary" societies have high numbers of assassination. Finally, "high mass consumption" societies have a low frequency of assassinations. Of the fourteen nations in this category only two, the United States and France, had more than two assassinations during a 20 years period.

326. Tarkunde, V.M. : State terrorism must end. *Statesman* 10 Sep 1985 ; 3.

327. Tate, Don. : Law agencies braced for possible years of terror. *Rocky Mountain News* 25 Jan 1976.

328. Taylor, G.R. : Terrorism : How to avoid the future. In *ITCW* ; 642-68.

The techniques of destruction are constantly improving. More powerful, more compact explosives are the most obvious example. I note that kidnappers now often inject their victims with a soporific drug-much more effective and reliable than old-fashioned chloroform. But no one is going to stop the march of technical progress, and I can readily imagine quite subtle wrecking techniques, such as feeding the wrong instructions to computers, while the CIA and KGB have shown what can be done in the way of concealed weapons, fancy gadgets which could be used for blackmail, and so on. And the case of Patricia Hearst shown what the technique of brainwashing can do.

The members of a closely knit community is somewhat inhibited from attaining his ends by force, not simply from fear of counterforce—meaning the law and punishment—but also by his need to live with the community afterwards, his dependence upon approval and acceptance, perhaps upon help if he is struck by illness and misfortune. In past times, to be an outcast was very serious for it deprived you of this vital support. In the modern world, the perpetrator of an antisocial act can get away to other communities where he can be anonymous, or even be approved. He may even call upon the state which he is attacking to care for him in the hospital, or to support him. It recently turned out that some of the Irish terrorists exploding bombs in Britain had been living on British unemployment insurance. Biting the hand that feeds you no doubt gives an extra kick. I'm sure you'll agree that social controls of this informal kind are becoming and will continue to become less and less effective against alienated individuals.

Perhaps the most important force restraining a person from the wanton wounding and killing of innocent third parties is the built-in restraint we call conscience. I can see that the "freedom fighter" who kidnaps a foreign diplomat in the hope of forcing his government to release his friends from prison (to take an example) can reconcile this with his conscience. I find it harder to understand the Irish Provisional who tosses bomb into a supermarket where innocent persons, children, and maybe even his own political supporters are shopping. The question needs more detailed discussion, but I think it is beyond doubt that some terrorists are pathological personalities, incapable of feeling, actually getting a kick from destruction, even attracted by the idea of a holocaust in which they may themselves perish.

I suspect that the number of such personalities produced by Western (and may be some Eastern) societies is increasing. The growth of schizophrenia, which is marked by emotional blunting, is a clue. Why this should occur is something I have written about at length in my book Rethink and elsewhere. Here I need only say that if the output of pathological individual is increasing, violence-including terrorism—will certainly increase, too.

To recap : All these five factors, to name no others, are likely to become more marked and thus promote an increase of terrorism and violence over the next twenty or thirty years education, freedom of movement, techniques of destruction and disruption, decay of social controls, decay of conscience Dont't overlook the obvious point that the terrorists of the year 200 have already been born. They are now undergoing experiences which will turn them towards terrorism.

329. Terekhov, Vladimir : International terrorism and the fight against it. *New Times* (Moscow) 11, 1974 : 20-22.

330. Terraine, John *et al* : Terrorism and the media. In *TYT* : 87-108.

331. Terrorisation. *Patriot*. 22 Apr 1984 ; 4.

President Ronald Reagan has signed a policy directive authorising pre-emptive strikes and reprisal raids against terrorists. And that's a laugh. If there is anything that is needed at the moment it is a world-wide alert against US terrorism. It is as insidious as cold steel in the dark and as blatant as a lynching at high noon. It is mindless and perverse in its logic. And who is a terrorist, who forfeits the right to life and liberty for his style of functioning ? Nicaragua, where a UN-recognised government has been laid siege to by former official cut throats led by a despot called Samoza ? The land of life, liberty and the pursuit of happiness is spending sleepless nights trying to blast the Sandinista government in Nicaragua into the dust by every means possible—mining of ports, bombardment from the air, infiltration and, terror. Libya, of course, is a prime attraction for the new directive, for pre-emptive strikes and reprisal raids. Several attempts have already been made to assassinate Libyan President Muammar Gaddafi and at least one to provoke him into suicidal military action in the Gulf of Sidra. But the directive while unleashing the dogs of war against all those who happen, by circumstance or by will, to cross the path of the US, has not defined assassination. Perhaps when an alleged terrorist is caught, his elimination would be an act of grace, "mukti" to be precise. To kill a terrorist is not assassination but to fight a war of liberation against the gain of US interests is terrorism. To be eliminated while doing so is to die the death of terrorist. There is no such thing as a freedom fighter or a nationalist. How would the late President of Panama Torrijos who was killed in an aircrash which, Panamanians believe, was engineered by the CIA, be classified ? And Ngo Dinh Diem of South Vietnam ? And Patrice Lumumba of the Congo ? Each one in a different category but victim of the same knife. It could be argued that the CIA did not hold the knife that did the deed nor pull the trigger. But it was "our own son of a bitch" who did it. Same difference, what ? And how does one explain the terror of "benign neglect" or the verbal naildigger which demands that if you take my aid you must vote for me—a task conducted with exemplary acerbity by the Defarge-Like Jeane Kirkpatrick at the UN ? President Reagan has already made out a hit-list of international terrorists which includes Iran and North Korea, Syria, Cuba and Nicaragua. It can only be said to be a quirk that China does not fall on the other side of the fence. China is supplying weapons to the arch-terrorists in Teheran not to mention the gene-bashers called the Khmer Rouge who are operating against Kampuchea from Thailand. To assist in the search for and destruction of designated terrorists the CIA and the FBI will be allowed to raise their own "hit squads". The thought is enough to curdle the blood.

332. Terrorism. *Madhya Pradesh Chromicle.* 18 Jul 1985;6.

333. Terrorism. *Democratic World* 19 May 1985; 3-4.

In general, terrorism is the outcome of despotic systems which do not allow the expression of dissent. Or it can be due to economic reasons where a section of the people, generally the poor, get no benefit from the national growth. But Sikh terrorism in India does not fall into either category. There is no suppression of dissenting opinion in the country. The Sikhs from a community that has done very well for itself from the green revolution and general industrial expansion. It is directed from abroad, by rich Sikhs who are above the battle and far removed from the places where terrorism occurs. Those who engage in terror are people without any political purpose or policy. Their only motivation seems to be to create trouble. They think Indian polity is so fragile that it can be blackmailed, into accepting any political formula. But they are reckoning without the people of India. There are many political factions in the country. But no one questions they are united. That is the unity and integrity of the country. From the extreme left to the far right they all stand for a united India. Terrorism is thus doomed from the start. The fate of the Naxalites is a case in point. They wanted to change the political system in favour of the poor and the dispossessed. They were willing to offer the greatest sacrifice. But they found that the people will not have it. Ultimately, after many years of travail and sorrow they have had to give up violence and are thinking of entering the mainstream of Indian politics. They have come io terms with reality. The Akali faction of the Sikhs have for long been a divisive force in Indian politics. While one section like the Ghadrs took to revolution to evict British colonialists, the official leadership tried to endear themselves with the British.

334. Terrorism. *Democratic World* 30 Jun 1985 ; 3.

335. Terrorism. *National Herald.* 29 Jun 1985; 7.

The declaration by the Canadian Government that it would not allow the terrorist gangsters to turn the country into a playground for their depredations is reassuring at a time when grave doubts have been cast about the effectiveness of the steps taken by the security staff at Ottawa and Montreal to prevent the air disaster despite prior warnings. The US and Canadian ambassadors in New Delhi met Foreign Secretary Romesh Bhandari promising full cooperation in countering the terrorist activities. These moves are indicative of a new awareness, however belated, to treat international terrorism as a threat to the civilised world as a whole. This point has been stressed time and again by India while urging the western countries not to allow any quarter to the terrorists. It is clear that the sabotage of the 747 Booling is not a matter of concern for any particular country. In the words of the UN Secretary-General Javier Perez de Cuellar, "this terrible phenomenon is beyond the capacity of any one country to handle it alone." Terrorism is a hydraheaded evil with roots in mafia violence which is no respecter of nations or individuals. Canada's determination to comb out the malcontents that pose a danger to the civilised societies needs to be backed with deeds and actions.

The US and Canada along with Britain have become the hotbeds of terrorist intrigue. It is time for different nations to put their heads together and evolve steps to meet the grave situation. The main point to be understood in this regard is that no country can go on providing refuge to the culprits without jeopardising its *bona fide* as to the seriousness of intention to fight the menace in credible terms.

336. Terrorism : A debate. *New Republic.* 27 Dec 1975.

337. Terrorism—a double edged weapon. *Hindustan Times* 20 Jul 1985 ; 3.

338. Terrorism—a global phenomenon. *Searchlight* (Patna) 6 Oct 1985 ; 5.

The country which has contributed vast sums of money and massive quantities of arms to terrorist is Libya. The recipients have been the Sandinistas of Nicaragua, Montoneros of Argentina, Topamaros of Uruguay, Spanish Basques as well as Irish, West German, Italian, Sardinian, Corsican, Palestinian, Nigerian, Turkish, Japanese, Egyptian and Filipino rebels.

Within Libya itself, Col. Gaddafi maintains terrorist training camps at El-Beida, near Tobruk, the Tokra naval base and at several locations near Tripoli. Libya's state assassination teams have been responsible for more than two dozen executions of Libyan dissidents abroad. Moreover, Col. Gaddafi has personally claimed responsibility for the assassination of the Egyptian leader, Mr. Anwar Sadat. Two years ago, the Libyan ambassador to Jordan, Mr Aziz Oman Shennib defected and then revealed that Col. Gaddafi had recalled him to discuss plans for assassinating King Hussein.

Libya's close ally, South Yemen maintains several international terrorist schools, including one on the Soviet-controlled island of Socotra, at the mouth of Red Sea and backs armed groups opposed to Oman and North Yemen.

Syria maintains several terrorist camps, including one located near Hamoura. Syria also provided support for radical Palestinian splinter groups during the showdown in North Lebanon. It is also one of the main supporters of the Lebanese and Turkis terrorists.

Iran is a comparative newcomer to international terrorism but what its terrorists may lack in training they make up by fanaticism—dying for the "Islamic cause". Iran is the home for the Armenian secret army for the liberation of Armenia and is a principal supporter of the Abu Nidal Arab terrorist group in Lebanon. It is also a principal backer of the Islamic Jihad organisation the Lebanese Shi'its Amal Militia, the Iraqi Al-Dawa Party and other fundametalist terrorist groups in West Asia.

There are reports of Iran having recently set up terrorist schools where 3,000 Islamic fundamentalists can be trained. These schools are located at Ahwaz, Qom, Marydacht and Zahedan.

Thanks to its fanatic Islamic fundamentalism Iran, like Libya, has ventured further afield. While Libya has gone as far as Latin America the Iranian terrorists have gone to the aid of Islamic fundamentalist forces in Burma, Malaysia, Philippines and Indonesia. Like the Libyans, the Iranians are also told that they are performing a 'sacred duty' in the cause of Islam and revolution.

339. Terrorism : The need to understand. *Caravan* (New Delhi) Jan (First) 1986 ; 12.

340. Terrorism and innocents. *Japan Times Weekly* 13 Jul 1985 ; 12.

341. Terrorism came to stay. *Newstime* 29 Nov 1984 ; 7.

342. Terrorism galore. *Egyptian Mail* 26 Apr 1986 ; 3.

343. Terrorism intercepted. *International Herald Tribune* 14 Oct 1985 ; 4.

344. Terrorism to rise by 2000. *National Herald* 4 Dec 1985 ; 7.

345. Terrorism unlimited. *Pioneer* (Lucknow) 25 Apr 1986 ; 6.

Let us be clear about one thing. Most of the terrorism that is making front page news these days has its roots in the Arab-Israel unresolved conflict in West-Asia. The present Libyan crisis is a fall-out of this bitter festering strike. Admittedly, terrorism is rampant elsewhere too. What is happening in Punjab is a gruesome business—many call it a national disgrace. Britain has its trouble spot in Ireland ; the IRA brand of terrorism keeps taking its deadly toll periodically in Britain and in Ulster. No Western country for the matter of that is free from this menace. It has to be combated on a global basis, not by repression alone but by removing the root causes of this monstrous strife. Of course there are a few isolated acts of terrorism in the world, such as the recent assassination of the Swedish Prime Minister Olof Palme and the religious fundamentalism that is unsettling many Islamic countries and causing turmoil in our sub-continent.

In the nature of things there can be no instant cure of this spreading malaise. But there is every reason to apprehend that it will spread and not be arrested by the application of any double standard in eradicating this evil. It is surprising to note that while the so-called Libyan brand of terrorism prompted a super power like the United States to respond with unbridled terror raids on a sovereign country, killing and maiming hundreds of people, the main western powers—Britain, France, and the United States, virtually endorsed Reagan's brand of terrorism by exercising their power of veto in the Security Council. In other words, what is sauce for the goose is not sauce for the gander. What is more, while Britain and France have been very prompt in packing off Libyans from their respective countries, on the bare suspicion that they are sympathisers if not supporters of the Libyan terrorists allegedly working under Col. Gaddafi, they have been very accommodating to the Sikh terrorist expatriates who are wanted in this country to face criminal charges in the Indian courts. And all this is happening while Britain claims "special relations" with India.

The United States of course has gone several steps ahead of its allies in launching vicious air raids on a foreign country without declaring a war. The world stands aghast at the blatant display of double standard by the big Western powers in their professed drive to root out terrorism.

In West Asia, as has been stressed earlier, the current terrorism springs from the unfinished war between Israel and its Arab neighbours. It would go on even if President Reagan could expunge Libya and its leader from the face of the earth with his nuclear warheads. The well springs of Palestinian terrorism, as the 'Christian Science Monitor' pertinently points out in a thoughtful article, are not in Libya. They are in the refugee camps where 1.9 million Palestinians live in conditions of squalour, humiliation and burning resentment against Israel. The primary target of virtually all violence in West Asia is Israel. The United States and its people are secondary and often incidental targets for the plain reason that the annual subsidy to Israel makes it possible for Israel to pursue an expansionist and aggressive foreign policy.

Without American weapons and the annual American subsidy from America Israel could exist only by coming to terms with its Arab neighbours Similarly, Pakistan would not indulge in anti-Indian activities, train and equip the Sikh terrorists if America refused all sophisticated hardware and fantastic economic aid to Islamabad on the ground that the hawks there were nursing terrorists to destabilise India and fan communal hatred and violence by conniving at indiscriminate killings in Punjab. To put it without frills, terror wherever you find it, and it has to be squashed rationally and firmly without fear or favour.

346. Terrorists and civilization. *Mid-Day* (New Delhi) 1 Sep 1986 ; 5.

347. Tewari, Manjul : Terrorism engulfs mankind. *Caravan* (New Delhi) Jan (First) 1986 ; 49-511.

348. Tent of the American draft convention on terrorism. *Survival* 15 (1) Jan-Feb 1973; 32-34.

349. Thadani, Jaya : Advert of terrorism. *Tribune* 20 Jan 1984 ; 4.

350. Thapar, Romesh : Terrorism calls for many responses. *Mid-Day* 11 Jun 1986 ; 6.

351. Thompson, Robert : Terrorism and security force requirements. In *TYT* ; 128-46.

352. Thornton, Thomas Perry : Terror as a weapon of political agitation. In *Internal War* Ed. by Harry Eckstein. London, 1964 ; 71-99.

353. Trantman, Frederic : *Voice of terror : A biography of Juhaun most.* Westport, 1980.

354. Trilok Nath : Against terrorism. *Patriot* 11 May 1986.

355. Trotsky, Leon : *Against individual terrorism.* New York, Pathfinder Press, 1974.

356. Trotsky, Leon : *Terrorism and communism.* Ann Arbor, Univ. of Michigan Press, 1961.

357. Tyagi, Yogesh : Cooperation vital for combating terrorism. *Times of India* 11 Jan 1987 ; 3.

358. Unity against terrorism. *Statesman* 19 Apr 1986 ; 6.

The fortuitous timing of the American bombing of targets in Libya gives the Non-aligned group, whose Coordinating Bureau is currently meeting in New Delhi, a chance to clarify its own stand on violent solutions of international disputes. There cannot, of course, be any two opinions on condemning US policy : even if the movement of Soviet warships does not necessarily support fears of a wider conflagration,

President Reagan's recklessly dangerous intervention suggests both an absence of normal restraint and a contempt for international norms that cannot possibly be condoned, even by those who may not entertain any particular sympathy for Col. Gaddafi or his views. While the reasons for Mr. Reagan's adventurism are of interest only to the American public, the question it has posed affects the entire world community and has to be faced by a movement that includes 101 countries. A special responsibility devolves on India in this context, not only as Chairman of the Non-aligned Group but also as a victim of repeated acts of terrorism.

This is not necessarily to suggest that President Reagan's allegations against the regime in Tripoli are well founded. Even if the latest specific charge is, the American response is so extreme as to win sympathy even for Col. Gaddafi. But persistent reports of Libyan help for a variety of guerrilla groups in places as far apart as Northern Ireland and Japan cannot be dismissed only on account of the USA's overkill retaliation ; indeed, Wednesday's reiteration of the pledge to incite "popular revolution" can only have strengthened misgivings. Nor, in the interests of their own security, can Non-aligned nations appear to act on the tacit assumption that the end always justifies the means. There are, of course, strong moral and historical reasons for arguing that a terroirst in one society is a freedom fighter in another ; the duality has invariably been pleaded in mitigation of offences committed by the PLO or SWAPO. But Mr Rajiv Gandhi's unambiguous denunciation of "all sorts of terrorist activities, whether by individuals or a State", suggests a less partisan approach that might be more effective in countering the threat in the longrun. This was also the message of India's draft political resolution for the Coordinating Bureau which urged all member nations to refrain from organizing, instigating, assisting or participating in terrorist acts in other countries, and calling on them to take speedy measures, both individually and collectively, at the national and international levels, to eliminate the danger.

Unfortunately, differing national perceptions have so far prevented any kind of multilateral action. Mr. Gandhi's discussions of the subject with President Reagan led nowhere, apparently because of the USA's obssession with Communists and, to a lessor extent, radical Arab instigators to the exclusion of other dangers. Last December's SAARC conference in Dhaka also ailed to agree on collective steps because of disputes over definition and the right to sanctuary. Many of the people in India regards as terrorists are treated as political refugees in Britain and granted asylum, Canada and the USA displaying equal insensitivity to this country's grave security problems. It is probably pointless to think of constructive collective action so long as individual Governments refuse to take into account the threat to the international community as a whole, or while guerrillas like the Contras are financially and militarily encouraged because their cause enjoys Washington's political blessings. But not having similar global stakes to defend, the Non-aligned Movement can afford to take a more objective view : its condemnation of American aggressiveness will be all the more telling for including dis-approval of certain aspects of Col. Gaddafi's policy and rhetoric. The careful balance of Mr. Gandhi's speech has already shown how this may be achieved.

359. Van Dalen. Hendrick : Terror as a political weapon. *Military Police Law Enforcement Journal* 2, 1975.

360. Van Den Bergh, Harry : Maintaining the balance. In *ITCR* ; 283-88.

361. Varma, Parpuranand : Terrorism : Worldwide phenomenon. *Hindustan Times* 19 Jul 1985 ; 9.

India is not alone in facing terrorism. Surveys reveal that nearly all democracies are faced with this scourge. Since in such countries criminal law and the judicial system is based on democratic principles, it is not as easy as in autocracies to eliminate this class. The select committee of the Council of Europe in "Violence in Present-day Society"—its voluminous report was released on February 19, 1985—has highlighted the difficulty in fighting terrorism thus : "Freedom of expression is a fundamental right in our democratic societies. Even the most serious crimes cannot justify restrictions other than those provided for in the Convention for the Protection of Human Rights and Fundamental Freedoms. It is mainly exercised through the mass media, those decision makers normally agree to abide by the rules of professional ethics."

Many democratics have now adopted laws legalising tapping of telephones and the recording of telecommunications to combat this scourge. Two judgments of the European Court of Human Rights have become a standard for all European courts. In the KLASS case, the Court had ruled : "Democratic societies nowadays find themselves threatened by highly sophisticated forms of espionage and by terrorism, with the result that the State must be able, in order effectively to counter such threats, to undertake the secret surveillance of subversive elements operating within its jurisdiction . . . . granting of powers of secret surveillance over the mail, post and telecommunications is, under exceptional conditions, necessary in a democratic society in the interest of national security . . . ." Para 49 of the long judgement was upheld in another case, 'Malone', in which the Court ruled : ". . . . . the resultant interference can only be regarded as 'necessary in a democratic society' if the particular system of secret surveillance adopted contains adequate guarantees against abuse."

362. Vas, E.A. : Special units to deal with terrorism. *Times of India* 27 Sep 1984 ; 8.

363. Veenaskay and Sahar Muarkasab : *Terrorism and Political deestabilisation*. Advance Research Enterprise, 1985.

364. Victor, Cecil : "International terrorism" : Larger perspective. *Patriot* 12 Jul. 1985 ; 4.

365. Vinci, Piero : Some considerations of contemporary terrorism. *Terrorism* 2(3-4) 1979 ; 149-58.

366. Vitink, Viktor : *Leftist terrorism*. Moscow, Progress Publishers, 1984. p. 236.

367. Vivechak. Source of international terrorism. *New Wave* 11 Aug 1985 ; 2.

368. Von Balyer-Katte, W. : Terrorism. In *Marxism, Communism and Western Society*. Ed. by C.D. Kerning. Vol. 8. New York, Herder and Herder, 1973.

369. Von Clausewitz, Carl : *On War*. Princeton, 1976.

370. Vncinic, Milan : Responsibility of states for acts of international terrorism. *Review of International Affairs* 236(11) 1972 ; 536-37.

371. Waging War on terrorism. *International Herald Tribune* 9 Sep 1986 ; 8.

372. Wagner, Joachim : Origin of terrorism. *Terrorism* 3(3-4) 1980 ; 349-51.

373. Walzer, Michael : New terrorists *New Republic* 173(9) 30 Aug 1975 ; 12-14.

374. Wardlaw, Grant : *Political terrorism : Theory, tactics and countermeasures*. Cambridge, 1982.

375. Warren, Robert Penn : *Night rider* New York, Bantam Books, 1948.

376. Way to counter terrorism. *Free Press Journal* 3 May 1986 ; 4.

377. Weakness promotes terrorism. *China Daily* 26 Jun 1985 ; 4.

378. Weger, M. : Terrorism and peace. *International Herald Tribune* 27 Jan 1986 ; 4.

379. Who's terrorist ? *Moscow News* 28 Dec. 1986; 6.

"Let representatives of different countries meet and define precisely all the aspects of the terrorism problem." This idea was voiced the other day by Syria in a message to the UN Secretary-General. If implemented, this timely initiative could finally separate the wheat from the chaff.

However, those who are most vocal in accusing others of international terrorism and who pose sometimes as victims, have reacted rather angrily to it. Summed up, the US and Israeli reaction is as primitive as this : "Damascus is the epitome of terrorism and there is nothing to discuss with it."

This position may make sense to a narrow-minded American. The rejection of the Damascus offer has more serious motives.

Some Western governments appear to be regarding it as disadvantageous to discuss the problem of terrorism. They would much prefer to continue to groundlessly call Libya, Syria, Nicaragua and other countries and organizations they don't like terrorists. They put the terrorist label, first and foremost, on national liberation struggles.

There is no doubt also that those who proclaim "struggle against international terrorism" to be their foreign policy objective (the US and Israel again) are practising flagrant lawlessness and violence on an international scale. Some of the instances of this are the American aggressive actions against Grenada and Libya and the slander campaign unleashed against Syria by a number of Western countries, the Israeli air raids at the nuclear centre in Baghdad, capital of Tunisia, the aggression in Lebanon, daily Tel Aviv reprisals against the population in the occupied Arab lands.

The real reasons for the West's, negative reaction to the Syrian initiative is the fear of disclosures, the attempts to prevent from disintegration the "conceptual" basis of the policy of blackmail and diktat, and the unwillingness to have ajust settlement of regional conflicts.

380. Wilkinson, Paul : Concepts of terror and terrorism. In *Political terrorism*. London, Macmillan, 1974 ; 7-9.

381. Wilkinson, Paul : *Political terrorism*. London, Macmillan, 1974.

382. Wilkinson, Paul : Proposals for government and international responses to terrorism. *Terrorism* 5(1-2) 1981 ; 161-93.

383. Wilkinson, Paul : *Terrorism and the liberal state*. London, Macmillan, 1977.

384. Wilkinson, Paul : Terrorist movements. In *ITP* ; 99-120.

385. Wilkinson, Paul : Three questions on terrorism. *Government and Opposition* 8(3) Sum 1973 ; 290-312.

386. Will, George : Calculating the public interest. In *ITCR* ; 208-13.

387. Willrich, Mason : Terrorists keep out. *Bulletin of Atomic Scientists*. May 1975.

388. Woetzel, Robert K. : Detente in action : A convention on international crimes. In *ITCW* ; 341-45.

French President Valery Giscard d'Estaing described detente in his address to Congress on May 18, 1976, as an attitude of remaining open to others' ideas without giving up one's own sense of values. Secretary of State Henry Kissinger most often equates detente with relaxation of tensions, and Soviet Party Chairman Leonid Brezhnev sees detente as cooperation when this is in the mutual interest. Former President Ford decided not to use the word for fear of misunderstanding.

Whatever connotation one ascribes to detente, it is clear that relaxation of tensions between any two parties in the world arena may not be considered relaxing by others. This explains the current Chinese nightmares about a United States-Soviet detente. Domestically, one leader may not consider relaxing what another one does ; Ronald Reagan's campaign against detente is a case in point. In a global context, detente to be truly relaxing to all must take into consideration mankind's interests as a whole. The following Convention on International Crimes, presented here for the first time, may speak more eloquently for global detente than any definition can. It was drafted by experts from different ideological and legal systems under the auspices of the Foundation for the Establishment of an International Criminal Court and edited by this writer who is also President of the foundation which is in consultative status with the United Nations. It represents an international code of conduct which prescribes certain actions which are in nobody's interest and which outrage the conscience of mankind. It is openended, and other categories may be added on later. It depoliticizes certain actions which constitute obstacles to peace and relaxation of tensions and establishes responsibility and accountability without denigrating states or state sovereignty.

Perhaps it seems ironic that this approach to global detente rests on defining obstacles to peace and categories of international criminal behaviour. But it must be remembered that since Cain slew Abel it has been outrages against civilized conduct that have caused war and blooshed. It is hoped that by isolating the worst of these and by bringing to justice their perpetrators, the causes of international tensions as well as their consequences may be diminished.

389. Wohl, J. ; Responses to terrorism : Self-defence or reprisal ? *International Problems* 28 Jun 1973.

390. Wohlstetter, Albert : Delicate balance of terror. *Foreign Affairs* Jan 1959.

391. Wohlstetter, Roberta : Terror on a grand scale. *Survival* May-Jun 1976.

392. Wolfenstein, M. : *Disaster* Glencoe, ill ; Free Press, 1957.

393. Wolpin, Miles D. : *State terrorism in the Third World.* Oslo, IPRI, 1983.

394. Yaari, Ehud. *Strike terror.* New York, Sabra Books, 1970.

395. Yarborough, William P. : Terrorism—The past as an indicator of the future. In *ITCW* 454-61.

For reasons known only to the Creator, terrorism has been with mankind since the beginning. Our own American Declaration of Independence refers to the use of terror by King George III of Great Britain in these terms :

> He has plundered our seas, ravaged our coasts, burnt our towns, and destroyed the lives of our people. He is at this time transporting large armies of foreign mercenaries to complete the works of death, desolation, and tyranny already begun with circumstances of cruelty and perfidy scarcely paralleled in the most barbarous ages, and totally unworthy of the head of a civilized nation.

> He has constrained our fellow citizens, taken captive on the high seas, to bear arms against their country, to become the executioners of their friends and brethren, or to fall themselves by their hands. He has excited domestic insurrections amongst us, and has endeavored to bring on the inhabitants of our frontiers the merciless Indian savages, whose known rule of warfare is an undistinguished destruction of all ages, sexes and conditions.

The deplorable conditions imposed by Great Britain on our American forebears seem almost wholesome when compared with the bloody chronicle spelled out carefully and painfully by Alexander Solzhenitsyn in The Gulag Archipelago. The terror of the truly evil base upon which the Soviet Union has been built rises from every page of Solzhenitsyn's epic work. Use of terror as a political instrument was a key element of Lenin's strategy for building the first Communist state. At Lenin's direction, the VECHEKA under Comrade Dzerzhinsky systematically brutalized the Russian public into accepting control by one Bolshevik out of every six hundred in the population of that time. As inhuman as the methods of the VECHEKA might have been, they were mild when compared with the scientific and sophisticated terror mechanisms which were brought into play by its successors : the OGPU (1922-34) ; the NKVD (1934-43) ; the NKGB (1943-46) ; the MGB (1946-53) ; the MVD (1953) ; and today's KGB. The tactics, techniques, philosophy, and inspiration for a major part of today's deliberate use of terror as a political weapon radiates from the carefully developed Soviet model. There is no indication on the horizon that Soviet political, military, and psychological power is on the wane. Thus the prospects for the continued flow of moral, physical, and conceptual assistance to terrorist activities inside the non-Communist states of the world are good.

Recent events on the continent of Africa illustrate the skillful orchestration of the Soviet psychological warfare strategy in that important area. Having focused upon an progressively inflamed the "contradictions" which still remain from former colonialism, the Soviet propagandists are again selling the doctrine that a new order can only "grow out of the barrel of a gun." Of even greater help to the proponents of violent resolution of sociological problems is the black-white dichotomy which seems to be made expressly for the architects of civil disorder.

It is ironic that much of the non-Communist world, which largely abhors imposition of the death penalty for even the most heinous crimes, looks with little concern at the mutilation and murder of black and white farmers in Rhodesia by Soviet-trained terror squads. With the help of massive Soviet propaganda, much of the Western world has been led to believe that the ends (black majority rule) do in fact justify the means (terror against innocent men, women, and children). This attitude seems to represent support for Lenin's repeatedly stated conviction that it is always the enemy who is to blame if terror has to be employed against him ! The use by revolutionary groups in Africa of Communist-supported terror mechanisms for political purposes should strike a familiar note particularly to students of war and conflict.

It was during the very early 1960s that American Army officers had their first chance to study the strategic and tactical uses of terror. Professor Bernard Fall, the eminent French author and historian, was a frequent visitor at the United States. Army's Speical Warfare School at Fort Bragg, North Carolina. As a guest lecturer he shocked, outraged intrigued, and stimulated military students who had assembled to try to unravel some of the mysteries surrounding the catastrophic French military failure in Indo-China. There were time when Fall concealed with difficulty his contempt for the purely conventional soldiers' view as to how irregular forces could be destroyed through classical fire and movement. He argued that the "People's Wars" of Mao Tse-tung, Ho Chi Minh, and Vo Nguyen Giap were multidimensional and thus only partially responsive to bombs and bayonets. There were other facets which the United States military would have to understand if they were to avoid the same pitfalls upon which the French had foundered.

Professor Fall invariably went to considerable lengths to trace the pattern of Vietcong terror and to show that it was aimed at very definite objectives. Both the geographic spread as well as the nature of the terrorists' targets were clues to the strategy which was developing. Vietcong and North Vietnamese terror activities were a clearly identifiable projection of psychological operations. Terrorist acts against certain village officials or Government functionaries had the calculated effect of placing varying degrees of psychological stress on others in the same categories as those who had been maimed or killed.

396. Yogasri. V : Tackling terrorism : A scientific approach. *Deccan Chronicle* 12 Apr 1987 ; 4.

397. Zawodry, J.K. : *Death in the forest : The story of the Kalyn Forest Massacre.* South Bend, 1962.

398. Zawodry, J.K. : Infrastructures of terrorism organizations. In *POT*, 61-70.

Anarchism

399. Abon, Alan : Anarchism and agriculture. *Anarchy* (41) Jul 1964 ; 197-202.

400. Adamiak, Richard : Withering away of the State : A reconsideration. *Journal of Politics* 32, Feb 1970 ; 3-18.

401. Albon, Alan : Anarchism and the needs of men. *Anarchy* (76) Jul 1967 : 197-202.

402. Alexander, A. John : Ideas of Lysander Spooner. *New England Quarterly*, 23, Jun 1950 ; 200-17.

403. Allen, Mary B. P.J. : Proudhon in the revolution 1848. *Journal of Modern History* 24, Mar 1952 ; 1-14.

404. Anarchism : A bibliography of articles, 1900-1975. *Political Theory* 4 (1) Feb. 1976 ; 113-27.

405. Anarchists tamed. *Economist* 208, 31 Aug 1963 ; 736.

406. Anarcho—Nihilison. *Economist* 237, 24 Oct 1970 ; 28-31.

407. Apter, David E. and James Joll. : *Anarchism today.* New York, 1972.

408. Apter, David E. : Old anarchism and the new *Government of Opposition* 5, Aug 1970 ; 397-409.

409. Avakumovic, Ivan : Books on anarchism and anarchists. *Russian Review* 33. Jan. 1974 ; 86-88.

410. Avrich, Paul : Anarchism and anti-intellectualism in Russia. *Journal of History of Ideas* 27, Jul-Sep 1966 ; 381-90.

411. Avrich, Paul : *Russian anarchists.* Princeton, 1967.

412. Avrich, Paul : Russian anarchists and the civil war. *Russian Review*, 27, Jul 1968 ; 296-306.

413. Bailie, William : *Josia Warren : The first American anarchist.* Boston, 1906.

414. Baty, Thomas : Can anarchy be a state ; *American Journal of International Law* 28, Jul 1934 ; 444-55.

415. Baylee, Machael D. : In defence of authority. *Personalist.* 52, Aug 1971 ; 755-819.

416. Berkman, Alexander : *ABC of Anarchism*. London, Freedom Press, 1964.

417. Berkman, Alexander : *Now and after : The ABC of Communist anarchism*. New York, Vanguard Press, 1929.

418. Berkman, Alexander : *Prison memories of an anarchist*. New York, Scholcken Books, 1970.

419. Bookchin, Murray : *Post-Scarcity Anarchism*. Berkeley, Ramparts Press, 1971.

420. Boston, Richard : Conversations about anarchism. *Anarchy* (85) Mar 1968 ; 65-75.

421. Brothers in anarchism. *Economist* 227, 29 Jun 1968 ; 24.

422. Buber, Martin : Society and the state. *Anarchy* (54) Aug 1965 ; 232-43.

423. Buchanan, James M. : Contractarian perspective on Anarchy. In *Anarchism*. Ed. by J. Ronald Peunock and John W. Chapman. New York, 1978 ; 29-42.

424. Bull, Hedlly : *Anarchical Society : A study of order in world politics*. London, 1977.

425. Cadogan, Peter : Politics of direct action. *Anarchy* (13) Mar 1962 ; 67-70.

426. Carter, April : *Political theory of anarchism*. New York, 1971.

427. Carter, April : Anarchism and violence. In *Anarchism*. Ed. by J. Ronald Peunock and John W. Chapman. New York, 1978 ; 320-40.

428. Chomsky, Noam : Notes on anarchism, *New York Review of Books* 14, 21 May 1970 ; 31-35.

429. Christie, Stuart and Albert Meltzer : *Floodgates of anarchy*. London, 1970.

430. Clark, John P. : On anarchism in an unreal world. *American Political Science Review* 69, Mar 1975 ; 162-67.

431. Clark, John P. : What is anarchism ? In *Anarchism*. Ed. by J. Ronald Peunock and John W. Chapman. New York, 1978. 3-28.

432. Commager Henry Steele : Nations have added to the anarchy. *International Herald Tribune* 28 Jun 1985 ; 6.

433. Currell, Melrille : *Gentle anarchists*. New York, 1973.

434. Dawa, Henry : Africans and anarchism. *Anarchy* (16) Jul 1962 ; 183-86.

435. De George, Richard T.: Anarchism and authority. In *Anarchism*. Ed. by J. Ronald Peunock and John W. Chapman. New York, 1978 ; 91-110.

436. Doctor, A.H. : *Anarchist thought in India*. Bombay, Asia, 1964.

437. Dubermann Martin B. : Anarchism left and right. *Partisan Review* 33 Fall 1966 ; 610-15.

438. Ellingham, Francis : Anarchism, society and the socialised mind. *Anarchy* (63) May 1966 ; 152-60.

439. Falk, Richard A. : Anarchism and world order. In *Anarchism*. Ed. by J. Ronald Peunock and John W. Chapman. New York, 1978 ; 63-90.

440. Fishman, W.J. : Anarchism. In *Glossary of political ideas*. Ed. by Maurice Cranston and Standford Lakoff. New York, Basic Books, 1969.

441. Gaus, Gerald F. and John W. Chapman : Anarchism and political philosophy. In *Anarchism*. Ed. by J. Ronald Peunock and John W. Chapman. New York, 1978 ; 15-65.

442. Gellner, Ernest : How to live in anarchy. In *Contemporary thought and politics*. Ed. by I.C. Jarvie and Joseph Agassi. London, 1974.

443. Goldman, Maurice : Anarchism and the African. *Anarchy* 16, Jun 1962 ; 179-82.

444. Grave, Jean : *Moriband society and anarchy*. San Francisco, Free Society Library, 1899.

445. Guerin, Daniel : *Anarchism : From theory to practice.* New York, Monthly Review Press, 1970.

446. Handlin, Oscar : Russian anarchist visits Boston. *New England Quarterly* 15 Mar 1942 ; 104-9.

447. Hedman, Carl G.: Anarchist reply to Skinner on weak method of control. *Inquiry* 17, Spr 1974 ; 105-11.

448. Hoffman, Robert *ed.* : *Anarchism.* New York, Atherton Press, 1970.

449. Holgate, P. : *Malatesta.* London Freedom Press, 1956.

450. Horowitz, Irving Louis : Theory of anarchism. In *Political ideologies.* Ed. by James Gould and William Truitt. New York, Macmillan, 1973.

451. Jacker, Corinne. *Black flag of anarchy : Anti-Stalin in the U.S.* New York, Scribner, 1968.

452. Jackson, Gabriel : Origins of Spanish anarchism. *South Western Social Science Quarterly* 36, Sep 1955 ; 135-47.

453. Jagger, Alison : Just state as a round square. *Dialogue* 11, Dec 1972 ; 580-83.

454. Joll, James : *Anarchists.* Boston, 1964.

455. Jordan, David. C. : Authoritarianism and anarchy in Argentina. *Current History* Jan 1975 ; 1-4.

456. Jourdain, M. Mikhail Bakunin. *Open Court* 34, Oct 1920 ; 591-92.

457. Krimerman, Leonard and Lewis Perry *eds.* : *Patterns of anarchy.* New York, Doubleday, 1966.

458. Kropotkin, Peter : Anarchism. *Encyclopaedia Britannica*, 1910.

459. Kropotkin, Peter : *Anarchism : Its philosophy and ideal.* London, Freedom, Pamphlets, No. 10, 1897.

460. Kropotkin, Peter : *Place of anarchism in socialist education.* London, W. Reeves, 1886.

461. Landauer, C. : From anarchism to reformism. *Journal of Modern History* 44, Mar 1972 ; 124-25.

462. Leibzon, B.M.: *Anarchism, Totskyism, Maoism.* Moscow, 1971.

463. Lerner, Michel : Anarchism and the American counter-culture. *Government and Opposition.* 5 Aug 1970 ; 430-55.

464. Liggio, Leonard P. : Anarchism—From theory to practice. *Liberated Guardian* 1, 14 Jul 1970 ; 13-16.

465. Mack, Eric : Nozick's anarchism. In *Anarchism.* Ed. by J. Ronald Peunock and John W. Chapman. New York, 1978 ; 43-62.

466. Madariaga : *Anarchy or hierarchy* ? New York, Macmillan 1937.

467. Madison, Charles A. : Anarchism in the United States. *Journal of the History of Ideas* 6, Jan 1945 ; 46-66.

468. Martin, James J. : *Men against the state* : *the expositors of individualist anarchism in America.* Dekalb, Ill. Adrian Allen Association, 1953.

469. Martin, Rex : Anarchism and Skepticism. In *Anarchism* Ed. by J. Ronald Peunock and John W. Chapman. New York, 1978 ; 115-29.

470. Marx, Engels and Lenin. *Collected works on anarchism and anarcho-socialism.* New York, International Publishers, 1972.

471. Masters, Anthony : *Bakunin* : *The Father of anarchism.* New York, Saturday Review Press, 1975.

472. Maximoff, G.P. : *Constructive anarchism.* Chicago, 1952.

473. Maximoff, G.P. *Political philosophy of Bakunin* : *Scientific anarchism.* Glencoe, Free Press, 1953.

474. Mazor, Lester J. : Disrespect for law. In *Anarchism.* Ed. by J. Ronald Peunock and John W. Chapman. New York, 1978 ; 143-59.

475. McClelland, Hardin T. : Anarchy and aspiration. *Open Court,* 36, Dec 1922 ; 753-60.

476. McIntosh, Donald : Dimensions of anarchy. In *Anarchism.* Ed. by J. Ronald, Peunock and John W. Chapman. New York, 1978 ; 239-72.

477. Miller, David : *Anarchism.* London, Dent, 1984.

478. Miller, Martin A. : *Kroptokin.* Chicago, 1976.

479. Miller, Martin, A. *ed.*: *Selected invitings on Anarchism and revolution : Peter Kropotkin.* Cambridge, 1970.

480. Molnar, George: Meliorism, *Anarchy* (85) Mar. 1968 ; 76-83.

481. Newton, Lisa : Propoundest for law and the case for anarchy, In *Anarchism.* Ed. by J. Ronald Peunock and John W. Chapman. New York, 1978 ; 160-66.

482. Novak, D. : Place of anarchism in the history of political thought. *Review of Politics* 20, Jul 1958, 307-29.

483. Nozick, Robert : *Anarchy, state and uptopia.* New York, Basic Books, 1974.

484. Ostergaard, G. and Melville Correll : *Gentle anarchists.* Oxford, Clarendon Press, 1973.

485. Ostergaard, G. : Indian anarchism. *Anarchy* (42) Aug 1964 ; 225-36.

486. Parsons, Albert R. : *Anarchism.* Chicago, 1887.

487. Peunock, J. Ronald and John W. Chapman *ed.* : *Anarchism.* New York University Press, 1978 ; p. 375.

488. Perlin, Terry *ed.* : *Contemporary anarchism* Edison, N. J., Transaction Books, 1977.

489. Plekhanov, Georgii: *Anarchism and Socialism* (Chicago), 1918.

490. Powell, W. : *Anarchist Cook Book.* New York, Lyle Stuart, 1977.

491. Pyziur, Eugene : *Doctrine of anarchism of Michael Bakunin.* Milwaukee, 1955.

492. Read, Herbert : *Existentialism, Marxism and anarchism.* London, Freedom Press, 1949.

493. Richards, Vernon *ed.* : Errico Malatesta : *His life and ideas.* London, Freedom Press, 1965.

494. Rilly, Patrick : On the "Kantian" foundations of Robert Paul

Wolff's anarchism. In *Anarchism* Ed. by J. Ronald Peunock and John W. Chapman. New York, 1978 ; 294-319.

495. Ritter, Alan : Anarchist justification of authority. In *Anarchism.* Ed. by J. Ronald Peunock and John W. Chapman. New York, 1978 ; 130-42.

496. Rocker, Rudolph : *Anarcho-syndicalism,* London, 1938.

497. Rothbard, Murray N.: Society without a state. In *Anarchism.* Ed. by J. Ronald Peunock and John W. Chapman New York, 1978 ; 191-207.

498. Runkle, Gerald : *Anarchism : Old and new.* New York, 1972.

499. Russell, Bertrand : *Proposed roads to freedom : Socialism, anarchism and syndicalism.* New York, 1966.

500. Schuster, Eunice M. : *Native American anarchism.* New York, AMS Press, 1970.

501. Stafford, David: *From Anarchism to reformism.* Toronto, 1971.

502. Stalin, Josif: *Anarchism or socialism* ? Moscow, 1951.

503. Stone, Christopher D : Some reflections on arbitrating our way to anarchy. In *Anarchism.* Ed. J. Ronald Peunock and and John W. Chapman, New York, 1978 ; 208-14.

504. Taylor, Michael : *Anarchy and Cooperation* London. 1976.

505. Walter, Nicolas : About anarchism. *Anarchy* (100) Jun 1969.

506. Wall, Grenville : Philosophical anarchism revisited. In *Anarchism.* Ed. by J. Ronald Peunock and John W. Chapman, New York, 1978 ; 273-93.

507. Ward, Colin : *Anarchy in action.* London, Allen & Unwin, 1973.

508. Ward, Colin : State and society. *Anarchy* (44) Apr 1962.

509. Wasserstrom, Richard: Comments on "Anarchism and authority." In *Anarchism.* Ed. by J. Ronald Peunock and John W. Chapman. New York, 1973 ; 111-14.

510. Weisbord, Albert : *Conquest of power : Liberalism, socialism, fascism and communism.* New York, Cavici-Friede, 1937.

511. Wertheimer, Alan : Disrespect for law and the case for anarchy. In *Anarchism.* Ed. by J. Ronald Peunock and John W. Chapman New York, 1978 : 167-90.

512. Wieck, David : Anarchist justice. In *Anarchism.* Ed. J. Ronald Peunock and John W. Chapman. New York, 1978 ; 215-38.

513. Woodcock, George and Ivan Avakumovic : *Anarchist Prince; Peter Kropotkin.* New York, Schocken Books, 1971.

514. Woodcock, George : *Anarchy or chaos.* London, Freedom press, 1944.

515. Woodcock, George : *Anarchism and morality.* London, Freedom Press, 1945.

516. Woodcock, George : Anarchism revisited. *Commentary* Aug. 1968.

517. Zenker, Ernst Victor, *Anarchism : A criticism and history of the anarchist theory.* London, Methuen, 1898.

APARTHEID AND RACISM

518. Apartheid—new move. *Deccan Chronicle* 16 May 1982 ; 6.

519. Apartheid denies human dignity. *China Daily* 9 Sep 1985 ; 4.

520. Apartheid faces mounting pressure. *Ta Kung Pao* 19 Sep 1985 ; 11.

521. Architects of apartheid are also its prisoners. *China Daily* 22 Aug. 1985 ; 4.

522. Arkhipov, A. : Many-faced racism. *New Times* (6) Feb 1986 ; 14-15.

523. Attar Chand : Apartheid. *Radiance* (Delhi) 2 Jul 1978 ; 7.

524. Attar Chand : Fight against racism. *Patriot* 12 May 1986 ; 4.

525. Austin, R. : *Racism and apartheid in Southern Africa ; Rhodesia.* New York, Unesco, 1975 ; p. 122.

526. Bhasin, Lalit : Apartheid is brutal colonialism. *Indian Review of African Affairs* (New Delhi), Oct. 1985 ; 3-6.

Twenty years ago, SWAPO had launched its armed struggle to liberate their country being plundered by a combine of the apartheid rulers and industrial-magnates. Notwithstanding the unimaginable sufferings and sacrifices, the freedom fighters are undaunted and they have fully exposed the brutality perpetrated by the Apartheid. Similarly, African National Congress (ANC) has spearheaded the struggle to the extent that almost the entire non-white population is in revolt against the oppression and exploitation of their country, South Africa. Their freedom struggle has now entered quite a serious and decisive phase. The white rulers in Pretoria on the pretext of emergency situation have declared a complete and total war against the freedom fighters in Namibia and South Africa as well as against the independent African States bordering these two colonial strongholds. The Pretoria regime has, however, failed either to convince the World or the freedom fighters. The world opinion has seen it as the complete defeat of Apartheid regime. The freedom struggle, on the other hand, has a new feather in its cap that despite the draconian laws and martialling its might by the Apartheid, the black labour is going on strike in Diamond and Coal Mines for regaining their lost freedom and equality before the law of their nation. In this struggle, the entire world is on the side of freedom of Namibia and removal of Apartheid laws which have subjected the Blacks to the worst type of colonialism in South Africa.

The struggle for freedom should have been over by now after humanity has paid heavily in fighting the two World Wars to saving democracy and enjoying self-determination and freedom of all the nations threatened by fascist forces. Ironically, it proved just a rhetoric of the Imperial Powers who exploited the support of the people in their colonies with false hopes of winning independence by defeating the fascist forces combined in the Axis. The colonial people had to sacrifice much more to get off the colonial yoke imposed upon them by the so-called saviours of democracy. The struggle of the colonial people emerged into a wind of change that stormed the colonial citadels in the 'forties in Asia and in sixties in Africa'. But the imperial machinations sought to frustrate the freedom struggle in the richest part of their colonial world in terms of mineral wealth of Southern Africa by planning a new strategy with the White settler community as its pivot.

Migration and adoption of the countries of their destination by the different races and people of the world has been a very common phenomenon from the beginning of human civilization. Our own country, India, is the abode of different races and people who came as traders, and as aggressors and conquerors. But more often they got settled and adopted India as their own country. This trend was reversed by the White traders, conquerors and settlers. They did not adopt the conquered territories as their own motherland. Rather they sought exploiting the human and natural wealth of the conquered territories in building their parent countries.

Sensing the emergence of nationalism in Asia and Africa as a formidable tide against their exploitation, the colonial powers pampered their White community by conceding their control over the land, economic and even polity of their colonies. This policy reached its logical end in the transference of power to White settlers in South Africa in 1909. It was not a Republic of South Africa as the imperial Britain claimed. It was continuation of colonialism, or neo-colonialism as one may like or propound. The White Settler rulers evolved the policy of Apartheid to perpetuate their hold over the country for all times to come. Therefore, they evolved a policy, known as Apartheid.

Apartheid is the most notorious system of national oppression, racial discrimination, and extreme repression. Under this policy, to quote Robert Davies and other : "Black people in South Africa are classified into three distinct 'racial groups'—Africans, the so-called Coloureds and Asians." Although the particular forms of racial discrimination of (the three sections) differ slightly, the racist system has placed them all in conditions of brutal oppression. They have no effective political rights, and no freedom of movement. The official state policy denies that they are even South Africans. White settlers continue controlling state machinery, economy and 87 per cent of the land of South Africa. Even in the rest of 13 per cent of the land earmarked as native areas, which as a rule is poor and fragmented into enclaves surrounded by the White lands, "Africans are not free whereto live, where to work, or where to send their children to school. Taken together, all the oppressive measures of Aparthied policy have produced a situation in which most of the wealth of South Africa is in the hands of five million White settlers, and overwhelming majority of 30 million blacks live in poverty. The advancement of the blacks is also regulated and could never be allowed to go beyond the "shoulder of the European". It is very repulsive to human conscience. Therefore, the General Assembly of the United Nations has declared that Aparthied is a Crime Against Humanity.

But defying the world criticism shamelessly, the Aparthied regime pushed its all the might and brutality against the advancing tide of freedom struggle. Fall of colonial citadel in Zaire, Kenya and Zambia—all considered at one time to be the heavens for the White settlers—intensified the Aparthied brutality. Therefore every inch of the liberated land in Zimbawe, Angola and Moazmbique is a witness to the bastial mentality of the settler—rulers in shedding the blood of freedom fighters in these countries.

But the Apartheid policy of scuttling the freedom of colonial people has not changed. It is out to destabilize the countries which have attained independence. It also does not hide any more its aggressive, and openly defends its right to raid and weaken the neighbouring states pleading that these states were helping the freedom fighters. The apoligists and all those vested interests who are hands in glove with the Apartheid regime in exploiting the wealth of the region, plead that any sanctions would help "our enemies" and they will be back pushing for more". Who are these enemies ? What for they would be pushing? Are these enemies not the indigenous African people who have been petitioning for long the conscience of the Big and small Powers for treating them the citizens of their own country, for treating them equal before the law of their nation : Is it not independence struggle against settlers' colonialism ?

Apartheid regime is pursuing openly a colonial policy by subjugating Namibia. It has no right to be in Namibia except as a colonial power. Defying the world opinion and unanimous Resolution 435 of 1978 adopted by the UN Security Council the Apartheid regime imposed a puppet regime in Namibia. It is an added injury to the mankind by the Apartheid which has deprived thirty million native coloured and Asian peoples of fundamental human rights.

The aggressive approach, the raids on the neighbouring countries on fabricated pre-texts, and the uncompromising attitude adopted by the regime in the Security Council has brought the struggle to the point of no return. The world has understood the Apartheid game of threatening the independence of all the countries of Southern Africa. Therefore, country after country is deserting the Apartheid regime to support the genuine cause of the freedom struggle in South Africa and Namibia. It is only Britain, West Germany and USA which are still arguing against imposing economic sanctions and exerting pressure upon the holders of Apartheid citadel. But the widespread violence and determined opposition by the people of South Africa and Namibia has swayed the opinion in these countries as well. Botha's intransigent stand in not lifting he emergency, which is nothing but a War against the non-

White people of Africa, has disappointed the majority of people even in Britain, West Germany and USA. France and other European countries are no more moderate to the Apartheid hold on South Africa and Namibia. It is for this reason that their representatives in the United Nations Security Council joined the other 12 members to adopt an unanimous Resolution demanding lifting of emergency and holding fair elections on the basis of One-man-one vote in South Africa.

It is also the time for France, other EEC countries to join NAM and the OAU in getting the UN Resolution calling for the withdrawal of occupied army of the Apartheid regime in Namibia implemented. It is imperative for Britain, West Germany and USA to get this resolution implemented if rulers in these countries are sincere in defending the freedom of the world. Independence to Namibia will be most appropriate and right step. Fall of Apartheid in Namibia, will be helping the people of South Africa who are struggling for their freedom. Their solidarity can stop the bloodbath in Namibia and South Africa and also in neighbouring states. Otherwise also, Pretoria regime cannot hold on for long. The resistance is widespread : even children have taken to resistance. Miners are restive and workers are getting defiant. How long Pretoria can stand the strike without outside support. Therefore, we call upon all the people who cherish freedom and rule of law to exert their pressure upon their nations to stop any type of support to Apartheid brutality. Fall of Apartheid will be a genuine service to the humanity.

527. Botha embalms apartheid. *International Herald Tribune* 3 Oct 1985 ; 6.

528. Bromley, D. G. and Ch. F. Longino *eds.* : *White racism and black Americans.* Cambridge, 1972.

529. Bunting, Brian : *Rise of the South African Reich.* London, Penguin, 1964.

530. Chhabra, Hari Sharan : India's contribution in anti-apartheid struggle. *Madhya Pradesh Chronicle* 11 Jan 1987.

531. Cherian, John : Of apartheid, arms and terrorism. *Deccan Chronicle* 2 Jan 1987 ; 6.

532. Conrad, Thomas: Half hearted assault on apartheid. *International Herald Tribune* 14 Nov 1985 ; 4.

533. Cowell, Alan : Apartheid foes debate the merits of investment. *International Herald Tribune* 4 Jun 1986 ; 1-2.

534. Cowell, Alan : No trial, no charge, but 101 days in Soweto prison. *International Herald Tribune* 19 Nov 1985 ; 1-2.

535. Cracks in apartheid's walls. *International Herald Tribune* 14-15 Sep 1985 ; 4.

536. Crisis of apartheid deepens. *Sechaba* Mar 1986.

537. Dewen, Xu : Apartheid meets its match. *Beijing Review* 13 Jan 1986 : 11-12.

538. Dolgov, A. : Racists manoeuvre. *New Times* (49) Dec 1983 ; 27.

539. Fighting apartheid. *Hindustan Times* 9 Apr 1986 ; 9.

540. Franco, Guido : Apartheid and the Pacific. *Asiaweek* 27 Sep 1985 ; 76.

541. Friedman, Milton : Apartheid : Disinvestment is popular, but is it wise ? *International Herald Tribune* 17-18 May 1986 ; 8.

542. Gerhart, Gail : *Black power in South Africa : the evolution of an ideology*. Berkeley, University of California, 1978.

543. Goonatilake, S. : Growth of racial prejudice. In *Crippled minds*. New Delhi, Vikas, 1982 ; 74-77.

544. Gupta, Vijay : United action against apartheid *Party Life* (New Delhi) 7 Dec 1983 ; 15-19.

545. Hanging in South Africa (Benjamin Moloise). *International Herald Tribune* 18 Oct 1985 ; 6.

546. Inskeep, R. R. : Archaeology, apartheid. *International Herald Tribune* 21 Mar 1986 ; 8.

547. Irvine, Keith : *Rise of coloured races*. London, Allen & Unwin 1972.

548. Klaaste, Aggrey : Still apartheid, even in the dark. *International Herald Tribune* 5 Nov 1985 ; 8.

549. Kohler, Gernot : *Global apartheid*. New York, World Policy Institute, 1978.

550. Lewis, Anthony : Apartheid splits the U S right. *International Herald Tribune* 7 Jan 1986 ; 4.

551. Lewis, Anthony : War against black children in S. A, *Amrita Bazar Patrika* 5 May 1986 ; 6.

552. Lustagarten, L. : *Legal Control of racism discrimination.* London, Macmillan, 1980.

553. Meer, Fatima : Indians' views on apartheid. In *south African dialogue.* Ed. by N. J. Rhoodie, 1972 ; 435-56.

554. Millions of Blacks protest apartheid. *International Herald Tribune* 2 May 1986 ; 5.

555. Mintz, Sidney W. *ed.* : *Slavery, colonialism and racism,* New York, 1975. p. 213.

556. Naidoo, L. V. : Apartheid and imperialism. *Secular Democracy* (New Delhi) Apr 1986 ; 21-22.

557. Nengbiow. Wang Rand pays price of apartheid. *China Daily* 5 Sep 1985 ; 4.

558. Omond, Roger : *Apartheid handbook.* Penguin, 1986.

559. Palme Seeks action against apartheid. *China Daily* 26 Feb 1986 ; 4.

560. Pavice Vic, Miso : Fight against apartheid. *Review of International Affairs* 5 Apr 1978 ; 12-14.

561. Pfaff, William : Speaking softly about racism won't make its evil go away. *International Herald Tribune* 17 Oct 1985 ; 3.

562. Philips, Norman : *Tragedy of apartheid.* London, Allen & Unwin 1976.

563. PM (Rajiv Gandhi) calls for quick action to end apartheid. *Patriot* 9 Jan 1987 ; 1.

564. Policeman kills man in South Africa. *International Herald Tribune* 21 Aug 1985 ; 2.

565. Price, Robert M. and Carl G. Rossberg. *eds.* : *Apartheid regime.* Berkeley, 1980.

566. Programme against racism (apartheid) adopted. *Statesman* (New Delhi) 11 Jan 1987 ; 8.

The anti-apartheid declaration adopted by the two-day International Youth Conference which ended in New Delhi on January 9, 1987 has chalked out a five-point programme to intensify the struggle against racism.

Criticizing the racist policies of the South African regime, the declaration said, they constituted a crime against humanity. It was an insult and challenge to the conscience of the international community.

The conference described the white minority regime of Pretoria as an "immoral" one and pledged the determination of the world youth to intensify the struggle for the elimination of the apartheid Government.

The first item on the programme of action pledged youth initiatives to create public opinion in their own countries in support of the struggle against apartheid and to create an awareness of the dangers posed by it to international peace and security.

It aslo promised "public action" in countries which were still-uncertain about measures against Pretoria.

"We will assist in a number of ways to give material assistance to the brave people of South Africa who are engaged in the struggle", the action programme said.

"We will include donation of clothing, blankets, medical supplies and means to achieve greater publicity for their struggle", it said.

"We will work to help to create the trained manpower that is necessary during the present struggle and will be essential for the future in a liberated South Africa," the declaration assured.

It also promised on behalf of youth delegations from 90 countries to try to provide scholarships and training facilities for the people of South Africa to acquire academic as well as practical skills.

567. Reagan's error on apartheid. *International Herald Tribune* 9 Sep 1985 ; 6.

568. Reddy, E. S. : *Apartheid.* New Delhi, Vikas, 1986.

569. Reddy, Sheela : Apartheid. How it works. *Mainstream* 23 Feb 1985 ; 13-14, 30.

570. Repression in South Africa. *Japan Times Weekly* 10 Aug 1985 ; 12.

571. Rubin, Leslie. *Apartheid in Practice*. New York, United Nations, 1976, p. 47.

572. Sachs, Albie : *Justice in South Africa.* Berkeley, 1973.

573. Safire, William : Apartheid : Other ways to fight it. *International Herald Tribune* 9-10 Aug 1986 ; 4.

574. Singh, S. P. : It's time to demolish apartheid. *Hindustan Times* 18 Jul 1986 ; 20.

575. Streek, Barry : Ruthless act of apartheid. *Tribune* (Chandigarh) 29 Jul 1983 ; 4.

576. Terreblanche, S. J. : Blacks in South Africa : A post-apartheid horizon ? *International Herald Tribune* 18 Sep 1985 ; 6.

577. Tutu calls apartheid a Hitler-like plan. *Patriot* 12 Jan 1987 ; 7.

ASSASSINATIONS

578. Abbas, K. A. : Mr. Camper, Mr. Camper. *Blitz* 21 Sep 1985 ; 24.

579. Abraham, Abu : Politics of murder. *Mainstream* 21 May 1983 : 7, 27.

'Murder' said Charles Chaplin in Monsieur Verdoux, 'to be successful must be committed on a large scale". Or, they might have added, it should be done through hired assassins, puppet dictators, summary courts or expert spies.

Political murders on the whole seem to be the easiest and the most successful, especially when committed by established governments. The last two decades were a peak period for these. Amnesty International's latest book, 'Political Killings by Government' is a chilling chronicle of horror, particularly when one thinks of the torture that has often preceded the killings. Indonesia and Kampuchea lead the rest of the nations in the scale of murder, according to Amnesty. A conservative estimate of people killed in Indonesia under Generals Suharto and Nasution in 1965 and 1966 is 5,00,000. In Kampuchea, at least 3,00,000 people were eliminated between 1975 and 1979 by the Khmer Rouge led by Pol Pot. Third comes Uganda under Idi Amin, with a score of 1,00,000. The total over the last twenty years must run into millions.

This report only deals with killings outside any legal or judicial process which probably explains why the execution of Bhutto doesn't figure in it. Nor is there any mention of the political opponents he is known to have got rid of. There is no mention either of the students, teachers and innocent women and children massacred in thousand by the Pakistani army in its effort to crush Bangladesh. There is no mention at all of Pakistan. But India figures prominently, with eight pages devoted to 'encounter killings' of Naxalites by the Indian police.

580. Assassination : Swedish shcoker. *Asiaweek* 16 Mar 1986 ; 28.

581. Assassination a severe blow to forces of unit. *Patriot* 22 Aug 1985 ; 6.

582. Assassins ; Hardcore or hired ? *International Meridian* (New Delhi) Oct. 1985 ; 4.

583. Bell, J. Bowyer : Assassination in international politics-Lord Moyne, Count Bernadotte and the Lehi. *International Studies Quarterly.* 16 (1) Mar 1972 ; 59-82.

584. Chopra, Nora : Intelligence fiddles as terrorism stalks. *Current* 14 Sep 1985; 11.

585. Conrad, Thomas R. : Coercion, assassination, conspiracy : Pejorative political language. *Polity* 6, 1974 ; 418-23.

586. Dutt, Dev. Political assassinations : How they changed the course of history. *Onlooker* (Bombay) 8 Sep 1986 ; 13-15.

587. Ellis, Albert and John Gulls : *Murder and assassination.* New York, Lyle Stuart, 1971.

588. Ford, Franklin L: *Political murder* : *From tyrannicide to terrorism*. Cambridge, Harvard University Press, 1985 ; p. 440.

"Political murder" can mean many different things—to a pacifist, war is a form of political murder—and in choosing the phrase for the title of his book, Franklin L. Ford has taken advantage of its flexibility. He is primarily concerned with assassination, as the word is commonly understood, and with tyrannicide, the slaying of an unjust or illegitimate ruler, in particular. But where appropriate he also feels free to discuss judicial murder and those forms of terrorism—bombings, hijackings and the like—that claim their victims more or less at random.

The subject is a vast one, but in his willingness to range across centuries and continents Ford, who teaches history at Harvard, shows himself equal to the task. The assassins or would be assassins he considers range from Jael in the Book of Judges to Squeaky Fromme, the victims or intended victims from Henry IV of France to Anwar Sadat. While he concentrates mainly on Europe and the West, he finds space to examine the role played by assassination in non-Western cultures as well—there is an interesting account of attempts to kill the Buddha, for example. And while he tends to dwell longest on the most celebrated episodes, on such figures as Julius Caesar, Thomas a Becket and Abraham Lincoln, he also explores less familiar territory.

Taken primarily as a narrative, "Political Murder" makes rewarding reading. Individual incidents—Orsini's attempt on Napoleon III, for instance—are skillfully reconstructed ; the motives of a variety of assassins and effects of their actions are carefully weighed ; there are succinct accounts of some of the more noteworthy movements that have been committed to killing their opponents, including the original assassins, the heretical Islamic sect of "Hashishiyyin."

The principal question the book poses is whether assassination is "good politics by either ethical or pragmatic standards." At the end of the inquiry Ford comes out and says that with a few exceptions, the answer is "no", but it is clear which way the wind is blowing as early as his chapter on the ancient Greeks, where he discusses the case of Harmodius and Aristogiton.

These two friends were honored by the Greeks for slaying the tyrant (or purported tyrant) Hipparchus—they were reputedly the first mortals to have status made of them, an honor previously reserved for gods. But both Thucydides and Aristotle took a cool view of the motives for the killing, and while Aristotle conceded that there could be such a thing as justifiable tyrannicide, he warned against the dangers of what Ford calls "pseudo-tyrannicide."

Ford also tries to trace the "peaks and valleys in the frequency curve for political murder." There have been several notable periods of remission, he argues, distinguished in their outlook by "a certain quality of balance, as between authority and forebearance"—most recently, the later 17th century and the 18th century until its final decade.

While it is possible to disagree about defining the boundaries of these periods and about their significance, what can hardly be disputed is that the last 30 years have seen a brutal increase in the number of major assassinations and assassination attempts. There have also been developments for which the past offers little guidance, the use made by terrorists of highly sophisticated technology, for example, and the growth of a "terrorist international."

Ford acknowledges that when he comes to deal with recent times he is also frequently dealing with unprecedented situations. But the same lessons apply, and he brings the same balanced judgment to contemporary disorders that he does to those of earlier epochs. He has written a thoughtful book, one that deserves to be carefully pondered.

589. Franziers, Eno : *History of the orders of assassins.* New York, 1969.

590. French Socialist (Philip Brochard) Slain in poster dispute. *International Herald Tribune* 10 Mar 1986 ; 1.

591. Gross, Feliks : Political assassination. In *ITCW* ; 307-15.

"Political" assassination as a systematic activity, a part, even a major one, of political tactics, advanced by an organized political group for achievement of an ideological goal, seems to be a nineteenth-century occurrence, a consequence of struggle against autocracy and foreign rule.

After the French Revolution, what is called "the reaction" in Central and Western Europe close to the avenues of peaceful development of representative and democratic institutions. Monarchies and autocracies representing the interests of the ruling classes lacked will and initiative to resolve the burning social problems of the new industrial society. Here, the traditions of the French Revolution suggested the onces established and effective type of revolutionary tactics. In Russia, however, which lacked this tradition of a popular revolution "from below", where the people—the peasantry—were either passive, or loyal to the Tsar, or rebellious at times, but without broader political goals of basic change, where the government was autocratic in the Oriental sense rather than in terms of contemporary European monarchs, assassination appeared as a political tactic. It spread to the Balkans, again as a tactic in response to foreign oppression and massacres.

During the second half of the nineteenth century, a theory of individual terror developed among revolutionary Russians in their struggle against autocracy. Unlike political assassination as an isolated act, individual terror—in terms of nineteenth century revolutionaries and later in terms of some resistance groups during World War II—is a systematic, tactical course of action with political objective. Individual terror attacked directly, above all, key decision makers or administrators, or acted in lieu of punishment against persons responsible for cruelties and oppression. One of its functions was retribution and deterrence. The leaders of the organization expected that assassination of an oppressive administrator would deter his successors from inhuman, oppressive acts.

Such was the goal of assassination of high German Gestapo officers in Poland during World War II. The major function of individual terror in Tsarist Russia was, however, weakening of the government and of the autocratic institutions of the Tsarist Empire.

Still, it was in this terroristic revolutionary group in autocratic Russia where democratic ideas flourished. There were several factions of course, some minor, whose objective was—as was said before—establishment of dictatorship, as the means or a transitory stage toward a true free society, free of any coercion. Here rationalism worked in harmony with perfect ideals and logical contradictions, impressive and convincing for novices. Theories were also advanced (by Morozov and Tkachev) that terror should continue under constitutional rule, since even under such rule a tyranny might appear ; they indicated contemporaries—Bismarck or Napoleon III. Individual terror by its power of intimidation and elimination of future tyrants would keep the future, perfect world free from autocracy. Those late regicides were, however, in a minority and formed an insignificant faction or separate party. The main party, the core of the "People's Will," had democratic traditions and clear democratic objectives. In 1878, the "People's Will" stated clearly and sharply in an "Urgent Note" its differences with the group which "indulges in Jacobinistic tendencies and methods of a centralistic organization." The Russian revolutionary movement of those times was not economic ; it was primarily political. As Thomas Masaryk put it, "It was an aristocratic struggle for freedom waged against Tsarist absolutism."

We found ourselves, rather suddenly, in an historical period of intellectual consuion and physical violence. The issue of violence and past experiences became of practical significance in a time of appeal to physical violence in domestic politics, as a way of interfering with the business of education and government.

592. Havens, Murray Clark *et al.* : *Politics of assassination*. Englewood Cliffs, N.J. Prentice-Hall, 1970.

593. Jain, Girilal : After the assassination (of Sant Longowal). *Times of India* 24 Aug 1985 ; 8.

594. Lander, Richard : 1985—The year when deaths dominated news. *Baghdad Observer* 18 Jan 1986 ; 4.

595. Mazrui, Ali A. : Thoughts on assassination in Africa. *Political Science Quarterly* 83 (I) Mar 1968 ; 40-52.

596. Peters R. : Terrorists at work : Report from Argentina. *National Review* 28 Jul 1964.

597. Political assassination of Jewish leader. In *WTAZIT* ; 15.

598. Politics of assassination. *Link* 4 Aug 1985 ; 3.

The murder of Lalit Maken, Delhi's young Congress (I), Member of Parliament, is yet another tragic reminder of the continuing threat of terrorism and the cult of assassination. The Punjab accord notwithstanding the danger of extremism remains and will continue. In this situation it is imperative that all steps are taken to ensure the Prime Minister's physical safety. Violent elements, and their alien patrons, have been emboldened by the success they have had in the murder of Indira Gandhi. These elements believe that murders and civil strife can force on India the changes they cannot persuade the people of this country to accept. But this country will frustrate their design, as it has done before.

President Ronald Reagan has declared war on terrorism : Yet, he would not close down the schools where terrorist mercenaries are trained. But, if we find a gap between his professions—or, should we say, his pretensions—and his practice, the fault is entirely ours. Mercenaries receiving training in US schools are in his lexican freedom fighters. For him, terrorists are people who stand up to him and assert the sovereignty of their respective countries. In his declaration of war on terrorism he has named five countries—North Korea, Libya, Iran, Cuba and Nicaragua. If his declaration had come earlier, he would have named Syria also. But the list was announced after Syria had secured the release of 39 American hostages of the hijacked TWA flight. Assad had received three telephone calls and three private messages from Reagan before that happened, and American officials familiar with the contents of these messages say that the President had literally "begged" the Syrian President for help. So Syria was kept out of the Reagan list.

Reagan's list is flexible. Today it includes five countries. Tomorrow it may have either more or less names. If some names are dropped from the present list, it would make no difference except that the so called freedom fighters whom we know as killers and saboteurs excluded from Reagan's list would be rendered unemployed. But if more names are included, the Americans would find themselves at a disadvantage because there would be no trained "freedom fighters" to operate against the countries which have freshly earned US ire. So the schools for terrorists will remain open, provided these seminaries cooperate with the FBI. The moral is evident. However, much we may protest, no purpose would be served. We have to deal with terrorists ourselves and leave to Reagan his own terrorists.

599. Rapport, David C. : Assassination and terrorism. Toronto, Canadian Broadcasting Corporation, 1970.

600. Sant's supreme sacrifice. *Amrita Bazar Patrika* 22 Aug 1985 ; 6.

601. Schmookler, Andrew : Assassinations : The problem is not that the world is sick. *Terrorism* 5 (4) 1982 ; 367-69.

602. Sergeyev, Fyodor : Pawn or queen ? Who orders coups and assassinations ? *New Wave* 23 Feb 1986 ; 8-9, 12.

603. Sethi, J.D. : Murder of reason. *Indian Express* (New Delhi) 2 Feb 1986 ; 4.

The assassins of Mahatma Gandhi and Indira Gandhi took upon themselves to punish two great personalities by murdering them for their victim's act of ommission and commission, not against the person of the murderers but against a political community. It was a personalised punishment for a collective injury, The personal and the collective were interwined to create "perceived relations of legitimacy between the punisher and the punished". When the mass killings of the Sikhs followed Indira Gandhi's assassination, it was also conceived by the killers as legitimate against the punishment inflicted on the victims for their personalised acts of commission as symbolised by the two Sikh security guards. Political legitimacy without a moral basis is itself illegitimate.

Bhindranwale empowered many assassinations though he himself did not kill anyone. He entertained the pathological fantasy that he could punish the collective entity, the Hindus, and the result was the system punishing him by acquiring total legitimacy. Bhindranwale might have been feared but, in the eyes of most Sikhs, he was a legitimate actor. But the defeated have no political legitimacy, particularly if they have no moral legitimacy. Mahatma Gandhi was a political failure but a moral triumph. The failure was epitomised in the vivesection of India ; his assassination exposed the moral bankruptcy of his opponents.

Mahatma Gandhi's murder had an intrinsic political value. It was difficult for the beneficiaries of imperialism and vested interests to close the Gandhian era without damaging Gandhi's political and economic philosophy. His murder gave his successors an opportunity to bypass him and destroy the Gandhian paradigms. But Nehru's failures were compounded by those of his daughter. No wonder, the violence, corruption and terrible debasement they left behind have set people to re-evaluate Gandhi. Of course, the global issues have already put Gandhi at the centre of things. Thirty seven years later, Gandhi is being resurrected as a global man who just happened to fight for India's freedom in his long battle for rescuing man's humanity and moral dignity.

These murders also exposed the sickness of society and the perversion of minds that had taken place through auto-intoxicating propaganda. Ironically, both murders paid handsome dividends to the jubilant mourners. Nehru, the political heir of the Mahatma, became the unquestioned ruler of India so much so that he continued to rule even after he was unable or unfit to do so and left India in humiliation and shambles when he died. Now Rajiv Gandhi has broken all electoral records. Longowal's murder gave victory to the Akalis in the elections.

604. Sharma, Rajat : Who next ? *Onlooker* (Bombay) 8 Sep 1985 ; 8-13.

605. Singh, Surendra P. : Grateful to assassins. *Indian Nation* (Patna) 15 Dec 1985.

606. Sterling, Claire : *Time of the assassins* : *Anatomy of Investigation*, New York, 1983.

607. Sunder Rajan, K.R. : Unanswered questions about Indira's assassination. *Amrita Bazar Patrika* 29 Jan 1986 ; 6.

608. Tarkus, Burton B. and Sid. Feder : *Murder inc.* London, Victor Golancz, 1953.

609. Thukral, Gobind : Assassination : Unwinding threads. *India Today* 15 Sep 1985 : 26-27.

610. Weiss, Peter : *Persecution and assassination of Jean-Paul*, Marat. New York, Atheneum, 1972.

ASYLUM

611. Weis, Paul. : Asylum and terrorism. *The Review* (19) 1977.

612. Goffman, Erving : *Asylums.* New York, Anchor Books. 1961.

BANKING

613. Godfrey, David : Terrorism and banking. *Terrorism* 5 (4) 1982 ; 353-61.

BIBLIOGRAPHY

614. Elliot, John D. and Leslie K. Gibson *eds.* : *Contemporary terrorism; Selected readings.* Gaithers burg, 1978.

615. Kress, Lee Bruce : Selected bibliography. In *ITCW* ; 469-502.

616. Lakos, Amos : *Bibliography of international terrorism.* Boulder, Westview Press, 1986, p. 450.

617. Mickolus, Edward F. : *Annotated bibliography on international and transnational terrorism.* Washington, CIA, 1976.

618. Mickolus, Edward F. : *Literature of terrorism : A selectively annotated bibliography.* Westport, 1980.

619. Norton, August and Martin Greenberg : *International terrorism : An annotated bibliography and research guide.* Boulder Westview, 1980.

620. Russell, Charles A. *et al* : Urban guerrillas in Argentina : A select bibliography. *Latin American Research Review* 9 (3) Fall 1974 ; 53-89.

621. *Select bibliography on international terrorism.* New York, United Nations, 25 Oct 1972, List No. 5.

622. Symser, Willis M. *et al* : *Annotated bibliography on internal defence.* Washington, Center for Research in Social System, 1968.

BODYGUARDS

623. Dev, S. : Bodyguards are in ? *Nagpur Times* 16 Mar 1986 ; 15.

Bodyguards are drawn from the army of the police and they are specially trained to meet the threat of terrorists. In the U.S.A. secret services personel are trained in swimming, fighting fire, face combat and in expert use of all kinds of fire arms.

These secret agents test the food and clothing of important leaders and they keep a close watch on doubtful persons. These secret agents also protect the US President and such other important persons. They are always prepared to face death. They receive bouquets presented to the leaders only to find out if any bomb is hidden in it ! They also investigate three to four thousand threatening letters received every year by the presidents. They are prohibited even to disclose their secrets to their wives.

Despite all these precautions it is not necessary that they can provide a foolproof security. The US President is surrounded every moment by such bodyguards. Despite this they could not save President Kennedy. The assassin had fired from the 6th floor of a seven storey house !

In India, Mrs. Gandhi was killed by her own bodyguards. So was murder of the Guatemalal President in 1967 by his bodyguard. The shortcomings of bodyguards in India have been exposed again and again. Metropolitan Councellor Arjun Dass was killed despite bodyguards. The bodyguard could not even fire a single shot. The assassins took away his piston rightaway. The same story was repeated during the murder of Longowal and Harbans Singh Manchanda two years ago. A sikh leader found his bodyguard sleeping with his pistol under his pillow ! For the last 5 years only 3 bodyguards were injured in U.P. and only one died. Some record !

BUREAUCRACY

624. Rayne, F. : Executive protection and terrorism. *Top Security* (England) 1 (6) Oct 1975 ; 220-25.

625. Saksena, N.S. : Terrorism by organised labour and public servants. In *THF* ; 189-98.

626. Sickman, Philip : When executives turned revolutionaries. *Fortune* Sep 1964.

627. Terrorist schools in Canada gurdwaras ? (Sikh temples). *Tribune* 9 Aug 1986 ; 16.

628. War on terrorism. *National Herald* 9 Nov 1985 ; 5.

The Canadian Government's move against the extremists is reassuring in the light of its commitment to India to help curb terrorism with a firm hand. It is a step which was overdue and though it falls short in terms of a formal extradition treaty between the two countries, the new regulation issued by the Canadian Government through its order-in-council does seek to expand its extradition act to include India. This would make possible for India to ask for extradition of the extremist fugitives. The order comes into effect from October 31 and will include cases only after that day. The overall issue was also a subject of discussion between the Prime Minister, Mr. Rajiv Gandhi, and his Canadian counterpart, Mr. Brian Mulroney at the CHOGM meeting in Nassau. Latest reports indicate that the Canadian police have carried out a swoop against several Sikh extremists in connection with the crash of Air India jet off the Irish Coast in June last. The reports suggest that the Canadian authorities are trying to find out the nature of the link between the "Kanishka" disaster and the explosion at Narita airport in Tokyo the same day.

Britain has also pledged to evolve a legal machinery to send back to India the extremists based in London. The US President, Mr. Ronald Reagan, had also assured Mr. Rajiv Gandhi of cooperation in fighting the terrorist threat. All in all, the Canadian step is in the right direction to contain terrorism at an international scale. It is to be hoped that the Canadian initiative would be followed up by vigorous action to root out the menace completely.

629. Warden, William : 'We will not allow our country to become a killing ground'. *Sunday Observer* (Bombay) 30 Jun 1985 ; 4.

CAPITALISM

630. Abbas, K.A. : Capitalism is the culprit. *Blitz* 20 Jul 1985 ; 24.

631. Aglietta, M. : *Theory of capitalist regulation.* London, NLB, 1979.

632. Alavi, Hamza *et al* : *Capitalism and colonial production.* London, Croom-Helm, 1982, p. 198.

633. Amin, S. : Expansion or crisis of capitalism. *Contemporary Marxism* 9(1) 1984 ; 3-17. *Third World Quarterly* (London) Apr 1983.

634. Amin, S. : Toward a structural crisis of world capitalism. *Socialist Revolution* 23(1) 1975 ; 7-44.

635. Bottomore, Tom : Theories of modern capitalism. *Tribune* 4 May 1986.

636. Capitalism : is it working ? *Time* 21 Apr 1980.

637. Desai, A.R. : How capitalism starves 100 million people, *Economic & Political Weekly* 12 Apr 1986 ; 619.

638. Douglas, Mike. *Regional integration on the capitalist periphery : The Central plains of Thailand*, The Hague, 1984, p. 231.

639. Edquist, Charles : *Capitalism, socialism and technology : A comparative study of Cuba and Namaica.* London, Zed Books, 1985. p. 195.

640. Farsaun, K. : *State capitalism in Algeria.* New York, 1975.

641. Frank, Andre Gunder : *Capitalism and under-development in Latin America.* New York, Monthly Review Press, 1967.

642. Friedman, David : *Machinery of freedom : Guide to a radical capitalism.* New York, 1973.

643. Harvey, D. : *Geopolitics of capitalism. In Space and social structure.* Ed. by D. Gregory and J. Urry. London, Macmillan, 1985.

644. Henry, Ernst : Modern Capitalism : Neo-Fascism : who needs it. *Socialism Theory and Practice* (Moscow) (5) 1985 : 29-39.

645. Keane, John : *Public life and late capitalism.* Cambridge, 1984. p. 348.

646. Krieger, J. : *Undermining capitalism*, Princeton, 1984. p. 333.

647. Lipton, Merie : *Capitalism and apartheid : South Africa, 1910-84.* London, Gower, 1985 p. 449.

648. Luxemburg, Rosa : *Accumulation of capital.* London, Routledge & Kegan Paul, 1963.

649. Mandel, E. : *Late capitalism*. London, 1975.

650. Nasud, Iqbal : Capitalism masquerading as socialism. *Indian Express* 6 Apr 1986.

651. Patel, Surendra J. : Economic crisis and the transition from capitalism. *Economic and Political Weekly* 29 Mar 1986 ; 536-45.

652. Peet, R. : Consciousness dimension of Fiji's integration into world capitalism. *Pacific Viewpoint* 21, 1980 ; 91-115.

653. Pirogov Grigony : Capitalism in the grips of structural crisis. *Party Life* (New Delhi) 22(4) Apr 1986 ; 22-31.

654. Przeworski, Adam : *Capitalism and social democracy*. Cambridge. 1984.

655. *Rights and freedoms in the capitalist world.* Moscow, Novosti, 1985. p. 87.

656. Ross, R.S.J. : Facing Leviathan : Public policy and global capitalism. *Economic Geography* 59, 1983 ; 144-60.

657. Rowley, Anthony : Capitalism's Comeback. *Far Eastern Economic Review* 30 Jan. 1986 ; 44-45.

658. Schumpeter, Joseph A. : *Capitalism, socialism and democracy*. New York, 1950.

659. Schumpeter, Joseph : *Capitalism, socialism and democracy*. New York, 1956.

660. Stoler, Ann Laura : *Capitalism and confrontation in Sumatra's plantation belt, 1870-1979*. London, Yale University, 1985.

661. Sweezy, P.M. : Present global crisis of capitalism. *Monthly Review* Apr 1978.

662. Vogel, Ezra : Kind of guided capitalism. *Look Japan* 10 Sep 1985 ; 11.

663. Walicki, A *Controversy over capitalism*. London, Oxford Univ. Press, 1969.

664. Wallerstein. I. : *Capitalist world economy*. Cambridge, 1979.

665. Westergaard, J.H. : Capitalism without classes. *New Left Review* (26) Sum. 1964; 10-32.

COLONIALISM

666. Barnett, Correlli : *Collapse of British power*. New York, William Morrow, 1972.

667. Chopra, V.D. : Neocolonial manoeuvres. In *Pentagon shadow over India*. New Delhi, Patriot Publications, 1985 ; 43-60.

668. Dugard, John : OAU and colonialism. *International and Comparative Law Quarterly* 16, 1967.

669. Goonatilake, Susantha : *Crippled minds : An exploration into colonial culture*. Delhi, Vikas, 1982. p. 362.

670. Kidwai, Anser : Terrorism and neo-colonialism. *National Herald* 16 Jan 1986 ; 5.

671. Nandy, Ashis : *Intimate enemy : Loss and recovery of self under colonialism.* Delhi, Oxford University Press, 1983. p. 140.

672. Nkrumah, Kwame : *Neocolonialism, the last state of state of imperialism.* New York, International Publishers, 1965.

673. Norbu, Dawa : Super-power competition : Links to decolonisation, anti-imperialism and anti-colonialism. *Shakti International Review* (New Delhi) Jan 1986 ; 3-4.

674. Perham, Margery : *Colonial reckoning.* London, 1961.

675. Popkin, Summel L. : Colonialism and the ideological origins of the Vietnamese revolution. *Journal of Asian Studies* 4(2) Feb 1985 ; 349-58.

676. Rai Singh : Rise of neo-colonialism. *National Herald* 29 Apr 1985 ; 7.

COUP D'ETATS

677. Afrifa, A.A. : *Ghana Coup.* London, Frank Cass, 1966.

678. Al-Sadat, A. : *Revolt on the Nile.* New York, John Day. 1957.

679. Brill, W.H. : *Military intervention in Bolivia : the overthrow of Paz Estenssoro and MNR.* Washington, Institute for the comparative study of political systems, 1967.

680. Carleton, A. : Syrian coups d'etat of 1949. *Middle East Journal* 4(1) Jan 1950.

681. Clapham, C. : Ethiopian Coup d'etat of December 1960. *Journal of Modern African Studies* 6(4) 1960.

682. Dalby, D. : Military take over in Sierra Leone. *World Today* 23(8) Aug 1967.

683. Daalder, H. : *Role of the military in the emerging countries.* The Hague, Mounton, 1962.

684. Dann, V. : *Iraq under Qassen : A political history. 1958-63.* New York, Prager, 1969.

685. Einaudi, L.R. : *Peruvian military.* Santa Monica, Rand, 1969. (RM—60480 RC).

686. First, R. : Barrel of a gun : *Political power in Africa and the coup d'etat.* London, Penguin, 1970.

687. Fisher, H.J. : Elections and coups in Sierra Leone, 1967. *Journal of Modern African Studies* 7(4) Dec 1969.

688. Fossum, E. : Factors influencing the occurrence of military coups d'etat in Latin America. *Journal of Peace Research* 3, 1967.

689. Garin, C. Dahomey : Another coup. *Africa Report* 15(1) Jan 1970.

690. Goodspeed, D.J. : *Conspirators : A study of the coup d'etat.* London, Macmillan, 1962.

691. Gurr, T.R. : *Why men rebel.* Princeton, 1970.

692. Khadduri, M. : Coup and counter-coup in the Yaman, 1948. *International Affairs* (London) 28(1) Jan 1952.

693. Khadduri, M. : Iraq, 1958 and 1963. In *Politics of the coup d'etat.* Ed. by W.G. Andrews and U. Raanan, New York, 1969.

694. Kim, C.I.E. : South Korean military coup of May 1961 : Its causes and the social characteristics of its leaders. In *Armed forces and society.* Ed. by J. Van Door. The Hague, Mounton, 1968.

695. Kraus, J. : Ghana. In *Politics of the coup d'etat.* Ed. by W.G. Andrews and V. Raanan. New York, 1969.

696. Kraus, J. : Men in charge. *Africa Report* 11(4) Apr 1966.

697. Lemarcharnd, R. : Dahomey : Coup within a coup. *Africa Report* 13(6) Jun 1968.

698. Levine, V.T. : Coup in the Central African Republic. *Africa Today* 15(2) Apr-May 1968.

699. Luttwak, Edward : *Coup d'etat : A practical handbook.* London, Allen Lane, Penguin Press, 1968.

700. Malaparte, Curzio : *Coup d'etat, the technique of revolution.* New York, 1932.

701. Morrison, D.G. and H.M. Stevenson : Social complexity, economic development and military coup d'etat. *Journal of Peace Research* 2(4) 1974 ; 345-47.

702. Needler, M.C. : *Anatomy of a coup d'etat : Educator, 1963.* Washington, ICSPS, 1964.

703. Nun, J. : *Latin America : The hegemonic crisis and the military coup.* Berkeley, IIS, 1969.

704. Nun, J. : Middle Class military coup. In *Politics of conformity in Latin America.* London, Oxford University, Press, 1967.

705. Payne, A. : *Peruvian coup d'etat of 1962.* Washington, ICSPS, 1968.

706. Ross, S.R. : Some observations on military coups in the Caribbean. In *Caribbean : Its political problems.* Ed. by A.C. Wigns. Univ. of Florida Press, 1956.

707. Stone, L. : Theories of revolution. *World Politics* 18(2) Jan 1966.

708. Thompson, Villiam R. : *Explanations of the military coup.* Doctoral Dissertation. Seattle, University of Washington, 1972.

709. Thompson, William R. : *Grievances of military coup-makers.* London, Sage Publications, 1973. p. 73.

DEATH AND SUICIDE SQUADS

710. Death Squads : Can they be stopped. *International Meridian* Oct 1985 ; 6-7.

711. Khurana, Anand : Death squads are here ? *Nagpur Times* 6 Apr 1986.

712. Khurana, Anand : Mass graves and death squads. *Free Press Journal* 21 Dec 1985 ; 4.

713. Kner, John : Armenians assert : Suicide squads are ready. *New York Times* 27 Sep 1981 ; 7.

714. Libya alerts suicide squads. *Daily* (Bombay) 27 Mar 1986 ; 10.

Libya called March 26, 1986 for Arab suicide squads to strike US Embassies and other interests "wherever they may be," after the armed conflict between the US Navy and Libyan forces.

A commentary broadcast by Libyan Radio and monitored by the British Broadcasting Corporation in London here exhorted the "Arab Nation" to be transformed "in its entirety into suicide squads and into human bombs, missiles and aircraft to deter and resist terrorism and destroy it for good."

"Oh heroes of our Arab nation," the commentary went on, "let your missiles and suicide cells pursue American terrorist embassies and interests wherever they may be".

715. O' Neill, Richard : *Suicide squads : Axis and allied special attack weapons of World War II : Their development and their missions.* London, Salamander Books, 1985.

DEMOCRACY

716. Danforth, John C. : Terrorism *versus* democracy. In *ITCR* ; 115-21.

Government in a democratic society, by its nature, respects the dignity of its citizens. The state exists to serve and protect the individual, which is the precise opposite of the relationship that exists in a totalitarian regime Totalitarianism, the total claim of the state on the lives and loyalties of its subjects, is in flat contradiction to the values of democratic society. The purpose of democratic government is not to bully people—to push them around for its own ends—but to provide individuals with the necessary structure so that their opportunities for personal fulfilment are enhanced. In the words of the United States Constitution, a function of the government is to "insure domestic tranquility." Thus, the democratic state restrains antisocial behaviour and prevents those outbreaks of destructiveness which would make a decent life impossible for the individual citizen.

While democratic governments must preserve order within their countries, they do not possess unlimited power to do so. They themselves are restrained, and this sets them apart from totalitarian regimes.

A totalitarian state can maintain order quite efficiently by the exercise of unrestrained power. By contrast, a democratic society must preserve order without abridging the individual rights of its citizens.

This tension between insuring domestic tranquility and avoiding excessive governmental power is heightened by the growing frequency of terrorism. On the one hand, violent extremists so disrupt the orderly workings of society that effective governmental action is a necessity if we are to enjoy the fruits of civilization. On the other hand, we must be watchful lest, in dealing with the actions of terrorists, the values of a democratic society are weakened by governmental excess.

Clearly, terrorism cannot be ignored on the theory that to deal with it effectively threatens the civil liberties of our citizens. A well-advanced sensitivity to civil liberties is an essential ingredient in a democratic society. Yet unchecked terrorism is, by itself, a threat to the values of a democratic society. Therefore, not to check it, and effectively, is to invite the destruction of a set of values which were centuries in the making.

Terrorism is the antithesis of democratic values. As democratic societies hold a common respect for the unique worth of each individual, terrorism rejects that concept of personal worth. Terrorism is inherently indiscriminate and arbitrary in its actions. Any innocent civilian killed will serve its purposes. It does not matter who the next victim is. All lives, combatant and, preferably, noncombatant are equally expendable. No matter whether violence produces dismemberment, maiming or death ; no matter whether the victims are young or old, male or female ; all serve the purpose of the terrorist.

When a locker in a busy airport explodes, it does not matter to the terrorist who may happen to be walking by. When an aeroplane is hijacked, it does not matter to the terrorist who is in that aeroplane.

Persons are, to the terrorists, not persons at all. They are not separate and distinct human beings, each possessing his own special value. They are only things—objects—numbers to be counted in some body count when the anonymous phone call is made claiming credit for the most recent outrage.

As terrorism is the antithesis of a democratic society's concept of man, it is obviously the antithesis of a democratic society's concept of the social order.

Unlike a democratic government, which depends for its authority on the consent of the governed, terrorists depend on no consent at all. They exist by stealth in tiny bands, sneaking from one secret hiding place to another to scheme about their next manoeuvre. With tiny followings, they reject the democratic process. They cannot operate openly. They do not appeal to the public. They hide from it. They are accountable to no one except themselves.

717. Ellenberg, Edward : *International Terrorism* v. *Democracy*. New York, 1972.

718. Ellenberg, Edward : *Western Demacracies* v. *Terrorism* : *A study of ineffectiveness*. New York, 1974.

719. Horowitz, I.L. : Can democracy cope with terrorism. *Civil Liberties Review* May-Jun 1977 ; 29-37.

720. Rattan, H.R. : Global terrorism : Democracy under Siege. *National Herald* 30 Jun 1985.

721. Rustin, Bayard : Democracy and terrorism. In *ITCR* ; 201-7.

722. Turner, Stansfield : *Secrecy and democracy* : *The CIA in transition*. Boston, Honghton Mifflin, 1985. p. 304.

723. Wolf, John B. : Terrorist manipulation of the democratic process. In *ITCW* ; 297-306.

Arab terrorist strategy is to claim that their people are unable to redeem their lost lands inside Israel through diplomacy, conventional warfare, or a Maoist-type guerrilla struggle. Thus they present themselves as people who are free to employ the tactics of terror against the Israelis and their international supporters everywhere. They use terror to intimidate the world community into believing that the cost of maintaining the *status quo* in the Middle East will be an eventual nuclear confrontation between the United States and the Soviet Union. Consequently, Arab terrorism supplements those aspects of conventional Arab diplomacy and propaganda which emphasize that a lasting peace in the Middle East is dependent upon a resolution of the "Palestinian Question".

Although aware of the threat posed by terrorist groups, the urban police departments, particularly of the United States, lack the resources and training required to control it. Furthermore, to combat the terrorist it is necessary for municipal American police departments to cooperate with every Federal investigatory agency in a pooled effort against this menace. The Federal agencies, however, have found it most difficult to effect cooperation among themselves, and consequently they are unable to develop any lasting and mutually beneficial liaison with local police departments.

Evidence of this shortcoming in American law enforcement is plainly visible. Eighteen Federal strike forces have been established to combat Mafia-dominated organized crime throughout the United States. The record of these forces has been mixed, and, until recently, the United States Attorney's Office had been urging their dissolution since it is known that the various Federal agencies pooled in the strike forces tend to be competitive and distrustful of each other. Included among the federal agencies normally grouped into the strike forces are the Federal Bureau of Investigation (FBI), Drug Enforcement Administration (DEA), United States Immigration and Naturalization Service (USINS) and Alcohol, Tobacco and Firearms Division of the United States Treasury Department (ATF).

There is some justification, however, for the competition and distrust which exist among these various agencies. One strike-force attorney who had been asked, for example, if he could show a reporter FBI charts on the Mafia, said cynically : "They'll hardly show them to us." "Why is that ?" he was asked. "Well, the Bureau has the attitude that one day you're a prosecutor, and the next day you're a defence attorney," he said. That is frequently true of the young attorneys who work in the Federal Strike Forces and the United States Attorney's Office, where a prosecutor's term averages three years.

Fettered both politically and economically, most American police departments also are unable to construct the top-level operational intelligence network which is required to keep records on extremist groups. Yet these same intelligence networks are an effective terrorist countermeasure since they consist of components which will allow rapid acquisition, analysis, and dissemination of current data from a specially constituted and specially skilled group. Once convinced of the need for sophisticated intelligence networks, however, most American police departments would still find it very difficult to conduct any intelligence operation of a prolonged basis which cannot be justified by the performance statistics required to support budgetary appropriations for additional financing. Thus, the drive of the American police for statistics tends to divert investigative energy to a succession of low-level arrests most of which have little or no impact on any organized criminal group. Furthermore, most urban American police commanders also realize that intelligence operations normally yield a low number of arrests ; consequently, they are often reluctant to undertake them as the size of their budget is often related to the total number of arrests made during the previous twelve-month period.

DIPLOMACY

724. Eayrs, James : *Diplomacy ar.d its discontents.* Toronto, University of Toronto, 1971.

DRUGS

725. Drugs and terrorism. *Pioneer* 1 Apr 1986 : 6.

A new dimension has been added to terrorism by the stepped up use of drugs on a global scale. Narcotics of the most beneful variety are being peddled all over the world, not only by drug mafias out to make a fabulous fortune through drug addiction of the young, but also by terrorists to collect sizeable funds quickly to finance their lethal trade. India, which is fast becoming a conduit for drug pedlars and narcotic merchants to smuggle millions of dollars worth of heroin abroad, is illustrative of this dangerous trend. It has now been established that terrorists in this country are receiving enormous funds from their compatriots abroad who are reaping a rich harvest by selling their smuggled wares at a fantastic price to the young and the not-so-young alike.

Attention to this mounting menace was focussed by Health Ministers around the world who recently met in London. They gave a warning that drug abuse had increased dramatically and seemed set to get even worse. They said new forms of drugs, which were more addictive were being increasingly used. The conterence also drew attention to possible links between drug traffickers and terrorists who sought to undermine society. The warnings came at the end of a three day conference called by the U. K. Government with the help of the World Health Organisation to discuss these global problems of the drug manace.

Delegates from about thirty countries, reports the 'Times' of London, were told that rough estimates put the number of people taking cannabis at more than 29 million. The number of people taking opium and heroin was nearly three million, with more than four million taking cocaine. Many others were taking barbiturates, tranquillisers and amphetamines or hallucinogens. Mr. Barnay Hayho, U. K. Minister of Health, said that the use of socalled "designer" drugs was beginning to spread from the United States to other countries.

In a joint statement the ministers "expressed great concern that health problems related to the misuse of narcotics and psycho-tropic substances have increased dramatically at a global level". The statement said that countries should encourage action to promote "healthy and personality fulfilling alternatives to drug-taking". In India and many other Third World countries tranquillisers of all kinds are openly sold across the counter without a doctor's prescription. The pharmacists often take upon themselves the responsibility of prescribing these drugs which are habit-forming and even dangerous with serious side effects for their worried customers. Unlike the heroin and hashish smugglers who ply their trade surreptitiously, many pharmacists keep their show cases openly and heavily stocked with drugs which have been banned elsewhere or can be procured only through registered and qualified doctors' prescriptions. The World Health Organisation keeps publicising periodically the lengthening list of such drugs, but over here and in several developing countries it seems to be nobody's business to interfere with this dangerous drugs business.

726. Drugs and terrorism. *Times of India* 26 Mar 1986 ; 4.

For the second time within a week the Delhi Police has seized a huge hoard of charas in a farmhouse, thus bringing the total haul to over 1000 kg. Laudable though the police operation has been, it throws light on a frightening aspect : the size of the trade in this deadly cargo and also the frequency of shipments. This fear is strengthened by the memory of a similar haul in Maharashtra in January when 615 kg of white heroin—the most valuable variety in the world today—was recovered from a farm. It was worth over $ 1 billion in the "retain market" of the U.S.A. and Europe. In operations last year over

8,000 kg. of various drugs like herion, ganja and charas were recovered either in transit to Bombay or from the city itself. There are several inescapable inference from the series of susccessful "catches". One, drug peddling and export have become the most profitable form of economic crime. Not only is the crime very lucrative but it gives to the participant access to ruthless criminals and thus vastly enhances his ability to "punish" critics and adversaries alike. Two, the movement of a huge volume of this contraband inevitably leads to a mushroom growth of addicts all along the route. This has happened earlier in other countries, and if Press reports are any indication, it is happening in India. The socalled "white plague"has infected an estimated 1,00,000 persons, with 15,000 new cases every year. The figure is frightening, although it is still likely to be on the conservative side. Three, with the near liquidation of the "golden triangle"—the vast stretch of land lying at the intersection of Thailand, Burma and China—in the mid-seventies, the drug scene has shifted to the "golden crescent" touching Pakistan, Afghanistan and Iran. The chronic unstable conditions in he last two countries and the eager cooperation of a set of military rulers in the first have led to a flourishing trade in narcotics in the region.

The alarming significance of the increase in the quantity of the contraband going through India is its close links with terrorism. The what and the why of this relationship have been detailed in an American weekly which has done extensive research in this field. It seems that drugs can pass undetected through a country only when it is rocked by a social and political upheaval and the law and order machinery is engaged in other work, leaving the field free for peddlers. The situation in the northern part of Thailand in the past decade and of Burma for several years now proves this point. The socalled civil wars in a few Latin American countries are actually waged between the authorities and drug smugglers. This is the prime motive behind the drug mafia encouraging terrorism. A secondary reason is financial : the narcotics trade provides ample resources to equip terrorists and they, in turn, serve their benefactors by unleashing chaos. It is a moot point if the several groups of Afghan tribesmen looked in a ferocious fight with the Babrak Karmal regime are interested only in asserting their fundamental rights. If this were indeed so, their bloody internecine fighting and well-documented links with heroin cultivation and commerce are hard to explain. The same goes for the Pathans of the North-West Frontier Province, the most fertile producer of high quality poppy. With Nepal joining the ranks of growers, India is hemmed in by Burma, Nepal and Pakistan (which itself is also a conduit for the stuff originating from Iran and Afghanistan). The "terrorist connection", more than the spectre of addiction, should spur the Government to root out the trade. The problem also provides a strong argument for sealing the border with Pakistan, at least in the Punjab and Jammu and Kashmir segments.

727. Meese, Edwin : Fighting drug as close to the source as possible. *International Herald Tribune* 6 Aug 1986 ; 4.

728. Mills, James : Eradication is way to fight drugs. *International Herald Tribune* 5 Sep 1986 ; 6.

729. On the heroin trail. *Amrita Bazar Patrika.* 31 Mar 1986 ; 6.

730. Riding, Alan : Colombian drugs : A problem at home. *International Harald Tribune.* 22 Aug 1986 ; 5.

731. Safire, William : Drugabuse hysteria has its political benefits. *International Herald Tribune* 16 Sep 1986 ; 5.

732. Sapru, Somnath and Devsagar Singh : Terrorism and drug trafficiking-II : Pakistan major source of drugs. *Indian Express* 19 Apr 1986 ; 1, 7.

733. Saksena, N. S. : Tackling the heroin menace. I & II. *Times of India* 28 & 29 Mar 1996 ; 8.

734. Singh, Devsagar and Somnath Sapru : Terrorism and drug trafficking—I : Commonwealth plans to fight menace. *Indian Express* 18 Apr 1986 ; 1, 9.

735. Terror of terrorists and drug peddlers. *Blitz* 18 Jan 1986 ; 6.

The determined initiative taken by Arun Nehru, Minister of State for Internal Security, to combat the drug menace is reaping rich dividends like the biggest-ever seizure of narcotice worth almost Rs. 6 crores on the Maharashtra-Gujarat border on January 9, last.

This and similar hauls in the course of the week are definitely the outcome of the countrywide alert sounded under the dynamic young minister following the smooth passage of the legislation on narcotics in Parliament last year.

This Bill in the drafting of which Arun Nehru played the key role, has vested necessary powers in the various agencies of our security and intelligence forces—the police, the CBI, the BSF, the CRP—with a view to effectively meet the challenge posed by drug peddling that is corroding a sizeable segment of our youth force.

Arun Nehru has all along been monitoring the operations being conducted against the elements behind drug trafficking, and issuing instructions to deal stringently with those responsible for the illegal transactions of hashish and heroin across our borders.

Within less than a year of Rajiv Gandhi's assumption of power, Arun Nehru has emerged as his principal task force and trouble-shooter. Today he symbolises the strength and potentiality of the Rajiv Gandhi Government. Even as the Minister for Power, Arun Nehru was a force to reckon with not merely because of his proximity to the Prime Minister, whose confidence he always enjoyed, but primarily due to his capability to display firmness with efficiency in tackling the chronic weaknesses plaguing the power sector.

As the Minister of State for Internal Security he demonstrated his characteristic no-nonsense attitude in his discussion with the Chief Minister of Punjab on extremists and secessionists in the State.

Meticulous in his approach to problems, Arun Nehru is one of the most competent personalities in the Union Ministry.

736. Terrorism and drugs. *Tribune* 11 Jun 1985 ; 4.

737. Triple nexus. *Madhya Pradesh Chronicle* 25 Mar 1986 ; 6.

A study published by the Executive Intelligence Review, a private U.S. organisation, says, there is convincing evidence to establish links between drug-trafficking, gun-running and terrorist activity. Drug-peddling is the quickest way to raise funds for arms smuggling and allied nefarious activities. The problem has been complicated by the presence of a large number of Afghan refugees in India, particularly in Delhi and Bombay. Arrests in Delhi reveal that the Mujahdeen are deeply involved in drug-trafficking as a means of financing their guerilla operations against Soviet troops present in the country.

The study shows further that the Khalistan movement has links with Ecuador which is connected with drug trafficking. In short, it has been found that where there is terrorism, there is usually a drug connection. Delhi police had also confirmed that some known terrorists were involved in drug-trafficking. This is proved by the arrest of a notorious extremist J.S. Narelawala from the house of another extremist known for drug-smuggling. Ishwar Chopra, a drug-peddlar, who was nabbed last year with 145 kgs. of charas and 45 kgs of smack, also confessed that he had close links with Sikh extremists.

The nexus between drug peddlers, arms smugglers and extremists is a matter of grave concern. It can, if not checked, destabilise the entire country, particulary the strategically important border states of Punjab and Jammu & Kashmir. Government must intensify patrolling on the borders and the excise staff be vigilant to curb the menace by nabbing those who indulge in these anti-national activities. The triple nexus must be broken at the earliest.

738. Weisman, Steven R. : India is becoming a stop on heroin transit route, giving rise to addictions. *International Herald Tribune* 18 Mar 1986 ; 9.

739. World war on drugs. *International Herald Tribune* 6 Aug 1986 ; 4.

ECOLOGY AND ENVIRONMENT

740. Adler, D.V. and J.H. Segre : Ecology of terrorism. *Survival* 15 (4) Jul-Aug 1973 ; 178-83.

ECONOMIC ASPECTS

741. Alexander, Yonah *ed.* : *Political terrorism aud business : The threat and response.* New York, Prager, 1979.

742. Dentsch, Antal : On the economics of terrorism. *Terrorism* 5 (4) 1982 ; 363-66.

743. Economic sabotage. In *WTAZIT* ; 16-17.

EDUCATION

744. Advani L.K. : for 'white paper on terrorists' training'. *Tribune* 31 Mar 1986 ; 12.

745. Bhambani, Kavita : Terrorist Schools. *Times of India* 19 Aug 1985 ; 8.

746. Camper reveals all. *Statesman* 15 Sep 1985 ; 6.

747. Camper school. *Times of India* 18 Sep 1985 ; 8.

748. Camper's confession. *Patriot* 11 Sep 1985 ; 4.

749. Chakravorti, Robi : Schools for mercenaries and arms bazaars in U.S. *Amrita Bazar Patrika* 25 Jul 1985 ; 6.

750. Frank (Camper) plays foul. *Daily* 12 Sep 1985 ; 8.

751. Lopez, George A. : Teaching about terrorism. *Terrorism* 3 (1-2) 1979 ; 131-46.

752. Mercenaries, *Patriot* 15 Sep 1986 ; 4.

753. Mukherjee, Sadhan : Terrorism school in United States. *New Age* (New Delhi) 27 Jul 1985.

754. Nandy, Pritish : Is camper real or just a CIA plant ? *Illustrated Weekly of India* 15 Sep 1985 ; 11.

755. Nandy, Pritish : Killing fields. *Illustrated Weekly of India* 15 Sep 1985 ; 6-17.

756. Nandy, Pritish : What will camper reveal during the New Orleans trial ? *Illustrated Weekly of India* 15 Sep 1985 ; 12-13.

757. Patra, Saral : USA : Training Centre of terrorism. *Hitawada* (Bhopal) 7 Jul 1985.

758. Plea to close down terrorism schools. *Times of India* 21 Jul 1985 ; 16.

759. Scholarships to Frank Camper Commando School. *Telegraph* (Calcutta) 11 Jul 1985 ; 6.

760. School for killers, *Indian Express* 1 Jul 1985 ; 6.

761. Terrorirm in exam. halls. *Deccan Chronicle* 13 Jan 1986 ; 6.

762. Training schools of terrorism. *Madhya Pradesh Chronicle* 5 Jul 1985 ; 4.

763. Training the world in terrorism. *Hindustan Times* 30 Jun 1985 ; 9.

764. US stand biased on terrorist schools. *Hindustan Times* 30 Jul 1985 ; 1-16.

765. Whodunit Camper. *National Herald* 13 Sep 1985 ; 5.

Whether it is Mr. Jack Anderson or Mr Frank Camper, we, Indians, have an extraordinary knack of over-reacting to the words they utter. Ever since the disclosure that two Sikhs had obtained training in the mercenary school being run by Mr. Camper, he has hit the headlines and indeed, a kind of a best-selling name. Otherwise where was the need to interview him by an Indian weekly ? The interview itself has been flashed across India in the media in a prominent manner. Mr. Camper spoke of many things without bothering the level of his own credibility. For a man running a mercenary school without any qualms, normal norms need not matter. Two things of his long interview deserve to be taken note of. First, that someone in the Prime Minister's Office was passing on all informations to the extremists ; secondly, his own admission that he runs the school with the connivance of the FBI and CIA.

The first assertion is meant to sow seeds of mistrust among the people about the functionaries in the Prime Minister's Office and make those occupying crucial positions suspect in the eyes of public. Mr. Camper's admission that he is in league with the FBI and CIA makes a lot of sense for after all one cannot run a mercenary school of, thus, this type without vast resources and powerful support. With this admission it is now possible to tie the loose ends and comprehend rather accurately how and perhaps, for what purpose extremists were being trained by Mr. Camper.

It is also possible now to understand why the U.S. State Department refused to advise Mr. Camper to close down his school on the fallacious ground he had the freedom to run it. But is that school expected to train people to undermine democracies ? If so, what happens to the great American dream and slogan of fostering democracies and what value one should attach to the U.S. leader's claim that they respect the unity and integrity of India ? Less said the better about his claim that he had tipped off Indian consulate in New York on the alleged planting of two bombs on the Kanishka. Is he trying to divert the attention of the world to the possible defects in the plane that could have caused the disaster ? No one can tell, but Mr. Camper's claim gives more credence to this suspicion. While there is no need to get rattled by what he said, it should be needed to get rattled by what he said, it should be read and understood between the lines. Who is this Mr. Camper, by the way ? As long as his own *bona fides* are in doubt, his observations will be treated with the contempt they deserve.

ELECTIONS

766. Bullets against ballot. *Statesman* 6 Sep 1985 ; 6.

ESPIONAGE

767. Abetting espionage. *Frontier* 26 Apr 1969 ; 3-4.

768. Copeland, Miles : *Without cloak or dagger : The truth about the new espionage.* New York, Simon and Schuster, 1970.

769. Thompson, James W. and Saul K. Padover : *Secret diplomacy, espionage and cyptography, 1500 1815.* New York, Ungar, 1963.

EXTREMISM

770. Methvin, Eugene H. : *Rise of radicalism* : *The social psychology of messianic extremism.* New York, Arlington House, 1973.

FASCISM

771. Aladyin, V.: Fascism : The monster imperialism breeds. *Soviet Land* (New Delhi) (9) May 1985 ; 24.

Mankind lost more than 50 million people during World War II. This is over 2.5 times more than that it lost in World War I. The dead cannot be brought back to life, but they do remind the living of their debt of gratitude, of their responsibility for the present and future of our planet. Fascism was condemned and sentenced at the Nuremberg War-Crimes Trials. Many believed at that time that one of the most terrible pages in human history had been turned over finally. However, the present day realities show that this is not so. That is precisely why it is so important to reveal the root causes of fascism as a historical phenomenon and the forces that are standing behind it.

The course of history between the Two World Wars graphically revels that, for 70 years now, fascism has been the chief bulwark of the most reactionary and aggressive circles of monopoly capital, which found in it an efficient tool for their salvation in history. As early as in the first years of its existence, fascism drowned in blood the workers' movement in Italy, Bulgaria and other European countries.

What is fascism ? Much has been written about fascism, there are many definitions of fascism. What is common to all of them is that fascism rests on the negation of intelligence of humanity ; it is characterised by hatred towards humanism, civilisation ; by worship of base instincts. One of the leaders of German fascism used to say that when he heard the word "culture", his hand reached for a pistol.

"One should not give power to the blind mass that is unable to think and possess a spark of God." Hitler wrote in this Mein Kampf (My Battle).

Fascism was the first form of bourgeois ideology which started to employ means of massive ideological brainwashing of the working people. The fascists portrayed themselves as fighters for social justice, while being financed by giant monopolies. After the 1922 "march to Rome" and capture of power, Italian fascists proclaimed the establishment in Italy of a "proletarian fascist state." The Spanish fascists, counting on the traditions of the Spanish workers' movement, called themselves "syndicalists". German fascists named their party National Socialist.

An important place in fascists ideology and propaganda belonged to the race theory. Fascists claimed that Germans and some "Nordic" peoples in Europe were the superior race. The fascists were especially hostile towards Jews and so called "coloured" peoples among whom they placed the peoples of Africa, Asia and Latin America. These peoples, the fascists maintained, were created for obedience and were to be slaves of the dominant race.

Of great importance for understanding the nature of fascism is the question of how fascist leaders—people who stood away from state authority in bourgeois society—were able to seize state power so fast and using so unusual methods. In Italy, for instance, the fascists came to power by outwardly "revolutionary" means allegedly directed against monopolistic bourgeoisie, but with its money and its interests. In other words, fascism is the greatest deception, in the history of mankind, of the broad working masses by the ruling class. Fascism is a form of struggle of monopoly capital against the working people. Open terrorist dictatorship—fascism—is exercised by elements of society hired by monopoly capital, as if beyond the forms of a capitalist state. The emergence and history of fascism in Europe, specifically in Germany and Italy, offers an example.

"Blackshirts", calling themselves fascists, appeared at rallies in Italy in 1919. It was conspicuous that many of them came from workers' organisations—the Socialist Party and Syndicalists. Mussolini himself, the chieftain of the Italian fascists, was considered to be a leader of Socialists before World War I. But, later, he and his associates were expelled from the Socialist Party for chauvinism. The hoodlum would have remained with the criminal world if they had not caught attention of Italian monopolists who were frantically looking for a way out of the revolutionary situation in Italy.

In Germany, fascism was financed by monopolistic circles from the very beginning. In 1919, the fascists in Germany numbered only 30 and possessed only one type writer. In 1920, they already owned a newspaper bought with "unaccountable" 64,000 marks. Contributions came not only from national monopolistic circles, but also from abroad, for instance, from Henry Ford. In 1923, before the first abortive putsch of German fascists, Fritz Thyssen, one of the richest man in Germany, handed over to the fascists 100,000 gold marks, which was one of the first "contributions" of German capital to fascism. German oil tycoon Deterding alone handed over to fascists, before they assumed power (in

1933), about 10 million marks. The IG Farbenindustrie concern transfered to German fascists on a voluntary basis more than 80 million marks between 1933 and 1944. The process can be described as the establishment of open terrorist dictatorship of monopolistic capital through its merger with fascism. Fascism "worked hard" to pay off : the revolutionary workers' movement was practically smashed and existed since 1933 in extremely difficult underground conditions.

The domestic problems of Germany, however, like any other fascist state, could not be resolved without restructuring society in a radical way. That is why fascism, after coming to power and consolidating its grip over the country, turned to capturing the outside world. Fascism means war, either internal or external. It cannot exist without war ; war is its specific feature as a form of power in a class of society.

In 1935, Hitlerite Germany announced its scrapping of the Versailles Treaty which limited its military potential. Universal military conscription was introduced. In October, Mussolini started the invasion of Abyssinia. In 1936, General Franco staged a fascist putsch aimed against the republican government, and the first 6,500 fascist "volunteers" landed in Spain : a year later, there were already 40,000 regular troops of fascist Italy in Spain. Japan started hostilities in China in 1937. In March 1938, the Hitlerites finally did away with Austria's independence, joining the country to the Reich.

Despite all these actions of the fascists, the Western governments pretended not to notice the threat to peace in Europe and the world at large. Nazi propaganda, wrote a British historian, "convinced" the West's capitalist states that Germany, the bulwark to struggle against Bolshevism, should be allowed to beef up its might. Italy, France and Britain signed a sentence passed on Czechoslovakia, at Hitler's dictation, in Munish in September 1938. It ceased to exist as an independent state in 1939. The Munich collusion between the capital states and German fascism paved the way for World War II.

Its course is remembered by all. Fascist Germany invaded Poland in September 1939. In 1940, it captured Denmark, Norway, Holland, and Belgium. France was captured on June 22, 1940. All these operations of fascism were, however, only preparations for fulfilling the chief mission of fascism—destruction of the Soviet state, of socialism as the main force opposed to imperialism.

The fascists treacherously attacked the Soviet Union on June 22, 1941. The Great Patriotic War of the Soviet people started. The fascists counted on a lightning war, but they were grossly mistaken in assessing their potentialities and the military-economic, moral and psychological potential of the Soviet people. The course of the war proved the mistake of fascist illusions. The war ended with the collapse of the fascist reich. Having swept from the face of the earth the brown plague of fascism, the Soviet Union saved the human civilisation.

772. Anti-Fascism. *Indian Express* 9 Dec 1974 ; 4.

773. Babani, Kirat : Is the monster rising again ? *Clavity* 19 May 1979 ; 7.

774. Becker, Jillian : *Hitler's children.* London, Panther Books, 1978.

775. Bondarevsky, G.L. : Fascism that spread to Iran. *Patriot* 20 Jul 1985 ; 4.

776. Bondarevsky, G.L.: Significance of fascist defeat for Asian peoples. *Patriot* 11 May 1985 : 6.

777. Borooah : 20-pt. programme to fight fascism. *Patriot* 2 Feb 1976, 1 & 9.

778. Bullock, A. : *Hitler* : *A study in tyranny.* London, 1964.

779. Chomsky, Noam and E.S. Herman : *Washington connection and Third World Fascism.* Boston, 1979.

780. Crooker, John : Fascist revival in Europe. *National Herald* 19 Dec 1980 ; 7.

781. Dimitroff, G.: *United Front—The struggle against Fascism and War.* New York, 1938.

782 Douglas, D.: Parent cell, 'some computer notes' on the composition of the first Nazi groups in Munich 1919-21. *Central European History* 10 (1) 1977.

783. Fascism. *Patriot* 12 May 1985 ; 4.

784. Fascism : A living threat. *Patriot* 23 Sep 1982 ; 2.

785. Gaur, Raj Bahadur: Working class and victory over Fascism. *New Age* 12 May 1985 ; 9.

786. Gohain, Hiren : Faces of fascism. *Telegraph* (Calcutta) 16 Mar 1983 ; 7.

787. Goyal, D.R. : Shadows of fascism. *National Herald* 6 Nov 1985 ; 5.

788. Joshi, K.K. : Will India go fascist ? *Pioneer* 3 Oct 1979 ; 5.

789. Karanjia, R.K.: Who's fascist and what is fascism ? *Blitz* 2 Dec 1978 ; 1.

790. Kidwai, Anser : Fascists—old and new. *National Herald* (New Delhi) 23 May 1985 ; 7.

791. Krishnan, N.K. : Fortieth anniversary of victory over Fascism. *Party Life* (New Delhi) May 1985 ; 1-4.

792. Mishra, Girish : Menace of fascism today. *Link* 22 Sep 1985 ; 19-22.

793. Neo-Fascism. *Democratic World* 19 May 1985 ; 4.

794. Noakes,, J. : *Nazi Party in lower Saxony, 1921-33.* Oxford, 1971.

795. Nolte, Ernst: *Marxism, Fascism and Cold War.* London, Methuen, 1982. p. 350.

796. Orlow, Deitrich : *History of the Nazi Party, 1919-33.* Pitsburgh University Press, 1969.

797. Salvemini, Gaetano : *Fascist dictatorship in Italy.* New York, 1967.

798. Shourie, Arun : *Symptoms of Fascism.* New Delhi, Vikas, 1978. p. 322.

799. Struggle against the modern fascists. *Baghdad Observer*, 6 Dec 1975, p. 1, 8.

800. Turner, H.A. : Fascism and modernization. *World Politics* 24, 1972.

801. Unite against fascism. *Link* 14 Dec 1975 ; 11-13.

802. War against fascism. *Blitz* (Bombay) 11 May 1985 ; 27.

803. Zhilin, P. : Historic victory over Fascism. *International Affairs* (Moscow) (6) 1980 ; 28-41.

FOREIGN AFFAIRS

804. Keohane, Robert O. and J.S. Nye *eds.*: *Transnational relations and world politics.* Cambridge, Harvard University Press, 1973.

GENOCIDE

805. Kulhanjian, Gary A.: Genocide studies : A benefit to all. *Armenian Weekly* 7 Jan 1984 ; 2.

806. Nazer, James : *First genocide of the 20th century.* New York, 1968.

807. Robinson, Nehemiah : *Genocide Convention.* New York, 1960.

808. Taylor, Simon: *Prelude to genocide : Nazi ideology and the struggle for power.* London, Duckworth, 1985. p. 228.

GLOBAL SURVEY

Afghanistan

809. Afghan guerrillas battle fiercely. *China Daily* 22 Nov 1985 ; 4.

810. Barron, John: Where children are trained as terrorists ? *Nagpur Times* 11 Aug 1985 ; 4.

811. Efros, Vladimir : *Afghanistan : US terrorism in action.* Moscow, 1985.

812. Genocide in Afghanistan. *International Herald Tribune* 16 Dec 1985 ; 4.

813. Goyal, D.R.: Pre-1978 origin of insurgency : Dark shadow of CIA. In *Afghanistan behind the smoke screen.* New Delhi, Ajanta, 1984 ; 75-96.

814. Guerrillas oust Afghan troops. *China Daily* 2 Dec 1985 ; 8.

815. Haqqani, Husain : Moles in high places : Afghan generals held for helping guerrillas. *Far Eastern Economic Review* 30 Jan 1986 ; 24-25.

816. Khan, Masood Ali : Terrorist crime in Afghanistan. *New Age* 27 Apr 1986 ; 13.

Another Terrorist Attack in Afghanistan has killed six school children. On April 21 a powerful bomb was laid by counter-revolutionary bandits in Kunduz in the 'Shirkhan' school and it exploded when the children came to attend classes in the morning.

Afghan security services managed to track and arrest the terrorist bandits who were found to be mercenaries of imperialist forces and were sent from Pakistan.

The question arises if Reagan and Thatcher would condemn this terrorism in their crusade. These criminals are being presented as freedom fighters and are being fed and equipped by the western imperialist powers.

In a speech in Moscow welcoming the Prime Minister of Afghanistan Soviet Premier Nikolai Ryzhkov said that in the case of both Libya and Afghanistan the source of aggression and terrorism was one and the same.

The only difference being that in one case it was perpetrated by the United States itself and in the other case by proxy. But aggression remained aggression and it created a threat to universal peace and an end must be put to it.

The undeclared war against Afghanistan, unleashed by forces of international imperialism and reaction headed by the United States and conducted mostly from the terriroty of Pakistan, was a great trial for the young republic.

The Democratic Republic of Afghanistan (DRA) is building its life on the principles of independence and progress, consistently carrying out socio-economic transformation in the interest of the working people, Ryzhkov said.

Soviet Union supports the DRA in its striving to achieve a settlement of the situation around Afghanistan by political means. "Our principled position on this question was outlined at the 27th Congress of the CPSU. As we were told by Prime Minister Sultan Ali Keshtmand, the Afghan-Pakistani talks have now approached a particularly important stage.

The Soviet Union wishes these talks success and would like substantial progress to be achieved already this year in the matter of reaching a political settlement that would ensure a reai termination and guaranteed non-resumption of armed interference from outside into the internal affairs of the DRA.

Sultan Ali Keshtmand in his speech declared that all attempts of the enemies of the April Revolution to bring Afghanistan back to the past grim times were doomed to failure. He said that the DRA and the Soviet Union had confirmed that the two countries agreed on the scheduled stage-by-stage withdrawal of Soviet troops from Afghanistan.

This will be done "as soon as a political settlement is achieved that will really put an end to outside armed interference in internal affairs of the Democratic Republic of Afghanistan and reliable guarantees that such interference is not resumed."

Keshtmand continued : "We have a right to expect the same sense of responsibility and realistic approach from the other side. Deplorably, while paying lip service to normalisation of relations with DRA, Pakistan steps up interference in Afghanistan's internal affairs from its territory, the interference which is masterminded by the USA, by its western allies and the reactionary circles in the region". All these attempts to turn the clock back in Afghanistan were doomed to defeat.

The masses of Afghanistan strongly support the aims of the April Revolution. The frontier tribes are also on the side of the revolution. This was shown by the Loyal Jirgah and the Supreme Jirgah of frontier tribes. They endorsed fully the home and foreign policy of the DRA, the policy of Afghan-Soviet freindship.

Over 100 facilities have been built in Afghanistan by Soviet help and they play a decisive role in the economy. 45 per cent of the revenue of the state budget from domestic sources and 75 per cent of the individual output of the state sector come from the enterprises built and operated by Soviet assistance.

817. Renfrew, Barry : At a cavern base, a show of Afghan revel strengthen. *International Herald Tribune* 13 Dec 1985 ; 7.

818. Steele, Jonathan : Under fire in Afghanistan. *Secular Democracy* Apr 1986 ; 46-47.

819. Tempest, Rone : Pakistan : A key to Afghan War. *International Herald Tribune* 25 Apr 1986 ; 5.

820. Ustinov, G. : Wholesale terrorism. *New Times* (Moscow) 20 Jan 1986 ; 23-24.

The counter revolutionary leaders regard sabotage and terror as one of the principal means of struggle against the people's government. Their main objective is to frighten the population and provoke unrest. Terrorist acts are carried out by groups specially trained for the purpose by experts from the secret services of the U.S., Pakistan and a number of West European countries. They kill or kidnap party and government officials and servicemen, conduct acts of sabotage in public places, at airports, fuel storages, pump houses, electric power stations, and on transport, and sheel housing estates from mobile guns, mortars and other weapons.

Not long ago the Afghan news agency, Bakhtar held a press conference to demonstrate the handbooks prepared by the CIA for the sabotage training centres in Pakistan and for the bands and terrorist groups operating in Afghanistan.

Among them was a pocket-size booklet, "Lessons of Guerrilla Warfare," distributed by the counter revolutionary Islamic Party of Afghanistan. Its table of contents includes the following chapters: "How to Use Small Arms," "Types of Weapons." "Chemical Agents and Their Practical Use," "Use of Anti-Tank and Anti-Personal Mines," "Anti-Aircraft and Rocket Weapons," "Ambushing," "Camouflage," "How to Hide in Mountains and Flat Country," "Destruction of Roads, Bridges and Communication Means," Combat with Superior Enemy Forces", "How to Behave When Arrested," "Ciphering and Smuggling Letters out of Prison."

Another manual, "War in the Enemy Rear," is intended for the fifth column, for the counter revolutionary underground. It contains instructions of an entirely different kind: how to become legalized, how to win people's confidence, to engage in subversion at the place of residence and work, how to set managers against their subordinates and tradesmen against buyers, sow panicky rumours, where and how keep arms, manufacture toxic agents and explosives.

New Times readers probably remember what an uproar was caused some time ago by reports about the manuals issued by the CIA for the contras fighting against revolutionary Nicaragua and how vehemently the CIA denied its complicity in the preparation and distribution of literature of this kind.

At the above-mentioned press conference the Bakhtar news agency also demonstrated by way of comparison the manuals put out for the Somozist bands in Nicaragua. It seems that the authors of manuals for the Afghan bands were not very imaginative—the same general outlines, the same recommendations, and even similar illustrations, but with a slight Moslem tint.

In their war against democratic Afghanistan the U.S. secret services closely cooperate with Pakistani intelligence. This was confirmed once again by a letter captured by Afghan public order forces and published in the Kabul newspaper Hakikate Enkilabe Thawr (Truth of the April Revolution). Here is the translation of this document:

"Top secret.

"From deputy head of the intelligence service of the Northwest Frontier Province, Peshawar.

"To director of the Central intelligence Service of Pakistan, Islamabad.

"February 6, 1985.

"In keeping with the decision on creating an atmosphere of chaos in Afghanistan and especially in Kabul, by March 21, 1985 (the Moslem New Year—G.U.) we had infiltrated five of our highly active and experienced men in the groups of mujahiddins and sent them to Afghanistan. Each had been provided with Afghan papers.

"Only group commanders know that we infiltrated these men.

"Secrecy must be observed at all stages of fulfilment of the plan.

"Muhammad Ahmed Khan, deputy head of Northwest Frontier intelligence.

"Copies sent to :

"The War Office of the President of Pakistan.

"The Chairman of the Afghan Refugee Committee."

It is easy to guess what decision the author of the letter had in mind. For several years now March 21 has been declared in the U.S. Afghanistan Day. On that day American TV reporters and highly-placed officials pour invective on the people's government of Afghanistan, prate about "solidarity with the courageous defenders of the faith," promise them aid of every kind and, simultaneously, urge them to continue the "holy war" against the revolutionary government without any scruples as to the means and methods used.

The instructors from US secret services incite the counter revolutionary bands to carry out particular brutal acts of sabotage and terrorism on the eve of the New Year festivities. So it was on March 21, 1984, when terrorists set off a bomb in a Kabul mosque during the service there. Four people were killed and 21 injured in the explosion. So it was on March, 20, 1985, when an explosive device went off in the rush hour on the crowded market square of the capital. Thirty people were taken to hospital. The lives of some of them could not be saved.

Terrorist acts and sabotage are often times to coincide with revolutionary and national holidays, festivities and other important dates. The aim is to spoil the holiday and mar the joy, and also to show that the counter revolutionary forces are still active.

The citizens of Kabul and the entire country condemn terrorist acts against innocent people. Whomever I talked with after the December explosions—victims and doctors, relatives of the dead, and public order officials—all spoke with anger and contempt of those who masterminded and committed these vile crimes. "Venal mercenaries of the CIA—Cowardly murderers—Vain are their hopes," they said. "They will be punished by revolutionary justice. They will never succeed in undermining our determination and militant spirit. They will not check the steady advance of the revolution carried out with the aim of ensuring a better future of the people."

Africa

821. Carey, Robert G. : Africa. In *Peace Corps*. New York, 1970 ; 136-49.

822. Carey, Robert G. : North Africa, the Near East and South Asia In *Peace Corps*. New York, 1970 ; 150-160.

823. Gupta, B. : Changing role of the major multinational oil firms. In *Multinational firms in Africa*. Ed. by C. Widstrand. Sweden Upsala, IDEP and SIAS, 1978.

824. Hodgkin, Muriel : *Nationalism in colonial Africa*. New York, University Press, 1957.

825. Mojekwu, Christopher C. : From protest to terror-violence : The African experience. In *ITCW* ; 177-81.

Africa had learned during these processes to submit to some of the atrocities in order not to be totally destroyed. She had learned to stoop in order to conquer. When protest, which is a legitimate political process, produces violence rather than political redress, as in the 1960 slaughter of Africans in the Sharpeville protest rally in South Africa, confrontation and greater violence are bound to follow. When the national power holders have reacted abnormally to these political processes, the socalled rebel groups, that is, the revolutionary heroes, would resort to terror and violence because they were never strong enough to overthrow such foreign domination by any other means. In such a situation terrorism becomes a technique in the overall strategy to remove the foreign authority and maintain Africa's independence. The successful overthrow of foreign regimes through guerrilla warfare, arson, sabotage, and terror-violence in Algeria, Guinea Bissau, Mozambique, and Angola are classical examples of the efficacy of this strategy.

But what about the situation in Zimbabwe (Rhodesia), Namibia, and the Republic of South Africa ? The white minority regime in Rhodesia has continued to use terror-violence and fear as a system of governing the majority African population. Mere political protests have led black

Africans nowhere. After several years of torture and death for the African majority in Rhodesia, the OAU and the United Nations finally sanctioned that the self-determination of the Zimbabwe people may be achieved by whatever means available to them.

From the Africans' point of view, the introduction of Cuban teachnicians and Russian assistance in nearby Mozambique, Zambia, and Tanzania at the request of the Zimbabwans in Rhodesia and by the OAU—Africa's regional body—must be viewed by unbiased political analysts as legitimate, desirable and. indeed, as humanitarian act.

The establishment of zones of terror in the Union of South Africa and Namibia, the creation of the native homelands of Bantustan in Zulu land are clearly aggressive acts by the white minority government of South Africa to enable it to apply the full rigors of fear and intimidation, which is characteristics of aparthied policy. Policy brutality against black South Africans is a commonplace event. The target is South Africa, the victims once more are black South Africans. Violence and fear, causing mental and emotional harm, have been and will continue to be applied in these terror zones where black South Africans will be forced to live and congregate. Neither the OAU nor the United Nations has been able, through diplomatic niceties or through international law, to effect any change of heart in South Africa. The ambivalence of some of the democratic superpowers is simply bewildering. It is therefore no wonder that Africans are skeptical about Vorster's concept of dialogue with African leaders. They are doubtful that it will ever produce significant results to assuage the course of violence—a course which South Africa has uncompromisingly set itself.

A survey of the activities connected with self-determination or liberation movements in Africa within the last two decades has shown that groups that have employed terror-violence were always successful in achieving their objectives : Algeria, Guinea Bissau, Mozambique, and Angola are cases in point. Those who either from public policy or for material inadequacy failed to employ the instruments of terror and violence lost in their bid for self-determination and political independence : Southern Sudan and Biafra, and the blacks of Zimbabwe and South Africa. In contrast, the success of Bangladesh but more especially Arafat's Palestinian Liberation Movement, with its supreme appearance at the United Nations, are concrete examples that international practice, if not international law, recognized the international effectiveness of terror-violence as the true "Real Politic." Africa has the capacity to learn fast. Events in Lebanon and in Angola are object lessons. The greater the terror, violence, and firepower, the quicker and more successful the goals will be reached.

But the situation does raise major issues of political sociology and political theory, especially in African domestic affairs. The ability of Afric a leaders to resolve African domestic problems without resort to violence and terror is called in question. These questions must be asked : In this terror and violence a carry over of the experiences of colonial terrorism practiced against them ? Are these the extension of practices, patterns, and measures cultivated during decolonization and during the liberation movements ? We must further ask whether all this terror and violence within the state and between states has come to stay. Is it really necessary ? Is this state of affairs endemic to Africa, as some historians are apt to speculate ?

Because transnational mugging has paid rich dividends from the days of the slave trade through the colonial period to the present, one must have the capacity to terrorize dramatically. It is my contention that terrorism—violence and terror—will stay with us and that it will be on the increase until human society learns to listen, to talk, and to compromise. So far, "effective" terrorism wins recognitions and friends. Power and influence can now be measured by the size and effectiveness of "the barrel of the gun" and all that implies.

826. Parry, Albert: Fire in the African bush. In *Terrorism.* New York, 1976 ; 469-87.

827. Venter, A.J.: *Africa at war.* Conn : Devin-Adair, 1974.

828. Walter, Eugene Victor : *Terror and resistance.* London, Oxford University Press, 1972.

829. Welfling, Mary B. : Terrorism in Sub-Sahara Africa. In *POT* ; 259-300.

Lacking material and human resources, political leaders are incapable of affecting the daily lives of most citizens. Power holders may inflict a "regime of terror" on a few but certainly not on the entire society. On the other hand, national populations that are largely unaffected by national political institutions develop little political interest and, hence, are not likely to become politically involved. A "seige of terror," or actions against the existing system of authority, becomes less likely. Gurr, in Chapter I in this volume, provided additional support for these assertions. His empirical evidence indicates that terrorist activity in the 1960s was more common in European and Latin American countries than in Afro—Asian ones ; more common in demoratic states than in autocratic or Third World ones ; and more common in richer countries than in poorer ones. He argues that these findings seem reasonable because terrorism is easier to carry out in open societies, in complex societies where organizational bases exist, and in areas where means are readily available and media attention assured. Terrorism on the part of officials and citizens cannot be discounted in Africa, but we must recognize from the outset that it may be far more limited than in more technologically developed societies where citizen and government are much more interdependent.

African states provide a variety of contexts within which terrorism has occurred and continues to occur. Although the continent now is decolonized, the bulk of sub-Sahara countries remained colonies of European powers until the early 1960s. Thus, terrorism at the national level was manifested first in the colonial context. The majority of sub-Sahara countries are now independent national-States ruled by indigenous blacks. This second context is the forum for most contemporary terrorism. Although events at the time of writing portend future change, a third situation currently exist in Rhodesia and South Africa, where minority whites of European origin (though generally not birth)rule the majority black populations.

Investigations of terrorism in these diverse contexts will reveal that, in spite of the diversity, portions of the population reject with terror the right of existing power holders to rule, and that those who control institutions of power use terrors to maintain their power. We shall not attempt to disentangle the "chicken and egg" problem of those who used terror first, for terrorism is recognized as an interactive process involving violence on both sides, reactions, on both sides, and social effects for all.

Before introducing the African context and outlining the organization of the chapter, we need to clarify the use of the term terrorism in this chapter. Terrorism involves violent acts designed to induce fear, which are indiscriminate, unpredictable, arbitrary, and destructive (Walter, 1969. Chap. 1 ; Wilkinson 1974, Chap. 1.) The concern here is with political terrorism ; that is, violent acts employed for political objectives. Finally, terrorism is carried out by organized groups, not by isolated individuals. Although this view of terrorism is conventional, two differences in the use of the term may emerge in comparison to other chapters. First, violent acts on the part of officials as well as violent acts against the state are considered terrorism. The second possible difference relates to the distinction of political terrorism from other forms of violence. In this volume, for example, Gurr separates terrorism from other forms of violence such as guerrilla activity, civil war and so forth, where activity is more continuous and where practitioners frequently control some territory. He considers terrorism to be a strategy or tactic, however, and as such it can be a part of more widespread guerrilla campaigns or revolutionary movements. In this chapter we shall be working with a definition similar to Gurr's, but in examining the African cases we will not exclude terrorist activity that is a part of other violent movements as Gurr chooses to do in his data collection. The reasons for this choice are largely practical. First, the infrequency of political terrorism in Africa limits the relevant material. Including terrorism related to other violent movements expands this relevant material and permits more interesting examples. Second, the problem of accurate journalistic reporting of events in Africa makes distinctions between terrorism and other violence difficult and arbitrary at best.

Although African historians have tended to slight the precolonial periods of the continent and our knowledge of these eras has been biased by the colonial belief that history did not begin until the European intrusion, as it is true that contemporary Africa has been unalterably affected by the European presence. Major kindoms such as Ghana, Mali, Kongo and Songai saw their days of glory in the tenth through sixteenth centuries. Other kindoms as well as a variety of other social and political units developed throughout the continent, but by the nineteenth century nothing equivalent to the European nation-state existed. It was the Europeans who created states in Africa and who introduced these states as members of the international system.

The Portuguese began their maritime explorations of Africa in the fifteenth century. Subsequent centuries saw other European powers enter the competition for the trade in slaves and commodities that Africa offered. Increasingly Indigenous systems were affected by outside powers, but it was not until European balance-of-power rivalries prompted the "scramble for Africa" in the 1870s and 1880s that real efforts were made by Europeans to claim, settle, and administer Africa. The Berlin Conference of 1884 set the ground rules for claiming territory and gaining recognition. By 1900 Africa had been carved up by the European powers. During this period major decisions on boundaries were made in Europe by Europeans with little knowledge of the territories they were creating.

Algeria

830. O' Ballance, Edgar : *Algerian insurrection, 1954-62*. London, Faber and Faber, 1967.

831. Saksena, N. S. : Algeria and South Vietnam are wrong parallels. In *THF* ; 129-30.

Angola

832. Alberts, Donald J. : Armed Struggle in Angola. In *IMW* ; 235-68.

Protuguese involvement in Africa started in the early fifteenth century as a result of the search for India, but penetration of the interior was slight until the latter half of the nineteenth century. Until then Portuguese were content to trade with the various tribal kingdoms of the interior. The main export from all of the Portuguese African territories was human beings. The slave trade was openly carried on from about 1510 until 1838, when the practice was declared illegal by the European powers. The Portuguese contented themselves with coastal trading posts until the turn of this century, when military conquest was undertaken. The final boundaries of Portugal's African territories were set at the Congress of Berlin, and confirmed in the aftermath of World War I. Angola was the largest and potentially the richest of Portugal's African territories. The other territories of note were Mozambique and Portuguese Guinea, or Guinea-Bissau as it became known in revolutionary circles.

The armed independence struggle in Angola against the Portuguese started in 1961, led by a group that came to be known as the Frente National de Libertacao de Angola (FNLA) under the leadership of Holden Roberto. Intial insurgent success, in a manner more reflective of ill-armed conventional war than guerrilla war, was followed by a fairly successful Portuguese counter attack. Stalemate set in, and other groups moved to create guerrilla forces to carry on the struggle. This pattern was essentially the same in all of Portugal's African territories ; the Portuguese were fighting what amounted to a four-front war. In Angola, the three main insurgent groups that dominated the preindependence struggle were FNLA ; the Movimento Popular de Libertacao de Angola (MPLA), which is the current ruling government party ; and Uniao Nacional para Independencia Total de Angola (UNITA). There can be little doubt that the original insurgent movement was a revolutionary insurgency, for all antigovernment groups involved sought to replace the Portuguese-dominated political values and structures with values and structures stressing nationalism, independence, "Africanness," and egalitarianism. The degree to which radical change was promised and hoped for beyond the granting of independence varied from faction to faction.

The Portuguese government and the colonial administrators of the African territories followed similar policies in each of the African territories. There were differences to be sure, but these differences derived more from the personalities and latitude allowed individual governors and general than from any legal or constitutional differences in the manner in which the territories were treated. Of particular importance was the stated Portuguese view of race. The concept, termed "Lusotropically," was one of equality on a theoretical level. This equal racial policy was not borne out by the dynamics and realities of life in the territories, especially in Angola. Lusotropicality was the combination of Portuguese culture and history with the Black African physique ; a new race uniquely suited to build and develop the African territories into modern states, all part of a Greater Portugal. Putting a name on this policy was a relatively recent innovation, perhaps borrowed from Brazil, another formed Portuguese colony (and one where substantial mixing of the races has occurred over times). But there were never any official distinctions among people in the Portuguese empire based on race. Rather, the class distinctions were based on levels of "civilization," that is, the speaking of Portuguese, education level, and other similar criteria. Natives of the territories were divided into two groups that were considered citizenship categories ; the assimilado and the indigena. The requirements for assimilado status were the ability to speak Portuguese, income from a job, good character, age (over 18), and noneffective of military or public service. The indigena were all other native-born black inhabitants. Settlers from Portugal and those of mixed blood seldom had to meet the official standards of the assimilado class. The indigena class had no real political or economic rights, and assimilado status was restricted to a very small proportion of the population. While the assimilado was little better off than the indigena, he did share some of the rights of Europeans. Like *de facto* segregation in the United States, class distinction was not on the basis of race, but rather on other factors that tended to break primarily on racial lines. Thus, the Portuguese could claim that race was not a factor, while the insurgents could point to the obvious racial overtones of all the inequities of life. Both sides thus claimed a superior moral position. The race problem has not gone away with the Portuguese and continued to be an issue of great sensitivity for all the political factions in Angola.

Early nationalistic tendencies in the colony resided more in the European sector than in the indigenous sector. These tendencies were tied to the citizenship distinction described above , as well as certain political facts of life arising out of the Portuguese political system. Even whites from Angola were not treated as full citizens of Portugal. Portugal, prior to the coup in 1974, was an authoritarian state where little dissenting opinion was allowed to surface. The precoup regime was based on a blend of fascist political values and highly centralized, authoritarian, "non-political," nationalistic, and bureaucratic organizational structures. Meaningful political participation, both in Portugal and in the overseas territories, was extremely limited. In an economic sense, the metropole can still be described as underdeveloped and backward, certainly by European standards.

833. Smith, James F. : In Angola, 'rebel territory' is wasteland. *International Herald Tribune* 5 May 1986 ; 7.

Argentina

834. Argentine military junta's final report on the war against subversion and terrorism April 1983. *Terrorism* 7(3) 1984 ; 323-40.

835. De Onis, Juan : Argentine funds aided terrorists : *New York Times* 6 Feb 1976.

836. Enough in Argentian. *International Herald Tribune* 16 Dec 1986 ; 4.

837. Graham, Bradley : Argentine torture convictions extend blame to lower ranks. *International Herald Tribune* 4 Dec 1986 ; 3.

838. Rock, David : Revolt and repression in Argentina. *Current History* Feb 1978 ; 57-60, 83.

839. Torture under dictatorship. *National Herald* 16 Dec 1985 ; 7.

Asia

840. Bryce, James. *Transcancasia and Ararat.* London, Macmillan, 1896.

Asia East

841. How Asia views terrorism. *Asiaweek* 15 Jun 1986 ; 42-43.

842. SAARC meet on terrorism. *Indian Express* 13 Jun 1986 ; 7.

843. Steps to curb terrorism mooted. *Newstime* 6 Dec 1985 : 7.

844. World cooperation urged in anti-terrorist campaign. *China Daily* 17 Dec 1985 ; 4.

845. Carey, Robert G. : East Asia and the Pacific. In *Peace Corps.* New York, 1970 ; 161-74.

Asia, South

846. Focus on terrorism. *Indian Express* 18 Aug 1986 ; 6.

847. SAARC and terrorism. *Patriot* 11 Aug 1986 ; 4.

848. Saxena, J.N. : Plea to South Asian nations to curb terrorism. *Times of India* 12 Jan 1987 ; 3.

The three-day conference on international law which concluded in New Delhi, on January 11, 1987 appealed to all the countries of South Asia to extend mutual cooperation and enter into bilateral agreements as was required to combat and condemn terrorism in the region.

The day's proceedings started with a paper on "the relationship between international terrorism, state terrorism and human rights in the world order," read out by Prof J.N. Saxena of the Delhi University.

In order to curb terrorism and protect human rights, Prof Saxena said, it was imperative that the world community in rejecting the proposition that all forms of violence were justified if supported by political goals, avoided the trap of supporting the other extreme that violent opposition to an established regime was never permissible by international standards.

"The remedies of rebellion and revolution that some people are adopting are not unknown in international law, but what is required is that the modalities of revolt should not violate the established norms. What has confused and confounded contemporary international practice is the refusal of those who claim the human right of self-determination to respect the human rights of innocent parties in the ensuring struggle for national liberation," the professor explained.

Asia West

849. Abir, Mordecai : A World, oil bar and terrorism. In *ITCR* : 135-40.

850. Blumenthal, Ralph : At airport gateways to the Middle East, Vigilance is the new watch word. *International Herald Tribune* 24 Apr 1986 ; 1-2.

851. Doran, Michael. Terror in the Middle East. *International Herald Tribune* 13 May 1986 ; 9.

852. *Efforts continue to check Arab terrorism.* Washington, Embassy of Israel, 1973.

853. Geyelin, Philip : Washington has adjusted its Middle East focus, *International Herald Tribune* 29 Jan 1986 ; 4.

854. Going after the killers, *International Herald Tribune* 27 Jan 1986 ; 4,

855. Gulf terrorism behind call for summit, *Egyptian Gazette* 11 Aug 1985 ; 3.

856. Heradstveit, Daniel : Role of international terrorism in the Middle East conflict and its implications for conflict resolution, In *ITWS* ; 93-104.

857. Ibrahim. A. Mohammed : Terrorism in West Asia, *Deccan Herald* 10 Dec 1985 ; 8.

858. *ICAO and Arab terrorists operations : A record of resolutions,* Jerusalem, Ministry of Foreign Affairs, 1973.

859. Khashaf, Al. : *Arab terrorism, American style.* Gaitherburg, Md., International Association of Chiefs of Police, 1974.

860. Meron, Theodor : *Some legal aspects of Arab terrorists, claims to privileged combatancy.* New York, Sabra Books, 1970.

861. Mushkat, Marion *ed.* : *Violence and peace building in the Middle East,* New York, K.G. Saur, 1982. p. 192.

862. *Nasser terror gangs : The story of Fedayun,* Jerusalem, Ministry of Foreign Affairs, 1956.

863. O'Balance, Edgar : Terrorism in the Middle East. In *ITCW* ; 160-64.

This paper excludes, except by way of brief reference, what may be thought of as battlefield or urban guerrilla warfare, as expounded by Mao Tse-tung and other authorities, and only the terrorism with a political motive will be considered. The hostage system, murder, torture, and terrorism in all forms are not new to the Middle East : they have been carried out for a variety of reasons, and particularly for political ends. In the Middle East terrorist acts probably date at least to the original old Man of the Mountains, Hassan ben Sabbah, who towards the end of the eleventh century organised and conditioned a fanatical sect, the Assassins, in the northern Iran. He later moved to Lebanon, where his followers committed many political murders.

The Arab fedayeen, or freedom fighters, came into prominence in 1965, when the Fatah organization began to raid Israel, but it was fairly ineffectual and failed, after the Six-day War of 1967, to instigate Mao Tse-tung-type guerrilla tectics in the occupied territories, where lived some 1.3 million Arabs. Then suddenly in late 1968, something seemed to snap in the Arab mind, and the cult of the fedayeen swept through Arab countries like wildfire and a crop of guerrilla groups sprang up almost overnight, mostly based in Palestinian refugee camps. Early in 1969, Yasser Arafat, the Fatah leader, became Chairman of the Palestine Liberation Organization, the PLO, which was supposed to control and coordinate their activities. By mid-1969, mergers and forcible take-overs had reduced the number of guerrilla groups from more than fifty to about a dozen, but they all had different aims, were of varying quality, and were very independently minded; Arafat's control in most cases was less than nominal. Fedayeen activities included terrorist raids acrcss Israeli borders, explosions inside Israel, assassination of Arabs suspected of collaborating with Israelis, attacks on Israeli embassies and EI AI offices abroad, and hijacking aircraft.

On December, 1 1968, Arab terrorists attacked an EI AI airliner at Athens Airport, causing death and injury. This incident provoked the Israelis, whose policy was one of hard reprisal, to mount a raid in helicopters on the Beirut Airport in which thirteen Arab airliners were destroyed. The first fedayeen hijacking of an aircraft had already occurred on July 23. Other incidents followed in quick succession, and soon the list became long.

Arab adulation, coupled with the fact that they tried to brush aside governments and reach the people directly, caused the fedayeen to become arrogant and to resist national restraints as they strove to become a "power witho t responsibility" in their host countries. In October 1969, this caused a clash with the small Lebanese army, which showed unexpected determination in preventing fedayeen expansion of its Fatahland base. In September of the following year, fedayeen activities and arrogance in Jordan brought about civil war, during which King Hussein eventually ejected them all from his country by the following July.

One of the more spectacular and dramatic incidents occurred at the World Olympic Games at Munich, on September 5. 1972, when members of the Black September Organisation, the BSO, which had arisen from the bitter ashes fedayeen defeat at the hands or king Hussein, and which had already assassinated the Hordanian Premier, were responsible for killing eleven Israeli athletes. This act caused attitudes of moderate Arab governments to harden against the fedayeen, and they took what restricting action they could.

864. Reich, Walter : Many losers of the Achille Lauro trial. *International Herald Tribune* 25 Jul 1986; 4.

865. Romaniecki, Leon : *Arab terrorists in the Middle and the Sovier Union.* Jerusalem, 1973.

866. Terror against Arabs. In *WTAZIT*; 39-40.

867. Terror against neighbouring Arab territory. In *WTAZIT*; 34-36.

868. Terrorist reprisals spread in Mideast and W. Europe. *Ta Kung Pao* 1 May 1986; 11.

869. Volsky, Dimitry : Spring of terrorism in the mechanism of tension. *New Times* (50) Dec 1985; 10-11.

870. Yahalom, Dan : *Fire on Arab Terrorism*. Jerusalem, Carta, 1973.

871. Yahalom, Yivtah. *Arab terror*. Tel Aviv, World Labour Zionist Movement, 1969.

872. Yariv, Aharon : Arab State support for terrorism. In *ITCR*; 73-78.

Australia

873. Horton, Dick C. : *Ring of fire : Australian guerrilla operations against Japanese in World War II*. London, Secker & Warburg, 1983. p. 164.

874. Lane, E.H. : *Dawn to dusk : Reminiscences of a rebel.* Brisbane, 1939.

875. Lang, J.T. : *Why I fight* ? Sydney, 1934.

Austria

876. Austria steps to fight terrorism. *National Herald* 10 Jan 1986.

Bahrain

877. Bahraini Prime Minister warns terrorists. *Pioneer* 31 Jul 1985;9.

878. Repression in Bahrain. *New Age* 7 Dec 1986; 13.

There are intensified repression, arrests and torture of political prisoners in Bahrain.

As a result of this violent campaign against progressive national patriotic forces, some brave fighters have perished, others have been made invalids for life.

Well-known leaders of the country's popular movement, Rahdi Mahdi Ibrahim and Hashim Ismail Al-Alawi have died under torture.

The campaign of repression against patriots is continuing. The main target are those who take an anti-imperialist stand and call for democratistion of life and betterment of conditions for the working masses.

The Bahrain National Liberation Front and other democratic organisations of Bahrain are banned but they continue to fight for the people's interests. The repression is meant to destroy all opposition to the anti-democratic regime. Another aim is to divert the attention of the people from rising social and economic difficulties.

Even the western press has noted the sharp fall in living standards of the people in Bahrain, growing unemployment and liquidation of all democratic freedoms.

Arab communist parties have issued a joint statement of solidarity with the patriots of Bahrain who are the victims of inhuman repressions and tortures.

Bangladesh

879. Dhaka to end insurgency. *Times of India.* 9 Jan 1987 ; 16.

880. Saksena, N.S. : Brutal terror in East Pakistan (Bangladesh). In *THF* ; 104-5.

Belgium

881. Belgium expels 7 Libyan envoys and restricts travel of others. *International Herald Tribune* 29 Apr 1986 ; 1.

Bolovia

882. Alexander, Robert J. : *Bolivian national revolution.* New Brunswick, Rutgers University Press, 1958.

883. Cyr, Anne V. : *Cuban revolutionary strategy : Lessons drawn from insurgency movements in Bolivia and Venezuela.* McLean, Va., 1970.

884. Gonzalez, Luis J. and Gustavo A. Sanchez Salazar : *Great revel : The Guevana in Bolivia.* New York, Grove Press, 1969.

885. Sullivan, George : Bolivia. In *Story of the Peace Corps.* New York, 1964 ; 96-102.

Brazil

886. DeGramont, A. : How one pleasant, scholarly young man from Brazil became a kidnapping, gun-toting bombing revolutionary. *New York Times Magazine* 15 Nov 1970.

887. Della Cava, Ralph : Torture in Brazil. *Commonwealth* 92, 24 Apr 1970 ; 129, 135-41.

888. Dulles, John W.F.: *Anarchists and communists in Brazil. 1900-1935.* Austin, 1973.

889. Marighela, Carlos : *For the liberation of Brazil. Tr. by John Butt and Rosemary Sheed.* Baltimore, Pengwin, 1971.

890. Quartim, Joao : Dictatorship and armed struggle in Brazil. *New Left Review*, 1971.

891. Quartim, Joao : Regis Debray and the Brazilian revolution. *New Left Review* Jan-Feb 1970 ; 61-82.

892. Riching, Alan : Former guerrilla on new path in Rio. *International Herald Tribune* 8 Aug 1986 ; 18.

Burma

893. Insurgencies : Rangoon in front. *Newsweek* 16 Aug 1985 ; 19-25.

894. Lintener, Bertil : Burma : A gathering of rebels. *Far Eastern Economic Review* 22 May 1986 ; 26.

895. Roy, Subir : Insurgents lose sanctuaries in Burma. *Telegraph* (Calcutta) 5 May, 1986.

Cameroon

896. Levine, Victor T. : *Cameroon Federal Republic.* Ithaca, Cornell University Press, 1971.

Canada

897. Alexander, Rajani : Canada and terror. *Hindustan Times* 23 Aug 1985 ; 9.

898. Canada sets up special anti-terrorist squad. *Tribune* 12 Jun 1986 ; 5.

899. Canada to help fight terrorism. *Free Press Journal* 19 Dec 1985 ; 5.

900. Canadian move against terrorism. *Deccan Chronicle* 20 Dec 1985 ; 6.

901. Canadian response. *Tribune* 20 Dec 1985 ; 4.

902. Hosenball Mark : Vancouver—Safe heaven for Sikh extremists. *Times of India* 21 Jan 1986 ; 9.

903. Jain, Ajit : Terrorists in Canada. *Statesman* 5 Aug 1986 ; 6.

904. Morf, Gustav : *Terror in Quebec* Toronto, 1970.

905. Move to curb terrorism. *Deccan Chronicle* 12 Feb 1986 ; 6.

The recrudescence, in Punjab, of terrorism engineered from abroad underlines the need for India to conclude extradition treaties, particularly with Britain and Canada. India has presented to Britain the draft of an extradition treaty designed to ensure extradition of terrorists from that country for trial in Indian courts. The Indian move is in pursuance of an understanding reached between Prime Minister Rajiv Gandhi and British Prime Minister Margaret Thatcher during the former's visit to Britain in October last. While Britain has offered to extend to India the provisions of its Suppression of Terrorism Act, India is of the view that there should be, between the two countries, a comprehensive treaty covering a wide range of offences. The Indian proposal for such a legislative measure is being studied by the British Government. Talks by legal experts from both countries have reportedly made good progress. There is a desire on both sides to reach an agreement on tackling terrorism. That desire, one hopes, will result in an early accord. Such a step is necessary in view of the fact that many separatist elements from Punjab and Jammu and Kashmir have, for some years now, been operating from London. The nexus noticeable between the separatist terrorists in Punjab and anti-national elements in the Kashmir valley appears to have been forged, to some extent, in London. Strangely, the two groups of separatist elements based in London became very active during the political turmoil in Punjab. And that was the time when the pro-Pakistan elements in Jammu and Kashmir surfaced. They tried to revive the plebiscite slogan. In London an Indian envoy was murdered allegedly by some members of a body known as the Kashmir Liberation Front. And there is now reportedly a move to hold an international conference on Kashmir in London. All this makes one feel that London has become a centre for separatist elements from Kashmir and Punjab. During the Punjab strife, some terrorists seemed to have been in daily contact with their supporters in London. This has been a major irritant in Indo-British relations for sometime now. And this is why the Prime Ministers of both countries have agreed on specific measures to tackle the problem.

Simultaneously with this, India is considering signing an extradition treaty with Canada, another country where Khalistan activists are based. Canada has assured India that it is determined to contain Sikh terrorism. Canada has already presented to the Indian Government the draft of an extradition treaty. During his recent visit to Delhi, Canadian Foreign Minister Joe Clark said that terrorism was a matter of common concern to the two countries. And Mr. Gandhi expressed satisfaction at the Canadian stand on terrorism. Khalistan activists operating from cities in Canada make no bones about their desire to scuttle the peace process in Punjab. Some of them have even undergone training for that purpose at mercenary schools. Therefore, India and Canada should conclude the proposed extradition accord as early as possible. Only close cooperation between the two countries could deter the trained saboteures. Peace in Punjab has again become fragile.

The time has now come for all nations to concert a plan to tackle terrorism, wherever it occurs. But the trouble with some big powers is that they do not mind turning a blind to terrorism if it subserves their foreign policy objectives. Only when they are hit by terrorism do they raise a hue and cry. It is this double-standard that has been responsible for the growth of terrorism in some parts of the world. What the situation calls for is an objective approach. This objectivity manifested itself, to some extent, in the unanimous resolution that the U.N. General Assembly adopted sometime ago. The member-States closed ranks and adopted the resolution condemning all acts of terrorism as criminal. That resolution called upon all nations to sign existing global treaties against terrorism and take steps to harmonise domestic legislation with those treaties. The proposed extradition treaties between India and Britain and between India and Canada are fully in consonance with the U.N. call to curb terrorism. There is urgent need for greater international cooperation in tackling terrorism.

906. Parry, Albert : Canada's White Niggers. In *Terrorism*. New York, 1976 ; 365-75.

907. Saywell, J. *Quebec 70*. Toronto, 1971.

908. Terrorism : Canada seeks India's help. *Tribune* 5 Jun 1986 ; 1.

909. Terrorism again. *Northern India Patrika*. 22 Oct 1985 ; 4.

Chile

910. Alterman-Santiago, Simon : Pinochet vows to stay in power. *Baghdad Observer* 26 Mar 1986 ; 4.

911. Angell, Alan : One year after the coup. *Current History* Jan 1975 ; 11-14.

912. Baryshev, A. : Pinochet on a Volcano. *New Times* (Moscow) (21) May 1983 ; 13.

913. Graham, Bradley : Communists step up violence in Chile. *International Herald Tribune* 20 May 1986 ; 3.

914. Hersh, Semore : Doubts on U.S. role in Chile. *New York Times* 17 Oct 1974.

915. Saksena, N.S. : Chile. In *THF* ; 50-51.

916. Sixty seven dead in Chilean violence. *National Herald* 2 Jan 1986.

917. Spooner, Mary Helen : Torture that never fails. *Amrita Bazar Patrika* 30 Oct 1985 ; 6.

A former Chilean security agent, arrested in connection with a court investigation into the 1977 disappearances of 13 Communist Party members, has described how political detainees were interrogated and tortured during the first few years of General Augusto Pinochet's regime.

Otto Trujillo, who worked under the Chilean Air Force Intelligence Unit, said he had witnessed electric shock and beatings against prisoners, but that psychological torture usually proved a more effective means of interrogation.

"I believe that the greatest torture is of the psychological variety," he told La Prensa Austral, a newspaper in southern most Chile. "For example, a prisoner would be forced to hear an imitation of his child crying, and this would break him."

An Appeals Court judge in Santiago ordered Trujillo to be jailed for his alleged involvement in the 13 disappearances. The court inquiry is one of several investigations by the Chilean judiciary into human rights abuses.

While the court investigations have concentrated on specific crimes and have not attempted to examine a specific pattern of abuses, the cases represent a growing willingness on the part of the Chilean judiciary to confront the country's security forces.

Trujillo is not the first former Chilean intelligence agent to disclose some of the inner workings of the country's videly feared security apparatus. Earlier this year an opposition news magazine published a cover story entitled "I Tortured", the detailed confessions of another ex-Air Force agent and member of the Central National de Informaciones, (CNI), Chile's secret police organisation. Andres Valenzuela, who fled the country late last year, recounted how officials sometimes disposed of the bodies of political prisoners by slitting open their abdomens and dropping them from helicopters into the sea.

Former Air Force chief and junta member General Gustavo Leigh has rejected the Trujillo statements, saying that the Chilean Air Force during his command "has nothing to fear".

918. Torture : Where a doctor's duty lies. *Baghdad Observer* 26 Jul 1985 ; 5.

Colombia

919. Dix, Robert H. : Implications of violence. In *Colombia.* New Haven, Yale University Press, 1967 ; 382-88.

920. Fals Borda, Orlando : Violence and the break-up of tradition in Colombia. In *Obstacles to change in Latin America* Ed. by Clandio Veliz. New York, Oxford University Press, 1965.

921. Gilly, Aldolfo : Guerrillas and peasant republics in Colombia. *Monthly Review* 17 Oct 1965 ; 30-40.

922. Hobsbawn, E.J. : Anatomy of violence. *New Society* (London) 11 Apr 1963, 16-18.

923. Sullivan, George Colombia : In *Story of the Peace Corps.* New York, 1964 ; 102-9.

924. Szulc, Tad : *Twilight of the tyrants.* New York, Herry Holt ; 1959.

925. Treaster, Joseph B. : Colombian Guerrilla War heats up again. *International Herald Tribune* 30 Nov-1 Dec 1985 ; 4.

926. Williamson, Robert C. : Toward a theory of political violence : the case of rural Colombia. *Western Political Quarterly* 18, Mar 1965 ; 35-44.

Cuba

927. Band, R.E. : Havana Knows : Castro's assassins strike again *American Opinion* 17 Jun 1974 ; 23-25.

Denmark

928. Lelyveld, Joseph : Danish Clinic finds keys to treating the tortured. *International Herald Tribune* 31 Mar 1986 ; 11.

When Luciano Vasquez landed in Denmark as a political refugee after three years in Chilean military prisons, he carried a double burden in addition to the anxieties that normally accompany exile.

First there was the problem of his feet, which had been partially maimed by interrogators who, he says, systematically broke his toes after having subjected him to a variety of other tortures.

The ordeals, he said, included forms of suffocation in which the victim's head is submerged in filthy water—known as the "wet submarine"—or the head is covered in a tight-fitting plastic hood—"the dry submarine."

But secondly, and ultimately more serious, was the problem of his mind. Like many torture victims, Mr. Vasquez suffered from chronic depression, nightmares and an inability to concentrate, making adjustment to exile all the more painful for himself and his family.

Mr. Vasquez, 33, who is in training as an electronics technician, still has problems with his feet, but the problems have been alleviated by three operations in Denmark. That was the relatively easy part of the thereapy designed for him in Copenhagen by the International Rehabilitation Center for Torture Victims.

But now, after a year and a half of intensive psychotherapy and physiotherapy, he is able to feel that he had come to terms with the experience of torture.

In the sense that they now live in the present and future as much as in their traumatic past, Mr. Vasquez and three other victims of torture in Chile who spoke about their treatment at the rehabilitation center can regard themselves as having recovered.

The center, which has treated about 50 torture victims a year since it was established in 1982 under the auspices of the Neurology Department at the University of Copenhagen, was the first institution of its kind. It is said to have been followed by similar programs elsewhere in Denmark and in Sweden, France and the U.S. State of Minnesota.

Dr. Inge Kempe Genelke, a neurologist who directs the program, said that torture victims have basically different problems from those of Danish psychiatric patients, even when their symptoms seem similar. Therefore, in the rare cases when it becomes necessary to hospitalize torture victims, they are never placed in psychiatric wards.

The difference, she said is that torture victims usually prove to be strong and healthy personalities. The pathology was in the situation they encountered, not in themselves. In all its aspects, the treatment program at the center is designed to get across that point to the victims, who tend to believe they have been permanently damaged physically and emotionally.

The first step in the therapy program is an exhaustive medical examination. Often torture victims report chest pains or chronic headaches; they need to be told their hearts and brains are functioning normally.

Often they have been sexually humiliated or abused ; they need to be assured that their capacity to have a normal sex life has not been physically impaired.

All these tests and subsequent therapy programs need to be conducted, Dr. Genefke said, with an awareness of the many ways that a medical examination might inspire an uncontrollable flow of memories. A person who has been subjected to electric shock torture is likely to balk at the wires and electrodes that are routine in taking an electrocardiogram.

Physiotherapists who customarily strap their patients to tables and use electric machines to stretch their spines dispense with the straps and machines in treating victims who were bound in prison or tortured by machines.

Exercise and massage are essential to the program. Nearly all torture victims suffer chronic pains from physical tension long after their bruises have healed.

In psychotherapy, torture victims are guided to the conclusion that it would be abnormal, given their experiences, not to manifest severe physical or emotional problems. Those who broke down under torture, providing information that they felt betrayed friends or relatives, need to be guided again through the choices they made so that they can see that they really had no choice. They are told, for instance, that they still would feel guilt if they had kept silent when that meant allowing a loved one to be tortured.

929. No refugee status for terrorists : Danish PM. *Hindustan Times* 15 Jan 1987 ; 8.

Dominican Republic

930. Dominican dangers. *International Herald Tribune* 22 May 1986 ; 4.

Egypt

931. Attacks on Egypt. In *WTAZIT* ; 73.

932. Craxi urges world action to contain violence : Egypt will ask U.N. to open international talks on terrorism. *Egyptian Gazette* 20 Apr 1986.

933. Kifner, John : Fear of terrorism weakens tourism in Egypt. *International Herald Tribune* 16 Jan 1986 ; 13.

934. Purposeless terrorism. *Egyptian Gazette* 22 Aug 1985 ; 3.

935. Sphinx loses out to terrorists. *Business Standard* (Calcutta) 14 Jan 1986 ; 5.

936. Terrorism : Hellish hijack. *Asiaweek* 6 Dec 1985 ; 18.

El Salvador

937. Anderson, Thomas P. : *Mantanza* : *El Salvador's Communist revolt of 1932*. Lincoln, University of Nebraska Press, 1971.

938. Bush, George : U.S. condemns Salvadoran death squads. *Terrorism* 7 (3) 1984 ; 347-49.

939. El Salvador : *Latin America Political Report* 6 May 1977.

940. New law lays base for mass repression. *El Salvador Reports* (New York) 1 Jan 1978.

941. Strong fighting in El Salvador. *New Age* 1 Jan 1986 ; 15.

Equador

942. Orme, William A.: Terrorism begins in cities. *International Herald Tribune* 13 Feb 1986 ; 8.

Equatorial Guinea

943. Sundiata, I.K.: Integrative and disintegrative terror : The case of Equatorial Guinea. In *ITCW* ; 182-94.

Equatorial Guinea possesses traits which are found in several other states in equatorial Africa, for example, Uganda, Zaire, and the Central African Republic. However, in Equatorial Guinea these are exaggerated by the republic's miniscule size, and peculiar diversity. Within narrow and, perhaps, nonviable confines, an indvidual and the interest he represents must defend his newly won economic and social position against a plethora of internal and external enemies.

At the time of its independence, there were few surface indications that the relations between President Francisco Macias Nguema's government and Spain would become unalterably embittered or that he would eventually eliminate the members of the ruling coalition which had been put together in the last year of Spanish rule. On October 12, 1968, the Spanish Minister of Information, Fraga Iribane, as representative of General Issimo Franco, devolved sovereign power to the government of Macias Nguema, saying that it was "the result of a peaceful, friendly, and constructive development" with Franco as its architect.

This seemingly auspicious beginning of Hispanic-Guinean relations was shattered the following year when anti-Spanish demonstrations and speeches by the new president materialized. The great breach between Spain and Equatorial Guinea is traceable to the efforts of Spain and the enemies of Macias Nguema to reverse these "anti-Spanish" tendencies. A former rival of the president, Foreign Minister Atanasio Ndongo, and the Equatorian delegate to the United Nations, Saturnino Ibongo, were asked by Spanish officials to stop supposedly inflammatory broadcasts. After the president refused to heed them, the two attempted a coup. Ndongo briefly took over the Presidency, but was soon routed. He and Ibongo were captured. The followers of the ill-fated putsch fled to the forest, while the President ordered the arrest of a number of political leaders.

The events of 1969 were something more than a conflict of personalities. They reflected the socio-economic tensions present in Equatorial Guinea and the problems inherent in the relationship between Fernando Po (Macias Nguema Biyogo) and the mainland enclave of Rio Muni. In 1968 it was estimated that Rio Muni, the poorer of the two major sections of the Republic, had a population of approximately 200,000, while Fernando Po had a population of around 62,612. Rio Muni, with a population composed mainly of fishermen and peasants, had an annual per capita income of $ 40.

There, as in neighbouring Gabon, the predominant ethnic group is the Fang. Fernado Po, together with the island of Annobon, had a more prosperous population, the annual per capita income being $ 250 to $ 280 at the time of independence. On the island at least 89 per cent of the indigenous population received a primary education. In 1960, exports from then Spanish Guinea totalled more than $ 33 million, the highest level of exports per capita in Africa ($ 135). This level was artificially maintained, since Spain bought Rio Muni coffee and Fernando Po cocoa at prices much above the world market price.

The independence of "Spanish" Guinea presented serious (as was to be seen later) conflict of economic motives and interests. Unified independence would favor the relatively disadvantaged mainland. Separate independence or continued rule by Spain promised to conserve the wealth of the island for its own use (with continuation of advantageous trade terms with Spain). In the year of independence the insular population consisted of roughly 15,000 Bubis (the indigenous Bantu-speaking population), 4,000 Fernandinos (descendants of freedmen landed by the British in the past century), 5,000 Fangs, and a force of 40,000 Nigerian migrant labourers (mostly from Eastern Nigeria).

The metropolitan government had by the 1960s resolved on unified independence for the island and the mainland. A 1963 Basic Law gave the two areas four counselors each in a central Consejo do Gobierno. Opposition to this arrangement was readily evident on Fernando Po where only 5, 340 Fernando Po voters voted yes on the new Basic Law, while 7, 150 voted no. On the eve of independence one commentator noted, "it seems reasonable to assume that the aggressive Fang (who outnumber the Bubi by a ratio of a least ten to one) will not be satisfied with this distribution of political power. much less economic power, once Spanish rule is lifted". The same writer noted :

> In contrast to the economic slowdown and tense relationships on the mainland, Fernando Po is booming with prosperity. The Bubi, who are indirectly benefiting from the flight of Spanish investment from Rio Muni, are disenchanted with continental nationalism. They are now convinced that independence in union with Rio Muni, and the loss of Spanish protection, would open their island to economic and political plunder from a flood of Fang. In the circumstances, this fear is thoroughly justified.

Organized separatist sentiment was not unknown on Fernando Po. In the sixties the Union Bubi was founded under the leadership of Enrique Gori Molubela. The Union Bubi advocated separation from Rio Muni and very strong links with Spain. In 1968, Wilwardo Jones Niger, former mayor of Santa Isabel, founded the Union Democratica Fernandina, a group which was prepared to accept independence for Fernando Po in a federal union with the mainland. An added, but most potent, force urging a separate status for Fernando Po was Spanish economic interests on the island.

Ethiopia

944. Bell, J Bawyer : Endemic insurgency and international order : the Eritrean experience. *Orbis* 18 (2) Sun 1974 ; 427-50.

945. Harden, Blaine : Slayings in Ethiopia hamper U.S. aid programme *International Herald Tribune* 29-30 Mar 1986 ; 2.

946. Legum, Colin. Ethopia : A regime of torture. *International Herald Tribune* 20 May 1986 ; 6.

947. Sullivan, George : Ethiopia. In *Story of the Peace Corps.* New York, 1964 ; 109-16.

Europe, West

948. Alexander, Yonah and Kenneth A. Myers. *eds.* : *Terrorism in Europe.* London, Croom Helm, 1982 ; p. 216.

949. Allies (of U.S) divided on terror. *International Herald Tribune* 18 Apr 1986 ; 6.

950. Armon, Moshe : Phoenix complex : Terrorism and the death of Western Civilization. In *POT* ; 13-18.

951. Corrado, Raymond R. : Ethnic and student terrorism in Western Europe. In *POT* ; 191-258.

Favourable conditions for ethnic and ideological terrorism exist when there is a highly visible social group that sees itself as oppressed in political and/or economic terms ; a monolithic and repressive government or political regime ; and few structural vehicles of redress. Another important factor in the existence of terrorism is the need for a concrete symbol of repression—a historical act of terrorism is the need for a concret symbol of repression—a historical act or acts that involved government violence against an ethnic or working-class group, especially if the structure of government has not changed substantially since the original violent act. In effect, it seems that ideological and ethnic terrorists need historical precedents that allow them to perceive recent history and contemporary government behaviour as continuously repressive and as requiring drastic and violent action.

One of the major themes in this chapter is that favorable conditions for terrorism are waning in Western Europe. It is increasingly difficult for terrorists to isolate the oppressed and the oppressor and to convince the former that violence is the solution to their oppression. The inability of terrorists to gain significant popular support reflects the gap between values and perceptions of the terrorist and those of most of the public. Chapter 7 will describe this value and perceptual gap and present an analysis of why it exists.

Since the French Revolution, terrorism has periodically affected European politics. As a result of Napoleon's attempts to rebuild the Internal political structures of various European states, a significant number of university students, the middle class, and the intelligents, although bitterly opposed to Napoleon's armies, were inspired to support revolutionary and nationalistic values. The reaction to this by the conservative elites and other segments of the European societies became an important factor in the violence and turmoil that frequently characterized European politics in the nineteenth century, particularly during the struggle for liberal reforms in the German states and the British Isles. Ideologies such as communism, anarchism, and fascism provided additional rationale for the terrorism that took place in the nineteenth and twentieth centuries, including the events that shaped World Wars I and II, the Russian Revolution, and the fascist dictatorships. Ethnic terrorism was also linked to the creation of the Irish Free State and Ulster in the British Isles.

Following World War II, there were few incidents of terrorism in Europe because fundamental change had occurred. The war experience was traumatic ; in addition to the physical devastation, there was the emotional shock of the savagery of Nazism. Major structural changes took place that affected every European country, such as the division of Germany and the onset of the Cold War. In addition, the creation of the European Economic Community (EEC) interlocked the economies and, to a lesser degree, the political systems of the key Western European countries. The North Atlantic Treaty Organization (NATO) joined the military forces of some of these countries as did the Warsaw Pact for Eastern European countries. The latter countries were also linked economically through COMECON and politically as satellites of the USSR. In addition, Britain, France, Belgium, and the Netherlands all lost their colonial territories. An equally dramatic economic change took place in Western Europe. While West Germany led the way with a complete material recovery, the economies of most of the other members of the EEC had also undergone impressive changes. Thus, the material standard of living had increased to the point that much of the classbased political conflict of the pre-World II period had been mitigated so that most political parties adopted essentially moderate positions on formerly bitterly contested class-based or ideological issues.

The conditions necessary for terrorism, an oppressed working class or a deprived ethnic group, were now waning. It was difficult to identify oppressed or exploited masses in any Western European country. The slums of the major European cities were only partially inhabited by indigenous people ; the majority were immigrants who, for the most part, were temporary workers. Depopulation often occurred among the more disadvantaged ethnic groups from the economically peripheral areas such as Wales and Scotland in the United Kingdom, Brittany in France, Galicia in Spain, and Calabria and Sicily in Italy. People were migrating from these ethnic regions to be absorbed in the expanding work forces of the more dynamic industrial regions of Western Europe. It appeared that cultural homogenization was the trend throughout Western Europe. Consequently, ethnically-based socio-economic and political interests were giving way to more functionally based interests. With rapidly expanding service economies, most Western European students were pragmatic toward the job market. They were named the "skeptical generation". wary of extremism because of the lessons of World War II and the continuing Soviet threat.

952. Dionne, E.J. : For many Americans, Europe is becoming a bunker in the shadow of terrorism. *International Herald Tribune* 29 Apr 1986 ; 6.

953. EC to Pool data on terrorism. *International Herald Tribune* 25 Apr 1986 ; 1-4.

954. Flenining, Marie : Propaganda by the deed : Terrorism and anarchist theory in late nineteenth-century Europe. In *TIE* ; 8-28 *Terrorism* 4 (1-4) 1980 ; 1-24.

It is hardly surprising that such unqualified approval could be given to Russian revolutionaries. Throughout Western Europe there was an awareness of the extend of Tsarist oppression, so that even liberals might in all conscience extend their sympathies. But for the ever-anxious anarchists (and most other socialists) in the dark post-Paris Commune days, there was at last a revolutionary spark, and it seemed all the stronger because it glowed in Russia, the darkest corner of the civilised world. Marx, too, who in this period is supposed to have supported the strategy of taking the parliamentary route to socialism, was cheered at the prospects for revolution. For anarchists in particular, insofar as Russia provided specific lessons, it is clear that these largely consisted in a reaffirmation of the importance of spontaneous acts of revolt within the context of propaganda by the deed. In spite of the enthusiasm with which anarchists might be expected to greet revolutionary events in Russia, however, their lack of anxiety over what constituted acts of revolt there may be taken to indicate that the ambivalence of 1878 was gradually abating. Many anarchists must have been thinking of events in Russia in July 1881, four months after the assassination of Tsar Alexander II, when they met in the famous London International Congress and officially recognised propaganda by the deed. The Congress pointed the direction to later events by advocating a study of the new technical and chemical sciences from the point of view of their revolutionary value.

Few leading anarchists understood so fully and accepted so readily the implications of propaganda by the deed, as did the German Johann Most. From late 1880 the pages of his Freiheit (published outside Germany) throbbed with articles inciting workers to rebel against injustice through violence and terrorism. Information and instructions were provided on the effective use of lead ; knives, poisons, fire and explosives. The journal urged the destruction of homes and churches, offices, shops and factories. All methods of achieving the social revolution were justifiable ; it was time to demand an 'eye for an eye'. 'Comrades of Freiheit". Screamed the pages of the journal, 'we say murder the murderers. Rescue mankind through blood, iron, poison, and dynamite. Freheit was intended for clandestine distribution in Germany and Austria, and in the early 1880s it had considerable influence among the anarchist groups there. Almost prophetic in terms of its response to propaganda by the deed, it no doubt also had an important influence in preparing the way for fuller acceptance of the role of violence and terror within later anarchist theory. This was true even though Most's enthusiasm for violence had begun to wane markedly by the early 1890s when the full force of the European anarchist movement was making itself felt. By this period Most had become so disillusioned with the role of violence that he publicly condemned Goldman and Berkman, provoking Goldman to the point where she physically attacked him.

By 1882 propaganda by the deed was becoming identified by anarchist theoreticians, such as Reclus, with any act of revolt, even when the act was not performed consciously to elicit support for the anarchist cause. On 24 March 1882 the young unemployed Fournier shot at an employer whom he considered responsible for the crisis in the weaving industry at Roanne in France. From August of the same year there was extensive terrorist activity by the Bande Noire (Black Band) directed against the mine owners of Montceau-les-Mines in the Lyons area. Fournier had not acted under the banner of anarchism, but none the less Le Revolte, the paper launched by Kropotkin in 1879, referred to his act as 'propaganda by the deed, the most fecund, the most popular'. The terrorism of the Bande Noire was likewise considered an event of 'immense significance, and hence the consequences from the socialist-revolutionary point of view, are inestimable'. There is little question that underlying such deeds was the unrest caused by a French economy which had been experiencing stagnation from

1873. But whether the cause was socio-economic or simply personal, the anarchists chose to regard these acts as encouraging and as indications that revolution was not entirely out of the question in Europe. For those who doubeted the power of popular protest there were the terrorist activities of the Spanish Mano Negra (Black Hand) in 1883. In Spain, as well as in France, police authorities responded with intense efforts to r und up anarchists, regardless of whether or not they were involved in the out bursts of terrorism.

955. Galor, Noemi: Council of Europe and its organs. In *International Cooperation to suppress terrorism.* London, Croom—Helms, 1985 ; 179-88.

956. Garcia, Robert : For a NATO Committee on countering terrorism. *International Herald Tribune* 10-11 May 86 ; 4.

957. Kriegel, Annie : Public opinion, intellectual and terrorism in Western Europe. In *ITCR* ; 172-79.

Leninism, it is true, condemns and repudiates the use of terrorism as an essential arm in the revolutionary struggle. This general censure depends on circumstantial reasons peculiar to the history of Russian Communism. There are also fundamental theoretical reasons : the ideas the Communists have developed of the necessary relationship between the Party, the working classess, the masses and the revolution. Thus, the Communist parties of Western Europe do not miss a chance to recall these positions which in principle are hostile to terrorism. One may read, for example, in a recent issue of New Times (put out by the Soviet Ministry of Foreign Affairs) an authorized study in which terrorism is once again denounced and condemned. Whatever the circumstances, the Communists cannot forget that they must conduct a permanent struggle of education and propaganda against the distortions and deviations of anarchists, leftists and ultra-leftists which constitute a constant threat to Leninism.

This being said, the concrete attitude of each Communist Party toward terrorist episodes in its own country is much less clear, more, blurred, more supple and often defined after the fact. Thus, it was that in the affair of Aldo Moro, the Italian Communist Party was in the lead of those demanding that the government resist all dealings with and yielding to terrorist blackmail. The Italian Communists discovered their "real vocation" – that of assuming the mantle of defending the constitutional government, after having spent of defending the constitutional government, after having spent the previous ten years deliberately trying to weaken it. On the other hand, the French Communist Party, whose Jacobin steadfastness is well-known, tends to assume positions which are more and more shaded and quasi—"objectivist" toward terrorists. L'Humanite, for example, discussed the recent trial of a Corsican terrorist in a neutral tone quite different from their usual preemptory voice expressing approval or rejection.

The third source of perplexity is the uncertainty as to a remedy. It is in seeking remedies that the propensity of intellectuals to play tricks with reality is revealed. As uncertain about the nature and limits of terrorism as they are about its significance—in short, about to both the diagonosis and the prognosis—they are naturally uncertain about the proper remedy against terrorism. Since they have not the slightest intention of taking real responsibility for evil, they find it comfortable to devote themselves to observation and denunciation of the possible excesses of any repression. This is a shrewd position because in the end, for these sort of people, all repression is excessive.

It is true that the proper response to indiscriminate terrorism is not indiscriminate repression. The necessary counter-measures—such as the dismantlement of terrorist cells, the arrest, trial and sentencing of terrorists—must all be carried out in such a way so that they could not appear to be the unique and exclusive weapon in the arsenal of the democracies.

All such countermeasures must be accompanied by a concerted intellectual attack bearing on the totality of the issues likely to supply the terrorists with a semblance of legitimacy and rationality. But this concerted effort should be conducted not with the terrorists, but with the general public. To believe, as the French government wrongly did for some time, that the delay in the development of Corsica could be the subject of negotiation, not with the Corsicans elected by universal suffrage, but with the clandestine representatives of the separatist terrorist movement, proved itself to be counterproductive. Democracy weakened when it is not respected, and when men who refuse to submit to the electorate (or when they do submit, receive a pitiful handful of votes) are dealt with as interlocutors. When, as in Corsica, electoral democracy is imperfect, it should be improved rather than pushed aside for the benefit of what is in essence anti-democratic.

958. Lall, John : Policing the world : New Western system and Indian response. *Statesman* 24 May 1986 ; 6.

959. Lenis, Flora : On terrorism, little signs of the new cooperation. *International Herald Tribune* 18 Jul 1986 ; 4.

960. Lodge, Juliet and David Frestone : European community and terrorism : Political and legal aspects. In *TIE* ; 79-101.

The problem of arms control was to become a preoccupation of the European Parliament during the second half of 1978. This can be attributed both to the realisation that combating abuses in arms procurement, supply and sales was an essential facet of the attempt to curb terrorism, and to parallel developments in the Council of Europe where, on 28 June 1978, the Committee of Ministers presented the European Convention on the Control of and the Acquisition and Possession of Firearms by Individuals for signature (endorsed by the United Kingdom, Ireland, Denmark and the FRG). While the Commission favoured EC action on this front, it was powerless and uncertain about the legal basis for any action over and above the co-operation, outside the EC's framework, of EC Ministers of the Interior which had begun in 1976. Devignon hinted that Commission action might be possible if the Nine agreed that article 235 of the Rome Treaty should be the basis for action. Failing this, the Commission might have recourse to article 100, although action would be difficult to justify since this article concerned the approximation of laws in so far as it was necessary to the functioning of the common market. Article 36, which provides for member states to take measures restricting free trade on a number of grounds, including public policy ('ordre public'), public safety or security, could possibly be invoked. Even so, action in this area was difficult.

While it is true that the legal basis for Commission action in this sphere was open to dispute, the problem lay with the unwillingness of EC member governments to compromise their national provisions on this and other matters relating to terrorism in the name of EC harmony. Their failure even to endorse the European Convention on the Suppression of Terrorism led to further pressure in 1979 from the European Parliament, and notably from its directly elected MEPs. At the same time, some progress towards a common EC attitude on combating and prosecuting terrorists was achieved, after a great deal of haggling, by the EC's Ministers of Justice using greater leeway than the Council of Europe in the interpretation of what acts constituted political offences justifying a refusal to extradite providing the case was referred to the appropriate national authorities for prosecution. In addition, to overcome French objections, the member states supported a Belgian compromise to follow up French proposals for a commong EC judicial or legal zone (un espace judiciare europeenne) where, *inter alia*, anti-terrorist measures would be tightly enforced. Henceforth, discussions about arms control, anti-terrorist measures based on EC accord regarding the extradition of terrorists, and the creation of a common judicial area proceeded in tandem with the broader and equally controversial debate concerning defence and a common arms procurement policy for the EC. This issue was complicated by the fact that not only was defence explicitly excluded from the Rome Treaty but Ireland was not a member of NATO, France had a special relationship with NATO, and the FRG's access to nuclear weaponry knowhow remained contentious.

In 1979 and 1980, EC initiatives against terrorism reflected external stimuli and, as before, largely translated themselves into pressure from the European Parliament on the EC's member governments.

Following the murder of Lord Mountbatten in August 1979, the whole issue of terrorism and EC action to combat it was debated, often acrimoniously, at the September Session of the European Parliament following the tabling of a question by Lady Elles on behalf of the European Democratic Group addressed to the Foreign Ministers concerning the nature of progress towards a common system of extradition. Lady Elles noted that terrorist crimes invariably involved a cross-national element and, therefore, made EC harmonisation crucial.

961. Menezes, S.L. : Face of Euro-terrorism. *Hindustan Times* 24 May 1985 ; 9.

962. Oreja, Marcelino: Chance for democratic Europe to oppose terror. *International Herald Tribune* 29 Oct 1986 ; 4.

963. Party, Albert : New Europe's old hatreds. In *Terrorism.* New York, 1976 ; 395—416.

964. Pilat, J. F. : European terrorism and the Euromissiles. *Terrorism* 7 (1) 1984 ; 63-70.

965. Pluchinsky, Dennis : Political terrorism in Western Europe : Some themes and variations. In *TIE* ; 40-78.

In France, the indigenous terrorist threat consists primarily of the activities of the separatist 'Corsican National Liberation Front' (FLNG). Other indigenous groups have periodically surfaced in France only to be quickly neutralised by French security forces. The more prominent ones have been the leftist, anarchist 'Armed Nuclei for Popular Autonomy', the leftist 'Direct Action Organisation', the separatist 'Front for the Liberation of Brittany' and the neo—Fascist 'Federation of European National Action' (FANE).

Only the FLNG has been able to mount a sustained, if limited, threat to the French government. The FLNC has restricted itself to date to bombings aimed at property damage. It has attempted to avoid casualties where possible. And although it has carried out periodic bombings in Paris and Marseille, it has concentrated its activities on the French Mediterr anean island of Corsica, where in 1980 it claimed responsibility for half of the more than 465 bombings on the island. The indigenous terrorist threat in France is less than in West Germany. In fact, more people have been killed in France over the last several years as a result of international terrorist attacks than by indigenous attacks.

Greece is another country which has faced a limited indigenous threat. According to a statement by the Minister of Public Order in March 1980, since 1974 there have been six political murders, 300 bombings, 80 molotov bombings and 180 vehicle fire—bombings. Some 81 persons have been arrested for 'terrorist activities with political motives'. Greek indigenous terrorist activity, like that in france, has focused on low—level bombings aimed at property damage. At present, the most active indigenous group in Greece is the leftist, anarchist 'Revolutionary Popular Struggle' (ELA), which first emerged on the terrorist scence in 1975. The ELA, which is similar in tactics and motives to the revolutionary cells in West Germany, has been responsible for the majority of bombings in Greece. It has also claimed responsibility for one assassination and is suspected of three more.

Although the ELA in the most active groups operating in Greece, other groups have attempted to surface. Some have failed for internal reasons, other because of arrests. One recent example was the 'Popular Frontal Initiative' (PFI). A leftist group apparently founded in November 1979, the PFI was broken up by police before it could carry out any operations. This group had planned to carry out a campaign of assassinations, bombings and kidnappings against public officials, the military and certain foreign embassies (including the American Embassy.)

Like most Western European countries, Greece has had some problems with rightist terrorist groups. In June 1979, twelve rightist terrorists were sentenced to prison for carrying out numerous bombing attacks during 1976-8. This group was called the 'Organisation for National Resistance', and, although it caused no death, it was responsible for injuring eleven people when it detonated over 50 bombs in Athens on 17 December 1978. Unlike Spain, Italy, France, Northern

Ireland and West Germany, Greece has not had any recent problems with right—wing terrorist groups.

The remaining Western European countries, especially the Netherlands, Portugal and Switzerland, have been faced with mere traces of indigenous terrorist activity which on occasion flares up to noticeable proportion. The Netherlands faced such a threat during 1975 to 1978 when South Moluccan extremists carried out several major terrorist attacks. They seized four Dutch establishments and an Indonesian consulate, were responsible for seven deaths and held a total of 328 people hostage, including 105 Dutch schoolchildren. This is the largest total number of hostages ever held by any contemporary European terrorist group. Since 1978, the South Moluccan extremists have been quiet, but certainly not eradicated.

In Portugal and Switzerland, occasional leftist extremist groups have carried out periodic low—level bombings. These groups have failed to develop into even a limited terrorist threat like the South Moluccan extremists. In 1980, one leftist group calling itself the 'Popular Forces of April 25' surfaced and claimed responsibility for several bank robberies, bombings, a kneecapping and an attempted kidnapping. It remains to be seen whether this group develops like the revolutionary cells in West Germany or the Revolutionary Popular Struggle in Greece, or is neutralised like the Direct Action Organisation in France and Front Line in Italy. If the conditions are right in Portugal, then the April 25 th group may survive and grow.

966. Russell, Charles A. : Europe : A regional review, 1970-78. *Terrorism* 3 (1—2) 1979 ; 157-72.

967. Sundberg, Jacob W.F.: Operation Leo : Description and analysis of a European terrorist operation. *Terrorism* 5 (3) 1981 ; 197-232.

968. Suro, Roberto : Experts slowly piece together the puzzle of how terrorists operate in Europe. *International Herald Tribune* 16 Apr 1986 ; 8.

969. Tagliabue, John : Europe faces new brand of terrorism. *International Herald Tribune* 2 Jan 1985 ; 2.

970. Tiltman, H. Hessell : *Terror in Europe* New York, 1932.

971. West encouraging terrorism : Bhasin (Lalit) *National Herald* 23 Jul 1985 ; 9.

Fiji

972. Naidu, Vijay : *Violence of indenture in Fiji.* Suva, World Univerity Series, 1981.

France

973. Bernstein, Richard : France. Syria join to prevent renewed terror. *International Herald Tribune* 30 Oct 1986 ; 1-2.

974. Carr, Reginald : *Anarchism in France : the case of Octave Mirbean.* Manchester, 1977.

975. Chirac bars talks, vows fight : Gunmen kill Paris attache in Lebanon. *International Herald Tribune* 19 Sep 1986 ; 1-2.

976. Coryell, Schofield: Lessons of Paris massacre. *Mainstream* 4 Sep 1982 ; 15-16.

977. Dasgupta, Punyapriya : Counterproductive terrorism by France. *Deccan Herald* 11 Sep 1985 ; 8.

978. Dumoulin, Jerome and Dinah Londa : Star Wars : A dilemma for France. *Intetnational Herald Tribune* 26 Feb 1986 ; 4.

979. Edwards, Stewart *ed.* : *Communards of Paris, 1871* London, 1971.

980. Fitchett, Joseph : Ambiguous record on terror comes back to haunt France. *International Herald Tribune* 17 Sep 1986 ; 2.

981. Fitchett, Joseph : Terrorism : Adding up a long, expensive bill. *International Herald Tribune* 17 Nov 1986 ; 8.

982. McManus, Doyle : U. S. officials assert France, Italy made pact with terrorists. *International Herald Tribune* 5-6 Apr 1986 ; 1.

983. Moisi, Dominique : Once-Smug France finds it's not immune to terror. *International Herald Tribune* 19 Sep 1986 ; 4.

984. O' Farrell, Rodrigo : State terrorists at work. *International Viewpoint* 16 Sep 1985 ; 7-8.

985. Ridley, F.F. : *Revolutionary syndicalism in France.* Cambridge, 1970.

986. Safire, William : Tough talk by France : Is it serious ? *International Herald Tribune* 19-20 Apr 1986 ; 4.

987. Smyth. Robin : Reign of terror panics Paris. *Tribune* 24 Sep 1986 ; 4.

988. Terror ; France caves in *International Herald Tribune* 5 Nov 1986 ; 4.

989. Terrorism in France. *Indian Express* (New Delhi) 7 Oct 1986 ; 8.

The recent wave of bombings in Paris has led to a new twist in the French Government's policy towards terrorists. The main demand for the group which claimed responsibility for the explosions was for the release of Georges Ibrahim Abdallah, a Lebanese militant arrested in 1984 in connection with the assassination of an American and an Israeli diplomat in the French capital two years earlier. He was, however, convicted only of possession of illegal arms and false identity papers. Following this, the authorities were apparently toying with the idea of releasing Abdallah under the guise of "expulsion". This attitude seemed to have been influenced to a considerable extent by the fact that Shiite extremists in Beirut have been giving a rough time to French diplomats and personnel of the French contingent of the UN peace-keeping force in Lebanon. For instance, these extremists have held four French hostages for quite some time. The French government, however, has now decided not to expel Abdallah but to start a fresh trial specifically for involvement in the murder of the American and Israeli diplomats.

Significantly, this came in the wake of reports about strong resentment within the French police and intelligence agency againt the government's failure to take a tough line towards the various Arab militant groups within France. Some elements in the security force are even reported to have planned a clandestine crack-down on these groups. It is a moot point whether the possibility of such a development was mainly responsible for the decision of the government to launch a new prosecution against Abdallah on a specific murder charge. What is beyond doubt is that the U.S. government exerted pressure on Paris not to let Abdallah go without facing such a retrial. While stiffening its attitude in the case of Abdallah the authorities have, however, conceded one demand of the Lebanese Shiite faction holding four French men hostage. They have arranged for the return to Paris of two radical Iraqi student opponents of the Iraqi government, who were earlier deported to Baghdad.

All this has underlined the complexity of the problem of combating terrorism faced by the French Government. It will not be easy for it to disentangle itself from the labyrinthine conflicts it West Asia. The eruption of terrorism in West Germany, Italy, Spain and England in the seventies was mainly the handiwork of local separatists and ultra-leftists. In West Germany and Italy, the authorities succeeded in crushing these groups while in the other two countries, terrorism has been checked to a great extent. While battling their own extremists West Germany , Spain and Italy had complained that they took shelter in France and urged the latter to ratify the European convention against terrorism. But, with its penchant for an independent stance on all issues, the French government refused to do so. West European critics have not failed now to make the point that the terrorist threat might not have been as serious as it is today if France had recognised it ealier as a common problem of all countries in the region. During debates in the UN, nowdays, every country calls for the closet possible international cooperation in curbing terrorism. But often there is a wide gap between precept and practice as India, at any rate, has discovered to its cost.

990. Thuchman, Barbara : Anarchism in France. In *Anarchists* Ed. by I. L. Horomitz. New York, 1964.

Germany, West

991. Acherson, Neal : Urban guerrillas of West Germany. *New Society* 10 Apr 1975.

992. Allies move against terrorist in West Berlin. *Baghdad Observer* 13 Apr 1986 ; 1.

993. Becker, Jillian : Another final battle on the stage of history. *Terrorism* 5 (1-2) 1981 ; 89-105.

994. Billing, Otto : Case history of a German terrorist. *Terrorism* 7 (1) 1984 ; 1.10.

995. Bonn to encourage terrorists to defect. *International Herald Tribune* 31 Oct 1986 ; 5.

996. Carlson, Andrew : *Anarchism in Germany*. Metuchen, N. J. Scrarecrow Press, 1972.

997. Cook, Schura : Germany : From protest to terrorism. In *TIE* ; 154-78.

The export of elements of the American counterculture to the rest of the Western World owed a large part of its success to the new technology of mass communication, which made it possible for the new music and pop culture to reach not only the masses of American youth through radio, television, films and records, but youth all over the world. This resulted not only in the adoption of the American counter-culture by the youth of most of the world, but also in an increased identification with American social and political problems, such as racism, the Vietnam War, etc. This supplied the student and youth movement in Germany, France, Austria, Scandinavia, Italy and Japan with political issues and an enemy to hate, resulting in the seemingly paradoxical situation of American problems becoming the problems of the international youth, who used them to legitimise protests against their own systems. The youth of Germany, Italy and Japan, the former Axis countires, especially appeared to 'over-identify' with the imported issues since they could not or did not want to identify with their own democratic system. Their history of Fascism may explain why political terrorism developed in these countries and not in others.

Juergen Habermas, a *German philosopher and social scientist,* analysed the German student movement in this context and points out that :

> Culture transmitted through electronic gadgetry never quite loses, its game character and superficiality, and has the inherent danger to portray the pseudo world of entertainment as reality. This results in an incapacity to see the difference between symobls and reality and corresponds on the psychopathological level to a state of paranoia.

Frederick Hacker thinks that the euphoric feeling of the counter-culture with its passion to revolutionise society owes a large part of its success to the mass media. He states :

> Events become socially effective and important through their mass-reproduced image. Often they take place only for the sake of the image; they are produced in order to be reproduced. The image is no longer only the reflection of reality; the image is reality, most likely the only one accessible to us.

Michael Baumann started his 'career' as a terrorist (he claimed to love only the funny and spontaneous aspect of terrorist protest, in the anarchist and nihilist tradition) as an early communard. He describes the communes as attempts to translate one's ideas about equality, justice and humanism into practice, where one had to share everything with everybody, and as a link from the youth movement to politics. In the communes the members actively and collectively engaged in political analysis and discussed sociological, cultural, political and psychological issues, problems, literature and theories. They considered themselves part sub-culture and part political underground. They read a lot, mainly leftist and revolutionary writers such as Reich, Marcuse, Marx, Fanon, Lenin, Che Guervara, Mao, Bakunin and Debray.

Communal activities, according to Baumann, comprised psychological self-finding processes using psycho-drama, discussions and readings of selected psychological theories. There were also attempts to decrease sexual restraints as well as a growing belief in activism, which they praised as creative living. The cultural significance of protest was emphasised by stressing spontaneity and fun. Eventually drugs became important, both to 'flip out' on or to raised consciousness. Political work meant to politicise delinquent youth. It also meant participating in demonstrations, sit-ins and destruction of property, while being careful not to injure people. The communards cherished funny terroristic acts which required 'chutzpah', courage and boldness. They had a slogan, 'terror without limit is limitless fun'. Later on, the RAF (Red Army Faction) composed of the Baader-Meinhof Group, criticised the methods of the communards as not being serious enough. Terrorism, the RAF believed, should not be enjoyable, but a hard job.

998. Extremists won't find a haven in FRG : Kohl. *Patriot* 25 Apr 1986 ; 7.

999. Glicksman, William: Violence and terror : the Nazi-German conception of killing and murder. In *ITCW* ; 423-29.

In Germany, the most fanatical Jew-haters have in the main been from among the urban rather than the rural population ; that is, they have been members of the so called educated class. According to Paul Massing, "The most virulent kind of anti-Semitism was spread throughout Germany by teachers, students, industrial and commercial employees, petty officials, professional people, and followers of cults of every variety."

It was this Mittelstand, with all its social and economic problems, that was the dominant factor in racial anti-Semitism. (It is a fact that Hitler's votes came from the urban element of the population.) Baptism and even total assimilation did not help Jews: To cite Massing again :

The exigencies of competition were such that many participants felt that no individual merit should enable Jews to gain access to spheres from which it was desirable to eliminate them altogether." It was the agricultural population who accepted Jews, whether willingly or unwillingly. The bestknown advocates of the anti-Semitic policy to rescind emancipation and foster discrimination were Treitschke and Stoecker. Wilhelm Marr, the creator of the term anti-Semitism, maintained that racial anti-Semitism was needed in order to destroy Jews and "Jewishness" and to prevent the verjudung of humanity.

One need only look at the catalogue of Jewish misdeeds, which the racial anti-Semite Theodor Fritsch compiled in his Antisemiten-Katechismus to recognize the founder and progenitor of Hitler's deeds. He merely followed the teachings of Treitschke and Stoecker, which became a Weltanschauung. Marr reinforced this in his "Sieg des Judentums uber das Germanentum." Toward the end of the nineteenth century, racial anti-Semitism in Germany was becoming an "organized myth."

"Aryan blood, embodying the secret of the highest creation, was glorified as the only guarantee of national survival in a hostile world, and consequently, as a providential promise of world domination" "Hitler's...... prediction that the nation of purest blood would eventually rule the universe was formulated in the anti-Semitic literature of the 1890's".

"The people which first and most thoroughly rids itself of its Jews and thus opens the door to its innate cultural development is predestined to become the bearer of culture and consequently the ruler of the world." Thus wrote Ahlwardt in 1890.

Hitler merely paraphrased this statement in Mein Kampf. "A state which in the days of race poisoning endeavors to cultivate its best racial elements is bound to become some day the master of the world."

Hitler expounded Ahlwardt's theory in this way : "This is the great significance of our long, dogged struggle for power, that in it will be born a new master class, chosen to guide the fortunes not only of the German people but of the world." It is no wonder, then, that the "basic principle formulated by Hitler (was) that man does not equal man, but is divided into gods and beasts."

This was his attitude toward the domination of the world. His theory about Jews is stated, so often that one would need volumes to document it. I will therefore limit myself to one of Hitler's statements, made during what Fest calls "The Incubation Period."

> The press, art, prostitution, land speculation, syphilis, capitalism as well as Marxism, but also pacifism, the idea of world citizenship and liberalism, these were all camouflages adopted at different times to conceal a world conspiracy : and behind all of them stood the figure of the Eternal Jew. The last obstacle to the Jew's plans was the German nation with its high proportion of Aryan blood."

What about Hitler's henchmen ?

"Goebbels found in the increasingly unrestrained practice of anti-Semitism by the state new possibilities into which he threw himself with all the zeal of an ambitious man worries by a constant diminution of his power."

"Heydrich set about seizing and herding together the Jews of Europe and sending them to gheir death, partly by 'national reduction,' that is to say, by hunger, exhaustion or disease, and partly by physical destruction, either with the aid of murder squads or by the so called 'special treatment' of mass gassing."

Franck is described as "the man who, in the vulgar phraseology characteristic of the officials responsible for the Final Solution, described his task as being to clean Poland of lice and Jews." "We must not be squeamish when we hear the figure of 17,000 shot."

Heinrich Himmler : "The Jewish people is to be exterminated, says every party member. That's clear, it's part of our program ; elimination of the Jews, extermination, right, we'll do it. . . . This is a glorious page in our history that has never been written and never shall be written."

We know by now that the Final Solution to the Jewish Problem was not adopted at the Wannsee Conference on January 20, 1942, but long before that. On January 24, 1939, Goering empowered Himmler and Heydrich "to solve the Jewish Problem." And on July 31, 1939, he requested them to prepare plans that would once and for all liquidate the Jewish Question. On September 21, 1939, Heydrich issued an order to the S.D. (Sicherheitsdienst—Security Service), a document known at the Nuremberg Trial as PS-3363, in which he differentiated between the final act, that is, the gas chambers, which still had to be kept secret, and measures like the concentration of Jews in ghettos, the establishment of

Councils of Elders, and "the ejection of Jews from their economic positions and property." Also, document NG-2586-F, dated December 12, 1941, issued by the Ministry of Foreign Affairs, gave detailed steps to be taken for the extermination of the Jews.

1000. Kren, George M. SS : A social and psychohistorical analysis. In *ITCW* 436-43.

History of childhood Quarterly 3 (1) Sum 1975.

The black uniform of the SS with its death's-head insignia has come to symbolize cruelty, while the organization's actions—most particularly its administration of the death camps—have come to identify it with a unique kind of evil.

The first stage in the analysis of the SS held that it was a collection of criminal and sadistic individuals. During World War II, Hollywood Productions consistently portrayed SS men as lacking all feeling and being sadistic—though the movie producer never seemed to be aware that this portrayal involved a contradiction. Ellie Cohen, in one of the first serious studies of the psychodynamics of the German concentration camp, defined the men as individuals with a criminal superego. This interpretation reached its logical conclusion during the Nuremberg trials which condemned the SS as a criminal organization and made membership in it *ipso facto* proof of criminal guilt. This almost demonic view of the SS was reinforced by the various memories memoirs of concentration camp inmates, who—with the exception various of Kautzky and Kogon—painted a radically undifferentiated picture of evil.

Nor was this view without a foundation, for the prisoner situation had produced a radical cognitive distortion which led inmates to see only the uniform. Thus, Reimund Schnable, who had, before became a prisoner, been a Hitler Youth leader and had some acquaintance with the system from another perspective than that of victim, wrote : "The brutal faces of the men in uniform with the symbol of death on their caps and collars, with a lack of expression, a whip in the hand and a pistol around the belt...made an unforgettable impression on the new prisoners." Or an academically educated Jewish prisoner comments : "For me they were all the same. If you asked me how they looked I can only reply : they all wore boots. These dull, evil and uncritical automatons, educated for murder in the school of Himmler will whenever they receive an order carry out their shameful craft." Or :

All SS officers have something dominating, almost like supermen.

> All SS noncoms are brutal individuals, sadists and robbers who attempt wherever possible to organize for themselves. They are convinced that prisoners are not human beings but rather embody all the evil in the world. The prisoner is some kind of animal for them which must be punished and which must be made to suffer with all means available before one finally exterminates it.

On the basis of the available evidence—memoirs of Wiesenthal, Kogon and, above all, Langebein, as well as the evidence from the Auschwitz trial, it becomes quite apparent that SS individuals were not uniform in their behaviour, in personality, and even in values. They included pathological sadists—though these were in a minority—a number who would fit an authoritarian personality, and even some who were able to relate empathetically to others and even within the structure of the camps attempted to help the victims.

1001. Kren, George and L.R. Waffen SS. *Armed Forces and Society* Nov 1976.

1002. Lowenthal, Gerhard: Case of West Germany. ITCR; 223-29.

In West Germany we have also experienced what Robert Moss calls the "Conspiracy of Silence." Very few in Germany would dare call the New Left a reactionary, dark movement. For years the members of the Baader-Meinhof Gang have been pictured as misled young people who were obsessed by their strong feelings for social justice, desperate, frustrated and lonely young men and women who could express their impotence and despair in no other way than in applying violence. And this in a country which gives everybody the utmost freedom to express himself and to work for the betterment of social and political conditions in the framework of the most liberal constitution in German history. In this country the internationally known writer Heinrich Boll could write an article in January 1972 in which he compared the criminal members of the Baader-Meinhof Gang to those persecuted under the Nazi regime. Boll wrote about a "merciless society" that hunted down those poor people at a time when leaders of that very society, far from being "merciless", had irresponsibily begun to renounce the vigorous defence of our democratic system. The article by Boll stirred up a heated controversy which even produced a book in which those who, like myself, had dared to criticize him were themselves bitterly attacked and dismissed as "fascists."

At the same time the head of the German Federal Office of Criminal Investigation stated in a meeting of the Ministers of the Interior that "the climate in the mass media had considerably deteriorated." He mentioned explicitly television, radio, Der Spiegel, Die Zeit, Vorwarts, Suddeutsche Zeitung and Frankfurter Rundschau as those media "that had adopted a distinctly negative attitude." The highest ranking police officer,of the Federal Republic quoted a public opinion poll which revealed that the sympathy for the Baader-Meinhof Gang had grown within the youth, and that the field of sympathizers had broadened in university circles and in the press.

I have a long list of concrete examples demonstrating how terrorism has been played down, minimized, explained away in a so called "objective" fashion. I shall for a moment concentrate on one publication. In 1975 I sponsored an investigation of its articles which were not simply journalistic reports or commentaries on terrorism but often sympathetic transmissions, at times verbatim, of terrorist demands, declarations and manifestos. My investigation revealed nine such articles between 1968 and 1975. Some came from wanted terrorists in hiding—one was even smuggled out of the famous Stammheim jail, for which this magazine paid DM 15,000 fee (the intermediaries were the lawyers of the gang). Most of the terrorist pamphlets were published by this magazine without any commentary or dissociating footnote. One striking example : On April 1972 that magazine published the famous pamphlet of Ulrike Meinhof "Serve the People-red Army Faction : Town Guerrilla and Class Struggle."

Well-known German magazines have in numerous articles dealt with the deplorable situation of misled young people, of terrorists who have become terrorists only because of their social "commitment." Most of these articles are uncritical or contain a barely hidden sympathy common to so many of these publications. If it is correct that the success of a terrorist action depends to a large degree on the extent of publicity it enjoys, then the German media have contributed a great deal to this success. Mahler, one of the early activists who received his terrorist training in a Fatah training camp, had the privilege of a 90 minute "portrait" on television—a mostly uncritical portrayal. It was only one of several devoted to him because he claimed to have left the camp of the terrorists. Many programs have been devoted to other terrorists, under the pretext of a "search for their motives" and "discovering the roots of terrorism"—but most of these exude sympathy for their subjects.

1003. Nair, Kunhanandan : Terrorism used as a cover—Racist spectre in W. Berlin again. *Blitz* 24 May 1986;11.

1004. Parry, Albert: Hitler's holocaust. In *Terrorism.* New York, 1976; 203-10.

1005. Saksena, M.S.: Attempts to murder Hitler. In *THE*; 45-46.

1006. Saksena, N.S.: Efforts made by West Germany. In THE; 55-57.

1007. Saksena N.S.: Genocide of Jews. In *THE*; 119-20.

1008. Saksena, N.S. Nazi Germany. In *THE*; 117-18.

1009. Violence in West Germany. *International Herald Tribune* 5-6 Oct 1985; 8.

1010. Wagenlehner, Gunther : Motivation for political terrorism in Germany. In *ITCW*; 195-203.

1011. Woman, U.S. : Soldier killed in bombing at Berlin nightclub. *International Herald Tribune* 7 Apr 1986; 1.

1012. Ward, James J. : Terror, revolution or control? The KPD's secret *Apparat* during the Weimar Republic. *Terrorism* 7(3) 1984; 257-98.

Ghana

1013. Afrifa, Colonel A.A. : *Ghana Coup 24th Feb* 1966, London, Frank Cass.

Guatemala

1014. Collazp-Davila, Vincente : Guatemalan insurrection. In *IMW*; 109-36.

Guatemalan government took strong, decisive action beginning in mid-1966 and that it adjusted its strategy as the insurgents varied theirs. The government successfully differentiated among the various types of threats and replied with various countermeasures based on a coordinated political, administrative, military, police, and intelligence efforts. The organisational and propaganda threat was countered by civic action, right-wing counteror, a low-level police effort, and a concerted intelligence effort. Terrorism was countered mainiy by a combination of intensive police action, tight security measures, and a continuous intelligence effort. Guerrilla warfare was met by defense of vital targets, mobile operations by company-sized units, and—once again-by a good intelligence effort. Furthermore, the government launched a national program aimed at eliminating many of the economic grievances used by the insurgents to gain support. As government success increased, it became easier to bring about desertion and defection among the insurgent forces. The government interrogators used techniques ranging from torture to bribes to get information from prisoners. It appears that near the end, the guerrillas lived in fear of the collaborators and government agents among their ranks. While the contribution of U.S. aid to the counterinsurgent effort should not be underestimated, it would not have been decisive without a Guatemalan government totally dedicated to the task at hand. The government made good use of current counterinsurgency doctrine and in fact added a new twist with the widespread use of the covert terror groups.

In the Guatemalan case the environment was generally a neutral factor. It held some advantages for the insurgents but, at the same time, it placed certain obstacles in their path and provided some advantages to the government forces.

The size of the country was certainly adequate to give the inrsurgents room in which to operate. In fact most of the 42,000 square miles of national territory is jungle and/or mountainous terrain, which many claim to be the ideal of insurgent operations. The road and communications network would also seem to favour insurgents since it is rather limited. There are only three major all-weather highways in the nation : the Pan American Highway ; the Pacific Coast Highway (which parallels the Pan American but runs along the coastal lowlands) ; and the Inter-ocean Highway (which runs east and west along Southern Guatemala). There are few, if any, roads in the northeastern region, but there are not many people living there either. Aurora Airport in Guatemala City is the best in Central America and there are 46 smaller airports, half of them unusable during the rainy season. There is one major railroad that parallels the Inter-ocean Highway. The quantity and distribution of the people is another factor that should have favoured the insurgents. Some 70 per cent of the almost 5 million population live in the rural areas, removed from the urban centers of government power. On the whole, these factors would tend to favour the insurgents ; however, they were offset by other key environmental factors.

The environmental consideration that hurt the insurgent casuse most was the cultural and ethnic composition of the rural population. The majority of these people are Indians, which posed serious obstacles to politicization by the insurgents. The first barrier was one of language. Even though Spanish is the official language, the majority of the Indians speak no Spanish, but rather one of some twenty different Indian languages. This not only hampered the insurgents' efforts to communicate with the Indians, but it also made them seem foreign to the Indians. The second problem was the political attitudes of the Indians. Simply put, they had none. Many of the Indians felt no loyalty to any

Social organization beyond their villages and saw the insurgents only as a threat to their isolation.

Local economic conditions were a factor that both helped and hindered the insurgents. The rural population in Guatemala is extremely poor and this, at least on the surface, tended to favour the insurgents by providing them with a forum for exoteric appeals. On the other hand, many of the Indians are so poor that are completely outside of the country's money economy and have time for nothing but subsistence farming. This, combined with the previously mentioned cultural factors, placed a stumbling block in the path of the insurgent propaganda and organizational efforts.

1015. Galeano, Eduardo : Footprints of terror. In *Guatemala.* New York, Modern Reader Paperbacks, 1969 ; 59-68.

1016. Geyer, G.A. : Blood of Guatemala. *Nation* 207 (1) 1968 ; 8—11.

1017. Guerrillas Claim kidnap credit. *Guatemala News* 6 Jan 1978 ; 1.

1018. Johnson, K. : *Guatemala, : From terrorism to terror.* London, Institute for strategic studies : Adelphi Papers.

1019. Johnson, Kenneth F. : On the Guatemala political violence. *Politics and Society* (4)1 Fall 1973 ; 55-82.

1020. Kinzer, Stephen : Crime is called threat to Guatemala's democracy. *International Herald Tribune* 11 Aug 1986 ; 3.

1021. Portes, Alejandro : Guatemala's right wing terror. *Nation* 10 Jan 1972 ; 48-55.

Haiti

1022. Mathur, Girish : US ditches baby doc the Haitian 'SOB' ! *Blitz* (Bombay) 5 Apr 1986 ; 11.

Honduras

1023. Anderson, C.W. : Honduras : Problems of an apprentice democracy. In *Political systems of Latin America.* Ed. by M.C. Needler. New York, 1970.

1024. Exploiting a flare-up. *International Herald Tribune* 28 Mar 1986 ; 6.

India

1025. Abbas, K.A. : Logic of terror. *Blitz* 13 Dec 1986 ; 24.

1026. Abhilash. Terror in Bihar. *Caravan* (New Delhi) Jan (First) 1986 ; 37-38.

1027. Abraham, Amrita : Feeding terrorism. *Sunday Observer* 26 May 1985 ; 4.

1028. Agony of Bihar. *Asiaweek* 6 Jul 1986 ; 11-17.

1029. Aiyer, S.P.: *Politics of mass violence in India.* Bombay, 1967.

1030. Ali, Salamat : India : A communal quandany—Hindu-Sikh killings put the Punjab regime in a bind. *Far Eastern Economic Review* 10 Apr 1986 ; 16.

1031. All hemmed in (Punjab). *Asiaweek* 2 Nov 1986 ; 6.

1032. Alleged terrorist (Daljit Singh) dies in police custody. *Times of India* 26 Jan 1986 ; 9.

1033. Amte (Baba) : Stamp out terrorism. *National Herald* 28 Mar 1986 ; 4.

1034. Angry Gurkhas. *Asiaweek* 1 Jun 1986 ; 34.

1035. Another assassination. (Arjun Dass). *Nagpur Times* 6 Sep 1985 ; 4.

1036. Arafat raps hijacking of Italian liner. *Ta Kung Pao* 10 Oct 1985 ; 12.

1037. Aravindakshan, P. : Occasional bursts. *Week* (Cochin) 18 Jan 1987 ; 24-25.

1038. Argov, Daniel : *Moderates and extremists in the Indian national movement, 1892-1923.* Bombay, 1968.

1039. Bali, Suryakant : Terrorist challenge to Indian democracy. *Caravan* (New Delhi) Jan (First) 1986 ; 13-15.

1040. Banerjee, Sumanta : *India's simmering revolution* : *The Naxalite revolution.* London, Zed, 1984. p. 332.
see also In *the wake of Naxalbari.* Calcutta, 1980.

1041. Banerjee, Sumanta. Naxalbari ; Between yesterday and tomorrow, *Frontier* 24 May 1969 ; 10-11.

1042. Banerjee, Sumanta : Ordinance to deal with terrorism. *Deccan Herald* 26 Jul 1984 ; 6.

1043. Barnala should act. *Daily* (Bombay) 28 Mar 1986 ; 10.

1044. Barnala's ineptness. *Daily* 24 Mar 1986 ; 8.

1045. Basu, Nupur : Bizarre drama of Kidnapping, torture. *Indian Express* 12 May 1986 ; 17.

1046. Berindranath, Dewan : Foreign hand in Punjab terrorism : who are the culprits. *Hitavada* (Bhópal) 11 Jan 1987 ; 2.

1047. Bhambhri, C.P. : India : the question mark over Punjab. *World Focus* (New Delhi) (74) Feb 1986 ; 19.

Political terrorism in India is directed against all the premises and assumptions underlying the Indian political system. The terrorists in India do not accept the basic postulates of participatory democracy and electoral system. The challenge of terrorists is directed against human rights, clivil liberties, universal adult franchise, and legitimacy of government through elections. Since terrorist attacks are on the democratic political system, the response of the Government of India has to be ruthless because if terrorism succeeds, democracy in India will collapse. The people of India have to make a clear choice, i.e. between democrarcy and terrorism.

The Naxalites in some parts of India and a section of Sikhs in Punjab are two terrorist groups which have to be confronted by the Indian State. During the middle sixties and early seventies, the Naxalite groups followed the policy of physical liquidation of the so called class enemies of the poor and the Indian State responded by effective use of state apparatus to curb the menace of Naxalism. All terrorist group pretend to have an ideology and they evolve strategies to achieve their goals. The ideology of the Naxal groups was that the exploiting classes in India are anti-people and the democratic legitimacy of the political system is a myth which can be exposed by rallying the poor in the task of physical liquidation of the representatives of the exploiting classes. The Naxalites proclaimed themselves as true revolutionaries and as self-appointed leaders of the poor. They employed guns to achieve their goals.

The Indian State confronted the Naxalities with the help of its law and order apparatus and these misdirected revolutionaries were contained and the politics of murder indugled in by the Naxalites were effectively checked by state intervention. At least three factors were responsible for this success. First, the Naxalities had a very limited and narrow social base. The Naxalite ideology did not enthuse the poor masses of India and this social isolation of the Naxalites facilitated the task of the Indian State in dealing with the Naxal phenomenon. Second, the Naxalites were isolated from other political parties of workers and peasants in India who had a much bigger mass base than the Naxalites. The Ideological battle of the Naxalites did not cut much ice because the organised communist movememnt which is committed to socialist revolution successfully exposed the hollowness of the so called revolutionary ideology of the Naxals. This isolation of the Naxals from the mainstream communist politics was based on ideological struggle where Naxals emerged only as murderers and not revolutionaries. Third, the Indian State was clear in its goal of physical liquidation of a so called political group which believed in the politics of aimless violence. Since the Indian State did not suffer from any ambiguity in dealing with the Naxalites, the anti-Naxal operations launched by the Indian State were successful.

1048. Bhardwaj, H.R.: Anti-terrorism and democracy. *Asiaweek* 5 Jul 1985 ; 70.

1049. Bhargava, G.S.: Rajiv and terrorism. *Free Press Journal* 19 Sep 1986 ; 4.

1050. Bid to Curb terrorism. *Deccan Chronicle* 9 Apr 1986 ; 6.

1051. Biswas, Nibedan : Foreign hand. *Caravan* (New Delhi) Jan (First) 1986 ; 43-45.

1052. BJP Nation Council meets ; Hard options must to combat terrorism. *Hitavada* (Bhopal) 3 Jan 1987 ; 1.

1053. Blow to terrorism. *Patriot* 27 Sep 1985 ; 4.

1054. Bose, Ajoy : Winds of War. *Sunday Observer* (Bombay) 2 Feb 1986 ; 4.

1055. Burki, S.J. : Social and economic detriments of political violence. A case study of the Punjab. *Middle East Journal* 25 Aug 1971 ; 465-80.

1056. Busting terrorism. *Pioneer* 14 Aug 1986 ; 4.

1057. Call for death sentence to check global terrorism. *Hindustan Times* 10 Jan 1987 ; 4.

1058. Chadha, Kumkum : Terror in Delhi. *Weekend Review* (New Delhi) 22 Sep 1985 ; 4.

1059. Chakravorthy, Nikhil : Maken's tragic end is a warning against complacency. *Telegraph* (Calcutta) 4 Aug 1985 ; 6.

1060. Chakravorthy, Sumit : Firm hand to end terrorism. *Daily* 7 Oct 1985 ; 8-9.

1061. Combating terrorism. *Deccan Herald* 22 May 1985 ;8.

1062. Compassion remedy for violence ; PM (Rajiv Gandhi). *Times of India* 13 Jan 1987 ; 1,16.

1063. Complex (Golden Temple, Amritsar) hotbed of terrorism? *Tribune* 21 Jan 1987 ; 1, 12.

1064. Cong-I and violence. *Hitavada* (Bhopal) 21 Jan 1984 ; 4.

1065. Congress leader, gunman shot in Ludhiana. *Times of India* 20 Jan 1987 ; 1.

1066. Countrywide call to fight terrorism. *Economic Times* (New Delhi) 16 Aug 1986 ; 4.

1067. Coup in the temple. *Tribune* 28 Jan 1986 ; 4.

1068. Crude awakening. *Asiaweek* 16 Mar 1986 ; 13.

1069. Crush terrorism or quit, Barnala told. *Times of India* 30 Mar 1986 ; 3.

1070. Cult of Violence. *Madhya Pradesh Chronicle* 2 Aug 1986 ; 4.

1071. Curbing terrorism. *Indian Observer* May 1986 ; 43-44.

1072. Dang, Satyapal: Who keeps terrorism alive in Punjab ? *Patriot* 17 Jan 1987 ; 4.

1073. Das, Binod S. : *Civil rebellion in the frontier Bengal, 1760-1805.* Calcutta, Punthi Books, 1973.

1074. Datta-Ray, S.K. : India after Mrs. Gandhi : Answer to politics of violence. *Statesman* (New Delhi) 1 Nov 1984 ; 6.

1075. Dayal, John : Happy hunting ground India. *Link* 31 Mar 1985 ; 7-8.

1076. Death for Mrs. Gandhi's killers. *Asiaweek* 2 Feb 1986; 11-12.

1077. Dhar, M.K. : Efforts for consensus against terrorists. *Hindustan Times* 23 Dec 1986 ; 1,16.

1078. Dichotomy of Akali terrorist ties. *Link* 6 Apr 1986 ; 4-5.

1079. Diwarkar, R.R.: Akali agaitation. *Gandhi Marg* (New Delhi) Jul 1983.

1080. Dubey, K.P. : Lingering shadow of terrorism in India. *Indian Nation* 11 Jan 1987.

Terrorism and Secessionism are the two dreaded ghosts haunting every Indian Mind in recent years. Terrorism-till recent past was absolutely foreign to the Indian system of life. The image that we find in the epics, scriptures and host of religious treatise depicted about India is that of a peace-loving and Godfearing country. From this sacred land of 'Bharatvarsha' spread the messages of Lord Buddha, Lord Mahavir and Mahatma Gandhi and stirred the mind of the whole mankind in the remotest corners of the earth. Their preachings have remained the perennial sources of solace to the people living in this strife-torn world. Unfortunately in this land of Buddha and Gandhi the cult of terrorism has found a suitable climate to survive. Politically 'terrorism' was not at all a chosen means for realisation of political ends in this country. Previously, we used to hear about sporadic acts of violence indulged in by goondas and mafias for basically economic gains but with the passage of time, organised terrorism has come to stay as a method for realising political ends. Terrorism, not in so acute form as it is now evident, was resorted to by the insurgents in the North-Eastern States like Nagaland and Mizoram. But during the recent years, this virus of terrorism has travelled to other parts of the country. Terrorism portends more dangers now because the secessionist elements have adopted it as a weapon against the Government. Be it Punjab, Kashmir or any other North-Eastern State, this element of terror has badly affected the lives of the people.

1081. End of terrorism near : Ray (S.S.). *Economic Times* (New Delhi) 18 Aug 1986 : 1.

1082. Ending terrorism. *National Herald* 17 Oct 1985 ; 5.

The two-day visit of Prime Minister Rajiv Gandhi to UK and his talks with his counterpart Margaret Thatcher may not have resulted in complete accord on all issues which the two discussed but there was one positive aspect. This pertains to the resolve of two countries to fight the cult of violence particularly terrorism. A treaty between the two countries to extradite terrorists is proposed for the propose whose details are being worked out by experts. This proposal has far-reaching importance and will go a long way in tackling a problem which has assumed alarming proportions. This decision must be appreciated in the context of Mr. Gandhi's observations on 'external' support to terrorist activity. Credit must also equally go to Mrs. Thatcher who has said firmly that the menace of terrorism must be destroyed. Certain developments which took place in the last couple of years had more than established that those who provided a clout to terrorism could go scot-free because of laws prevalent in the West which gave them a measure of protection and which are exploited by the malcontents to carry on their nefarious activities. Now, that the British Government has offered to review its law and tighten it, it is to be hoped that it will act as a deterrent. The revised British anti-terrorist law will cover those from India operating there.

The growing menace of terrorism cannot be treated in isolation. The increasing incidence of highjacking which has spread to the high seas makes it all the more important that there should be cooperation among different nations. In the case of Punjab it has now been confirmed by independent observers that the situation would not have been so explosive but for the support a handful of mischief-mongers got from outside. The very fact that a peaceful poll took place and there was a large turn-out of the voters reveals that the people of the state have full faith in the democratic process. Yet, some elements from outside have continued to present a distorted picture. The plot that was unearthed prior to the Prime Minister's UK visit and the anti-India propaganda launched by some people who thrive abroad show how the hospitality they enjoy on foreign soil could be misused by them. This state of affairs cannot be allowed to last long.

Mr. Gandhi has made it clear that violence in any form must be condemned. India and Britain can go in for joint ventures. India has indicated the areas of possible cooperation between them. Mrs. Thatcher has the highest regard for Mr. Gandhi and has displayed a measure of understanding that augurs well for the future relations between the two countries. There remain differing perceptions on the issues of sanctions against South Africa. But one may still hope that the British capacity to move with time-spirit will prevail.

1083. Escape of terrorists. *Hitavada* (Bhopal) 6 Jan 1987 ; 3.

1084. Europe-trained 'elite' killers have crossed into Punjab. *Current* (Bombay) 5 Apr 1986 ; 3.

1085. Explosive sabotage (of Air India). *Times of India* 14 Oct 1986 ; 8.

The Kirpal Commission inquiring into the crash of Air India's "Kanishka" in the sea off the Irish coast has confirmed what everyone had believed all along. On the submission of the report to the Government last March the minister of civil aviation, Mr. Tytler, had informed Parliament about the main finding that an explosion was responsible for the crash. Though, all circumstances were responsible for the crash. Though, all, circumstantial evidence, including the almost simultaneous blow-up in the Canadian Pacific Airways plane at the Narita airport in Tokyo, the sizes of the Kanishka fragments and the area over which they were spread, pointed towards sabotage, the theory of structural damage was also advanced. This gained credence when the flying fitness of Boeing 747 became suspect in the wake of a Japanese Airlines accident last year. Even the manufacturers admitted that the tail section of the aircraft was prone to metal fatigue. However, all the experts that the commission questioned, with the sole exception on a British engineer, said unequivocally that the nature of damage observed in the wreckage must have been due to shock waves and penetration of high velocity fragments following an explosion. In arriving at its conclusion the commission has justly relied on this expert testimony as well as the technical data provided by the cookpit-voice.recorder (CVR) and the digital-fiight-data-recorder (DFDR). This should set at rest the doubts expressed by the sceptics who had questioned the wisdom of retrieving the wreckage by pressing into service sophisticated robotic devices at very high cost.

1086. Extremists' challenge. *Times of India* 28 Jan 1986 ; 8.

1087. Extremists pose open challenge : Sparrow (R.S.). *Times of India* 30 Jan 1986 ; 16.

1088. Extremists put the clock back. *New Wave* 9 Feb 1986 ; 5.

1089. Fight against terrorism : Opposition, Centre back Barnala. *Tribune* 1 Apr 1986 ; 1, 12.

1090. Fighting terror. *Times of India* 22 May 1985 ; 8.

1091. Fighting terroı in India. *International Herald Tribune* 2 Sep 1985 ; 4.

1092. Fighting terrorism. *Free Press Journal* 22 May 1985 ; 4.

1093. Fighting terrorism. *Patriot* 5 Aug 1985 ; 4.

1094. Flushing out traitor (from Golden Temple). *Nagpur Times* 2 May 1986 ; 4.

1095. Focus on terrorism. *Statesman* 18 Jul 1986 ; 6.

1096. Foreign had behind Punjab terrorism—Dharmendra. *Daily* 16 Jan 1987 ; 4.

1097. Fornaro, Robert J. : Naxalbari Uprising : the cultural variables. *Asian Profile* 14 (2) Apr 1986 ; 175-80.

1098. Four women among 6 killed in Punjab. *Times of India* 13 Jan. 1987 ; 1.

1099. Franda, Marcus F. : *Radical politis in West Bengal.* Cambridge, M.I.T. Press, 1971.

1100. Fuches, Stephen : *Rebellious prophets : A stuy of Messianic Movements in Indian religions.* New York, Asia, 1965.

1101. Gandhi (Rajiv) urges action on terrorism. *International Herald Tribune* 8 Jul 1985 ; 5

1102. Gandhi, Arun : Rajiv's forthnight stand against terrorism. *Pioneer* 1 Nov 1985 ; 6.

1103. Gandhi, Maneka : Terrorism. *Onlooker* (Bombay) 23 Sep 1985 ; 40-41.

1104. Gandhi, Rajmohan : Acceptable terrorism ? *Indian Express* 10 Sep 1985 ; 6.

1105. Gaur, Sanjeev : Is there a method in the terrorist madness ? *Telegraph* 6 Apr 1986 ; 7.

1106. Gaur, Sanjeev : Sikh extremists kill a renegade. *Telegraph* (Calcutta) 17 Feb 1986 ; 1.

1107. Genesis of terrorism. *Deccan Chronicle* 15 Oct 1985 ; 6.

Hitting the nail on the head, a study on international terrorism by

an Israeli university has criticised the Western nations for having recourse to terrorist methods, while condemning them when they hurt their interests. This finding applies not only to the Western, but also to many other nations, including Israel. The naked truth is that most nations adopt a double standard in dealing with terrorism. When terrorism, wherever it occures, is in conformity with the foreign policy objectives of a big power, that nation tends to soft-pedal it. But if the violence affects the interests of that big power, it will self-righteously condemn it and even call upon all nations to make a concerted effort to save the world from anarchy. It is this double standard that is the root-cause of growing international terrorism. In recent years, some big powers, as part of their global policies, have tolerated, even surreptitiously encouraged, terrorism, in varying degrees, in one part of the world or another. This has come to be known as the game of destabilisation. A country whose foreign policy is not in tune with those of some big powers is likely to be subjected to the game of destabilisation. A recent case in point is India, whose foreign policy, needless to say, is much resented by many big powers, especially Western. These powers see a pro-Soviet tilt in India's non-aligned foreign policy. Surprisingly, separatist trouble broke out in two of India's sensitive border States—Punjab and Jammu and Kashmir—when the international situation took a turn for the worse in 1981. It was in this year that the spirit of international detente died away. Was it a mere coincidence? A dispassionate review of the events in that year would make one feel that the eruption of separatist terrorism in India had something to do with the sudden worsening of the international situation. That was the time when one superpower indulged in much belligerent rhetoric. Confrontation replaced detente. This had an adverse effect on peace and stability in the Indian sub-continent because India's neighbour, Pakistan, chose to become a strategic outpost of the West in the East-West confrontation.

That this development should have also triggered separatist trouble in Punjab and Jammu and Kashmir is very intriguing. That was the time when pro-Pakistan elements in the Kashmir valley surfaced with impunity. They openly indulged in anti-national activities. Simultaneously, terrorists in Punjab played havoc with the traditional communal amity. There was a diabolical move to create a rift between Hindus and Sikhs in Punjab. It is now well known that most of the separatist terrorists had received training as well as material help from Pakistan. And, what is more, that was the time when some leaders in the West, known for their resentment of India's foreign policy, predicted eventual balkanisation of India. Where are those prophets of Indian doom now?

A local grievance was dovetailed into global politics. Whoever did it aimed at destabilising and weakening India. This was the refrain of many of the speeches that Mrs. Indira Gandhi made before her assassination. This reading of the situation in the Indian sub-continent from 1981 to 1984 is corroborated by the findings of the Israeli university's study on international terrorism.

It is the relativity of terrorism that is responsible for growing anarchy. The problem needs to be looked at objectively, particularly by the big powers. There is no heroism in terrorism. Whoever exalts a terrorist for whatever reason must know that terrorism is a double—edged weapon. Some big powers seem to have made terrorist methods a part of their global policies. It is time the powers involved in the East-West confrontation refrain from encouraging terrorism for strategic objectives. So long as this does not happen, the world will be plauged by terrorism of one ideological hue or another. Unless all the nations cooperated, terrorism could not be tackled. The time has now come for some such initiatives. The initiative could be taken by the world leaders now participating in the 40th anniversary of the United Nations. The U.N. is the best forum for concerted action against international terrorism.

1108. Ghosh, S. : Ideological setting for terrorism. *Hindustan Times* 28 Jun 1985 ; 9.

1109. Gill, P.P.S. : Succour for terrorist-hit families. *Tribune* 20 Jan 1987 ; 9.

1110. Glading, Percy : *India under British* terror, London, 1931.

1111. Gough, Kathleen : Indian peasant uprising. *Economic and Political Weekly* Aug 1974.

1112. Govt. funding terrorists ? *Current* (Bombay) 12 Apr 1986 ; 7.

1113. Grewal, Nahar Singh : Combating terrorism. *Tribune* 15 Oct 1985 ; 4.

1114. Griffith, Percival : *To guard my people : The history of the Indian police.* London, 1971.

1115. Guns in gurdwaras (Sikh shrines). *Patriot* 23 Aug 1985 ; 4.

1116. Gupta, Ranjit : Dangerous differences (Khalistani terror a and Naxalite insurgency). *India Today* 30 Jun 1985 ; 142.

1117. Gupte, Pranay : Punjab : Cooperation might still avert a bloodbath. *International Herald Tribune* 8 Dec 1986 ; 4.

1118. Gupte, Pranay : *Vengeance : India after the assassination of Indira Gandhi.* W.W. Norton, 1985.

In his introduction to Vengeance : India after the assassination of Indira Gandhi, Pranay Gupte tells his readers : "I wanted to see for myself what lasting impact her (Mrs. Gandhi's) style had on the lives of everyday Indians, and where they now saw their lives going. I wanted, if not a portrait, then at least a sense of where my country stood at a particular point in time."

And so Gupte undertook an "extensive reporting trip", travelling from the "snow-capped' heights of Kashmir to the sandy beaches and lazzling green paddies of Kerala", meeting people of "all religions and ethnic persuasions", rediscovering the "hugeness" of his land—and alas, the shallowness of his own mind.

Opening with the assassination of Mrs Gandhi, a section written in the best tradition of the American best-seller, with people waking up in different cities and converging on the capital, the book goes on to deal with the aftermath—an acknowledge rehash of the PUCL-PUDR report on the Delhi riots of 1984.

Then Gupte makes his "passage through India" to the trouble-torn states of Punjab, Kashmir and Andhra Pradesh. While there is nothing terribly objectionable in these chapters, there are no fresh insights, no sense of immediacy or effort at scrutiny ; only a cut-and-paste job, padded liberally with conversations with a varied section of people. The author makes no attempt to sort out and organise his material. It, therefore, reads more like a reporter's jottings than a well-considered analysis.

Then there is a chapter entitled "Expectations" on the country's "Yuppies" (Young Urban Professionals) most of whom feature in Bombay's glossies, western-educated professionals who seem all set to inherits India. Also included in this section are the dedicated physician and the medical system, the courageous cop and the police force, industrialists, Rajiv Gandhi's budget, the country's nuclear programme, the Oil and Natural Gas Commission and economic policy. To offset all these heavyweights and weightier policy matters are Dr. Mahendra Jain, product of the municipal school system, who takes a medical degree at an obscure college because his parents can't affort the "donation" needed to get admission to a better college ; and Hemant Khairay, who runs an "agribusiness" in Lonavla and with whom Gupte shares a "delicious lunch of dal—a lentil curry—rice and a dry concoction of potatoes, peas and onions."

Assaulted by the sights, smells, sound and stresses that are in this country, many a western writer retreats to take the easy way out. He presents India as exotica. When the surface skimmer happens to be a foreigner, it is annoying. But when he is an Indian, as in the present case, it is unforgivable—even if that Indian happens to have spent only 18 of his 46 years in the land of his origin.

1119. Gurider Singh : Punjab : Congress leaders supporting terrorism ? *Onlooker* (Bombay) 23 Jun 1985 ; 53-55.

1120. Harbhajan Singh : Pak-China-US axis behind terrorism in Punjab. *Indian Observer* May 1986 ; 30-32.

1121. Hardev Singh : Terrorism wins again in Punjab. *Business Standard* (Calcutta) 30 Jan 1986 ; 8.

1122. Harminder Kaur : State as terrorist. *Caravan* (New Delhi) Jan (First) 1986 ; 46-48.

1123. Hazarika, Sanjay : Indian leaders learn to live under menace. *International Herald Tribune* 12 Aug 1986 ; 1-2.

1124. Hula, Richard C. : Political violence and terrorism in Bengal. In *POT* ; 351-72.

The coming of independence to India was viewed throughout the country as an occasion for hope and optimism for the future. In Bengal, however, independence was viewd with a distinct ambivalence. There was a general delight taken in the fact that the British had been driven from the country. Yet the terms of independence had been harsh for Bengal. Once again Bengal had been partitioned. What was worse, the present partition created two provinces that were not under the same political administration but rather under two separate and hostile national governments. The economic effect on West Bengal was profound. Calcutta found itself cut off from its major source of raw goods ; the entire region found its transportation system severely disrupted. There was also a political component to the unrest in West Bengal after independence, and that was an unhappiness with the make up of the new political leadership in the state. Much of the radical elements of the Bengali independence movement remained out of power. A common response was to define the new Congress government as simply an extension of the order and to call for a continued revolution.

Following independence, leadership for continuing turmoil in West Bengal came from the Communist Party of India (CPI). Franda has described the activities of that party :

> The most intense party activity in Bengal took place in an eighteen-month period that extended from October 1948 until March 1950, during which time innumerable trams, busses, trains, and buildings were either bombed or set on fire. Demonstrations by students, mass organizations, and cultural front groups took place at the rate of one or two a week in Calcutta, and deaths from the activities of the revoluticnaries were estimated to be in the hundreds.

Acts which were specifically traced to the CPI or related organizations included : an attack on the West Bengal labour minister, an attack on a public meeting held by the same minister, the complete destruction of the Calcutta telephone exchange, an attempt to blow up the Calcutta waterworks, a number of raids on the home of the state Congress Party, attacks on a number of Congress officials, an attack on Prime Minister Nehru, and large scale raids on Dum Dum Airport, in which a number of airline employees were killed. Late in 1950 communal violence in which some units of the CIP were thought to be involved flared in Calcutta.

The New government of West Bengal reacted in what by now could be called a traditional response. The state government moved against the party with a series of laws very similar in content to those that the British had used against the nationalist movement. Leaders of the party leadership assumed a strategy of seeking power through the electoral process. It is important to note, however, that an electoral strategy in Bengal does not preclude violence. Indeed, violence had proved to be an effective vote-getting technique. Throughout the mid-1950s, the party was involved in numerous public demonstrations that were broken up only after police fired into the crowds. Bayley has argued that throughout the entire decade of the 1950s, public disorder was increasing on an all-India level. Alan Watts has argued that a similar trend has continued for India into the 1960s.

Public disorder reached new levels in the mid-1960s with the coming to power of a United Front government in West Bengal. The United Front was a collection of leftist parties, dominated by the state's two major Communist Parties. The coalition's major point of agreement was the desirability of removing Congress from political power in the state. An immediate impact of the United Front government was a sharp increase in labour unrest. The number of strikes rose sharply. Moorhouse reports that in 1967 there were 438 labour disputes reported in West Bengal involving 1,65,000 workers with a loss of 5 million manhours. By 1969 this figure had increased to 710 industrial disputes involving 6,45,000 workers with a loss of 8.5 million man-hours. From the numerous labour agitations a new form of protest emerged—the "gherao," in which a target individual is surrounded for a prolonged period by a group making demands on him. The person facing the gherao can either give into the demands being made of him or hope for rescue from the police. It is unlikely that he would be able to escape unaided. The use of the *gherao* increased sharply in the state after the Communist state labour minister announced that police were not to intervene in gheraos without specific instructions from his office. Although, this restriction was later removed by the courts, the morale of the police was severely damaged.

1125. Hutchinson, Lester : *Conspiracy at Meerut*. London, 1935.

1126. Inder Jit : Growing menace of terrorism. *Deccan Chronicle* 30 Aug 1985 ; 6.

1127. India, Pakistan discuss terrorism. *Statesman* 21 Dec 1986 ; 1.

1128. Inhumanity of Khalistani terrorists. *New Age* 28 Dec 1986 ; 5.

1129. Insaf : New efforts against terrorism. *Deccan Chronicle* 7 Apr 1986 ; 6.

1130. Issar, D.K. : Terrorists get more Pakarms. *Hindustan Times* 6 Oct 1986 ; 1, 16.

1131. Iyengar, Shobitha R. : How to counter terrorists' bombs. *Caravan* (New Delhi) Jan (First) 1986 ; 50.

1132. Jain, Praveen : Longowal was a traitor. Interview with Harinder Singh Kahloon. *Delhi Recorder* Sep 1985 ; 19.

1133. Jaisingh, Hari : Wages of violence. *Indian Express* 19 Feb 1986 ; 6.

1134. Joshi. H.M. : Challenge of terrorism. *National Herald* 12 Jul 1984 ; 7.

1135. Kak, B.L. : 'Terrorist' being worshipped. *Newstime* (Hyderabad) 17 Jan 1986 ; 5.

Sardar Sarbjit Singh, a Sikh "terrorist" devoted to the idea of a separate Sikh State in India, has become an object of worship among scores of Sikhs, mainly youth, in parts of the Jammu district. His photographs have, of late, become valued things for several Sikh dwellings, especially in the Nanak Nagar area on the outskirts of the principal town of Jammu. His detention in a police look-up notwithstanding, a number of Sikh activists have been found loyal to him and insisting on the need to keep alive and kicking the state wing of All-India Sikh Students Federation (AISSF) of which he is the President.

Even Sardar Sarbjit Singh's impact on several Sikh girls and women in the area has not been reduced with a section of the members of the local Sikh community opposed to his alleged involvement in acts of violence and terrorism. A Sikh girl, who had, without any condition, agreed to become his life-partner, is said to have decided against deserting him, for she has been quoted as having told her parents that she would not snap her married in mid-September last. Their marriage did not take place with the unexpected arrest of Sardar Sarbjit near Amritsar in August.

Sardar Sarbjit had expected to go scot-free after he managed to pass a word on to the former Governor of Punjab, Mr Arjun Singh about his (Sardar Sarbjit's) "altered" plan of keeping himself aloof from the rest of the terrorists. He walked into the police trap before Mr. Arjun Singh could be satisfied by his reported plan to behave properly in future. Sardar Sarbjit was transferred to Jammu and, in the wake of sustained interrogation conducted by the local police and two Indian intelligence agencies, he confessed : "I spent several months in Rawalpindi before returning to Amritsar." His involvement in anti-India activity at a training centre in Rawalpindi could not remain a secret as he himself told his investigators of how he and some Sikh activists had engaged themselves in the task of picking up new techniques of causing disruption and subversion.

1136. Kalathil, Mathew : Gujarat : Cover-up of gang rape by policemen. *Economic and Political Weekly* 22 Feb 1986 ; 329-330.

1137. Kannabiran, K.G. : State as terrorist. *Indian Express Magazine* 23 Jun 1985.

1138. Kannabiran, K.G. : State cannot resort to violence to curb violence. *Sunday Observer* (Bombay) 2 Jun 1985 ; 20.

1139. Kapur, Pratap : Bid for political consensus on terrorism. *Newstime* 31 Mar 1986 ; 1, 12.

1140. Khalistan danger. (Punjab), *Hitavada* (Bhopal) 2 May 1986 ; 3.

1141. Killers unlimited. *Pioneer* 26 Mar 1985 ; 6.

1142. Killings in Tripura on increase. *Times of India* 18 Feb 1986 ; 22.

1143. Kling, B.B. : *Blue mutiny : The indigo disturbances in Bengal, 1859-1862.* Phil. University of Pennesylvania, 1966.

1144. Krishan Kant : Perceptions of Sikh extremists. *Mainstream* 3 May 1986 ; 5-8.

1145. Krishna Kumar, B. : Terrorism : Bombs, bombs everywhere. *Week* (Cochin) 18 Jun 1987 ; 18-23.

1146. Kullkarni, V.B. : Violent workers. In *Conflict in Indian Society*. Bombay, 1981 ; 276-99.

1147. Let the Centre not meddle, we can handle terrorism. S.S. Barnala. *Current* (Bombay) 5 Apr 1986 ; 3.

1148. Longowal, H.S. : I don't fear anything. *India Today* 31 May 1985 ; 34-35.

1149. Loss of nerve. *Times of India* 29 Mar 1986 ; 8.

1150. Maini, Darshan Singh. : How terrorism became 'holy' for some in Punjab. *Sunday Observer* (Bombay) 19 May 1985.

1151. Majumdar, B.B. : *Militant nationalism in India.* Calcutta, 1966.

1152. Malhotra, Avtar Singh. : Punjab Terrorists desperate as mass campaign picks up. *New Age* 4 May 1986 ; 15.

1153. Massive violence. *Tribune* 25 Jan 1986 ; 4.

1154. Mathur, Girish. : Akalis and extremists. *Link* 2 Feb 1986 ; 13-14.

When Chief Minister Surjeet Singh Barnala and his colleagues in the Akali Government and political leadership initiated the offensive against the extremists and frustrated their call for a "rasta roko" in the State, it appeared that they would carry the fight to its logical end. But they did not, and the result is that they have lost the second round.

Today the extremists are in command. They are in control of the Golden Temple complex which has been the headquarters of Akali politicals all these years, they have "dissolved" the SGPC, and now the Akali Dal and the SGPC have been compelled to hold their meeting at the Anandpur Saheb gurdwara to plan their counter-measures. The extremists have won the second round not merely by their audacity, but also because of a basic weakness of the Akali position.

The Akalis had defeated the extremists convincingly when they fought with them on the political—secular plane during the elections. The extremists call for boycott of the polling failed and extremist candidates opposing the Akali nominees were defeated. The election outcome provided an opportunity to the Akali leadership to consolidate its hold over the Sikh peasantry and isolate the demoralised and shattered extremists.

However, the Akalis chose the path of appeasement of the extremists, making one compromise after extremists, another. To be fair to Barnala, two purely political secular factors pushed him on the slippery path of appeasement. He was afraid that his rival and former Chief Minister P.S. Badal might gang up with the extremists. And, secondly, his ally Tohra has to keep one leg in the extremist camp and the other in the Akali leadership in his political secular anxiety to retain his feudal, mahant-like control over the vast properties of the SGPC, and so Tohra too pushed Barnala along the appeasement course.

1155. Mathur, Girish : Barnala's panthic rhetoric and surrender to terror. *Link* 6 Apr 1986 ; 7-8.

1156. Mathur, Girish : Punjab terrorism and Arun Nehru's Department of Internal Security. *Link* 6 Oct 1985 ; 9-11.

1157. Mathur, Girish : Terrorists trained in Pak bases. *Link* 20 Jul 1986 ; 9-11.

1158. Mathur. S. M. : Terrorism in India : A profile. *Pioneer* 25 Mar 1986 ; 6.

1159. Men behind VIP killings. *Delhi Recorder* Sep 1985 ; 20-26.

1160. Minister (Punjab's Revenue Minister Major Singh Uboke) abetted terrorism. *Blitz* 17 Jan 1987 ; 1.

1161. Mishra, Prafulla : Terrorism stepped up by Tripura extremists. *New Age* 28 Dec 1986 ; 7.

1162. Mishra, R.K. : Punjab ; The destabilisation design. *Patriot* 29 Mar 1986 ; 1.

1163. Misra, Rahul : Terrorism and Punjab. In *India's northern security*. Ed. by Gautam Sharma and K.S. Nagar, New Delhi, Reliance Publishing House, 1986 ; 75-86.

1164. Mitra, Chandan : Class war in the Panth : Extremism's challenge from below. *Statesman* 1 Feb 1986 ; 6.

1165. Mobilisation against terrorism. *Mainstream* 12 Apr 1986 ; 1-2.

1166. Mohan Ram : Shift in naxalite tactics. *Economic and Political Weekly* 21 Aug 1971.

1167. Mohan Ram : Security scandal. *Far Eastern Economic Review* 16 Oct 1986 ; 14-15.

1168. Mohanty, Manoranjan : *Revolutionary strategy; Maoist outlook and India's naxalites. Ph.D. Thesis.* University of California, 1971.

1169. Mojumdar, Modhumita : Violence unlimited. *Hindustan Times* 4 Dec 1986 ; 9.

1170. Multi-faced subversion in India. *New Wave* 10 Feb 1985 ; 1, 14.

1171. Mustafa, Seema and Nirmal Mitra : Terror unlimited. *Sunday* (Calcutta) 14 Dec 1986 ; 21-27.

1172. Nabbed terrorists lionised in Jammu. *Current* 25 Jan 1986 ; 3.

1173. Nanda, H. S. : Incompetent or frightened. *Delhi Recorder* Sep 1985 ; 32-33.

1174. Nath, Shaileshwar : *Terrorism in India* (The study of revolutionary movement in Bihar, 1902-1935). New Delhi, National Publishing House, 1980, p. 350.

1175. Nayar Kuldip : Challenge of extremists : Rajiv's gesture goes unheeded. *Free Press Journal* (Bombay) 30 Jan 1986 ; 4.

1176. Nayar, Kuldip : PM writes to Zia on terrorists. *Tribune* 30 Mar 1986 ; 16.

1177. N. E. insurgency. *Patriot* 21 Feb 1985 ; 4.

The latest Naga ambush, the second in the Ukhrul district of Manipur within three months which took a toll of 14 military personnel, is the price of vigilence in the troubled north-eastern portion of the country. It coincides with reports of welcome signs of rapprochement between another rebel of the region—Laldenga of Mizoram—and the Central Government. It is possible that the pro-Beijing National Socialist Council of Nagaland led by T Muivah is trying to signal the Government that he too is a force to reckon with. Judging from the mayhem and murder his group is responsible for on both sides of the India-Burma border ; he does have nuisances value and his activities underscore the continual vigilance that anti-insurgency forces must maintain in their pursuit of peace in the region. The last attack was on Chief Minister Rishang Keishing himself in which his bodyguards were killed but in the interregnum there has been systematic liquidation of eminent political personalities with the obvious intention of influencing the elections in December. Former Chief Minister Yongmaso Shaiza fell to NSCN bullets. It appears that having failed to stem the tide of a pro-Congress upsurge by a two-track policy of underground support for certain political personalities backed by the hit squads and sustained pressure on the security forces the NSCN has intensified its activities and in a region where the terrain is ideal, for insurgency ambushes are not difficult to set up.

While it is widely recognised that insurgency is best controlled by a judicious policy of combining socio-economic improvement of the lot of the peoples with relentless pursuit of the insurgents by the security forces, not a little depends, on the terrain in which the whole exercise is conducted. Manipur borders on Burma where the insurgents are able to secure sanctuaries through terrorism of the local population or appeals to their tribal affiliations (several hundred Burmese tribals were slaughtered last April by the NSCN for refusal to cooperate with it). Going by the empirical mathematics of insurgency the Government would have to deploy about 50,000 personnel to tackle 1000 insurgents. Such deployment, given the state of security in various parts of the country, is not practicable hence greater emphasis must be put on winning over the hearts of the people so that they do not succumb to the blandishments and threats of the insurgents while at the same time provide enough forces to keep the insurgents on the run.

It is an insidious, dirty kind of war and efforts to eradicate it are not helped by sweeping accusations of alleged brutality by the security forces. There can be objections to the sweeping powers available to the security forces under the Distrubed Areas Act but few can deny that the extraordinary situation prevailing in the north-east require extraordinary measures. The foreign-inspired elements cannot be allowed the benefit of considerate action because of the treasonous nature of their activities. True, much of the efficacy of the anti-insurgency operations is lost by unnecessary harassment to the people of the area but it is best to avoid the pitfall of binding the security forces too much. Insurgency in the north-east can and has been controlled. Nagaland is an example. With a glimmer of hope of a similar development in Mizoram, the NSCN will find itself sandwiched between two quiescent States and increased military pressure.

1178. New legislation to control terrorism urged. *Patriot* 6 Nov 1985.

The Government should enact an emergency legislation to control terrorism, according to a paper presented at the four-day All India Police Science Congress inaugurated in Shillong on November 5, 1985.

The paper, entitled "Management of terrorism" presented by V. Kannupillai, Deputy Inspector General of Police, Police Computer Centre, Gandhinagar, Gujarat suggested that through searches of aircraft before flight should be made compulsory for the prevention of terrorist activities.

The paper broadly dealt with the trend of national and international terrorism and said cooperation of news media was essential to cope with terrorism.

It also suggested that terrorists should not be portrayed as "freedom fighters" and at the same time police should not resort to indiscriminate repression to control them.

The paper suggested that police officers should be trained to combat terrorism, study its growth, target selection, strategies, threat assessment and develop tactical capabilities, to prevent terrorism.

Analysing the profile of terrorists the paper said most urban terrorists were young, unmarried males less than 25 years and belong to middle class families. Most of them were well educated and imbibed terrorist ideology while in universities.

The paper found a definite link between terrorists and smugglers. To obtain funds terrorists had a nexus with smuggling and drug trafficking in India. Most terrorists had links with international smugglers, the paper said.

1179. Nijhawan, P.K. : No end of terrorism in Punjab. *Times of India* 22 Aug 1985 ; 8.

1180. No brooking terrorism. PM (Rajiv Gandhi). *Times of India* 25 Apr 1986 ; 9.

1181. No religion involved in extremism. *Hindustan Times* 16 Feb 1986 ; 9.

1182. *Note on terrorism in India except Bengal.* Simla, Government of India Press, 1933.

1183. People asked to fight terrorism. *Tribune* 9 Apr 1986 ; 6.

1184. PM (Rajiv Gandhi), Barnala agree on stern steps to curb terrorism. *Patriot* 17 Jan 1987 ; 1.

1185. PM Calls for unity : Foreign powers behind terrorism. *Tribune* (Chandigrah) 12 Dec 1986 ; 1, 12.

1186. PM (Rajiv Gandhi) for mass campaign to combat terrorism. *Financial Express* 8 Apr 1986 ; 1.

1187. PM reiterates resolve to crush terrorism. *Patriot* 20 Aug 1986 ; 1.

1188. PM (Rajiv Gandhi) unhappy at Barnala handling of terrorism. *Hindustan Times* 15 Jan 1987 ; 1.

1189. PM's (Rajiv Gandhi) call to fight terrorism. *Tribune* 6 Dec 1985 ; 1.

1190. Prabhakar Rao, A. : Naxalite rampage in AP. *Link* 9 Mar 1985 ; 12-13.

The problem of the violent and terrorist activities of the Naxalites, often referred to as extremist groups, had become so common in the state that the people of the state had come to learn to live with them. Despite the protestations of the Government to eradicate corruption, it continues unabatedly with varying degrees of intensity and people had developed the cynicism to accept it as a part of life.

This erosion of moral standards on the part of the administrator's as well as the administrative machinery and the utter disregard for the rights and liberties of the ordinary people on the part of the extremists are having a beneful influence in that they are undermining the faith of the people in the democratic set-up. It is in this context that the activities and political postures of groups who still maintain a "revolutionary" and leftist posture in public, and who often proclaim that they derive their inspiration from Marx, Lenin and Mao, deserve to be examined and exposed. Whatever they may call themselves, they have nothing in common whether with communist ideology or the strategy and tactics of revolution intended to usher in a socialist society.

During the last few months, a number of incidents occurred which had raised the issue to one of immediacy and the steps taken by the Government so far in controlling the violent activities of these groups, had yielded little results. The educative and intense political campaign of the more responsible leftist parties, like the two communist parties, had also not succeeded much in isolating the Naxalites from the people and to make them realise that their understanding of the socialist revolution was totally wrong. That these were individual terrorist activities of revolution, and thus inhibit their growth. Terrorist acts, whether indulged in by individuals or small groups, have the effect of making the masses passive. Revolution can be successful only when massesparticipate actively and do not remain mere witnesses, the fact of which has not been realised by these groups.

1191. Public support against terrorists sought (in Punjab). *Statesman* 15 Feb 1986 ; 10.

1192. Punish terrorists severely : Sikh leaders. *Hindustan Times* 29 Mar 1986; 3.

1193. Punjab crisis : The return of terrorism. *India Today* 31 May 1985 ; 22-37.

1194. Punjab police aiding terrorists : Billa. *Tribune* 30 Mar 1986 ; 16.

1195. Punjab terror. *Hitavada* (Bhopal) 29 Mar 1986 ; 3.

1196. Punjab terrorism. *Deccan Chronicle* 7 Apr 1986 ; 6.

1197. Punjab terrorism. *Deccan Chronicle* 30 Apr 1986 ; 6.

1198. Punjab votes against terrorism. *Blitz* 28 Sep 1985 ; 2.

1199. R. Venkataraman's call to fight terrorism unitedly. *Times of India* 10 Jan 1987 ; 3.

1200. Rahul Singh : New dimension to Punjab violence. *Indian Express* 29 Mar 1986 ; 7.

1201. Rahul Singh : Terrorist challenge. *Indian Express* 2 Apr 1985 ; 6.

1202. Rajan, Sundar : Political approach to Punjab terrorism. *Mid-Day* (New Delhi) 21 Jul 1986 ; 6.

1203. Rajiv assures Punjab all help to curb terrorism. *Patriot* 9 Dec 1986 ; 1.

1204. Ramachandran, K.S. : Getting tough with terrorism. *Financial Express* (New Delhi) 13 Jan 1986 ; 4.

1205. Ranganathan, L.R. : India's role in rise of terrorism. *Free Press Journal* 19 Sep 1986 ; 4.

1206. Rao, T.S. : State terrorism. *Link* 3 Nov 1985 ; 2.

1207. Rapists in uniform. *Times of India* 31 Mar 1986 ; 8.

1208. Ravindranath, P.K. : Reign of terrorism. *Industrial Times* (Bombay) 17 Mar 1986 ; 44.

1209. Ray's (S.S.) call not to back terrorists. *Tribune* 17 Jan 1987 ; 10.

1210. Ray, Shankar : Naxalites : Power from barrel of guns. *Caravan* (New Delhi) Jan (First) 1986 ; 33-35.

1211. Recrudescence of Punjab terrorism. *Deccan Chronicle* 5 Sep 1985 ; 6.

1212. Religio-political tussle led to Nirankari Baba's assassination : He virtually invited it. *Indian Observer* 15 May 1980 ; 26-27.

1213. Revelation among Hindus and Sikhs on killings. *New Age* 27 Apr 1986 ; 4.

1214. Ribeiro, J.F. : Motivated forces can match terrorists. *Blitz* 10 Jan 1987 ; 7.

1215. Rise of terrorism in Punjab. *Caravan* (New Delhi) Jan (First) 1986 ; 16-18.

1216. Roots of terrorism. *Tribune* 18 Sep 1985 ; 4.

1217. Rustamji, K.F. : Closing in on terrorists. *Indian Express* 13 Aug 1986 ; 6.

1218. Sabherwal, O.P. : India : Target of International terrorism. *Daily* (Bombay) 9 Dec 1984 ; 11.

1219. Saffron tigers—Khalistani terrorists. *Searchlight* (Patna) 11 Oct 1985 ; 1.

1220. Saha, B.P. : Security cover ; A myth. *Amrita Bazar Patrika*. 1 Sep 1986 ; 6.

1221. Saksena, N.S. : Terrorism : Fire fighting won't do. *Times of India* 12 Aug 1986 ; 1-9.

1222. Salamat Ali : India : Lebanon in Punjab. *Far Eastern Economic Review* 23 Jul 1986 ; 30.

1223. Salamat Ali. No end to the terror : Sikh militants step up violence to abort planned election. *Far Eastern Economic Review* 19 Sep 1985 ; 34.

1224. Sareen, Rajendra : Tackling the terrorists. *Tribune* 7 Apr 1986 ; 4.

1225. Sareen, Rajendra : Terrorism and Punjab poll. *Tribune* 26 Aug 1985 ; 4.

1226. Satindra Singh : Roots of Sikh extremism. *Free Press Journal* 1 Apr 1986 ; 4.

1227. Saksena, N.S. : Back to square one in Punjab. In *THF* ; 187-88.

1228. Saksena, N.S. : Dangerous illusions about terrorism. *Times of India* 10 Apr 1984 ; 8.

1229. Saksena, N.S. : Early history of terrorism in India. In *THF* ; 25-27.

1230. Saksena, N.S. : Exhaustive criminal records must for combating terrorism. In *THE* ; 254-55.

1231. Saksena, N.S. : Foreign gunmen on Indian soil. *Times of India* 2 Apr 1985 ; 8.

1232. Saksena, N.S. : Insurgency and terror in Manipur Valley. In *THF* ; 138-39.

1233. Saksena, N.S. : Investigations of Delhi riots—unpardonable lapses. In *THE* ; 185-86.

1234. Saksena, N.S. : Many facets of Assam carnage. *Times of India* 20 Apr 1983 ; 8.

1235. Saksena, N.S. : Meghalya-Government promoted terrorism in Dec 1979. In *THE* ; 157.

1236. Saksena, N.S. : Nagaland—Terrorism pays politicians. In *THF* ; 154-56.

1237. Saksena, N.S. : National efforts to fight terrorism. In *THF* ; 33-35.

1238. Saksena, N.S. : Naxalite terrorism in India. In *THF* ; 123-27.

1239. Saksena, N.S. : PAC mutiny of May 1973 in U.P. In *THF* ; 193-94.

1240. Saksena, N.S. : Right-wing terror. In *THF* ; 30.

1241. Saksena, N.S. : Rise in political murder. In *THF* ; 237-38.

1242. Saksena, N.S. : Root of terrorism in Punjab—I & II *Times of India* 5, 6 Dec 1983 ; 8.

1243. Saksena, N.S. : Terror and counter-terror in Tripura. In *THF* ; 144-45.

1244. Saksena, N.S. : Terror and insurgency in North-East of India. In *THF* ; 128-60.

1245. Saksena, N.S. : Terror against Sikhs in Delhi, Kanpur etc. in early November 1984. In *THF* ; 183-84.

1246. Saksena, N.S. : Terrorism. In *THF* ; 182.

1247. Saksena, N.S. : Terrorism becomes a political game. In *THF* ; 30-31.

1248. Saksena, N.S. : Terrorism in Assam. In *THF* ; 161-74.

1249. Saksena, N.S. : Why bare we failed to check terrorism ? In *THF* ; 226-55.

1250. Sebastian, P.A. : Terrorist act against democratic rights activist : case of K. Balagopal. *Economic and Political Weekly* 7 Dec 1985 ; 2148-49.

1251. Selbourne, David. : CIA and the Congress. In *Through the Indian looking-glass*. Bombay, Popular Prakashan, 1982 ; 157-60.

1252. Sen, Mohit : Multi-pronged strategy of destabilisation. *Patriot* 8 Apr 1986 ; 4.

1253. Senseless terrorism. *Deccan Chronicle* 22 Dec 1986 ; 6.

1254. Sethi, J.D. : India and Arab terrorism. *Indian Express* (New Delhi) 17 Jan 1986 ; 6.

India therefore should be very concerned with the fallout of Arab terrorism which has taken on a messianic character and has spread from Iran to Beirut. Col. Gaddafi has called it a *jihad* which he has defined as a permanent war against the non-Muslims.

Linkages already exist and more are being built among diverse groups of terrorists operating in different countries and for different objectives. It is well known that many terrorist groups are indirectly supported by Communist nations with weapons and even training. The linkages have been built between such Soviet-sponsored groups as the Red Brigade of Italy and the Red Army function of Germany, the Japanese Red Army and some Arab groups.

India is a democracy. In recent years our fragile democratic norms and institutions have been subjected to attacks from the forces of domestic and international violence. Sikh extremism is one such force. India's unrequited support for Arabs and its silence on their terrorism have encouraged them to pour in money into this country and fan religious fanaticism. Col. Gaddafi had a base in Pakistan and has now moved in a big way into Bangladesh. His lobby in India is of no mean importance. Mr. Rajiv Gandhi cannot afford to remain blind to the potential mischief of Arab terrorism for India.

This is the time and opportunity for India to begin an anti-terrorist diplomacy. First of all New Delhi should privately tell Libya that it does not approve of terrorism for any reason and then, also privately, let the victims know about India's stand and intentions. Subsequently, at some appropriate forum, India, independently and jointly with others, should denounce terrorism, letting it be known to everyone concerned where it stands. The third logical step would be to come out with a strong statement from Rajiv Gandhi deploring the US aggressive postures.

1255. Shameful lapse (Attack on Prime Minister Rajiv Gandhi at Raj Ghat). *Hindustan Times* 3 Oct 1986 ; 1.

1256. Sharma, Piare Lal : War on terrorism. *Hindustan Times* 24 Jan 1987 ; 9.

1257. Should India have bombed the terrorist camp at Alabama ? *Blitz* 3 May 1986 ; 2.

1258. Singh, Arjun : It was not entirely an intelligence failure. *Sunday Observer* 26 May 1985 ; 3.

1259. Singh, B. : Terrorist's mind. *Patriot Magazine* 20 Oct 1985 ; 1

1260. Singh, Baba Joginder : Terrorist acts are the will of God. *Telegraph* (Calcutta) 13 Sep 1985 ; 6.

1261. Singh, Khushwant : Declare war against terrorism. *Hindustan Times* 17 Jan 1987 ; 9.

1262. Singh, Parduman : CPI Challenge to terrorists. *Link* 15 Jun 1986 ; 12.

1263. Singh, Sardar Mahindar : Sikhism does not teach terrorism. *Spokesman* (New Delhi) 34 Annual Number 1985 ; 37.

1264. Six cops shot dead ; 3 terrorists freed. *Times of India* 6 Apr 1986 ; 1.

1265. Sumir Lal : Terrorists' split led to Khalistan. *Telegraph* (Calcutta) 5 May 1986 ; 4.

1266. Sundar Rajan, K.R. : Terrorism's deepening shadow. *Sunday Observer* 7 Dec 1986.

1267. Sundar Rajan, K.R. : Together against terrorism. *Amrit Bazar Patrika* 2 Oct 1985 ; 6.

1268. Surendra Mohan : Challenge of terrorism. *Free Press Journal* 1 Jun 1985 ; 6.

1269. Surendra Mohan : Countering terrorism : Reprisals not the answer. *Free Press Journal* 13 Aug 1986 ; 4.

1270. Surendra Mohan : Unlearnt lesson: Futility of violence, terrorism. *Free Press Journal* 9 Nov 1985 ; 4.

1271. Tackling terrorism. *Hindustan Times* 9 Nov 1985 ; 9.

1272. Tackling terrorism. *Hindustan Times* 9 Apr 1986 ; 9.

1273. Tackling terrorism. *Madhya Pradesh Chronicle* 6 Feb 1986 ; 4.

Violent extremism continues to raise its ugly head all over the world. Advances in science and technology have been pressed into service by terrorists to hold the innocent public to ransom. The Sri Lankan President asked in an interview the other day : "Who is dying ? Not the terrorist leaders ; not the government leaders but innocent people". This picture painted by Mr. Jayawardene applied to all situations where the terrorists are active. Therefore, the External Affairs Minister expressed concern at the spurt of terrorist activity in Britain and said that if this is not contained the close ties between India and Britain would be adversely affected. Protection has to be provided for Indian residents there against the activities of the Sikh terrorists. There is a lot of hari-splitting about the extradition of Sikh extremists based in Britain. The Government of India, it is argued, never applied for extradition which it could do under the Commonwealth Fugitive Offenders Act. An extradition treaty is proposed between India and Britain. Meanwhile it is stated that security is being provided to moderate Sikh elements in South hall after the assassination of Indian overseas Congress General Secretary Tarsem Singh Toor. But it is no use bolting the stable after the horse is stolen. Britain must act more vigorously to save the situation.

It is sad to note that the Barnala government has not been able to tackle the terrorists as well, as it was expected to do. The latest report says that four people were killed and five wounded in the curfew bound Nakodor town of Jalandhar district when police fired into a crowd of All India Sikh Students Federation. A magisterial inquiry has been ordered into the incident. The terrorists opened fire at the residence of the Punjab Assembly Speaker Nirmal Singh Kahlon. About 800 activists of the Sikh Students Federation tried to force their entry into the curfew bound town when the police had to open fire. Earlier a Punjab Roadways bus was burnt and another one hijacked. The United Akali Dal led by Baba Joginder Singh has warned government of the dangerous consequences if the culprits are not arrested and the Dal is prevented from organising Akhand Path.

Mr. Barnala and his colleagues in the Akali Dal will have to act because of the imperatives arising out considerations of their political survival. The extremists who had failed in the past to dislodge the Akali Dal have now taken complete control of the Golden Temple. But because of its past, the Akali Dal will not be able to persuade itself to send the police inside the Golden Temple. Such a step will put the Akali Dal on the defensive and give a certain amount of credibility to the extremists. The Akali Dal thus faces a dilemma. Firm action through police entry into the Golden temple will take away from the efficacy of the political offensive it proposes to take. The Centre for constitutional and political reasons had left it to the Barnala government to tackle the terrorists. The State authorities had taken a grave view of the situation. It is to be hoped that the Barnala government would take prompt and pertinent action to rid the state of terrorism and the terrorists.

1274. Tamilnadu : Police atrocities at Nadukkuppam. *Economic and Political Weekly* 22 Feb 1986 ; 330-31.

1275. Task force to curb terrorism. *Mid-Day* (New Delhi) 18 Dec 1986 ; 1.

1276. Tegart, C.A. : *Terrorism in India.* London, 1932.

1277. Temple "liberation". *Tribune* 4 Feb 1986 ; 4.

1278. Terror stalks Delhi : *Weekend Review* (New Delhi) 22 Sep 1985 ; 2.

1279. Terrorism a "threat to India's existence" (Zail Singh). *Patriot* 29 Dec 1986 ; 3.

1280. Terrorism can be wiped out if people give help. *Hindu* (New Delhi) 12 Jan 1987 ; 9.

1281. *Terrorism in India 1917-1936 documents.* Simla, Govt. of India Press, 1937.

1282. Terrorism in Northeast. *Times of India* 12 Dec 1986 ; 8.

1283. Terrorism in Punjab. *Deccan Herald* 30 Nov 1985 ; 6.

1284. Terrorism in Punjab and Sri Lanka. *Pioneer* 14 Jul 1986 ; 6.

1285. Terrorism in the valley. *New Wave* 5 Jan 1986 ; 5.

1286. Terrorism par excellence. *Amrit Bazar Patrika* 1 Sep 1986 ; 6.

1287. Terrorism vs. mob terrorism. *Daily* 28 Jul 1986 ; 8.

1288. Terrorism will wither away : Ray. *Hindustan Times* 15 Jul 1986.

1289. Terrorist links. *Times of India* 1 Apr 1986 ; 8.

1290. Terrorists gun down five in Punjab. *Searchlight* (Patna) 25 Mar 1986 ; 1.

1291. Terrorists in Punjab. *Hitavada* (Bhopal) 21 Feb 1986 ; 3.

1292. Terrorists kill top Punjab jail official. *Hindustan Times* 11 Jan 1987 ; 1.

1293. Terrorists plan to provoke war to achieve Khalistan. *New Wave* 6 Apr 1986 ; 2.

1294. Terrorists regroup in Punjab. *Blitz* 9 Nov 1985 ; 10.

1295. Terrorists shot dead 13 in Ludhiana. *Patriot* 29 Mar 1986 ; 1.

1296. Terrorists should be isolated : PM (Rajiv Gandhi). *Times of India* 9 May 1986 ; 7.

1297. Thapar, Romesh : Poison of terrorism. *Economic and Political Weekly* Sep 1985 ; 1585.

1298. Threat from extremists. *Northern India Patrika* 1 Feb 1986 ; 4.

1299. Three top terrorists shot. *Times of India* 24 Jan 1987 ; 1.

1300. Tidal Wave of terrorism. *Pioneer* 27 Jul 1986 ; 4.

1301. Together on terrorism. *Hindustan Times* 29 Oct 1985 ; 9.

1302. Torture of political prisoners in Bengal (West). *Hindustan Times* 13 Feb 1986 ; 8.

1303. Treat terrorists as traitors : Arjun Singh. *Hindustan Times* 9 Apr 1986 ; 16.

1304. Tripathi, Amalesh : *Extremist Challenge*. Bombay, Orient Longmans, 1967.

1305. Tripura terrorism. *Indian Nation* 25 Dec 1986 ; 4.

1306. Triumph and tragedy (Murder of Sant Harcharan Singh Longowal). *Deccan Herald* 22 Aug 1985 ; 8.

1307. Two terrorists among 14 killed in Punjab. *Patriot* 6 May 1986 ; 16.

1308. Two terrorists killed in Amritsar. *Daily* 2 Apr 1986 ; 2.

1309. Vajpayee, A.B. : Anti-terrorism and democracy. *Asiaweek* 5 Jul 1985 ; 70.

1310. Violence and communalism. *Hitavada* (Bhopal) 24 Feb 1986 ; 3.

1311. Violence, order of the day in Gujarat. *New Wave* 9 Feb 1986 ; 6.

1312. Viswam, S. : Killing of the Makens : Terror stalks again. *Deccan Herald* 2 Aug 1985 ; p. 8.

1313. Weiner, Myron : Violence and politics in Calcutta. *Journal of Asian Studies* 20 May 1961 ; 275-81.

1314. Weisman, Steven R. : Assam Moslems haunted by fear of new violence. *International Herald Tribune* 7-8 Dec 1985 ; 1, 5.

1315. Weisman, Steven R. : India ponders widening strife. *International Herald Tribune* 5 Jan 1987 ; 1-2.

1316. Who is the next (after assassinations of Indira Gandhi, Arjun Das, Lalit Maken, H.S. Longowal). *Indian Observer* Oct 1985 ; 20-21.

1317. Wig, A. R. : Delhi's snub to terrorists. *Hindustan Times* (New Delhi) 7 Apr 1986 ; 3.

1318. Zail (Singh) condemns terrorism. *Newstime* 4 Nov 1986 ; 1.

Indonesia

1319. Frederick, William H—*ed.* : *Reflections on rebellion* : *Stories from the Indonesian upheavals of 1948 and 1965.* Ohio University, 1983, p. 168.

1320. Hughes, John : *End of Sukarno* : *A coup that misfired* : *A purge that ran wild.* London, Angus & Robertson, 1968.

1321. Ranson, David : Berkeley Mafia and the Indonesian massacre. *Ramparts* Oct 1970.

1322. Terrorism : A jarring day in Jakarta. *Asiaweek* 25 May 1986 ; 25.

Iran

1323. Abrahamaian, Ervand : *Iran between two revolutions.* Princeton, 1982.

1324. Al-Hadithi, Naji : Iran : State-run terror. *Iraq* 15 Aug 1984 ; 5.

1325. Amin, Y.M. : Ugly form of alliance (Between, Iran, Israel, Syria, Libya and South Africa). *Baghdad Observer* 12 Feb 1986 ; 4.

Collusion between the terrorist regimes in the region has been high on the record recently. Such collaboration was not common before then ; it has been taking shape to appear in the ugliest possible form.

The Zionist entity, Iranian, Syrian and Libyan regimes have not only focussed in their schemes on liquidating opponents, opposition movements and organisations in their spheres of influence alone, but they also extended their collusion to cover countries in the region and in Europe.

Not long ago reports diclosed that the Zionist entity's intelligence service "Mossad" had formed a number of hit teams assigned the task of assassinating and liquidating Palestinian leaders. Other reports said that the Iranian regime had prepared its hit squads who were trained to carry out assassinations and acts of terrorism in a number of European capitals.

News also reported that the Libyan regime had reinforced its own hit squads to eliminate opposition outside Libya and to liquidate other "enemies". Meanwhile, the Daily Express quoted a British official as saying that London, Birmingham and Manchester would be springboards for Libyan terrorists to attack European countries Syria, by no means the fourth on the list, is spearheading them all.

Is this all a mere coincidence ? Are the roles assigned to these regimes coordinated ? Or could they be the outcome of the talks held by the regimes of Iran, Syria, Libya very recently in Tripoli ?

For the charge to be well substantiated, a quick glance at the regimes, very recent history can show a lot. (a) The Zionist raid against Iraq's Tummoz peaceful nuclear reactor was timed when the Iranian regime culminated its aggression against Iraq ; (b) the Zionist raid on Hammat Al-Shatt in Tunisia came exactly after Muammer Gaddafi threatened to attack Tunisia ; and (c) the Zionist invasion of South Lebanon and Beirut was accompanied with the Syrian troops withdrawal from the "red lines" in the Bekaa Valley without the least confrontation with the Zionist forces.

These are not the only evidence which unveil collusion between the regimes of Iran, Israel, Syria and Libya. Their ambitions are corelated now that all those parties have their own defined objectives as some wanted to export "revolution", some wanted to adversely influence the Palestinian struggle and to overthrow its legitimate leadership and as others wanted to lay down new maps for the region.

A few months ago, in a meeting held and attended by Iranians in Tripoli the regimes of Syria and Libya insisted on nothing else but pursuing the course of treason and conspiracy by "blessing" and supporting the aggression against Iraq.

The outcome of this illfated meeting mirrored, if nothing else, the bulging volume of resistance, indignation and hate among their people against the rulers. And the failure of Khomeini to achieve any of his set "objectives" both at the front and inside Iran, and the failure of his regime to alleviate the suffering of the Iranians is the same failure afflicting the regimes of Assad and Gaddafi.

As for Syria, after its unsuccessful scheme to contain the Palestinian decision, its set aim was to liquidate the Palestinian leadership as a prerequisite for its own version of a political settlement for the Middle East.

Now Syria's isolation, its conspiratorial course, its anti-Arab policies, unlimited support for the Iranian aggression against Iraq and its crimes in Lebanon which have extended over more than a decade all led to severe cracks in the structure of the regime and to a fierce struggle among its rulers.

However, such anti-Arab acts by Syria and Libya, and the course of terrorism of Iran were all welcomed by the Zionist entity because they eroded the image of the Palestinians and alienated world public opinion from the Palestinian cause as they were used to cover more Zionist acts of terrorism.

The joint coordination between the four entities signals new dimensions in their developed relations now that it benefits them all to keep the Iranian aggression against Iraq, cripple the Palestinian struggle, and keep the Lebanese question without solution.

Very recently the Libyan and Syrian regimes which were crying for Arab help, according to the Joint Arab Defence Pact, against an "expected American aggression" have militarily and politically allied themselves with Iran against Iraq.

Yet, few days ago Gaddafi was the focus of world media as new scandal of arms running was being unveiled by Austrian press. This time, he did not only send Iranians surface-to-surface missiles from his own arsena, but also brokered arms deals and purchased as many weapons as he could to prop up the tumble-down and shaky Iranian armed forces. And, in behaving in such a manner, he is no longer a head of state, rather a boss of gun-runner gang.

Not long ago, the British press uncovered another slice of Zionist-Iranian cooperation. The Sunday paper, the Observer underlined that Israel did not stop supplying Iran with conventional arms after the downfall of the Shah in 1979 and that it is still supplying Iran with weapons according to deals ratified by the Shah and renewed by Khomeini.

In an attempt to disguise military ties between these regimes, this arms-for-oil deal was arranged through a Swiss company.

Israel and Iran negotiated a one-billion-dollar arms-for-oil agreement in 1977 to jointly develop a nuclear missile system. The Observer said that Iran made its first down payment of 260 million dollars in oil to Israel in 1978.

Financial co-operation in the project, code named Operation Flower continued even after the Shah was replaced by Khomeini. Documents about the project show that it was designed for nuclear war.

The two countries agreed that Israel's nuclear scientists would continue to develop surface-to-surface Jerichotype missile. When completed, the missiles were to be airlifted for final assembly at Sirjin in central Iran and for long-range testing 70 miles to the north in a barren area near Rafsanjan. Collaboration between Iran and Israel was portrayed as emerging when Israel agreed to supply its missiles to Iran in return for a guaranteed supply of 80 million barrels of oil, but all facts prove that such co-operation has come into existence only to weaken Iraq.

No sane man would now deny collusion between these doomed regimes, whose main ambitions were only to create centres of tension in the region to protect their own survival.

1326. Ayoub, Ghassan A. : Iranian embassies—terrorist networks. *Baghdad Observer* 29 Dec 1984.

1327. Bill, James : Power and religion in revolutionary Iran. *Middle East Journal* 36(1) Win 1982.

1328. Brutal torture in Iranian prisons. *Tribune* 19 Jan 1983.

1329. DePerlac. Khomeini, a ring leader of international terrorism. *Baghdad Observer* 23 Nov 1986 ; 4.

Khomeini created a terrorist force two years ago to wage a campaign of terror in the United States, Europe and the Middle East.

According to a secret report leaked out in the topselling West German magazine "Allegmeine Frankfurt" some 25 terrorit units are directly under the orders of Khomeini.

Five Israeli military advisers are in charge of conducting the attacks in key areas. But none of the attacks have so far been successful.

The Moroccan daily "Risalat al-Umma" has revealed that Iran signed a secret pact with Israel which guarantees it a constant supply of arms to keep up its six-year war against Iraq.

The Moroccan daily said that under the pressure of unfavourable developments of the Gulf War, Iran had been pushed to buy arms from anyone.

A large network of international arms dealers, including an Iranian known in the trade as Hashimi, are making multi-million profits by channelling US-made weapons to Iran via Israel, the magazine "Aldustur" reported from London.

The Israeli government may not openly take part in the sale of the US-made weapons to Iran but has framed out instructions to its intelligence agents not to interfere in the transactions, the magazine said.

As arms dealer Hashimi told "Aldustur", Israel is the only one that really benefits from the War.

Referring to the Iran-Israel connection, the Paris-based magazine "Kul al-Arab" charged that Khomeini's Iran has moved away from real Islam to become an oppressive regime.

The proven sale of arms from Israel to Iran is only the tip of the iceberg, the magazine said.

Khomeini's regime employs terrorists tactics both at home and abroad to pursue its aims, to push Arab civilization back 1,000 years. And it does not stop short of dealing with Israel to achieve its target, the magazine said.

1330. Fischer, M. : *Iran : From religious dispute to revolution.* Cambridge, 1980.

1331. Four pillars of Islamic terrorism—Libya, Iran, PLO and now Pakistan. *Organiser* 19 Jan 1986 ; 13.

The Mediterranean water are hotting up with US resolve to teach the high-priest of terrorism a lasting lesson, Gaddafi showing visible signs of nervousness and the Soviet Union waiting to extract its own pound of diplomatic flesh from the crisis.

The Soviets have warned the United States to weigh "seriously the dangerous consequence" of its action againsts Libiya. The Soviet threat has come in the wake of the hollow rhetoric of Libyan dictator

Gaddafi that World War III will break out of the US took military action against Libya. The massive Arab support to him would be of little consequence if the US persists in its reprisal or eggs on Isreal to chaste Gaddafi.

It may be racalled that 15 innocent passengers including children were slaughtered and over a 100 injured at Rome and Vienna airports recently and the consequent dragnet led the investigating authorities straight to Libya. It was pointed out that the horrendous shootings were the handiwork of Muslim arch-terrorist Abu Nidal (having 300 hardcore followers) and his comrades who are based in Libya. It has been established, beyond doubt, that Gaddafi was aware of Abu Nidal's macabrous intents well in advance.

However ignoring all the evidence the Soviets are busy playing political games in order to derive as much propaganda mileage as possible, and re-establish their lost foothold in west Asia. Though they have condemned terrorism per se including the December 27 shootings at Rome and Vienna for obvious reasons the Soviets have not condemned its perpetrators. Instead, they have exonerated Arab terrorists and put all the blame on the United States and Israel. This is not unnatural in view of the Soviet poistion as leader of one of the two power blocs. In this context an official Soviet statement said :

"The real responsibility for rampage of terrorism in the world rests not with the Arab states which steer an independent course......(instead the responsibility lay with) those who having elevated terrorism to the status of their state policy, trample upon the legitimate rights of sovereign countries and peoples."

It further said that the Soviet Union most resolutely condemns the US and Isreali actions and added that "such kind of actions cannot be regarded otherwise than as posing threat to peace and security not only in the Mediterranean area but outside it as well."

1332. French police hunt Iranian terrorists. *Baghdad Observer* 10 Feb 1986 ; 3.

1333. Halliday, Fred : *Iran : Dictatorship and development.* New York, 1979.

1334. Ibrahim, J. : Iran's terrorist gangs : Another ailing tactic. *Baghdad Observer* 31 May 1985 ; 5.

1335. Iran missions as terrorist-support bases. *National Herald* 17 Apr 1984.

1336. Iran threatens Arab Gulf countries. *Iran Review* 1 Apr 1986 ; 16.

1337. Iran to open more terrorist centres in Western Europe. *Baghdad Observer* 11 Sep 1986 ; 1.

1338. Iran's guerrillas. *Sunday Observer* 12 Oct 1986.

1339. Islamic revolution in Iran. *Basheer* (New Delhi) Sep 1984 ; 19-23.

1340. Jenkins, Hubert : Mid-East terrorism : Iran Link. *Hindustan Times* (New Delhi) 19 Jan 1984 ; 9.

Iran's involvement with the group charged in the December 12 Kuwait bombings came as little surprise to analysts familiar with the growing terrorist problem in the Middle East.

Kuwaiti officials say that the multiple bombings directed against French, American and local targets, which took five lives and wounded more than 60 persons, were the work of the *Al Dawa* political party, a group of radical Shite Moslems with close ties with Iran.

Evidence of the Iranian hand in the Kuwait terrorism has strengthened the views of many Mideast officials who believe that Iranian-directed organisations are now engaged in a regional terrorist campaign. The objectives, these officials say, are to strike out at Iran's political enemies, to disrupt moderate Arab regimes and to create fertile ground for the spread of the Islamic Revolution.

To acheive these aims, Midest analysts believe, Teheran has re-introduced an ancient form of Persian Political violence, the "Hashishin" or suicide-killers of the 12th century. The Hashishin were religious radicals with a thirst for blood and a total belief in the assurances of their founder, Hassan Ibn Al-Sabbah, that death in a "Holy War" was a direct passport to heaven. The Hassen terrorist network embraced all of Persia and Iraq and extended into Syria, where no political or military leader, Moslem or Christian, was safe from the Hashish-smoking murderers. Invading Mongols destroyed the Hashishin in 1256, leaving behind the source for the English word, assassin, and the conviction among radical Shite Moslems that terrorism was a highly effective instrument of State policy.

When Shiite leader Ayatollah Ruhollah Khomeini seized power in

Iran, the Hassan view on terrorism was revived. It played a highly effective role in the revolution which brought down the Shah of Iran. Following victory, intensive police terror was used by Khomeini's followers to destroy any remaining political opposition within Iran.

The external phase of Iran's political terrorist campaign began with the 1981 bombings of the Iraqi Embassy in Beirut. It established a pattern wherein terrorist bombs were placed in untended cars, to be detonated by remote control from a safe distance. By 1983 when bombs destroyed the American Embassy in April and took hundreds of lives in the October blasts at the barracks of US and French peackeeping forces in Lebanon, a new method of operation had evolved.

In these terrorist strikes, as in the Kuwait bombings, the explosive-laden trucks were driven into the targets by terrorists who died in the blasts. These tactics revealed a new and dangerous twist in 20th century terrorism : Suicide bombers willing, even eager, to die for their cause.

A group which calls itself the Islamic Jihad has claimed credit for the suicide bombings in Lebanon. Western intelligence source are convinced that the leader of the militant Islamic Amal, Hussein Musavi, is behind the deadly attacks. Syria and Iran, they add, provide the assistance which makes the attacks possible. Musavi operates out of Baalbek, Lebanon, an area controlled by Syrian forces and where as many as 1,000 Iranian revolutionary guards have set up bases from which to attack the legitimate Lebanese Government.

In March 1982, newspapers in Lebanon revealed that the Khomeini Government had decided to train thousands of Moslem militants from more than 20 Islamic nations in revolutionary tactics. For this purpose a special school was set up near the Iranian Holy city of Qom. According to Iranian officials, graduates of the school would return to their home countries as "messengers of true Islam.'

Following the October bombings in Lebanon, Teheran's official newspaper, Kayhan, warned that a "New" powerful force has entered the Islamic "Holy War," and that "suicide attacks would multiply under different forms."

In the Kuwait bombings, Mideast observers say, this "powerful new force" achieved most Iranian objectives. Two of Teheran's leading political enemies, France and the United States, were hit. Shown as unable to prevent terrorist attacks the moderate, Iraq-supporting Sahad ruling family was embarrassed. More important the success of the attacks demonstrated that among the 10 per cent of Kuwait's population who are members of the Shitte sect, the violent Islamic revolution of Ayatollah Khomeini has found favour.

1341. Keddie, Nikki R. : *Roots of revolution : An interpretative history of modern Iran.* New Haven, 1981.

1342. Khomeini men behind Beirut blast. *Hindustan Times* 26 Oct 1983 ; 1.

1343. Komarov, V. : Reign of terror against patriots. *New Times* (Moscow) (21) May 1983 ; 10-11.

In early May the Iranian authorities announced the disbandment of the People's (Tudeh) Party. The move, behind which are the Rightwing conservative wing of the rulling Shiite Moslem clergy and the bourgeois and land-owning element associated with it, signifies the outlawing of Iran's oldest patriotic political party, a party that for more than 40 years was in the forefront of the Iranian people's struggle against the despotism of the Shah and the domination of imperialism and the reaction, for national independence and social progress.

The harsh repressive action taken against the People's Party follows more than two years of pressure exerted on it by the Right-wing forces. The leaders of the Party arrested in February this year are facing trial on trumpted-up charges of "spying for Eastern countries" and "forging documents". The threat of judicial murder now hangs over them. Not long ago President of the Iranian Supreme Court Abdolkarim Moussavi-Ardebili publicly declared that the penalties would be severe, all the way to death sentences. Recently a television spectacular was staged in order to make it appear as if some of the arrested People's Party leaders had confessed to "crimes" they could not have committed.

What such "confessions" are worth is plain to see. The French L' Humanite says that the imprisoned Party leaders were "subjected to moral and physical torture." This is confirmed also by reports corried by the capitalist press, for instance, the Paris Le Monde. The People's Party's Foreign Committee published in the Persian-language Rahe Tudeh the (People's Road) put out in West Berlin a statement refuting the accusations levelled against the Party leadership. Pointing out that members of official Iranian agencies "had recourse to torture and used the 'confessions' obtained under duress for their own ends," the statement condemned the "barbarous" inhuman and amoral" methods employed "with the connivance of the CIA, Intelligence

Service, Mossad (Israeli intelligence) and 'experts' from the SAVAK (the Shah's secret police)."

Official propaganda is doing its utmost to discredit the People's Party, maintaining that it does not uphold the national interests of the Iranian people and is dependent on the Soviet Union.

However, even a cursory survey of the Party's history testified to the contrary. The People's Party was founded in October 1941 at a time of upsurge in the general democratic movement in the country. Its core consisted of Communists who had survived the Shah's prisons and other progressive democratic-minded people who advocated socio-economic reforms in the interests of the working people. The programme the Party adopted at its inaugural congress called for an end to the stronghold foreign monopolies had on the country, for democratic reforms, the granting to the working people of such civil rights as free speech, freedom of the press and assembly, the introduction of an 8 hour working day and the transfer of the land to the peasants free of charge. From the outset the People's Party conducted extensive work to rally the masses to fight for their rights. By the end of World War II it had become a mass party.

When the Iranian reactionaries, frightened by the growth of the democratic movement, mounted in the late forties an offensive against the progressive forces, repressive action was taken first of all against active members of the People's Party. Thirteen of its leaders were sentenced to death in absentia. In 1949 the Shah's regime outlawed it. Its organizations were disbanded and its newspapers closed. The party had to go underground.

By the early 1950s the People's Party had rebuilt its organizations and again came out in the forefront of the anti-monarchy and anti-imperialist struggle. When the U. S. Central intelligence Agency staged through its agents in August 1953 a military coup which overthrew the Mossadegh government and suppressed the national democratic movement, a new wave of repressions was let loose against the People's Party. Many members of its Central Committee and other activists were arrested, its newspapers closed, and its print shops wrecked. For many years Iran was ground down by a monarchy dependent on U.S. imperialism which ruthlessly suppressed all progressive elements.

Throughout the nearly 25 years it functioned in the difficult conditions of illegality, the People's Party remained an active political organization of the working people and waged a persevering struggle against the regime of the Shah and the dependence of the country on imperialist powers, primarily the United States. In these years of reaction, thousands of the Party's members and supporters died in the Shah's dungeons and in exile. The name of Khosrov Rouzbeh, a member of the People's Party Central Committee, who died at the hands of the Shah's butchers, became the symbol of courage and heroism for all Iranian patriots. He is rightly regarded as a national hero.

In 1975 the People's Party was the first among all the Iranian opposition parties and organizations to call on the people to join in mass struggle to overthrow the despotism of the Shah. A new important stage in the Party's activity was ushered in by the growth of the broad anti-Shah and anti-imperialist movement which overthrew the monarchy in February 1979. It took a most active part in this struggle. Its members were in the front ranks of the massive strike actions and demonstrations and fought on the barricades during the armed uprising. On March 11 the same year its Central Committee announced the restoration of its legal status.

As an exponent of the interests of wide sections of the Iranian working people, the People's Party called for the building of a United Popular Front for defence of the gains of the revolution. It put forward a comprehensive programme of action for all contingents of the revolutionary forces fighting for the liberation of the country from foreign dependence and for guarantee of democratic rights and freedoms for all working people. It declared in support of those aspects of the socio-political programme of Ayatollah Khomeini, the leader of the Iranian revolution, which were objectively progressive in character and imposed restrictions on the big capitalists and landed interests and made for genuine national independence. However, when the implementation of the programme of reforms in the interests of the dispossessed notably slowed down, the Party saw this as the result of the strengthening of the positions of the counter-revolutionary elements. It came out for a radical land reform in the interests of the mass of the peasants, the abolition of large-scale land tenure, and nationalization of foreign trade with a view to strengthening economic independence. At the same time it underscored the need for a just solution interwoven in so dangerous a tangle that even some American military leaders, according to the Washington Post, see in the situation a "time bomb" that could go off at any moment.

If Pentagon generals have begun to think in these terms there is good cause for growing concern on the part of the public. For in a situation such as this the detonation might be set off even spontaneously, by accident, owing, say, to a computer error. Nevertheless the main danger lies elsewhere. A staff member of the American Foreign Policy Research Institute has described the strategy evolved by U.S. Defence Secretary Caspar Weinberger as being projected at deliberately involving the Soviet Union in hostilities not only in Europe but in the Persian Gulf, Northwest Asia and the high seas. This was written in March 1982, and roughly a year later U.S. Navy Secretary John Leman put it even more bluntly : "There is a tremendous tactical advantage" in getting the signal to fire first. To fire first, deliberately to provoke war, moreover, along the entire length of the vast land mass of Eurasia ; What fate is being prepared for the countries lying on the perimeter of this land mass ? Weinberger and Leman prefer to remain silent on this score. The facts, however, speak for themselves. For instance, the fact that the United State is producing on the quiet the neutron bombs, from which the West European countries recoiled in horror and revulsion, and intends to station them in Asia, South Korea for example. The South Korean authorities, in the opinion of the well-informed news analyst Jack Anderson, will not dare refuse to grant Washinton this modest request. Or, say, at the Diego Garcia base, where some Asian newspapers suspect they are already installed.

Can thinking people believe after this the contention that the "growth of tension in the Third World is uncontrollable," or the allegation that the U.S. is only replying there to some supposed "heightening of Soviet military activity". The actions of the Reagan Administration reveal even more clearly a consistent trend towards the instigation of armed conflicts. And not only local conflicts. Was not the West German magazine Der Spiegel right when it discerned in the Weinberger policy a "wartime strategy" according to which, if things in the Persian Gulf area come to an armed collision, NATO is to start a war also in other places ? This, the magazine says, is a strategic postulate in view of which no responsible leader should agree to the siting of the Pershing IIs in West Germany.

Thus, the icy breath of what would seem to be element seas is reaching the very centre of Europe. The participants in the Nicosia symposium were keenly aware of that chilling breath. On the eve of the meeting the Algerian Al-Moudjahid put it in these words : "The sum total of the nuclear potentials of the military bases and warships of the United States and NATO make the Mediterranean a unique concentration of lethal weaponry...... The mailed first' created by imperialist quarters in the Mediterranean was from the very outset designed for use against both the U.S.S.R. and the Arab liberation and revolutionary movements. Such actions are consonant with the global strategy of U.S. imperialism, which is seeking to keep the Arab peoples in the darkness of backwardness and illiteracy so as to enable the multinational corporations to plunder their natural wealth. For the U.S. and Israeli militarists the Mediterranean is also a proving ground for the latest and most barbarous engines of death such as, for instance, the vacuum bomb used last summer in Lebanon.

An explosive situation has developed over a vast area from the Indian Ocean to the Mediterranean where a great many widely different countries are situated. Their representatives met in Nicosia to voice their growing concern—concern, not despair and pessimism. The tocsin sounded by the Nicosia meeting is a call to action, to strengthen solidarity in the struggle against the United States' militarist designs. The document adopted by the participants in the symposium qualifies the establishment of Centcom and the expansion of the American presence as a direct threat to the national independence and social progress of the peoples. They also declared that the "settlement" in Lebanon imposed by the United States runs counter to the demand for the complete and unconditional withdrawal of Israeli troops from that country. Tel Aviv's threats to Syria were likewise condemned.

Important too is the fact that the participants in the symposium spoke up in support of the forthcoming World Assembly "For Peace, For Life, Against Nuclear War." Thus, they consider their initiative as inseparable from the principal common task of makind. They condemned America's efforts to use the "Soviet threat" myth, and underscored the importance of Soviet-Arab co-operation.

The Soviet proposals for talks on a range of questions connected with the reduction of military activity in the seas and oceans, the idea of making the Indian Ocean a zone of peace put forward by the non-aligned states and supported by the socialist countries, the initiatives advanced for normalizing the situation in the Persian Gulf zone and the Mediterranean--all this lays a solid groundwork for the further development of the mass movement to which the Nicosia meeting gave an impulse.

Of the national question through ensuring the right of all the national minorities in Iran to self-determination and self-government within the framework of a united independent state. All the practical activity of the People's Party was directed at these objectives.

These, then are the facts. The People's Party was subjected of fierce attacks by the Right-wing forces even before this. In 1981 its headquarters in Teheran was seized and wrecked by ultras and the newspaper Nameye Mardom, the organ of the Central Committee, was closed. Now the Party has been disbanded. At the same time an anti-Soviet propaganda campaign is being whipped up. The Soviet Union is accused of having had contacts with "subversive elements," meaning the members and supporters of the People's Party. In order somehow to "substantiate" the allegation that the Party's members have engaged in "spying," the Iranian authorities went so far as to expel from Iran a number of staff members of the U.S.S.R. Embassy and other Soviet institutions. A strong protest had been lodged in connection with this totally unfounded and provocative action.

The repressive action taken by the Iranian authorities against the People's Party has evoked legitimate indignation on the part of world progressive opinion. This action is rightly seen as an attempt by the Right-wing forces instigated by imperialist special services, not only to strike at the Iranian working people's vanguard party, but also to undermine the confidence of the masses in the Soviet Union, Iran's northern neighbour, and to damage Soviet-Iranian relations. More than 70 Communist Workers', Socialist, and Social-Democratic parties have already condemned the persecution of the People's Party of Iran. They declare their solidarity with the Iranian patriots and demand that the arrested People's Party, leaders be released.

1344. Kowait arrests pro-Iran group of terrorists. *Baghdad Observer* 31 Dec 1985 ; 1.

Four men have been arrested here on charges of conspiring to sabotage vital economic installations in Kuwait, security officials reported on Dec 30, 1985.

These officials refused to divulge details. But the independent newspaper Al-Anbaa identified the Lebanese suspects as Abdel-Azia Ali Karim, his brother Abdullah, and Suleiman Ahmed, and the Syrian as Walid Tewfix Suleiman.

It said the Lebanese belong to a sectarian militia operating in Lebanon, in a reference to pro-Iran Amal militia.

When the two Lebanese brothers were apprehended, the paper said, police found in their Kuwait apartment a letter from their uncle Hassan Karim asking them to blow up the Doha power stations 15 miles (25 km) north of Kuwait city.

Al-Anbaa added that quantities of explosives, molotov bombs, gas cylinders and detonation devices were captured by police at the apartment of the Lebanese brothers.

The four suspects were referred to the State Security Court for trial, security sources said.

That court on Sunday sentenced a 30-year-old man to five years in jail for a bomb hoax at Kuwait's Disneylandtype entertainment park. *The Court found him guilty of rumour mongering and causing public* panic after a hoax call to police on August 20.

Kuwait and other Arab Gulf states have always been the target of Iran's terror campaign. Press reports have frequently revealed that the Iranian regime is planning to carry out sabotage in a number of Arab countries including Saudi Arabia, the United Arab Emirates, Kuwait and Jordan.

On May 25th the Emir of Kuwait Sheikh Jaber Ahmed al-Sabah narrowly escaped an assassination attempt when a car laden with explosives smashed into his motorcade. A pro-Iranian terrorist organisation claimed responsibility for the attempt which drew worldwide denunciation. The blast killed two of his security guards and a passer-by and injured 12 others.

A series of explosion went off in December 1985 at the American and French embassies as well as government buildings in Kuwait killing six people and wounding more than 80.

Some 17 terrorists were arrested for the bomb attacks. Pro-Iran elements continued to threaten Kuwait's security by further carrying out twin blasts at Kuwaiti seaside cafe's killing and wounding more than one hundred people in a desperate attempt to free the terrorists responsible for the December bombings.

Kuwait's response was clear. In his statement on the incident Sheikh Jaber stressed that "such incidents will not dissuade me or Kuwait from continuing to work for the prosperity of our people as well as the Arab and Islamic nations."

The list of Iranian terror in the Gulf is so wide that it reveals the real intentions of the expansionist regime in Teheran.

In the early days of Khomeini's rule, Bahrain discovered a plot to topple its government.

In 1983 security authorities in Qatar discovered a plot engineered by Iran, in cooperation with other countries to blow up the Gulf Cooperation Council (GCC) headquarters during a summit. At that time, the Qatari authorities siezed guided missiles, arms and explosives which were smuggled to Qatar for this purpose.

The Iranian regime has often incited disturbances during Haj (pilgrimage) in Mecca, Saudi Arabia. A pro-Iran terrorist group claimed responsibility for two bomb blasts in the Saudi capital in which one person was killed and three others were wounded.

During their recent summit, leaders of the Arab Gulf state reviewed measures to combat the escalation of terrorism in the region.

1345. Malik, Ahmed : Executions : An untold story. *Link* 4 Sep 1983 ; 30.

1346. Prashar, A.S. : Torture of Khomeini opponents. *Tribune* 21 Jan 1983 ; 5.

1347. Pro-Iran terrorist group arrested in Turkey. *Baghdad Observer* 7 Jan 1986 ; 8.

Turkish authorities arrested in a pro-Iran terrorist group closely linked with the Iranian Embassy here. The aim of the group was to incite sectarian strife in Turkey.

A statement by Turkish Security Office said that the 12-member group aimed at establishing a Khomeini-style regime in Turkey. The statement added that the group has contacts with the Iranian Embassy here which has frequently supplied them with books and publications. The statement said that the first terrorist act, which was committed by the group, was the cutting off electricity from a suburb in Ankara during the New Year. The statement added that the group was planning to commit a series of sabotage acts throughout Turkey.

Turkish authorities, meanwhile, said that four Iranian infiltrators trying to enter Turkey near the Turkish province of Van were killed.

Turkish newspapers also said that the Iranian infiltrators were carrying military equipment to carry out sabotage acts. The newspapers added that the infiltrators were killed in a clash with Turkish patrols last week near the Iranian Turkish border.

Since coming to power the Iranian regime, has been exporting chaos, anarchy and terrorism abroad.

A considerable number of Iranian and pro-Iran terrorist groups were exposed in Arab Gulf countries, Yugoslavia, Indonesia and other European countries. They have been sent to carry out terrorist and sabotage acts and incite sectarian strife particularly in the Arab and Islamic countries. Those terrorists were operating under direct instructions from Iranian embassies in these countries.

Because of their complicity with such terrorists, a number of Iranian Embassy staff in Arab, Islamic and Western countries were declared persona-non-grata and were ordered to leave these countries because their work was incompatible with their diplomatic immunity.

In Teheran, the Iranian authorities fired 400 officials and workers at electricity offices in Tabriz because the regime was unable to pay them salaries, radio Mujahed said.

The radio, mouthpeice of Mujahedin Khalq opposition organisation, said another 50 teachers were also fired for the same reason. The radio added that a great number of officials and workers have recently been sacked by the regime because of the deteriorating financial and economic situation in Iran.

The radio, meanwhile, said that a Mujahedin member, Hussein Negfar was executed last month in Evin prison in Teheran after three years of arrest during which he received various types of torture.

In Cologne, West Germany, more than 1200 anti-Iranian regime protesters gathered in commemoration of the death of Ghulam Hussein Sa'di, who is a prominent Iranian resistance writer.

During the gathering, many speeches were delivered uncovering Khomeini regime's arrest, torture and execution campaign through Iran.

1348. Rajavi discloses more Iranian terrorism. *Baghdad Observer* 11 Feb 1987.

President of the Iranian Resistance Council, Mr. Masoud Rajavi said that the Iranian Embassy in West Germany was the centre of terrorist networks in Europe.

In an interview with a number of journalists, Mr. Rajavi said that one of the twenty-two terrorist networks which were run by the Iranian Embassy in West Germany launched the recent bomb attacks in Paris.

He added that Haddadi, the new Iranian Charge,' d Affairs in Paris was behind the wave of bombings in the French capital.

He said that Haddadi was also responsible for the bloody incidents in India in 1982.

Mr. Rajavi said that another terrorist centre in West Germany was based in the city of Cologne and run by a well-known Iranian terrorist called Sa'eed Mustafa.

The Iranian leader added that the terrorists used the mosque of Hamburg as a centre for their sabotage and terrorist activities.

He concluded that Mustafa's networks included 41 terrorists, who had previously been expelled from West Germany and then returned secretly one after the other.

1349. Ramazani, R.K. : Iran : Burying the hatcher. *Foreign Policy* (60) Fall 1985 ; 52-74.

1350. Reagan stance on Iran angers allies after calls to combat terrorism. *International Herald Tribune* 21 Nov 1986 ; 5.

1351. Ronfeldt, David : Hubris-nemesis dynamic : Gadhafi, Castro and Khomeini attack the Ogre. *International Herald Tribune* 23 Jan 1986 ; 6.

This month it is Moamer Qadhafi. Soon it may be Fidel Castro again, or Ayatollah Ruhollah Khomeini. Through them the ancient forces of hubris and nemesis are trying to fear the modern world apart in a way that Greek mythology never warned us about.

Mr. Castro, Colonel Qadhafi and Ayatollah Khomeini have all shown themselves to be filled with hubris, and perhaps they, too, will eventually bring about their own downfall. But that is not the point here.

The three leaders embody the spread of a new dynamic that we are only beginning to understand : a hubris-nemesis compels. In addition to having hubris, they have internationalized the role of the gooddess Nemesis. Each is committed to beg the nemesis of the United States ; for these men, America is the epitome of hubris, and hence the chosen enemy.

In this rare pathology, the two forces, which normally contradict one another, have become one, a fusion that generates awesome energy and ambition. To be as powerful as their hubris requires, these leaders must defy and attack the United States. To play the role of Nemesis, they must possess total power at home and project themselves on to the world stage. The two forces, now compatible, feed on one another.

Mr. Castro, Colonel Qadhafi and Ayatollah Khomeini might not be alone in having this affliction. Liberal and conservative analysts might have other candidates to add to the list. And a broader discussion of the complex might have to include a few Western leaders who, besides displaying vain glorious apetites for power, have shown themselves to be dead set on perpetual vengeance against the Soviet Union, the Palestenians or some other chosen enemy.

We must be on guard against the complex no matter what country, government, military, ideology or religion the leader belongs to. Even Mr. Castro, Colonel Qadhafi and Ayatollah Khomeini are important to single out because of the violent ways in which they have transcended the limitations of their small countries to become globe-shaking crusaders against the world's greatest power.

1352. Sabotage brigade formed in Iran, document says. *Baghdad Observer* 29 Dec 1984.

1353. Sainath, P. : Iran in agony. *Blitz* 5 Nov 1983 ; 11.

1354. Saksena, N.S. : Iran—Terrorism by Shab's Savak and Khomeini's Shia Fundamentalists. In *THF* ; 111-13.

1355. Sciolino, Elaive : U.S. aides say Iran uses terrorism, as policy tool. *International Herald Tribune* 25 Nov 1986 ; 1-2.

1356. Seale, Patrick : Iran behind terrorism in Lebanon. *Times of India* 23 Oct 1985 ; 8.

1357. Sharma, Nasira : Terror, disorder, chaos rule Iran. *Baghdad Observer* 1 Sep 1983 ; 5.

1358. Simes, Dimitri K. : Don't bribe terrorists. *International Herald Tribune* 11 Nov 1986 ; 6.

1359. Syria envoy kidnapped in Teheran. *China Daily* 4 Oct 1986 ; 1.

1360. Teheran's intransigence enlarges Gulf war. *New Wave* (New Delhi) 2 Mar 1986 ; 11-13.

1361. Top US official confirms Iran still involved in terrorrism. *Baghdad Observer* 26 Nov 1986 ; 1.

1362. Torture-killings continue under Khomeini regime. *New Age* 11 Jan 1986 ; 15.

Repression, Torture and executions of Tudeh party and OIPF (Majority) comrades continue unabated in the republic of Iran. After the murder of Tudeh Party leader Reza Shaltoki more news has come up of execution of six OIPF (Majority) comrades and death due to torture of Tudeh politbureau member Taghi Kaimanesh.

These comrades sacrifice their lives for freedom and justice in their native land. The savage repression unleased by the barbaric anti-people Iranian regime has only strengthened the resolve of OIPF (Majority) and Tudeh party comrades to fight for a better Iran.

Taghi Kaimanesh was tortured to death in the dungeons of Khomeini's Islamic republic. The regime tried to suppress the news but failed to cover up the sordid deed.

Born in 1923, Kaimanesh joined the Tudeh party at the age of 21. His arrest in 1954 came following the MI-6-CIA manipulated coup in 1954. He spent the next 25 years in Shah's jails resisting torture and in appalling conditions.

Widely seen as a figure symbolising resistance throughout the brutal rule of the Shah, he was released with the victory of the Iranian revolution—only to be rearrested in February 1983 following the onslaught on the Tudeh party by the treacherous Khomeini regime.

He was then subjected to the most severe physical and psychological repressions. Taghi Kaimanesh's heroic life came to an end in the torture chambers of the Islamic republic.

Despite appeals from democratic forces all over the world, six leaders of the Organisations of Iranian People's Feedian (Majority) were executed by the Islamic regime of Ayatollah Khomeini.

The latest group of patriots to be shot by a firing squad includes OIPF (M) political bureau alternate member Mohammad Reza Qebraii and alternate central committee member Razieddin Taban and OIPF (M) leaders Jahangeer Behtaji, Mohammad Amin 'Sheerkhani' Ebraheem Lotfollahzadeh and Mohamad Shiroodi.

The executed leaders were not allowed to be defended before the 'Islamic court'. After the execution neither were their names released nor their bodies handed over to their families.

Others who are being tortured in Khomeini's dungeons and await execution include OIPF (M) political bureau member Anooshiravan

Lotfi and other leaders and activists of the party as well as the Tudeh party of Iran.

Unconfirmed reports have also raised fears that during the last few months as 300 political prisoners may have been executed by the regime.

The Tudeh Party has asked for widespread protests against this latest wave of repression. Letters of protest in India may be sent to the Iranian Embassy, 5 Barakhamba Road, New Delhi-110001.

1363. Torture in Iranian prisons disclosed. *Baghdad Observer* 30 Jan 1986 ; 1.

Three political prisoners recently fled Iran for France disclosed various types of torture and maltreatment practised against prisoners in Iranian notorious prisons.

A spokesman for the Iranian Mujahedin Khalq Opposition Organisation said in Paris on January 29, 1985 that Mashkin Hamayoun Far, a 24-year old mathematics teacher was kidnapped by the Khomeini Guards and sent to the notorious prison of Evin where she was brutaly tortured and sentenced to death.

The spokesman added that another prisoner, Narjis Shwesta, a 27-year old mathematics teacher was arrested and sentenced to death after a summary trial.

A third prisoner, Hussein Datkha, an engineer was arrested with his wife and child. He was imprisoned at Evin and undergone various types of torture together with his wife was executed shortly after her arrest.

Datkha was moved to another prison in Mashhad in order to be executed but he managed to fleet to Denmark and then joined Iranian opposition forces in France.

The three prisoners attended the recent UN session and disclosed the deteriorating situation in Iran in general and conditions in Iran's prison in particular.

They also drew the world's attention to the ordeal of more than 150,000 political prisoners in Iranian prisons.

The UN had adopted a decision in which it condemned Iran regime's violations of human rights.

1364. U.S. had clues that Iran funded bombings in 1983. *International Herald Tribune* 8 Dec 1986 ; 5.

Iraq

1365. Terror on top. *Pioneer* (Lucknow) 27 Dec 1986 ; 6.

Terrorist have struck again in the air killing 62 passengers and maiming and injuring many more. The same syndrome has repeated itself in the hijacking of the Iraqi Airways Boeing 737 jetliner, which was hijacked en route from Baghdad to Amman in Jordan. Four hitherto unidentified gunmen enacted abizarre drama trying to hijack the airliner. According to a survivor's eyewitness account : It all happened like lightning about an hour after we took off from Baghdad. The captain had just announced that we had entered Saudi airspace, when one passenger (hijacker) from the economy class jumped up with a hand grenade and ran towards the cockpit. Three security men jumped up and tried to stop him and wrestled him to the floor, but he slipped out of their grasp and crawled into the cockpit. The door was slammed shut and then three loud noises and screaming from the cockpit and behind in the economy class there was another explosion."

The recent hijacking of the Iraqi plane which claims such appeallingly heavy casualties is reported to be the handwork of an unknown group which call itself "Revolutionary Action". It claims to be responsible for the blowing up of the Iraqi plane. A gulf news agency reports from Baghdad that the two hijackers who survived the plane disaster and have been taken into custody are agents of the Iranian regime travelling on-Lebanese passports.

The moral need not be heavily underscored. United the world can light the scourge successfully, disunited country after country will continue to be listed as "targets" for tomorrow by soulless terrorists.

1366. Arfa, Hassan : *Kurds : A historical and political study*. London, Oxford University Press, 1966.

1367. Hamilton, A.M. : *Road through Kurdistan*. London, Faber 1958.

1368. Iraq against terrorism. *Iraq* 1 Nov 1982 ; 10-11.

1369. Johns, Richard : No peace for Kurdistan but will there be war. *New Middle East*. Jan-Feb 1973 ; 48-50.

1370. O'Ballance, Edgar : *Kurdish revolt ; 1961-1970.* London, Faber & Faber, 1973.

1371. Safrastian, Arshak : *Kurds and Kurdistan.* London, Harvill Press, 1948.

Ireland

1372. Banks, Michael : Army in Northern Ireland. *Brassey's Annual*—1972.

1373. Barry, Tom : *Guerrilla days in Ireland.* Iralee, Anvil Books, 1968.

1374. BBC's Irish troubles. *Times* (London) 16 Mar 1977.

1375. Begin, Menachem : *Revolt.* Los Angeles, 1948.

1376. Bell, J. Bowyer : Chronicles of violence in Northern Ireland. *Review of Politics* 34 (2) Apr 1972 ; 147-57.
36 (4) Oct 1974 ; 521-43 & 38 (4) Oct 1976 ; 510-33.

1377. Bell, J. Bowyer : Escalation of insurgency. *Review of Politics* 35 (3) Jul 1973 ; 398-411.

1378. Bew, Paul : Britain's modern Irish question. *Economy and Society* 10 (4) 481-87.

1379. Bochringer, G.H. : Beyond hunt : A policy for Northern Ireland of the future. *Social Studies* 2 (3) 1973; 399-414.

1380. Boserup, Anders : Contradictions and struggles in Northern Ireland. *Socialist Register* 1972.

1381. Bowden, Tom : IRA and the changing tactics of terrorism. *Political Quarterly* 91, Oct-Dec 1976 ; 428-36.

1382. Brudaigh, Ruairio : Restore power to the people. *Guardian Weekly* 24 Feb 1980 ; 5.

1383. Byrne, Kevin : Attacking Irish myths of violence. *Macleans* (Toronto) 14 Jan 1980.

1384. Clark, Dennis : Terrorism in Ireland : Renewal of a tradition. In *ITCW* ; 77-83.

Although the Anglo-Irish war of the 1920s produced many civilian casualties, the attitude towards purposeful assaults on civilians by the Irish Republican Army of the time was quite clear. Such assaults were seen to be a secondary result of military action, not, a primary target to produce political results. The English forces, however, did pursue purposeful assaults on civilians in attempts to cow the Irish population. The change in priorities between the 1920s and the 1960s on the part of the IRA might be explained by several factors. In Ireland, as elsewhere, modern social influences have changed the context of life. Urbanization has proceeded, although at a slower rate than in most other European countries. Yet, it was from the towns and cities that the leadership for the modern Irish revolutionary movement arose. This same urbanization has contributed in Ireland as elsewhere to an increasing impersonality in local life. Northern Ireland is the most modernized portion of Ireland, and it is here. I believe, that the forces of impersonality have proceeded furtherest. This has had two effects. It has made it easier for those engaged in the fighting to depersonalize their efforts and to inflict civilian casualties. And this same depersonalization has made the tribalization or retribalization of Ulster society into religious and local groups of antagonists easier. Finally, the violence itself has acted as a polarizing influence, for its horror, shame, and brutality have helped to dissolve the bonds of sociability in North Ireland. If the Ulster struggle can be characterized as a "civil" struggle, then the savagery of the conflict is commensurate to that kind of fighting.

Second, the media coverage of the Ulster violence has dramatized it according to the vastly increased capacity of modern communications. This is especially true of television and film coverage of the violent events. The magnifying effect of this coverage has been enormous, and the respective propaganda uses of the media have been duly pursued by all parties. While the dissidents in the Tyrol and the Basques in Spain have been largely barred from media exposure, those in Northern Ireland have been able to achieve broad exposure. Although Irish agitation often received worldwide support in Westminister, and although the news media have often dramatized the IRA, the power of television has enhanced even further the profile at Irish agitation in our time. This development has made the Irish issue more acute than it might have been without televised scenes of bombings and arson. It has added to the political potency of the situation.

Third, within the framework of modern Irish history, the countries of Ulster have played a particularly vibrant role. Many of the leaders of the independence movement in the 1920s were of Ulster origin. Ulster was traditionally the hope of the battle sagas of Irish Literature and of the great clan leaders, the O'Neills and the O'Donnells. As such it held a special place in the nationalist hagiography and sentiment. The exclusion of six of the traditional Ulster countries from an independent Ireland had a particular irony and provocative effect for a nationalist traditon that had looked to Ulster for so many models. The events since 1969 have served to reaffirm the Ulster nationalist leadership and to reactivate one of the traditional slogans of Irish rebellion; "The North began......" Within Ireland, then, the nationalists of the North, who have always felt they were oppressed in a special way, have asserted again their intense localism and their claim to nationalists primacy, a primacy that would be a threat to Dublin and a rejection of the bureaucratization of the nationalist tradition under the government of the present Irish Repulic. This is an elaboration of the indigenous insurrectionary tradition.

Fourth, the intellectual isolation of Northern Ireland nationalist insurgents a change from the revolutionary pattern of the past. While it would be unrealistic to expect a renewal of that extraordinary literary and artistic upsurge that accompanied the burst of Irish nationalism in the early part of this century, the isolation of the Provisional IRA from the intellectual leaders of Ireland today is notable in a nation where nationalism and intellectual leadership have long been strongly intertwined. It is true that some of the artistic brilliance extolling the 1916 Easter Rising and the struggle for independence was an exercise in retroactive creativity, yet much of it was also contemporaneous with the actual events of the struggle. Today there are few writers, indeed, who are partisans of the Provisional IRA, and it does seem that the hard-pressed men of the North are estranged from the most powerful current of modern Irish cultural life. Perhaps this is due to a lack of intellectual leadership among the Provos themselves. Perhaps it is due to the narrowness of the Ulster conflict and its reference to religious loyalties that contradict human sentiments.

1385. Cluskey, Frank : Irish response. In *ITCR*, 180-86.

Terrorism in Ireland has posed a direct threat to the institutions of our state. In the Republic, the men of violence have made it clear that their targets are not confined to the situation across the border. If they were, that fact would in no way alter the wrongness of what they are doing. But, as a matter of history, these people have rejected with total arrogance of the very constitution of the Irish state and have set themselves up as a force quite prepared to oppose in arms the legitimate government of Ireland.

Such a situation is clearly intolerable and it has been necessary for the Irish government to take serious and, at times unpalatable, steps to deal with it. The past ten years have been a period in which the terrorist threat, and the overspill of the total Northern Ireland scene, have dominated our political and economic life to a most unhappy degree. Much political energy has been diverted to the essentially sterile area of counter terrorism. Economic progress has been damaged, with the tourist industry above all suffering grave setbacks. Resources have been diverted to the areas of policing and security—in 1968/69 our total spending under these headings was £ 23 million while in the current year it will amount to £ 28 millions.

A number of major political, legislative and administrative steps have had to be taken to deal with the existing threat of paramilitary activity. I shall refer briefly to these.

Strong action against illegal paramilitary groups has been taken under the terms of the Offences Against the State Act of 1939 which was originally introduced at a time of internal terrorist activity and obvious external threat. Membership of certain organizations has been prescribed and many IRA activists and others who belong to illegal bodies have been arrested, tried and jailed. A special non-jury Criminal Court was established in 1972 to deal with serious offences of a paramilitary nature in connection with which a serious history of intimidation of witnesses had been experienced. This Court is presided over by three civilian judges who decide on the cases brought before them after nominal criminal court proceedings.

1386. Coogan, Tim Patrick : *I.R.A.* New York, Prager, 1970.

1387. Dillion, Martin and Dennis Lehane : *Political Murder in Northern Ireland*. London, Penguin Books, 1973.

1388. Dunne, George H. : Irish sea of troubles. *America* 126, 4 Mar 1972 ; 227-29.

1389. Edwards, Dudley : *Sins of our fathers*. Dublin, 1970.

1390. Enloe, Cynthia : *Ethnic soldiers*. Harmondsworth, Penguin Books, 1980.

1391. Enloe, Cynthia : Police and Military in Ulster : Peace keeping or peace-subverting forces. *Journal of Peace Research* 15 (3) 1978 ; 243-58.

1392. Fisk, Robert : Effect of social and political crime on the police and British army in Northern Ireland. In *ITCW* ; 84-93.

In early 1970, the Ministry of Defence began publication of a four-page card to be issued to every soldier serving in Northern Ireland. It was printed on yellow paper, marked "Restricted"—the lowest security classification—and carried a long and occasionally confusing list of instructions about when a soldier may or may not open fire on a cilvilian in the province. It began with sensible enough advice. "Never use more force than the minimum necessary to enable you to carry out your duties," was one of the general rules. If a soldier had to open fire, the card said, "fire only aimed shots." But a warning should be given before opening fire, "preferably by loud hailter." If a guard is approached by a stranger who is behaving suspiciously, the Card went on, the soldier is at the second challenge to apply the safety catch of his weapon and shot : "Stand still I am ready to fire." But soldiers could fire without warning in certain circumstances ; when hostile firing was taking place, where delay could lead to serious injury (but then only if the person had a fire arm), or at a vehicle if the occupants were opening fire.

The disclosure that such a document existed created a predictable burst of anger from the Ministry of Defence at the time. The Guardian reporter responsible for breaking the story was virtually sent to Coventry by the army in Northern Ireland, and complaints were made to his editor about his lack of "responsibility." But then something very strange emerged from the government—an admission that while the card's instructions had been drawn up by civil servants at the Ministry of Defence, a soldier who obeyed them to the latter could still find himself in court charged with manslaughter. In other words this carefully worded document had no legal standing. Nothing could have more dramatically illustrated than the quasi-legal functions (as opposed to the legal role) of the army in Northern Ireland nor the vagueness with which these functions were conceived.

A glance at James Callaghan's memory of the first British military involvement in Belfast during the current war is enough to illustrate the speed with which the military authorities were, quite unprepared, plunged into the latest Irish conflict. When the first troops entered Derry in August of 1969—they belonged to the Prince of Wales's

Own—they crossed the Craigavon Bridge with bayonets fixed to their self-loading rifles. Officers at that time thought that their presence would be a very temporary one and for two years afterward their superiors announced (at least to the press) that the Irish Republican Army could be beaten by military means. The army, after all, knew that they themselves were only in the province "in support of the civil power" ; they were temporarily propping up the Royal Ulster Constabulary because for a number of reasons the police were unable to cope.

But from the start, there was an ambiguity not only about the army's functions but also about its enemy. The IRA, when they clearly emerged in the shape of the Provisionals in 1970, were described in fashionable if slightly easy terms as "thugs and murderers" ; they were—and the RUC still repeat this—common criminals with no genuine political aspirations. Merlyn, Rees, the Northern Ireland Secretary of State, has repeated this within the past six months, comparing the sectarian murders along the Irish border with the work of the Mafia in the United States. Yet British ministers and their civil servants found within three years that it was politically expedient to treat with the IRA. The men condemned as "thugs and murders" were invited to talk to senior British ministers in Cheyne Row. Men like Frank Steels, one of the Foreign Office's most able negotiators, were chatting amiably to the IRA within eight days of the resumption of hostilities in Belfast. Indeed, Sean MacStiofain remembers Steele approaching him on the secret flight back to Ireland with the words : "I hope you're not going to start your bloody stupid campaign again." It was only five days later that a British colonel in the Royal Artillery found himself negotiating directly with Seamus Twomey, then the IRA Brigade Commander in Belfast, in an army post in the Lenadoon housing estate.

It was little wonder, then, that as the years went by in Northern Ireland the army's activities became not less but more complex and confusing. Yet from the start of their campaign against the IRA—a campaign which gained some veracity for the IRA when a British general actually said the army was "at war" with them, thus giving extremists the dignity of a legitimate army—there was an extra legal dimension to the military actions. The Special Powers Act in Northern Ireland—which has since been replaced by the slightly less draconian Emergency Provisional Act—enabled soldiers to search houses almost at will, to arrest men and hold them for longer periods than would be allowed in Britain, to draw up massive intelligence files, to carry out spying operations in plain clothes and, in August of 1971, to assist in the internment of hundreds of people without trial. On the day after internment at least eleven men were subjected to a severe form of interrogation involving sensory deprivation. This was carried out by experts in deprivation techniques who came from the Ministry of Defence in London. To this day, the government has not been prepared to say who gave permission for this treatment of prisoners nor where the interrogations even took place. At least three of the men have since received 30,000 pounds compensation from the British government.

1393. Gale, Richard : Old problem : New setting. *Journal of the Royal United Service Institute for Defence Studies.* 117 (665) Mar 1972 ; 46-58.

1394. How hopeless is the Irish problem ? *Encounter* (London) Feb 1980.

1395. Lippman, Mathew : Abrogation of domestic human rights : Northern Ireland and the rule of British Law. In *TIE* ; 179-208.

The Secretary of State for Northern Ireland may issue interim custody orders authorising the detention of persons in Northern Ireland 'concerned in the commission or attempted commission of any act of terrorism, or in directing, organising or training persons for the purpose of terrorism". The case must be referred to an adviser for a report and if the Secretary of State is then 'satisfied' that the person has been 'concerned' in such activities and that the person's 'detention is necessary for the protection of the public', the Secretary of State 'may make a detention order for the detention of that person' for an unlimited duration.

The Prevention of Terrorism (Temporary Provisions) Act 1974 (and 1976) authorises the Secretary of State to exclude individuals from Great Britain, Northern Ireland and from the United Kingdom if the Secretary of State is 'satisfied that the person' is or has been concerned (whether in Northern Ireland or elsewhere) in the 'commission, preparation or instigation of acts of terrorism, or the person is attempting or may attempt to enter Great Britain or Northern Ireland with a view to being concerned in the commission, preparation or instigation of acts of terrorism'. The police may detain an individual, on their own authority, for up to seven days in order to determine whether to recommend to the Secretary of State that an exclusion order be issued against an individual.

The major arguments which were used by the proponents and by the opponent of the Northern Ireland (Emergency Provisions) Act and the Prevention of Terrorism (Temporary Provisions) Act are, in part, summarised below.

The violence in Northern Ireland is not 'politically motivated'. The Northern Irish terrorists are 'common criminals' with no altruistic motives', 'the terrorists have no realistic political cause' and they are an 'unyielding band of subversives led by "godfathers". They are "………bloody murderers………the fixed look of malevolence on their faces, ………' who engaged in 'horrifying assassinations………senseless sectarian violence………provocative marches………crimes for personal gain'.

In short, the terrorists are 'dishonourable enemies of democracy, of liberty, of Christian religion' who would 'do well to keep the word humane out of their mouths' and they are 'Fascist hoodlums who must be considered as criminals of the lowest type'.

The horror and cruelty of these terrorists is apparent to anyone who has to visit 'the home of the little girl who was blown to peices, and to anyone who has to visit the home of a young man of 25 who was slaughtered and in someway, try to find words of comfort for a widow of 25 left with two children'.

In another incident 'a council workman—a Protestant who volunteered to assist in the repair of bomb-damaged homes in the Catholic Lower Falls was beaten to death by a Provisional IRA gang'.

The Terrorist Threat is so Great that if it is non Halted in Northern Ireland it will Spread to Great Britain.

Government speakers offered statistical summaries of the 'terrorist threat' :

> In only the past three months, 178 bombs were exploded by terrorists and there were 909 shooting incidents, 581 involving the security forces, six soldiers, 28 policemen and 458 civilians were injured and treated in the hospital……
>
> In the last month, there have been 12 punishment shootings……… nearly all by knee-capping………'

If the violence in Northern Ireland is not halted, it may create a "Congo" in Ireland which would spill over into Britain………'

Thus, the Acts provide a framework to combat a 'continuing threat' which may 'escalate tomorrow' in Great Britain.

1396. Malik, K.N. : U.S. aid to N. Ireland to fight terrorists. *Times of India* 18 Nov 1985 ; 16.

1397. Mansfield, Don : Irish Republican army and Northern Ireland. In *IMW* ; 45-86.

That the conflict in Northern Ireland has been a never-ending one is beyond dispute. What is subject to question, however, is when it began. To some the starting point is 1968, when the civil rights demonstrations erupted ; to others the point is 1922, when Ulster and the Irish Free State, as the Republic of Ireland was then called, decided to go their separate ways ; and to still others—perhaps most—the origin of the troubles can be traced back to 1690, the date of the Battle of the Boyne, or even to 1603, the year of the "flight of the Earles" and the start of the Ulster plantation. Because each of these dates is important, a brief analysis of Irish history is necessary if a complete understanding of the struggle is to be obtained.

Ireland (the whole island) is approximately the size of West Virginia and has a total population of four and a half million. Six of Ireland's northern countries (corresponding to two-thirds of the historic province of Ulster) are an integral part of the United Kingdom. Northern Ireland, as it is called, has a population of approximately one and a half million. The rest of the island is the independent Republic of Ireland, or Eire, with an area four times that of Northern Ireland and a population twice as large. For centuries now the northern countries have been different from the rest of Ireland, above all with respect to their inhabitants.

The northeastern edge of Ireland is only a few miles from the Scottish coast and in the early years of the seventeenth century Scots settled in the area.

These Scots brought with them many different cultural traits compared to the native, or Irish. This helped to explain why it is frequently asserted that the Protestants of Northern Ireland belong to a race different from that of the rest of the Irish. It also illustrates why the Irish problem is as much a problem of different nationalities as of different religions.

"Ireland would not be the problem country that it is if it had ever been properly conquered." Ireland's history is one of a series of attempts at colonization and conquest, none of them completely successful and each one contributing a new element to the general confusion. Her history is also one of bloodshed.

During the sixteenth century, England extended its authority over Ireland, and by 1607 the conquest was completed by James I. However, although England had become Protestant (and the same metamorphosis was prescribed for Ireland), the native Irish remained Catholic. Indeed, the fact that the ruling English were Protestant only confirmed the Irish in their attachment to the Roman Church.

Following their defeat by James I, the Earls of Tyrone and Tyrconnell chose to exile themselves from Ireland and handed their Ulster lands over to English and Scottish settlers. The most important plantation in Ulster history was begun. Many of the "Irish" Irish were driven into the poorer lands in the south and west. Thus Northern Ireland firmly attained the characteristics it has today—largely Protestant and closely aligned to the rest of Britain.

Twice more during the seventeenth century Ireland was to experience large-scale warfare, and on both occasions the Irish chose the losing side, a choice dictated by religion. They supported Charles I against Cromwell and James II against William of Orange.

During the civil war in England in 1664, the Catholic Irish massacred many of the Protestant settlers in Ulster. After Cromwell won the civil war he put down the rebellion in Ireland with great ferocity and it was the Catholic's turn to be massacred. Cromwell's campaign was extensive and left lasting grievances in the hearts of the "Irish" Irish. However, their cause looking to be improving when the Catholic James II came to the English throne in 1685 and anti-Catholic laws were discontinued. But in 1688, the English Parliament invited William of Orange to become king in place of the "too Catholic" James. The "Irish" Irish rose on behalf of King James. The Protestants stood firm for King "Billy" and took their stand at Londonderry. For fifteen weeks the defenders of Londonderry held out against successive attacks by the Catholic army, until an English ship broke into the harbor to raise the siege. The Orange Order derives much of its mythology from this period and the defenders ("apprentice boys") of Londonderry are its legendary heroes.

1398. McCarthy, Colman : Victims in Northern Ireland. *Washington Post* 16 May 1979.

1399. McGuire, Maria :*To take arms.* London, 1973.

1400. McIntyre, Colin : Extradition of Irish Republican guerrillas under a cloud. *Baghdad Observer* 11 Jan 1986 ; 4.

The extradition of suspected Irish Republic guerrillas from the south to the British-ruled north, a key element in cross-border cooperation envisaged by last month's Anglo-Irish accord, is under a cloud after a series of embarrassing setbacks.

Some legal experts and politicians fear that unless the present 20-year-old Irish extradition law is amended, courts will stop sending suspects to the north, leading to a new freeze in Anglo-Irish relations.

The latest problems began in October, when Dominic McGlinchey, once described as the most wanted man on both sides of the Irish border, was freed by a Belfast court after becoming the first person to be extradited from the South for what were previously considered "political" offences.

This followed a landmark ruling by the Dublin supreme court which redefined political actions, for which people cannot be extradited under the Irish constitution, as "what reasonable civilized people would regard as political activity."

McGlinchey was extradited with what many politicians regarded as indecent haste, only hours after being captured in a shootout with police in south-east Ireland.

But when he eventually came to trial charged with the 1977 murder of a 67-year-old pastmistress, he was freed after the court ruled that fingerprint evidence was not sufficient to convict him. He was immediately sent back to the south, where he faced trial on other charges.

A few weeks later Brendan Burns, wanted in the north in connection with the deaths of five British soldiers in 1981, was freed by the Dublin high court after extradition warrants were ruled to be defective because of an elementary legal blunder.

The northern police inspector who put the warrants before a Belfast magistrate was not under oath at the time.

Then, in a virtual re-run of the McGlinchey case, the second suspected guerrilla to be extradited from the Republic to the north, Seamus Shannon, was cleared of the murder of a former leading Northern Ireland politician. Once again it was fingerprint evidence that was found wanting.

Shannon, accused of the 1981 murder of the 86-year-old former speaker of the Northern Ireland parliament, Sir Norman Strong, immediately announced he planned to sue the Irish government and the Northern Ireland secured forces for the time he had spent in jail.

Of the three cases, that of Burns was being followed with the most interest. He was the first person to be sought for killing British soldiers.

The three incidents came as cross-border cooperation in combatting republican guerrillas fighting to end British rule in the north was being highlighted by the new Anglo-Irish accord.

Signed in November, it gives the Dublin government a limited say in Northern affairs for the first time.

Since the Irish authorities have been accused by Britain in the past of providing a haven for guerrillas, a clear willingness to extradite suspects was seen as an essential part of any Northern Ireland agreement.

However extradition of activists whose goals many Irishmen would share, even if they did not support their methods, is still a sensitive subject.

The respected Irish press newspaper, voicing widely-felt concern, said the McGlinchey and Shannon extraditions appeared to have been the product of "an unseemly panic".

"Extradition was one of those grand gestures some of our politicians were anxious to make—at someone else's expense—to reassure the northern unionists".

The paper added : "It has proved to be a disaster area for all concerned and threatens to bring our courts into disrepute and create antagonism towards the police."

The Sunday Tribune newspaper, noting that those awaiting extradition normally ended up spending considerable time in jail accused the northern authorities of operating a system of internment on remand for suspects and added : "We should not be aiding and abetting such an abuse".

1401. Moodie, Michael : Patriot game : The politics of violence in **Northern Ireland. In *ITCW* ; 94-110.**

Like beauty, patriotism in Northern Ireland is in the eye of the beholder. Those who are committed to the creation of a thirty-two county Irish republic claim it as readily and as self-righteously as those who affirm their loyalty to the British crown. It is only one of the differences that has divided the Ulster community for the last four centuries and continues to make it a province of the United Kingdom where governing without consensus remains the rule.

In 1839 Gustave de Beaumont remarked that "Ireland is a small country where the greatest questions of politics, morality and humanity are fought out." The period between the collapse of the Sunningdale power-sharing agreement in May 1974 and the dissolution of Ulster's Constitutional Convention in March 1976 might lead one to conclude that the problems of Northern Ireland remain as far from resolution today as they were in the nineteenth century. Events in Northern Ireland during that period, however, may prove to be a turning point in the history of the province, providing the impetus for action that shatters the existing stalemate.

Political developments in Northern Ireland during these two years follow a pattern of action and reaction between three sets of actors : the Ulster Protestants, the Catholic faction in the province, and the British government. It has been said that the Catholics in Northern Ireland are preoccupied with the British Army, while the Protestants are preoccupied with the Catholics. During the past year, however, both communities in Ulster have been keenly conscious of the British government's policies emanating from Westminister. It is the interaction of these three groups, therefore, that is the focus of this analysis. While the discussion concentrates primarily on the acts of violence relating to the Ulster troubles, it must place those acts in the political context created by the interactions of Protestant, Catholic, and British politicians.

The British government had made a number of attempts to resolve the conflict in Northern Ireland through political channels. As recently as November 1973 a resolution of the Ulster dispute appeared to be in sight. In July 1973, following a poll in which a majority of the Northern Ireland electorate voted to remain part of the United Kingdom, the British government passed the Northern Ireland Constitutional Act. The purpose of the act was to replace direct rule of the province from London with an Assembly and an Executive representing both the Catholic and Protestant communities of Ulster.

Despite strong opposition to the provisions of the act by hardliners in both Protestant and Catholic communities, plans for its implementation went ahead into 1974. To fulfill the act's provision for a Council of Ireland, a tripartite conference at Sunningdale, including both the British and Irish prime ministers, agreed to establish a Council of Ministers and a Consultative Assembly to deal with such non-controversial issues as tourism and transportation between the Irish Republic and Northern Ireland.

Ratification of this agreement by the Northern Ireland Assembly in May of 1974 prompted militant Protestant leaders in control of Ulster's labour unions to call a general strike. Appealing to Protestant fears that the Council of Ireland would be a first step toward unification of Ulster with the Irish Republic, the Protestant leaders enlisted mass support for their action. Supported and policed by Protestant paramilitary groups, they strike all but shut down the province.

Brian Faulkner, leader of the provincial government's coalition of moderate Protestants and Catholics, favoured negotiations with the strikers. This course was resolutely opposed, however, by Secretary of State for Northern Ireland Merlyn Rees, who refused to be coerced into talks by the strikers. Faulkner and his fellow Unionists in the government resigned, and the power-sharing agreement outlined in the Sunningdale Agreement collapsed. London was forced to abandon its new arrangements and revert to direct rule.

In July 1974 the British government announced new plans for Ulster, calling on the people of Northern Ireland to devise a settlement themselves by holding a Constitutional Convention the following year. Both Britain and Northern Ireland were back where they had started in March 1972 when direct British rule was first imposed on the province. No prospects to an end of the stalemate were in sight.

1402. Moxon-Browne, E. : Water and the fish : Public opinion and the Provisional IRA in Northern Ireland. *Terrorism* 5(1-2) 1981 ; 41-72.

1403. Murray, Russell : Killings of local security forces in Northern Ireland 1969-81. *Terrorism* 7(1) 1984 ; 11-32.

1404. *Northern Ireland : A report on the conflict.* New York, Random House, 1972.

1405. O'Ballance, Edgaur : IRA leadership problems. *Terrorism* 5 (1-2) 1981 ; 73-82.

1406. O'Day, Alam : Northern Ireland, terrorism and the British State. In *TTP* ; 121-36.

1407. Parry, Albert : Crimson in the Irish Green and Orange. In *Terrorism* 1976 ; 376-94.

1408. Rees, Merlyn : Terror in Ireland and Britain's response. In *ITCR* ; 276-82. *Terrorism* 5 (1-2) 1981 ; 83-88.

The use of violence for political ends has been a feature of Irish history for over two hundred years. Since the establishment of Northern Ireland itself in 1920 there have been four distinct terrorist campaigns; in the 1920's, during the 1939-45 world war, between 1956 and 1962 and the present campaign which began in 1969. In 1972, following the propagation of the Northern Ireland Parliament and the imposition of direct rule from Westminster, the United Kingdom Government appointed a Committee under the chairmanship of Lord Diplock, the eminent jurist, to consider "what arrangements for the administration of justice in Northern Ireland could be made in order to deal more efficiently with terrorist organization........." Diplock found that the main obstacle to dealing with terrorists in the ordinary courts was the intimidation of jurors and witnesses by terrorist organizations, and the principal recommendations in his report were embodied in the Northern Ireland (Emergency Provisions) Act 1973. This provided for :

* all terrorist-type offences to be categorized as "scheduled" offences ;
* trials of scheduled offences to be by a senior judge, sitting alone, but with more than the usual rights of appeal ;
* bail in scheduled cases to be given only by the High Court (rather than by a magistrate) and then only if stringent precautions were made ;
* the arrest without warrant and detention by the police for up to 72 hours of any person suspected of being a terrorist (the normal requirement in Northern Ireland is that arrested persons must be brought before a court within 48 hours of arrest) ;
* the arrest and detention of a suspect for up to 4 hours by members of the Army ;
* wide powers of search and seizure by members of the security forces ;

* reversal of the normal onus of proof in relation to offences of possession of arms and explosives;

* a fresh system of detention by the executive.

(Detention orders could be made by the Secretary of State on the basis of information which the security forces believed to be valid, whereas conviction for offences under the normal criminal law is of course on the basis of evidence tested in court. I should add that, although the emergency legislation in Northern Ireland still provides for a system of detention, this power has not been used since 1975; all persons in custody in Northern Ireland have thus been convicted of criminal offences or are awaiting trial for criminal offences).

For the first time in United Kingdom statute law, terrorism was defined as the use of violence for political ends, including any use of violence for the purpose of putting the public in fear.

1409. Ross, Richard : *Northern Ireland : Time of Choice.* Washington, AEI PPR, 1976.

1410. Schmitt, David : *Violence in Northern Ireland : Ethnic conflict and radicalization in an international setting*. New Jersey, 1974.

1411. Souza, George : Irish Chaplain reveals jail horrors. *Herald American* 29 Apr 1979.

1412. Stetler, Russell : IRA : Beyond the barricades. *Ramparts* 10, Mar 1972.

1413. Tugwell, Maurice : Politics and propaganda of the Provisional IRA. *Terrorism* 5 (1-2) 1981 ; 13-140.

1414. Villiers, Peter J. : Where Angels fear to tread : An excursion into Irish politics. *Journal of the Royal United Services, Institute for Defence Studies* 124(3) 1979.

1415. *Violence in Ireland.* Dublin, Veritas Publications, 1977.

1416. Walsh, Sean Patrick : To England : Leave Ireland. *New York Times* 8 Nov 1979.

1417. Wells, Warren B and N. Marlowe : *History of the Irish Rebellion of 1916*. Dublin, 1916.

1418. Winchester, Simon : Provisional IRA in confident mood. *Guardian* (Manchester) 20 Dec 1971.

Israel

1419. Birendranath, Dewan : Zionist aggression on Tunisia—The real culprit. *Democratic World* (New Delhi) 13 Oct 1985 ; 5-6.

1420. Challenge of Israel : *International Herald Tribune* 7 Oct 1985 ; 4.

1421. Colebrook, Joan : Israel with terrorists. *Commonweal* 58(1) Jul 1974.

1422. Copeland, Miles : Israeli cause and effect. *International Herald Tribune* 14 Oct 1985 ; 4.

1423. Culter, Lloyd : Israel's air raid on Tunisia cannot be condoned. *International Herald Tribune* 10 Oct 1985 ; 4.

1424. Dershowitz, Alan M. : Terrorism and preventive detention : The case of Israel. *Commentary* 50, Dec 1976.

1425. Eitinger, Leo : *Concentration camp survivors in Norway and Israel.* University of Oslo Press, 1964.

1426. Frankel, Glenn : Israel is embroiled in torture changes. *International Herald Tribune* 18 Sep 1986 ; 5.

1427. Friendman, Thomas L : Experts say terrorists' closest link may be hatred. *International Herald Tribune* 29 Apr 1986 ; 6.

1428. Grouss and Sevrge : *Blood of Israel.* New York, William Morrow, 1975.

1429. Harkabi, Y. : *Arab attitudes to Israel.* Jerusalem, Keter, 1976.

1430. In Israeli character. *Telegraph* (Calcutta) 3 Oct 1985 ; 6.

1431. Inciting violence. *Egyptian Mail* 7 Sep 1985 ; 4.

1432. India flays Israel's state terrorism. *National Herald* 6 Nov 1985 ; 2.

1433. Israel. Spying on a friend. *International Herald Tribune* 28 Nov. 1985 ; 4.

1434. Israel does it again. *Deccan Herald* 3 Oct 1985 ; 8.

1435. Israel's state terrorism. *Tribune* 4 Oct 1985 ; 4.

1436. Israeli air terror. *Indian Express* 8 Feb 1986 ; 6.

The skyjacking international air space and forcelanding of civilian aircraft by Israeli war planes last Tuesday is the latest instance of state terrorism for which successive X governments in Jerusalem have rightly earned notoriety. Belonging to the Libyan Arab Airlines, the executive jet was carrying nine Syrian politicians, including a leader of the ruling Ba'ath Socialist Party, from Tripoli to Damascus when the Libyan pilot reported to Cyprus air control that two Israeli air force jets had intercepted it and "signalled the plane to follow them". The plane was diverted to Israel and forced to land at a military air base. It was released after seven hours of detention, search and interrogation.

This brazen act of lawlessness by Israel would be bad enough if it were the first of its kind. In fact, however, it represents what has become a routine. The reprisals and "punitive attacks" against various Arab countries and peoples resulting in widespread destruction and death, often of innocent civilians, as in the Tunis bombing, or acts of aggression against its neighbours constitute a deplorable record of military arrogance and state terrorism. The reason given for the latest episode was the Israeli suspicion that the plane carried "Palestinian terrorists". Even if that was so, Israel had no right whatsoever to act in the manner it did against a civil aircraft in international skies. This is air piracy on par with the skyjacking of an Egyptian plane by US navy jets following the Achille Lauro episode last October or Israel's own action in 1973 when it forced another Arab passenger plane to land on its soil in the belief that the Palestinian leader, George Habbah, was on board.

The Israeli Prime Minister has admitted that the interception was an error. But what Mr. Peres has said is not an admission of wrongdoing but merely of wrong information of who was on board. It is precisely these acts that fuel anti-Israeli terrorism, that provide the basis for President Gadafi of Libya to denounce the Israelis and their mentor, the United States, and that are increasingly causing discomfiture and disillusionment in the West. The failure of the UN Security Council to act on Syria's request for a resolution denouncing the Israeli action reinforces the belief of Arab and Palestinian extremists that they have no option but to resort to violent means to air their grievances.

1437. Israeli raid. *China Daily* 7 Oct 1985 ; 4.

1438. Israeli terror. *Patriot* 15 Oct 1985 ; 6.

1439. Israeli terrorism. *Indian Express* 3 Oct 1985 ; 6.

1440. Israeli varsity flays West for terrorism. *Telegraph* (Calcutta) 12 Oct 1985 ; 3.

1441. Israeli warplanes hijack Libyan jet. *Hindustan Times* 5 Feb 1986 ; 1.

1442. Kriyama, T. : Terrorism at Tel Aviv airport and a 'new left' group in Japan. *Asian Survey* 13 (3) Mar 1973 ; 336-46.

1443. Lilienthal, Alfred M. : Israeli counter-terror. In *Zionist connection* : What price peace ? New York, Dodd, Mead, 1978. Chapter 10.

1444. Lustig, Robin : In territory of terror. *Tribune* 23 Jul 1985 ; 4.

1445. Massacre of Israeli Arabs : Kafr Kassem. In *WTAZIT* ; 37-38.

1446. Maurer, Marvin : TWA hijack-Television embraces terrorists. *Midstream* Nov 1985 ; 10-12.

1447. New Zionist outrage : *Patriot* 3 Oct 1985 ; 4.

1448. Not just a terrorist raid. *Times of India* 4 Oct 1985 ; 8.

1449. Peace making Vs. terrorism. *Egyptian Gazette*. 29 Sep 1985 ; 3.

1450. Salzmann, Ariel : Sharon and terror. *International Herald Tribune* 16 Oct 1986 ; 5.

1451. Smith, M. S. : Palestinian leaders face deportation. *International Viewpoint* 24 Feb 1986 ; 23-24.

1452. Starr, Joyce R : For Peres, the issue is terrorism. *International Herald Tribune* 14 Oct 1985 ; 4.

1453. State terrorism. *New Age* 6 Oct 1985 ; 2.

The State-sponsored Terrorism of Israel, backed by the United States, has chalked up yet another barbarous crime against humanity. Israel and its patron Ronald Reagan have been violating all accepted norms of international behaviour and ordinary human decency. The attack by Israeli warplanes—the F-15s supplied by the USA—on the PLO headquarters at Tunis, Tunisia, destroying the building and killing 156 civilians is one more proof that Israel which is one of the terror squads of USA in the West Asian and North African region is simply running amuck using its sheer military might against civilisation.

It is obvious that the Israeli maraunders aimed to kill PLO chief

Yasser Arafat. Only a last minute change of mind on the part of Arafat to go somewhere else instead of going directly to the PLO headquarters saved him. But what is ominous is that the Israelis obviously had inside information and therefore could plan not only a precise pinpoint attack but also time it to the dot. It is quite clear that some one is feeding the Israelis with Arafats detailed intinerary and other PLO moves.

The state-sponsored terrorism of Israel with the support of US began long ago. Israel's former prime minister Menachem Begin had described the Palestinian freedom fighters as "two-legged animals" and asserted that force was the only basis on which they could be dealt with.

Since then Israel has been carrying on most inhuman acts against the Palestinians and other countries which supported the PLO. The Israeli attack on the Iraqi nuclear facility, the invasion of Lebanon in 1982 and the perpetration of the horrible mass murder in Shabra and Shattila of Palestinian refugee camps, and now the attack on PLO headquarters are all parts of a continuing chain of depredation, want only demonstrating military might, violating the independence and sovereignty of nations. Not only has the PLO headquarters been attacked ; earlier the Israeli war planes also attacked the Bekka valley PLO men led by Abu Moussa. Fortunately, the Israeli bombs there fell on uninhabited areas without causing much damage.

Only the United States has called the Israeli terrorism "legitimate", which, of course, is understandable, for its President Ronald Reagan, only on July 8 this year, has declared some countries as "outlaws" and threatened to launch "acts of retaliation" against them and their leaders. On August 7 Reagan signed the socalled international security and development cooperation act authorising an expenditure of 25,400 million dollars for the 1986-87 fiscal years, of which as much as 7,500 million dollars have been allocated to Israel.

What the UN security council is now going to do about Israel's terrorism remains to be seen. But one thing is clear—Israel and its mentor USA are not interested in a peaceful solution of the West Asian, especially the Palestinian issue. Violence will now naturally be responded to by violence. PLO chief Arafat has already warned : "My people will respond to this official terrorism and to the Israeli military junata...We will continue our long hard march against terrorism and oppression."

In the southern tip of Africa, the apartheid regime of South Africa is behaving in the same manner as Israel, defying the world opinion. Synchronising with Israel's attack on Tunis, South African airforce carried out yet another attack on Angola. This is in addition to the reign of terror and killings unleashed against black people within the country. Like in case of Israel, the USA is the chief backer of South African racist regime.

The 18th annual meet of terrorist gangs—patronised by USA, Israel, South Africa and others—was held in Dallas, USA. President Reagan in a message to these cut throats declared : "I commend you all for your part in this noble cause. Our combined efforts are moving the tide of history toward world freedom". This is not surprising. He had earlier paid homage to nazi butchers' cemetry at Bitburg and last year his CIA organised a terrorist workshop at a BNITA camp where ring-leaders of terrorist gangs operating in Afghanistan, Nicaragua, Angola and several other countries were present. To the Dallas meet came Savimbi, the UNITA gang leader, whom the USA, Israel, South Africa and China are backing in a bid to get the present revolutionary government of Angola overthrown, and also to cut off support to the Namibian and ANC freedom fighters. The roots of international terrorism really stem from USA.

Yet another sort of terrorism has taken place in Beirut in which four Soviet dilpomats have been abducted by the guerillas of the socalled Islamic Liberation Organisation and one of the abducted Soviet diplomat has since been killed. This group is seeking a ceasefire in Lebanon's northern city of Tripoli where fighting is going on between Muslim fundamentalist Tawheed movement and the militias. The Soviet Union has nothing to do with it and has fallen a victim to the crossfire of vendetta. The act of abduction and the brutal killing are most reprehensible and must be strongly condemned. And what is worse, the Soviet embassy itself in Beirut has been threatened to be blown up.

A peaceful and urgent solution of the West Asian problem is imperative and all democratic governments must come out for ending the state-sponsored terrorism. Complete and immediate economic sanctions and cutting of all relations—political, military and economic—is the only way to bridle the brigands of Tel Aviv and Pretoria.

1454. State terrorism by Israel condemned. *Patriot* 6 Nov 1985 ; 7.

1455. Terror against Israeli Arabs. In *WTAZIT* ; 29-30.

1456. Terror against Jews. In *WTAZIT* ; 33-34.

1457. Web of the spider : Israelis design a sophisticated remote control robot for dealing with terrorist devices. *Industrial Times* (Bombay) 24 Jun 1985 ; 36.

1458. Which terrorist ? *Pioneer* 17 Feb 1986 ; 6.

Italy

1459. Drake, Richard : Red brigades and the Italy political tradition. In *TIE* ; 102-40.

Red Brigade violence did not diminish after the Moro affair. Indeed, during the early months of 1979 terrorist violence and beatings reached levels of intensity and ferocity not seen in Italy since the days when Balbo's blackshirts clubbed the opponents of Fascism into submission. There was a lull after that, as the Red Brigades suffered personal and tactical losses. Nevertheless, the dramatic kidnapping of the American general, James L. Dozier, on 17 December 1981, affirmed that the group was far from being moribund, contrary to the optimistic predictions of some analysts in 1980 and 1981. The general spectacular rescue, on 29 January 1982, was certainly a severe blow to the Red Brigades, but only a rash prophet would undertake now to say whether or not it was a decisive setback.

The boldness and tactical brilliance of the Moro kidnapping astonished the imprisoned Curcio as much as anyone, and he remarked at the time, 'we did not do things in such grand style'. His statement underscores the great change that occurred in the Red Brigades around 1975 ; until then the movement retained a romantic; post 'flower child' character, at least in comparison with its later actions. The murders began on a systematic basis only in 1976 when Curcio was in prison and others had taken hold of the movement's reins. The names of Semeria and Moretti have already been mentioned, but another name must be mentioned now : Antonio Negri, a political sincere professor at the University of Padua and, at the request of Louis Althusser, a guest lecturer and the Ecole Normale Superieure.

The precise nature of Negri's relationship with the Red Brigades is not completely clear. This question has been the subject of a complicated legal since Negri's arrest on 7 April 1979, and given the ponderous character of Italy's court system, in all probability the matter will not be fully resolved for some time. The legal point, however, is not the most important consideration here ; the intellectual one is, for whatever the nature of Negri's direct involvement in Red Brigade actions his indirect involvement, through his books, has been enormous.

In short, Negri provides a leftist rationale for sabotaging and terrorising the capitalist state. This rationale is revealed most unambiguously, in a short work entitled II domino eil sabotaggio : sul metodo marxista della trasformazione sociale (1978).

Negri begins his analysis by protesting that he does not want to give an anarchis interpretation of Leninism but at the same time he insists on necessary connection between 'destabilization and destructuralization' in all revolutionary Marxist thought, i.e. : 'To destabilize the regime cannot be a thing distinct from the project of destructuring the system'. For the authentic Marxist 'then, there cannot be any question about the strategy of tension' in the war against capitalism. The struggle between capital and labour has not, in its essentials, become any more complex or less implacable since Marx's time : what is good for the capitalist state is bad for the worker. To put this another way, the Communist revolutionary should no more compromise with this state than a God-fearing Christian should compromise with the Devil. Good lies on the side of those who work for the 'self-valorization' of the proletariat ; evil is done by anyone who directly or indirectly maintains 'the process of capitalist production', 'Self-valorization of the proletarian class,' he writes, 'is above all the destructuralization of the enemy totality.' There can be no compromise, no dialogue, no commerce of any kind with the representatives of the system. In the capitalist world, the state structures and the workers destructure ; that is all.

Naturally, Negri cannot find a single redeeming feature in the present day eurocommunist policies of the PCI. In eurocommunist he is overwhelmed by the stench of reformism, for 'reformism radically negates this sense of rapport between self-valorization and structuralization.' In his mind this is nothing other than the Evolutionary Socialism (1899) heresay of Eduard Bernstein and of all the other 'soft' Marxists who in their cowardly longing to avoid a fight end up as prisoners of the enemy system.

1460. Fiorillo, Ernesto : Terrorism in Italy : Analysis of a problem. *Terrorism* 2 (3-4) 1979 ; 261-70.

1461. Francesco Piperno case. (Documents). *Terrorism* 4 (1-4) 1980 ; 293-309.

1462. Henze, Paul : B. *Plot to kill the Pope.* New York, 1983.

1463. Italy : Threat assessment. *Terrorism* 2[(3-4) 1979 ; 283-96.

1464. Italy offers to help fight terrorism. *Hindustan Times* 27 Aug 1985 ; 5.

The seventh United Nations congress on prevention of crime and treatment of offenders opened here today with Italian Prime Minister Bettino Craxi offering co-operation to nations facing organised violence and terrorism.

The conference held after every five year is being attended by 1,500 delegates from 120 nations in this industrial heart of Italy. The Milano conference will address itself to arms and dry trafficking, computer crime, government corruption, terrorism, hijacking and torture. A host of ministers from Europe and other continents are also attending the meet.

Inaugurating this "biggest-ever" crime congress of the United Nations, Italian Prime Minister Bettino Craxi told a packed house that "we can give a beacon of hope to peoples and nation experiencing great social upheavels as a result of development."

Mr Craxi said the Italian society was virtually a proving ground for many of these problems. "It is a society that has undergone a profound and frequently a turbulent process of economic and social development in the course of which it has had to tackle many problems involving a radical adjustment of behaviour patterns, values and normative provisions."

"We have been confronted with a growth in organised crime, where the crime, the behaviour, the power, the systems of operation, cannot be attributed to individual malefactors but to an organisation run by a corporate type of "management" such as the Mafia and the Camorra, the barbarous tumours that affect our society."

Mr Craxi stated that "every Government in such a situation has met the temptation to establish special organisations to deal with the growth of specialised criminal organisations, by modifying legislation aimed at preventing and repressing associative offences and by integrating more closely the police forces and the organs of justice."

"Italian society has already overcome many assaults upon its democratic stability, whether from collective violence or political terrorism. The effective victory of the State over terrorism and many victories against organised crime have been achieved through the work of the police and judiciary, without exceptional dramas and without special or anomalous forms of intervention."

The Italian Minister for Justice Martinazzoli, who was elected president of the congress, said that the "power of law can be kept alive if the minds of crime are overcome." He said that crime through the world was increasing at two per cent rate annually, even though expenditure on law enforcement in some countries had doubled. The Minister said there was need for international cohesion and polling of *knowledge to overcome the transnational terrorist violence sweeping the* world.

1465. Lesson of Rome and Vienna. *Egyptian Gazette* 6 Jan 1986 ; 4.

It is of course understandable that there should be outrage throughout world, or at least those parts of it where people are free to express honest opinions, at the airport massacres in Rome and Vienna on December 27. But the all-important aspect of the situation is not to allow anger to result in counter-violence. Immediately following the attacks on passengers waiting at EIAI check-in desks at the two airports Israel said that it would punish the Palestine Liberation Organisation for the terrorist actions. The statement took no account of any investigation into the attacks, particularly whether the PLO was actually responsible or not. It has now emerged without any shadow of doubt that the PLO played no part, and interrogation of the surviving terrorists has revealed the responsibility of the Abu Nidal group of Palestinian dissidents who enjoy the support of Libya.

Mr. Yasser Arafat, the PLO Chairman, has himself denounced the airport attacks and has made it very clear that he seeks a political solution of the Palestinian problem. In an interview with "The Washington Post" published yesterday Mr. Arafat pointed out that more attacks could be expected until such a solution, providing for an end to Israeli occupation of Palestinian land and freedom of the Palestinians in their own country, became a reality. In coming out again in favour of peace on such a basis he blamed the United States for the deadlock in the peace process.

In the meantime, however, while Israel has now for once seemingly backed off from military retaliation, the US is making bellicose noises against Libya, has sent an aircraft carrier to water off the Libyan coast, has placed two other warships on alert and has prepared an analysis of targets which it could hit in Libya. This is inflammatory reaction and the Arab League has rightly accused the US of increasing tension in the Middle East and Mediterranean. What is above all necessary is to rule out any form of reprisals against Libya or other quarters and to answer terrorism with moves to push for peace while of course stepping up security. It is true that there may be more terrorist attacks until there is an overall Middle East settlement but retaliation is only going to lead to a circle of increasing violence and put back the peace process, perhaps indefinitely.

It surely cannot escape the knowledge of the United States and Israel that recent terrorist actions have been directed as much against the PLO as against Israel and those who may support it. But it should be the prime task of the US policy on the Middle East to spike the guns of people who think that "armed struggle" and terrorism are going to solve problems and give the Palestinians their rights. The only solution lies in a fair Middle East settlement which would give terrorists no excuse for further action.

The lesson of Rome and Vienna is therefore not to escalate violence but to accept the mainstream PLO at its face value and respond to its peace overtures. The main responsibility must lie with the US which can and should oblige Israel to talk peace.

1466. Phenomenological and dynamic aspects of terrorism in Italy. *Terrorism* 2 (3-4) 1979 ; 159-70.

1467. Pisano, V.S. : Red Brigades : A challenge to Italian democracy. *Conflict Studies* (London) (120) Jul 1980.

1468. Pisano, V.S. : Survey of terrorism of the Left in Italy, 1970-78. *Terrorism* 2 (3-4) 1979, 171-212.

1469. Possony, Stefan, T. : Giangiacomo Feltrincelli : the millionaire Dinamitero. *Terrorism* 2 (3-4) 1979 ; 213-30.

1470. Rieser, Vittorio : Struggle against capitalism in Italy : A political manifesto. In *New revolutionaries.* Ed. by Taraq Ali. London, Peter Owen, 1969 ; 202-18.

1471. Russell, Charles A. : Statistics Italy, 1978. *Terrorism* 2 (3-4) 1979 ; 297-300.

1472. Sheehan, Thomas : Italy behind the Skimask. *New York Review of Books* 16 Aug 1979.

1473. Silji, A. : *Never again without a rifle* : *the origins of Italian terrorism.* New York, Karz Publishers, 1979.

1474. Stobart, Janet : How Italy tamed the terrorism. *Pioneer* 22 Apr 1984 ; 6.

The terrorism that plagued Italian society for so long is a shadow of its former self. The danger once posed by the Red Brigades and allied movements, seemingly unbeatable, remains. But for many reasons not least the strong measures taken over a number of years by the authorities the attempts to create a revolution have failed. On that everyone is agreed—ministers, magistrates, police and jailed terrorists alike.

"The armed struggle is defeated, but not definitively," Red Brigade terrorist Prospero Gallinari wrote to an Italian provincial newspaper ; Gallinari, once an ultra-leftist leader, is serving a life sentence for his part as executioner in the kidnapping and killing in 1978 of Christian Democrat politician and ex-Prime Minister, Aldo Moro.

Interior Minister, Oscar Luigi Scalfaro, says a recent sudden increase in kidnappings for ransom is partially the work of residual groups of terrorists seeking means to finance their re-organisation. Most magistrates involved in trials over the last few years believe the reduction in terrorism will continue.

What began as a potential revolutionary movement under Red Brigades in the students unrest of 1968 gained sympathy at first from young leftists dissatisfied with the Italian Communist Party and other existing leftwing parties considered too conciliatory towards Italy's capitalist ruling parties.

A founding member of the Red Brigades, jailed since 1974, Alfred Buonavita, wrote a public letter to his terrorist comrade in the summer of 1980, announcing his disassociation from political violence : "A long period of reflection has led me to consider armed struggle as contrary to the interest of the proletariat......this is the season of darkness of political blindness, masked by machine guns and assassins."

Spontaneous disintegration of the terrorist movements is not without its problems. The government law which took advantage of offenders ready to collaborate lasted only a year, but its effects will last much longer as those who invoked it are now beginning to be released.

Public outcry on the release last November of two terrorists directly responsible for the killing of a young journalist in Milan in 1980, was immense. So were the threats from their former comrades, victims of their confessions.

Peci, whose confessions began before the law existed, was repaid by ex-comrades with the kidnapping and assassination of his innocent brother. The brutal reprisal was filmed and publicised as a warning to other would-be collaborators.

The government, too, is trying to restore some sort of normalcy after the draconian laws enforced between 1976 and 1979 when terrorism was at its height. Parliament has approved a new eight clause law modifying some of the present measures governing arrest and detention prior to trial.

Main changes are the reduction of maximum preventive detention from ten years eight months to six years and suspects can now be held for questioning before formal charges are made for ten days, not 40, unless the investigating magistrate has valid reasons for prolonging the period.

While judicial attention is turning more towards organised crime offenders, the government is wary of relaxing vigilance on terrorism especially as the signs are, say the authorities, that terrorist forces, or what is left of them may be availing themselves of help from the Mafia.

A recent police report says terrorists at large number about 400, many living outside Italy, mainly in France. About 150 are said to be re-organising activist groups, especially in Rome and Naples. Interior minister Scalfaro says : Terrorism is not finished. We have had without doubt much success in defeating it, but, I repeat, it is not over.

1475. Vigna, Piero Luigi : Italian responses. In *ITCR* ; 196-200.

Allow me first to describe in a cursory way the situation in Italy, where terrorism has recently met with some serious defeats.

* In Italy there exists terrorism of the extreme right and of the extreme left. The latter is, at present, the most active.

* Both these groups of terrorists aim at provoking an authoritarian transformation of the State.

* However, while this is the final aim of the extreme right terrorism, the extreme left aims, instead, at provoking the revolution through the authoritarian involution of the democratic state.

* Extreme leftist terrorists include, in addition to the Red Brigades, about another 150 groups.

* The Red Brigades have a clandestine structure, a rigid military one, inspired by Marxist-Leninist principles. The other groups are more fluid and have various ideologies based on "social needs." They

have a "Philosophy" that is similar to that of the American Weathermen.

* There are proven international connections among terrorist groups of the same political camp, and occasionally even of opposing camps. Here are a few examples drawn from my personal experience :

— Judge Occorsio was killed in Rome in 1976 by a group of the extreme right, with an automatic Ingram gun, which had been sold to the Madrid police, a city where some extreme rightist activists were taking refuge.

— The Palestinian Arab terrorist movements have established contacts with Italian groups of the extreme right.

— Mario Tuti, an extreme right terrorist, who killed two policemen near Florence in 1975 and who had carried out sabotage operations against the railway system, wrote in his diary that he had received from Libya.

— Judge Coco, Judge Palma, and the Honorable Aldo Moro, who were murdered by the extreme left terrorists of the Red Brigades, were all killed with Skorpion automatic guns of Soviet make. The Red Brigades are conclusively linked with the Rote Arme Fraktion.

— Last year, a terrorist of the extreme left, arrested near Florence, had on him a map with directions to reach a Lebanese training camp near Baalbek, Lebanon.

All this gives some idea of the gravity and nature of the problem.

1476. Weinberg, Leonard : Patterns of neo-Fascist, Violence in Italian politics. *Terrorism* 2 (3-4) 1979 ; 231-60.

1477. Wilson, Derek : Italy sees itself in front line. *Amrita Bazar Patrika* 1 May 1986 ; 6.

1478. Zoppo, Ciro E. : Never again without a rifle. *Terrorism* 2 (3-4) 1979 ; 271-82.

Japan

1479. Apple, R.W. : Genesis of Tokyo statement on terrorism. *International Herald Tribune* 7 May 1986 ; 7.

1480. Bomb attack on Hirohito palace (by Red Army Guerillas). *Newstime* 26 Mar 1986 ; 11.

1481. Burgess, John : 5 rockets fire at site of Summit (of 7 big nations) but no one is injured as shells miss. Leaders plan statement on terrorism. *International Herald Tribune* 5 May 1986 ; 1 : 6.

1482. Haberman, Clyde. Japan girds for violent summit : Tokyo awash with police over threats by terrorists. *International Herald Tribune* 22 Apr 1986 ; 5.

1483. Hane, Mikiso : *Peasants, rebels and outcastes : the underside of modern Japan.* London, Scholar Press, 1982.

1484. Japan : Dismay over Israeli action. (the release of a Japanese Red Army terrorist). *International Meridian* (New Delhi) Oct. 1985 ; 47-48.

The release of Japanese Red Army terrorist from an Israeli jail has invited strong official protests from Tokyo without avail.

The release of Kozo Okamoto, who took part in the 1972 massacre at Tel Avivi's Lord Airport, was the only Red Army guerilla known to be jailed abroad though nine of his colleagues including his elder brother, Takeshi, have lived in exile in North Korea since their hijacking, of a JAL flight from Tokyo to Pyongyang in 1970. As of now, as many as 17 Red Army terrorists are wanted by Tokyo but the latter have no idea about their whereabouts. "They are mightly potential threat", said an official spokesman in Tokyo.

Okamoto, who with two other Red Army terrorists used Czech VZ-58 machine-guns and grenades to kill 26 civilians and wound another 70 at Lod Airport, was freed on 20 May in a swap of three Israeli soldiers for 1,154 Palestinian guerillas. Okamoto, now aged 37, was the sole survivor of the attack : one guerilla was caught in the indiscriminate fire of his colleagues and the other put a grenade to his chest.

Okamoto has never repented the crime, and felt insulted when an Israeli court denied his request to be executed, instead sentencing him to life imprisonment. He was tricked into confessing with an offer of a pistol and a single bullet with which to take his life.

On 16 May the Japanese Government received a report that Okamoto would be among the guerillas in the controversial exchange to be conducted in Geneva. On the same day, Japan sought confirmation from the Israeli authorities, and urged Israel to reconsider Okamoto's inclusion in the swap. In the end the Japanese appeared to have accepted Israel's explanation that Okamoto's release was unavoidable, given that the Syrian backed Palestinian group, with which the swap was negotiated, had listed him as a high priority candidate.

After the release, Foreign Minister Shintaro Abe expressed Japan's regret at the decision, and the National Police Agency put out a "blue notice" through the Paris-based interpol in the hope of obtaining information of Okamoto's subsequent movements. But Foreign Ministry officials do not expect the notice to Interpol will produce immediate results. Okamoto arrived in Libiya to a hero's welcome, and, after resting, is expected to join other Red Army terrorists in Syria and possibly Lebanon. None of those countries is known to volunteer information on guerillas fighting for the Palestinian cause.

Nobuo Miyamoto, a Foreign Ministry official dealing with international terrorism, gives three reasons for Tokyo's displeasure at the Israeli Action. First, it would leave an international terrorist at large. Secondly, it could boost the morale of the Red Army and other international terrorists. Thirdly, it brought into question the corrrect role of the International Red Cross ; which negotiated the prisoner swap.

The Japanese Government has twice totally succumbed to the demands of the Red Army, releasing five Japanese terrorists from Jail inside Japan when a Red Army squad took hostages within the United States and Swedish embassies in Kuala Lumpur in 1975, and a further six in the 1977 hijacking of a JAL flight between Bombay and Dhakka. Such a record, it may be argued, weakens Tokyo's case against Israel's decision to set Okamoto free.

In the Dhakka incident, the Japanese Government also agreed to a ransom of US $6 million for the safety of 151 passengers and crew, and provided the terrorists with a number of blank passports. At the time, Japan has no fixed policy on terrorist acts nor even an anti-hijacking legislation, which has since been enacted. There was, however, the precedent of the West German Government yielding to the demand for US $5 million by a squad of the Popular Front for the Liberation of Palestine which hijacked a Lufthansa Boeing jet in 1972.

Japan's decisions in those incidents and its concern for the whereabouts of Okamoto, even 15 years after the crime, are perhaps best explained by the Japanese Government's reasoning that it knows the minds of its fanatical radicals better than any non-Japanese. The officials knew that the terrorists, who were capable of the most brutal of tortures and did not blink once at the prospect of suicide, were not bluffing and that prolonged negotiations would lead to certain death for most, and perhaps all, of the hostages at stake.

Perhaps the Red Army's most vicious work was witnessed at a mountain villa in Japan, in 1872, where members "purged" at least 12 fellow radicals who disagreed with them, binding them with ropes, stabbing them with knives and icepicks, choking and beating them, and then leaving them to die outside in the icy cold. It is against a background of terrorist acts such as this that Japanese officials wonder where Okamoto might be.

1485. Kuriyama, Y. : Terrorism at Tel Aviv Airport and a "New Left" group in Japan. *Asian Survey* 13, Mar 1973.

1486. Naoi, Takeo : Japan after the assassination. *New Leader* 43, 7 Nov 1960 ; 8-9.

1487. 'Red Army' killer freed by Israelis. *Japan Times Weekly* 8 Jun 1985 ; 1.

1488. Rockets hit Tokyo palace and embassy. *China Daily* 26 Mar 1986 ; 1.

1489. Roscoe, Bruce : Japan : The Red Army threat. *Far Eastern Economic Review* 6 Jun 1985 ; 21.

1490. Saksena, N.S. : Very strict control in Japan and U.K. In *THF* ; 219-20.

1491. Sase, Masamori : Fighting back against terrorism. *Look Japan* 10 Sep 1986 ; 28.

1492. Taylor, Robert W. and Byong-sub Kim. Violence and change in post-industrial societies : Student protest in America and Japan in the 1960s. In *ITCW* ; 204-22.

The impact of technology on society has produced a new stage of socio-economic development. In advanced technological societies, the industrial revolution is being replaced by what a group of scholars call "postindustrial society." As preindustrial society was based on the extraction of primary resources from nature, and industrial society was organized around nature fabricated for the efficient production of goods, postindustrial society depends upon the large-scale transmission of knowledge between individuals through cybernetic processes, new telecommunications, and jet transport. The postindustrial society is an analytical construct, not a picture of any specific or concrete society. It is an ideal-type to denote a social framework that identifies a new form of social structure which has a particular set of tendencies ; codification of theoretical knowledge as sources of innovations, creation, and productive force ; a new character of work which is focused on services among individual persons rather than production of goods and the change of scale in institutions created by the role of technology.

Thus, in the postindustrial society, a new stratification is structured by a service economy, a technologically based industry, and the rise of new technical elites based on codified knowledge. According to sociologist Daniel Bell, the United States, Japan, western Europe, and the Soviet Union will take on such aspects of postindustrial society by the end of the century, and they have to confront the management of these new dimensions. Some scholars stress the advent of the "technetronic age" where society is shaped culturally, socially, and economically by the impact of technology and electronics, and by the bureaucratically structured process of cybernetic gadgetry. As technological change profoundly alters the nature and centrality of industrial activity as a major social institution, capital and heavy industry will no longer generate wealth and productive force. Instead, in the future society, the codification of theoretical knowledge obtained through technetronic, cybernetic processes which are transformed into many systematized forms of physical and social activities becomes the primary productive force and wealth generator.

Critics of the concept argue that postindustrial society is a result of transitional historical forces that can be traced back over a hundred-year span. Postindustrialism, according to their notion, is merely an advanced stage of industrialism and problems imputed to be post-industrial are also endemic to capitalist societies. While we recognize that some conceptual ambiguities exist, as the critics point out, we maintain that the conceptual construct of the postindustrial society is a useful analytical scheme, and as an ideal-type it presents a particular set of tendencies which emerge in advanced technological societies. This discussion, therefore, does not deal with the specific historical details of change in advanced industrial societies, but attempts to synthesize the three tendencies of social structure noted above which emerge in postindustrial society in order to analyze violence and functions of conflict in such a societal transformation.

The codification of theoretical knowledge is the growth of the science-based industries of computers, electronics, telecommunications, and optics which were mostly developed after World War II. The utilization of intellectual technology in the form of cybernetics, electronic data retrieval systems, and systems research produce an exponential growth in knowledge. As industrial society was organized around technological efficiency in the production of goods, post-industrial society focuses upon knowledge accumulation and dissemination.

Due to their centrality to theoretical knowledge, the university and the "think tank" such as the Rand Corporation and Brookings Institute in the United States become key institutions. Knowledge is intrinsic to power relations in postindustrial society, and it becomes the controlling factor in decision-making processes, as the technocratic elite administers and manipulates this knowledge.

1493. Tsuzuki, C. : Anarchism in Japan. *Government and Opposition* 5(4) Aug 1970 ; 501-22.

1494. Yamamoto, Soji : Japanese enactment for the suppression of unlawful seizure of aircraft and international law. *Japanese Annual of International Law* 15, 1971.

1495. Yamane, Hiroko. Will Japan do more than talk tough on terror? *International Herald Tribune* 24-25 May 1986 ; 4.

Jordan

1496. Attacks on Jordan. In *WTAZIT* ; 70-71.

1497. Malawer, Stuart S. : United States foreign policy and international law : The Jordanian civil war and air piracy. *International Problems* 10, 1971.

Kampuchea

1498. Kiljunen, Kimmo *ed.* : *Kampuchea : Decade of genocide : Report of a Finnish Inquiry Commission.* Bath, Pitman Press, 1984.

1499. Raghavan, Sudha : Kampuchea factor and nonalignment. *Patriot* 16 Apr 1986 ; 4.

1500. Saksena, N.S. : History of capsule form-scale of terror. In *THF* ; 100-2.

1501. Shubin, Valentin : *History condemns genocide conducted under Pol Pot.* Moscow, Novosti, 1985, pp. 56.

Kenya

1502. Karinki, Josiah : *Man Man detainee* London, 1963.

Koreas

1503. Saksena, N.S. : Korean war used to kill opponents. In *THF* ; 97.

1504. State Violence in South Korea. *New Age* 1 Jun 1986 ; 15.

Kuwait

1505. Kuwait blasts. *Patriot* 16 Dec 1983 ; 4.

1506. Pro-Iran terrorists arrested in Kuwait. *Baghdad Observer* 19 Dec 1983.

Ten persons belonged to the pro-Iranian al-Da'wa party were arrested, the Kuwaiti Minister of State for Cabinet Affairs, Abdul Aziz Hussein said here today.

He added, following a Kuwait Cabinet meeting, that all those arrested had admitted involvement in the bomb blasts carried out in Kuwait last Monday.

The Kuwaiti News Agency quoted the Minister as saying that Kuwaiti authorities had seized a number of weapons and bombs smuggled into Kuwait by sea, referring to Iran.

It is to be mentioned that the reactionary al-Da'wa party has taken from Iran a place to train its members and supply them with weapons to be used for committing terrorist acts in the neighbouring countries.

The Kuwaiti authorities recently declared the arrest of a number of Iranian infiltraters came to Kuwait by sea.

Half a dozen bombs went off in a 90-minute period in Kuwait last Monday, with the United States and French Embassies among the targets. At least five people died at the U.S. embassy, including the driver of the bomb truck, and one in a separate bomb attack at Kuwait Airport.

The Kuwait government identified the dead driver of the suicide truck as a pro-Iranian agent who belonged to the banned "Da'wa" party.

The agency quoted the Minister as saying one more suspect wanted in connection with the bombings was still at large.

In 1981, an Iranian-backed plot was discovered by Bahraini authorities. The conspirators were trained on various types of arms inside Iran by Khomeini's guards. Many Iranian saboteaurs were arrested.

The plot was planned to take place during Bahrain's National Day and to start with the assassination of senior Bahraini officials and the occupation of vital installations in the capital.

Bahraini government angrily reacted and set a strong-worded protest to the Iranian regime and summoned the Iranian Ambassador to Bahrain and handed him over a protest.

In North Yemen, in 1981, authorities there confiscated leaflets circulated by Iranian Charge d'Affaires in North Yemen calling for the overthrow of the government and inciting sectarian strife in the country. North Yemen government expelled the Iranian Charge d'Affaires for carrying out illegitimate acts.

On October 14, Indonesian authorities discovered an Iranian-backed onspiracy to overthrow the government of Indonesia.

Reliable sources in Jakarta said that the conspiracy's ring leader was a former member of an Iranian terrorist organisation. Indonesia's army intelligence said that the plot was discovered in the central Indonesian island of Java.

Quoting informed sources in the Indonesian intelligence, the Indonesian newspaper, Sinar Harapan said that five people were arrested and thousands of leaflets were confiscated from the Iranian Embassy in Indonesia.

Indonesian Foreign Minister expressed concern over the acts of an "Islamic country" to incite sectarian strife in the Islamic countries. Informed sources said that the Foreign Minister meant the Iranian regime.

On November 10, Lebanon broke diplomatic relations with Iran, an official source said.

The decision was made by the cabinet at its weekly session, the source said. There was however no official announcement after the cabinet meeting.

Relations between Beirut and Teheran have been strained since an estimated 400 Khomeini's guards came to eastern Lebanon last June.

Iranian-Lebanese ties suffered further after suspicion of Iranian involvement in bomb attacks against U.S. marines and French troops in Lebanon.

On November 14, press sources disclosed that the embassies of the Iranian and Libyan regimes in Vienna were financing extremists in Yugoslavia to overthrow the government.

The Austrian newspaper, Karntner Tageszeitung said that the two regimes' embassies put all their potential at the disposal of the Yugoslav extremists by exploiting their diplomatic status.

The Yugoslav authorities informed Austria of a Yugoslav organisation headed by a Yugoslav refugee in Vienna and financed by the Libyan and the Iranian embassies, aiming at inciting strife in Yugoslavia and spreading anarchy.

The paper added that the Yogoslav authorities were able to get this information following the trial of a number of extremists in the Yogoslav city of Sarajevo who admitted that they were working according to certain instructions by the Iranian regime.

The paper concluded that security authorities in Yugoslavia and Austria were conducting intensified contacts to investigate and know the organisation's members and its activities inside Austria.

1507. Terrorists trying to wreck Kuwait's Security. *Iraq* 1 Aug 1985; 18-19.

Iraqi Ambassador in Kuwait, Abdul Jabbar Omar, told Kuwait's Deputy Prime Minister, Sheikh Sabah Al-Ahmed Al-Sabah who received him on July 13 that Iraq denounces the blasts and reaffirms support for Kuwait.

Agents of Khomeini regime committed other terrorist acts in some Arab capitals.

On May 18 two explosions occurred in Riyadh, Saudi Arabia causing the death of one person and injuring three. An anonymous caller in Beirut told western media there that "Islamic Jihad" cells carried out the subversive acts.

Several people were also killed when a few fundamentalists staged mob crimes at "Al-Hasa" area towards the end of 1979 and the beginning of 1981.

Over 80 fundamentalists were arrested in Bahrein in 1981 involved in a coup attempt. They were trying to install a regime similar to that in Teheran.

Fundamentalists acting on instruction from Teheran rulers performed several subversive acts in other Arab capitals, namely, Amman, Beirut and Baghdad.

In Baghdad, Al-Da'wa members tried to kill Deputy Premier

Mr. Tareq Aziz when he was attending an international student gathering in the Spring of 1980. Their bomb killed a few innocent students. The perpetrators persisted in their crime and tried to murder others on the following day during a funeral procession of the martyrs. The criminals were unable to escape their destiny, they were killed instantly.

Al-Da'wa or so-called Islamic Jihad or Hezballah (party of God) or any other group carrying similar names are known of their close contacts with Khomeini regime.

According to many observers the terrorist group members are being trained and indoctrinated by Teheran rulers in a special camp near the capital as part of their plan to export so-called "Islamic revolution" forgetting that terrorism does not pay.

"Such incidents will not dissuade me or Kuwait from continuing to work for the prosperity of our people as well as the Arab and Islamic nation", Sheikh Jaber al-Sabah, the Emir of Kuwait told his people when the unsuccessful attempt on his life was made.

Observers also recalled that a terrorist group hijacked a Kuwait airliner to Teheran on December 4 last year while on a regular flight from Kuwait to Karachi enroute Dubai and threatened to blow up the plane with its 161 passengers and crew unless Kuwait releases the criminals. The skyjackers killed a few hostages and finally surrendered to the Iranian authorities. The Iranian rulers surrendered to the Iranian authorities. The Iranian rulers never bothered themselves to try the skyjackers who are punished by death in all countries of the world, according to an international agreement signed by the UN members.

At the same time, the terrorist group "Islamic Jihad" said it is holding four Americans and two Frenchmen in Lebanon and will free them only when Kuwait releases the prisoners.

Kuwaiti officials have stressed they are not ready to surrender to the terrorist demands. Furthermore, Iraq has reiterated that Kuwait's security is part of its own and anything happens there affects it.

Several terrorist groups in Europe and Asia whether called Badre-Meinhov or the Red Japanese Army attempted to realise their narrow goals by adopting same methods, i.e., terrorising senior officials, kidnapping or killing others but finally their members ended in jails and their groups disappeared.

Although there was no official indication to the perpetrators of the two Kuwait blasts, no doubt the only side which is known of harbouring terrorists and encouraging them to carry out such vicious crimes is Khomeini regime.

"What can we say to these terrorists who, instead of mounting suicidal attacks on Israeli enemy targets, are murdering innocent civilians, men, women and children," one Kuwaiti newspaper said in an editorial. "Is that your brand of holy war ? Kuwait will never bend to your blackmail and intimidation," the paper added.

1508. Threat to Kuwait of further terrorist, attacks. *Times of India* 24 Jan 1984.

1509. Wallace, Charles ? Terrorist attacks bring siege mentality to Kuwait. *International Herald Tribune* 15 Aug 1985 ; 4.

Laos

1510. Dommen, Arthur J. : Kong Le's conp d'etat. In *Loas* ; Bouldern, Westview Press, 1985 ; 63-66.

Latin America

1511. Alsina, Geronimo : War and the Tupamaros. *Bulletin Tricontinental* Aug 1972.

1512. Anderson, Thomas, P. : Ambiguities of political terrorism in Central America. *Terrorism* 4 (1-4) 1980 ; 267-76.

1513. Anderson, Thomas P. : Political violence and cultural patterns in Central America. In *ITCW* ; 153-59.

One aspect of violence which is very Central American is the machete culture of the area. There is a surprisingly complete and technical vocabulary concerning the types and usages of machetes. In lands which raise maize, cane, and fruits, the machete is a very useful tool. But is more than that. The highly decorated scabbards and the loving care of the blades would tell you that this was primarily a weapon, even if you had never witnessed a Saturday brawal in a rural village. It is the mark of the lower classes that they carry these weapons, just as it is the mark of the upper classes that most men carry pistols. To a Central American peasant the machete is closely tied up with his manhood and his honor. During the Communist uprising of 1932, the participants largely disdained guns in favour of their familiar and beloved weapons. Even today, the Guardia in El Salvador carry the machete rather than the billy-club, along with automatic rifles.

In short, this is an armed society. Such societies, whether in the Middle Ages or today, are noted for their excessive politeness in everyday address with acquaintances and strangers. Theodore Roosevelt noted the same thing in the 1880s among his cowboys, and correctly remarks that excessive politeness is always the rule where every man is armed.

A machete society, by its very nature, lends itself to machetisomo which William S. Stokes characterizes as "a crude, primitive mobilizing violence primarily in local, rural politics but occasionally in national urban areas as well." And, as he points out, "Whoever can command the authority represented by the machete in rural areas possesses political power of an important nature and automatically constitutes a factor to be reckoned with in the affairs of government." Both Maximiliano Hernandez Martinez in El Salvador and his rival Jorge Ubico in Guatemala were masters of exploiting the rural, machete-wielding populace.

Too often, however, sociologists and political scientists tend to focus on violence and terrorism as if they were exclusively lower-class manifestations, linked to the rural village backwaters and to the shanty towns of the cities. In reality, the present wave of Marxist terrorist in Central America is actually a product of the universities and the colegios, a violence perpetrated in the name of the masses, but not necessarily always implicating them.

The educationasl system of any culture is a microcosm of the society itself. It is hardly surprising that the Central American educational establishments, surrounded by a world which legitimizes the violent response to social and political situations, takes on itself the aspect of a warfare society. The same sort of politicization that Hugh Thomas has discussed in regard to the University of Habana in the 1930s and 1940s has gone on in the Central American universities. A university strike, attended with considerable violence, was a key factor in the overthrow of General Martinez in El Salvador, and similar incidents marked the downfall of Ubico in Guatemala and that of many later leaders. The degree in which institutions of higher learning serve as breeding grounds for gunmen suggests that the privileged student is not as remote from the national life as he might like to think. It is not even unheard of for university intellecturals such as Abel Guenca in El Salvador to end up as leaders of a machete-wielding uprising.

The politics of the university community tend to more extremes than that of the society as a whole. So the combination arises of a cultural tradition of violence, in which the attitudes of the elite are only slightly removed from those of the masses, coupled with a strong revolutionary idealism. When one adds to this the fact that the intellectual demands of Central American universities are often not very great, and the prospects of a career arising out of one's education per se rather slim, one sees the potential for violence becoming more of an academic way of life than the taking of examinations.

So far, this paper has focused on various aspects of Ladino society; the macho character of both the poor, machete-carrying peasant and that of the pistol-packing university student. At this point it might be well to remember that one of the distinctive features of society in part of Central America is the existence of a relatively separate Indian society. In Guatemala, the various Maya peoples make up more than half of the population, and while El Salvador and Honduras are Mestizo nations, there remain, especially in the former, isolated Indian communities, such as the Izalco region's Pipil.

In communities among the Indians where social institutions like the leadership of the cacique and the brotherhood of the cofradia remain intact, there appears to be less violence and tension than in communities which follow the Ladino patterns of culture. Age-old bonds of cooperation and the still prevailing pre-Hispanic cults maintain a civility not found in the surrounding world. This is not to say that such peoples are not potential participants of left-wing revolutionary movements.

1514. Andreski, Stanislav : *Parasitism and subversion : the case of Latin America*. New York, Panthson, 1967.

1515. Carey, Robert G. : Latin America. In *Peace Corps*. New York, 1970 ; 123-35.

1516. Davis, Jack : *Political violence in Latin America*, London, 1972.

1517. Debray, Regis : Latin America ; the long march. *New Left Review* 33 Sep-Oct 1965.

1518. Debray, Regis : *Revolution in the revolution? Armed struggle and political struggle in Latin America*. New York, Grove Press, 1967.

1519. Dharte, Moises De Jesus Ulloa : Terrorism in Central America. *Terrorism* 7 (1) 1984 ; 57-62.

1520. Duff, Ernest A. and John F. McCamant : *Violence and repression in Latin America*. New York, Free Press, 1976.

1521. George, Andrew : How the U.S. got Che. *True* Apr 1969.

1522. Gott, Richard : *Guerrilla moven ents in Latin Americo* London, Nelson, 1970.

1523. Halperin, Ernst : *National liberation movements in Latin America.* Cambridge, MIT, 1969; p. 85.

1524. Halperin, Ernst : *Peaceful and the violent road : A Latin American debate.* Cambridge, MIT, 1965 ; p. 22.

1525. Halperin, Ernst : *Terrorism in Latin America*, Baverly Hills, Sage, 1976.

1526. Hodges. Donald C. : *Legacy of the Guevara : A documentary study.* London, Thames & Hudson, 1977, p. 216.

1527. Kohn, James and John Litt : *Urban guerrillia warfare in Latin America.* Cambridge, 1974.

1528. Lamberg, Robert F. : Latin America's urban guerrillas. *Swiss Review of World Affairs* 20 (3) 1970 ; 18-19.

1529. Lavretsky, I. : *Ernesto Che Guevara.* Moscow, Progress Publishers, 1977. Pp. 308.

1530. Mansilla, H.C.F. : On some psychological and cultural aspects of Latin American guerrilla warfare. In *UG* : 139-41.

Guerilla movements always pretend to have made a careful Marxist class analysis before beginning with fighting actions. Writings and other available material display the same Manichean and simplistic view about the class structure supposed to exist in every Latin American country. They assume the existence of two main classes only : the feudal-agrarian aristocracy together with some representatives of the monopolistic industry on the one hand and the very poor paseantry together with some small urban proletarian sectors on the other. This dualistic conception of class structure allows no place for a nation, rather autonomous bourgeoisie, or for middle class sectors and for landowning middle and small peasantry. It has been assumed that the failure of the rural guerilla movements in Latin American is due to this over-simplification of the social structure and to an extreme one-sided strategy oriented towards this dualistic scheme. The urban guerilla movements have only produced a shift within the over simplification from the rural to the town scene. They deny also the relevance of middle class sectors in the urban areas, assume a non-existent extreme polarization of income levels, neglect the reformist attitudes of the working masses and trade unions, and suppose a non-existent extreme polarization of income levels, neglect the reformist attitudes of the working masses and trade unions, and suppose a non-existent solidarity of the working classes towards urban guerillas.

This dualistic and undifferentiated conception of society has led the urban as well as the rural guerilla movements to stress the importance of technical-military matters. Political issues have been subordinated to military-strategic tasks. It is well known that this subordination leads to an extreme militarization and technicalization of the so-called liberation struggle and it becomes therefore an affair separated from the daily problems and daily hopes of the working masses. It is not surprising that the Latin American population did not cooperate too much with all the guerilla movements after the Cuban experience, for the rural and urban masses of the working classes did not identify themselves with armed movements which were mainly concerned with the technical perfection and the presumed omnipotence or a certain fighting system. The theories, of Regis Debray on rural guerilla and of Carols Marighela on urban guerilla are only the intellectual expression of the widely practised ways of guerilla warfare. It is possible to blame this technical onesideness on the failure of the guerilla movements, at least to a very important extent. This onesidedness displays also a very clear correlation with a voluntaristic and activistic tendency, which is peculiar to the elitist, pettybourgeoise extremist movements. These characteristics have also been criticized by some guerilla leaders who have published their experiences under a selfcritical intention : Jaime Arenas of the Columbian ELN, Hector Bejar of the Peruvian ELN and Humberto Vazquez-Viana of the Bolivian ELN. According to them there was an extremely high proportion of student and professionals of middle and upper class background in the movements especially at all commanding levels. This applies to the Uruguayan and Argentine urban guerilla groups too. The elitist background correlates with the typical conspirative, dogmatic and paternalistic mentality of all socialist inspired guerillas. The paternalistic attitude can be found in their behaviour towards the peasantry. The peasants were allowed to support and supply the guerilla forces, not, however, to influence the strategy of the armed struggle. Like the Leninist party conception, the guerilla is a movement for the masses but not by the masses themselves. The conspirative and elitist tendency leads to an extremely hierarchical structure within the movements, whose commanding level has very large powers and privileges at its disposal. These negative aspects have been largely amplified in Latin America by the permanent validity of some aspects of the Spanish-Creole tradition : the cult of the hero, of the heroic death and of masculine honour. Guevara and Debray have stressed the importance of daily heroism, of correct, honourable masculine behaviour and, above all presumed absolute truth of the own mission. The dogmatic conception of the only and unique truth, namely the own one, avoids a critical appraisal of errors and the thinking and implementation of alternatives ; this aspect makes any guerilla movements inflexible and contributes to the probable isolation of the revolutionary elite from the masses. Although dogmatism they are not very likely to renounce it, for dogmatism satisfies in revolutionary and religious movements some indispensable moral, ideological and psychological necessities.

1531. Mercier, Vega, Luis : *Guerrillas in Latin America : the techniques of the counter-state*, London, Pall Mall, 1969.

1532. Mieres, Francisco : Lessons of October and contemporary revolutionary movements in Latin America. *World Marxist Review* (Toronto) 10 (11) 1961 ; 77-81.

1533. Needler, M.C. :*Political development in Latin America : Instability, violence and evolutionary change*. New York, Random House, 1968.

1534. Parry, Albert : Wanton romantics : Guevara, Debray, Marighella. In *Terrorism* New York, 1976 ; 244-60.

1535. Petras, James : New forms of struggle in Latin America. *New Politics* 6 (1) 1967 ; 80-94 ; 6 (2) 1967 ; 58-72.

1536. Reif, Linda L. : Women in Latin American guerilla movements. A comparative perspective. *Comparative Politics*. 18 (2) Jan 1986 ; 147-70.

1537. Russell, Charles A. : Latin America : Regional review. *Terrorism* 4 (1-4) 1980 ; 277-92.

1538. Simon, S. Fanny : Anarchism and anarcho-syndicalism in South America. *Hispanic American Historical Review* 26, Feb 1946 ; 38-59.

1539. Sloan, John W. : Political terrorism in Latin America : A critical analysis. In *POT* ; 301-22.

The problem for Latin American revolutionaries is to make successful revolutions. According to their Marxist analyses of objective conditions—the disparity between the rich and the many poor, the unemployment and underemployment, the exploitation of the peasant, and the economic and political dominance of the United States—each of the Latin American states is ripe for revolution. The dilemma is in creating the subjective conditions for fomenting revolution. Most young revolutionaries have lost faith in the orthodox Latin American Communist parties, who are accused of waiting for the Godot of a progressive national bourgeoisie that will fulfill its historic mission of industrializing in Latin America so that a proletarian revolution can take place. The revolutionaries want the revolution now.

There are two broad streams of revolutionary thought in Latin American, one urging that the revolution should be initiated in the countryside, the other that the principal battleground should be in the cities. Both rural and urban guerrillas agree that the principal enemies of the revolution are U. S. imperialism, the landowners, and the wealthy bourgeoisie. In the words of a Peruvian revolutionary group. "We realize that the greatest scourge of the peoples of the earth is North American imperialism, and that our country's wealthy bourgeoisie and landowners debase themselves in the slavish pursuit of its interests and are there to exploit the people and to keep them in a state of poverty and backwardness.

Both revolutionary groups recruit mainly from the young, especially the university populations. In Debray's words, "there is a close tie between biology and ideology....An elderly man ...... will not easily adjust himself to the mountains nor– though this is less so—to underground activity in the cities. In addition to the moral factor—conviction—physical fitness is the most basic of all skills needed for waging guerrilla war...." The primary recruiting centers for guerrillas are the university centers of Bogota, Buenos Aires, Lima, Mexico City, and Montevideo. With the exception of Bolivian tin miners, the exploited groups of peasants and workers have generally not been attracted to participate in the guerrilla cause.

Both revolutionary groups also agree that fundamental social change can be brought about only by armed revolution. There cannot be any alliances with the progressive bourgeoisie, as advocated by the Communist parties, because there is no progressive bourgeoisie. They believe that the bourgeoisie is aligned with the traditional oligarchy because of its fear of socialism. The perspective of the revolutionaries is a stark dichotomy : either death (physical or spiritual) under the enforcement terror of colonial fascism or life under a liberating socialist revolution. A Venezuelan revolutionary explains :

> To create a world where the peasants, workers, students and the people in general can share in material benefits and advantages, requires war. This is not because the revolutionaries have so

decreed it, but because the reactionaries, the rich, and those who are bolstered by North American imperialism force the people and the revolutionary armies to wage this war and induce the people to take up arms.

Similarly, a Guatemalan revolutionary writes, "They (the Guatemalan Communist party) do not see that armed struggle is the highest form of political struggle, and that our motto of 'to conquer or die for Guatemala' is not a juvenile or leftist boast."

The rhetoric, morality, and behaviour of the terrorists suggest that they share certain traits of what Daly calls the revolutionary. personality. According to Daly, "The distinctive characteristic of the revolutionary is that he apparently combines extreme dogmatism with extreme cynicism and extreme populism with extreme elitism—that he appears to be a genguine combination of zealo and power-hungry butcher."

The agitational terrorist is continually trying to justify (for others and possibly himself) the use of antihumanistic means to attain humanistic ends.

1540. Social and cultural roots of political violence in Central America. *Aggressive Behavior* 2, 1976 ; 249-55.

1541. Tarasov, K and V Zubenko : *CIA in Latin America.* Moscow, Progressive Publishers, 1985.

1542. Terrorism takes left turn. *International Herald Tribune* 16 Sep 1985 ; 6.

Lebanon

1543. Attacks on Lebanon. In *WTAZIT* ; 72-73.

1544. Hostage to terror. *National Herald* (New Delhi) 2 Jul 1985 ; 5.

1545. Ominous development. *Free Press Journal* 25 Oct 1983 ; 4.

Terrorists have struck again in Lebanon, this time with unprecedented ferocity. American Marines and French troops stationed in Beirut as part of the UN peace-keeping force have been the targets of repeated sniper attacks. But nothing like the latest bomb blasts that wrecked the camps of the Marines and French forces in Lebanon's embattled capital have occurred before. According to Washington's own version, more than 160 Americans were killed while the French lost some 60 of their men in the blasts. The devastating explosions apparently were the handiwork of death squads deployed by the same mysterious organisation as the tactics adopted by them at the two bases were almost identical. By any reckoning, the-death dealing assault was well planned and executed with utmost precision.

Without question, this ominous development throws bleeding Lebanon into a deeper mire. It has at once smashed whatever faint hope there was of a negotiated settlement between the warring factions in the tragic country in the wake of last month's U.S. initiated cease-fire. After the initial wranglings over the choice of an acceptable site for the reconciliation committee meeting, as provided for in the cease-fire accord, all parties had at last agreed to hold the talks at a neutral venue in Geneva later this month. But now there is a danger of the entire peace process being derailed. And that precisely seems to have been the set goal of the perpetrators of the savage strikes.

Predictably, President Reagan has vowed to retaliate against those responsible for the killings once their identity is established. U. S. Defence Secretary Weinberger has blamed Iranian revolutionaries for the crime. Other quarters see the Syrian hand behind the lethal blows. It is also possible that both the regimes might have acted jointly when one takes into account the warm freindship that subsists between the two militant leaders. Syria is one of the few Arab countries that has consistently been on Iran's side in the Gulf war. Khomeini has not viewed kindly to Reagan's threat of military action in the event of Iran's reported decision to block the Hormuz Strait if Iraq destroys its oil wells with French-supplied planes and missiles. The Iranian Imam has an equal grouse against France for its move to arm Iraqi forces with its most modern planes and missiles. In the context, the possibility of Khomeini pressing his suicide squads against both the American and French forces in Lebanon cannot be ruled out. Assad has a long standing grouse against Washington for keeping him out of the negotiating process in Lebanon where he still has a sizeable military presence. What is more, Reagan's reported proposal to provide C-130 transports and other logistical support for a Gulf strike force that would be created by the Jordanian army has further widened the Damascus-Washington gulf. Evidently, Assad's hands have been stregthened by Moscow's supply of its latest missiles and other military hardware.

Sunday's massacre of the Marines, the worst since Vietnam, has predictably sent shockwaves across the U. S. The cry for the withdrawal of the U. S. forces from Lebanon will now gain added momentum. In any event, Reagan is left with no choice but to get more and more directly involved in the Lebanese quagmire, and that is what he has threatened in the wake of the killings. He cannot ignore the fall-out from the massacre even as he is all set in his quest for a second term in the White House. All these spell continuing instability and strife in Lebanon, already bled white by conflicting sectarian and religious forces.

1546. Peace antidote to terrorism. *Egyptian Gazette* 7 Jul 1985 ; 3.

1547. Saksena, N. S. : Shiite terror in Lebanon. In *THF* : 46-47.

1548. Stand up to terrorism. *International Herald Tribune* 26 Jan 1987 ; 4.

1549. State terrorism. *Times of India* 22 May 1985 ; 8.

The CIA denial of its involvement in training terrorist squads in Lebanon is quite unconvincing. The Washington Post has marshalled impressive evidence to indicate that after the killing of 241 U. S. marines in October 1983 by a suicide squad, the CIA with the approval of the White House decided to train certain Lebanese groups in these very techniques of terrorism. Thus an attempt was made this March to kill a prominent Shiite religious leader, Mr Mohammed Fedlallah by causing a car bomb which not only missed him but killed 80 innocent bystanders and injured 200 more. According to the newspaper account, it was only after this horrible fiasco that the White House abandoned these attempts at sponsoring "counter terrorism". There was not even adequate proof that Mr Fadlallah was or is a terrorist. Indeed his help had been sought to trace Americans kidnapped in Lebanon. All that the CIA (and the White House) have done by indulging in such activities is to confirm their contempt for due processes of law, remove the moral barrier between terrorism and legitimate state response and sow suspicions among other countries about the willing ness of the Reagan administration to use any means it sees fit to get its way. For if the CIA can be used to support terrorism in Lebanon what reason is there for not believing that it can behave similarly elsewhere ?

Indeed, the CIA might still be at it in Lebanon were it not for the car bomb tragedy and the divisions within the CIA. The latter is almost certainly responsible for the damning leaks to The Washington Post. There is a strong lobby which wants to remove the present director of the CIA, Mr. William Casey. Hampered by official decrees which prevent the agency from directly resorting to assassination or bombings it now seeks to achieve these ends by utilising existing groups which are prepared to engage in such activities. The United States is the most powerful country in the world. But it must exercise its immense power with restraint. However serious the menace of terorrism, to tackle it by using similar means is to play into the hands of terrorists, to obliterate the supposed difference in the goals pursued. Mr. Reagan, as so often before, has allowed himself to become the prisoner of dangerous rhetoric. For it is hardly a surprise that CIA counter-terrorism should be so endorsed when the declared official policy of the White House is to support "pre-emptive self defence" against global terrorism.

1550. Suitcase bomb kills two women in east Beirut. *Baghdad Observer* 13 Feb 1986 ; 1.

Lesotho

1551. Cowell, Alan : Lesotho will end role as haven for Guerrillas. *International Herald Tribune* 25-26 Jan 1986 ; 1, 5.

1552. Cranston, Maurice : Sartre and violence. In *The Mask of Politics and other essays.* London, Allen Lane, 1973.

Liberia

1553. Buying brutality in Liberia. *International Herald Tribune* 25-26 Jan 1986 ; 4.

Libya

1554. Ajami, Fouad : American as 'Demon' ; Qadhafi a terror. *International Herald Tribune* 19-20 Apr 1986 ; 4.

1555. Alford, Jonathan : European are scared of Qadhafi. understandably. *International Herald Tribune* 17 Apr 1986 ; 4.

1556. 'Arab friends back US action." *Times of India* 29 Mar 1986 ; 1.

1557. Armies of the night. *Asiaweek* 4 May 1986 ; 15-13.

1558. Ashford, Nicholas : World's most dangerous man (Colonel Gaddafi). *Statesman* 11 Jan 1986 ; 9.

1559. Baiting Libya. *Patriot* 15 Apr 1986 ; 4.

1560. Berman, Paul *ed.* : *Quotations from the anarchists.* New York, Prayer, 1972.

1561. Better late than never. *Egyptian Mail* 19 Apr 1986 ; 3.

1562. Bombs don't stop terrorists. *International Herald Tribune* 24 Apr 1986 ; 4.

1563. Calling Libya's bl ·ff. *Times of India* 26 Mar 1986 ; 8.

1564. Civilians are unfair game. *International Herald Tribune* 25 Apr 1986 : 6.

1565. Clash over Sidra. *Japan Times Weekly* 12 Apr 1986 ; 12.

1566. Cordesman, Anthony H. : Why America erred in the Gulf of Sidra. *International Herald Tribune* 2 Apr 1986 ; 4.

1567. Dangerous games at Sea. *International Herald Tribune* 25 Mar 1986 ; 8.

1568. For international action. *International Herald Tribune* 16 Apr 1986 ; 6.

1569. Gaddafi to train Arab terrorists. *Telegraph* (Calcutta) 17 Jan 1986 ; 1.

The Libyan leader, Col Muammer Gaddafi, last night offered to train Arab soldiers in "terrorism and suicide missioms" and make Libya a base for liberating Palestine.

In a two-hour speech to thousands of young Libyans, Col. Gaddafi said he was ready to accept members of pro-Libyan Arban groupings in Libya for such training.

"I accept all their decisions and declare that we shall train them on terrorist and suicide missions and allocate trainers for them and place all the necessary weapons needed for such missions and their disposal....... (I) offer them my personal protections because Libya is a base for the liberations of Palestine," he told a cheering crowd.

He also said Libya would accept volunteers from among Arab soldiers and invited young men and women to join the Libyan armed forces.

1570. Gaddafi will help end terrorism. *Hindustan Times* 10 Jan 1986 ; 1.

1571. Gains and risks off Libya. *International Herald Tribune* 27 Mar 1986 ; 4.

1572. Goshko, John M. Libya would retaliate abroad, US says. *International Herald Tribune* 28 Mar 1986 ; 6.

1573. Grave provocation. *Amrita Bazar Patrika* 29 Mar 1986 ; 6.

1574. Gupte, Peranay : Terror : the third world should react. *International Herald Tribune* 10-11 May 1986 ; 4.

1575. Harden, Blaine : Qadhafi works to increase his influence in Sudan. *International Herald Tribune* 28 Mar 1986 ; 4.

1576. Hiatt, Fred : Nightmare over Libya : 'Man, what a target'. *International Herald Tribune* 26 Apr 1986 ; 8.

1577. Hijack planner residing in Libya : Mubarak : Terrorist acts won't pass unpunished. *Egyptian Gazette* 27 Nov 1985 ; 1.

Presicent Hosni Mubarak on November 26, 1985 condemned the brutal massacre of innocent passengers at the hands of blood-thirsty air pirates and said ; "We will never leave a terrorist act unpunished." The President emphasised that Egypt wants peace not war.

President Mubarak told reporters the hijackers of the Boeing 737 seized from Athens, Greece, to Cairo, belong to a renegade Palestinian group, one of whose leaders is staying in the Grand Hotel in Tripoli, Libya.

Asked whether Egypt planned a military strike against in retaliation, President Mubarak said : "We are not callers for war. We are callers for peace."

"War *is not* a *simple thing," President Mubarak added.* "We cannot take that decision simply, and whoever punishes one person does not punish, a whole people".

He said Egypt's next move in the crisis "will be discussed sometime in the future."

Mr. Mubarak, briefing reporters for the first time since the hijack drama, said, Egypt took the decision to storm the aircraft after all efforts to establish a dialogue with the hajackers failed.

"The pilot told Malta Airport : 'Please do something, they're going to kill us all,' President Mubarak said. "If we had been any later. They would have killed a large number of people. If there had been any possibility of a dialogue, we would have waited for two or three days."

Mr. Mubarak said Foreign Minister Esmat Abdul-Meguid had telephones his Libyan counterpart Ali Abdul Salaam Treiki shortly after the plan has seized to convey Cairo's suspicions of Libyan involvement.

"The Libyan Foreign Minister said : "It couldn't be us' and said he would call back in 15 minutes," President Mubarak said. "We tried to call back again but there was never any answer."

Mr. Mubarak said the hijackers issued no demands except for fuel to fly on to Tunisia or Libya.

"Libya seems to have refused to keep away any suspicion from it," Mr. Mubarak said.

President Mubarak said only six Egyptian commandos stormed the plane, firing seven bullets exactly. Three bullets were fired at the chief terrorist and four bullets against the other hijackers, he said.

"Seven bullets could not cause this high number of casualties," President Mubarak said. "Our six commandos were very careful about safeguarding the lives of passengers," he added.

The President said the victims died in the fire started by the 'phosphoric' grenades which the hijackers exploded.

Mr. Mubarak said the Egyptions decided to storm the plane "because the pilot said there is not other solution."

"We were ready to delay (the attack) if there was room for a dialogue," he said. But there was none.

1578. Ideas for dealing with Libya. *International Herald Tribune* 13 Jan 1986 ; 4.

1579. "If Arafat and Gaddafi are terrorists, so were Washington, Lincoln and Garibaldi." *Times of India* 19 Jan 1986 ; IV.

1580. Korshunov, Evgeny : Who the terrorists are. *New Times* (14) 14 Apr 1986 ; 11-12.

1581. Legum, Colin : Scruitiny to reform the world. *International Herald Tribune* 26-27 Apr 1986 ; 9.

1582. Leuis, Flora : Alliance in need of confirmation. *International Herald Tribune* 28 Apr 1986 ; 4.

1583. Leuis, Flora :Don't just do something—think first. *International Herald Tribune* 28 Mar 1986 ; 6.

1584. Leuls, Flora. What to do about Qadhafi : The unhappy dilemma. *International Herald Tribune* 11-12 Jan 1986 ; 4.

1585. Libya : A target of US state terrorism. *National Herald* 15 Apr. 1986 ; 4.

In early May 1981 Washington decided to close down Libya's

People's Bureau (Embassy) in the US and to expell its staff. A spokesman for the State Department ocered Libyan diplomats and auxiliary personnel to quit Libya in five days. At the same time he charged the Libyan Government with "violating the rules of conduct" and supporting international terrorist without citing any evidence to prove this as usual.

Breaking normal diplomatic relations with Libya, an equal and sovereign member-state of the UN, the US *administration* was planning to make short work of it by proxy. The New York Times wrote in May 1981 that the Reagan administration was working out a secret plan to use Egypt and other Arab States for overthrowing the Libyan leader Mummar Al-Gaddafi. The paper noted that Washington intended to encourage conservative Arab regimes, above all, Egypt to take independent action—either engineer a coup in Libya or invade it.

At the same time CIA Director, William Cassey personally endorsed the plan for the physical destruction of the leader of the Libyan revolution Gaddafi, while President Reagan set up in June 1981 a special task group of the administration to monitor the developments in Libya.

In August-September 1981 prominent American analyst Jack Anderson published in the WASHINGTON POST a series of articles about secret activities of the CIA, nothing that it was preparing covert anti-Libyan operations via Egypt. He described the CIA plans to dispatch to Libya a hired assassin who would kill Gaddafi with slow poison. In the first 38 hours there would be no signs of poisoning whatsoever, Anderson wrote. Then Gaddafi would fall ill, and it would be impossible to tell his ailment from those caused by viruses. Then a partial paralysis would hit him, followed by coma and death. But there would be no traces of poison in his body. The American authorities did not make any official denials of these publications, thereby tacitly admitting that accusing Libya of "encouraging international terrorism", it was preparing an act of terror against its leader itself.

In August 1981 the US decided to show its military muscle off Libyan shores. The US Sixth Fleet launched provocative-manoeuvres in the Gulf of Sidra. On August 19, 1981 eight American fighters from the fleet's deck aviation which took part in these manoeuvres downed two Libyan planes that were patrolling the coasts of their country. Throughout the day American aviation simulated variants of air thrust to Libyan town. The US department of State urged American citizens staying in Libya to leave that country.

In September 1981 Washington began the intensive conditioning of the Egyptian and Sudanese beaders into acting against the Libyan Jamahiriya with US logistics support. According to the US press, complete agreement with the Sadat regime was reached on this sore. Only Sadat's death prevented the implementation of the plan of Egypt's attack against libya.

After the failure of the plan to make short work of Libya with Arab hands. Woshington decided to intensify its own pressure on that country. In late 1981 carried out a series of manoeuvres aimed against Libya. From November 11 to 24 the US conducted joint exercises with Somalia on the latter's territory in the Bright Star framework. From November 14 to 24, 1981 the US staged Bright Star exercises with Egypt on Egyptian terrory. From November 27 to December 15, 1981, Us-Sudanese manoeuvres took place in Sudan.

In the end of the year Reagan banned all trips of US citizens to Libya. It tried to involve its NATO allies in the economic blockade against Libya, persuading them to boycott Libyan oil which is the country's chief export item.

The Italian press reported that in late 1981 the US was preparing for an overt armed action against Libya with the use of the RDF.

In subsequent years the US administration kept launching provocations against Libya and subjecting it to pressure. In February 1982 two carrer-based planes from the US Sixth Fleet intercepted a civilian Libyan airliner on a regular flight from Athens to Tripoli. In the summer of the same year US Navy Secretary John Lehman speaking about US Naval exercises off Libyan coasts, stressed once again that the show of force has become one of the favourite means of US pressure on Libya and other Arab nations. The US stays in the Middle East and intends to remain there said he. It is going to use military force if this is necessary for defending its interests. During 1983 and 1984 the US administration sent to the shores of Libya an atomic aircraft carried and escorted by other ships. Since that time the presence of US aircraft-carriers off Libyan shores has become all but permanent. The US also sent to this region four AWAS, aircraft, thereby subjecting Libya continuous radar observation.

In the summer of 1984 the US air Force simulated an air raid on Libya. For 13 hours its fighters were entering Libya's air space in three waves and intimidated the bombing of El-Beida Benghazi and Sirte. In late 1984 the CIA prepared for the US President a classified report assessing Libya's vulnerability. The report proposed carrying out a broad programme of political, economic and paramilitary actions against *it President Reagan issued a decree banning the US imports of oil products from Libya.*

The year 1986 is witnessing incessant military and other provocations of the US set up a 200-strong commando unit for subversion against it.

On January 7 and 8 President Reagan signed two decrees, banning trade and all transactions with Libya and arresting all Libyan property in the US. The decrees went into force immediately. The US dispatched two attack carrier-based units to Libyan shores. When they were joined by a third one led by the America aircraft-carrier, the US launched exercises which developed into an armed provocation against Libya.

To sum up, the policy of State Terrorism against Libya which the US administration has pursued for years resorting to diplomatic and political pressure. economic blockade and the threats of overt armed interference in Libyan home affairs has produced very dangerous results.

The Soviet Governing circles warned about the possibility of this turn and expressed the hope that realism would prevail in the US that it would seriously consider the dangerous consequences to which such policy towards sovereign Libya could lead.

By such actions the US is challenging the entire world public and trampling underfoot the norms of universally recognised civilised relations, declared Soviet leader Mikhail Gorbachyov at the dinner in the Kremlin in honour of Chadli Benies did. Such policy provokes regional conflicts and threatens international peace and security. It is directed against all independent nations and is contrary to the interests of the American people as well.

"We are strongly denouncing the aggressive anti-Libyan actions of the US", said Mikhail Gorbachev. "The Soviet Union is solidly with the Libyan people who are upholding their sacred right to freedom and independence against imperialists' ecroachments".—APN.

1586. Libya for talks with U.S. on restricting terrorism. *Egyptian Mail* 19 Apr 1986 ; 1.

1587. Libya linked to terrorism on Cyprus, *International Herald Tribune* 8 Aug 1986 ; 3.

1588. Libya was behind bombing, Kohl says. *International Herald Tribune* 17 Apr. 1986 ; 6.

1589. Mageoin, Denis : Coming of the barbarian. *Free Press Journal* 4 May 1986.

1590. Middleton, Drew : Who approved the Sidra Caper ? *International Herald Tribune* 27 Mar 1986 ; 4.

1591. Mount, Ferdinand : Raid on Libya : Why Europeans are angry. *International Herald Tribune* 21 Apr 1986 ; 4.

1592. Mr. Reagan's ill-considered attack. *Japan Times Weekly* 3 May 1986 ; 12,

1593. Mummar Khadafy : Libya's prophet of terrorism. *Newstime* 27 Apr 1986 ; 4.

1594. Muravchik, Joshna : Attack on Libya : Necessary blow against terror. *International Herald Tribune* 18 Apr 1986 ; 6.

1595. Of mad dogs and bums. *Deccan Chronicle* 5 May 1986 ; 6.

1596. Ottaway, David B. : Qadhafi has a love hate attitude on U.S. *International Herald Tribune* 10 Jan 1986 ; 2.

1597. Out terrorising the terrorist. *Radical Humanist* May 1986 ; 1-3.

1598. Parasuram. T.V. : US-Libyan ballet. *Deccan Chronicle* 31 Jan 1986 ; 6.

Eventually, the Reagan method of graduated pressure may pay off. Certainly Gaddafi, instead of talking tough, went out of his way to call foreign diplomats and disassociate himself at least publicly from the acts with which he is charged.

But if mild measures do not work, public opinion will compel Mr. Reagan to use military force. Before force is resorted to, the U.S. may try to persuade the Europeans again to join in the economic sanctions. Mr. Oakley estimated that the loss of the tourist trade due to terrorism is costing the Europeans a billion dollars a year.

Another way of putting it is that if the Europeans keep saying 'no', Mr. Reagan may put Europe out of bounds for American tourists—a loss they cannot afford, apart from the fact that the Allies cannot indefinitely say 'no' to the leader. At present Mr. Reagan has, so to speak, issued only a one-line whip on sanctions. Soon it may be a two-line or even a three line return home) ; and a freeze on Libyan assets in the U.S. and in U.S. banks and branches.

The man who coordinates the worldwide anti-terrorist efforts of the U.S. is Rober B. Oakley, currently acting ambassador-at-large for counter-terrorism. He answered the question why the U.S. is focussing on Libya when according to its own statements, Damascus is equally involved with Abu Nidal. His answer was that Damacus has recently asked Abu Nidal's people to adopt a low profile. Gaddafi on the other hand glorifies his contacts.

According to Mr. Oakley, for a long time Gaddafi has been embracing quite a number of movements around the world. For instance, one of the sons of Z.A. Bhutto, hanged Prime Minister of Pakistan, is said to be in Tripoli directing the movement against President Zia in Pakistan. Gaddafi is also said to be funding the opposition in Bangla Desh. Anyone who is pro-American is Gaddafi's enemy. However, he did not score too many successes in any of the continents until Abu Nidal joined forces with him. It is this combination that is regarded as deadly.

But one complication is that one man's terrorist is another's liberation fighter. However, on one matter President Reagan has been absolutely right : a nation that support acts of terrorism against another's whip.

1599. Pfaff, William : After the attack on Libya : NATO needs rethinking. *International Herald Tribune* 24 Apr 1986 ; 4.

1600. Pfaff, William : Europe can justify its policy on Libya ties. *International Herald Tribune* 16 Jan 1986 ; 4.

1601. Qadhafi, in shift, condemns attacks, vows to fight terror. *International Herald Tribune* 10 Jan 1986 ; 1, 6.

1602. Randal, Jonathan C. : Arab moderates caught in the Middle of Sidra Clash. *International Herald Tribune* 28 Mar 1986 ; 4.

1603. Randal, Jonathan C. : U.S. aid to Sudan is threatened by presence of Libyans linked to terrorism. *International Herald Tribune* 16 Jul 1986 ; 5.

1604. Reagan hints at more measures. *Patriot* 29 Mar 1986 ; 7.

1605. Reagan plays a love hand. *International Herald Tribune* 11-12 Jan 1986 ; 4.

1606. Restov, James :Unpredictable holy war in holy week. *International Herald Tribune* 27 Mar 1986 ; 4.

1607. Richardson, Michael :Libya is said to fund, train radicals in New Caledonia. *International Herald Tribune* 7 Apr 1986 ; 5.

1608. Rvot Cause needs addressing. *Egyptian Gazette* 9 Jan 1986 ; 4.

The US President Ronald Reagan's imposition of sweeping economic sanctions against Libya is likely to be ineffective for the simple reason that none of the United States' allies appears to be willing to follow suit and certainly no country of the Soviet bloc will do any thing against Libya. This is not to say that Libya deserves any kid-glove treatment. On the contrary, Colonel Gaddafi, the Libyan leader, has openly espoused terrorism and has made no secret of his aim to eliminate his opponents by sending hit-squads to kill them. No country is more aware of this than Egypt which has foiled several Libyan plots.

The massacres at Rome and Vienna airports on December 27 were further proof of Libya's support of terrorism. All the evidence goes to show that the killing of innocent passengers waiting to board Israeli aircraft was work of the Abu Nidal group of Palestinian dissidents who have Libyan backing. The claim that the murders were in retaliation for the Israeli raid on the Palestine Liberation Organisation headquarters in Tunis on October 1 can have no justification because international airline passengers, even if including Israelis, cannot in any way be collectively responsible for actions of the Israeli government, however, reprehensible such actions may be. But Libya had no hesitation immediately after the airport killings in hailing them as "heroic". If that is what they were, then dictionaries should revise their definition of heroism. Later, perhaps in reaction two world revulsion and the fingers of accusation, Libya toned down its comment and sought to dissociate itself from the incidents. But Colonel Gaddafl remains unrepentant and cannot absolve his government from support of, if not actual participation in the murders.

It would certainly be desirable to isolate Libya as long as it uses terrorism as a political weapon. A complete international boycott of the country would have a serious effect on its economy and would force Colonel Gaddafi to revise his policy or go. But US sanctions alone will hardly have an impact. What is essential is to attack the root causes of terrorism—in the case in point, the Palestinian question.

Once again therefore the situation points to the need for an overall Middle East settlement. It is a pity that President Reagan made no mention of this in his announcement of sanctions against Libya. It is vital to look beyond the cycle of violence and revive the Middle East peace process because a just settlement, which gives the Palestinians their rights, will deprive terrorists of any reason to carry on their murderous activities. But as long as Israel remains in illegal occupation of Palestinian and other Arab land there is unlikely to be an end to the use of terrorism whether by Libyan-supported dissidents or others, including those who do not really care about a Palestinian settlement but seek to exploit the unstable situation for their own purposes.

Whatever some people may say and despite inter-Arab divergences, the mainstream PLO remains committed to the cause of peace by means of negotiations with Israel. This is the aspect which President Reagan should have before him. It is totally wrong to lump the PLO into the terrorist camp with Libya and Palestinian dissidents. If President Reagan wishes to end Middle East terrorism the best thing he could do would be to oblige Israel to meet the PLO at the negotiating table, either at an international conference or in any other suitable forum, and insist on its reaching a settlement that would give all Middle East peoples, particularly the Palestinians, their freedom within their own borders following Israeli withdrawal from all occupied land. Until this happens terrorism in some form or other will doubtless continue.

1609. Rostow, Eugene V. : Attack on Libya : A break through for the West. *International Herald Tribune* 28 Apr 1986 ; 4.

1610. Seale, Patrick and Peter Pringle, Gaddafi : Man and myth. *Tribune* 24 Jan 1986 ; 4.

Libya's Colonel Gaddafi is today where he most likes to be—in the eye of the storm.

President Reagan calls him a "pariah" and seeks to have him outlawed. Israel's Premier Shimon Peres describes him as a "clown, a murderer and a liar".

But threats and verbal diatribes make him rather than break him. Gaddafi thrives on crises, on media attention and on blazing public rows.

The more he is attacked and villified by Irsael and the U.S.A., the more influential he becomes in his wide Third World constituency.

Gaddafi is not mad nor even unduly eccentric, as the West often tends to see him. He has, on the contrary, proved exceptionally shrewd, retaining power for 16 years and seeing off whole battalions of internal and external enemies.

His challenge to the international oil companies in the early seventies pioneered the oil price explosion which turned the world's economy upside down and resulted in the greatest transfer of wealth ever seen.

He is a rebel against the international system, a permanent revolutionary, a restless spirit impatient with the Arabs' weakness and devoured by dreams of greatness. A great influence on him was the late President Nasser of Egypt.

Gaddafi grew to manhood in the Libyan desert with a transistor radio stuck in his ear, listening to the inspiring speeches of the Egyptian leader. Nasser became his hero and pan-Arabism his cult.

When in 1969, at the age of 27, he seized power in Tripoli, overthrowing the mild and benevolent King Idris, he immediately put himself at Nasser's service. But Nasser, weakened by defeat in war, died in 1970, leaving Gaddafi—or so the yough thought—to inherit his mantle.

"Zionism" and "imperialism" have been his enemies ever since—in other words Israel and its American ally.

Just as Nasser was carried to the pinnacle of his fame by the Suez war of 1956 waged against him by Britain, France and Israel, Gaddafi has benefited hugely by his depiction as a bogeyman. He could benefit still further if Israel or the U.S.A. were rash enough to attack him physically. The backlash against western and Jewish interests could be horrendous.

Original to Gaddafi is his skilful use of irregular warfare—terrorism if you will—as an expression of Third World revolt. What has set the world by the ears is not Libya's real power, but the fear Gaddafi's methods widely inspire. The true victims of an act of terror are not only the people slain or maimed but many others who think they may be nest.

In this war of nerves Gaddafi is a master, scaring African despots, causing Arab princes to tremble, and even creating nervous tremors in the White House. Threats of bombs and rumours of prowling suicide teams can be as effective as the explosions or the gunmen themselves.

Terrorism is the traditional weapon of the poor. In the hands of Gaddafi it has become a weapon with which a very small State, led by a bold repel, can cock a snook at the great fleets, air force units and nuclear arsenals of the guardians of our world order.

But Gaddafi's influence does not rest on feat alone, or on his ability to spring surprises. It rests on the fact that in Arab eyes at least he has a case.

1611. Seale, Patrick : Qadhafi is a small part of a big problem. *International Herald Tribune* 25 Apr 1986 ; 6.

1612. Setback for terror. *International Herald Tribune* 9 May 1986 ; 6.

1613. Shastri, Ravi : Libya and Third World Security. *Pioneer* (Lucknow) 6 May 1986 ; 6.

1614. Sidra Showdon. *Asiaweek* 6 1986 : 20.

1615. Slamming a door on Libya. *International Herald Tribune* 10 Jan 1986 ; 4.

1616. Suro, Roberto : Qadhafi offers to curb terrorists if U.S. bars attack against Libya. *International Herald Tribune* 29 Jan 1986 ; 1-5.

1617. Taming Terrorism. *Madhya Pradesh Chronicle* 11 Jan 1986 ; 4.

1618. Terrorism : We did what we had to do. *Asiaweek* 27 Apr 1986 ; 30.

1619. Terrorist organisations owing allegiance to Col. Gaddafi. *Industrial Times* (Bombay) 31 Mar 1986.

1620. Third World countries reject Ragan's Libya sanction. *Ta Kung Fao* (Hongkong) 16 Jan 1986 ; 11.

1621. Unjustified act. *Egyptian Gazette* 6 Feb 1986 ; 4.

1622. US adventurism. *Patriot* 28 Mar 1986 ; 4.

1623. Vanaik, Achin : USA's attack on Libya : Nothing to do with stopping terrorism. *Times of India* (New Delhi) 23 Apr 1986 ; 8.

1624. Washington obliges Col. Gaddafi. *Telegraph* (Calcutta) 28 Mar 1986 ; 6.

1625. Woodward, Bob : CIA reportedly plans to undermine Qadhafi. *International Herald Tribune* 4 Nov 1985 ; 1-2.

Malaysin

1626 Clutterbuck, Richard : *Conflict and violence in Singapore and Malaysia 1945-1983.* New York, 1985.

1627. Crossette, Barbara. Sabah violence raises questions on democracy in Malaysia. *International Herald Tribune* 22-23 Mar 1986 ; 2.

1628. O'Ballance, Edgar : *Malaysia : The communist insurgent War, 1948-1960.* Hamden, 1966.

1629. Pyc, Lucian : *Guerrilla Communism in Malaysia.* Princeton, 1956.

Mexico

1630. Stevens, Evelyn P : *Protest and response in Mexico. Cambridge* 1974.

1631. Womack, John : *Zapata and the Mexican revolution. New York,* Knopf, 1969.

Mozambique

1632. Mondlane, Eduardo : *Struggle for Mozambique.* Baltimore, Penguin, 1969.

Nepal

1633. Abdi, S.N.M : Chinese factor (in Nepal). *Illustrated Weekly of India* 21 Jul 1985 ; 22.

1634. Abdi, S.N.M. Terror in Shangri-La. *Illustrated Weekly of India* 21 Jul 1985 ; 20-23.

1635. Beri, H.M.L : Terrorism in Nepal. *Pioneer* 30 Jun 1985 ; 6.

Nepal the Himalyan Hindu Kingdom, has also become a victim of political terrorism. Recently bomb explosions "ripped through" the centre of the Nepalese capital and its surroundings. On June 20 five bombs exploded at government buildings, a hotel lobby and the Royal Palace ; and as a result of it six persons were killed and 28 were injured. Thereafter on June 21 three blasts rocked a police station, a government store and customs office in southern town of Birgunj near the Indo-Nepal border.

It is strange that the bomb blasts coincided with growing demands for change by outlawed opponents of the Himalayan kingdom government. In the recent weeks banned opposition Nepali Congress led a civil disobedience movement and seven thousand people were arrested. It had been campaigning for a return to multi-party politics. When in mid June Parliament began its annual session, the Nepali Congress Party spokesman Chakra Bastola said : "We are trying to make His Majesty (King Birendra) realise that the destiny of the country is at stake. The people are disillusioned—this could lead ultimately to chaos and disintegration of the country."

Apart from this, it was only on June 19, 1985 (a day before the bomb explosion) while addressing the National Assembly King Birendra warned the political opponents who were demanding a revival of Western style democracy and said it was "the bounden duty" of all supporters "to counter those who seek to create an atmosphere of *instability in the country by spreading unnecessary confusion about the system chosen by the people themselves in free exercise of their will*".

1636. Clampedown in the Kathmandu. *Newstime* 31 Oct 1985 ; 12.
1633. Lal, Dilip : Evidence of extremist infiltration : Centre (New Delhi) approves UP Plan to secure border with Nepal. *Current* (Bombay) 15 Feb 1986 ; 16.

Netherlands

1638. Dutch PM defends steps against terrorism. *Indian Express 25* Jan *1986* ; 8.

The Dutch Premier Mr. Ruud Lubbers, on January 23, 1986 defended the European stance against international terrorism, saying it would be "a fundamental mistake" to underrate European efforts to curb it.

"Sometimes I have the feeling that they (the United States) think they are the tough guys and we (Europeans) are the weak guys," Mr. Lubbers told reporters.

"But it would be a fundamental mistake to see the United States as taking terrorism more seriously than Europe," said Mr. Lubbers whose Government holds the current six-month presidency of the European Economic Community (EEC).

Mr. Lubbers' remarks came only hours before the U.S. Deputy Secretary of State, Mr. John Whitehead, was due to arrive in The

Hague, concluding a nine-nations European trip focusing on combating international terrorism.

The Dutch Premier claimed that the justice ministries in the EEC's 12 member nations are working closely together to treck the movement of terrorist groups. He noted that the issue of international terrorism would figure high on the agenda at a meeting of common market foreign ministers week next in Brussels.

Mr. Lubbers called for "efficient action" as a response to terrorist activity in recent years.

"An efficient reply (to terrorism) is to discourage, those countries that host terrorist from doing so," Mr. Lubbers said without elaborating on the nature of such a response.

But earlier this month, Mr. Lubbers said it was 'highly improbable' that the common market would decide to impose economic sanctions against Libya as the United States did in retaliation for the December terrorist attacks on airports in Rome and Vienna.

Asked whether he had seen proof of Libyan involvment in recent terrorists attacks, Mr. Lubbers said : "It is simplifying the matter to say this country (Libya) is the only source" of terrorism.

But he noted that Italy and Spain, which joined the EEC on January 1, May have better insight in the kind of pressures that can be applied to Libya because of their closer historical and georaphical links with the North African nation.

Mr. Lubbers added that efforts to encourage the West Asia peace process were an important part of trying to deal with the terrorist problem.

1639. Herman, Valantine and Rob Van Der Laan Bouma : Nationalists without a nation. South Moluccan terrorism in the Netherlands. *Terrorism* 4 (1-4) 1980 ; 223-58.

1640. Uyl, Joop den : Dutch response. In *ITCR* ; 165- 71.

The Netherlands has been faced with much terrorist violence during the 1970s. As Prime Minister during that time, I had to cope with six major acts of violence, the taking of hostages in my country, and with four cases of hijacking of Dutch civil aircraft.

In those years the Dutch government developed a certain strategy of dealing with terrorist acts. The essence of this strategy, as see it, could be formulated thus : The duty of governments is to save the lives of captured innocent people, without given in one any essential point to the terrorists. It is also our duty to prove that terrorist crimes do not pay.

In my view, the essence of the problem with which we are dealing in this conference is just how can we prove that terrorist crime does not pay ? In some ways I think I differ from opinions that have been formulated during the last two days of this conference, and that will become clear.

Though I do not think that what we achieved in Holland in the fight against terrorism is anything to the particularly proud of, I do think that, compared with some other countries, we did not do badly.

1641. Wittermans, T. and N.P. Grist : Ambonese Nationalist Movement in the Netherlands : A study in status deprivation. *Social Forces 40*, 1962 ; 309-17.

New Zealand

1642. Act of state terrorism. *Deccan Herald* 23 Sep 1985 ; 8.

Nicaragua

1643. Bell, Peter, D : Helping the rebels in Nicaragua is wrong. *International Herald Tribune* 5 Mar 1986 ; 4.

1644. Brumberg, Abraham : "Sham" and "Farce" in Nicaragua ? *Dissent Spr* 1985 ; 226-36.

1645. Guerrillas' crimes don't matter. *International Herald Tribune* 10 Mar 1986.

1646. Harris, Richard : Revolutionary process in Nicaragua. *Latin American Perspectives* 12 (2) Spr 1985 ; 3-22.

1647. Lernoux, Penny : Somozas of Nicaragua. *Nation* 23 Jul 1977 ; 72-77.

1648. Millett, Richard : *Guardians of the dynasty : A history of the U.S. Created Guardia Nacional de Nicaragua and the Somoza Family.* Marynoll, N.Y., Orbis Books, 1977.

1649. Nicaragua : The autumn of the Patriarch. *Latin America* Political Report 21 Oct 1977.

1650. *Report on the situation of human rights in Nicaragua.* Washington Inter-American Commission on Human Rights, Organisation of American States, 1978.

1651. Somoza, A and Jack Cox : *Nicaragua betrayed* Belmont, 1980.

1652. Subversion in Nicaragua. *New Age* 1 Jun 1986 ; 15.

1653. Walker, Thomas W. ed : *Nicaragua in revolution.* New York, Praeger ; 1981.

1654. U.S. aiding terrorism in Nicaragua. *Northern India Patrika* (Allahabad) 14 Jan 1986 ; 4.

While the U.S. was denouncing Gaddafi's terrorism and subversion worldwide, the "New York Times" published a letter from Mr. Edgar Chamoro, the former contra Director, pointing out that the U.S. is doing subversive activities of its own in Central America against the Nicaragua Government.

Mr. Chamoro, who resigned from the Directorate of the United Nicaraguan Opposition wrote : "The Contras based in Honduras, were and are a proxy army controlled by the United States government".

'If U.S. support were terminated, they would not only be incapable of conducting any military activities against the Sandinistas, but would also immediately begin to disintegrated. I resigned rather than continue as a Central Intelligence Agency puppet, Mr. Chamoro said.

'It is cynical to assert that the Contras respect human rights. During my four years as Contras director, it was premidiate policy to terrorize civilian non-combinats and to prevent them from cooperating with the Government. Hundreds of civilian murders, multiliations, tortures and rapes were committed in pursuit of this policy, of which the Contra leaders and their superiors were well aware', the letter said.

Only when these practices were revealed in the U.S. Press and by human rights groups did the Contra leaders feel compelled to give lip service to ending them.

'But no serious effort to stop them has been made because terror is the most effective weapon of the Contras', Mr. Chamoro asserted.

Mr. Chamoro gave an example of August 1986, when the Contras briefly occupied the town of Cuapa, gathered the residents in the town square, selected those civilians they suspected of sympathising with the Government, and shot them in cold blood as a lesson'.

'It is a gross fabrication to claim that the Contras are composed of democratic groups who joined in the revolution against Anastano Somoza', the former Contra leader said.

'As I can attest, the Contra military force is directed and controlled by officers or Somoza's national guard, who fought at the dictator's side until the very end and then fled to Honduras', he said.

Mr. Chamoro said my knowledge is confirmed by an April 1985 congressional study that shows 46 or the 48 positions in the FDN's (Fuerza Democratic Nicaraguense, the principal U.S.-backed counter-revolutionary group) military leadership were held by ex-national guardsmen'.

'At U.S. urging, some former Somoza oppenents ; including Mr. Arturo Cruz and Mr. Alfonso Robeo, have now been affiliated with the Contras to make them more palatable to the Congress', he said.

'But real power in this military organization rests with those who have the guns—the ex-guardsmen, he added.

"The Sandinistas, for all their faults, have made enormous advances in education, housing and health care', Mr. Chamoro said adding 'unfortunately, the Contras burn down schools, homes and health centres as fast as the Sandinistas build them'.

1655. Walkers, Thomas W. *ed* : *Nicaragua* : *Land of Sandino*. Boulder, Westview Press, 1981.

1656. Weinraub, Bernard : Reagan says Sandinists give refuge to terrorists. *International Herald Tribune* 24 Apr 1986 ; 3.

Nigeria

1657. Sullivan, George Nigeria : In *Story of the Peace Corps*, New York, 1964 ; 116-24.

Non-Aligned Movement

1658. Attar Chand : SDI, terrorism and NAM. *National Herald* 28 Feb 1986 ; 5.

1659. Chakravartty, Sumit : NAM Ministers' meeting : Place for global efforts to curb terrorism. *Daily* (Bombay) 28 Mar 1986 ; 10-11.

1660. Goyal, D.R. : NAM to discuss terrorism. *National Herald* 2 Apr 1986 ; 5.

1661. NAM for joint bid to end terrorism. *Tribune* 28 Aug 1986 ; 12.

1662. Zivic, J. : Nonaligned and the problem of international terrorism. *Review of International Affairs* (Belgrade) 24, 20 Jan 1973 ; 6-8.

Norway

1663. Eitinger, Leo : *Concentration camp survivors in Norway* and Israel. University of Oslo Press, 1964.

Oman

1664. Azzi, R. Oman : Land of frankinscense and oil. *National Geographic* 4 Feb 1974.

1665. Bondarevskiy, G.L. Continuing Western interest in Oman—as seen from Moscow. *New Middle East* Aug 1971.

1666. Fiennes, Ranulph : *Where soldiers fear to tread.* London, Hodder and Stronghton, 1975.

1667. Hudson, Michael : *Arab politics* New Haven, Yale University Press, 1977.

1668. Kelly, J.B. Prevalence of furies ; Tribes, politics and religion in Oman and Trucial Oman. In *Arabian Peninsula : Society and Politics* Ed. by Derek Hopwood. N.J., Rowman and Little Field, 1972 ; 107-44.

1669. O'Neill, Bard E : Revolutionary war in Oman. In *IMW*. 213-34.

Patrimonial monarchies, such as the one in Oman, have been under almost constant attack in the modern era. Thus, it should come as no surprise to find that the Omani regime also has its share of enemies. Since 1968 the most prominent of these has been the Popular Front for the Liberation of Oman (PFLO), a revolutionary insurgent movement that has sought, through violent means, to supplant the traditional political values and structures of the current regime with Marxist-Leninist ones. The strategy chosen to accomplish this ambitious task has been the familiar Maoist protracted revolutionary warfare approach that was successfully employed (albeit with local modifications) in China and Vietnam. Through a blend of political organization and propaganda, terrorism, and guerrilla warfare, the PFLO gradually has tried to erode the regime's will to resist, the morale of the Sultan's armed Forces (SAF), and what popular backing the regime enjoys. While the influence of Maoist doctrine and strategy has been pervasive in all of this, an examination of the origins of the violence directed at the sultanate reveals other elements, such as strong tribal and religious indentification, which have had a major impact on the struggle. To better understand the interaction of Maoism and tribalism, as well as other aspects of the current insurgency, it is important that the conflict be placed in its historical context.

Opposition to the sultan has been endemic for more than a century and has reflected a basic societal cleavage between the conservative ibadhi Moslems of the interior and the rulers located in the coastal region of Muscat. The Ibadhis, who settled in Oman during the seventh century, long have resented efforts by Muscat to control them, in part because the sultans were perceived as corruptors of the faith.

The spiritual and temporal leaders of the Ibadhis, known an imams, data as far back as 1749, when the first was elected. Following the creation in the seventeenth century of an Omani empire (which extended to the coast of East Africa), civil conflict ensued between rival contenders for the office of imam. The outcome was a victory for Ahmed bin Said, who was elected iman in 1749, thereby establishing the Al Bu Said dynasty that has ruled all or part of Oman until the present. Though the head of the Al Bu Said family took the title of sultan, he also was often the imam.

In 1786 the capital of Oman was moved to the coastal city of Muscat, a development that led eventually to a political cleavage between the interior and coastal areas that was reinforced by tribal and religious differences. As a result of the division of the empire into the sultanates of Zanzibar and Oman following the death of Sultan Al Bu Said, in 1856, and a reduction of revenues (due to a curtailment of the slave and arms trade), Oman entered a period of considerable violence and unrest. However, because of tribal rivalries and British assistance, the Al Bu Saids were able to maintain their rule."

Nevertheless, the tribes of the interior increasingly had grown disaffected with the rulers in Muscat, who had established a hereditary basis for rule that contradicted Ibadhi traditions. In protest against the secularization of the imamate by the Al Bu Saids, the interior tribes elected another imam in the late eighteenth century. Although in the years thereafter the sultan occasionally was accepted as imam and sometimes there was no imam at all, the general pattern was to have an imam of Oman and a sultan of Muscat and Oman.

Whatever the case, distrust and tensions continued to be the halmarks of relations between the regime and the people of the interior. These differences finally gave rise to a general revolt against Sultan Taimur bin Faisal Al Bu Said in 1913 that was triggered by tribal objections to cooperation with Great Britain and restrictions on the arms traffic in the area. When it became apparent that the sultan would be unable to maintain his rule without outside help, he turned to the British who promptly dispatched troops to Oman. Attempts to reconcile the differences between the two sides culminated in the Treaty of Sib (1920) in which the sultan recognized the Imam's spiritual authority and granted him political authority over those who would accept his jurisdiction. The sultan, however, retained his claim to sovereignty and continued to control main posts and the coastal regions.

1670. Owen, R.P. Developments in the Sultanate of Muscat and Oman. *World Today* Sep 1970 ; 379-83.

1671. Phillips, Wendal : *Oman : A history*. New York, Revnal, 1968.

1672. Price, Raymonds : *Oman : Insurgency and development*. London, Institute for the Study of Conflict, 1975.

1673. Rentz, George : Sultanate as under. *National History* Mar 1974 : 59-65.

1674. Secret war in the Persian Gulf. *Atlas* Apr 1972.

1675. Skeet, Ian : *Muscat and Oman*. London, Faber and Faber, 1974.

1676. Wilkinson, J.C. : Oman question : the background to thepolitical geography of South East Arabia. *Geographical Journal* Sep 1971.

1677. Wilkinson, J.C. : Origins of the Omani state. In *Arabin peninsula : Society and politics*. Ed. by Derek Hopwood. N.J., Rowman and Little Field, 1972.

Pakistan

1678. Abbas, K.R. : Organised terror ! (Pan Am Plane Hijacked). *Blitz* 20 Sep 1986 ; 24.

1679. Akhtar, Jamna Das : Thousands of extremists waiting in Pakistan. *Patriot* 17 Sep 1985 ; 4.

1680. Chowdhary, S.S. : *I was a prisoner of war in Pakistan*. New Delhi, Lancer International, 1986. Pp. 94.

1681. Cross-border terrorism, *Patriot* 23 Dec 1986 ; 4.

1682. Debate demanded on Pak training camps. *Hindustan Times* 8 Apr 1986 ; 11.

1683. Hard choice for M.R.D. (Movement for Restoration of Democracy). *Pioneer* 6 Feb 1986 ; 6.

1684. How Pakistan trains Punjab extremists. *Hindustan Times* 11 Feb 1986 ; 4.

1685. Infiltrators from Pak behind terrorism : PM (Rajiv Gandhi) *Times of India* 17 Sep 1985 ; 1.

1686. Kak, B.L. : Pakistan did help Sikh terrorists. *Newstime* 6 Jul 1985 ; 6.

1687. Mvsterious 'hammer' murders. *Asiaweek* 4 May 1986 ; 26.

1688. Pak aid to terrorists. *Deccan Chronicle* 8 Feb 1986 ; 6.

The Indian intelligence authorities are now in possession of enough evidence to prove that Pakistan and some other external forces have, for some years now, been providing sophisticated arms training to Sikh extremists and fomenting separatist-feelings in the Kashmir valley. It would be naive to think that the recrudesence of terrorism in Punjab has no foreign dimension to it. This dimension, which was shockingly evident during the Punjab turmoil, seems to persist still. The two sensitive States of Punjab and Jammu and Kashmir are the special target of the foreign forces out to destabilise India. If the information gathered by the Indian Intelligence is correct, then Pakistan is indulging in much double-talk. And Punjab Chief Minister Surjit Singh Baranala was right when he said sometime ago that Pakistan was an unfriendly neighbour. One is utterly at a loss to understand the secret training of the saboteurs in Pakistan territory and Islamabad's periodic assertions that it is very serious about normalising relations with India. Even if Pakistan is not directly involved in training Sikh terrorists, it certainly is guilty of allowing its territory to be used by some other foreign force out to create anarchy in Indian border States. The determination with which the terrorists are carrying on their nefarious activities makes one think that they have full foreign backing. What could be the motive behind this ? Some grievances of Pakistan against India seem to have diabolically been dovetailed with the anti-India activities of some forces. The nexus was noticeable during the Punjab crisis. And since then Indian, intelligence authorities have been very few days, stumbling upon fresh evidence of that connection. Last month, the Uttar Pradesh and Jammu and Kashmir police arrested a four-member gang of terrorist near Varanasi. This arrest provided the police with clues to a mercenary groups of terrorisis operating in Northern India, particularly Punjab and Jammu and Kasmir. The four-member gang had reportedly been operating from its headquarters in Canada.

And in Canada there are many Sikhs separatists who have vowed to scuttle the peace process in Punjab. They are at it now. Some of them have undergone training at mercenary schools. They may be using Pakistan territory as a spring-board to create communal and political strife in Punjab. They outbreak of separatist trouble in Kashmir and Punjab about four years ago was no mere coincidence. There was a powerful foreign hand behind it. Unfortunately, the foreign forces allegedly involved in the separatist violence have not yet reconciled themselves to the peaceful and democratic settlement of the Punjab problem. Terrorists continue to commit murders in Punjab. As the international border in Punjab has been secured against infiltration, saboteurs, trained in Pakistan seem to be infiltrating into India through Kashmir. They have strong links with the pro-Pakistan elements in the Kashmir valley. These people are trying to revive the demand for a plebiscite.

After the Punjab and Assam ordeals, India has become stronger. This may be causing much concern to the foreign forces hostile to India. A stable strong and democratic India is not to the liking of some forces. Our neighbour's decades-old desire to achieve, for whatever reason, military partly with India is well known. And this must be one of the reasons for Pakistan's secret plan to make atomic weapons. The strains in Pakistan's relations with India have, many times in the past, come in handy for the some big powers which see a pro-Soviet tilt in India's foreign policy. They continue to see the alleged tilt. Since the partition of the sub-continent, Pakistan has become a stick in the hands of some big powers to beat India with. But whoever is orchestrating and financing the plots to weaken India had better give some thought to the way India has solved the Punjab and Assam problems. And in the process, India has emerged stronger. The people of neither Punjab nor Jammu and Kashmir will not tolerate the foreign machinations in their states. Let there be an end to these dangerous games. There is the danger of whoever is playing the games getting destabilised.

1689. Pak aiding terrorists ; PM (Rajiv Gandhi). *Times of India* 13 Oct 1986 ; 1.

1690. Pak and terrorists. *Hitavada* (Bhopal) 5 Apr 1986 ; 3.

1691. Pak camps to train extremists. *Patriot* 15 Jun 1985 ; 5.

1692. Pak, China back Sikh terrorists ; Camper. *Tribune* 11 Sep 1985 ; 11.

1693. Pak involvement. *Times af India* 16 Sep 1985 ; 8.

1694. Pak meddlers. *Current* 21 Sep 1985 ; 2.

1695. Pak support to terrorists hindrance to relations (with India). *Deccan Chronicle* 26 Feb 1986 ; 9.

1696. Pak-trained terrorists. *Deccan Chronicle* (Secundrabad, A.P.) Aug 1985 ; 6.

While Pakistan keeps on denying that it is extending help to the Punjab terrorists, reports continue to trickle in from one source or another about training camps for terrorists in the areas bordering on India. According to the latest reports, more than 600 terrorists are being trained at six camps organised by the Pakistan military authorities in occupied Kashmir and other places. In January last, more than 30 heavily armed extremists were nabbed by the Jammu and Kashmir police while trying to sneak into India. Highly sophisticated arms and ammunition, including antitank rockets and medium machine guns, were seized from the extremists. And now it is learnt that a group of terrorists trained in Pakistan has slunk into Delhi to create panic on or before August 15. In recent months, terrorists have surfaced surprisingly. This definitely has something to do with the recent Punjab accord. Ever since they started their murderous activity in Punjab more than two years ago, they have been hell-bent on scuttling all moves to settle the Punjab tangle, Unfortunately for the nation, they succeeded in their nefarious plan which culminated in the two cataclysmic tragedies last year. Even after the assassination of Prime Minister Indira Gandhi, intelligence reports indicated that extremists continued to get training in the use of arms and organisational tactics in Pakistan. One report said that the training period had been reduced from three months to three weeks. And in the second week of November last year, when India was still in mourning, Pakistan authorities allowed Khalistan activists to misuse a religious occasion to carry on an anti-India tirade. This was disconcerting and Prime Minister Rajiv Gandhi was constrained to express strong resentment against Islamabad's open encouragement to the Khalistan activists from other countries visiting Pakistan. Whenever such resentment is expressed, Pakistan promptly deines that it is fuelling the Khalistan campaign. Pakistan's support for the campaign has a long history. Pakistan's involvement in the campaign in some Western capitals, particularly London, is well known. About two decades ago, Pakistan intelligence agencies are believed to have prepared a plan to alienate the Sikhs from the Hindus in the border State of Punjab with the ultimate aim of delinking the State from India. If the latest reports about Pakistan's support to terrorists are correct—and there is no reason to believe that they are not so—that wicked plan is still in operation. Indeed, the outbreak of separatist tendencies in a violent form in the two Indian border States of Jammu and Kashmir and Punjab over two years ago had carefully been engineered, from across the international border. And that was the time when one superpower became openly critical of, and even hostile to India's alleged tilt towards the other superpower. Coincident with this was the finalisation of the U.S. arms aid to Pakistan. Strangely, the terrorists in Punjab started getting not only training but sophisticated arms from mysterious sources. That mystery still persists. On the Pakistan side of the Line of Actual Control in Jammu and Kashmir there has not only been hectic military activity but also much training for saboteurs.

Therefore, Indian Minister of State for External Affairs did well the other day to tell the *Lok Sabha* that Pakistan's denial of the charge of supporting terrorists was not satisfactory. The Punjab accord must have surprised the foreign forces out to create trouble for India on its borders. The occurrence of terrorism even after the accord is a clear indication that the extremists and their foreign supporters are still hard at their devilish game. It is now dawning on those investigating the recent brutal murder of a member of the Lok Sabha and his wife that it was a terrorist act. Pakistan would do well to set its house in order instead of fishing to India's troubled waters. From the political and communal turmoil created by the terrorists, India has now emerged more united. Any further evidence of Pakistan's support for terrorists out to create disturbances in India would hamper the already slow-paced normalisation of bilateral ties. Pakistan's secret support for terrorists is not only an unfriendly but a provocative act.

1697. Pak's hidden hand. *Free Press Journal* 23 Aug 1985 ; 4.

1698. Pak's killer gangs. *Daily* (Bombay) 12 Oct 1985 ; 11.

1699. Pakistan and terrorism. *Hitavada* (Bhopal) 24 Dec 1986 ; 3.

1700. Pakistan's assurance on terrorism (to India). *Hindu* (New Delhi) 23 Dec 1986 ; 8.

1701. Raghavan, A. : US bolsters Pak was machine for Balbanisation of India. *Blitz* (Bombay) 5 Apr 1986 : 9.

1702. Terrorism abetted by Pakistan (in India) ; Jack Anderson. *Current* 12 Oct 1985 ; 4.

The American columnist Jack Anderson is positive that Pakistan has had a hand in the extremist activity in India and had been supplying equipment to terrorists and training them.

Anderson, who is making a one-hour movie on modern India, said he would try to depict the damage caused by the terrorists in Punjab. His efforts will be to show briefly what happened there.

The movie, to be widely televised in the US, Europe and the Far East, will also include an exclusive interview with Rajiv Gandhi.

A champion for the cause of India, Anderson believes that the US should encourage democracies elsewhere. "Terrorists in India and the US represent nobody," he said. "I do not know how the US supports the dictatorship in Pakistan and turns its back to democracy in India."

1703. Terrorists' bid to flee to Pakistan. *Deccan Chronical* (Secundrabad) 30 Jan 1986 ; 6.

1704. Terrorists' link with Pak. *National Herald* 18 Oct 1985 ; 4.

1705. Terrorists' links with Pak proved. *Deccan Chronicle* 3 Apr 1986 ; 1, 11.

1706. Torture and killings in Pakistan. *New Wave* 2 Feb 1986 ; 11.

More than 130 political prisoners, most of them civilians, are now serving sentences of between seven and 42 years after being denied fair trials by military courts in Pakistan, says Amnesty International.

Publishing a memorandum it sent to the Pakistan regime in June 1985, Amnesty International called for new trials for all prisoners convicted of political offences and politically motivated crimes by special military courts.

Many prisoners spend a year or more a leg irons and in chains before appearing at the special military courts, often held in closed sessions in prisons, according to accounts collected by Amnesty International.

They were then denied internationally recognised rights to fair trial including the right of appeal to a higher court, it said.

Trials before special military courts are regularly reported to use as evidence "confessions" extracted under torture. Among methods of torture reported to have been used are prisoners being hung upside down and beaten, given electric shocks, burnt with cigarettes and deprived of food while incriminating statements were forced from them, the organisation said.

Amnesty International's memorandum also called for the prompt abolition of special military courts. The organisation noted that the government promised to end martial law by January 1, 1986 and that military courts would stop functioning then.

However, prisoners serving sentences imposed by special military courts have no leagal redress, as a result of a constitutional amendment which bans judicial jurisdiction over decisions of military courts.

Amnesty International also published information received after the memorandum has sent including a detailed account of the case of Abdul Razzaq Jharna, accused of a 1981 political assassination and reportedly tortured during incommunicado detention into making a "confession".

Two of the prosecution witnesses presented in the trial were detained until they testified. The court bearing his case is to have headed to acquit him but before the verdict was announced the president of the court was removed. Under the new presiding officer, the second court relying on the first court's record of the trial, convicted him. He was hanged in May 1983.

Amnesty International said it knew of more than 130 political prisoners convicted by special military court since 1979 and at least 38 awaiting verdicts. More than 100 have faced these courts in the past year.

In addition, hundreds of political prisoners have received sentences of up to three years from summary military courts, which deal with offences considered less serious.

The courts were established under martial law after the military takeover in 1977. The civilian judiciary, purged when constitutional changes were introduced in 1981, has no jurisdiction over them.

Many prisoners have been held incommunicado for months after their arrest. This is the period when torture or other ill-treatments has been regularly reported.

Amnesty International said it was also concerned about short-term political arrests, cruel punishments and the use of the death penalty in Pakistan.

It noted that the total number of prisoners of conscience was believed to be lower than in earlier years, when thousands were sometimes in custody. Among those arrested now are people held for trying to engage in non-violent political activity and members of the Ahmadiyya community—who have been banned from calling themselves Muslims.

More than 140 people are reported to have been sentenced to death, most of them on criminal charges, in 1983 and 1984 ; over two thirds of them were condemned by special military courts. Flogging is frequently imposed by summary and other courts, and sentences of amputation have been handed down, though Amnesty International has not received confirmation that any have been carried out.

1707. Venkatesh, S. : Terrorists a Pak headache too. *Statesman* 26 Jan 1986 ; 1, 9.

1708. Sullivan, George : Pakistan. In *Story of the Peace Corps.* New York. 1964 ; 125-30.

1709. Terrorism Probing the Karachi hijacks. *Asiaweek* 21 Sep 1986 ; 36.

Palestine

1710. All in the same boat. *International Herald Tribune* 10 Oct 1985 ; 4.

1711. Alon, Hanon : *Countering Palestinian terrorism in Israel.* Santa Monica, The Rand Corporation, 1980.

1712. Bailey, Clinton : Political concessions aren't the way to snuff out Palestinian terrorism. *International Herald Tribune* 23 Jan 1986 ; 6.

Viewed from Britain, the main outcome of the Palestinian terrorist attacks at the Rome and Vienna airports last month was to strengthen Colonel Moamer Qadhafi's position in Europe. It was first apparent in the readiness of the British media to highlight and give credence to the Libyan leader's denial of implication in these attacks and to his belated condemnation of them as U.S. warships steamed toward his coast.

This despite Colonel Qadhafi's known sponsorship of the Abu Nidal groups, the alleged perpetrators, and despite Egypt's identification of the very hotel in Tripoli from which Abu Nidal has engineered the hijacking of an Egyptian airliner to Malta—'November—not to mention initial applause for the Rome and Vienna attacks when they occurred.

The second indication of the European's concern for Colonel Qadhafi was their rejection of President Reagan's request for economic sanctions against Libya. It immediately became clear that Europe's dependence on the colonel for billions of dollars in exports and much of its oil endows him with strategic importance.

Economic interest so not full account for the European reluctance to take emphatic action against terrorism. John C. Whitecheed, dered in the Palestinian terrorist attacks that provoked the raid was pointedly suggested as the reason for the Rome and Vienna assaults. The illogic of Abu Nidal avenging the restruction of the headquarters of his supposed archenemy, Yasser Arafat, did not deter the various pundits. Nor did they stop to ponder whether the Romeand Vienna attacks would have been avoided that Israel retaliated only against the exact number of persons that it had lost.

1713. Caute, David : *Fanon*, London, 1970.

1714. Chabetz, Zev : Unfolding catalog of Arab violence. *International Herald Tribune* 10 Oct 1985 ; 4.

1715. Cabban, Helena : PLO faces new pressures. *Middle East International* May 1978 ; 10-12.

1716. Dyer, Gwynne : Strategy of massacre. *Hindustan Times* 21 Jan 1986 ; 9.

1717. Ellenbreg, Edward S. : PLO and its peace in violence and terror. In *ITCW* ; 165-76.

With their numbers continuously increasing and the misery of the conditions in the refugees' camps growing, the Arab refugees became an easy prey to those who, refugees themselves, decided to make a political career. In 1956 a Palestine Arab nationalist organization, the Al Fatch, was created in the Gaza Strip. The word Fatah, which means conquest, was formed by the Arabic initials in reverse order of

"Harakat all Therir al Falastia" or Palestine Liberation Movement, In 1959, Fatah, led by Yasser Arafat, created the military commando organization of al Assifa which, in 1964, developed into an operational force trained cheifly on Syrian territory. In the meantime, in Cairo, under Egyptian auspices and following an agreement at the Arab Summit Conference, the late Ahmed Shukairy, a Palestinian lawyer who represented Saudi Arabia and later Syria in the UN, prepared the charter of the PLO and became the organization's first president. In May 1964, the National Convenant of the PLO was drawn up, suspending the charter launched only a year before. The PLO was proclaimed as "a mobilizing leadership of the forces of the Palestine Arab people to wage the battle of liberation, as a shield for the rights and aspirations of the people of Palestine."

At the time of its proclamation, it was clear that this National Covenant of the PLO was influenced by the political aims of Gamal Abdul Nasser, who as leader of Egypt dreamt of becoming the leader of all Arabs. But Article 24 of this covenant specified that "this Organization (PLO) does not exercise any regional sovereignty over the Western Bank in the Hashomite Kingdom of Jordan, or the Gaza Strip or the Himmah Area." In other words, the PLO did not want to or was not allowed or supposed to exercise any sovereignty over those parts of Palestine that were considered parts of an Arab Palestine state but which had been already annexed by other Arab states. The PLO was only allowed to fight against Israel. The conclusion is a clear one : the PLO was meant to be an organization aimed at pushing the Arab refugees to fight against the Jewish State but not at resettling them in the territory of historic Palestine. According to the wishes of Nasser and of Hussein of Jordan, the PLO was not entitled to proclaim an Arab state on the territories that belonged to the initial Arab parts of Palestine—as mentioned by the UN Partition Resolution—that were not yet occupied by the Isrselis, but was only to fight the Jewish state. Again the refusal of the Arab leaders to find a solution for a large number of the Arab refugees by helping them to create an Arab Palestinian state was evident. They had divided the Arab Palestinian territories among themselves in an effort to maintain the plight of the refugees and to play them against Israel. And the whole world did nothing to step this shameful action.

After the Israeli victory in the 1967 war and the occupation of the Western Bank, Fatah retreated into Jordanian territory, making Jordan its base of guerrilla operations against Israel. Shukairy was forced to resign as the PLO's president and was succeeded by Fatah's Yasser Arafat, as the head of the already biggest Palestinian organization. The Seven

Points adopted in 1969 by the Central Committee of Al Fatah made it clear again that the struggle was against Israel and only in the second place towards "restoration of the independent democratic State of Palestine." In 1967, another guerrilla organization dedicated to the destruction of Israel was founded—the Popular Front for the Liberation of Palestine, led by Dr. George Habash, an avowed Marxist. The second aim of this organization was the creation of a revolutionary socialist Palestine Arab State. Habash decided that his organization must conduct a campaign of terror directed not only at Jews but designed to attract international attention to the plight of the Palestinian Arabs. The Al Fatah, the Popular Front for the Liberation of Palestine, the Syrian, sponsored al Saiqa, the Popular Democratic Front, and five other smaller groups, despite their ideological differences are formally united in the PLO. But each is waging its own war against Israel and acting upon orders of different Arab states. In this struggle, the younger Palestinian generations of refugees are used as soldiers, and their camps have become centers of recruitment. In Cairo, under Egyptian auspices and following an agreement at the Arab Summit Conference, the late Ahmed Shukairy, a Palestinian lawyer who represented Saudi Arabia and later Syaia in the UN, prepared the charter of the PLO and became the organization's first president. In May 1964, the National Covenant of the PLO was drawn up, suspending the charter launched only year before. The PLO was proclaimed as "a mobilizing leadership of the forces of the Palestine Arab people to wage the battle of liberation, as a shield for the rights and aspirations of the people of Palestine."

At the time of its proclamation, it was clear that this National Covenant of the PLO was influenced by the political aims of Gamal Abdul Nasser, who as leader of Egypt dreamt of becoming the leader of all Arabs. But Article 24 of this covenant specified that "this Organization (PLO) does not exercise any regional sovereignty over the Western Bank in the Hashomite Kingdom of Jordan, or the Gaza Strip or the Himmah Area." In other words, the PLO did not want to or was not allowed or supposed to exercise any sovereignty over those prats of Palestine that were considered parts of an Arab Palestine state but which had been already annexed by other Arab states. The PLO was only allowed to fight against Israel. The conclusion is a clear one : the PLO was meant to be an organization aimed at pushing the Arab refugees to fight against the Jewish State but not at resettling them in the territory of historic Palestine. According to the wishes of Nasser and of Hussein of Jordan, the PLO was not entitled to proclaim an Arab state on the territories that belonged to the initial Arab parts of Palestine—as mentioned by the UN Partition Resolution—that were not yet occupied by the Israelis, but was only to fight the Jewish state. Again the refusal of the Arab leaders to find a solution for a large number of the Arab refugees by helping them to create an Arab Palestinian state was evident. They had divided the Arab Palestinian territories among themselves in an effort to maintain the plight of the refugees and to play them against Israel. And the whole world did nothing to stop this shameful action.

After the Israeli victory in the 1967 war and the occupation of the Western Bank, Fatah retreated into Jordanain territory, making Jordan its base of guerrilla operations against Israel. Shukairy was forced to resign as the PLO's president and was succeeded by Fatah's Yasser Arafat, as the head of the already biggest Palestinian organisation. The Seven Points adopted in 1969 by the Central Committee of Al Fatah made it clear again that the struggle was against Israel and only in the second place toward "restoration of the independent democratic State of Palestine." In 1967, another guerrilla organization dedicated to the destruction of Israel was founded—the Popular Front for the Liberation of Palestine, led by Dr. George Habash, an avowed Marxist. The second aim of this organization was the creation of a revolutionary socialist Palestine Arab state. Habash decided that his organization must conduct a compaign of terror directed not only at Jews but designed to attract international attention to the plight of the Palestinian Arabs. The Al Fatah, the Popular Front for the Liberation of Palestine the Syrian-sponsored Al Saiqa, the Popular Democratic Front, and five other smaller groups, despite their ideological differences, are formally united in the PLO. But each is waging its own war against Israel and acting upon orders of different Arab states. In this struggle, the younger Palestinian generations of refugees are used as soldiers, and their camps have become centers of recruitment.

1718. Foxman, Abraham H. and Kenneth Jacobson : Arafat has yet to renounce Palestinian terrorism. *International Herald Tribune* 21 Fep 1986 ; 6.

1719. Friedman, Thomas L. : Nidal-a mercenany or a nationalist ? *Amrita Bazar Patrika* 21 Jan 1986 ; 9.

1720. Gazit, Shlomo : Myth and the reality of the PLO. In *ITCR* ; 443-49.

1721. George Habash to Oriana Fallaci. *Life* 22 Jan 1970.

1722. Gerbasi, Frank : Terror in Palestine. *Colliers* Aug 1945.

1723. Golan, Galia : Terrorism. In *Soviet Union and the Palestine Liberation Organization.* By Galia Golan. New York, Praager, 1980 ; 210-27.

1724. Hansen, Emmanuel : *Frantz . Fanon : Social and political thought.* Columbus, Ohio State University Press, 1977.

1725. Hart, Alan : Arafat : *Terrorist or peacemaker* ? London 1985. Pp. 480.

1726. Hoffman, Bruce : Recent trends in Palestinian terrorism in *ITDC* : 241-50.

1727. Jansen, G.H. : Portrait of Abu Nidal ; Self-defeating Obssession. *Deccan Herald* 16 Jan 1986 ; 6.

1728. Laffin, J. *Fedaveen.* New York, 1973.

1729. Meron, Ran : Soviet concept of Guerrilla warfare and retaliation : The case of the Palestinian guerillas and Israel. *International Problems* (Tel Aviv) 16 (3-4) 1977 ; 78-91.

1730. Nisan, Mordechai : PLO messianism : Diagnosis of a modern gnostic sect. *Terrorism* 7 (3) 1984 : 299-312

1731. O'Neill, Band E. : Towards a typology of political terrorism. The Palestinian resistence movement. *Journal of International Affairs* Spr-Sum 1978 ; 17-42.

1732. Parry, Albert : Arafat and other sacrifices. In *Terrorism* New York, 1976 ; 449-68.

1733. Schiff, Z and R. : Rothstein *Feyadeen.* New York, 1972.

1934. Seale, B. : *Seize the time ; the story of the Black Panther Party.* London, Arrow Books 1968.

1735. Seale, Patrick : PLO shifts back to terrorism. *Amrita Bazar Patrika* (Calcutta) 23 Jan 1986 ; 6.

1736. Sharabi, Hishan : *Palestine guerrillas : their credibility and effectiveness.* Beirut, Institute for Palestine Studies, 1970. Pp. 64.

1737. Sobel, A. Lester *ed.* : *Palestinian impasse : Arab guerrillas and international terror.* New York, Facts on File, 1978.

1738. Suro, Roberto : Terrorists are suspected of using new networks, new tactics. *International Herald Tribune* 15 Sep 1986 : 2.

1739. Weisband, Edward and Damir Roguly : Palestinian terrorism : violence, verbal strategy and legitimacy. In *International Terrorism.* By Yonah Alexander ; 283-308.

1740. Yaniv, Avner : Phoenix or phantom ? the PLO after Beirut. *Terrorism* 7(3) 1984 ; 313-22.

1741. Yodfat, Aryeh : USSR and the Palestinians. *New Outlook* 19 Jun 1976.

People's Republic of China

1742. China, Pak aiding terrorists. (Frank Camper) *Times of India* 17 Mar 1986 ; 16.

Frank Camper, who runs a private paramilitary training camp near Birmingham, Alabama, says he has been told by Sikhs who had undergone training in his school that China and Pakistan were "aiding the Sikh cause, providing both money and weapons, as well as safe areas inside their own borders, for training or hiding."

In an article in "Penthouse" magazine, Camper quoted an unidentified Sikh as telling him that Chia had given "equipment and some money" and "we have a camp in China."

Camper wrote that he tried to mentally picture a map of India, and recall where the borders with China were. "The Punjab did touch China—an almost perfect situation". Had Pakistan offered any help ? "Of course," he was told. "The Pakistanis hate the Indians. They do what they can. We have friends."

Mr. Camper said a Sikh who had identified himself as Balraj Singh had approached him with three others who were introduced as Sukvinder Singh, Avraj Singh and Lal Singh, seeking training in his camp. They had told him that they needed training in special techniques, such as the making bombs, like time bombs, and how to assassinate or capture government officials.

"We need to know how to make grenades, silencers for firearms, and how to sabotage factories," Balraj Singh was quoted as saying.

Camper wrote : „Good grief, I though. 'Okay' I told him. Let me think about that. Just stay in the training." " I made a decision to enter into an operation to stop the Sikhs in the US who were planning violent acts."

Camper is to testify before a federal district judge in New York currently trying Gurparatap Singh Virk, a 35-year-old computer scientist on a charge of conspiring to assassinate the Prime Minister, Mr Rajiv Gandhi during his visit to the US last year.

Defence counsel, Mr. William Kunstler, had told the Judge on the opening day the of trial last week that Camper was profiting from his involvement in the case and that he was "making a mint" by publishing articles in the "Penthouse" magazine.

In his article Camper detaile what the magazine called "the complete history of the Sikh terror plot—and of his involvement with the plotters and the U. S. authorities who were determined to stop them."

The magazine said Camper would conclude in the May issue the "dramatic and tragic conclusion" of his story.

Camper says the Sikhs had told him they wanted to blow up the all the three nuclear plants in India. "If we would create another Bhopal, it would be perfect," one of them was quoted as saying.

"Did you have anything to do with the Union Carbide plant at Bhopal ?" Camper said he asked the Sikhs. "No, that was an accident, but a bloody good one," he was told. "That is what we need, another Bhopal."

Camper, who was keeping an FBI agent informed of his encounters with the Sikhs, said in his article, the Sikhs had formulated a plan to contaminate their nation's food and water, to destory its nuclear reactors, and to assassinate at will which trained hit teams.

"The hatred from both sides (Sikhs and Hindus) was almost a tangible thing. Now, I was going to become part of it.... I began to structure my notes, I would have a report for the FBI of a kind they did not see every day," Camper wrote in concluding his first article.

1743. Dirlik, Arif : Vision and revolution : Anarchism in Chinese revolutionary thought on the eve of the 1911 revolution. *Modeır China* 12 (2) Apr 1986 ; 123-65.

1744. Epstein, Israel : Mensories of the war. *China Reconstructs* Sep 1985 ; 25-29.

1745. Fung, Edmund S. K. : Anti-imperialism and the left Ghomindang. *Modern China* 11 (1) Jan 1985 ; 39-76.

1746. Lang, Olga : *Pa Chin and his writings.* Cambridge, Havard University Press, 1967.

1747. Party, Albert : Mao's muzzle. In *Terrorism.* New York, 1976 ; 223-33.

1748. Saksena, N.S. : Large Scale terror in China, 1920-70. In *THF* 91-99.

1749. Scalapino, Robert : *Chinese anarchist movement.* Berkeley, 1961.

1750. Scalapino, Robert A. and George T. Yn : Emergence of anarchists. In *Modern China and its revolutionary process.* Univ. of California, 1985 ; 231-59.

1751. Seybolt, Peter J. : Terror and conformity : Rectification and mass movement, 1942-43. *Modern China* 12 (1) Jan 1986 ; 39-74.

1752. Shuanliang, Hu and Han Zengxing : Safety first flying. *China Reconstructs* Dec 1985 ; 60-61.

1753. Soviet bloc and China training Sikh terrorists ? *Organiser* 1 Sep 1985 ; 1-2.

1754. Tie, Yan : China's part in the victory over the fascist powers. *China Reconstructs* Sep 1985 ; 11-15.

1755. Tson, Tang : Back from the brink of revolutionary 'feudal' totalitarianism. In *Cultural revolution and post-Mao reforms.* Chicago University, 1986 ; 144-88.

Peru

1756. Bennett, Philip : Peru : Corner of the dead. *Atlantic* May 1984 ; 28.33.

1757. Goodsell, Charles T. : That confounding revolution in Peru. *Current History* Jan 1975 ; 20-23.

1758. Guerrillas kill top Peruvian naval officer. *Times of India.* 7 May 1986 ; 24.

1759. Indian embassy in Peru attacked. *Daily* 28 Jan 1987 ; 2.

1760. Kidnapping reaps big profit in Peru. *Telegarph* (Calcutta) 2 Jan 1986 ; 9.

A wave of kidnappings is spreading fear and uncertainty in Peru Now-a-days more and more businessmen are sending members of their family abroad to protect them from the kidnappers.

Recently, for example, the head of the Peruvian branch of the West German chemical firm Bayer left the country with his wife and three children after his family had spent six days held by kidnappers. It was believed that ransom of at least 2.6 million marks (over one million dollars was paid to secure their release.

The influential newspaper El Comercio here said that the series of kidnappings is "shaking the foundations of our society". It warned that foreign firms' interest in investing in Peru could drop to a level lower than that already caused by the economic crisis.

Another publication, Caretas, estimated that each month around 50 persons are being kidnapped in Peru : Industrialists in front of their factories, their children outside the schoolyard, and their wives at home while opening the garage door.

In about 80 per cent of the cases, the families or companies affected do not seek help from the police. Caretas said that there was a good reason for this fact : In many cases it had turned out that policemen belonged to the kidnapping gangs.

Beyond this, the Lima Chamber of Commerce believes that the gangsters may have contacts working in Peruvian banks who provide them with information about the size of a potential victim's bank account. In the negotiations for ransom money, the kidnappers often seem to be excellently informed about the family's ability to pay.

In one case it turned out that a member of a kidnapping gang was employed with the tax authorities. The circle of "potential customers" from which he could choose is relatively small, since only about 70,000 persons out of Peru's population of 20 million pay taxes. The biggest taxpayers are foreign firms and their employees.

Most foreign companies have now started providing private police protection to their top managers. At a time when unemployment is running beyond 50 per cent, the payrolls of private security firms are surging. In Lima alone 20,000 private police are now employed.

Meanwhile Peruvian police, aided by British experts, have set up a special department to deal with kidnapping.

But the officers there, who on average earn only about $ 80 a month, have so far had only limited success against the kidnappers, who by Peruvian press estimates, have taken over $ 100 million's worth of ransom money since the end of 1984.

Among other incidents, police found on a beach the sand-covered corpase of industrialist Alex Municher, 34, for whom the first "instalment's—10 per cent of the total ransom demand of just over one million dollars—had already been paid.

In view of the apparent helplessness of the police, some kidnapping victims have begun to strike back by hiring armed groups to capture relatives of those known leaders of kidnapping gangs.

For example, at present two daughters and a sister of the Sanchez Bedon brothers—known to lead one of at least eight kidnapping bands in Lima—are being held.

The most feared kidnappers are the tree Reynoso Augilar brothers, who are chiefly known for cutting off a finger or an ear of their victim and sending it to his family to press their ransom demands.

Peruvian police say that the wave of kidnappings has no political background. They believe that many of the bank robbers of bygone days have gone over to kidnapping as a more profitable and less dangerous crime. In 1984, when crime rose by 9.1 per cent, the number of bank robberies declined.

1761. Massacre in Peru. *International Herald Tribune* 23 Jun 1986 ; 6.

1762. McClintock, Cynthia : Democracies and guerrillas : The Peruvian experience. *International Policy Report* Sep 1983.

1763. McClintock, Cynthia : Why peasants revel. *World Politics* 35, Oct 1984 ; 48-84.

1764. Palmer, David Scott : Rebellion in rural Peru. *Comparative Politics* 18 (2) Jan 1986 ; 127-46.

1765. White terror in Puno : *International Viewpoint* 19 Nov 1986 ; 21-22.

Philippines

1766. Aquino, Corazon : I want to avert violence. *Asiaweek* 23 Feb 1986 ; 17.

1767. Blejwas, Stanislaus, A. : Big powers hold key card in popular revolutions. *International Herald Tribune* 13 Mar 1986 ; 6.

1768. Hundred Filipino rebels lay down arms. *International Herald Tribune* 12-13 Apr 1986 ; 5.

1769. Mood in Mindano, *Far Eastern Economic Review* 30 Jan 1986 ; 12-13.

1770. Philippines : Murder City. *Asiaweek* 9 Sep 1985 ; 6-18.

1771. Sacerdoti, Guy and Jose Galang : Resorting to violence to ensure victory. *Far Eastern Economic Review.* 20 Feb 1986 ; 16.

1772. Sullivan, George : Philippines. In *Story of the Peace Corps.* New York, 1964 ; 131-37.

Portugal

1773. *Insight on Portugal* ; *The year of the Captains.* London, Andre Deutsch, 1975.

1774. Pottinger, Ken: Prortugese Hero of '74 Coup on trial Monday as *International Herald Tribune* 20-21 Jul 1985 ; 2.

1775. Venter, A.J. : *Portugal's guerrilla War.* Capetown, John Malherbe Pvt. Ltd., 1973.

Seychelles

1776. Nambcodiri, P.K.S. : Seychelles Coup bid in perspective. *Strategic Analysis* 5 (10) Jan 1982 ; 557-64.

Singapore

1777. Clutterbuck, Richard : *Conflict and violence in Singapore and Malaysia, 1945-1983.* New York, 1985.

South Africa

1778. Benson, Mary : *South Africa : The struggle for a birthright.* London, Penguin, 1966.

1779. Black rule in South Africa inevitable. *China Daily* 7 Feb 1986 ; 8.

1780. Bochikarvov, V. : Backing the terrorists. *New Times* (6) Feb 1986 ; 8.

A regular red-carpet was accorded to Jonas Savimbi, the leader of the UNITA terrorists, on his arrival in Washington on January 30, He was received by the President the Secretary of State, the Secretary of the Defence, the Chairman, of the Joint Chiefs of Staff, and the director of the CIA. The ultra-Right organizations that have taken him under their wing bent over backwards to ensure him as much publicity as possible. He was given the opportunity to appear on TV programmes, diverse "seminars" (I) were planned for him and meetings and interviews of all kinds. All this could serve as the plot of an amusing vaudeivilee were it not for the sinister schemes concealed beneath the surface.

Savimbi was brought to Washington from the depths of Africa at the moment when the question of rendering him military and other aid is being considered. As a matter of fact the question has long been settled in principle. All that remains is to haggle with Congress over the exact amount of dollars to be allotted Savimbi for the purchase of arms. Initial reports put the sum at $ 27 million, but now there is talk of double that figure. The sum of $ 300 million is even mentioned ?

Reagan has never concealed his hostility towards the People's Republic of Angola, and the desire either to overthrow the government of the republic or to force it to enter into negotiations with the UNITA leaders has become something of an obssession with him. South Africa, acting in compact with the U.S., has been giving every support to the UNITA bands. Its troops have invaded Angolan territory several times to save them from being wiped out in the course of offensive operations by the People's Liberation Army of Angola. But the racists are finding this too much for them. Pretoria needs troops at home to put down the anti-racist actions that have swept all provinces of South Africa. It needs troops also in Namibia to keep that country under its heel. Besides, there are also the terrorist bands operating in Mozambique to be supported. And all this at a time when the South African economy is splitting at the seams. UNITA, for its part, has to have constant help, for without it Savimbi's bands would have been routed long since. Hence Washington's decision to hasten to his assistance.

In the U.S. Congress, however, there are a good many opponents of the Administration's intentions. More than 100 Congressmen have apppealed to the President to stop helping UNITA. There is also considerable opposition to that reckless policy outside Congress. The New York Times, for instance, says that Savimbi is not a "freedom fighter", as Reagan depicts him, but merely an unscrupulous politican and terrorist. He has a reputation as a South African puppet, the paper says, and to render him assistance would only bind the U.S. closer to South African policy, which would evoke the anger of the whole of Africa. But the Administration remains adamant. Reagan received Savimbi and promised to hold UNITA in its struggle against the Marxist government in Luanda. Savimbi himself has said he will not be leaving the US. empty-handed.

The U.S. Administration's decision to aid UNITA is in line with its "new globalism" strategy which consists in resorting to strong-arm methods against Third World countries which do not wish to submit to Washington's diktat, are pursuing their own independent policy and building their own life as they see fit. U.S. policy towards Angola give the lie to Washington's assurances of its desire for a peaceful settlement of regional conflicts. In reality it is seeking to incite such conflicts, headless of the fact that this can only lead to more bloodshed, to more loss of human life.

But Angola will not be brought to its knees. It has loyal friends who are always ready to help it withstand all trials. The Soviet-Angolan-Cuban consultations held on January 27 in Moscow testify to this. The participants in the meeting, reviewing the world situation in general and the situation in southern Africa in particular denounced Pretoria's attempts to legalize its colonial domination of Namibia and voiced their unfailing support for the ANC-led struggle of the South African people against the detested apartheid regime. They noted the "timeliness and usefulness" of the consultations for the "further coordination of the actions of the three countries to defend the independence, sovereignty and territorial integrity of the People's Republic of Angola and to achieve a fair and honest settlement in southern Africa."

1781. Call for sanctions against S. Africa. *China Daily* 23 Nov 1985 ; 4.

1782. Conyers, John : Getting tough with. Pretoria. *New York Times* 23 Jan 1985 ; A23.

1783. Crary, David : Violence a fact of South African life. *Baghdad Observer* 11 Sep 1986 ; 4.

1784. Eliason, Marcus : Slipping through the cracks of apartheid's walls. *Baghdad Observer* 25 Mar 1986 ; 4.

1785. Fossedal, Gregory A. : Morality test for South Africa's opposition. *International Herald Tribune* 6 Feb 1986 ; 4.

1786. Frankel, Glenn : South Africa's disappeared tales of torture, deprivation. *International Herald Tribune* 14 Jul 1986 ; 1, 6.

1787. Frankel, Philip H. : *Pretoria's pretorian : Civilmilitary relations in South Africa.* Cambridge 1984. Pp. 230.

1788. Horrell, Muriel : *Terrorism in South Africa.* Johannesburg, South African Institute of Race Relations, 1968.

1789. Imperialist collusion with racists. *Iraq Today* 16-31 Oct 1979 ; 13.

1790. Jacobs, W.D. *et. al.* : *Terrorism in Southern Africa* : *Portents and prospects.* New York, American-African Affairs Association, 1973.

1791. Latest wave of violence claims 13 in S. Africa. *China Daily* 20 Nov 1985 ; 8.

1792. Legum, Colin : New South African conflict ; Black versus. Black. *International Herald Tribune* 20 Dec 1985 ; 6.

1793. Mathews, A.S. : Terrorism of *South African Law Journal* 41, Aug 1974.

1794. Moola, M. : Reign of terror continues. *Indian Review of African Affairs* Oct 1985 : 15-19.

The declaration of another State of Emergency in 36 towns and cities by the South African racist regime is a desperate attempt to stem the growing tide of resistance against its inhuman and oppressive policies. The Emergency is another act of violence against an oppressed, voiceless and voteless majority. But it must be seen as a panic and stopgap measure aimed to bolster a week and tottering regime in the throes of an ever-deepening economic and political crisis.

For nearly ten months the world has witnessed the growing determination and mass upsurge of an unarmed people against a brutal and sophisticated state machinery. The assertion of their human dignity and striving for fundamental freedoms has earned our people the deserved respect and admiration of the universal community. Over five hundred have been killed and thousands injured during this year alone and yet the movement against an oppressive system continues unabated.

The South African racist regime can never fully suppress this movement of resistance unless it addresses itself to the fundamental question of the total dismantling of the apartheid system and the granting of unfettered freedoms to all South Africans, irrespective of race, colour, sex or creed. For, the seeds of violence and racial conflict are to be found in the very nature and structure of the apartheid system—a system declared by the United Nations as constituting a crime against humanity.

It might be recalled that a state of emergency was imposed 25 years ago in the wake of the Sharpeville and Lanka massacres when unarmed Blacks protesting against the hated pass laws were brutaly murdered by a trigger-happy police force. In Sharpeville alone 69 were killed and over 200 wounded, many of them maimed for life.

The African National Congress (ANC) was declared illegal and 20,000 people of all nationalities were detained throughout the country. Every form of political dissent or activity was banned and severely curtailed.

During the period of the emergency when virtually its entire leadership and activists were in detention the ANC made its position abundantly clear that no amount of repressive measures, strong-arms tactics or muzzling of individuals and organisations can prevent an oppressed and determined people from attaining its cherished objectives. In a clarion call to the people of South Africa the ANC declared that the arbitrary ban will in no way deter it from its firm resolve to continue the battle for a free, democratic and non-racial South African Society.

A year later, and as a direct consequence of further repressive measures the African National Congress announced the formation of its military wing—Umkhonto we Sizwe (The Spear of the Nation). On the 16th December, 1961 by means of co-ordinated acts of sabotage in the four major centres of the country—Johannesburg, Cape Town, Port Elizabeth and Durban—the movement warned the white-minority regime of grave consequences of its ill-conceived policies and of the emergence of a new era in black policies and resistance. In clear terms it procailmed that unbridled state violence shall be met by armed revolutionary violence from a long-suffering and an oppressed people. The emphasis, henceforth, shall be on the armed struggle for liberation and all South Africans—black and white—were called upon to join the peoples' army and meet the growing repression and violence of a brutal, sophisticated and fully-armed and equipped state machinery which does not hesitate to kill and maim an unarmed black majority which had been deliberately denied basic human rights and fundamental freedoms taken for granted elsewhere. Nelson Mandela, the charismatic leader of the ANC, was elected its first Commander-in-Chief. That Mandela has been incarcerated for the past 23 years for "plotting the overthrow of the racist regime by violent means" and his consistent, courageous and principled opposition to racial tyranny is a matter of current history. He remains a beacon of inspiration to countless South Africans of all nationalities and political persuasion to redouble their efforts in the common endeavour to eradicate the racist scourge.

The period between the 1960 and 1985 emergencies has been marked by a general upsurge and has been punctuated by violent and non-violent campaigns of resistance—strikes, boycotts of schools, universities, buses, etc ; open defiance of aparthied institutions and discriminatory laws ; resistence to forced removals of settled communities and struggles for better wages, trade union rights and living conditions. A specific feature of this period has been an escalation of armed guerrilla activity and sabotage of government installations and the virtual unbanning of the ANC by hundreds of thousands of its members and supportes who refused to be bludgeoned into submission.

Perhaps the most significant development during the past two-and-a-half decades has been the growing awareness and realisation by thousands of our people (particularly youth and students) that the regime is not invincible and can be removed by the combined efforts of all those opposed to apartheid and racism ; that the struggle for liberation can and must be intensified on all fronts and levels—political, economic, military, etc.—if the objective of total liberation is to be realised within a relatively short period of time.

It is precisely this awareness that explains why millions of our people have unbanned the ANC, adopted its programme—The Freedom Charter—as their own vision of a new South Africa, sing its songs, unfurl its banners and shout its battle-cry AMANDLA NGAWETHU (Power to the People) when facing the armed might of a police State that hundreds of thousands of Coloureds and those of Indian decent rejected the pseudo-reforms and over-whelmingly boycotted the elections for separate "parliaments." This was an impressive display of solidarity with their African brothers who were totally excluded by the so-called constitutional reforms. It is this realisation of their inherent strength and the justness of their cause that impels countless numbers of our people to carry on the struggle regardless of the consequences.

Viewed against the backdrop of continuing unrest, violence and turmoil against a patently oppressive, unjust and an exploitative system the adoption of more draconian measures cannot, in the final analysis, restore "calm and tranquility" which the emergency hopes to do. The violence and killings are bound to escalate so long as the basic causes of unrest are not squarely famed and honest attempts are made to resolve them.

Reaction to the imposition of a state of emergency has been adverse. Both nationally and internationally sane and civilised voices have condemned the action of the Government and South Africa's image has been at an all-time low. The demand for the imposition of comprehensive and mandatory sanctions and the tolal isolation of the racist regime has been reinformced and given greater urgency. The French Government declared a ban on further investments and the possible application of sanctions unless real and genguine changes are effected by the Botha regime within the next 18 months. And for the first time in the history of the Security Council has a country that in the past consistently exercised the veto to block sanctions agains South Africa now initiated a move, supported by Denmark, calling for a freeze on foreign investments and the application of voluntary sanctions by member-States of the U.N. Notwithstanding its shortcomings the French resolution must be seen as positive step. Today the Reagan and Thatcher administrations stand exposed, as never before, as unabashed supporters of a regime which continues to flout with impunity virtually every cannon of justice and principle of the UN Charter and the Universal Declaration of Human Rights.

The withdrawal of the French Ambassador and lesser diplomatic personnel of other western countries are strong signals to the Botha regime that its policies are becoming more and more repugnant and indefensible and that the West will have no distance itself from policies and practices which assault the very dignity and worth of the human personality. For its onwn credibility and long-term economic political and other interests the Western world connot be seen as remaining silent in the fact of unbridled barbarism and terror in a country which prides itself as a socalled Western Christian outpost, a staunch supporter of "Western democratic values" and a bulwark against the "Communist menace" in Africa.

It is against this backdrop that Denmark's closure of her Consulate General and the initiative taken by her, France, Greece, and the Netherlands, within the European Economic Community, calling for disinvestment and stringent action against Pretoria assume special significance. Every anti-apartheid move, no matter how small, is another nail in the coffin of racism.

It adds to the groundswell of condemnation of apartheid tyranny in all corners of the world and strengthens the demand for Pretoria's total isolation and for the imposition of comprehensive and mandatory sanctions against South Africa. And, it reinforces the resolve and determination of our embattled people to fight on regardless.

It is imperative that international pressure be kept up and intensified for it undoubtedly contributes to the weakening of the apartheid system and enhances the anti-colonial and anti- apartheid struggle. It should, however, be underscored that the main thrust and burden of dismantling and eradicating the apartheid system rests upon the South African people themselves—both black and democratic-minded whites. International pressure is important and necessary but for obvious reason can only be complementary. The point is repeatedly emphasised lest our people become excessively dependent on external help only and lapse into complacency.

The emergency in indeed a desperate and drastic act to suppress a growing resistance movement. Unfortunately for the upholders of white overlordship these measures can no longer save their criminal and despicable system from eventual doom and destruction. There are moments in the history of oppressed people when the old tyrannical system finds itself besieged, in an untenable situation and with its back against the wall. This moment might, just have arrived in South Africa. And White South Africa has but few options before it : suffer and die fighting a lost cause or recognise the reality with courage that the days of white domination are indeed numbered : that it has no alternative but to concede to the just demands of our people for total emancipation and unfettered freedoms for all South Africans irrespective of race, colour, sex or creed. There is no alternative to this basic reality facing the racist regime. The writing is writ large on the wall.........and the ball is in Botha's court.

1795. Morrock, R. : *South Africa's Bantustans : Illusion and reality*. Lusaka, IDEP Feb 1974. Pp. 28.

1796. Multinationals in South Africa. *People's Democracy* 2 Feb 1986 ; 8.

1797. Ottaway, David B. : U.S. aide backs majority rule in South Africa. *International Herald Tribune* 14 Mar 1986 ; 1-2.

1798. Parks, Michall : Forced boycott splits South African blacks. *International Herald Tribune* 20 Dec 1985 ; 4.

1799. Parks, Michael : South Africa's private wars. Frightened white communities turning to vigilantism. *International Herald Tribune* 19 Mar 1986 ; 1-5.

1800. Pretoria main base of terrorism. *National Herald* 6 Jan 1986 ; 10.

1801. Pretoria's cautions change. *International Herald Tribune* 6 Feb 1986 ; 5.

1802. Raspberrg, William : Botha's style, Boesak says much of the problem. *International Herald Tribane* 13 Dec 1985 ; 6.

1803. Raspberry, William : South Africa ! Who will Salvage the youngsters ? *International Herald Tribune* 16 Dec 1985 ; 4.

1804. Rudolph, Harold : *Security, terrorism and torture detainees' rights in South Africa and Israel : A Comparative Study*. Cape Town, 1984. Pp. 288.

1805. Safire, William : Time for terrorism's victims to organize. *International Herald Tribune* 4-5 Jan 1986 ; 4.

1806. Saxena, S.C. : Armed struggle enters a decisive phase. *Link* 29 Sep 1985 ; 28-29.

1807. Selbourne. David : Racism and hypocrisy. In *through the Indian looking glass*. Bombay, Popular Prakashan, 1982 ; 107-9.

1808. South African scene. *International Herald Tribune* 19 Dec 1985 ; 6.

1809. State terrorism in South Africa, *Deccan Chronicle* 23 Jul 1985 ; 6.

The racist regime of South Africa has stepped up the use of raw military power, against the majority blacks. About 500 people have been killed druing, the unrest in the past 17 months. President P.W. Botha has now assumed emergency powers to maintain law and order in the black townships. But the more the suppression of the black aspiration for democratic freedom the greater the danger of the white minority government getting engulfed by the volcanic black anger. The declaration of emergency has proved counter-productive because rioting in the black townships is reportedly continuing unabated. It is unfortunate that Mr. Botha should still be ignorant of the historical fact that state terrorism can never suppress people's genuine aspirations. By defying international opinion and satanically repressing the freedom struggle, Pretoria remains sadly isolated from the comity of nations. Even the U.S. Government, known for its constructive engagement with Pretoria, is deeply troubled by the situation in South Africa. Black anger is spreading like wild fire. Whatever the military might of the government, that fire cannot be extinguished. The sooner Mr. Botha realises this the better for the white minority. Transition to majority rule in South Africa is historically inevitable. As the general secretary of the South African Council of Churches, Mr. Beyers Naude, has said, the awful bloodbath, long prophesied, is upon the people. Anti-government rioting has spread to the Soweto township near Johnnesburg, for long centre of unrest. If the suppression of the blacks continues, a blooodbath is sure to occur. Will the world be a silent spectator of the explosive situation in South Africa ? Should the situation go out hand and result in a bloodbath, the accusing finger would point to the Western nations which have hypocritically supported Pretoria.

And it is this support that has emboldened the racist government to make apartheid more rigid. It is a despicable system. For some time the Government has been undertaking one reform or another with a view depriving the black majority of its national identity. Through the use of naked military power, the government has uprooted millions of blacks from the homes of their ancestors and forcibly relocated them in strange and inhospitable lands hundreds of miles away. This has been going on for some months now and the Western champions of democracy and human rights are not at all perturbed by it. This large-scale forcible resettlement of the blacks reminds one of some of the actions of Nazi Germany. Strangely, the world is unable to do anything to end the political atrocities against the South African blacks. At last, the U.S. Government is feeling deeply troubled by the events in south Africa. But there is no sign yet of any change in its policy of constructive engagement with Pretoria. It is this constructive engagement that is responsible for the political destruction of the blacks in South Africa.

By resorting to terrorism, the minority government has provided the black rioters with justification for indulging in violence. There is an international consensus that efforts to end apartheid should be redoubled. Apartheid is rightly condemned as a crime not only against South African blacks but against humanity itself. Therefore, international forces supporting the freedom struggle in South Africa would be perfectly justified in extending all kinds of help, including military, to the fighters. Let not the covert supporters of Pretoria still dilly-dally. Their economic opportunism and political hypocrisy vis-a-vis South Africa have exposed them for what they really are. Now is the time for them to take a decisive step to dissociate themselves from the hateful racist regime. Feeble and sanctimonious criticism of Pretoria's reign of terrorism will be of little avail. What is needed is a concerted international more to liberate the majority blacks from the racist rule. This could happen only if the Western powers supported the move. The world cannot remain passive in the face of mounting atrocities against the blacks. Regrettably, most African States are not in a position to support openly the freedom fighters. The tornado of black anger is rising ominously. Even atomic weapons, which the racists are supposed to be in possession of, will not avail against the black hurricane.

1810. Torture of prisoners. *Nagpur Times* 29 Oct 1985 ; 4.

1811. Ungar, Sanford J and Peter Vale: South Africa: Why constructive engagement failed ? *Foreign Affairs* Win 1985-86 ; 234-58.

Spain

1812. Bookchin, Murray: *Spanish anarchists : The heroic years. 1868-1936*. New York, Free Life editions, 1977.

1813. Carline, Luis : New move to combat violence in Spain. *Baghdad Observer* 25 Mar 1986 ; 4.

1814. Clark, R. P. : *Basque insurgents, ETA, 1952-80*. Madison, Univ. of Wisconsin Press, 1984.

1815. Saksena, N.S. : Long history of terror in Spain, In *THF* ; 120-22.

1816. Schumacher, Edward : French terror controls stir Spain to curb Arabs. *International Herald Tribune* 2 Oct 1986 ; 1.

1817. Thomas, Hugh : Anarchist agrarian collectives in the Spanish Civil War. In *Century of conflict, 1850-1950*. Ed. by Martin Gilbert. New York. Atheneum, 1966.

1818. Torture of prisoners in Spain. *Statesman* 3 Jul 1985 ; 7.

1819. Trevino, Jose A. : Spain's internal security : The basque antonomous police force. In *TIE* ; 141-53.

The legal basis for the autonomous police force in Euzkadi lies in the Spanish constitution and the 1979 Basque Home Rule Statute. Questions arise, however, as to how these provisions should be implemented in a way that will satisfy both sides. The Spanish government's incumbent political party UCD (Centre Democratic Union) tried to reconcile two principles which appear to be mutually exclusive. One principle which holds that as part of the overall to be mutually exclusive. One principle which holds that as part of the overall settlement Basques are entitled to their own security force, may clash with the principle that Spain's central government should retain ultimate control over public order and security matters throughout the country. After the Basque police have taken over, the central forces will try to lower their visibility in Euzkadi or withdraw altogether according to a specific timetable. Basque radicals and ETA demand the latter programme of total withdrawal. The government, however, appears to be more inclined towards the former alternative.

Undoubtedly the question of who exercises ultimate control over the security forces is crucial to the success of the autonomy programme. The Spanish constitution in Art. 154 envisions a government appointed delegate (Marcelino Creja, former Foreign Minister in the Suarez administration was appointed to that position on 10 October 1980) who would direct the central state's administration and act as a liaison point between the autonomous region and the central government. He is called Governor General of Euzkadi. The Basque Home Rule Statute (Art. 17) in turn envisions a Joint Commission for Security which is supposed to co-ordinate Basque security with the central government. Membership in this Commission is to be divided equally between representatives from the central state administration and the Basque autonomous region. Although the Basque Home Rule Statute officially went into effect on 11 January 1980, necessary legislation which will elaborate on the provision of Art. 17 of the statute regarding Basque autonomous police forces is still pending. When completed, this legislation will specifically define the role of the central security forces in the Basque provinces under the new legal configuration.

Theoretically, the mechanism for the transfer of police powers and their subsequent interface with the central government appears to be sound and workable, under ideal conditions. The reality and actual application of this mechanism, however, are much more complicated. In May 1980 the central government apparently tried to strengthen its hand within the Basque security scheme. In the draft legislation which the goverment was required to submit to Parliament concerning the specific provisions for the Basque police force, the government proposed that the delegate appointed by Madrid, the Governor General of Euzkadi, also preside over the Joint Security Commission. It is obvious this arrangement would give the central government undisputed superiority on security matters. There was strong opposition to this proposal, however, both in Parliament and among the public in the Basque provinces. The government withdrew the draft legislation from Parliament rather than risk facing the rising opposition.

There is little doubt that not only internal security but the entire autonomy issue turns on the intended or actual future role of the central security forces in the Basque region. The mechanism which will bring them into play is still untested and fraught with uncertainity. The government apparently intends to maintain a substantial police presence in Euzkadi, albeit a less visible and active one. The Civil Guard and the National Police, the two uniformed national police bodies, will spend more time in their respective garrisons and curtail their patrolling duties. The functions of the Superior Police Corps, comprised of plainclothes investigators, will remain relatively unchanged however. Under the central direction, they will continue to carry out investigations of major crimes, including terrorist mateers, in Euzkadi. No one seems to know with certainty, however, what will be the result if the internal security situation in Euzkadi deteriorates to such an extent that the central government regards it as intolerable. What will happean for instance when terrorism slides into guerrilla operations to include take-overs of government installations ?

Srilanka

1820. Bandarage, Asoka : *Colonialism in Sri Lanka.* Berlin, Mouton, 1983. Pp. 420.

1821. Conflicts : the battle for Jaffna. *Asiaweek* 1 Jun 1986 ; 36-40.

1822. Dastardly act (Bombing Air Lank a Tristar jet). *Free Press Journal* (Bombay) 6 May 1986 ; 4.

The bomb blast that killed twenty-two passengers abroad an Air Lanka Tristar jet at the Colombo international airport last Saturday indeed adds an ominous and tragic dimension to Sri Lanka's mounting troubles. The Liberation Tigers of Tamil Eelam (LTTE), the largest' and the most violent-prone of the innumerable Tamil separatist groups, was quick to own responsibility for the blast, though its spokesman in Madras subsequently denied it. But all signs point to the inevitable conclusion that the dastardly crime was committed by Tamil extremists whichever group they belonged to. Needless to say, such reprehensible acts, involving the lives of innocent air passengers, will in no way advance the cause for which the misguided and blind fanatical elements are professedly fighting for. On the other hand, they will lose whatever support and sympathy of even the people of India who are gravely concerned over the killings of innocent Tamils by the security forces and are earnestly hoping for an early breakthrough from the latest New Delhi-Colombo dialogue. The majority of those who lost their lives in the bomb blast were foreign holidaymakers en route to Male. There is no question that attacks on civilian aircraft carrying foreign tourists by Tamil militants will steadily dry up the considerable fund of sympathy for the minority community that exists particularly in the western countries at the present time. To be sure, the tragedy would have reached horrendous proportions had the bomb exploded after take-off from Colombo for Male, as the perpetrators had clearly planned none of the 121 passengers of crew would have survived a mid-air explosion.

It is most puzzling that the aircraft blast occurred even as a high level Indian delegation was engaged in crucial talks with the Sri Lanka leaders in a bid to break the ethnic logjam. It is on cards that the extremist elements ; whether belonging to LTTE, TELO or any such group, who are opposed to the moderate TULF, want nothing sort of a separate Tamil State in the island. Significantly, the latest terrorist act came in the wake of bloody violent clashes between the followers of

LTTE and TELO resulting in the death of some 150 people. New Delhi is already treading a very delicate path in a bid to solve this sensitive problem, of course commensurate with the Tamils' legitimate aspirations. Such senseless terrorist acts by extremist groups would clearly make its task extremely difficult. Thereby they are only playing into the hands of hardcore Sinhala elements and freewheeling security men who can now justify the use of greater force to curb terrorism.

1823. Dastardly incidents. *Indian Express* (New Delhi) 6 May 1986 ; 6.

The bombing of the Air Lanka flight from London to Male in the Maldives at Katunayake airport on May 3, 1986, killing at least 22 of the 121 passengers, mostly international tourists, and injuring several others, including two Indian Airlines pilots who were on the tarmac, is another of those ghastly and despicable terrorist attacks that nothing can extenuate. The precise sequence of events is not yet known and responsibility cannot yet be fixed. It would, however, appear that the explosives were loaded in Colombo and placed in the rear cargo-hold, packed in a large consignment of betel nuts, vegetables and meat carcasses intended for Male. Fortunately the Tri-star jet was delayed by a few minutes in Colombo or else it would have exploded in mid-air with fatal consequences for all on board.

The motive was clearly political and suspicion has fallen on the Black Tigers, described as a militant Tamil hit-squad, as a badge and some uniforms used by them were found. However, definite proof if lacking and another report would cast suspicion on the Liberation Tigers of Tamil Eelam (LTTE) which is said to have put up a poster in Jaffna, later torn down, suggesting that the bombing was its handiwork. The LTTE in Madras and some other Tamil militant groups have, however, disowned responsibility. The Government of India has unequivocally condemned the incident "in the event of its having resulted from a terrorist act". Of this there can be no doubt, and the finger points at one or other Tamil militant group, tarnishing them all until culpability is pinpointed. The object could well have been to disrupt the latest round of high-level Indo-Lanka talks that were in progress in Colombo at the time. Neither side was, however, deflected from this path and at the end of the current round of discussions on Sunday evening exuded guarded optimism that meaningful progress had been made.

Meanwhile, it is extremely disconcerting that the LTTE in a fatricidal attack on a rival militant group, TELOm conducted at various points in northern and eastern Lanka killed 100-150 or more of its rivals in a bid to settle scores. It should surely disturb India that the LTTE leadership resides in Madras and that such blood-letting endorses

Sri Lankan complaints that some Tamil militant groups have been responsible for grave acts of terrorism. The Indian all-party Tamil Eelam Supporters Organisation, let by Mr Karunanidhi, met in Madurai on Sunday but does not appear to have had anything to say on this aspect of the matter. If Mr Chidambaram's mission to Colombo has succeeded in breaking new ground, then the Tamil groups must equally observe certain norms and discipline and adopt a practical and flexible negotiating position which has to be more positive than all or nothing attitude.

1824. De silva, Meruyn : Refression in the guise of stability. *International Herald Tribune* 22 Apr 1986 ; 6.

1825. Escalating violence : *Economic and Political Weekly* 22 Mar 1986 ; 462-63.

1826. Government and guerrillas : *Statesman* 5 Feb 1986 ; 6.

The cancellation of Mr Romesh Bhandari's visit to Colombo can only play into President Jayewardene's hands if it is interpreted as a victory for the Eelam underground. New Delhi's role in the crisis must be limited to urging the two parties to exercise restraint and helping them to work out a mutually acceptable compromise. This objective demands that Mr Rajiv Gandhi retain the trust of the Sri Lankan Government as well as of the various militant Tamil organizations without, however, forfeiting the trust of the Tamil United Liberation Front. The moderate TULF still offers the best bet for a negotiated settlement though it was unrealistic to expect an immediate positive response to its alternative proposals. President Jayewardene's 57-page rejoinder, which amounts to a total rejection according to Mr Amirthalingam, in effect tries to cut the TULF down to size. It was a shrewd move in consonance with Colombo's entire strategy to discredit the moderates, expose their inability to fulfil the minority community's expectations, and demonstrate that the long-term solution can only be between the Government and the guerrillas.

What passes understanding, however, is that New Delhi should appear to fall into the trap. The Government could have waited for Colombo's reply before announcing the Foreign Secretary's visit ; having travelled as far as Madras, he might have continued the journey to ask President Jayewardene to clarify his objections to the TULF formula. True, the abrupt last-minute decision may have a salutary effect by conveying in to the UNP regime that India's patience is not unlimited, and that there can be no constructive talks while the Sri Lankan security forces indulge in massacres such as the latest outrage in Killinochchi. But, the cancellation may also enable President

Jayewardene to claim that the TULF proposals provide no basis for discussion and that any settlement must, therefore, be negotiated only with the Tamil secessionist. That plea can only strengthen his further argument that the guerrillas must first be completed compelled, by the use of even greater military force if necessary, to give up their Eelam demand.

Direct talks between the two may be unavoidable ; they may even be necessary since the Tamil militants are, in a sense, hand in glove with the Colombo authorities in the effort to marginalize the TULF. But discussions on the only basis that seems to be acceptable to President Jayewardene—with the guerrillas on their knees—will not solve the social and economic problem of discrimination against Tamils. The separatist threat is certainly not to be condoned, and New Delhi will perform a useful function if it can persuade the militants to desist from wanton depredations. But only the TULF can call Colombo's bluff and oblige it to abandon legalistic quibbling like the specious argument that it is impossible to amend Sri Lanka's unitary constitution. And the TULF needs New Delhi's support to arrive at a compromise that satisfied Tamils without jeopardizing Sri Lanka's territorial integrity. That is something that President Jayewardene seems still unable to recognize.

1827. Groping for a policy. *Times of India* 9 Jan 1987 ; 8.

1828. Growing Climate of fear. *Asiaweek* 15 Jun 1986 ; 19-20.

1829. Guerrilla action takes toll on Sri Lanka tourism. *International Herald Tribune* 5-6 Apr 1986 ; 5.

1830. Jack, Ian : Official terrorism in Sri Lanka. *Times of India* 4 Jun 1986 ; 8.

1831. Jayewardene terror. *Hitavada* 22 May 1986 ; 3.

1832. Kulkarni, V.G. : Tamil separatists also fight among themselves. *Far Eastern Economic Review* 12 Jan 1986 ; 28.

1833. Kulkarni, V.G. : Terrorist scourge puts up the ante. *Far Eastern Economic Review* 12 Jun 1986 ; 27-28.

1834. Massacres in the East. *Asiaweek* 8 Jun 1986 ; 34.

1835. Menon, Sadanand : Tamil militants to release English hostage only to Red Cross. *Sunday Observer* (Bombay) 2 Feb 1986 ; 3.

1836. Moorty, D.N. : Will the killings stop ? *Indian Express* 4 May 1986.

1837. No end in sight to Sri Lanka violence. *International Herald Tribune* 1 Apr 1986 ; 2.

1838. Peril in Sri Lanka. *International Herald Tribune* 14-15 Jun 1986 ; 4.

1839. Torture of Tamils continues unabated. *Patriot* 23 Oct 1985 ; 6.

1840. Vije, Mayan : Terrorists or liberators ? *Far Eastern Economic Review* 15 Aug 1985 ; 4.

St. Lucia

1841. Sullivan, George : St. Lucia. In *Story of the Peace Corps*. New York, 1964 ; 138-42.

Sudan

1842. Wright, Jonathan : Sudan's rebels turn to mass attacks in bush war. *International Herald Tribune* 5 Mar 1986 ; 8.

Surinam

1843. Surinam expels Dutch envoy (favouring terrorist acts). *Hindustan Times* 12 Jan 1987 ; 11.

Sweden

1844. Assassination : Swedish Shocker. *Asiaweek* 16 Mar 1986 ; 28.

1845. Gustafsoon, Tom : Murder that shocked the entire world (Olof Palme) *Clavity* 20 Apr. 1986 ; 6. *International Viewpoint* 24 Mar 1986 ; 3.

1846. Mosey, Chirs : Swedish connection. *Tribune* 24 Sep 1986 ; 4.

1847. Neutrality of Sweden an advantage. *International Herald Tribune* 15-16 Mar 1986 ; 4.

The quintessential memory of Olof Palme is in Stockholm in 1970. There was that magnificent democratic informality that was to lead to his death ; while waiting for an elevator at his party headquarters, my wife was joined by a man who walked in from the street, the prime minister.

Later, at the University at Lund in southern Sweden, there was "Prime Minister's Night." The gem was packed and the chief of state walked in alone and sat down at a little table. The students had elected 10 of their number to question him. Most were : as befit those hectic times, Maoists.

They denounced Mr. Palme as a sell-out, a social democratic traitor to the working class, and demanded that he advocate violent and radical overthrow. Mr. Palme replied patiently but with great force. He was not, he said, a pacifist. Yet he understood the limits of violence, the fact that socialism itself could be built only by non-violent cooperation.

That memory of a wonderful, rumpled, impeacably logical and infinitely compassionate man makes it all the more utterly senseless that he was taken away from a world that desperately needed him. And still does.

When the leader of a small country engages the imagination and the respect of leaders around the world, he must have special qualities of character. His persuasiveness comes not from power but from himself. Olof Palme was such a person. What was it about this Swedish politician that touched so many people of diverse cultures and ideas? There was no great external drama about him. His voice was soft, his manner unassuming. He relied on reason.

"Complacency is a terrible danger," Mr. Palme said. "A politican shouldn't say everything's fine. He should talk about what is wrong. We in Sweden can be happly about not having the excitement of Northern Ireland, or the race problem. But there is a real risk for us. You have to try to activate people." He made his people care.

To many Americans, Olof Palme was the democratic leader who most consistently criticised U.S. policy in the world. But he was much more than that. Over a period of nearly two decades, he performed a highly unusual role as a global statesman, acting on many ocassions in the interest of the United States and other Western democracies.

His stands against U.S. action in Vietnam, against South Africa's policy of apartheid, and for a more equitable distribution of the world's wealth between rich nations and poor were viewed with admiration by leaders not usually friendly to the West. That Mr. Palme represented a neutral country, with nothing to gain from these stands, enhanced his credibility.

1848. Power, Jonathan : Palme : Shadow on the wall was his fear. *International Herald Tribune* 15-16 Mar 1986 ; 4.

Mr. Palme proposed the concept of preemptive peacekeeping, using forces of the United Nations. The problem with traditional UN peacekeeping operations is that the troops are sent in after a conflict has broken out. While this is valuable, averting as it has full-scale continuing war between India and Pakistan, in Cyprus and the Middle East, prevention of the conflict in the first place is much better.

The Commission was debating this as the Falklands dispute was coming to the boil. It studied why UN forces had not been sent into the Falkland Islands before Argentina moved to grab it.

Russian members were wary about any proposal which implied a diminishing of Soviet freedom of action. Mr. Palme was aiming for the creation of standing UN force that could be rushed into a Third World trouble spot on the orders of the secretary general. This would compel both sides to seek arbitration unless they were prepared to kill an international contingent drawn from the armies of several member countries.

A strong compromise proposal was finally agreed on. Although the secretary-general would not have a free hand—the UN Security Council would still have to approve deployment—there would be a "concordant" among the permanent members of the security council that would commit them to support collective security action.

Its a pity that this idea has never been formally taken up. It is imaginative, bold and, above all, absolutely necessary. Too much of the Third World is in danger of being torn apart by petty conflicts which could at any time get out of control because of a lack of cooling off and arbitration mechanisms.

If the world wants a monument to Olof Palme and the ideas he fought for, it could at least open a full-scale debate on preventive peacekeeping. It might well be the alternative to us all becoming merely a shadow on a well.

1849. Rudbeck, Carl : Sweden loses immunity from world violence. *International Herald Tribune* 15-16 Mar 1986 ; 4.

"They shoot prime ministers, don't they ?" could sum up the national reaction to the assassination of Prime Minister Olof Palme as he was walking home after a movie late at night in Stockholm on Feb 28.

Swedes are as much stunned as gried stricken. They are also angry. It is as if a snake finally turned up in their Garden of Eden. For Swedes had thought their country to be free from the taint of violence that plagues other countries. Jan Carlzon, Chief executive officer of Scandinavian Airlines, summed up typical Swiss feelings : "My reaction is two-sided. I am deeply affected by the fact that Olof Palme has been murdered, but also because public figure has been slain in my home town, in my own country. That we are not as safe here as we imagined with grave consequences."

The site of the murder in Stockholm has been covered with flowers left by mourning citizens, and the street where the shooting took place is to be renamed after Mr. Palme. People have been gathering there, some crying silently but others speaking. The usually shy and reserved Swedes dare suddenly to show their emotions and talk to each other, to verbalize their amazement and horror. It is a horror which is not only caused by the fact that Mr. Palme has been shot but also by the fact that the action took place in Stockholm, the capital of a country where no political leader has been murdered since 1792, when King Gustav III was killed.

Political assassinations, it has been thought, happened out there, in the big world, in America, may be in Germany and France. Swedes had every reason to believe that they were still immune. We live in a country where controversies were resolved by reasoned arguments and compromise, not guns. Swedes reacted like people whose homes have been burglarized ; they feel violated, their security destroyed.

1850. Saxena, Neeraj : Tragic assassination (of Olof Palme) *Industrial Times* (Bombay) 17 Mar 1986 ; 46.

1851. Sundberg, Jacob : W.F. Anti—terrorist legislation in Sweden. In *ITCW* ; 111-121.

It may be suggested that this list or organizations has in reality only a limiting function. Nobody can be put on the list as a presumed terrorist without his membership in one of the listed organizations first being positively established. By the end of 1975 the list included slightly fewer than eighty persons, all of them residing abroad. This list was, in all its versions, approved by the National Police Board in pleno and copies thereof were, successively, submitted to the king in council.

It has been asserted that the question of membership in terrorist organizations alone seldom acquires decisive importance. This was ascribed to the fact that "it is a characteristic feature of the organizations and groups in question that they are of an extremely secret nature. Experiences has shown that it is primarily other circumstances relating to the relationship of the person concerned to the organization and its activity that becomes decisive." By this is meant, presumably, that information coming from foreign police departments is always directed at a certain individual and includes material on his past activity in connection with acts for which a certain listed organization has taken credit, so that membership by itself cannot be said to have independent importance.

Expulsion of presumed terrorists has been an issue in twelve cases. Board requests for expulsion have been submitted to the king in council and have been granted in about half the cases. In 1974 decisions to expel were taken against three Yugoslavs and one Japanese (Akira Kitagawa). In 1975, the decision was taken to expel another Yugoslav as well as the five-member band of Germans that took the West German embassy in order to extort the release of the Baader-Mein of defendants. In six of these cases, the requests were either turned down or withdrawn, the latter presumably because the alleged terrorists had left the country anyway.

The decision to expel could not be executed in any of the Yugoslav cases because the persons concerned enjoyed political refugee status. Instead, the presumed terrorists were subjected to directives which imposed certain limitations and conditions for their continued presence in Sweden. These directives established limitations relating to residence and employment which were not to be changed without prior permission. The presumed terrorists were also to register regularly with the police.

The basic weakness in the Swedish approach to terrorism has turned out to be the existence of the status of political refugee because it has often prevented the exeuction of a decision to expel. This comment by the chief prosecutor in Stockholm seems pertinent :

> Since it justifiably can be said that in most cases under the new Act those foreigners to whom it applies are such as may invoke political refugee status, the conclusion seems warranted that the Committee has attempted to make political activity at one and the same time a ground for returning and expulsion, on the one hand, and a bar for such measures on the other.

Political refugee status was to be granted to the presumed terrorist if he, in the country to which he was sent, risked "political persecution." What was meant by this extremely imprecise formula was very unclear ; till, it was pivotal. The heavily leftist Swedish mass media were almost able to limit the application of the act to the Baader-Meinhof group by singling out the Federal Republic of Germany. They focused on the societal monopoly on violence and on attorney privileges in communicating with clients and accused-of being a country that had abandoned the rule of law. If that was synonymous with "political persecution", the murder squad could look forward to some time in a Swedish jail (probably no longer than the master-spy Col. Wennerstrom, who eventually was pardoned by the Palme government) and thereafter remain in Sweden on social welfare, if not otherwise. So that was meant by "political persecution"?

To take the Swiss example relating to the former prohibition barring women from taking part in general elections, this certainly was a violation of the declaration of human rights, but it could not be considered persecution, since the prohibition was not based on race, nationality, and so forth, but on sex, which is not mentioned by the Refugee Convention as a basis for persecution.

"It is difficult to understand," says Dr. Melander, "why a violation of human rights should not be considered to be persecution—of course on conditions that this violation is founded on..............political opinion."

It was considered advisable to look more closely into the matter of "political persecution" in Japan. Eventually, after some on-the-spot research, it was concluded that people could be expelled to Japan without risking political persecution.

With such definitions of "political persecution" it is hard to send a presumed terrorist anywhere. Daniel Patrick Moynihan, the United States delegate to the United Nations, has reminded us that there are no more than two dozen genuine democracies remaining in the world. The rest are nations that have adopted or accepted autocratic forms of government, socialist or not. He was prepared to produce a list of forty-five military governments and thirty-five governments installed by coups. Certainly all of these would fail to meet the Human Rights test. On the other hand, the rule of law might conceivably be a lot better in some of these countries (for example, Switzerland) than in the genuine democracies because the rule of the majority is no guarantee that the majority will stick to the laws it has enacted.

1852. Violent death of a Champion of peace. (Olof Palme) *Japan Times Weekly* 22 Mar 1986 ; 12.

Syria

1853. Attacks in Syria. In *WTAZIT* ; 73.

1854. Boyd, Gerald M. : Reagan warns Syria, Iran on trrorism. *International Herald Tribune* 25 Apr 1986 ; 1.

1855. Dionne, E.J. : Italy sees caution by Syria on terrorism. *International Herald Tribune* 16 Jun 1986 ; 3.

1856. Gelb, Leslie H. : Terrorist in Rome links Syria to airport attacks. *International Herald Tribune* 22 May 1986 ; 1-2.

1857. Goyal, D.R. : Syria : Target of U.S. terrorism. *Mainstream* 24 1986 ; 41-42.

1858. Kemp, Geoffrey : Isolating Syria solves very little. *International Herald Tribune* 4 Nov 1986 ; 4.

1859. McCartney, Robert J. : Bonn indicates Berlin terrorist trial will not cause break in Syrian ties. *International Herald Tribune* 21 Nov 1986 ; 5.

1860. Ottaway, David B. : Shultz says El Al bombing attempt proves Syrian role in terrorism. *International Herald Tribune* 3 Nov 1986 ; 6.

1861. Parker, Richard B. : On Syria, no answer but the agony of diplomacy. *International Herald Tribune* 31 Oct 1986 ; 4.

1862. Pffaf, William : You get the anti-terrorism you deserve. *International Herald Tribune* 11 Nov 1986 ; 6.

1863. Schiff, Z. : Syrians are playing a dangerous game. *International Herald Tribune* 27 May 1986 : 4.

1864. Sciolino, Elaine : U.K. Eaves dropped on Syria : Analysts say violence is used as policy. *International Herald Tribune* 27 Oct 1986 : 1, 6.

1865. Strategy for the isolation of Damascus. *International Herald Tribune* 31 Oct 1986 ; 4.

1866. Syria abetting terrorism. *Mid-Day* (New Delhi) 22 Jan 1987 ; 16.

US Defence Secretary Cahpar Weinberger has charged that Syria, Iran and Libya are still supporting international terrorism to promote their political goals.

Speaking at an international conference on terrorism in Washington on January 21, 1987, Mr. Weinberger said the US bombing raid on Libya last April had "a clear effect" on Libya's terrorist activities though its overall goals had remained unchanged.

He also said the United States will still consider military measures as a last resort against states which support terrorism.

"Despite the collective actions of the west, there appears to be no substantial modification of Syria's overall support to terrorist groups or its use of terrorism to support Syrian political goals", he said.

1867. Syria gets off the hook. *International Herald Tribune* 31 Oct 1986 ; 4.

Taiwan

1868. Amnesty International. *Taiwan* London, Russell Press, 1976.

1869. Gregor, A. James : Terrorism : the view from Taiwan. *Terrorism* 5(3) 1981 ; 233-64.

1870. Violence in the name of reason. *Far Eastern Economic Review* 28 Dec 1979 ; 27.

Tanzania

1871. Sullivan, George Tanganyika : In *Story of the Peace Corps*. New York, 1964 ; 142-46.

Thailand

1872. Fire over Phuket : *Far Eastern Economic Review* 3 Jul 1986 ; 12-13.

1873. Heaton, William R and Richard MacLeod : People's war in Thailand. In *IMW* ; 87-108.

Four separate areas of insurgency exist in Thailand : North, Northeast, Central and South. While there has been an effort to link these by the CPT, each enjoys considerable autonomy, according to reliable observers.

The insurgency has its greatest stronghold in the Northeast, where a near classic insurgency environment prevails. There, about 11 million people, roughly 25 percent of Thailand's 44 million, live in fifteen provinces comprising the Korat Plateau which extends to the borders of Laos and Cambodia. The great majority of these people are ethnically akin to the Lao and speak a distinct of Thai known as Isan. The area is poor economically, having few natural resources, poor soil, inadequate moisture, and a poor drainage system. More than 90 per cent of the people are engaged in subsistence farming ; in the early 1970s the average per capital annual income was about $ 42 compared with the national average of about $ 100. Moreover, the income of more than 75 percent of the people of the Northeast was only about $ 15-$ 30 annually, indicating broad disparity between the more wealthy landholders and the peasant farmers. The birth rate has been very high—about 3.5 percent annually—but the population is slightly less dense than the national average. Most people live in relatively isolated hamlets and villages dispersed throughout the countryside. Laos and Cambodia from time to time have both claimed portions of Northeast Thailand. The relative poverty, geographic isolation from Bangkok, proximity to Laos, Cambodia, and Vietnam (countries from which the insurgents derive support), and ethnic and social diversity from the remainder of Thailand have contributed to the development of insurgency in the Northeast.

North Thailand is also an ideal area for insurgency. Bordering on Northern Laos and on Burma, the North is inhabited by several hundred thousand tribesmen (primarily Meo and Yao) who have little allegiance to the government in Bangkok. The provinces of Chiangrai, Nan, and Uttaradit are mountainous with heavy jungle. There are few roads and only limited communications in many areas. The Meo are slash-and-burn agriculturalists and many grow opium as a cash crop. The anti-insurgent campaign in the North has a distinctively anti-Meo flavor owing to traditional Thai-Meo animosity. For example, a 1969 survey in Bangkok asking how to deal with the "red Meo" drew responses ranging from "kill them all" to "use napalm......but don't set the forest afire, it is bad for the economy." Indiscriminate bombing of Meo villages by the Thai military has sometimes contributed to the expansion of the insurgency in this region.

The insurgency in Central Thailand has also drawn support from Meo tribesmen. The three provinces of Pitsanulok, Loei, and Petchabun which are affected by the insurgency, are not as remote from Bangkok as the North and the Northeast regions ; however, they are plagued by similar problems. The area lacks sufficient water and has poor soil, with the attendant serious agricultural problems. As in other areas, the Thai government, in spite of a host of land reform programs, has done little to solve problems of tenancy, taxes, and other matters close to the needs of the villagers. Many people in this area feel that the government has neglected education and other services. Also, previous government counter insurgency programs have been regarded by the populace as little more than official banditry.

Perhaps the most complicated and intense area of insurgency is in the provinces bordering Malaysia in the South, where some 85 percent of Thailand's nearly 2 million Malay-Muslims live. The terrain, social and economic diversity, and other cleavages characteristic of this region also favour insurgency. Yet is it difficult to discern which of the many groups offering resistance to the government are true insurgents and which are merely bandit gangs. There are Muslim separatist groups, groups linked with the Malaysian Communist party. Thai communists, and bandits, to mention a few. The situation is not helped by the tendency of Thai authorities to lump them all as "communist terrorists" While the Thai Communist party often claims credit for the activities of these various groups, there is some question as to how many actually operate under communist auspices.

All of the insurgent areas are geographically separate and fairly remote from the Bangkok Area, the heartland of Thai society. Social cleavages stemming from diverse ethnicity, religion, customs, and language dialects have prevented full integration of the Thai policy. The insurgent areas generally are characterized by a lower standard of living and occasionally a different means of livelihood than that of most Thais. The areas tend to be poorly penetrated by roads of other forms of transportation and communications are sparse. They are frequently characterized by jungle or mountainous terrain. Furthermore particularly in the North and the Northeast, they border on countries from which external support for insurgency is derived.

Tunisia

1874. Moore, Clement H. : Tunisia : the prospects for institution alization. In *Authoritarian politics in modern society*. Ed. by clement H. Moore. New York, Basic Books, 1970.

1875. Tunisian is said to admit, London bombings. *International Herald Tribune* 13 May 1986 ; 1.

Turkey

1876. Adams, James : Ring Lessons and links of anti-Turk terrorism. *Wall Street Journal* 16 Aug 1983 ; 32.

1877. Armenian question ; the roots of terror. *International Herald Tribune* 10 Mar 1983 ; 9, 14.

1878. Ataov, Turkkaya : Procurement of arms for American terrorism : Realities based on Otooman documents. In *ITDC* ; 169-78.

1879. Berberogln, B. : *Turkey, in crisis : From State Capitalism to neo-colonialism*. London, Zed Press, 1982.

1880. Cooley, John K. : Turkey fears involvement in other people's war. *International Herald Tribune* 18 Sep 1986 ; 6.

1881. Corun, Andrew : Armenian terrorism : A profile. *U.S. Department of state Bulletin* Aug 1982.

1882. Dionne, E.J. : Armenian terror : Tangle of motives. *New York Times* 1 Aug 1983.

1883. Fisek, Sinan : Torture of Suspects : Centuries-old issue. *International Herald Tribune* 10 Mar 1983 ; 14.

1884. Gunter, Michael M. : Armenian terrorist campaign against Turkey. *Orbis*, Sum 1983.

1885. Gunter, Michael M. : Contemporary aspects of Armenian terrorism. in *ITDC* ; 103-146.

1886. Gurun, Kamuran : Causes and prevention of Armenian terrorism. In *ITDC* ; 251-60.

1887. Henze, Paul B. : Long effort to destabilize Turkey. *Atlantic Community* 19, 1980-81.

1888. Henze, Paul B. : Roots of Armenian violence. In *ITDC* ; 179-202.

1889. Hewsen Robert H. : Who speaks today of the Armenians ? In *ITCW* ; 444-46.

The Nazi Holocaust is considered by many to be a purely Jewish experience but this was not entirely the case. While some six million Jews were, indeed, murdered in Hitler's death camps, it has been estimated that at least another six million non-Jews perished in the same camps under identical circumstances. Not all of these were merely miscellaneous victims ; non-Jews were to a certain extent the victims of genocide as well. It was the usual Nazi policy to exterminate gypsies for example, while a conscious and deliberate attempt was made to "thin out" the Slavic populations of both Poland and Russia during the German occupation. Nazism, as the world knows, was a racist philosophy, and while this racism, applied to the Jews, resulted in genocide, genocide—actually, in part, and potentially, in toto—could be practised by the Nazis upon all so-called inferior peoples.

It is natural, of course, for many Jews to think of the Holocaust largely in terms of its Jewish victims, a situation akin to a newscaster identifying only the casualties from his local community when describing a plane crash occurring in another city. But to limit the Holocaust to an anti-Jewish phenomenon, as is sometimes done, is not only historically inaccurate but also unwise. Not only does this ignore the sufferings of other people who were victims of the same atrocity, but it also ignores the fact that the Holocaust was in actuality an atrocity committed against all mankind.

To neglect this does the Jews themselves a disservice, too, for limiting the Holocaust to a solely Jewish experience tends to cut non-Jews off from the real lesson of this monstrous episode in recent history and creates at times in some non-Jews one of the following three responses :

1. The Holocaust was a uniquely anti-Semitic phenomenon, another example of the age-old streak of anti-Jewish sentiment which has run throughout Western history and which would not and could not happen to another people.

2. The Nazis were dynamic, efficient, exciting, and even glamorous figures, except for their unfortunate aberration of being anti-Semitic. This is an attitude—in part fostered by Hollywood films—which I have often encountered among my students.

3. Or, finally, the attitude I have heard, occasionally in Germany and once in Russia, that the massacre of the Jews was not such a bad idea after all and that "it is too bad they didn't get the rest of them."

It is my position that no one could take any of the three attitudes just cited if the true extent and nature of the Nazi atrocities were fully realized.

I once doubted if a plan aimed at genocide, however terrifying it might appear, could be classed as an act of terrorism in and of itself. However, I have changed my view. Apart from the fact that the Holocaust can be seen as an attempt to terrorise the opposition both in Germany and in the occupied territories, and apart from the step-by-step terror inflicted upon the victims in particular, there is also, I believe, an implicit long-term terror imposed upon humanity at large by the realization that such a monstrosity could take place in modern times and in one of the supposedly most civilized states of Western Europe—perhaps of Christendom, itself. If the land of Goethe, Schiller, and Beethoven could raise to supreme power a man like Adolf Hitler, whose views had been openly presented in his notorious testament Mein Kampf, might we not all be potential victims of the would-be Hitlers and their followers who must surely exist in every civilized state not excluding our own.

1890. Itil, Turan : Terrorism in Turkey with special consideration of Armenian terrorism. In *ITDC* ; 29-48.

1891. Jordan, Robert : Proud Armenians. *American Geographic* Jun 1978.

1892. Kevorkyan, Dikran : Armenian terrorism within the framework of terrorism. *ITDC* ; 95-102.

1893. Lowry, Heath W. : Nineteenth and twentieth century Armenian terrorism : Threads of continuity. In *ITDC* ; 71-84.

1894. McCarthy, Justin : Armenian terrorism : History as poison and antidote. In *ITDC* ; 85-94.

1895. Nihilism in Turkey. *International Herald Tribune* 10 Sep 1986 ; 4.

1896. On Armenian activities. *Economist* 6 Feb 1980 ; 20.

1897. Parry, Albert : Red Samurai and Turkey's rihilists. In *terrorism,* New York, 1976 ; 433-448.

1898. Shiragian, Arshavir : *Legacy : Memoirs of an Armenian Patriot.* Boston, Hairenik Press, 1976.

1899. Somer, Tarik : Armenian terrorism and the narcotic traffic. In *ITDC* ; 19-28.

1900. Songar, Ayhan : Terrorism in general and psychiatric evaluation of terroristic events in Turkey. In *ITDC* ; 147-54.

1901. Szaz, Z. Michael : Armenian terrorist ironies. *Washington Times* 2 Sep 1982 ; 8A.

1902. Taneri, Aydin : Turks—Byantines—Armenians. In *ITDC* ; 281-88.

1903. Torture persists in Turkey, rights group says. *International Herald Tribune* 31 Mar 1986 ; 5.

Although the Turkish authorities recently have allowed greater exercise of civil liberties, prisoners in Turkish police stations and prisons continue to be subjected to torture and inhumane cell conditions, a human rights organization has asserted.

The report, issued last week by the New York-based organization Helsinki Watch, said that despite increased freedom of expression, Turkey continues to detain political prisoners and to restrict many publishers and scholars.

The organization noted that the military-backed government of Prime Minister Turgut Ozal had lifted martial law in all but nine of the country's 67 provinces and permitted open parliamentary debate and wider press coverage of reported instances of torture.

The group cited new laws to punish torturers and to provide a partial amnesty for political prisoners.

But it reported recent incidents of torture involving electric shock, rape and severe beatings.

It also reported police raids in which literature was confiscated. The independence and quality of universities, severely damaged by punitive dismissals of many professors during martial law, had not been restored, the study said.

"Repressive legislation remains in place," the study said, "and is being utilized in a seemingly haphazard fashion that serves to keep a degree of intimidation alive."

Responding to the report, the Turkish Embassy in Washington said : "The Turkish Constitution, Turkish law and Turkish government policy categorically prohibit inhumane treatment of detainees and prisoners, Torture of detainees is a felony crime, and security and correctional officials suspected of perpetrating such offences are prosecuted and subjected to severe sentences when found guilty."

The embassy's statement said that all allegations raised in the Helsinki Watch report would be investigated, but it denied all assertions of illegal detention of political prisoners.

"Capital sentences have been reduced to 30 years, life sentences to 20 years and all other have been reduced by half," it said. "It is expected that 70 to 80 percent of all prisoners will be released forthwith."

1904. Wohlstetter, Albert and Nancy Virts : Armenian terror as a special case of international terror. In *ITDC* ; 261-80.

Uganda

1905. Axelrad, Albert S. : Uganda, the terrorists and us. *New Outlook* Sep-Oct 1976 ; 59-61.

1906. Gargan, Edward A. : Violence, decline ingrain Ugandans with pessimism. *International Herald Tribune* 3 Jan 1986 ; 13.

1907. Leibovitz, Yeshiyalun : Occupation and terror. *New outlook* 19(6) Sep-Oct 1986 ; 56-58.

1908. Mamdani, Mahmood : *Imperialism and fascism in Uganda*. London, Heivemann, 1983. PP. 115.

1909. Sullivan, George : Turkey. In *Story of the Peace Corps*. New York, 1964 ; 146-51.

Union of Soviet Socialist Republics

1910. Bergman, Jay : Vera Zasulich, the shooting of Trepov and the growth of political terrorism, in Russia, 1878-81. *Terrorism* 4(1-4) 1980 ; 25-52.

1911. Broido, Vera : *Apostles into terrorists : Women and the revolutionary movement in the Russia of Alexander II.* New York, Viking Press, 1977.

1912. Devikar, D.R. : Soviet Union and terrorism. *Clarity* (Bombay) 18 May 1986 ; 4.

The Soviet Union has declared war against terrorism. Rejection of terrorism in any form is the Soviet Union's principal stand.

Terrorism cannot be wiped out unless its causes are removed. These causes are the striving to impose alien will on sovereign peoples, the interference in the affairs of other countries nnd reigons and attempts to perpetuate inequitable conditions of the existence of capitalist states at the expense of others interest.

These are actually manifestations of terrorism. The latest manifestations of state terrorism are well known. They were with regard to Nicaragua, Libya, other countries and regions.

The US intention to take weapons and mercenaries to Ghana is an example of international terrorism. This anti-Ghanian action was prepared and planned in the US and mercenaries were recruited in America.

1913. Gross, Feliks : Political violence and terror in 19th century and 20th century Russia and Eastern Europe. In *Assassination and Political Violence.* Ed. by James F. Kirkham *et.al.* New York, Prayer, 1970.

1914. India, USSR decry terrorism. *Indian Express* 15 Jun 1986.

1915. Kropotkin, Peter : *Terrorism Russia.* London, Methmen, 1909.

1916. Markham, James M : Soviet said to seek role in fighting terrorism. *International Herald Tribune* 20-21 Dec 1986 ; 1-2.

1917. Parry, Albert : Stalin's arhipelago. In *Terrorism.* New York, 1976 ; 187-202.

1918. Saksena, N.S. : Soviet Union's viewpoint of terrorism. In *THF* ; 72-90.

1919. Saksena, N.S. : Tsarist Russia. In *THF* ; 43-44.

United Kingdom

1920. Airports prime targets of terrorist. *Tribune* 12 Jan 1987 ; 5.

1921. Apple, R.W. : Britain in the 1980's : Portrait of a society in decline *International Herald Tribune* 10 Oct 1985 ; 1, 6.

1922. Attacks against British civilian, police and military personnel. In *WTAZIT* ; 26-27.

1923. Bhatia, Prem. : Maharaja of South-hall (Tarsem Singh Toor). *Tribune* 27 Jan 1986 ; 4.

1924. Buchan, Alastair : Britain debates the "balance of terror" *Reporter* 3(4) 1958.

1925. Chandran, Ramesh : Tackling terrorism. *India Today* 30 Nov 1985 ; 63-64.

1926. Combating terrorism. *National Herald* 11 Apr 1986 ; 5.

Only a comprehensive extradition treaty can provide an effective deterrent to the activities of Sikh terrorists that are operating in Britain with impunity. It is unfortunate that the British foreign secretary, Sir Geoffrey Howe, during his talks in New Delhi early this month could give little hope on such a treaty being worked out. He talked in terms of strengthening the "braces" instead of having a "belt". He missed the obvious point that the present system required firm curbs and his "extra buttons" won't just do in the present situation. The present laws need an altogether fresh look and a drastic change to make them tangibly effective. There is no denying that Sir Geoffrey's prescriptions fell much short of Indian expectations.

A meeting between the legal experts of India and Britain is likely to be held in London to discuss the issue in details. This will be another opportunity for the British authorities to come to grips with the core of the problem and help evolve fool-proof measures. It is clear that the existing laws have not been efficacious and Sikh terrorists have been able to thrive and preach their gospel of hatred against India and her democratic system in a perverted measure. The self-style "khalistani defence minister", Jaswant Singh Jathedar, was even granted a council house However, the latest reports suggest that his application for political asylum has been rejected and he has gone in an appeal against the decision. The issue at stake is not legalistic and has far-reaching dimensions. The foreign-based terrorists must not be allowed to carry on their nefarious activities against India and any let-up in checkmating them would be legitimately construed as an unfriendly act here. We are sure that those at the helm of affairs in the United Kingdom would not abdicate their responsibility for the sake of a set of loony gangsters.

1927. Easier extradition. *Tribune* 11 Mar 1986 ; 4.

As a long time victim of terrorism within its frontiers Britain ought to be more responsive to the pleas of other nations with similar problems. But the British Government has remained largely insensitive to outside protests (including those from India) about its indulgent attitude to persons accused of criminal acts on its soil. It is in this connection that the Thatcher Government's decision to amend the 116-year old extradition law represents a significant step forward. It must be clarified at the outset that the new proposals were not the result of British deference to India's recent complaints against that country being a ready sanctuary for pro-"Khalistan" terrorists. The new proposals, which form part of a comprehensive White Paper on the system of criminal jurisprudence in the United Kingdom, are an attempt to bring the British law in line with laws in the rest of Western Europe and will enable Britain to sign and ratify the European Convention of Extradition.

India recently submitted a draft extradition treaty to Britain seeking prompt deportation of persons wanted for crimes in each other's territory. The latest proposals meet India's demands only part of the way. Under the existing British law, the onus is on the foreign government concerned to convince a British judge that there is prima facie evidence to launch extradition proceedings. The British judiciary has always opted for a very liberal interpretation of the term "political refugee" and rarely went into the nature and gravity of the crimes for which extradition is sought. It has been a major irritant between the two countries that Britain has not done all it could to send back to India suspected extremists and propagators of "Khalistan" against whom there are valid cases. According to a Delhi estimate, there are about 500 Sikh extremists resident in England, most of them engaged in the supply of arms and funds to promote terrorism in Punjab. In recent months these militants have also taken advantage of British leniency towards them to mount attacks on Indians living abroad. Hopefully, the amended law will not insist on the "prima facie satisfaction" of the British judge for granting extradition. Any offence attracting a penalty of one year's imprisonment will be adequate to start extradition proceedings. The Indian Government will have no complaint about this because most of the terrorists whose extradition has been sought are wanted for murder and crimes against the State.

India, however, should press its case for a comprehensive treaty on the subject. British reluctance, so far, is explained by the fact that there are no fugitives from justice from that country hiding in India. On the other hand, Britain is asking the U.S.A. to do exactly what it refuses to do in the case of India. Delhi will do well to continue pressing for a treaty because terrorism in Punjab draws some of its sustenance from sources in such far a way places as Birmingham, San Francisco and Montreal. It will not be long before Britain realises that funding terrorism is as great a menace to peace and friendship as actual acts of terrorism. The interests of Indo-British relations depend on recognition of this basic fact.

1928. Extradite the terrorists. *International Herald Tribune* 4 Nov 1985 ; 6.

1929. Extradition treaty (India-U.K.) draft given to U.K. *Times of India* 9 Feb 1986 ; 1.

1930. Extremists abroad. *Deccan Herald* (Bangalore) 30 Jan 1986 ; 8.

British Home Secretary Douglas Hurd's reported assurance to Indian High Commissioner P.C. Alexander that his Government is determined to bring to book those responsible for the murder of moderate Sikh leader Tersem Singh Toor is reassuring. Mr. Toor, General Secretary of the Indian Overseas Congress since its formation 18 years ago, was a marked man because of his vigorous opposition to the extremists, who are very active in Britain. At the height of the Punjab crisis he received several threats to his life and his business premises in London were attacked more than once. According to eye-witness accounts, Mr. Toor was seated in his liquor shop at Southall, which has a large Indian population, when he was shot at point-blank range by a well-built white man in his twenties who spoke with a London accent. The incident occurred on January 23, only a week after the unsuccessful attempt on the life of Mr. Sangtar Singh Sandhu, Chief Organiser of the Akali Dal (Longowal) in Britain. Mr. Harbans Singh Ruprah, President of the Indian Overseas Congress, described Mr. Toor's killing as a political murder, pointing out that no attempt was made to burgle the shop. He also expresssd the view that the killer might have been hired by Sikh extremists. Although Scotland Yard immediately launched a manhunt, the killer was not found. The Indian envoy called on the Home Secretary after a newspaper quoted police, sources as saying there could be a drug angle. Mr. Hurd's statement that the Government was proceeding on the basis that this was a political murder should still doubts that interested parties might lead the investigators astray by drawing a red herring across the trail.

When Dr. Jagjit Singh Chauhan launched his campaign of separatism he found the ground fertile in Britain, Canada and the

United States, thanks to the powerful support extended by some influential people. The assistance he could muster abroad played a critical role in the aggravation of the situation in Punjab immediately before and after Operation Bluestar. Since then there has been some evidence of rethinking in the Western capital concerned. But in the absence of any serious attempt to apprehend the terrorist elements, forces hostile to this country feel free to operate from hospitable terrains abroad. Following the establishment of a Khalistan outfit in the Central American republic of Ecuador, extremists have now announced the opening of "diplomatic missions" in the Canadian cities of Toronto and Vancouver.

1931. Forward or backward ? *Hindustan Times* (New Delhi) 14 Feb 1986 ; 9.

What does British Home Secretary Douglas Hurd's offer to co-operate with India in extraditing terrorists amount to ? The only firm step that he indicated Britain was ready to take was to extend the Suppression of Terrorism Act to India for this purpose. The rest was soft soap about India being the first country outside Europe to which such an offer had been made and about warning those settled in Britain not to disturb the peace "in pursuit of quarrels which have nothing to do with this country".

When it is seen that such an offer had already been made and rejected by India as not being far-reaching enough and that only a few days before India had presented the draft of an extradition treaty that it felt could more effectively deal with the problem of terrorists, the announcement seems strange indeed. The draft was given following an agreement in principle between the Prime Minister of India and Britain last October to have such a treaty which reportedly was to be modelled on the existing Anglo-American extradition pact. Moreover, one meeting of Indian and British legal officials had already taken place in New Delhi as a follow up to the agreement and more discussions were agreed upon. It was following these that India gave the draft to the British Government.

By no stretch of imagination can the British Home Secretary plead ignorance of these developments which included the fact that Britain was supposed to be carefully studying India's proposals. Does Hurd's statement, at the Indo-British Association's annual dinner, imply a rejection of these ? Another mystery is Industry Minister N.D. Tiwari's reactions to Hurd's offer in his address later at the meet. For, he said this would be widely welcomed in India. One can only suppose that he was not properly briefed on India's stand. It is up to the Indian Government to clear the air.

1932. Goodhart, Philip : *Climate of Collapse* : *The terrorist, threat to Britain and her allies*. Richmond, England, Foreign Affairs, Pub. Co., 1975.

1933. Gregory, F.E.C. : British police and terrorism. *Terrorism* 5(1-2) 1981 ; 107-23.

1934. Howe, Geoffery told of India's concern over terrorists. *Times of India* 1 Apr 1986 ; 1.

1935. India for firm U.K. action. *National Herald* 19 Jul 1985.

1936. India wants U.K. to curb terrorism—B. R. Bhagat. *Tribune* 6 Feb 1986 ; 1.

1937. Kirkland, Lane. : Terrorism and the Gulag. In *ITCR* ; 330-31.

1938. Lessing, Doris : *Good terrorist*. New York, Afred A. Knopf, 1985. Pp. 375.

1939. Mackenzie, W.J.M. : *Power Violence and decision*. Harmondsworth, Penguin, 1975.

1940. Malik, K.N. : India, UK to discuss extremist issue. *Times of India* 26 Mar 1986 ; 16.

1941. Malik, K.N. : UK may amend law to curb terrorism. *Times of India* (New Delhi) 28 Mar 1986 ; 16.

1942. Murder abroad. *Amrita Bazar Patrika* 28 Jan 1986 ; 6.

1943. Osterhamnnel, Jurgen. : Imperialism in transition : British business and the Chinese authorities, 1931-37. *China Quarterly* (98) Jun 1984 ; 260-86.

1944. Plan to kill Indian diplomat. *Times of India* 29 Jan 1986 ; 1.

1945. Protecting murderers. *Patriot* 30 Jan 1986 ; 4.

Britain, which talks so glibly about curbing international terrorism, has much to answer for the campaign of cold-blooded murder that has been launched against moderate Sikhs and Indian diplomats in that country. All its excuses on behalf of the terrorists have been exposed to be nothing short of blatant collusion in the attempts to destabilise India by affording refuge to Khalistanis and Kashmiri separatists and encouragement in their nefarious deeds. Just one fact speaks for itself : the protection afforded to self-styled "President of Khalistan" Jagjit Singh Chauhan by Scotland Yard. Chauhan's goons are roaming about Britain murdering those who are not prepared to joining them in their anti-national activity while their mentor enjoys Scotland Yard's protection. Protection from whom ; one may ask. It is he who is the fountainhead of murder and mayhem. It raises serious doubts about Scotland Yard's efficacy in giving protection to the victims when it is so deeply committed. The threat to murder a senior Indian diplomat posted in London comes soon after a prominent moderate Sikh Tarsem Singh Toor was shot dead. This follows the murder of Sohan Singh Lidder at Luton in November and Sangtar Singh Sandhu at Cransford in mid-January. Since then a man with a shotgun has been looking for Toor's nephew.

Another alarming aspect of this sordid affair is that reports indicate that the killer is a "white" man, that is, not a Sikh. This could mean either of two possibilities : that Jagjit Singh Chauhan and his like are using hired killers to further the Khalistan cause because they will not be suspected by the prospective victim ; or, that western intelligence agencies (which are known to have done such things before) are taking a direct hand in extremist violence in pursuit of the larger game-plan to destabilise India. In this context, the arrest in India of some foreigners who are alleged to have links with the Khalistanis takes an added significance and perhaps points to a renewed attempt, scotched by Operation Blue Star, to revive separatism and for this mercenaries are recruited in much the same manner as is being done against Nicaragua, Afghanistan and some of the frontline African States that oppose the racist regime in South Africa.

The Government of India must tell the British Government in no uncertain terms that enough is enough ; that it must now produce evidence to bolster its claims to be a protector of democratic values by taking action against the Khalistanis. It is not for the Government of India to prove their guilt, it is for Britain to prove that they are innocent. Their "prophecy" over the British Broadcasting Corporation could be the first information report of their murderous intent. Apparently, the waffling over the Westland helicopter deal has given the British Government the impression that it can get away with its pampering of the Khalistani killers.

1946. Ramachandran, K.S. : Bid to clip terrorism. *Financial Express* (New Delhi) 21 Oct 1985 ; 4.

1947. Saksena, N.S. : Britain—History of Irish revolts and terrorism. In *THF* ; 65-71.

1948. Shackleton, Lord : *Review of the operation of the prevention of terrorism (temporary provisions) Acts of 1974 and 1976.* London. PMSO, 1978.

1949. Sharma, V. D. : Terrorists : Double-faced British policy. *Patriot* 17 Mar 1986 ; 4.

Legal experts of Britian and India are reportedly meeting at Delhi next month to discuss ways and means to control the activities of Sikh extrimsts in Britain. But so far the policy of the UK Government on this issue has not only been double-faced but also hypocritical. Many concrete examples can be cited.

Those who are aware of even a little about the procedures of political asylum applications know quite well that the British Home Office exhaustively interviews the applicant to get full facts and satisfy themselves as to why the person is not able to stay in his own country. Only then is political asylum granted. It is obvious, that the protagonists of 'Khalistan' applying for political asylum in UK must have told the British immigration authorities during their interviews about their grounds to justify their applications for political asylum, and as to why the Government of India wants them. They must have also submitted documentary evidence to establish their cases. The British Covernment must have also inquiries about them through their official channels. Thus,it is quite clear that the British Government knows full well about the antecedents of these persons.

British is a country which has granted political asylum to a large number of 'Khalistani' extremists. In its capital, London, not only does the office of the so-called "government of the Republic of Khalistan" function openly, but it also acts as an international anti-India centre. Pro-Khalistanis have delivered public speeches in Britain for murdering the late Prime Minister of India, Mrs Indira Gandhi.

Violent and extremist speeches are being published in 'Khalistani' newspapers in Britain, and no action whatsoever has been taken against them. British Minister of State David Maddington has been meeting pro-Khalistanis at their residences, enrolling them as forged members of the Conservative Party and seeking their help to fight the election to the Indo-Conservative Society. He has even promised to issue instructions or guidelines to the police that the 'old' leadership of the Sikhs in UK has lost its influence, and that they (the police) should adopt a sympathetic and lenient attitude towards the 'youthful' leadership. (see 'Charcha' August-Septemper, 1985).

1946. Sheltring terrorism. *Patriot* 7 Apr 1986 ; 4.

1947. Shipley, Peter : *Revolutionaries in modern Britain*, London, The Bodley Head, 1976.

1952. Sikh terrorists to face Sharper UK laws, *Amrita Bazar Patrika* 2 Apr 1986 ; 1.

1953. Toft on terrorists. *Tribune* 6 Feb 1986 ; 4.

Indo-British relations have been put under fresh strain by what seems to be a strange obstinacy in London over the treatment of known terrorists and campaigners for "Khalistan." The Indian resentment over the British attitude, which appears to be a blend of casualness and sympathy for killers and saboteurs, is not a new development, but it has become deeper since the murder last month of Mr. Tarsem Singh Toor, General Secretary of the Indian Overseas Congress. There is plenty of evidence to suggest that Mr. Toor's assassination was arranged by extremists, possibly through an agent. The incident caused great shock in India, and the Government's concern was reflected by the decision to send two senior Congress (I) leaders to attend the murdered leader's funeral. Instead of expressing a sense of shame the outrage, an unnamed British spokesman was wicked enough to suggest that Mr. Toor's death was connected with a drug racket : Such statements are unforgivable, and the British authorities ought to know that Mr. Toor was a highly respected Indian immigrant with business interests which were open to public inspection.

To make things worse for both countries, it was later claimed on behalf of the British authorities that India had never made a specific application in the past 10 years for the return of extremists to the land of their birth. If such an assertion is not a white lie, it comes fairly close to it. The Ministry of External Affairs in Delhi has described the British statement as baseless. India's informal requests, made through diplomatic channels, were rejected as far back as November 25, 1984. According to the External Affairs Ministry, Britain has not yet given any formal indication of a change in its position. A suspect is occasionally chosen for questioning but nothing is heard about follow-up action if any. The matter has now become serious enough for sharp official notice in Delhi. This is clear from certain remarks made by the Minister for External Affairs during a brief stopover, in London on his way to Washington on Tuesday. Expressing his Government's "serious concern" at the spurt in Sikh extremists' activities in Britain, Mr. B. R. Bhagat went to the extent of warning the host country that Indo-British relations may be adversely affected in the absence of prompt and effective action by the Thatcher Government to deal with the situation. India's Cabinet Ministers do not go around using such strong language without cause. There is no doubt that the Indian community in Britain is genuinely scared over the freedom with which assassins are allowed to operate. An unfortunate feeling has been growing in India that Britain is quietly encouraging the "Khalistan" movement and its Government thinks nothing of making excuses about its own helplessness to tackle Indian immigrants hostile to India's national interests and integrity.

If, as the British Government claims, the difficulty about extradition or deportion arises only from the absence of a formal request by India, the fact should have been known to the Government in Delhi. The British explanation that the Government of that country has to follow its own laws and regulations is a valid argument which India cannot question. But the impression in Delhi that guilty or suspected immigrants receive protection at the hands of the local authorities in London, Birmingham and eleswhere is widespread. If there is truth in that suggestion, Britain is guilty of an outrageously unfriendly attitude towards India. Mrs. Margaret Thatcher's role in the whole business shuld extend beyond words of sorrow and sympathy when an innocent Indian settler is gunned down by terrorists who receive shelter in her country.

1954. Terror against the British. In *WTAZIT* ; 6-10.

1955. Terror against the general public (Jews, Arabs and British). In *WTAZIT* ; 11-14.

1956. Terror on London streets. *Statesman* 26 Mar 1986 ; 8.

1957. Terrorism condemned by Queen Elizabeth. *Statesman* 19 Feb 1986 ; 8.

Queen Elizabeth on Febuary 17, 1986 condemned terrorism and shared Nepal's "revulsion at the bomb explosions which took place in Kathmandu last year,".

At a banquet hosted in Kathmandu honoured by King Birendra and Queen Aishwarya, he said : "Britain abhors terrorism and condemns it wherever and whenever it occurs".

"Despite the differences in our cultural and political evolution, we share a belief in the fundamental principles of independence and stability, backed by economic development".

On foreign affairs, the Queen said : "Britain appreciates Nepal's role as a moderate member of the Non-Aliged Movement and we hold same views on many important issues that come before the United Nations".

King Birendra in his speech stressed the need for peace and harmony in the world and hoped that the South Asian Association for

Regional Cooperation would become an instrument of peace and collaboration for the countries of the region.

He said Nepal and Britain, despite geographical distance, "have been close and trusted friends because Nepal has nurtured her friendship with Britain and Britain too has appreciated Nepal's will to live in freedom and dignity."

Queen Elizabeth had a special word of praise for the Nepalese soldiers. She affirmed her Government's support to King Birendra's earlier proposal that Nepal be declared a zone of peace.

The Queen also announced an increase in Britain's development assistance to Nepal.

1958. Toor : Man with a mission. *National Herald* 30 Jan 1986 ; 5.

1959. Toynbee, Polly : Horror as business. *Telegraph* 25 Aug 1985.

1960. Vivekanandan, B. : Riots in Britain : An analysis. *India Quarterly* (New Delhi) Jan-Mar 1982 ; 52-63.

1961. Wade-Gery, Ropert : There is very little or no support for Sikh terrorists in Britain. *Telegraph* (Culcutta) 3 Feb 1985 ; 6.

1962. Williams, Shirely : Terrorism. *Indian Express* 11 Jan 1986 ; 3.

1963. Wisdom downs on Britain after all. *Indian Observer* May 1986 ; 39-50.

United Nations

1964. Attacks on U. N. personnel. In *WTAZIT* ; 27-28.

1965. Containing terrorism. *Madhya Pradesh Chronicle* 11 Dec 1985; 4.

1966. Gupta, Vishwa Bandhu : International terrorism and role of U. N. *Mainstream* 14 Jan 1986 ; 12.

The United Nations, through innumerable but ineffective resolutions has tried to curb this intransigence. But now faced with a much greater adversary than puny Israel, which has got away with so much, what will it do with the crushing hammer of the veto ?

We saw, recently, the veto being used in the Security Council, both on the American raid on Libya and South African raids on Botswana, Zimbabwe and Zambia.

The cruel truth is that the United Nations set up once with such fervour and dreams of a new world order based on justice and peace has been cynically abused by the great power who gave to themselves not only "uniting for peace" enablement but also the veto, precisely to prevent any division in uniting. But as we all know the veto has been an instrument of blockage and sabotage.

What is alarming is that recently there is even an attack on the United Nations itself and demands for its dismantling. The alarm is further enhanced because the demands are not by some lunatic fringe but by powerful interests capable of carrying out such a programme. Their clout was seen in their success in getting the USA, Britain and Singapore to quit UNECO. A vases and shrill campaign has been unleashed to spell out the inadequacies of the United Nations, its capture by small and struggling netions whose crime is that they want a place in the sun. The monopoly of hegemony enjoyed for forty years by a minority is now threatened and therefore the United Nations has become a liability.

1967. Harrassment and intimidation of U. N. personnel. In *TAWZIT*; 31-32.

1968. Jack, H.A. : Terrorism : Another U. N. failure. *Americo* 20 Oct 1973.

1969. Killing and intimidation of U. N. personnel. In *WTAZIT*; 49-50.

1970. McWhinnery, Edward : International terrorism : United Nations projects for legal controls. *Terrorism* 7 (2) 1984 ; 175-84.

1971. Morello, Ted : Terrorism and the U. N. *Tribune* 1 Aug 1985 ; 4.

1972. Morello, Ted : Terrorism back on U. N. agenda. *Tribune* 28 Nov 1984 ; 4.

1973. Murphy , John. F. : *United Nations and control of International Violence.* Totowa, Allanheld, Osmun, 1983. Pp. 212.

1974. U. N. ban on torture. *Patriot* 12 Dec 1984 ; 6.

1975. UN. Condemns terrorism : *Deccan Herald* (Bangalore) 11 Dec 1085 ; 11.

1976. UN Condemns terrorism. *Madhya Pradesh Chronicle* 23 Dec 1985 ; 4.

Looking at the world-wide escalation in terrorism, it was in the fitness of things that the UN General Assembly took up the issue for discussions and a solution. Consequently an unanimous resolution was passed by the Assembly condemning "all acts, methods and practices of terrorism". The resolution further declared that terrorism "where-ever and by whomsoever committed" was "criminal". The resolution pleaded that world governments should take stern steps to curb terrorism. It also urged them to refrain from instigating or assisting terrorist activities in other countries, it is heartening to note that there was encouraging show of unanimity on the issue.

Behind almost every organised act of international terrorism there is a grievance either political or otherwise. More often than not it is political, as between the Israelis and the Arabs. Both sides in this case accuse each other of resorting to terrorisms. This raises the question as to who is terrorist and who is not. The sequence of events in West Asia, which has become the originating point of various kinds of terrorist activities, establishes that at times such criminal and heinous acts move in a vicious circle. Violence is retaliated by greater violence.

In order to work betterat at this place to live in it is imperative that good sense should prevail on all and an united effort be made to curb terrorism once for all. The UN resolution in this context is a step in the right direction. It is welcome that the General Assembly has at least spoken out in strong terms against this crime against humanity. How far the involved nations act on the UN's appeal will be a test of their sincerity.

1977. UN Council decries airport attacks. *Times af India* 1 Jan 1986 ; 16.

1978. UN member condemn US (over attacks on Libya). *Patriot* 29 Mar 1986 ; 7.

1979. UN Move to curb terrorism. *Deccan Chronicle* 12 Dec 1985 ; 6.

The United Nations has taken a momentous step by unanimously adopting a resolution condemning all acts of terrorism as criminal. At last there is a remarkable consensus among the member-States on the urgent need to curb international terrorism. Almost every country has in recent years become vulnerable to terrorism in one form or another. India is a case in point. The cataclysmic events in India in the recent past were the direct result of terrorism. The tragedy is that much of the murderous terrorism that rocked India, particularly the border

State of Punjab, had been engineered from abroad. Even after the people of the State have voted overwhelmingly in favour of democratic, rule, peace and stability, terrorists, undoubtedly very few in number, are trying to create distrubances in the State. That the terrorists have no local support is there for all to see. And there are grounds for believing that the terrorists, wherever they are, are being inspired and supported from aborad. There are some hardcore separatists terrorists operating from some Western countries. These terrorists, for long out of touch with the political realities in the State, are bent upon sabotaging the peace process that began after the historic Punjab accord. Many are of the view that the recrudescence of extremism in Punjab is part of international terrorism. Which means that destabilisation of India through terrorism is one of the foreign policy objectives of some forces envious of India's stable democracy and its emergence as an assertive regional power. And there are many countries in the world which are guilty of adopting a double standard on the question of terrorism. These countries are known to have supported terrorism in some parts of the world when it subserved their foreign policy objectives. Many big powers, obssessed with their global strategies, have not been objective in their approach to terrorism.

And this is the root-cause of increasing terrorism in the world. Some powers donot scruple to fuel terrorism aimed at toppling a regime whose foreign policy in at outs with theirs. This seems to have happened to some extent during the Punjab turmoil. How some terrorists got training facilities in India's neighourhood is now an open secret. Expectedlly, the country concerned keeps denying the charge. But there is enough circumstantial evidence to prove how the separatist sentiment in Punjab was sought to be meshed with the foreign policy objective of some powers maliciously wishing for balkanisation of India. And the recurrence of terrorist violence in Punjab should be a warning to the Indian people. It is in this context that one welcomes the UN General Assembly resolution condemning terrorism. Only through cooperation can the member-States rid the world of terrorism. The consensus should be given a concrete shape in bilateral and multilateral arrangements to curb, and ultimately, eliminate terrorism in all its forms. The unanimous resolution augurs well for world peace and stability.

Consonant with the UN resolution is the setting up of a group, by the recently formed South Asian Association of Regional Cooperation (SAARC), to examine the problem of terrorism and the stability of the member-States. Such regional cooperation is what international terrorism warrants. Whatever be the cause of terrorists, they deserve to be condemned. Soft-pedalling of terrorism with an ulterior motive. which is the case with many countries now, is dangerous. And no country is immune from this danger. Regretably, there is much relativity in terrorism. There have been instances of some countries lauding terrorism as an act of heroism. There is no university acceptable definition of terrorism. Such a definition should be the aim of the Un member-States which have unanimously condemned acts of terrorism as criminal. A consistent stand by all countries on the problem of terrorism is essential.

1980. United Nations. *U.N. General Assembly* : *Report of the Adhoc Committee on International Terrorism.* New York, Official 28th Session Supp no. 28 (A/9028) 1973.

United States of America

1981. Abraham, A.S. : Fighting global terrorism : U.S. moral posture crumbles. *Times of India* 5 Dec 1986 ; 8.

The arms-for-hostages scandal has demolished all the assiduous PR type of which the Reagan administration has been so skilful a purveyor But it has been hurt most on the moral front, which it sought to appropriate through sustained and sanctimonious rhetoric that could, as turns out, camouflage the shabbiest actions.

Nowhere has the lofty moral stance the Reagan White House regularly strikes been more in evidence than on combating global terrorism. This was Mr. Reagan's very own latter-day crusade against "murder incorporated". as, ever the wit, he once labelled it. It was to be waged, like the crusades of old, with a single-minded ferocity inspired by a Manichaean concept of good and evil. "So there we have it," he said in July 1985, "Iran, Libya, North Korea, Cuba, Nicaragua ....The growth of terrorism in recent years results from the increasing involvement of......these......outlaw states run by the strongest collection of misfits, looney tunes, and squalid criminals since the advent of the Third Reich". They had to be stopped in their tracks by a combination of measures : diplomatic ostracism, economic punishment, the denial of arms ("Operation Staunch", another Reagan coinage) and, when push came to shove, a punch in the nose.

The country Mr. Reagan chose to make an example of in the enforcement of his anti-terrorism policy was Colonel Gaddafi's Libya. As it happened, the colonel was not exactly the darling of the Third World. He had rubbed so many poor countries especially those in his immediate vicinity, the wrong way that when the Americans kicked him in the shin, not everyone was unhappy. But they dressed their punishment as intended, not merely to cut him down to size, but to proclaim their determination to snuff out what they were convinced were the sources of global terrorism.

1982. Abrham, Thomas : Price of power. *Frontline* (Madras) 17-30 May 1986 ; 47-48.

1983. Ackerman, Mike : Take the fight into the terrorirsts' nether-world. *International Herald Tribune* 19 Sep 1986 ; 4.

1984. Acting against terrorism. *International Herald Tribune* 19 Apr 1986 ; 6.

1985. Adamic, Louis. : *Dynamite : The story of class violence in America.* New York, Viking Press, 1934 & New York Chelsea, 1968.

1986. Adams, Velma : Future of the Peace Corps. In *Peace Corps in action.* Chicago, Follett, 1984 ; 205-67.

1987. Adams, Velma : *Peace Corps in action.* Chicago, Follett, 1964. Pp. 318.

1988. Agee, Philip : *Inside the company : CIA diary.* London, 1978.

1989. Agee, Philip and L. Wolf. *ed.* : *Dirty work : The CIA in Western Europe.* Secancus, Citadel Press, 1978.

1990. Aiyar, Shahnaz Anklesaria : US wants India to help curb terrorism. *Indian Express* 24 Apr 1986 ; 1-9.

1991. Allied against terror. *International Herald Tribune* 22 Jul 1986 ; 6.

1992. American spy for China (Mr. Larry Wu-Tal Chin) commits suicide in jail. *International Herald Tribune* 22-23 Feb 1986 ; 1.

1993. Arab-Americans protest against discrimination. *Baghdad Observer* 13 Feb 1986.

Arab-American leaders asked the U.S. Commission on Civil Rights Tuesday to investigate "an ugly, racist type of anti-Semitism" against Americans of Arab descent.

The leaders, in a briefing for the Commission, accused President Ronald Reagan, the news media, the film industry and Zionist Organizations of fostering the discrimination by generally portraying Arabs as terrorists.

"We are not terrorists. We are not supporters of terrorism", said Dr. James J. Zogby, Executive Director of the Arab-American Institute.

Zogby and former U.S. Senator Jamas Abourez, Chairman of the American-Arab Anti-Discrimination Committee, contended the FBI is more interested in political surveillance of Arab-Americans than in investigating crimes against them.

Commissioners took no immediate action on the request, and pointed out their obligation under U.S. law to allow those criticized to respond.

Abourezk told the eight-member Commission, "Arab-Americans have experienced a wave of harassment and violence directed against them personally, their communities and their businesses and property".

Zogby asked the commission to investigate "the extent to investigate" the extent to which acts of discrimination and political exclusion and instances of harassment and violence against Arab-Americans, constitute a serious infringement of civil rights.

1994. Arrogance of power. *Patriot* 7 Apr 1986 ; 7.

1995. Ashley, Mick : How US arms to Iran feed terrorism. *Baghdad Observer* 14 Jan 1987 ; 4.

1996. Attacks against American and British institutions, and concerns outside Palestine. In *WTAZIT* ; 22-32.

1997. Babu, R. : Terrorism unclothed. *People's comment* (New Delhi) 15 Feb 1987 ; 35-37.

1998. Batronkha, Dean : Terrorism by a superpower. *International Herald Tribune* 5 Dec 1986 ; 3.

1999. Bell, J. Bowyer and Ted Robert Gurr : Terrorism and revolution in America. In *Violence in America.* Ed. by Hugh Graham and Ted Gurr. London, Sage. 1979 ; 329-47.

2000. Bennett, W. Tapley : United states initiatives in the United Nations to combat international terrorism. *International Lawyer* 7 (4) Oct 1973 ; 752-68.

2001. Berg, Eric N. : Terrorism trims number of U.S. students abroad. *International Herald Tribune* 26 Jun 1986 1.

2002. Berger, Harry W. : American labour overseas. *Nation* (New York).

2003. Boyd, Gerald M. Reagan warns terrorists about 'cowardly acts.'. *International Herald Tribune* 28 Apr 1986. ; 1-6.

2004. Braden, Tom : I am glad that the CIA is immoral. *Saturday Post* (London) Jul 1987.

2005. Bruck, David I. : Teen-age killers : Draw the line at 18 for execution. *International Herald Tribune* 17 Sep 1985 ; 8,

2006. Buckley, William F. : No-nonsense programme against terror. *International Herald Tribune* 24 Jul 1986 ; 5.

2007. Bush, George : U.S. and the fight against international terrorism. In *ITCR* ; 332-37.

2008. Butler, Sharon : US rich befriend right-wing rebels abroad. *Telegraph* (Calcutta) 12 Jan 1986 ; 6.

2009. Button, James W. : *Black violence : Political impact of the 1960s riots.* Princeton, 1978.

2010. Carey, Robert G. : *Peace Corps.* New York, Prayer, 1970. Pp 274.

2011. Chalmers, D.M. : *Hooded Americanism.* New York, Quadrangle, 1968.

2013. Chandler, Christopher : Black Panther killings in Chicago. *New Republic* 162 (2) 10 Jan 1970.

2014. Chernyavasky V. *ed.* : *CIA in the dock.* Moscow, Progress Publishers, 1983. Pp. 176.

2015. Chopra, Suneet : Anatomy of US terror in Nicaragua. *Patriot* 30 Aug 1986 ; 4.

2016. Chopra, V.D. : *Pentagon shadow over India.* New Delhi, Patriot Publishers, 1985. Pp. 223.

2017. CIA hand (in India) *Daily* 21 Jan 1985 ; 10.

2018. CIA radio flops. *New Age* 9 Feb 1986 ; 11.

2018. CIA record of terror. *Blitz* (Bombay) 6 Jul 1985 ; 3.

CIA chose a civilian airliner, the KAL flight from Anchorage to Seoul, for spying over Soviet missile sites in the Far East, plunging to death 269 passengers on September, 1, 1983.

In 1955, CIA blew up Air-India's "Kashmir Princes", vainly hoping to kill Chinese Premier Chou Enlai, a day before the opening of the Bandung conference.

CIA placed bombs and blew up C ban airliner in a Latin American flight.

Reagan directed the CIA late last year to train and support "special units" for strikes against suspected Arab targets "before they could attack US targets in Lebanon." In accordance to this plan, one of the units, "hiring others in Lebanon", planted a car bomb outside the residence of Sheikh Mohamed Hussein Fedlallah, leader of "the Hezballah" (Party of God), a militant Shiite faction on March 8 this year, killing 80 people in Beirut (report in Washington Post).

2019. CIA unifies Nicaraguan counter-revolution. *Frontline* (Oakland, Ca) 25 Jun 1984.

2020. Chine, Raj S. : *Secrets, spies and scholars.* Washington, 1976.

2021. Cohen, Richard : Innocent will suffer from call for reprisals. *International Herald Tribune* 10 Jul 1985 ; 6.

2022. Cordes, Bonnie : Armenian terrorism in America. In *ITDC* ; 155-68.

2023. Dahl, Robert A. : *Pluralist democracy in the United States. Conflict or consent.* Chicago, 1967.

2024. Das, Tapan. : High moral principles or a manual on terrorism. *Link* 1 Feb 1987 ; 28-29.

2025. Das, Tapan : Terrorism world over : US foreign policy weapon. *Daily* 10 Apr 1985 ; 10-11.

2026. Davidson, Alfred E. : Toug talk on terror. *International Herald Tribune* 14 Nov 1285 ; 4.

2027. Dealing with terrorism. *Patriot* 23 Sep 1986 ; 6.

2028. Dieterich, Jeff. : How to attack terrorism : the view from skied row. *International Herald Tribune* 15 Jan 1987. ; 5.

2029. Dual US policy on terrorism. *Daily* (Bombay) 6 Jul 1985 ; 12.

2030. Dulles, A. : *Craft of intelligence*. New York, 1963.

2031. Eastern airlines adopts takeover safeguards. *International Herald Tribune* 3 Feb 1986 ; 7.

2032. Evans, Ernest H. : American policy response to international terrorism : Problems of deterrence. In *ITCW* ; 376-88.

There have been several American efforts to deter acts of international terrorism. Among them are the Latin American Diplomats Convention, the United Nations Convention on the Protection of Diplomats and Diplomatic Agents, and the policy of "no negotiations, no ransoms" with terrorist groups. Of particular interest, however, was one specific effort, namely, the 1972 Draft Convention on International Terrorism, which was introduced by the United States in the fall of 1972 in the General Assembly of the United Nations, debated in the Sixth (Legal) Committee, and finally quite effectively killed by that committee.

The 1972 American Draft Convention and the accompanying debates are interesting because they provide an answer as to why it has been so difficult to negotiate a general multilateral accord to deal with the problem of transnational terrorism. There are, to be sure, numerous extradition treaties between states that provide for the extradition or punishment not only of common criminals, but also of certain categories of political offenders, such as individuals who have assassinated or attempted to assassinate a head of state or a member of a head of state's family. (This is the so-called Belgium clause in extradition treaties). In addition, there are several multilateral conventions in effect that deal with certain specialized forms of international terrorism : the Latin American Diplomats Convention (negotiated in 1971), the United Nations Convention on the Protection of Diplomats and Diplomatic Agents (adopted by the General Assembly in 1973), and the three conventions on aircraft hijacking : the 1963 Tokyo Convention, the 1970 Hague Convention, and the 1971 Montreal Convention. However, the two major efforts to negotiate multilateral conventions against the general problem of international terrorism have both failed. The first was the 1937 League of Nations Conference on the Suppression of Terrorism, which produced a convention for that purpose. The convention never received sufficient ratification to be enacted and so has remained a dead issue. The second was the previously mentioned 1972 American Draft Convention on International Terrorism.

I will concentrate on explaining the 1972 convention's failure to be accepted. The 1937 convention is not without interest, but it was considered in a very different era and by a far more limited number of nations than the 1972 convention ; an analysis of why it failed would shed light only indirectly on the problem of the response to terrorism in the contemporary world.

The American Draft Convention on International Terrorism was formulated with the intention of securing maximum possible support. Thus those who drew it up took care to exclude from its scope of domestic terrorism. The convention applied only to terrorist acts of "international significance". For a terrorist act to be of international significance four conditions had to be fulfilled ; First. the act had to take place or have effects outside of the terroritory of the state of which the offender was a national ; second, the victims of the attack had to be citizens of a state other than the one on whose soil the attack took place ; third, the attack had not to be committed against a member of the armed forces in the course of military hostilities ; fourth, the attack had to be intended to damage the interests of or to obtain concessions from a state or international organization. Even with these fairly precise guidelines, exactly what acts the convention would have covered is open to dispute, but the drafters went to great pains to note that wars being waged by indigenous rebels in such places as South Africa were not within the jurisdiction of the convention.

The key provision of the convention pledges its signatories to either extradite or punish any individuals within their territory who were deemed to have committed an act of international terrorism as defined by the convention. The convention's articles dealing with what constituted an extraditable offence were to be considered as being included in the existing extradition treaties of the signatory states.

Accompanying the draft convention, the United States introduced a resolution which urged states to ratify the three antihijacking conventions and which called for prompt measures against international terrorism. It soon became apparent in the debates in the legal committee that the American resolution commanded little support, so the United States switched its support to a second resolution that had been introduced by some West European and Latin American states. This resolution, unlike the American resolution, had a paragraph reaffirming the right of national self-determination, and therefore it was hoped it would meet the objections concerning wars of liberation raised by the Arab, African, Asian, and Communist states to the original American resolution. However, this coalition of Third World and Communist states refused to accept the second rcsolution either, and instead introduced and passed a resolution of their own which condemned racist and repressive regimes as terroristic and called for an ad hoc committee to meet in 1973 to consider the problem of international terrorism.

2033. Evans, Ernest E. : *Calling a truce to terror : the American response to international terrorism.*

2034. FBI analysis of terrorist incidents in the United States—1982. *Terrorism* 7 (1) 1984 ; 87-96.

2035. For a declared war on terror. *International Herald Tribune* 28-29 Dec 1985 ; 4.

2036. Freed Donald and Fred Simon Landis : *Death in Washington* Westport 1980.

2037. Fuchs, Lawrence H. : *Those peculiar Americans.* New York. Meredith Press, 1967.

2038. Galbraith, John Kenneth : 1985 : the year of the spy (in a manner of speaking). *International Herald Tribune* 8 Jan 1986 ; 4.

2039. Gandhi, Nelima : FBI hinders terrorists hunt. *Hindustan Times* 31 Jan 1987 ; 1.

2040. Getting tough. *Asiaweek* 19 Jan 1986 ; 18.

2041. Geyellin, Philip : Blow to the credibility of Presidential discourse. *International Herald Tribune* 13-14 Jul 1985 ; 4.

2042. Geyellin, Philip : In drawing a line against terrorism, beware of nasty surprises. *International Herald Tribune* 26 Jan 1985 ; 8.

2043. Geyelin, Philip : Life at the top : Trust must outweigh fear of spies. *International Herald Tribune* 26 Dec 1985 ; 4.

2044. Gleason, John : Poison model of incidents of International terrorism in the United States. *Terrorism* 4 (1-4) 1980 ; 259-66.

2045. Global policeman. *Newstime* 15 Oct 1985 ; 7.

2046. Goleman, Daniel : Making of a terrorist could begin in childhood. *International Herald Tribune* 12 Sep 1986 ; 5.

2047. Goshko, John M. : Great game of spying intrades at UN. *International Herald Tribune* 18 Mar 1986 ; 6.

2048. Graham, H.D. and Ted Robert Gurr *eds.* : *Violence in American : Historical and comparative perspectives.* Washington, 1969.

2049. Greenhouse, Linda : U.S. measure would pose response to terrorism. *International Herald Tribune* 19-20 Apr 1986 ; 6.

2050. Gupta, Rakesh : Terrorism of US radical rift. *Patriot* 31 Jul 1985 ; 4.

2051. Gwertzman, Bernard : U.S. sees new wave of terror : Exports expect indiscriminate acts in Europe. *International Herald Tribune* 14 Jul 1986 ; 1, 6.

2052. Half, Marvin and Elie Abel : *Roots of involvements : The US in Asia, 1784-1971.* London, Pall Mall, 1971.

2053. Halloran, Richard : Pentagon, citing terrorism, tells personnel to hide identity of overseas. *International Herald Tribune* 17 Oct 1985 ; 5.

2054. Hofstadter, Richard and Michael Wallace *eds.* : *American violence* New York, Hintage Books, 1971.

2055. Homer, Frederic D. : Terror in the United States : Three perspectives. In *POT* ; 373-406.

Many individuals believe that the United States is an open democratic society where grievances can be heard and where alternatives are presented (both candidates and policies) and, after open deliberation, decided upon by the people. Few believe democracy in this country functions ideally, but proponents of this perspective feel that despite delay, obstruction, and even corruption, groups and individuals can peaceably air their views and, if acceptable to the majority, get these views forged into law. Therefore, with an operable democratic society that allows for peaceful change, one cannot tolerate terrorism. Irving Howe states this position succinctly : "In a society where reasonable (which is necessarily to say, an imperfect) measure of freedom to speak and organize is available, we must regard it as utterly impermissible to resort to terrorist methods or to give the faintest encouragement to them" (1976, p. 60). Terrorism is intolerable when other modes of expression are available. "And if (terrorism) is wrong because minorities in a democratic society, as long as their freedom to dissent is largely protected, do not have the right to impose their will upon the majority through violence" (1976, p.60). Howe also reasons that terror is intolerable for pragmatic reasons as well as on moral grounds. "In countries with highly developed and articulate class structures, terrorism has never succeeded, nor is it likely to succeed, in effecting any basic change of power—though it may through an art of sudden blackmail achieve a limited end such as forcing the release of prisoners, etc." (1976, p. 60).

The democratic perspective has often been used to suggest the limits to which a group can go in articulating its grievances even when terrorism is not in the forefront as a tactic. As an example, in the 1960s, many were concerned with the establishment of acceptable limits of nonviolent protest in a democratic society. People argued as to whether nonviolent protest should be carried so far as to provoke a violent response from the opposing side. The democratic perspective can also focus on acts of terror by government officials that might threaten the existence of democratic institutions. Joseph Schumpeter raised this problem when he asked whether in a democracy the people have the right to dissolve a democratic system, or if the government may by undemocratic means, restore a democratic system (1950, pp. 242 243). For instance, James Burnham believes that a democracy is worth saving even at the cost of counter-terror and other activities that may temporarily abridge freedom : "......if terrorism is both serious and long-continued—(it) apparently also requires a certain amount of counter-terror. A contemporary anti-terror strategy that did not include many sorts of undercover surveillance, infiltration, enemy and potential enemy lists, secret search and serizure, etc., would be ludicrous" (1974, p. 365).

The perspective of terror in a democratic society is useful for its attempts to establish permissible limits of terror in a system for government and its opposition. Adherents of this perspective, including those like Burnham whom advocate strong measures in response to terrorists, seem to agree that terror should be limited as much as possible. Thus, terror as defined by this perspective in a pejorative term : It is something to be avoided in a democratic system if at all possible. To define terror further, we shall examine a typology of acts that Feliks Gross (1970) calls terrorist and shall elaborate upon it. His categories will be analyzed to see if, according to democratic theorists, some acts are more repugnant than others and thus less tolerable in a democratic system. The acts Gross is concerned with involved death to victims, normally thought of as less desirable than threats of violence, unsuccessful attempts at terror, and the destruction of property.

Gross suggests the objective of dynastic assassination is the "elimination of a family, as well as a change of ruling elites, and usually a change of political orientations" (1970, p. 533). We are all too familar in this country with assassinations of our presidents. John F. Kennedy was the eighth presidential victim of a violent attack and the fourth to be killed (Kirkham, Levy, and Crotty, p. xv). This country seems to be victimized by lone assassins for the most part, even though some may have been part of complex conspiracies, as rceent speculations on the Kennedy assassination seem to indicate. The assassins' objectives have been elimination of a "bad" leader or covert takeover of the country be elites. There has been no overt show of force in this country after an assassination, although in many other countries dynastic assassinations are preludes to power plays by conspiracies.

Individual assassination is the murder or attempted murder of someone "taken to be crucially represntative of autocratic power" (Howe, 1976, p. 60). In this senator part of the ruling elite or the opposition ? Are cabinet members, dissident members of the federal bureaucracy, or Supreme Court justices part of the opposition to government ? It depends upon one's definition of such concepts as power, elite, and opposition. We shall define individual assassination as the murder or attempted murder of someone taken to be crucially representative of autocratic power, whether or not the person holds a formal office.

2056. Hoopes, Roy : *Complete peace corps guide*. New York, *Dial Press*, 1961.

2057. Howe, Russell Warren : Means fair or foul : Confessions of a veteran terrorist (William colby) *Statesman* 25 Feb 1986 ; 6.

2058. Huggins, Martha : Police : U.S. training programes haven't worked. *International Herald Tribune* 1 Apr 1989 ; 4.

2059. Hunter, Robert E. : Anti-terrorism has to be pro-peace. *International Herald Tribune*13 Jan 1986 ; 4.

2060. Hunter, Robert E. : U.S. rhetoric will not help to eradicate terrorism. *International Herald Tribune* 12 Sep 1986 ; 4.

2061. Jansen, G.H. : Terrorism : Reagan rhetoric ignores causes. *Deccan Herald* 15 Jul 1935 ; 6.

2062. Jesuran, C.G. : Super power terrorism. *Mid-Day* (New Delhi). 3 Sep 1986 ; 5.

2063. Kamath, P. K. : Sikh extremists in the US : Need for effective lobbying. *Radical Humanist* Sep 1985 ; 11-14.

2064. Karnad, Bharat : US resolve against terrorism stiffens. *Hindustan Times* 17 May 1985 ; 16.

2065. Keniston, Kenneth : *Uncommitted : Alienated youth in American society*. London, Pall Mall, 1968.

2066. Keniston, Kenneth : *Youth and dissent : The rise of a new opposition*. New York, 1960.

2067. Kirsanov, Yuri : Terrorism and U.S. hypocrisy. *Indian Observer* Jan 1986 ; 26.

The Legal committee of the UN General Assembly has approved a resolution denouncing terrorism as a criminal act. This document calling on all the countries to fulfil their obligations under international law, refraining from incitement, assistance or participation in terrorist acts in other countries, was voted for by 118 countries, including the USA.

Taking into account the fact that last year the USA abstained from voting on a resolution on the same issue, the present position imposes a high responsibility.

The international community expects now that the USA will abandon, at long last, its policy of state-sponsored terrorism, that is stop hatching new Grenades, renounce officially proclaimed tactics of "support" for anti-communist forces "throughout the world" and wars "by proxy" waged by the USA against Angola Mozambique, Nicaragua and Afghanistan. It also expects that the USA will stop assisting South Africa and Israel in their acts of terror against neighbouring states. The world community also expects that the USA will stop training, inside the country and in dependent satellite countries, terrorists, Nicaraguan "contrast" and Afghan bandits.

The US delegate voted for the resolution condemning terrorism as a criminal act at the time when two terrorist acts against civilians were committed in Kabul. These were a powerful mine explosion at the Kabul international airport on December 8, 1985. As a result, over 60 people were killed or wounded and in another explosion at a laboratory of the Kabul polytechnic the next day over 20 students were wounded. The US administration has not uttered a single word of condemnation as it there were no terrorist acts at all. This is understandable, since the USA itself is to blame for them. Back in 1981, the Afghan authorities confiscated from counter-revolutionaries a CIA-issued map with marked objects for acts of sabotage. They included all Afghan civil airports, major enterprises, power plants and food storages. In 1982-83, Afghan and Indian authorities arrested terrorists from Afghan counter-revolutionary organisations who had been instructed to carry out saboteur acts on civil planes in these countries.

In 1984, saboteurs trained at a special Pakistani camp and supplied with instructions by a US Embassy staffer as well as with the latest explosives, detonated a bomb near the Kabul airport building. Over 200 people were killed or wounded as a result of this act. The same year, two months later, an abortive attempt was made to down an Afghan liner DC 10 carrying 308 passengers. Terrorists used a US ready missile.

The terrorists activities remained continue in 1985. In the summer, President Reagan announced his decision to supply Pakistan with modern stinger anti-aircraft missile system. and in September terrorists shot down an Afgan airliner by such a missile in Afghanistan. All passengers and the crew were killed. This "operation" was directed by a group of Americans, and one of them (Charles Thornton) was killed in Afghanistan.

Apart from its crimes in Afghanistan, the USA was also an accomplice in the destruction of an Indian airliner Boeing—747, the barbaric Israeli air raid on Tunis and the interception of an Egyptian passenger airliner by the US air force. The list of the American terrorists acts could be continued.

A US State Department spokesman expressed "satisfaction" with the adoption of the UN resolution denouncing terrorism. But the above facts show that terrorism and hypocrisy are a characteristic feature of the UN administration's conduct in the world arena.

2068. Klein, Milton M. : Fact of violence in America : A historical perspective. *Social Education* 37, 1973.

2069. Krauthammer, Charles : It takes a hard man to make nonviolence work : *International Herald Tribune* 28 Jan 1986 ; 4.

2070. Krauthammer, Charles : U. S. allies' passivity underscores NATO rift. *Internotional Herald Tribune* 29 Apr 1986 ; 8.

2071. Kroes, Rob : Violence in America ; Spontaneity and strategy. In UG ; 81-93.

This essential allofness from the world of experience of 'the other America', especially in its moments of outcry, would, a fortiori, account for official views of violence as conscious strategy rather than unplanned outburst. Books by ranking Black Power spokesmen illustrate whate specific 'official' reactions this strategy may elicit. Yet, in this context, the distinction between spontaneity and strategy may seem unduly stark. There is a twilight zone where the one concept shades over into the other and which we propose to highlight here. For one thing, the riots which have occurred urban riots. Originally the scene of violent invasions by whites of recently populated black neighbourhoods—forays in retaliation against the penetration of Negroes on to the urban scene—riots became more strictly a black phenomenon during the thirties, when looting and plunder of stores came to prevail. Janowitz refers to the first type as communal riots, meant to clearly demarcate urban neighbourhoods against the tide of black migration; the second he refere to as commodity riots. Riots in the sixties, finally, do display patterns of rationally directed violence, of acts inspired by a glimmering political awareness of who are to be held responsible for prevailing oppression and misery. They still display, to be true, the characteristics of cammodity riots : yet the first signs are appearing of the use of political violence. Therefore, next to the aspects of violence as protest—as an expressive outburst—aspects can be discerned of the instrumental use of violence. Janowitz alternatively referes to this as political violence, political terror, or even conspiratorial violence. The trend was for more specific, more premeditated, and more regular use of force to appear. Janowitz refers to the harassment of white school teachers active in union work, sniper fire at, or downright shootouts with police personnel and the subjecting of integrated housing projects to rifle fire and fire bombings. These incidents are created for the purpose of developing solidarity in local gangs and in paramilitary groups'. Janowitz does not refer to what I would consider an instance of commodity riots shading over into politically conscious riots : the selectivity of looting his directed at the local bridgeheads of the oppressor—his stores, pawn-shops—while at the same time sparing black-owned businesses. Yet another intermediate case would be the use of sniper fire in support of looters, aimed at diverting the attention of the police.

The term conspiratorial violence in particular conjures up the image of a confluence of spontaneous breakdowns of order and ideologically motivated violence—a confluence, in other words, of a dissatisfied following and an articulate radical vanguard. All too easily, it would seem, Janowitz dismisses the use of the guerrilla concept to describe these trends. According to him, 'the guerilla concept is not relevant since guerrillas are part of an organization, proceed with a plan, prepare paths of withdrawal, and develop sancturaries.' Grandet that, similar to political violence, no more than the first glimmering of guerrilla tactics has been apparent, yet the very aspects of organization, planning, and the establishment of an underground network for purposes of withdrawal and sanctuary, can be discerned. It would seem that the secession of the black wing from the broad Civil-Rights movement as well as its concomitant radicalization, have led various black-power organizations, most notably Black Panthers, to provide for these elements of organization, planning, leadership, and strategic analysis. In the radical rhetoric of these groups, for instance, the police (or 'the pigs') were singled out as the very embodiment of racist oppression and a ready target for political terror. Moreover, the very adoption of the rhetoric of 'picking up the gun', and the brandishing of arms by black students at Cornell University, may have served, more than any actual use of arms, to bring home to the nation the awareness of a definite escalation in protest and resistance. On the lavel of strategic analysis, ever since Cruse coined the concept of 'domestic colonialism', it has served as a powerful tool for analysis and a ready vehicle for translating the domestic struggle of the blacks into the larger framework of the liberation of the Third World from 'colonialist' oppression.

Similar trends can be discerned in white protest, especially student protest. A few main factors of radicalization have been at work. The early Civil-Rights workers had to confront the repression of Southern whites and, more ominously, of Southern law-enforcing agencies, such as the police and the courts. There, incidentally, it had led some non-violent activists to adopt practices of armed self-defence, and to come up with concepts such as civilian defense. In Northern cities, the community-organizing work of SDS (Students for a Democratic Society) gave some of its participants first-hand experience of riot-quelling tactics of the police, as for instance in the ghetto riots in Newak in 1967. Finally, the importance of anti-war protest in the face of steady escalation of the Vietnam war has, perhaps more than any other single factor, served to radicalize segments of the student body. Here again, patterns of confluence of spontaneity and strategy can be discerned.

2068. Leaderer, William J and Eugene Burdick : *Ugly American.* New York. W. W. Norton, 1958.

2069. Leuis, Anthony : Campaign by Reagan is perilous. *International Herald Tribune* 5 Mar 1986 ; 4.

2070. Lewis, Flora : Sounding off doesn't hurt terrorism. *International Herald Tribune* 13-14 Jul 1985 ; 4.

2071. Lewis, Flora : Ulster : Is America serious about fighting terror ? *International Herald Tribune* 16-17 Nov 1985 ; 6.

2072. Losev, S. : International brigandage and terrorism—weapons of US imperialism. *International Affairs* (Moscow) Jan 1984 ; 12-19.

2073. Mad dog on rampage. *Mainstream* 19 Apr 1986 ; 1-3.

2074. Marchetti, Victor and John D. Marks : *CIA and the cult of intelligence*. New York, 1974.

2075. Marcus, Ruth and Fred Hiatt : U. S. spy suspect said to steal house transcripts. *International Herald Tribune* 28-29 Dec 1985 ; 1, 5.

2076. Marchetti, V and John D. Marks : *CIA and the cult of intelligence*. New York, 1974.

2077. Mishra, R. K. : Reagan's terrorism. *Patriot* 16 Apr 1986 ; 1.

Ronald Reagan has, without doubt, entered his name in the annals of contemporary history as the Godfather of state terrorism. The US bombing raid on Libya has proved that Reagan respects no international norms ; he believes only in one law—the law of the jungle. The US Air Force was assigned to murder Col. Gaddafi—there is no other explanation of bombing the Libyan leader's residence. Prime Minister Rajiv Gandhi has strongly condemned the reprehensible American aggression against a non-aligned country. Reagan, we know, treats world opinion with indifference. Even for America's allies, the US President has nothing but utter contempt.

According to former American Ambassador to UN Andrew Young, Ronald Reagan behaves like a heavyweight boxing champion who enters a kindergarten and beats up a child to prove his manliness. "It is not manliness but evidence of a sick mind", Andrew Young said in course of conversation during his visit to Delhi last month. Reagan is brazenfaced in inventing alibis for his acts of brigandage ; in Grenada then and Libya now. Every time he suffers a setback, Reagan acts like a maniac running amuck on the international state. The American reverses in Lebanon, according to Andrew Young, spurred the US President to display his "manliness" by raping Grenada. The opposition in the American Congress to his demand for funds for counter-revolution in Nicaragua might have induced him to launch the naked aggression against Libya. Reagan hates non-alignment, he is flexing muscles not only against the human race, he is also at war against the US Congress, Andrew Young added.

Whatever the reasons, the fact remains that the action of the chief executive of one of the mightiest military powers in the world has become a menace to the security of all countries, particularly the smaller, non-aligned countries. By striking Libyan targets from the American base in Britain, Ronald Reagan has demonstrated the real purpose of establishing these military outposts—to intimidate every nation which has the courage to assert its independence and raise its head in defiance of US threats.

The American aggression against Libya is a warning to the Arab world to the non-aligned countries and to America's allies. In fact every national which values its sovereignty and freedom cannot but take notice of the grave threat inhrent in this act of state terrorism. So far, the US administration preferred covert action against countries and government it wanted to destabilise and dislodge. Now it has given up all pretences. It has made state terrorism an instrument of foreign policy. Every international forum which the US fails to bend to its wishes faces the threat of destruction by Reagan's machinations. Security Council will be made impotent by veto, the United Nations rendered helpless by arms-twisting of weaker nations and defiance of international opinion.

True, where Hitler failed, Reagan cannot succeed. It is, however, inportant that no civilised government should vet the maniac's appetite by acquiescence or endorsement of this aggression. Though Margaret Thatcher has chosen to follow it the footsteps of Neville Chamberlain, not many others will join her in this display of disgusting surrender to Reagan's crime against humanity. The world is witnessing the most dangerous turn of events in recent times. India has shown the courage of her convictions. The snowballing effect of this fearlessness is the only hope in an otherwise grim situation.

2078. Morley, Jefferson : Terrorist link to North's cowboys. *International Herald Tribune* 24-25 Dec 1986 ; 1.

2079. Morris, Roger : Aftermath of CIA intervention. *Society* 12 (3) 1975.

2080. Mr. Reagan turns to terror. *Telegraph* (Calcutta) 17 Apr 1986 ; 6.

2081. Mukherjee, Sadhan : Terrorism school in United States. *New Age* 7 Jul 1985 ; 1.

2082. Mukherjee, Dilip: Terrorism unlikely to level off. *Deccan Herald* 12 Dec 1985 ; 8.

2083. Muravchik, Joshua : Terrorism : Reagan is sounding more like center. *International Herald Tribune* 16 Jan 1986 ; 4.

2084. Nair, Kunhanandan : US, Father of international terrorism. *Blitz* 27 Jul 1985 ; 17.

2085. Nair, Kunhanandan : Who promotes world terrorism ? *Daily* (Bombay) 20 Jul 1985 : 8-9.

2086. Nandy, Pritish : Camper's Story. *Times of India* 23 Sep 1985 ; 8.

2087. Nanes, Allan S. : Congressional developments. *Terrorism* 7 (1) 1984 ; 71-72.

2088. Nelson, W. Dale : U. S. will act again if terrorism continues : Regan issues new warning. *International Herald Tribune* 24 Apr 1986 ; 1-2.

2089. Nokes, R. Gregory : Why is US aiding terrorism ? *Telegraph* (Calcutta) 9 Apr 1984 ; 6.

2090. Omang, Joanne : Report says terrorism is almost routine, calls nuclear action unlikely. *International Herald Tribune* 5 Dec 1985 ; 5.

2091. O'Toole, Thomas : U. S. increases security at nuclear facilities as fear of terrorists grows. *International Herald Tribune* 29 Aug 1985 ; 3.

2092. Overt covert meddling. *International Herald Tribune* 2 Dec 1985 ; 8.

2093. Pejman, Pegman : Envoy's anti-terrorism course draws fire in U. S. *International Herald Tribune* 11 Sep 1935 ; 11.

2094. Pfaff, William : Americans are aiding terrorism. *International Herald Tribune* 10-11 May 1986 ; 4.

2095. Pfaff, William : Dealing with dictators : the test before Reagan. *International Herald Tribune* 22 Apr 1986 ; 6.

2096. Pfaff, William : Dramatic retaliation is not a real option. *International Herald Tribune* 10 Jul 1985 ; 6.

2097. Power Thomas : *Man who kept the secrets* : *Richard Helms and the CIA*. New York, 1979.

2098. President (Ronald Reagan) has a list of his own. *International Herald Tribune* 13-14 Jul 1985 ; 4.

2099. Pressler, Larry : This extradition treaty is an occasion. *International Herald Tribune* 16-17 Nov 1985 ; 6.

2100. Price, Raymond : Terrorism : A case for new rules. *International Herald Tribune* 9-10 Nov 1985 ; 4.

2101. Price, Raymond : Ways to halt epidemic of terror. *International Herald Tribune* 6 Jan 1986 ; 4.

2102. Prouty, F. : *Secret team : the CIA and its allies in control of the United States and the world.* Prentice-Hall, 1973.

2103. Raghavan, A. : Reagan's legalised terror. *Blitz* 1 Jun 1985 ; 9.

2104. Ray, Ellen and William Schaap : Vermon Walters : Crypto diplomat and terrorist. *Mainstream* 20 Sep 1986 ; 15-20. *Covert Action Information Bulletin* (26) Sum 1986.

2105. Reagan and terrorism. *Link* (New Delhi) 30 Jun 1985 ; 3.

And what about the USA & FBI ? It took credit for foiling the conspiracy to kill the Prime Minister and America wanted India to be grateful for this piece of information. But the plot to kill the PM was only one part of the conspiracy which included a whole lot of other acts of terrorism about which the FBI has claimed knowledge. Though its own men trained the terrorists, the FBI has refused to give India all information it has in its possession. Had the US agency arrested the two it wanted for the conspiracy against Rajiv Gandhi probably the Air-India tragedy would not have occurred. In any event, the terrorists both from Punjab and their collaborators from Kashmir, have been operating in the US, and the FBI has done very little to curb their activities. The authorities in the UK have done even less, although there too these elements have long been active.

The Government has asked the US, Britain and Canada to restrain these killers and saboteurs. But, seen from India, this is not enough. Friendly relations with these countries should hinge on the extent of cooperation they give in countering terrorism directed against this country. In the case of America, India should invoke the agreement which pledges US cooperation in the fight against terrorism. India can validly demand firm action by the Reagan Administration in this matter. The process of improvement in bilateral relations initiated by the Prime Minister's visit ought to be regulated by the earnestness the Administration displays in this area. India cannot be infinitely patient with the countries that harbour open conspiracies and avowed killers whose designs are directed against Indian leaders and citizens.

2106. Reagan Terrorism. *New Age* 20 Apr 1986 ; 2.

No Words Are Strong Enough To Condemn US President Ronald Reagan's mad act of state terrorism against Libya. The US bombing raid of Libyan establishments and the brazen manner in which Reagan justified it and threatened to repeat it again shows that he respects no international norms. Even if Libyan President Muammar Gaddafi was in some way involved with the West Berlin club explosion—Libya has denied this and even West Germany discounts it—there is no grain of justification for the kind or barbaric retaliation which 'Rambo' Reagan had ordered.

Reagan and his cronies like secretary of state George Shultz and secretary of defence Caspar Weinberger have claimed that the laser-directed poinpoint attacks were against installations connected with training of terrorists. Why was then Gaddafi's residence bombed? Clearly, the orders included the bombing to death of Gaddafi himself. Luckily, Gaddafi did not perish in the attack but his adopted baby daughter has died and his two sons injured. Does Reagan think that by such official terrorism against individual leaders he can bring to heel nations which do not sing Uncle Sam's tune?

It is good that whole India has come out with strong condemnation of the US imperialists' crime against humanity. External affairs minister B.R. Bhagat's statement in parliament conveyed India's deep shock over the US action which was, he said, a clear cut act of aggression against the sovereignty and territorial integrity of Libya. As chairman of non-aligned movement, prime minister Rajiv Gandhi has also deplored the attack, pointing out that NAM was against terrorism whether by individuals or by a state. The entire spectrum of political opinion in parliament was one in condemning the US imperialism's high-handed action.

The NAM foreign ministers who had assembled in New Delhi for the scheduled April 16 coordination bureau meeting, held an unscheduled session on April 15 to condemn the US action. They called it "blatant and unprovoked act of aggression" against a fellow non-aligned state. The socialist countries have also squarely condemned the US crime. CPSU general secretary Mikhail Gorbachyov termed it "lawless and arbitrary action" and said that the raids "signify deliberate aggravation of Soviet-American relations".

Reagan today stands alone, condemned by the entire humanity for his philosophy that might is right and that he would enforce his "Pax Americana" with the armies at his command. Not even his NATO allies have backed his attack on Libya, except for Maggie Thatcher of Britain who is deridingly called in her country as "Reagan's poodle". France and Spain refused permission for the US warplanes from bases in Britain to overfly them on their deadly mission to Libya.

It is not only against Libya that the Reagan administration is striking ; it is against peoples of the whole world, humanity itself. That is the only meaning of the nuclear tests it has recently undertaken in the Nevada desert. After the first test this year on March 22, Gorbachyov had warned on Soviet TV that if USA coutinued nuclear tests after March 31, the Soviet Union would be forced to resume nuclear tests. Unheedingly, USA again made a nuclear test on April 10, and the result is that the Soviet Union has declared that "from now on it is free from the unilateral commitment made by it to refrain from conducting any nuclear explosions."

Not that the current series of tests are absolutely necessary for USA to complete its present program of nuclear research and updating nuclear technology, as claimed by Reagan and his cronies. Eminent scientists in USA itself have pointed out that the tests are not scientifically necessary. The national laboratories at Livermore and Alamos had such super-computer complexes as to make available simulated results of nuclear tests. It is only Reagan's mad rush to set up his strategic defence initiative—star wars—that makes it necessary for him to continue nuclear tests as in Nevada.

2107. Reagan terrorism denounced. *New Age* (New Delhi) 25 May 1986 ; 10.

2108. Reagan's terrorism round the world. *New Age* 9 Feb 1986 ; 11.

2109. Rositzke, Harry : America's secret operations. A perspective. *Foreign Affairs* 53(2) Jan 1975 ; 334-51.

2110. Safire, William : Enough 'Mad-dog' talk on Libya : Let Reagan explain the danger. *International Herald Tribune* 15 Apr 1986 ; 6.

2111. Safire, William : Some ways for American to fight back. *International Herald Tribune* 5 Jul 1985 ; 6.

2112. Safire, William : Terror : Has Reagan really lost his nerve ? *International Herald Tribune* 10 Jan 1986 ; 4.

2113. Sareen, H. K. : *Subversion incorporated : A case study of CIA* New Delhi, Sterling, 1982.

2114. Schlesinger, Arthur : Negotiating with terrorists can make sense. *International Herald Tribune* 28 Jun 1985 ; 6.

2115. Schubeler, Peter : Variants of terrorism. *International Herald Tribune* 16-17 Nov 1985 ; 6

2116. Schwarz, Urs : *America strategy : A new perspective.* London, 1967.

2117. Sharma, Madan Lal : CIA : State terrorism. In *Terrorism : American Style*. New Delhi, 1982 ; 57-78.

2118. Shipler, David K. : Spy case seen to affect sharing of intelligence by U.S., Israel. *International Herald Tribune* 14-15 Dec 1985 ; 5.

2119. Shuttle (Challenger) was never routine. *International Herald Tribune* 30 Jan 1986 ; 4.

2120. Smith, Brent L. : Anti-terrorism legislation in the United States : Problems and implications. *Terrorism* 7(2) 1984 ; 213-31.

2121. Soviet defector says CIA tortured, drugged him. *International Herald Tribune* 8 Nov 1985 ; 1, 3.

2122. Sponsoring terrorism. *Patriot* 8 May 1986 ; 7.

2123. State sponsored terrorism. *New Wave* 7 Jul 1985 : 13.

Recently the CIA, with President Reagan's personal approval, organised a conference of anti-government rebels of Angola, Nicaragua, Afghanistan and Laos in an Unita camp on the Angolan territory. The purpose of the conference was to work out a common strategy of "struggle against communism".

In Washington this gathering was described as "the first world congress of anti-communist rebels." President Reagan sent a message of greetings to the mercenaries conference and described it as an "unique event."

It is by no means accidental that the recruitment and training of mercenaries to destabilise the government the Reagan administration considers unfriendly has become an official policy of the U.S.

Again it is not a coincidence that a resolution on the inadmissibility of the policy of state terrorism, adopted by the 39th General Assembly of the United Nations, was opposed by the United States and some of its allies. For many years the U.S. is obstructing the drafting of an international convention on combating recruitment, use, financing and training of mercenaries.

The fifth session of the special U.N. Committee on drafting the anti-mercenery convention, which ended in May could not accomplish its task due to the opposition of the U. S. and other western countries.

2124. State terrorism on trial. *New Wave* 20 Oct 1985 ; 3.

2125. Statement by Senator Jeremiah Dentor before the Subcommittee on security and Terrorism Feb 2, 1983. *Terrorism* 7(1) 1984 ; 73-80.

2126. Subramanyam, K. : Terrorism : An analysis. *Pioneer* 16 Jun 1985 ; 4.

2127. Sullivan, George : *Story of the Peace Corps*. New York, Fleet Publishing Corporation 1964. Pp. 156.

2128. Taft, Philip and Philip Ross : American labor violence : Its causes, character and outcome. In *Violence in America*. Ed. by Hugh Davis Graham and Ted Robert Gurr. New York, 1969.

2129. Terrorism : Why U.S. is vulnerable. Interview with Robert H. Kupperman. *U. S. News and World Report* 10 Apr 1978.

2130. Terrorism and the CIA. *International Herald Tribune* 17 May 1985 ; 4.

2131. Terrorists abroad may be abducted by US. *Indian Express* 21 Jan 1986 ; 1.

2132. Tierney, John J. : Terror at home. *Stanford Journal of International Studies* 12 Apr 1977 ; 1-20.

2133. Tolchin, Martin : In U. S , private guards widen role in public safety. *International Herald Tribune* 2 Dec 1985 ; 3.

2134. Toner, Robin : Mrs. Klinghoffer pleads for fight on terrorism *International Herald Tribune* 1 Nov 1985 ; 5.

2135. Tyler, Patrick, E. : CIA covert role flourishes under "Reagan Doctrine". *International Herald Tribune* 10 Mar 1986 ; 3.

2136. Tyler, Patrick E and David B. Ottawa : CIA officer reportedly was tortured in Ethiopia. *International Herald Tribune* 26-27 Apr 1986 ; 1-2.

2137. Unusual alliance on terror. *International Herald Tribune* 21-22 Dec 1985 ; 4.

2138. U. S. breeds terrorists. *Pioneer* 3 Nov 1985 ; 4.

2139. US, Canada search for terrorists. *Hindustan Times* 4 Nov 1986 ; 6.

2140. U.S. Congress Okays. Sweeping. *Economic Times* (New Delhi) 20 Mar 1986 ; 8.

The U. S. Congress has approved a $ 4.3 billion plan aim at

protecting U.S. embassies and other diplomatic missions around the world against terrorist attack.

The measure was passed last night by 389 votes to seven in the House of Representatives but must still be considered by the Senate.

"This Bill represents an unprecedented effort by Congress to update U. S. security measures across the board," said congressman Olympia Snowe who co-sponsored the Bill.

Most of the money would fund a five-year programme to upgrade or rebuild 254 embassies, consulates, missions and other official build-missions and other official buildings, including a new embassy in Tel Aviv, a consular building in Jerusalem and a chancery in Vienna.

The measure incorporates recommendations made last June by a panel on overseas security chaired by retired Admiral Bobby and by vice-president George Bush's task force on fighting terrorism.

The plan would also authorise $ 10 million next year in rewards for information on international terrorism or drug trafficking. It creates a fund for the victims of terrorism and their families.

2141. U.S. hypocrisy in terror. *International Herald Tribune* 11 Nov 1986 ; 6.

2142. US manoeuvers off Libyan coast. *Times of India* 25 Jan 1986 ; 16.

2143. US move for war on terrorism. *Statesman* 10 Dec 1985 ; 1.

2144. U. S. move to assassinate terrorism. *Times of India* 13 Jul 1985 ; 1.

2145. U. S. muscle-flexing against Libya. *New Wave* 2 Feb 1986 ; 13.

2146. US State terrorism. *Deccan Chronicle* 16 Apr 1986 ; 6.

2147. US supporting extremists in Punjab. *Times of India* 1 Feb 1987 ; 1.

2148. Vasfi, Ausaf Saled : Focus on Frank Camper School : What is really extraordinary ? *Radiance* 22 Sep 1985 ; 1.

2149. Vibhakar, Jagdish : U. S. Style of combating terrorism. *New Wave* 24 Nov 1986 ; 11.

2150. Wicker, Tom : Reagan's 'Contra' advisers evoke Vietnam and terror. *International Herald Tribune* 4 Sep 1986 ; 5.

2151. Wills, G. : CIA from beginning to end. *New York Review of Books* 22 Jan 1976.

2152. Wingenbach, C. E. : *Peace Corps : Who, how and where.* New York, John Day, 1961.

2153. Wise, D and B. Ross : *Invisible government.* New York, Random House, 1964.

2154. Yakovlev, Nikolai ; *CIA target : The USSR.* Moscow, Progress Publishers 1983. Pp 264.

2155. Yoder, Eelwin M. : Quiet advocate of fighting fire with fire. *Telegraph* (Calcutta) 3 Feb 1986 ; 6.

The internal US administration argument over when to use military force in the face of less than life-or-death challenges—first Lebanon and now Libya—has been noticed. But probably not in proportion to the damage the wrong winner could do.

The antagonists are Caspar Weinberger and George Shultz, secretaries of defence and state. Their across-the-river argument began in earnest with the US marine mission to Lebanon, to which Mr. Shultz stood godfather.

Mr. Shultz was warned by professionals more familiar with Lebanon than he that it was a snakepit, but he pushed on with the drive of a man resolved not to be enfeebled by facts.

A "peace-keeping"mission by US marines widened almost imperceptably into an intervention in a murderous civil war. And by an evil act of terrorism on October morning, 246 marines lost their lives. Those who supported the commitment have repented at leisure, but it isn't clear from his speeches that Mr. Shultz absorbed any lessons in Beirut. Certainly he emerged with a smoldering anger about terrorism.

Who doesn't share it ? Yet who can help wondering if the thirst for vindication against terrorism is a suitable foundation for a really successful foreign policy ?

Th Shultz-Weinberger debate violates conventional wisdom about who usually wants what. Conventionally, Pentagon people are through to be rashly eager to use their dangerous toys on even the most speculative pretext, while state department types would wear out the knees of their striped trousers groveling, sooner than raise a finger in anger.

2156. Wicker, Tom Terror : What makes America so vulnerable. *International Herald Tribune* 27 Jun 1985 ; 8.

Uruguay

2157. D'Oliveria, Sergio L. : Uruguay and the Tupamaro myth. *Military Review* 53(4) 1973 ; 25-36.

2158. Miller, James A. : Urban terrorism in Uruguay : The Tupamaros. In *IMW*; 137-90.

What is Uruguay's physical and human environment ? After the Rupamaros decided to base their movement in Montevideo's urban environment, Uruguay's terrain (predominantly tall-grass prairies, with a considerable mixture of forests and some hills, 1,000-2,000 feet above sea level) and climate (temperature with rainfall distributed evenly throughout the year) had little bearing on the Tupamaro insurgency. The nation's good pattern of railways, all-weather roads, and electronic communications all coverage on Montevideo, the capital and the center of the nation's good commerce, manufacturing, fishing, and resort activities. The smallest nation in South America in area, Uruguay is still six times as big as Belgium. The total population of Uruguay was an estimated 2,800,000 in the mid 1960s ; about 1,400,000 lived in Montevideo. The population is homogeneous, primarily white and European and nominally Roman Catholic. There is no population explosion—the rate of expansion of 1.4 percent is the lowest on the continent. There are no large uninhabited or undeveloped areas. The nation has the best public health record on the continent, and shares the highest literacy rate (91 percent) with Argentina. Living standards are high by South American terms, and there is a strong middle class with no pronounced extremes between rich and poor. The nation also had, until recently, a sound tradition of political democracy and stability.

These are some of the major environmental characteristics of Uruguay in effect in the mid and late 1960s, when the Tupamaros began their intensive campaign of violence directed against the government. Two additional environmental factors—economic conditions and attitudes of the population are treated below.

Popular support was crucial in determining the degree to which the Tupamaro insurgency was successful in attaining its goals. The Tupamaros were from the outset concerned with publicity and their public image, and they stated that popular support was essential to the success of their movement.

The Tupamaros had two types of popular support—active and passive. Active support refers to the actual participation of people who were engaging in MLN activities, either as combatants or as service personnel. Passive support included all of those engaged in such non-combative activities as logistics, intelligence, and propaganda. The distinction between combative and non-combative is artificial, however, because, for example, some types of logistics and propaganda activities were integral parts of armed operations. In any case, as its maximum srength, the MLN consisted of an estimated 3,000-4,000 combatants and service personnel. In considering persons to be members, we assume they had acted on behalf of the movement and did not merely hold sympathetic views toward the movement.

"Passive popular support" refers to the persons who were either sympathetic to, indifferent to, or intimidated by the MLN, to the extent that their behaviour either benefitted or failed to hinder MLN activities. What this means is—to use the distinction pointed out by Andrew M. Scott—what is crucial to insurgents is the behavior of the general populace and not their attitudes. When the people look with favor on the guerrillas as romantic, Robin Hood-type individuals "expropriating" from a corrupt and inefficient government and its rich domestic and foreign business allies and passing proceeds to the poor, then these people are in effect passively benefitting the insurgency by embarrassing the government and by reducing the likelihood that individuals will report suspicious activities and persons to the authorities. Popular indifference can be especially valuable to an insurgent. The converse is of course true with regard to passive popular support. When people no longer marvel at insurgent activities but are instead repelled by them, when they stop pressing for changes in government leaders or policies and start pressing the government to fight the insurgents more aggressively, or when they begin actively to report suspected insurgent activity to the government and otherwise assist the authorities in counter insurgency efforts, the lack of passive popular support takes its toll by diminishing the insurgency's chances of success.

The Tupamaros' attempt to gain active and passive popular support will be examined in terms of esoteric and exoteric appeals ; demonstration of potency ; terror ; and provocation of government counter terror.

Although the Tupamaros themselves apparently never articulated a concise, internally consistent political ideology and strategy, they nevertheless sufficiently publicized their view of Uruguayan society and its ills, as well as ways in which the society could be transformed.

2159. Nunez. Carlos. : *Tupamaros : Urban Guerrillas of Uruguay*. New York, 1970.

2160. Porzecanski, Arturo C. : *Uruguay's tupamaros*. New York, Prayer. 1933.

2161. Uruguay : Confrontation : *Latin America* 6(27) Jul 1972.

2162. Uruguay : Military mystery. *Latin America* 6(31) 4 Aug 1972.

2163. Uruguay : People's war : *Latin America* 6(24) 16 Jun 1972.

2164. Uruguay : In *Amnesty International Report*. London, 1983 ; 176-80.

Venezuela

2165. Alexander, Robert J. : Experiment with violence. In *Communist Party of Venezuela*. Stanford University, 1969 ; 48-113.

2166. Callanan, Edward F. : Terror in Venezuela, 1960-64. *Military Review* 49(2) Feb 1969 ; 49-56.

Vietnam

2167. Hosmer, Stephen T. : *Viet Cong. repression and its implications for the future*. Lexington, 1970.

2168. Mallin, Jay : *Terror in Vietnam*. Princeton, 1966.

2169. Mathur, Girish : Riots rock Vietnam, China, Kazakhstan : Regional tensions in Socialist World. *Blitz* 10 Jan 1987 ; 11.

2170. Maurer, Marvin : Ku Klux Klan and the National Liberation Front : Terrorism applied to achieve diverse goals. In *ITCW* ; 131-52.

Understanding the phenomenon of political terror entails more than realizing that unarmed civilians are the main target. Terrorism is a tool which enables insurgents to disrupt moderate, decentralized social political systems. It is especially effective against weak, pluralist, democratic regimes. Political terrorism is associated with those historical periods when sharply divergent value systems are clashing for power. In the nineteenth century a democratic America was unable to thwart a racist insurgency ; while in the 1960s the same nation was unable to stem "a war of liberation." In both cases the United States government was not defeated military. Its withdrawal symbolized its considered opinion that the government it supported could not halt their respective insurgencies.

Two ideologically different insurgencies were selected for this study to determine whether their tactics and ethics were similar. Both overcame weak, pluralist, or fragmented, and even partially democratic governments. Both deliberately utilized terror as part of an effort to reach their goals and both sought and received the support of powerful groups and leaders outside their territories. Their opponents were no match for nor were they able to grasp the significance of these insurgencies. This study seeks to review the events of two different areas and eras and link them together on a comparative basis in order to determine how political terrorist groups armed with different ideologies were capable of determining the fate of millions of people as well as the course of history.

The key problem can be expressed either in the form of a question or as a hypothesis. Given a weak, rural, decentralized, pluralistic political system, what techniques would an insurgency adopt to topple it? Or, given a similar situation—a rural society, weak leaders, ineffective and insufficient military forces backed by a powerful democratic state—then similar organizational responses can be expected from opposing insurgencies.

The NLF is an easier organisation to deal with because its organizers and leaders were theoretically oriented. Their insight into the sociology of power and organization, albeit from a Marxist-Leninist view, can be counted as original contributions to social thought. The Klan's leaders and their supporters did not have a theory of insurgency. At best they came up with apologies and moral declamations. However, thanks in part to the excellent study by Allen W. Trelease, it is possible to describe the Klan's actions and subsequent successes in terms utilized to examine the NLF.

Thomas Perry Thornton's ideas are extremely useful in studying both insurgencies. Insurgency terror is designed to disrupt a social order allegedly having superior conventional military forces. The insurgents seek to secure the support of the population or neutralize it so that the power of the government is undermined. Insurgents not only propagandize the populace but seek to break their connection with the government by whatever means possible. Thornton suggests that terrorism is a form of "investment". An effective, but limited application of terror enables its users "to project an image many times larger than their actual strength." Terrorism is a variant of classical guerrilla warfare. The latter consists of hit-and-run tactics against a superior armed force. Terrorism is a form of warfare aimed at civilians or individuals—whether they be police or military. Its purpose is to secure a socio-psychological victory in that a cowed populace accepts its version of events and disclaims or is hostile to those set forth by the government.

Both the defeated Confederacy and SVN were in a state of leaderless confusion after 1865 and 1954 respectively. Both were susceptible to the claims of opposing groups seeking to press their plans for reconstruction. Both areas had a pool of fighting talent from having fought the French and the Union armies respectively.

After 1954 Vietnam was divided in half. The Vietminh, led by the brilliant and redoubtable Ho Chi Minh, defeated the French. As a result the latter ceded control of North Vietnam to the Democratic Republic of Vietnam (DRV). The transfer of power was ratified in July 1954 in Geneva. The peace agreement was signed by the Communists and the French. In the South, Ngo Dinh Diem came from the United States to replace the French and their puppet administration. Diem and his American supporters hoped to develop a nationalist regime independent of Hanoi. According to Philippe Devillers, assumption of leadership by Ho Chi Minh and Diem "decisively marked the end of the colonial period in Vietnam history and the beginning of its modern period of independence."

The Geneva agreement called for a nationwide election in two years. Apparently there was a consensus that the DRV would win the elections and by 1956 Vietnam would be completely under Communist rule. With some reluctance the DRV accepted the partition which roughly divided Vietnam's 127,000 square miles and some 32 million people in half. Hanoi mistakenly hoped that their "democratic" (that is, Communist) friends in France would pressure the French government to live up to the terms of the Geneva agreement. Also, Hanoi figures there was no capable leadership to unify fragmented Vietnam or to lead what Robert Scigliano describes as a collection of "states within states".

2171. Osborne, Robin : Vietnamese and violence. *Far Eastern Economic Review* 25 Jul. 1985 ; 7.

2172. Parry, Albert : Vietnam and other jungles, other pyres. In *Terrorism* New York, 1976 ; 417-32.

2173. Sansom, Robert L. : *Economics of insurgency in the Mekong Delta of Vietnam.* Cambridge, MIT Press, 1970.

2174. Smith, John Russell : Vietnam and Rap Groups. Boston, American Psychiatric Association, Sep 1980.

Yugoslavia

2175. Binder, David : Yugoslavia displaying ambivalence on terror. *International Herald Tribune* 21-22 Dec 1985 ; 2.

Zaire

2176. Wagoner, Fred E. : *Dragon rouge : The rescue of hostages in the Congo.* Washington, National Defense University, 1980.

2177. Weiss, Herbett : *Political protest in the Congo.* Princeton, 1967.

Zambia

2178. Dresang, Dennis : Ethnic politics, representative bureaucracy and development administration : The Zambian case. *American Political Science Review* 68, Dec 1974 ; 1605-17.

Guerilla Warfare

2179. Aaron, Harold. R. : Anatomy of guerrilla terror. *Infantry* 58, Mar-Apr 1967 ; 14-18.

2180. Bacheller, Don : Guerrillaism and peasantry and the N.L.F. *Independent Socialist* Apr 1968.

2181. Bayo, Alberto : *150 Questions to a Guerrilla.* Montgomery, Alaj Air University, 1978.

2182. Beres, L.R. : Guerrillas, terrorists and polarity : New Structural models of world politics. *Western Political Quarterly* 27, Dec 1974.

2183. Calvert, Michael : Characteristics of guerrilla leaders and their rank and file. *Practitioner* (London) Dec 1973.

2184. Carr, Gordon : *Angry brigade : A history of Britain's first urban guerrilla group.* London, Gollancz, 1975.

2185. Chaliand, Gerard *Ed.* : *Guerrilla strategies : An historical anthology from Long March to Afghanistan* Berkeley, 1982 Pp. 353.

2186. Chjsters, Edi. : Guerrilla warfare as a means of confrontation in stabilizing big power structure, In *UG* ; 69-80.

In less-developed countries, the established authorities do not have at their disposal a large margin for concessions since they are themselves subordinate to the vested interests of other nations or of multinational corporations. In technologically advanced, rich countries, on the contrary, potential conflicts, especially along the socio-economic conflicts line, are much less of a threat, and even when they are actualized, the established authorities have a much larger range of purely material concessions to offer. They can thus be much more flexible in their approach and handling of challenges—or at least succeed in giving the impression of being so. In most modern democracies, the vast majority of the population believes that political activity along traditional, 'bourgeoise-democratical' lines and by non-violent means is still possible and efficient, and that a just cause stands a fair chance, even when it requires a fundamental change in the nature of the society. The possibility of political and socio-economic change by non-violent means is continuously stressed by establishment that has at its disposal a wide range of media to impregnate the public with this idea. Together with the condemnation of violence, (exerted by anybody else than the questioned authority......) one tries by all means to obscure the structural violence, inherent to the system. In such a context any form of violent opposition is met with deep hostility by the masses. And as long as the methods of the guerilla group are not politically accepted by a large fraction of the population, it will not have any political basis or impact. Since a sound political basis is elementary for any serious form of guerilla, one must conclude that a guerilla group that lacks this basis—regardless of what the reason may be—is therefore fundamentally wrong in its practice. Groups starting an urban guerrilla in technologically advanced countries may justify their premature attempts by claiming that people who more or less radically oppose the existing regime must prepare themselves to oppose the growing fascination of that regime ; or they may point out that no real change was ever obtained without violence, or that their action intends to provoke the establishment to the point where it will show its 'real face'. All these arguments undoubtedly have some value in themselves, but they cannot make up for the vital lack of a sufficiently nature political background—the water in which the guerrilla-fighter must be the fish.

One inevitably arrives at the conclusion that violent and non-violent action are not so contrasting as it is often said—not always without some underlying interest. On the contrary, violence and non-violence must be considered as two different points on one scale, going from absolute submission to over-all armed conflict. It becomes highly important, then, to analyse which forms of 'political guerilla' on this continuum can best be used in a specific situation, instead of blindly transferring to a technologically advanced socio-economic setting a series of guerilla-directives that were conceived for another type of society and that may have been successful there.

To sum up we can say ;

— that the value of war as a means of imposing certain policy, of reaching certain goals, is seriously reviewed ;

— that the relations between major powers among themselves, and between major powers, intermediary powers, small powers and non-powers are continually changing ;

— that this change is more often than not in favour of more powerful nations—or rather : of a small elite within these nations ; but

— that the very intensification of the exploitation of the less powerful creates the basis for some outburst, and that such an outburst in many cases seems to develop into some form of armed guerrilla ;

— that in many technologically advanced countries, however, such a form of struggle is made virtually senseless by the existing political climate, and moreover, met by the authorities with far more sophisticated means of integration of repression ;

— that therefore, groups striving towards a fundamental change of the regime had rather re-examine the various possibilities of a 'political guerrilla'.

2187. Clutterbuck, Richard : *Protest and the Urban guerrilla.* London, Cassell, 1973.

2188. El-Rayyes, Riad and Dunia Nahas : Commandoes, China and the USSR. In *Guerrillas for Palestine.* London, Croom Helm, 1976 ; 127-32.

2189. Greene, T.N. : *Guerrilla—and how to fight him.* New York, Prayer, 1960.

2190. Griffith, Sammel B. : *Mao Tse-tung : On guerrilla warfare.* New York, Prayer. 1961.

2191. Grundy, Kennete : *Guerrilla struggle in Africa.* New York, Grossman, 1971.

2192. *Guerrilla war fare advocates in the United States.* Washington, U.S. Govt. Printing Office, 1968. Pp. 90.

2193. Guevara, Che : *Guerrilla Warfare* . Harmondsworth, Penguin, 1969.

2194. Hueting, Johan E. : Some cliches about guerrilla warfare and the proposal of psychological models explaining so-called excessive behavior. In *UG* ; 142-47.

2195. Janke, Peter : *Guerrilla and terrorist organisations : A world directory and bibliography.* New York, Macmillan, 1983. Pp. 550.

2196. Jenkins, Brian : *Soldier versus gunman : the challenge of urban guerrilla warfare.* Rand Paper Series, 1974.

2197. Lanvan, George, *ed.* : *Che Guevara speaks* New York, Grove Press, 1969.

2198. Laquer, Walter : *Guerrilla reader.* New York, Meridian Books, 1977.

2199. Larteguy, J. : *Guerrillas*, New York, Signet, 1970.

2200. Leiser, Burton M. : Terrorism, guerrilla warfare and international morality. *Stanford Journal of International Studies* 12, Spr 1977 ; 39-66.

2201. Lowy, Michael : Guerrilla, Warfare. In *Marxism and Che Guevara.* New York, Monthly Review Press, 1967 ; 86-99.

2202. Lowry, Michael : *Marxism of Che Guevara : Philosophy, economics and revolutionary warfare.* London, Monthly Review Press, 1973. Pp. 127.

2203. Mao, Tse-tung : *Selected military writings.* Peking, 1963.

2204. Marighella, Carlos : *Guerrilla tactics and operations*, New World Liberation Front.

2205. Nasution, Abdul H. : *Fundamentals of Guerrilla warfare.* London, 1965.

2206. O'Ballance, Edgar. : *Arab Guerrilla power, 1967-72*, Hamden, Archon Books, 1973.

2207. Orlon, A. : *Handbook of intelligence and guerrilla warfare.* Ann Arbor, University of Michigan Press, 1963.

2208. Parel, Peter, and John W. Shy : *Guerrilla in the 1960's.* New York, Prayer, 1962.

2209. Pawan : One man's guerrilla is another man's freedom fighter. *Times of India* Sunday Review 12 Jan 1986.

2210. Pomeroy, William *ed.* : *Guerrilla warfare and Marxism.* London, Lawrence and Wishant. 1869.

2211. Reid, Charles J. : Reflections on the failure of the spartacan slave revolt. In *UG* ; 94-110.

2212. Rojo, Ricardo : *My friend Che.* New York, Grove Press, 1968.

2213. Rostow, W.M. : *Guerrilla warfare in the underdeveloped area.* (Address delivered at graduation ceremony at the U.S. Army Special Warfare School, Fort Bragg, N.C., Jun 28, 1961.

2214. Sangal, S.K. : Shivaji's guerrilla tactics under study. *Economic Times* 13 Jan. 1984 ; 4.

2215. Sarkesian, Sam C *ed.* : *Revolutionary guerrilla warfare.* Chicago, Precedent Publishing, 1975.

2216. Sinclair, Andrew : *Guevara.* New York, Viking Press, 1970.

2217. Tellez, Antonio : *Guerrilla extraordinary.* London, Davis – Poynter, 1974.

2218. Thayer, Charles W. : *Guerrilla.* London, Michael Joseph, 1963.

2219. Tringquier, Roger. : *Modern warfare.* New York, Prayer, 1964.

2220. Wiberg, Hakon : *Are guerrillas possible* ? In *UG* ; 11-21.

During the last few years urban guerrilla movements have become rather widespread, according to the impression we get from the press. The first problem to merit consideration when dealing with the phenomenon at a scientific conference might therefore be : to what extent is urban guerrilla a product of the press ?

In one interpretation of this question, we are asked to what extent urban guerrilla movements are simply freely invited by the press, albeit on the basis of some actual events. There are good reasons for putting the question even in this strong form, since the type of events that are seen as urban guerrilla activities certainly rank high on 'news value', according to several of the criteria laid down by Galtung and Ruge. They are therefore likely to be overinterpreted, in the sense that the reporting will present events of the same type as forming much more of a coherent pattern than they do in reality. For example, a recent study found that the Indian press, and, consequently foreign correspondents in India, has a tendency to report any acts of violence in the country as actions of the 'naxalites', inexpective of whether there are any specific indications of the acts being political and organized.

Another interpretation of the question above will be rather to what extent urban guerrilla movements are products of mass media, in the sense that the patterns of action commonly so designated are inspired by and learnt from mass media, as are apparently some other forms of protest. In asking this question, no assumption is made as to the underlying social conflicts being 'created' by mass media; it only concerns the issue why we find one rather than another expression.

Neither of these questions can be answered in this paper; but they should serve as a fair warning that its object is problematical as to its existence as well as to its character and causes. As the heading indicates, we shall discuss rather the possibility of urban guerrilla as a phenomenon with strong social impacts, starting from some very general sociological considerations. To begin this discussion we will have to consider some problems of definition.

It appears that the word 'guerrilla', which literally means 'small war' was generally spread in connection with the Spanish resistance against the Napoleonic occupation of 1808-14. The phenomenon referred to by that word is very much older, if we take the word to mean 'irregular warfare on low level': Tacitus describes the Numidians as using it against the Romans, and Mao Tse-tung in his military writings cites even older examples of a nominally weaker party defeating a stronger one by means of we would now call guerrilla warfare.

If the phenomenon of guerrilla is nothing new, neither is the theory of guerrilla warfare: classical European literature dates back to the seventeenth and eighteenth century. It should be noted, however, that the main interest at that time was devoted to the area of using light but highly mobile troops, for example cavalry, to harass and eventually destroy an enemy stronger in numbers, and firepower. What is still missing is the 'people's war' element, which was a highly 'modern' factor in warfare in Napoleon's time. Just as the regular armies started being systematically recruited by leves an masse at that time people also start getting involved in irregular forces. The American revolution contains several examples of this, and the phenomenon has gradual spread, scoring some notable successes in our century.

Before going further, one ambiguity in the notion of guerrilla warfare should be pointed out : it may refer to warfare using exclusively guerilla tactics, and it may refer to warfare where guerrilla tactics are one important element, although not necessarily the dominating one throughout the whole war. Only in some cases does it appear that guerilla tactics alone were reasonably successful against a stronger enemy—Albania, Algeria, Cuba and Yugoslavia appear to come close to this whereas in other cases conventional warfares has eventually become decisive : the defeats of Chiang Kai-shek and of the French in Indo-China may be good examples. The importance of going over eventually to fighting conventional warfare is also stressed both by Mao Tse-tung and by Vo Nguyen Giap.

Our remarks further on are limited to cases of exclusively urban guerilla, i.e. forms of struggle which, at least in their use of military and paramilitary violence, on the one hand to guerilla rather than conventional tactics, and, on the other hand, are restricted to cities with little or no connection with the countryside.

So far we have tried to define the concept of urban guerilla by reference to tactics and location alone. While many other dimensions are of central importance, it may not be necessary to make more than one additional dimension a component of the definition : that of organization.

While we find a number of different taxonomies of collective violence proposed in the literature, most of them appear to be empirical rather than theoretical in origin ; and even this appearance is often deceptive, since such aspects as social recruitment, dominant ideology, and others are often only possible to assess on the basis of a thorough study of the concrete case under consideration, and are therefore ill-suited as parts of working definitions to be used for a preliming sorting out of the objects of the study.

However, it would appear appropriate to make a distinction between more organized and more spontaneous cases of collective violence for example because different models of explanation tend to be employed for the different cases here. We shall return to this at a later stage. We shall therefore include as one more element in the concept of urban guerilla the conditions that it is based on a movement with some common goal and some continuous organization. This condition is not a stringent one : the common goal may not be more specific than ending tyranny, or driving the foreign invader away, and the organization does not by any means have to be hierarchical ; it may well consist of weakly coordinated and mutually anonymous calls.

We feel that this delimitation of the object helps the theoretical discussion without making it less general in scope, as our focus is one the possibility of urban guerrillas being-socially effective ('successful'), and it appears to be a fairly credible hypothesis that the violence which has a goal and organization is more likely to have durable social impact than outburst which lack both.

High Seas

2221. Drama on high seas. *Statesman* 12 Oct 1985 ; 6.

2222. New forms of terror. *Amrita Bazar Patrika*. 12 Oct 1985 ; 6.

2223. Now it's ship hijacking. *Newstime* 10 Oct 1985 ; 7.

The hijacking of the Italian cruise ship, Achille Lauro, gives a new twist to "direct action" politics. Till now plane hijacking and hostage taking were the preferred forms of making a point. The 420 hostages on board Achille Lauro have been threatened with death if Israel does not release some 50 Palestinian prisoners. Two of the hostages have already been killed pour encourager les autres. While Italian and Egyptian naval forces are standing by for an assault should the need arise, it does not seem at the present moment that this would be advisable. The hijackers appear to be too desperate to bother about consequences. In the event, the lives of the innocent hostages must take precedence over all other considerations.

There are doubts about whether the Palestinian Liberation organisation is involved in this incident. Though the hijackers claim to represent the Palestine Liberation Front, a constituent of the PLO, a spokesman for Mr. Yasser Arafat has denied that any constituent of the PLO had anything to do with the hijacking. But the PLO is an umbrella organisation and includes many people and units of whom evev Mr. Arafat is not fully aware. In the event, it would be prudent to assume that some Palestinians are involved in the hijack, at least as a working hypothesis. The question that then arises is this : what do the Palestinians hope to gain from this rash adventure. While the hijack drama continues, all sympathy will be on the side of the victims rather than on the side of the perpetrators. The Palestinian cause will not gain measurably, and indeed it might suffer.

As for Israel, it repays terrorism with more terrorism. The recent air attack on Morocco is an example of the lengths to which Israel will go in defence of its expansionist policies. In the event, the present hijack might lead to an Israeli attack on some undefended Palestinian settlement somewhere at a time of Israel's choosing. Surely, the misguided souls who hijacked Achille Lauro could not have been oblivious to these consequences. Perhaps the only course open to them now is to give up their mad endeavour in exchange for promises of safe conduct. The Palestinian cause is a worthy one. But is not strengthened by acts of blatant terrorism.

2224. Piracy on high Seas. *Pioneer*, 11 Oct 1985 ; 6.

2225. Terror for smugglers in sea. (in India) *Hindustan Times* 1 Feb 1986.

2226. Terrorism on seas. *Times of India* 4 Feb 1987 ; 6.

International shipping circles have given a guarded welcome to the UN secretary general's assurance that soon a UN navel patrol would be made available to escort and protect from missile attack unarmed merchant vessels in the Persian Gulf. The optimism is tempered by the fact that so far, despite the personal efforts of Mr. Perez de Cuellar, the UN security council had found it impossible to agree on effective measures to end these attacks whether from Iran or Iraq.

Since mid-1984, some 30 ships have been lost, about 100 seamen killed in the missile attacks launched on a total of 200 merchant vessels. Both Teheran and Baghdad have claimed exclusion zones in which shipping may be subject to attack. But in actual fact, most of the attacks have taken place well outside these zones. What is galling is that vessels with no connection with either of the belligerents have been attacked with impunity in contravention of the universal right of navigation on the high seas.

Shipping interests aver that they are not blind to the political complexities of the situation in the Gulf region or oblivious to the huge loss of life in the Iraq-Iran war entering its seventh year. But attacks on ships affect the interests of third parties. To go about their legitimate business in the Gulf of Hormuz, it is vital, the shippers argue, that adequate protection is available under international auspices.

Some ships, it is said, get due protection from their own naval vessels in the Gulf region but the bulk of the bustling trade is on bottoms which have no such assured protection. Clearly, there are both political and financial problems to overcome before the international community can assume responsibility for safety and freedom of navigation. Some shipowners agrue that the attacks on third parties doing their business in the Gulf is nothing but terrorism on the high seas and must be condemned accordingly. However, few governments or agencies have done that, so far.

2227. Terrorism on the seas. *Tribune* 10 Oct 1985 ; 4.

Hijacking

2228. Abbas, Mohammed : refutes US allegation. *Ta Kung Pao.* 17 Oct 1985 ; 12.

2229. Acharya Purushan : Valletta massacre. *Financial Express* (New Delhi) 3 Dec 1985 ; 4.

Death in flight is bad enouh. But when mass death occur as a result of attempts to neutralise hijackers, and that too on the ground, there is unspeakable revulsion. And though whether the grisly end to the Egyptian hijack could have been prevented will be debated for long, there will no longer be any doubt in people's minds that the rules of the game, if one may call it that, have now changed.

Gone are the days when hijackers were content with blowing up aircraft. Gone, too, are the days when they generally sought no more than to focus world attention on their cause.

Today's hijackers are different—they kill first and then begin talking. Experts on political violence and terrorism believe that this is because a mere hijack is no longer taken very seriously. In order to show that they are deadly earnest, hijackers now quickly kill a hostage so that the negotiators come under even greater pressure.

This has been the pattern in the last several hijacks and the Egyptian incident was no different. While reports are not unanimous about how many were actually killed by the hijackers—some say just one, others as many as seven—there is no dispute about the fact of the killing itself.

2230. Aggarwala, Narinder : Political aspects of hijacking. *International Conciliation.* DLXXXVI Nov 1971.

2231. Air terrorism can be curbed. *International Herald Tribune* 2 Jul 1985 ; 4.

2232. Akbar, M. J. : Innocent victims of lunatic terrorism. *Telegraph* (Calcutta) 93 Jun 1985 ; 1.

2233. Balasubramanium, K. M. : Only human vigilance can prevent air disasters. *Sunday Observer* 30 Jun 1985 ; 20.

2234. Barrie, G. N. : Crime committed abroad aircraft. *South African Law Journal* ,83, 1968.

2235. Bekes, Imre : Legal problems of hijacking and taking of hostages. In *ITCW* ; 346-53.

In the decade following World War II, new forms of behaviour appeared and spread to the field of criminality. Airplanes were diverted and both passengers and crew were subjected to terrorism. Diplomats were kidnapped and held as hostages compelling governments to make decisions whether or not to pay for their lives and release. Bombs were exploded on busy streets, in department stores, at railway stations, in amusement places, and entire buildings were destroyed. During the last decade, these actions became an epiphenomenon of regional wars and other international conflicts. But they also showed themselves in civil wars and in some other social, political, and religious conflicts within states as methods and means of belligerent activity.

The circle of potential victims has constantly widened becaue terrorists have captured and taken as hostages not only diplomate but ordinary citizens without influence. Kidnappings and assassinations became a way of expressing political power. As we know from experience, victims of these terrorist attacks were innocent civilians, diplomats, members of international boards, members of international civil air crews, members of international mass media services, members of nonbelligerent armed forces or members of nonbelligerent governments. Simultaneously, kidnapping has appeared in countries free of civil war or other armed crisis, such as Italy, and has become a lucrative form of criminality. Similarly, since 1951, not only political motives but ransom have played a part in some hijackings.

This diversity of motives has made it more difficult to understand these actions. The political question has been raised whether or not hijacking, kidnapping, or assassination aimed at helping rational and justifiable national goals should be considered as legitimate national wars or struggles for freedom. If the answer is affirmative, the terrorist should be regarded as a hero instead of a criminal. If terrorism can be conceived by the law as a political crime, there should be no extradition. The terrorist who escapes to another country should be granted political asylum. Acceptance of this conception would lead us to perceive hijacking, kidnapping assassination as common crimes or as political crimes according to the motive of the offender.

In an earlier century and in another situation, this problem had appeared already. Sea law made a distinction between piracy and privateer. The pirate was seeking private and lucrative goals in his use of illegal force, holding up and looting on the open seas ships of any nationality. Privateers, however, being authorized or commanded by a belligerent partner, applied force on the open seas against ships of an enemy nation only. But in spite of the historical analogy, assential differences exist. The privateer got his authority from a belligerent partner and was subject to international law, but the modern terrorist acts according to the instructions of a secret organization.

To this day no common definition or interpretation of terrorism has been agreed upon. A satisfactory legal definition covers only one part of terrorism, namely, hijacking.

The fight against terrorism has been carried on now for over two decades. Apart from technical means, this fight has another important aspect—and this is in the area of criminal law. The first offenders in these crimes appeared as adventures seeking their own personal goals. Typical personal goals frequently drove them to reach a land or a country which could not be reached by any other means. The unexpected success of this activity called the attention of criminals to the advantages ransoming both the passengers and crew of a plane. The insufficient defence against kidnapping and the willingness of flight companies to give in to criminal demands then drove illegal political organizations to add this method to their political arsenal. They could, for example, use hostages to have their own confined members released. Their first actions meant the criminalization of domestic politics. After the Arab-Israeli war in 1967, hijacking was applied by Arab guerillas to help freedom fighters and to acquaint foreign politicians about the Palestinian movement. Attacks were thus made on planes and passengers of countries that were completely uninvolved in the Middle East conflict. International air transportation was menaced by a serious crisis.

Countries which had international airlines sought effective legal defence against the attacks through conventions held in The Hague and Montreal. Special equipment was set up in national and international airports, and preventive control over passengers become universally accepted. These are effective means of security to which legal enforcement has supplementary importance. Nevertheless, one can trust in the effectiveness of criminal law especially in cases when the offender is motivated by a private aim, and the crime was committed alone or by a small group. According to experience, the criminal punishment could not have preventive force since attackers are persons who volunteered for death and who even in the case of capture often have a chance to get out of prison in exchange for hostages from other hijackings.

2236. Ben-Ari, Mordecai : Protecting the airways. In *ITCR* ; 289-93.

2237. Beristain, A. : Terrorism and aircraft hijackings *International. Journal of Criminology and Penology* 2, 1974.

2238. Boyle, Robert P. : International action to combat aircraft hijacking. *Lawyer of the Americas* 4, Oct 1964.

2239. Boyle, Robert P and Roy Pulsifer : Tokyo Convention on offenses and certain other acts committed on board aircraft. *Journal of Air Law and Commerce* 30, 1964.

2240. Camper's stunt : *Indian Observer* Oct 1985 ; 35-36.

2241. Chaturvedi, S.C. : Hijacking and the law. *Indian Journal of International Law* 11, 1971.

2242. Chauncey, Robert : Deterrence : Certainty, severity and Skyjacking. *Criminology* 12, Feb 1975.

2243. Cheng, Bin : Crimes on board aircraft. *Current Legal Problems* 12, 1959.

2244. Commandos storm hijacked Pan Am jet at Karachi : 15 killed *Patriot* 6 Sep 1986 ; 1.

2245. Countries condemn Israeli air piracy. *China Daily* 8 Feb 1986 ; 4.

2246. Dangerous gamble : *International Herald Tribune* 7 Feb 1986 ; 4.

2247. Dasgupta, Punyapriya : Terrorist attacks at airports : Logic behind the terror. *Deccan Herald* 15 Jan 1986 ; 8.

2248. Datta, Surinder K. : Terror in the air. *Democratic World* 14 Jul 1985 ; 5-6.

Back to air terrorism, the question is why should an aircraft be so vulnerable to terrorism ? Is it just the publicity alone ? Is it the impracticability of fool-proof safeguards ? Do would be hijackers cash in on the deterrence of unnecessary harrassment of air travellers to exploit loopholes in security ? The same way they use innocent people to shield them ? Gone would be the days of showing up ten minutes before flight time. And so far the terrorists have perhaps taken advantage of the airline industry's dilemma of balancing security with smooth functioning.

Already bizzarre new technologies are on the horizon (Newsweek July 8) 'nuclear magnetic resonance' for instance to check cargo and "thermal neutron activation" in which baggage is bombarded with radiation. There might also be structural redesigning of cargo holds to dissipate the effect of an explosion. These are, however, welcome practical solutions, costs permitting. Equally welcome are moves to anticipate nuclear terrorism which might be the scourge of the future. US Vice President George Bush is reported to have warned in Geneva recently about the danger of nuclear terrorism. According to the same report in a meeting in June of the Geneva-based Standing Consultative Commission, the superpowers signed a "common understanding" whereby they will inform each other immediately everything they know about any 'unauthorised' nuclear explosion or threat. (Rakshat Puri in *The Hindustan Times* July 9).

Terrorism is a perversity that has no beginning or end. It is random violence any time anywhere. The main aim of the terrorist is perhaps to make others cowardly. To stop children playing in the public park ? Have people boycott the crowded cinema hall ? Avoid the marriage pandal and may be even the railway station and the airport ? The answer is that there are no clear-cut or final answers to the problem than are already known. It is in the face of the knowledge of evil that faith (in the ultimate beauty and goodness of things) takes over and one leaves the area of the problematic to mystery (the inscrutability of things). From the realm of politics to philosophy.

2249. Dinstein, Yoram : Criminal jurisdiction over aircraft hijacking. *Israel Law Review* 7, 1972.

2250. Dody, Lawrence : Anti-hijacking drive gains impetus. *Aviation Week and Space Technology*. 19 Oct 1970.

2251. Evans, Alona E. : Aircraft and aviation facilities. In *LAIT* ; 3-148.

Hijacking, or the diversion of an aircraft from its scheduled destination by force or threat thereof, is a form of terrorist attack against international and domestic civil aviation. Having achieved spectacular success between 1968 and 1972, it continues to pose a threat, albeit a declining one. But aviation terrorism may also take the following forms : sabotage of aircraft on the ground or in the air ; forced flights or the demand that terrorists be flown to an asylum state from the state in which they have committed an act of terrorism, a situation that may involve the extortion of ransom or release of "political" prisoners as well as the use of hostages ; interception of aircraft by state authorities for reasons other than the protection of a state's jurisdiction over its airspace ; and abduction of persons from aircraft that have landed routinely, by force majeure or by interception.

The reach of terrorism to civil aviation also comprehends what may be broadly described as "aviation facilities," including air terminals, cargo buildings, maintenance facilities, apron passenger vehicles, aprons, cargo areas, runways, taxiways, and off-airport processing facilities such as urban airline terminals and ticket agencies. Whatever the motive, an attack on aircraft and related facilities not only serves to "produce fear"—the distinguishing characteristic of terrorism—but it is also peculiarly heinous because innocent persons dissociated entirely from the terrorist's personal or political ambiance are the victims. In addition, in an increasingly interdependent world, a major form of communication is subjected to disruption and often to destruction. Whatever the motive-escape from self, family, criminal process, or the furtherance of real or imaginary political objectives—interference with international and national civil aviation must be recognized as a crime and treated accordingly.

Politics is the persistent theme running through most instances of aircraft hijacking and related offences against international civil aviation. Politics appears overtly in hijackings by seekers of political asylum ; in hijackings, forced flights, and attacks on aviation facilities by persons seeking to dramatize their opposition to colonialism, particular regimes, or personally unpalatable ideologies ; in extortion of ransom or the release of convicted criminals in furthering these acts ; and in Cuba's denunciation of the Anti-Hijacking Agreement with the United States. Politics appears covertly in the denial of extradition of fugitive offenders qua political refugees on the ground that the territorial state has jurisdiction over their act ; in the persistent grant of asylum to perpetrator of attacks on civil aviation, whether terrorists, fugitives from justice, or psychopaths, as has been the case with Cuba vis-a-vis the United States, Venezuela, Columbia, and Mexico with which its relations have been broken or strained from time to time or Libya vis-a-vis states whose policies do not coincide with current Libyan policy ; or in the aiding and abetting of a hijacking involving the threat of death to 103 hostages, as demonstrated by the government of Uganda in June 1976 for reasons, possibly of foreign policy, possibly of domestic policy, if not simply the personal whim of Ugandan President Idi Amin.

Responses of states that have been victimized by terrorist attacks on civil aviation have also been affected by the political factor, although here the aim has been to reconcile politics with the humanitarian consideration of protecting hostages. The concessionary attitude taken between 1970 and 1975, when a number of convicted terrorists were released by various states—including the Federal Republic of Germany,

Greece, Japan, Sweden, Switzerland, and the United Kingdom—contrasts with the vigorous intervention by Israel on behalf of the hostages held at Entebbe Airport. This latter action raises the question whether humanitarian intervention is the latest alternative when states fail to fulfil their general obligation to control international criminal activity or to fulfil, as in the case of Uganda, their obligations under the Hague Convention. Entebbe was followed by the West German commando attack in October 1977 on a hijacked Lufthansa aircraft at Mogadishu, Somalia, for the purpose of rescuing hostages, and the ill-fates effort by Egyptian commandos at Larnaca in February 1978 to rescue hostages held on board a Cyprus Airways aircraft that had been subjected to an abortive forced flight. Humanitarian intervention is not only another phase of the hardening of government attitudes towards treating with terrorists, especially where the lives of hostages are at stake, but it also introduces a technique that can have a dangerous impact on the relations of the states involved. The course of action now appears to be to negotiate with terrorists for as long as feasible, then to take vigorous measures, but not to concede to extortionate demands or threats against hostages. This procedure has at least two disadvantages : (1) it makes the hostages victims of both the hijackers and the negotiators, and (2) it works best in the limited ambiance of a national hijacking, i.e., where the incident is confined to an airport within the state in which the incident begen, so if necessary, local authorities can bring pressure to bear on their own responsibility. Where a negotiation has to be carried out in a state other than the states of registration, of destination, or of take off of the hijacked aircraft or in a state whose relations with these states or with the states of nationality of the hostages is strained or broken—i.e., at long distance—force as the last resort is not likely to be a realistic choice for most countries ; nor are the suggestions—advanced during the Entebbe incident—that a prisoner demanded by the hijackers should be killed for every hostage killed, or that all terrorists should be subject to the death penalty so that none would be available for purposes of extortion. Such draconic measures would only reduce civilized states to the level of the terrorists. Methods short of force—ranging from boycott of air transport with an offending state, suspension of trade or economic aid, to severance of diplomatic relations—are the most practicable techniques, certainly for large industrial states, which are the common victims of offenses against aviation. These techniques can be usefully applied unilaterally, but they would have more impact if they had multilateral backing—i.e., in a particular instance of hijacking, if the principal air transport states united against the offending state. The use of these measures is legitimate under the United Nations Charter and should not be relegated to wishful thinking in chancelleries.

There is always an offending state, one that does not respect its obligations relative to the protection of international civil aviation. It is interesting to note that among the states that have condoned or have temporized with aircraft hijackers or terrorists who have committed offences against aviation facilities, Egypt, Iraq, Lebanon, Libya, and Tunisia are bound by one or more of the three relevant conventions. These states, along with Algeria, Cuba, Kuwait, Syria and Yemen (Aden), are also party to the Chicago Convention, which provides the basis for the facilitation of international air transport. All of them, and most of the states that choose to follow their lead, have some international commitment to protect the integrity of international communications as represented by international civil aviation.

It is argued that "freedom fighters" or proponents of "wars of national liberation" are exempted from the onus of criminality, no matter how barbaric their acts. This is the political stumbling block that has led the United Nations to abdicate its responsibilities as a law-making and law-enforcing agency with respect to the control of international terrorism.

2252. Fick, Ronald L. *et. al.* : Aircraft hijacking : Criminal and Civil aspects. *University of Florida Law Review* 20, 1969.

2253. Fitz Gerald, G.F. : Development of international rules concerning offences and certain other acts committed on board aircraft. *Canadian Year book of International Law* 1, 1963.

2254. Fitz Gerald, G.F. : Offences and certain other acts committed on board aircraft : The Tokyo Convention of 1963. *Canadian Year Book of International Law* 2, 1964.

2255. For aviation sanctions : *International Herald Tribune* 15 May 1986 ; 6.

2256. Gantzer, Hugh & Colleon : Security mess at airport. *Indian Express* 29 Sep 1985 ; 12.

2257. Gertler, Z.J. : Amendments to the Chicago. Convention, lessons from proposals that failed. *Journal of Air Law and Commerce* 40, 1974.

2258. Geyelin, Philip : Awarding the arch-terrorist a network audience. *International Herald Tribune* 14 May 1986 ; 6.

2259. Green, G. : Derogation of human rights in emergency situations. *Canadian Year Book of International Law* 16, 1978.

2260. Green, L.C. : Extradition Vs. Asylum for aerial hijackers. *Israel Law Review* 207, 1975.

2261. Greene, W and A. Cookburn : Case of the Paranoid hijacker. *Esquire* Jul 1975.

2262. Horowitz, Irving L. : Political terrorism and state power. *Journal of Political and Military Sociology* 1, Spr 1973 ; 147-57.

2263. Hotz, R. : Hijacking turns murderous. *Aviation Week* 100, 21 Jan 1975.

2264. Hotz, R. : Rising tide of terror. *Aviation Week* 97, 7 Oct 1972.

2265. How Iraq foiled Iranian bid to hijack Iraqi plane. *Iraq* 1 Oct 1984 ; 11-12.

Iraq foiled an Iranian attempt to hijack an Iraqi passenger aircraft on September 15.

The Iraqi plane, Boeing 737, which was carrying 110 passengers from different nationalities was making its regular flight from Larnaca (Cyprus) to Baghdad when a man sitting in the first class opened the cockpit door crying that the plane was skyjacked but no one answered him. He was killed a few moments later by one of the Iraqi security men inside the plane.

In describing the hijacking event, Minister of Transport and Communications, Mr. Abdul Jabbar Abdul Raheem said that an Iranian attempt to hijack an Iraqi plane was foiled.

The Minister added that three Iranians carrying forged passports tried to hijack an Iraqi Airways plane, a Boeing 737, while it was on a regular flight from Larnaca (Cyprus) to Baghdad. The abortive hijacking attempt was made while the plane was flying through the Syrian air space, he indicated.

The Minister further said ; the vigilance of the Iraqi security men and their swift movement thwarted the attempt. The three hijackers were killed amidst the chanting and clapping of the passengers."

Mr. Abdul Raheem described the abortive hijacking attempt a cheap effort by the Iranian regime to cover up for the hijackings of Iranian planes by Iranian citizens.

"The Iraqis are determined to consolidate their victories over the Iranian enemy, liquidate any such attempts and out off the hand which stretches to encroach upon Iraq's pride and prestige," the Minister concluded.

Security men of the aircraft told Iraqi News Agency (INA) that the abortive hijack attempt started one hour after the plane had left Larnaca and was frustrated only one minute after the attempt.

The security men added that the three hijackers took positions at the front, middle and rear of the plane. One of the hijackers who was carrying a bottle wrapped in paper as a hand grenade, announced that the plane had been hijacked, one of the security men shot him dead in one bullet, while the other Iraqi security men killed the other two hijackers at once.

The security men said that no passenger was injured and that the plane fuselage was not damaged.

One of the security men told Iraqi TV viewers that the three hijackers were under surveillance when the plane took off because their movements raised suspicion.

He said he was slightly wounded when he was hit from the back by one of the skyjackers who carried an empty bottle.

The security man told "Al-Jumuriya" daily that one hijacker was carrying an explosive device and a lighter while another was brandishing a knife.

The plane's four hostesses said when the passengers felt there was something happening they were told there was a sick men in the plane in order to avoid any panic. They were also asked to fasten their seat-belts.

The hostesses stressed that the three hijackers were in a state of embarrassment when they made their attempt.

One hostess said that one of the hijackers said he was ill and she gave him orange juice and before one of the security men came, the hijacker threw the glass at her face pushing her colleague and headed to the cockpit.

In appreciation of their bravery, President Saddam Hussein honoured the three security men who courageously prevented the three Iranians from attaining their goal.

Baghdad TV showed its viewers on September 16 the corpses of the three hijackers fallen in different places.

It is noteworthy, that three Iranian planes (two civilians and one military F-4) were defected to Iraq late August and September. The Iranians who skyjacked the Iranian aircraft were of different ages and positions.

The skyjackers expressed their disgust over the situation in Iran. They said that the majority of Iranians opposed Khomeini regime.

2266. Hubbard, D.G. : *Skyjacker* : *His flights of fantasy.* New York, Macmillan, 1971.

2267. India condemns hijacking. *Indian Express* (New Delhi) 6 Feb 1986 ; 1.

India on February 5, 1986 condemned the hijacking of a Libyan lane by Israel in the international air space and termed the action as "complete violation" of international law.

Replying to a question, the Foreign Secretary, Mr Romesh Bhandari, said the Government of India "condemns terrorism in all its forms and thinks that hijacking of the Libyan plane as a means of attracting attention has been a misguided ploy of terrorists."

Mr. Bhandari said that the Indian Government was quite disturbed by the trend of the terrorists for the last few months. It was shocked to know how the states could stand so low to yield to the tactics of the terrorists.

Syria on February 5, threatened retaliation and said Israel's action in forcing down a Libyan airliners could trigger a blow-up in West Asia.

The official Damascus Radio said Israel could not escape punishment and accused the United States of fuelling tension.

"The United States is encouraging Israel to pour oil on the fire," it declared.

Israel was widely condemned throughout the Arab world for intercepting a Libyan executive jet carrying senior Syrian officials from Tripoli back to Damascus on February 4.

The Israelis, seeking to capture a Palestinian guerrilla leader, forced the plane down at an airfield in northern Israel. The 2 passengers were allowed to leave after being interrogated and Israel admitted the operation failed. The Israeli Prime Minister Mr. Shimon Peres, said the operation was "an error".

When the U.N. Security Council failed to act on Syria's request for a resolution denouncing the action. Damascus Radio warned Israel : "To those who think they can play with international law and freedom of air navigation, if they think they can escape punishment, they must be living in an illusion".

The Syrian threat came amid strong condemnation of Israel by various Arab countries like the United Arab Emirates (UAE), Kuwait and Morocco as well as Iran.

In Tripoli, the Libyan Government of Col. Muammar Gaddafi said on Feb 5, it is joining Syria in seeking a formal United Nations condemnation of what it said was a case of "air piracy" by the United States and Israel.

2268. Jiwa, Salim : *Death of Air India flight 182*. London, W.H. Allen, 1986.

The crash of Air-India's Kanishka on June 23, 1985, is undoubtedly one of the most controversial air mishaps in the world. It has divided the world into two camps—India and the United States versus Europe. While both India and the US have maintained that Kanishka was a victim of sabotage, the general opinion amongst European aviation experts is that the explosion could have been caused by "various other factors" too.

In The Death of Air-India Flight 182, the Vancouver-based journalist, Salim Jiwa, attempts to support the Indo-American theory that the aircraft was blown up by a suitcase bomb. The evidence he has gathered by relying mainly on the records of the Royal Canadian Mounted Police (RCMP) is, however, purely circumstantial. He is critical of the Canadian authorities for their failure to enforce a strict airport security system. He says : "Tragically, though, the twin disasters (Kanishka and Narita) could have been averted if the Canadian authorities had listened to the Canadian Airline Fight, Attendants Association in 1983."

2269. Kahn, R. : Hijacking and international law. *Africa Quarterly* 10, 1971.

2270. Kaplan, Howard : Arafat must not be blamed for airport massacres. *International Herald Tribune* 6 Jan 1986 ; 4.

2271. Lessons from the hijack : *Deccan Herald* 2 Jul 1985 ; 6.

2272. Loy, Frank E. : Department of transportation reviews problem of aircraft hijacking and proposals for international action. *Department of State Bulletin* 60, 1969.

2273. Lynn, Robert H. : Air hijacking as a political crime—who should judge ? *California Western International Law Journal* 11, 1971.

2274. Malbmborg, K.E. : New developments in the law of international aviation : the control of aerial hijacking. *Proceedings of American Society of International Law* 1971.

2275. Malnie, Eric : Moving toward air safety. *International Herald Tribune* 17 October 1986 ; 7.

2276. Martin, Peter : Unlawful seizure of aircraft. *Law Society's Gazette* 66, 1969.

2277. McClintock, Michael C. : Skyjacking : Its domestic Civil and criminal ramifications. *Journal of Air Law and Commerce* 39, 1971.

2278. Mendelsohn, A.I. : In-flight crime : The international and domestic picture under the Tokyo convention. *Virginia Law Review* 53, 1967.

2279. Miller, Judith : Palestinians threaten U.S. and Israeli airlines. *International Herald Tribune* 7 Feb 1986 ; 1.

2280. Mohan Ram : Bolt out of the blue. *Far Eastern Economic Review* 4 Jul 1985 ; 12-13.

2281. Needs of national security. *Madhya Pradesh Chronicle* 19 Jul 1985 ; 4.

2282. New air terrorism. *Egyptian Gazette* 25 Nov 1985 ; 3.

2283. Owne-Davies, J. : Problems in the Middle East take their tool on Arab airlines. *International Herald Tribune* 3-4 May 1986 ; 7, 14.

2284. Pachisia, Pratibha : Fear of flying ? *Sunday Observer* 7 Jul 1985 ; 20.

2285. Path to safer air travel. *International Herald Tribune* 27 Jul 1985 ; 8.

2286. Piracy in the skies. *Telegraph* (Calcutta) 13 Oct 1985 ; 8.

2287. Piracy in the sky. *Hindustan Times* (New Delhi) 6 Feb 1986 ; 9.

International laws and conventions were flouted once again by Israel on Tuesday when it committed an act of air piracy in hijacking a Libyan aircraft. That it allowed the executive jet to leave Israel a few hours later with all the passengers on board cannot mitigate the criminality of the action. For it only did this because the man it was out to capture, believed to be George Habash, the leader of the Popular Front for the Liberation of Palestine (PELP), was not on board. This Israeli action follows almost on the heels of its terrorist act of bombarding the Palestinian Liberation Organisation's headquarters near Tunis last October in which action it had also failed to hit its target, Yasser Arafat of the PLO. Instead it had on its conscience the deaths of some sixty innocent persons including women and children who were killed in the bombardment.

These two actions, its Lebanese invasion fiasco and other recent happenings reveal that the once much wanted Israeli Intelligence is developing feet of clay. This is, however, by the way. The main point is what, if anything, the world will do to stop such "official terrorism". India and the vast majority of the countries will no doubt condemn the piratical act in the strongest terms. But as long as Israel has the US behind, it can cock a snook at the rest of the world. Even if by chance, wisdom has dawned on the U.S. that such actions can only escalate the already grim cycle of retribution in the Middle East, it cannot protest. For Israel can turn round and point to the U.S. act of air piracy last October when it forced an Egyptian airliner to land in Sicily. Its justification that it was to capture the hijackers of the Achille Lauro ship does not stand scrutiny. For apart from other factors, two wrongs cannot make a right. The world, instead of moving towards peace, seems to be fast overthrowing what little sanctity was left in international laws. The outlook for 1986 looks bleak indeed.

2288. Protect the aircraft industry. *China Daily* 15 Feb 1986 ; 4.

2289. Raghuram, A.C. *et. al.* : Death in the Air *Science Age* Aug 1955 ; 32-39.

2290. Rama Rao, T.S. : Hijacking : More stringent measures needed. *World Focus* (74) Feb 1986 ; 11-13.

Hijacking of aircraft has in recent years become a convenient method for organised terrorists all over the world, to draw attention to their cause, and to try to secure their demands including release of their colleagues in custody, payment of ransom money, etc. as a condition for the release by them of the detained crew and passengers. The phenomenon began possibly in 1948; and from 1948 to 1967, there were 45 successful hijackings, according to Prof. Alona Evans. In those early years, such hijacking was mainly done by people in eastern Europe, who sought refuge in the West, and it was also extended to Cuba, after the revolution in that country. From 1968, there was a dramatic increase in the number of hijackings, as the Palestinians resorted to hijacking as an instrument of indirect warfare against, and harassment of Israel. In 1968, there were 30 hijackings. India also has been a victim of aircraft hijacking as planes from Srinagar were taken to Lahore by the terrorists there, and also by Sikh terrorists in recent memory.

Hijacking posed a grave threat to international aviation and there was soon a demand for its legal control and for steps for punishment of the culprits of their extradition to the country of registration of the aircraft by the country where they had taken refuge. Paradoxically in the initial stages, it was the western states which were reluctant to extradite the hijackers who were mainly political refugees from East European countries. But when Arab terrorists took to hijacking on a large scale, the western states began to press for the conclusion of international treaties for dealing with the menace of hijacking. It was now the turn of the Afro-Asian states to drag their feet, as they were reluctant to extradite Arab hijackers to Israel or the western countries, whose planes had been hijacked. But since hijacking affected civil aviation and the lives of the crew and passengers, subjecting them to the ordeal of harassment and sometimes torture by the hijackers and to uncertainty about their very survival, the necessity of tackling this menace by national and international measures came to be felt by all nations.

2291. Rein, Bert : Government perspective. *Journal of Air Law and Commerce* 37, 1973 ; 183-94.

2292. Rubin, Alfred P. : Terrorism and piracy : A legal view. *Terrorism* 3 (1-2) 1979 ; 117-30.

2293. Safety : Year of the crash. *Asiaweek* 19 Jan 1986 ; 57.

2294. Salpukas, Agis : For travellers, new fear of flying. *International Herald Tribune* 16 Apr 1986 ; 8.

2295. Saksena, N. S. : How to cope with Hijacking ? *Times of India* 29 Aug 1984 ; 8.

2296. SchWarzenberger, Georg : Terrorists, hijackers, guerrillas and mercenaries. *Current Legal Problems* 24, 1971, 257-82.

2297. *Select bibliography on aerial piracy.* New York, United Nations, 20 Nov 1972. List no. 6.

2298. Sagarmann, Josh : Exciting news for hijackers : Plastic handguns. *International Herald Tribune* 29-30 Mar 1986 : 6.

2299. Tarred with the same brush. *Pioneer* 11 Feb 1986 ; 4.

2300. Tiwari, B. K. : Terrorism in the air. *Indian Express* 27 Jun 1985 ; 6.

2301. Volpe, J. A. and J. T. Stewart : Aircraft hijacking : Some domestic and international responses. *Kentucky Law Journal* 59, 1970-71.

2302. Zartman, I. William. *ed.* : *50 per cent solution.* New York, Anchor Books. 1976.

2303. Wurfel, Seymour W. : Aircraft piracy—Crime or fun? *William and Many Law Review* 70, 1969.

2304. Zia Ullah, Syed : Karachi massacre—ACIA Connection ? *Madhya Pradesh Chronicle* (Bhopal) 20 Sep 1986 ; 6.

Hostages

2305. Aston, Clive C. : Political hostages taking in Western Europe : A statistical analysis. In *POT* ; 99-130.

2306. Aston, Clive C. : United Nations Convention against the taking of hostages : Realistic or rhetoric ? *Terrorism : An International Journal* 5 (1-2) 1981 : 139-60.

2307. Crelinsten, Ronald D. and Denis Szabo : *Hostage taking.* Lexington Books, 1979.

2308. Culley, John A. : Hostage negotiation. *FBI Law Enforcement Bulletin* 43, Oct 1974 ; 10-14.

2309. France's hostage crisis. *International Herald Tribune* 12 Mar 1986 ; 4.

2310. France's hostage dilemma. *International Herald Tribune* 13 March 1986 ; 4.

2311. Friedland, Nehemia : Hostage negotiations : Dilemmas about policy. In *POT* ; 201-12.

2312. Goldlaber, I. : Typology of hostage takers. *Police Chief* 46, 1979 ; 21-23.

2313. Green, G. : *Hostage Heart* Chicago, 1976.

2314. Green, Gilbert : *New radicalism* : *Anarchist or Marxist* ? New York, International Publishers, 1971.

2315. Hanben, Robert : Hostage taking : The Dutch experience. In. *POT* ; 131-42.

2316. Hillman, Robert G. : Psychopathology of being held hostage ? In *POT* ; 157-68.

2317. International Convention against the taking of hostage. *Terrorism* 5 (3) 1981 ; 293-300.

2318. Jenkins, Brian : *Hostage Survival.* Santa Monica, Rand Corporation, April 1976.

2319. McClure, Brooks : Hostage survival. In *ITCW* ; 276-81.

Of all the tactics used by political terrorists, kidnapping has probably been the most effective. During the past four years, as much as $ 80 million in ransoms for hostages have been collected in Latin America alone. Other returns also from kidnapping have been substantial : scores of prisoners have been released ; governments have been embarrassed ; relations between nations have been strained ; and worldwide publicity for terrorist causes has been realized.

All this social disruption hast been accomplished at relatively small cost to the perpetrators. About 80 percent of the terrorists involved in political kidnapping have gotten away unscathed, although the odds for success have diminished in several countries during the past year. Countermeasures are improving, but kidnapping remains a low-risk, high-return activity for many terrorist groups.

Further progress in dealing with the kidnap weapon depends in large measure upon improved anti-subversion tactics by governments, still more effective protection of prime targets, increased international cooperation, and the elimination of terrorist safe-havens. Until more of these adjustments can be made, political kidnappings are likely to continue.

It the face of this threat, therefore, it has been necessary to take a look at the problem from the other end, that is, what can be done to help prepares a prospective kidnap victim and improve his chance of surviving the experience ? To answer this question, a number of researchers have analyzed hostage situations to see whether defence measures can be devised for vulnerable individuals—particularly international businessmen, diplomats, and military officers.

The result is interesting. Anyone with experience abroad might assume that cultural factors alone would create vastly different conditions for terrorist operations in different parts of the world. And to this fact must be added a multitude of other variables, such as the personality and temperament of the victim, the character of his captors, the nature of the terrorist cause, the immediate objective of the kidnapping, and the reaction of the authorities.

Indeed. the key question is whether hostage incidents are subject to so many diverse influences that each case must be considered basically unique. If so, any standard approach to the problem would appear nearly impossible.

Fortunately, the study of more than two dozen cases of political kidnapping in Latin America, Europe, and the Middle East indicates this is not so. While it is certainly no easy matter to develop concrete hostage counter-measures, and there is a danger of trying to set hard-and-fast rules, the task of providing useful guidelines for political kidnap victims is feasible. There are, in fact, several significant similarities in widely desperate incidents from which general lessons can be learnt.

The first of these similarities is the psychological reaction of almost any individual to being kidnapped. It does not matter much who the victim is, or where he is taken ; he will nearly always react in a predictable fashion. And it helps him to understand in advance what his reaction will be.

Second, again in the psychological realm, the confrontation of prisoner and captor follows a pattern. When the victim knows the basic dynamics of this type of encounter, he can assume his "prisoner role" in such a way as to make the most of what is, at best, an exceedingly difficult situation.

Third, there are basic types of hostage situations with different stresses and challenges to the victim. By understanding the nature of these different circumstances and being able to assess the character and aims of his captors, the hostage can act intelligently in his own interest.

Some hostages have held their own lives because of this ability to analyze their predicament.

Fourth, ideologically motivated terrorists often follow the same thought process and use similar operating techniques—they, in fact, have all that had much the same Marxist-activist schooling. An understanding of this mentality can be a help to any hostage.

Finally, there is a set of prisoner survival techniques which can help a hostage to maintain his mental stability and physical condition wherever he may be held.

It is possible, therefore, to give a potential hostage a certain amount of useful training so that he is better able to endure the truly traumatic experience of political kidnapping. The danger, of course, is that the instruction may become over-systematized, resulting in dogmatic "answers" to infinitely varied problems. The most valuable single point that can be made to a possible victim is that he cannot be prepared for precisely what he will encounter ; he must above all remain flexible and mentally alert. He has to make his own decisions. But he can draw from the experiences of earlier victims, and he can put his predicament into a framework for effective analysis, again based on the experiences of others.

2320. Mickolus, E.F. : Negotiation for hostages ; A policy dilemma. *Orbis* 19, 1976 ; 1309-26.

2321. Miller, Abraham H : Hostage negotiations and the concept of transference. In *TTP* ; 137-58.

2322. Miller, Abraham H. : *Terrorism and hostage negotiations*. Boulder, Colorado, Westview Press, 1980.

2323. Reiser, Martin and Martin Sloane : Use of suggestibility techniques in hostage negotiation. In *POT* ; 213-24.

2324. Shaw, Eric : Political hostages : Sanction and the recovery process. In *POT* ; 143-56.

HUMAN RIGHTS

2325. Green, J.F. : Human rights and the colour problems. *Current Legal Problems* 1(3) 1950.

2326. Saddy, Fehmy : International terrorism, human rights and world order. *Terrorism* 5(4) 1982 ; 325-51.

HUMANISM

2327. Merleau-Ponty, Maurice : *Humanism and terror*. Boston, Beacon Press, 1969.

IDEOLOGY

2328. Morton, Marian J. : *Terrors of ideological politics.* Cleveland, Press of case-Western Reserve University 1972.

IMMIGRATION

2329. Avriel Ehud : *Open the gates ? The dramatic personal story of "Illegal" immigration to Israel.* London, 1975.

IMPERIALISM

2330. Amin Samir : *Imperialism and unequal development.* New York, Monthly Review Books, 1977.

2331. Arright, G. : *Geometry of imperialism : The limits of Hobson's paradigm.* London, 1978.

2332. Bairoch, Paul : Historical roots of economic underdevelopment : Myths and realities. In *IAA* ; 191-216.

2333. Brewer, Anthony : *Marxist theories of imperialism.* London, Routledge and Kegan Paul, 1980.

2334. Brewer, Anthony : Theories of imperialism in perspective. In *IAA* ; 325-32.

2335. Brotel, Dieter : Imperialist domination in Vietnam and Cambodia. A long-term view. In *IAA* ; 167-90.

2336. Campbell, A.E. : Paradox of imperialism : the American Case. In *IAA* ; 34-40.

2337. Chopra, V.D. : India and world imperialism. In *Pentagon shadow over India.* New Delhi, Patriot Publications, 1985 ; 1-5.

2338. Demand for a forthright stand against imperialism *People's Democracy* (New Delhi) 30 Mar 1986 ; 9.

2339. Fieldhouse, David : New imperial system ? The role of the multinational corporations reconsidered ? In *IAA* ; 225-40.

2340. Frankel, Charles : Human rights and imperialism. *Proceedings of the Columbia University general education seminar* 6(1) 1977.

2341. Galtung, J. : Structural theory of imperialism. *Journal of Peace Research* 8, 1971 ; 81-116, 173-206.

2342. Geyer, Dietrich : Modern imperialism ? The Tsarist and the Soviet Examples. In *IAA* ; 49-62.

2343. Hobson, John Atkinson. *Imperialism : A study.* London, Allen & Unwin, 1968.

2344. Imperialism's new big stick. *People's Democracy* 2 Feb 1986 ; 8.

2345. Kulkarni, V.B. : Challenge to imperialism. In *Conflict in Indian Society.* Bombay, 1981 ; 74-103.

2346. Lenin, V.I. : *Imperialism : The highest stage of capitalism.* New York, 1969.

2347. Leys, Colin : Conflict and convergence in development theory. In *IAA* ; 315-24.

2348. Lipietz, A. : Imperialism or the best of the abocalypse *Capital and Class* 22, 1984 ; 81-109.

2349. Low, D.A. : *Lion rampant : Eassys in the study of British imperialism.* London, 1974.

2350. Martin, Berned : Politics of expansion of the Japanese empire : Imperialism or Pan-Asiatic Mission. In *IAA* ; 63-82.

2351. McGowan, P.J. and B. Kordan : Imperialism in World-system Perspective. *International Studies Quarterly* 25, 1981.

2352. Menzel, Ulrieh : Newly industrialized countries of East Asia : Imperialist continuity or a case of catching up ? In *IAA* ; 247-66.

2353. Midgley, J. *ed.* : *Professional imperialism : Social Work in the Third World.* London, Heinemann, 1981.

2354. Mommsen, W.J. : End of empire and the continuity of imperialism. In *IAA* ; 333-58.

2355. Mommsen, W.J. and J. Osterhammel : *Imperialism and after.* London, Allen & Unwin, 1986. Pp. 368.

2356. Mommsen, W.J. : *Theories of imperialism.* London, 1981.

2357. Munro, J. Forbes : Third World in the international economy. In *IAA* ; 217-24.

2358. Mish, Ian H. : Some thought on Japanese expansion. In *IAA* ; 83-89.

2359. Osterhammel, Jurgen : Semi-colonialism and informal empire in twentieth-century China : Towards a framework of analysis. In *IAA* ; 290-314.

2360. Robinson, Ronald : Executive idea of imperialism, with or without empire. In *IAA* ; 267-89.

2361. Robinson, Ronald and J. Gallagher : Imperialism of free trade. *Economic History Review* 6, 1953.

2362. Rothermund, Dietmar : Legacy of the British-Indian empire in independent India. In *IAA* ; 139-153.

2363. Schwabe, Klaus : Global role of the United States and its imperial consequences, 1898-1973, In *IAA* ; 13-33.

2364. Smith, Tony : American imperialism in anti-communism. In *IAA* ; 41-48.

2365. Smith, W.D. : *European imperialism in the 19th and 20th Centuries.* Chicago, 1982.

2366. Terrorism insurance on the increase. *Daily* (Bombay) 27 May 1986 ; 13.

2367. Tomilnson, B.R. : Continuities and discontinuities in Indo-British economic relations : British multinational corporations in India. In *IAA* ; 154-66.

2368. Von Lane, Theodore H. : Human rights and imperialism. *Bulletin of Atomic Scientists* Aug-Sep 1983 ; 32-35.

2369. Von Strandmann, H.P. Hartmut Pogge : Imperialism and revisionism in interwar Germany. In *IAA* ; 90-122.

2370. Wallerstein I. : Imperialism and development. In *Studies of the Modern World System* New York, Academic Press, 1980 ; 13-24.

2371. Wirz, Albert : Imperialism and state formation in Africa ; Nigeria and Cherd. In *IAA* ; 123-38.

Indian Ocean

2372. Anand, V. Eshwar : Theatre of conflict : Political rivalry in the Indian Ocean. *Statesman* 2 Apr 1986 ; 8.

2373. Attar Chand : Militarization of Indian Ocean. *National Herald* 31 Mar 1986 ; 5.

2374. Concern over Ocean militarisation. *Madhya Pradesh Chronicle* 13 Feb 1986 ; 4.

2375. Leonidov, D. : Diego Garcia being turned into U.S. nuclear arsenal. *Madhya Pradesh Chronicle* (Bhopal) 19 Jan 1986 ; 6.

Individualism

2376. Lukes, Stephen : *Individualisms.* Oxford, Basil Blackwell, 1973.

2377. Nedava, Yosef : Some aspects of individual terrorism : A case study of the Schowartzbard affair. In *TIE* ; 29-39. *Terrorism* 3(1-2) 1979 ; 69-70.

On 25 May 1926, Shalom Schwartzbard, a Jewish watchmaker, assassinated Simon Petliura, the chief Ataman of the Ukranian Republican Army. During Petliura's reign, prior to his defeat by the Red Army in 1920, the Jews in the Ukraine were subjected to slaughter on a scale unknown since the massacres of 1648-9 under Bogdan Chmielnicki Petliura was killed in rue Racine, in the Latin Quarter of Paris ; Schwartzbard surrendered to the police, and following a dramatic trial was acquitted on 27 October 1927. The verdict was almost universally acclaimed. Following his release, he expressed his wish to settle in the Land of Israel (Palestine at the time), but the British Mandatory authorities viewed his deed with disfavour and, fearing further trouble from a 'temperamental' type in a 'troubled' area, refused him permission to land. He died in March 1938, in South Africa, and his remains were transferred to Israel in 1967.

Schwartzbard's trial turned on one pivotal issue : could Petliura be held responsible for the programes in the Ukraine, and, consequently, be accountable for their grim results, as claimed by the defence : or was he innocent of the crimes imputed to him. For, the prosecution maintained, he had tried his best to stop the massacres by publishing exhortary proclamations to his soldiers. As was to be expected, Schwartzbard turned from accused to accuser ; yet in spite of this change of roles, the onus of proof still rested on him. The prosecution and its witnesses persisted in their argument that Petliura had been a friend of the Jews ; his proclamations to the army had denounced the pogroms unreservedly. The prosecution further claimed that he had contribued from the funds of the Directory, which he had headed, towards relieving the sufferings of the victims' families, and that he had manifested in diverse ways his resentment of the activities of the 'irregulars' who had joined his forces in the struggle against the Bolsheviks and for the independence of the Ukraine. The defence rejected these claims in toto, yet found it difficult to produce in court any written incriminating evidence. It lacked clear-cut documentary proof definitely to condemn the 'Chief Hangman', as Schwartzbard's attorney, Henry Torres, called Petliura.

It seems that from time imm morial, perpetrators of genocide have tended to hid behind the backs of their assistants and henchmen in order to be able to wash their hands of any responsibility when called to account. The Wansee Conference (January 1942), which was held in the presence of some of the highest officials of the Nazi hierarchy, refrained from putting down in writing any of its deliberations. It was ostensibly a 'social' gathering, although the lines were laid down for co-ordinating efforts to carry out the 'Final Solution' of the Jewish Problem. Among those present was Adolf Eichmann, who to the very end never admitted being anything but a minor functionary in any decision making. It was his consistent practice to avoid putting his signature to incriminating documents. He, too, like Petliura, pretended to have been a friend of the Jews bent 'on finding a piece of land that they could call their own'. But he was naturally unable to safeguard himself entirely against all 'foolhardy' actions on the part of his minor subordinates. Following a telephone conversation with Franz Rademacher, an expert on Jewish affairs at the German Foreign Office inquiring what should be done to some Yugoslav Jews, Rademacher noted : 'Eichmann says no possibility of reception (of Jews) in Russian and General Government.......Eichmann proposes shooting.

In Schwartzbard's case, too, the defence had to a great extent to rely on circumstantial evidence. This problem was dealt with by the well-known historian of the Ukrainian pogroms, Elias Tcherikower, in his comprehensive work. Tcherikower was invited to Paris by the Zionist leader, Leo Motzkin in order to preside over the preparation of the background material for the defence. From the numerous testimonies and documents collected, Petliura's culpability clearly stood out, but it was established somewhat indirectly, for the defence could lay its hand on no single document bearing the Ataman's signature incriminating him in the massacres.

A special chapter in Tcherikower's book deal with 'Petliura and the Proskurov Pogrom (February 1919)'. The shadow of this pogrom in particular hovered over the entire proceedings of Schwartzbard's trial because of its savagery and ferociousness. For three and a half hours on 15 February ('The Proskurov Sabbath'), over 1,500 Jews were slaughtered and more than 1,000 wounded. Hetman Semesenko's soldiers, who belonged to Petliura's Haidamacks, showed no mercy towards the old, women or children. On the eve of the pogroms they swore to deviate from their customary rule of conduct—to refrain from robbing their victims and content themselves with their killing. As usual, the massacre was carried out under the slogan: 'Kill the Jews and save the Ukraine', and the pretext was what that the Jews were Bolsheviks and ought to be eradicated mercilessly.

INSURANCE

2378. GIC policy to cover loses due to terrorism. *Times of India* 24 Dec 1986 ; 3.

Insurgency

2379. Ahmad, Eqbal : Theory and fallacy of counter-insurgency. *Nation* 213, 1970.

2380. Anand, J. P. : Insurgency in Burma and Sino-Indian repprochement. *Strategic Analysis* May 1979 ; 39-43.

2381. Arms for Sikh terrorists : Pak leaders' admission. *Hindu* (New Delhi) 2 Feb 1987 ; 9.

2382. Barrantes, M. G. : Bloody counter-insurgency operation. *International Viewpoint* 27 Jan 1986 ; 11-13.

2383. Barthakur, P. B. : Countering insurgency. *Hindustan Times* 11 Apr 1986 ; 9.

2384. Blaufarb, Douglas S. : *Counter-insurgency era : U. S. doctrine and performance, 1950 to the present*. New York, Free Press, 1976. Pp. 356.

2385. Buch, M. N. : Is insurgency the only way. *Times of India*. 26 Jul 1986 ; 8.

2386. China's role in growing insurgency in Tripura. *New Wave* 9 Feb 1986 ; 5.

Subversive forces are, as usual, active in Tripura. The underground Tribal National Volunteers (TNV) is the most active force of this kind in the area.

Recently the TNV extremists overtly showed some inclination to negotiate with the Centre on the basis of a five point chapter of demands. The charter includes promulgation of an inner line permit system in Tripura and Union Territory status of the Tribal Autonomous District Council.

Three other points in the TNV charter of demands are detection of foreigners with October 15, 1949, as the cut off date, appropriate rehabilitation benefits at par with those accorded to other insurgents groups in the North-Eastern region and grant of general amnesty to TNV gu·rrillas, besides the restoration of all alienated tribal lands take away by non-tribal settlers since 1960.

Interestingly, the charter of demands was drawn up by the TNV at their underground "capital" in Singhlam in Bangladesh and Chittagong hill traits in November last.

The very fact that the charter was drawn in Bangladesh made it obvious that the TNV is following the guidelines of its 'godfathers' which include Bangladesh, Pakistan, China and the USA. The US interests were explicitly exposed during the late 1985 visit to Dhaka by the US Deputy Secretary of State, John Whitehead which was an upshoot of the White House's long-standing desire to turn the Chittagong port into its naval base in the Bay of Bengal. This would naturally enable the US intelligence to extend all kinds of necessary help to the TNV and create destability in India.

China's vicious role in the north-eastern region is no secret to India. Though the Chinese leadership has declared time and again that it does not subscribe to secessionist elements in India, it has been substantiated with facts that China is doing its worst to create destability in India, and hence is providing every kind of help to all the subversive forces, including the TNV. Military-training of guerrilla warfare to TNV has already been reported a number of times.

Bangladesh's involvement is demonstrated from the fact that TNV has its underground "capital" in Singhlam in Bangladesh.

Now let us examine the mischievious role played by Islamabad. Recently the under cover agents of Pakistan's elite intelligence outfit, the Special Service Group (SSG) established links with the TNV extremists based in Bangladesh.

Three Pakistani SSG officials, masquerading as businessmen and based in Chittagong, contacted TNV underground leaders through some pro-Pakistani "repatriate" commanders in Bangladesh army, who were still reportedly loyal to Islamabad.

A top secret meeting was held at Rangmati with TNV "president" Bijoy Kumar Hrangkhawl and four of his close confidents, "general" Kartik Koloi, "home minister" Ananta Debbarma and "foreign secretary" Haripada Harangkhawl in December last. The involvement of Bangladesh was further exposed with the presence in the meeting of some officers of the Bangladesh National Security Intelligence Department.

It has been reported that the Pakistani officials assured TNV leaders of regular arms and ammunition supplied. Hence, Islamabad has agreed to supply 50 pieces of double barrel and single barrel guns to the TNV by late February. The "payment" would be made to an arms dealer based in Chittagong.

The Pakistani officers also assured the TNV rebels of training facilities once the "whole source" is settled.

However, one more damaging fact has come into limelight. The Pakistani officers have also established links with the 20-odd pro-Khalistani Sikhs now based in Chittagong. There are about ten army deserters amongst the group, who slipped out of their units after "Operation Bluestar" and made it to Bangladesh. One Subedar Balbir Singh is said to be leading the pro-Khalistan group.

So far it was established that the US, China, Pak, etc., were actively supporting the pro-Khalistan movement. The support extended by Bangladesh to this movement is a new phenomenon which has to be analysed very carefully by the centre. The TNV-Khalistan alliance in league with the USA, China, Pakistan and Bangladesh has created a new threat to India's integrity.

There is no doubt that the TNV charter of demands is nothing but IMV (Its Masters' Voice) from abroad. The Centre should be vigilant against such forces and their machinations.

2387. Chinese insurgency in India. *New Wave* 18 Jan 1987 ; 1, 11.

2388. Condit, D. M. *et. al.* : *Counter-insurgency bibliography*. Washington, American University 1963.

2389. Conley, Michael C. : Strategy of Communist-directed insurgency and the conduct of counter-insurgency. *Naval War College Review* 21 9) 1969 ; 73-79.

2390. Hutchinson, S. : Police role in counter-insurgency operation. *Royal United Services Institution Journal* 114 (656) Dec 1969.

2391. Insurgencies : Once more, violence in the hills. (in India). *Asiaweek* 13 Jul 1986 ; 20.

2392. Insurgency and CPM's dilemma. *New Wave* 11 Jan 1987 ; 5.

2393. Khurshid, Salman : Politics of insurgency. *Delhi Recorder* Aug 1985 ; 14-16.

2394. Kitson, Frank : *Low intensity operations : Subversion, insurgency, peace-keeping* London, Faber and Faber, 1972.

2395. Leites, Nathan and Charles Wolf : *Rebellion and authority : An analytic essay on insurgent conflicts* Chicago, Markham Publishing 1970. Pp. 174.

2396. Long, David E. : *Persian Gulf.* Boulder, Westview, 1976.

2397. Maoists hand in NE insurgency. *Hindustan Times* 28 Jan 1987 ; 8.

2398. Mohan Ram : Tense tribal tract : Separatist Nagas and Mizos remain restive. *Far Eastern Economic Review* 19 Dec 1985 ; 29.

2399. Molnar, Andrew R. : *Human factors considerations of undergrounds in insurgencies.* Washington, SORO, American University, 1966.

2400. O'Neill, Bard E *et al. eds* : *Insurgency in the Modern World.* Boulder, Westview Press, 1980. Pp. 291.

2401. O'Neill, Bard E. : Insurgency : A framework for analysis. In *IMW* ; 1-44.

It is hardly an exaggeration to suggest that a good deal of conceptual confusion obtains in the existing corpus of literature on internal political violence. In large part, this is due to the lack of agreement on the definitions of major terms such as insurgency, revolution, guerrilla warfare, terrorism, protracted struggle, and the like. As a result, it is not uncommon to find these terms used imprecisely, indiscriminately, and, at times, interchangeably,

In view of this unhappy situation and the problems it engenders for those interested in the systematic study of internal political violence, it is imperative that the principal concepts employed in our comparative analysis of insurgency be defined as carefully as possible. Accordingly, we begin by addressing the meaning of insurgency, its *relationship to the political system, and six types of insurgency.* Thereafter, we turn to a commentary on the political resources and forms of warfare the insurgents utilize. Once the discussion of terminology is completed, we are ready to proceed to the principal foci of the framework for analysis : the variables that have a major bearing on the outcomes of insurgent conflicts, and insurgent strategies.

Insurgency can be defined as a struggle between a non-ruling group and the ruling authorities in which the former consciously employs political resources (organizational skills, propaganda, and/or demonstrations) and instruments of violence to establish legitimacy for some aspect of the political system it considers illegitimate. Legitimacy and illegitimacy refer to whether or not existing aspects of politics are considered moral or immoral (or, to simplify, right or wrong) by the population or selected elements therein. For our purposes politics is defined as the process of making and executing binding decisions for a society; therefore, all behaviour associated with this enterprise comprises the "political system." On a general level the major components of the system may be identified as : the political community, the regime, the authorities, and policies. Any or all of these may be considered immoral by insurgents, and it makes a great deal of difference precisely which one is at stake.

The political community consists of those who accept interacting together in a situation where binding decisions will be made for all. In the contemporary international system this is, for the most part, equivalent to the nation-state. On this very basic point, violent conflict may result from considerations of legitimacy. The current uprising in the Eritrean sector of Ethiopia is illustrative here since the insurgents reject any notion that they should be an integral part of Ethiopia. Consequently, the Eritreans have sought through violent means to separate themselves from existing arrangement and to etablish a separate political community. In the United States, Great Britain, France, and Japan, by contrast, there is a general acceptance of the morality of the political community rooted in common history, tradition, and language.

Where a consensus on the morality of the political community obtains, there may be other grounds for violent internal conflict. For instance, there can be considerable discord over the salient values and structures that provide the basic framework within which binding decisions and policies are made. Thus, while the Marxists in Afghanistan accepted the political community, they used violence to expunge the traditional political values and patrimonial structures of the regime in order to replace them with a system in which binding decisions would be made within the framework of a one-party regime, in which the value of equality would replace ascriptive values that reflect private and aristocratic interests.

On another level some groups may grant legitimacy to the regime but reject the specific individuals in power. This is exemplified by coups in which insurgents seize the key decision making offices without changing the regime of their predecessors. Besides the well-known Latin American cases of the 1950s, one could point to the 1970 overthrow of the Sultan of Oman, Said Bin Taimur, by his son Qabus in this regard.

Finally, violence may be used by non-ruling groups in an effort to change existing policies that they believe have prevented them from acquiring their fair share of the collective political and economic product. One example is the terminal phase of the recent insurgency in the Sudan, where the blacks in the south demanded a change in policies to enable them to obtain a greater share of the political and economic benefits in society. Another is provided by the periodic attempts by Muslim and Druse elements in Lebanon to redress the perceived mal-distribution of political and economic assets that clearly favours the Christian community.

The important thing to remember up to this point is that insurgency is essentially a political legitimacy crisis of some sort. The first task of the analyst, therefore, is to ascertain exactly what the issue is. In seeking an answer to this question, it is useful to carefully examine the articulated long term aims of the insurgents.

By focussing on the ultimate goal of the insurgents and relating it to the aspects of politics discussed above, one can identify six types of insurgent movements : secessionist. revolutionary, restorational, reactionary, conservative, and reformist. Secessionist insurgents, such as the aforementioned Eritreans in Ethiopia, reject the existing political community of which they are formally a part ; they seek to withdraw from it and constitute a new autonomous political community. Revolutionary insurgents seeks to impose a new regime based on egalitarian values and centrally controlled structures designed to mobilize the people and radically transform the social structure within an existing political community (e.g., Marxist insurgents). While restorational insurgents also seek to displace the regime, the values and structures they champion are identified with a recent political order. In this case the values are ascriptive and elitist while the structures are oligarchical caes that have little or no provisions for mass participation in politics. The national Front for the Rescue of Afghanistan and Sultan Ali Mirrah's Afar Liberation Front in the Haoussa region of Ethiopia are contemporary manifestations of this type. Historical examples are provided by noncommunist partisans in Europe during World War II. Although reactionary insurgents likewise seek to change the regime by reconstituting a past political order, their destination relates to an idealized, golden age of the distant past in which religious values and authoritarian structures were predominant. The Moslem Brotherhood in Egypt and other Arab countries, which seeks to recreate the flowering Islamic society of centuries ago, is a case in point. Conservative insurgents, on the other hand, seek to maintain the existing regime in the face of pressures on the authorities to change. it. This type of insurgent movement was exemplified in the early 1970s by Protestant organizations in Ulster that wished to retain the regime in Northern Ireland that they saw as threatened by the Irish Republican Army, Catholic moderates, the Irish Republic, and "British capitulationists". Finally, reformist insurgents. such as the Kurds in Iraq and the Anayanya guerrillas in the southern Sudan, have attempted to obtain more political, social, and economic benefits without necessarily rejecting the political community, regime, or authorities. They are primarily concerned with policies that are considered discriminatory.

2402. Paget, Julian : *Counter-insurgency compaigning.* London, 1967.

2403. Pardesi, Ghanshyam : North-east : No end to insurgency. *Indian Nation* 28 Nov 1986 ; 4.

2404. Pustay, John W. : *Counter insurgency Warfare.* New York, Free Press, 1966.

2405. Pye, Lucian W. : Roots of insurgency and the commencement of rebellions. In *Internal War.* Ed. by Harry Eckstein. London, 1964 ; 157-79.

2406. Sengupta, Prasun : Internal security : Effective steps to counter insurgency. *Daily* 10 Jan 1987 ; 8-9.

2407. Silverman, Jerry M and Peter M. Jackson : Terror in insurgency warfare. *Military Review* Oct 1970 ; 62-64.

2408. Sinha, P. B. : Afghan insurgency and drug trafficking. *Strategic Analysis* Jul 1982 ; 226-30.

2409. Sinha, P. B. : Insurgency in Afghanistan : Problems and prospects. *Strategic Analysis* Feb 1979 ; 392-98.

2410. Solarz, Stephen J. : When to intervene. *Foreign Policy* (63) Sum 1986 ; 20-39.

2411. Thompson, Robert : *Defeating communist insurgency.* New York Prayer, 1970.

2412. Wilkinson, Anthony R. : *Insurgency in Rhodesia, 1957-73 : An account and assessment.* London, International Institute for Strategic Studies ; 1973.

2413. Zawoony, J. K. : How to capture a city by insurgency and how to combat insurgents fighting for such a city : Two combat reports from World War II. *Terrorism* 3 (1-2) 1979; 147-56.

Intelligence Agencies

2414. Berman, Jerry J. *et. al. ed.* : *Abuse of the intelligence agencies.* Washington, 1975.

2415. Cooper, H. H. A. : Terrorism and the intelligence function. In *ITCW*; 287-96. *Chitty's Law Journal* 24 (3) Mar 1976.

Terroristic activities are planned and organized by small, highly protective groups in the highest degree of secrecy they can attain. The illegality of their activities is unquestionable and their purposes are to inflict damage in human and material terms, to create disorder and panic with a view to affecting the normal workings of society. Before any action at all can be taken against such persons, there is a need to know who they are and what they are doing, and to relate it to what may be known of their earlier activities. Here we come up against what might be called the intelligence mystique. Those engaged in these functions logically have to collect a great deal of information, by a variety of techniques, much of which will be quite valueless for strict law-enforcement purposes. This part of the intelligence operation might be compared with panning for gold or mining diamonds from Kimberly Lode. The problem is what to do with the dross.

It should be borne in mind that terrorists do not, generally, advertise themselves before the event ; they hide, they masquerade, they put up a false front. It is part of the War of the Flea tc hop and hide and cause the authorities to scratch and to treat as fleas those who are not and thereby cause all to become uncomfortable. There has been a massive attack on all intelligence gathering in the United States during the past few years as part of the post-Watergate syndrome and the general public disquiet over "dirty tricks." There has been a wholesale dismantling of the intelligence-gathering apparatus of many law-enforcement agencies and an indiscriminate purging of much vital information which is now wholly lost to those entrusted with the tactical responses to terrorism. This has seriously impeded law-enforcement efforts in a number of important cases. Law enforcement has, naturally, become very sensitive to these issues and much misguided effort has been directed at embarrassing the intelligence community still further. It is not difficult to see how this has enabled the flea not only to survive but to multiply. The terrorist can only be detected by a proper use of diligent and sophisticated intelligence. Just as the law-abiding have learnt to accept for their own better protection the inconvenience of standing in line at airports to be searched, we must all be prepared to allow these instructions in order that the terrorist be discovered before the Slaughter of the Innocents.

Here we start to tread upon more controversial ground. We enter the realm of the informer, the police spy, and undercover activities of a wide and ingenious nature designed to attack and break up these movements before they can cause harm. That great tactician of the urban guerrilla movement, Carlos Marighella, has said :

> The urban guerrilla lives in constant danger of the possibility of being discovered or denounced. The chief security problem is to make certain that we are well hidden and well guarded, and that there are secure methods to keep the police from locating us or our whereabouts. The worst enemy of the urban guerrilla and the major danger we run in infiltration into our organization by a spy or an informer. The spy trapped within the organization will be punished to death. The same goes for those who desert and inform the police.

2416. Kerstetter, Waryne A. : Terrorism and intelligence. *Terrorism* 3 (1-2) 1979 ; 109-16.

2417. Mackenzie, Norman I. *ed.* : *Secret societies.* London, Aldus Books, 1967.

2418. May, Ernest R. *ed.* : *Knowing one's enemies : Intelligence : Assessment before the two world wars.* Princeton, 1984. Pp. 574.

2419. Sinha, M.K. : Intelligence, not guns : Only way of tackling terrorism. *Statesman* 2 Sep 1985 ; 6.

Kidnapping

2420. Alves, Marcio Moreira : Kidnapped diplomats ! Greek tragedy in a Latin State. *Commonweal* 92, 26 Jun 1970 ; 311-14.

2421. Baumann, Carol *ed.* : *Diplomatic kidnappings : A revolutionary tactics of urban terrorism.* Hague, Martinius Hijhoff, 1973.

2422. Cassidy, Anthony A. : Lloyd's Kidnap/ransom insurance. *Risk Management* Sep 1976.

2423. Clutterbuck, Richard : *Kidnap and ransom : the response.* London Faber & Faber, 1978.

2424. Clutterbuck, Richard : Management of the kidnap risk. *Terrorism* 5 (1-2) 1981 ; 125-37.

2425. Cooper, H.H.A. : Terrorist and his victim. *Victimology* 1, 1976 : 229-39.

2426. Cornwell, Rupert : Kidnapping—the peculiarity Italian crime. *Financial Times* 14 Nov 1979.

2427. Dortzbach, Karl and Debbie : *Kidnapped.* New York, Harper & Row, 1975.

2428. Fattah. E.A. : Use of the victim as an agent of self-legitimation *Victimology* 1, 1976 ; 29-53.

2429. Jackson, Geoffrey : *People's prison* London. Faber and Faber, 1972.

2430. Jackson, Geoffrey : *Surviving the long night.* New York, 1973.

2431. Kidnapping terrorists ? *International Herald Tribune* 16 Jun 1986 ; 6.

2432. Means, J. : Political kidnappings and terrorism. *North American Review* Win 1970.

2433. Murphy, John F. : Protected persons and diplomatic facilities. In *LAIT* ; 277-340.

A variety of security controls for the protection of diplomats have been introduced unilaterally by national governments. In some cases diplomats have permanent bodyguards riding with them in their limousines or following them in trailing vehicles. Embassy and consulate staffs have been reduced in size to lessen the potential number of targets.

In other cases, unnecessary travel has been eliminated and essential trips have been shrouded in secrecy. To keep potential terrorists off balance, work hours have been switched and staggered on a daily basis.

Similarly, embassy limousines, equipped with oversize rearview mirrors for travel in convoys, have been employed to pick up entire staffs from their homes, deliver them to the mission, and return them home after work. This technique has run into difficulty in congested urban areas, where convoy groupings can easily become separated. Efforts have also been made to reduce diplomatic visibility, such as the removal of diplomatic license plates from cars and the use of smaller and less ostentatious vehicles. Some diplomatic personnel carry arms, although others regard this as dangerous and provocative to terrorists. Security measures for U.S. diplomats have reportedly been carried to such an extreme in places like Nicosia, Beirut, and Buenos Aires that U.S. embassies there resemble fortresses.

The U.S. government has also become increasingly concerned with the security of foreign missions located in Washington and New York. According to the Department of State, from January to October 1971 ; 79 major documented incidents against foreign diplomatic, consular and semi-official officers and personnel occurred in the United States. These incidents were a prime motivating factor in the State Department's support of the 1972 legislation and the establishment of a 700-man Executive Protective Service set up to increase security for diplomats in the Washington area.

During the early 1970s the security of foreign missions to the United Nations and that of their personnel became an issue in the wake of numerous attacks on mission premises (especially those of the USSR and Eastern European countries) and on individual diplomats. In response to charges from some member states that security measures at the missions were inadequate, the United States described in detail steps taken under federal and state law by federal and New York City authorities to provide security for the missions. At the conclusion of discussions on the subject, the United Nations secretariat summarized proposals for improved security that various member states had submitted. These included, *inter alia,* :

1. extending the federal ban on picketing and demonstrating before foreign missions from a distance of 100 to 500 feet in order to bring it into accord with the situation in the District of Columbia;
2. 24-hour police protection, employing special guards, if

necessary, or, at a minimum, the use of additional guards who would participate in frequent but irregularly timed patrols;

3. the introduction of electronic surveillance systems such as security alarm systems ;

4. the creation of special security zones with notices stating that the premises are the object of special police protection ;

5. more intensive education of the public regarding the principle of diplomatic inviolability.

Partly in response to these suggestions, the Secret Service has reportedly created 23 additional fixed posts at U.N. missions in New York, and Congress has enacted legislation that extends the protection of the Executive Protection Service to foreign diplomatic missions located in metropolitan areas other than the District of Columbia where there are 20 or more such missions headed by full-time career officers, and that increases the maximum number of EPS officers from 850 to 1200. The secretary of the treasury may utilize, on a reimbursable basis and with their consent, the services, personnel, equipment, and facilities of state and local governments. No more than $ 3.5 million is authorized to be appropriated for purposes of reimbursement for any fiscal year, and is to remain available as provided in appropriation acts.

Most recently, the Soviet Union has complained to the Committee on Relations with the United States as Host Country about a series of demonstrations at the Soviet Mission to the United Nations by people carrying placards saying "Russian Blood in the Streets of New York" and "Seize Soviet Diplomats as Hostages" and about several violent attacks against Soviet diplomatic facilities, responsibility for which has been claimed by an underground group called the Jewish Armed Resistance. In response to these attacks, U.S. embassy officials and their families in the Soviet Union have also come under harassment.

In committee debate, the Soviet delegate charged that the harassment of Russian officials in New York was increasing because U.S. authorities had not taken effective countermeasures and, in spite of advanced criminal detection methods, had failed to find the guilty persons. William M. Scranton, the U.S. ambassador to the United Nations, responded by reporting that additional police security measures had been arranged for Soviet facilities and that intensive investigations were being conducted by the New York police and federal authorities. He also reported that the 1972 amendments to the federal law concerning the protection of diplomats were being re-examined to determine whether the display of placards with inflammatory calls for violence would constitute an offence under that law.

2434. Namruddin, D. : Kidnappings of diplomatic personnel. *Police Chief* 40, Feb 1973.

2435. O'Mara, Richard : New terror in Latin America : Snatching the diplomats. *Nation* 210(17) 1970 ; 518-19.

2436. Palmer, G. : *Kidnapping in the South seas, being a narrative of the cruise of H.M.S. Rosario.* Edinburgh. 1971.

2437. Paust, Jordan J. : Nonprotected persons or things. In *LAIT* ; 341-96.

One of the problems of implementing criminal sanctions concents acts of terrorism that produce a terror outcome by threats of violence, without actual physical injury to any human or non-human target. Criminal lawyers might view this problem through legalistic lenses framed by concepts of attempt, assault, and conditional assault, and the penalties, if any, might be conditioned upon such a focus. Standard criminal law treatises advise that "threatening words alone, without any overt act to carry out the threat" will not create the crime of assault. Take, for example, a situation where a terrorist group phones a person to inform him that his family will be bombed if he does not support the terrorist objectives. Many criminologists may find that there has been no crime of assault because there is no overt act to carry out the threat. Intimidation may create criminal responsibility in some states if a felony is involved, which is highly likely in the case of threats of violence, but state and federal law can be supplemented to include a specific offence of terrorism to meet this and other problems (e.g. degrees of penalty and gravity of demonstrated concern). The following discussion shows how this might be possible.

Legislative efforts to create a crime of terrorism, at the international or state level, should include a definition that realistically mirrors the terror process. An effort to punish terroristic conduct by using an overly broad definitional or jurisdictional focus (viz. as simply murder, attempted murder, threats, or assault) is unwise and unworkable in the long run. At the national level, an attempt to prosecute as "terrorism" many types of conduct that produce no actual terror outcome would seem politically and functionally unwise and constitutionally unsound. A generally accepted definition of terrorism required an element of "terror" and a coercive purpose.

Due process required some minimal connection between criminal distinction and reality. Furthermore, any legislative draft should mirror expectation and fact. The alternative is to regulate activity without attaching the term "terrorism" to the legislative provision. But any definition of terrorism should mirror expectation about "terrorism," or else constitutional restraints on the criminal sanction may be compounded by popular expectations. As social scientists are becoming increasingly aware, the effective implementation of law requires some deference to common expectation in the community. Overly broad definitions or criminal enactments against conduct that cannot be properly viewed as "terrorism" could reduce respect for authority and undermine attempts at prohibiting such conduct. This would be contrary to the goal of preventing and deterring terrorism. Legislative or executive pronouncements, for example, that characterize conduct or attitudes that "damage the interests of a state" as impermissible forms of "terrorism" are unrealistic and may also isolate the "state" from new attitudes, beliefs, or change by any means.

International and domestic political effects may also thwart the overall goals by overly broad prescriptions against terrorism. Attempts by certain state elites to control nearly all counter-attitudes and behavior in the name of antiterrorism may be a greater threat to law, authority, and human rights than most forms of terrorism. This type of legislative or executive control can lead opposition groups to feel less restrained in using any means appropriate to serve their ends. Furthermore, overly broad state attempts can control conditions and attitudes in at least two negative ways : (1) towards an undermining of governmental authority due to the belief that the government has gone too far ; and (2) toward an acceptance of terrorism by recognizing that power seems to take precedence over "law". Again, state responses are ideologically and politically significant.

2438. Poulantzas, Nicholas : Some problems of international law connected with urban guerrilla warfare : The kidnapping of members of diplomatic missions, consular offices and other foreign personnel. *Annals of International Studies* 3, 1972 137-67.

2439. Sinuon, Douglas W *et. al.* : *Simulation of the seizure of heads of state.* Drew University Jan 1977, (Mimeographed.)

2440. Simons, Marlise : Foreign demand for babies spurs kidnappings. *Nagpur Times* 29 Dec 1985 ; 5.

2441. Torture, kidnapping still rife. *Patriot* 6 Feb 1987 ; 7.

2442. Vayrynen, Raimo : Some aspects of theory and strategy of kidnapping. *Instant Research on Peace and Violence* 1, 1971.

Legal Aspects

2443. Bishop, Joseph W. : Legal measures to control terrorism in democracies. In *ITCR* 294-306.

2444. Crelinsten, Ronald D. *et. al.* : *Terrorism and criminal justice.* Lexington Books, 1978.

2445. Evans, Alona E and J.F. Murphy *eds.* : *Legal aspects of international terrorism.* New York, American Society of International Law, 1978.

2446. Galor, Noemi : Central legal issues concerning the suppression of terrorism. In *International cooperation to suppress terrorism.* London, Croom Helms 1985 ; 121-74.

2447. Green, L.C. : Legalization of terrorism. In *TTP* ; 175-200.

2448. Hall, George : Terrorism : International law isn't the answer. *International Herald Tribune* 18 Dec 1984 ; 6.

2449. Kapetanonic, Goran : International terrorism—Legal and political aspects. *Review of International Affairs* 5-20 Jul 1985.

2450. Kumar, S.R. : Terrorism and the law. *Searchlight* (Patna) 6 Apr 1986 ; II.

2451. Livingstone, Neil C. and Terrell E. Arnold. : Court action not words, needed to fight terrorism. *International Herald Tribune* 21-22 Dec 1985 ; 4.

2452. Moore, John Norton : Toward legal restraints on international terrorism. *Proceedings, American Society of International Law* 67, 1983.

2453. Murphy, John F. : Introdution : Legal aspects of international terrorism. *Terrorism* 7(2) 1984 ; 119-22.

2454. Murphy, John F. : International legal controls of international terrorism : Performance and prospects. *Illinois Bar Journal* 63, Apr 1975.

2455. Murphy, John F.: Legal controls and the deterrence of terrorism : Performance and prospects. *Rutgers Law Journal* 13, 1982.

2456. Pal, B.K. : Terrorism and law. *Mainstream* 17 May 1986 ; 29-30 ; 34.

2457. Pande, D.C. : National law : The lumpen element. *World Focus* (New Delhi) (74) Feb 1986 ; 3-6.

Terrorism is a word coined by society to deplore a particular kind of political violence that lies wholly outside accepted conventions of warfare. The term is most frequently used to describe revolutionary violence, but established governments are certainly no strangers to the systematic terrorizing of entire populations.

The aim is to destroy the morale of a nation ; the method is the random murder of innocent people. Randomness is the distinctive trait. Harm must come by chance to unremarkable men and women, whether Americans of Britons or Jews, simply because of their nationality, religion or political affiliation. They must feel themselves fatally exposed, and demand that their governments negotiate for their safety.

Since medieval times, philosophers have recognized the distinction between jus ad bellum, the justice of war, and jus in bello, justice in war. Terrorism is more a civilian strategy than what we commonly call war, but the distinction remains meaningful in this area as well. The moral reality of war is divided into two logically independent parts. We make judgments about the broader issues of aggression and self-defense ; but, employing a separate calculus, we make judgements about the observance or violation of the customary and positive rules of engagement.

2458. Saksena, N.S. : Way to pose law and order questions. *Times of India* 11 Sep 1985 ; 8.

2459. Sharma, Surya P. : International law : Consensus still elusive. *World Focus* (74) Feb 1986 ; 7-10.

The occurrence, with dramatic rapidity, of terrorist activity transcending national boundaries is a grave challenge to humanity at large. With increase in aerial hijacking, bomb explosions in aircraft and at airports, attack on diplomatic, missions, kidnapping of diplomats and the possible threat of nuclear terrorism, the situation has reached a saturation point. The current situation highlights the urgency for legal regulation of international terrorism.

Since the acceleration of international terrorism from the late sixties onwards, the international legal process has adopted important measures in the direction of formulating legal rules and policies. These efforts have been manifested in newly formulated treaty law to regulate specific forms of international terrorism and in efforts of international authorities to energise traditional legal institutions of general international law in order to tackle the problem of international terrorism. It will be useful to examine the main trends of the growing contribution of international law to the combating of international terrorism.

International efforts to combat terrorism began soon after World War I, as there was in upsurge an terrorist activities. A series of international conferences for the unification of penal law were convened under the auspices of the International Association of Penal Law, and the third to sixth of such conferences held between 1931 and 1935 specifically considered the issue of terrorism and adopted appropriate texts. The term "terrorism", explicitly employed for the first time in the Third International Conference held in Brussels, was spelled out as "the deliberate use of means capable of producing a common danger" to commit "an act of imperilling life, physical integrity or human health or threatening to destroy susbtantial property". The list of such acts included arson ; explosion ; flooding or submersion ; ignition or asphyxiating or noxious substances ; interruption of the normal operation of means of transport or communication ; damage to or destruction of government property and public utilities ; pollution, fouling, or deliberate poisoning of drinking water or staple foods, causing or propagating contagious or epidemic diseases, any wilful act which endangers human lives and the community and so on.

2460. Sliwowski, George : Legal aspects of terrorism. In *ITWS* ; 69-77.

International terrorism is a phenomenon which has been much in evidence in modern times. Its features, its essence and its origins are complicated. Later we will try to analyse these aspects in more detail. Here it is appropriate to mention only that acts of terrorism are often linked by their authors with wars or movements of liberation. This creates problems for international lawyers. In every case we must distinguish two strategies of terrorism : that involving acts directed against specific enemies and that involving acts directed against persons extraneous to the conflict. On the face of it. the latter have every right in international law to be left in peace and thus in such circumstances no terrorist would seem to be entitled to claim immunity from punishment on the grounds that he is engaged in a just liberation struggle. But only an International Criminal Court is likely to be able to resolve the complicated problems involved.

The problem of terrorism has concerned criminal and international lawyers for more than one hundred years. The first important sign of such interest was the well-known 'Brussels Clause" of 1856. Its origin lay in a series of attempts on the lives of heads of states and their families. This clause was narrowly concerned with the problem of extradition. It still retains validity and remains of great importance.

In the field of criminality there remain of course several offences, whose existence we acknowledge but for which it is very difficult to provide a precise legal definition. This problem has arisen, for example, in countries which have sought to combat 'hooliganism'. And this same difficulty evidently applies to terrorism. For all the attempts to establish a legal definition of this phenomenon have more or less failed ; and it is indeed quite possible that we may never establish such a definition with any legal precision. Different reasons for this may be cited. But optimists would stress the relatively novel character of the offence and hence argue that the scientific analysis of the problem of international terrorism is in itself a form of progress, if so far without great practical results.

It is obvious that terrorism involves the spreading of fear by threats to a large part of the population as a means of realising their goals. Terrorism may be carried out in various ways and each way has its own peculiar significance. Such operations may include the elimination of certain persons ; or the kidnapping of certain persons ; or the seizure of valuable objects. The aim is to compel individuals and ultimately states to adopt a certain manner of conduct.

In spite of their different characteristics terrorist activities have some common features. In almost all cases the terrorists are seeking their goals by spreading fear and by undermining confidence in accepted human values. Often among the specific goals are : a change in the head of state ; or a change in the direction of current policy ; or a change in the political regime ; or the liberation of arrested persons ; or the payment of a ransom. But all these specific acts are designed exlusively to further a general strategic goal, the 'social goal', which the terrorists acknowledge as the principal aim of their activity. This 'social goal' distinguishes terrorist acts from similar or identical acts by ordinary criminals.

The character of terrorist methods has been subject, however, to some evolution. In particular, in recent times the main accent has been placed on jeopardising general security, while the destruction of particular targets seems to be in decline. This of course does not imply that the elimination of individuals is no longer even considered by terrorists. It signifies only that a general threat is in the majority of cases quite sufficient to achieve at least the tactical goals of terrorists—a proposition which has been totally vindicated in practice. Individual persons, organisations, public authorities and even states have often surrendered in the face of terrorist threats, thereby rendering other measures such as homicide and destruction of property unnecessary. Human fear and insecurity have then been demonstrated to be more successful and useful in promoting the aims of terrorists than the acts of destruction. Obviously this phenomenon has been linked to the great advances in means of communication and the growth of mass media.

LETTER BOMBS

2461. Letter bombs : In *WTAZIT* ; 36-37.

Liberation Movements

2462. Attar Chand : Terrorism : A bird's eye view. *Indian Nation* 24 Jan 1974 ; 4.

2463. Graham, Gordon : Terrorism and freedom fighters. *Philosophy and Social Action* Oct-Dec 1985.

2464. Gupta, Vijay : Liberation movements : the means of violence. *World Focus* (74) Feb 1986 ; 14-18.

LITERATURE

2465. Gros, Bernard : Terrorism and literature. In *ITCW* ; 447-53.

In Modern Times (Sartre's periodical), in November of 1972, a certain Christian Zimmer reviewed an American film by Gordon Davidson "The Most Beautiful Day of Our Lives". Zimmer praised the theme of the film, that is, the re-enactment of the trial of nine citizens who had the files of the Catonsville recruitment office as a protest against the war in Vietnam. He also praised the production and then came to what he called the weakness of the film. They show us—this is essentially what he said—defendants who are after all reincorporated into the capitalist system ; they fall into the trap which consists of accepting trial and the legal system. What, according to our brilliant journalist, should have happened ? The film should have shown us violence—and I quote : "Everything would have doubtlessly been different, if they had not been content with an illegal action, one which did not imperil the authorities, and if they had had recourse to violence (illegality simulates violence). In short, 'The Most Beautiful Day of Our Lives' illuminates the insufficiency of protests which do not include the necessity of personal, individual violence, that is, they are divested of ideologies, acquired beliefs, accepted principles. . . ."

The second example is a newspaper commentary concerning the criminal arson of a school in Paris in February of 1973. Briefly, here are the facts : Some youngsters had set fire to their school, which burned rapidly and caused the death of some twenty children. This is the commentary which appeared in the newspaper Combat under the byline of Rene Scherer :

> These children affirmed themselves by taking vengeance for the meanness and humiliating constraints they suffer each day. Their gesture has obviously nothing to do with ordinary murder. It is rigorously confined : a symbol of exasperated protest against an institution where, as a matter of principle, the child can never take the initiative, be enterprising, or speak up, where the child dies from lack of social responsibility.

As far as I am concerned, those who died are the children caught in the fire, innocent victims of what I call in my book terrorism by imitation.

The final example concerns the murder of some diplomats, including an American charge d'affaires, George Moore, in Khartoum by Palestinian commandos. The journalist and "catholic" writer, Jean-Marie Domenach, wrote in Le Monde on March 4 and 5, 1973 :

> Perhaps the spread of terrorism will result in leading us to an examination of our individual political responsibilities. Also. . . . . we should consider that terrorism denounces the generalized immobility of societies and institutions, both national and international. . . . . . Technical proliferation is paid for by immobilization and the reduction of other factors in human development. . . . . . If, tomorrow, anyone can become a target for believers in a cause which he despises or is ignorant of, this is a sign that no one can henceforth escape his responsibility in deciding which world order is to die and which one it is urgent to create. . . . . . .

We should, as we say in France, make a scrupulous explication of these three texts, that is, a commentary in which each word would be studied and illuminated by the total context. I cannot do that there and therefore must take recourse in the more expeditious : I wonder how literature has reached the point of praising crimes which the entire world detests ?

It was Albert Camus who supplied the first answer to this question when he wrote in The Fall (1956) : "The Truth is that every intelligent man. . . . . . dreams of being a gangster and of reigning over society through violence alone. As that is not quite as easy as reading novels might lead one to believe, one generally has recourse to politics and joins the cruelest party." Oh well, I guess that's how it is, Literary terrorism is a sort of aggressive dream ; it is the manifestation of mental imperialism. It is also, doubtlessly, an attempt to come to terms with a neurosis. Every intellectual is an unquiet soul, tormented by the absolute, who bears, only with difficulty, the given order of the world. To write about terrorism, to write in favour of terrorism, is in some way to enter into a fantastic world which, at least in appearance. offers escape from the everyday. It is—in dream or in thought, it's all the same—to go from nothing to everything, to live the event in a sort of verbal orgasm, to allow oneself to play out sadistic or masochistic fantasies. It is to "make a habit of the unusual," as Paul Virilio, one of the intellectuals most excited by May 1968, said (in Common Cause, no. 2, 1972). The petty hoodlum chooses, as the locale for this terrorism by imitation, Saturday night dances, subway corridors or nightclubs ; the writer chooses a sheet of paper.

2466. Winegarten, Rence : Literary terrorism. *Commentary* (New York) 57 (3) Mar 1974 ; 58-65.

MASS MEDIA

2467. Aggarwal. A.K. : Press and the terrorism. *Security Controls* (New Delhi) 1 (2) Nov 1986 ; 11-13.

Is Press responsible for the increasing terrorism ? Has Indian Press cooperated with the respective authorities in preventive acts of terrorism ? To a large extent, it has acted with considerable restraint in the interest of safety and security.

Who is Jinda ? Ask anyone in Punjab or Haryana or Delhi or Maharashtra. He or she knows who Jinda is ! Why ? Is Jinda as important as the Prime Minister of India ? or a Chief Minister ? Or a prominent opposition leader ? None, of course. Then what is Jinda famous or notorious for ? One word answer is :

"TERRORISM". But is he so well known because of his terrorist activities or is the "excessive" media projection that has made him a celbrity ? The answer is somewhere between the two extremes.

This raises an important issue. What is the role of the media in abetting or combating terrorism ? Since radio and television, though becoming increasingly popular, especially the latter, are under total control of the Government, the discussion here is confined to the Press only i.e. role of the Press in abetting or combating terrorism.

In the West, media has come in for much official criticism for its role vis-a-vis terrorism. Abraham H Miller, a specialist on political violence, says terrorism is the media's stepchild. Walter Lequeur thinks media is "a terrorists best friend". Paul Johnson, a noted British writer and historian, holds that without the collaboration of the mass media, terrorism would be important. IMH Smart accused media of assisting terrorists at every step. Smart writes in the International Journal that the media informs the terrorist of his potential targets and reports his acts of violence, "according to him some apparent status, giving credibility to his subsequent menaces and communicating his achievements to his own constituency, inside or outside the country in which he acts." Frederick J Hacker believes that the mass media serves as "propaganda agent of terrorism". The Task Force on Disorders and Terrorism organised by the Department of Justice of the US Administration echoed Abraham Miller's allegation by saying. "In many ways the modern terrorist is the very creation of the media."

2468. Alexander, Yonah *Role of communications in the Middle East. Conflict*. New York, Prayer, 1973.

2469. Alexander, Yonah : Terrorism and the media : Some considerations. In *TTP* ; 159-75.

2470. Alexander, Yonah : Terrorism and the media : Some observations. *Terrorism* 3(3-4) 1980 ; 179-83.

2471. Alexander, Yonah and S.M. Finger : Terrorism and media. *Terrorism* 2 (1-2) 1979 ; 55-147.

2472. Ascherson, Neal : Grappling with terrorism : Media role in retrospect. *Newstime* 31 Jul 1985 ; 7.

2473. Baker, Robert K and Sandara J Ball : *Mass media and violence.* Washington, Government Printing Office, 1969.

2474. Barber, Benjamin R. : *Death of communal liberty : The history of freedom in a Swiss mountain Canton.* Princeton, 1974.

2475. Cherif Bassiouni, M. : Problems in media coverage of nonstate-sponsored terror-violence incidents. In *POT* ; 177-200.

2476. Chawla, N.L. : Terrorism, violence and media. *Mainstream* 20 Jul 1985 ; 7-34.

2477. Clutterbuck, Richard : Power to the people—media. In *Britain in agony.* London, Faber and Faber, 1978 ; 265-80.

2478. Code of terrorism : *Madhya Pradesh Chronicle* 3 Aug 1985 ; 4.

2479. Cooper, H.H.A. : Terrorism and the media. *Chitty's Law Journal* 34(7) Sep 1976 ; 226-32.

2480. Davidson, W. : Philips. *International political communication.* New York, Prayer, 1965.

2481. Decter, Midge : Need for clarity. In *ITCR* ; 242-44.

2482. Elkins, Michael : Caging the beasts. In *ITCR* ; 230-34.

I have been reporting from Israel for twenty three years. I have been deafened by the bomb and splattered by the blood, and believe me—I am not interested in political theologies or intellectual explorations.

The point is that the killers are loose in the world, and the first priority is to cage them. The esoterics can come later. What we need now is not more intellectual light on the subject, but more heat. We need to generate in the world passionate revulsion to terror ; and we need always and everywhere to deny them acceptance, to deny them dignity, and to deny them victory.

In this effort, in what ought to be this common cause, the media—press, radio, television—have in large measure abdicted their responsibilities, and have done so far reasons ranging from mistaken judgment to moral bankruptcy.

They have adapted and adopted the sour and sterile aphorism, "He is a terrorist, you are a guerilla. I am a freedom fighter," as though there were no criteria other than those reflecting personal predilection and political bias by which a terrorist may reasonably be identified and labelled as such, and by that label seen to be abhorrent.

I am not prepared automatically to define all liberation movements as "terrorist". I reject the concept that because terrorists call themselves "freedom fighter," we must call all freedom fighters terrorists. I cannot in simple decency condemn all use of violence as terrorist. One may not deny to oppressed people the weapon available when the ballot box is stolen and the democratic process does not exist. It we espouse such blanket denial, this Pavlovian reaction will separate us inevitably from oppressed peoples and will compel them to find their allies among the terrorists and only there. This cannot be useful to the struggle against terror.

But there are such criteria which, if not perfect, are at least reasonable and useful. The old adage; "by their actions you shall know them," still has a compelling logic. Those who take civilian hostages and kill them, or threatened to do so, are not guerrillas, or commandos or freedom-fighters. Within any reasonable judgment enabling democracy or even civilization to survive—they are terrorists. Those who put bombs in market places—are terrorists. Those who butcher children to death—are terrorists.

Within this context, it does not matter what their ultimate political purpose is—if such purpose they have. What matters is what they do, and if what they do is beyond the pale—well then, so are they.

I must mention the appalling truth that organized societies have engaged, and are still engaged and with increasing violence, upon the slaughter of the innocents and that this is not called terrorism, but war. It is true. It is appalling. And it is irrelevant to my argument. Because we are not able, or are not yet able, to banish all evil cannot mean that we must condone every evil.

The difficulty that the media have in identifying terrorist acts as such, and in holding their perpetrators up to public contempt, arises for the most part out of assumptions of "objectivity", and in some cases out of its opposite—an acknowledged "non-objectivity" that has gone askew.

2483. Epsteim, Edward C. : Uses of "terrorism". A study in media bias. *Stanford Journal of International Studies*. 12, Spr 1977 ; 67-78.

2484. Graham, Katharine : Media and terrorism. *International Herald Tribune* 10 Dec 1985 ; 5-6.

2485. Hacker, Frederick, J. : Terror and terrorism : Modern growth industry and mass entertainment. *Terrorism* 4 (1-4) 1980 ; 143-60.

2486. Heron, Paddy : Television's role in reporting Ulster Violence. *Harrongue* (Belfast) 1, Sum 1974.

2487. Mankekar, D.R. : Press and terrorism : Persistent dilemma. *Mainstream* 21 Sep 1985 ; 8-10.

2488. Mickolus, Edward F. : *Assessing the degrees of error in public reporting of transnational terrorism*. Washington, CIA ; 1976.

2489. Mosse, Hilde L. : Media and terrorism. In *ITCW* ; 282-86.

2490. P.M. (Rajiv Gandhi) : urged media to help fighting terrorism. *Indian Observer* Oct 1985 ; 29.

2491. Podhoretz, Norman : Subtle Collusion. In *ITCR* ; 235-41.

2492. Redlick, Amy Sands : Transnational flow of information as a cause of terrorism. In *ITP* ; 73-98.

2493. Saksena, N.S. : Terror and crude propaganda. In *THF* ; 114-15.

2494. Soustelle, Jacques : Liberty or license ? In *ITCR* ; 250-52.

2495. Sundar Rajan, K.R. : War on terrorism or press ? *Amrita Bazar Patrika* 13 Jun 1984 ; 6.

2496. Terraine, John *et. al.* : Terrorism and the media. In *RUSI. Ten Years of terrorism.* London, 1979.

2497. Wattenberg, Ben : Politics of freedom is the answer. In *ITCR* ; 245-49.

Medical Centres

2498. Attacks on hospitals. In *WTAZIT* ; 50-51.

Militarism

2499. Bagts, Alfred : *History of militarism, Civilian and military.* London, 1959.

2500. Bell, J. Bowyer : *Secret army* Cambridge, MIT Press, 1970.

2501. Mallin, Jay : Terrorism as a military weapon. In *ITCW*; 389-401.

Terrorism cannot be explained by psychologists who construct facile theories. It cannot be countered by police who view it as simply one more type of criminal activity : Identify the culprits, arrest them, throw them in prison, or perhaps shoot them, and the problem is solved. Nor can terrorism be handled by conventional military men who scoff at it as being beneath their notice. Even the academician who wishes to study terrorism dispassionately finds theories, explanations, and chronological statistics, but little else. Penetrating interviews with genuine terrorists, for example, are minimal in availability.

Terrorism is indeed a tangled skein, and any observer attempting to unravel and separate even one thread leaves himself open to criticism, justified criticism. For example, one might say terrorism is a military weapon. But what about the kidnappings solely for financial gain in Italy and the brigandage in Argentina motivated by monetary profit ?

Thus, the skein is a mess of threads ; it may not be possible to separate cleanly any one. Nevertheless, the effort is worth the attempt if it contributes even a pinpoint of light in what is certainly a long and dark tunnel. This discussion will attempt to focus on one thread : terrorism as a military weapon.

In September of 1972, the world as stunned to hear that the Twentieth Olympic Games, a symbol of international harmony, had been attacked by political terrorists. A group of urban guerrillas belonging to the Palestinian Black September movement had forced their way into the Israeli quarters at the Olympic site and seized nine hostages.

The guerrillas issued a number of demands, including one for the release of 200 Palestinian prisoners in Israel. Day-long negotiations took place between the guerrillas and the West German government, and eventually the government appeared to accede to the Palestinian demands. An accord was reached whereby the terrorists, together with their hostages, were to be taken to an airport and there provided with air transportation to Egypt. At Fuerstenfeldbruck Airport, however, German snipers opened fire on the terrorists, and in the resulting battle all Israeli hostages died, as well as four guerrillas, a police officer, and a helicopter pilot.

Thanks to the miracle of modern communications, people in many lands were kept abreast of developments minute by minute. Americans watched television in fascination as events unfolded before their eyes. When the final holocaust occurred at the German airport, shock, horror, and revulsion swept the civilized world.

The question was repeatedly asked, what did the Palestinians hope to gain by their action ? Did not the kidnappings—and the resultant killings—do their cause far more harm than good ? The actions of terrorists, however, cannot be measured in the way other acts of war or revolution are appraised. Urban guerrillas do not march to the same drummer as regular soldiers, or even rural guerrillas. Colonel William D. Neale (USA, ret.), the previously quoted observer stated :

> Terroristic violence must be totally ruthless, for moral scruples and terror do not mix and one or the other must be rejected. There can be no such thing as a weak dose of terror. The hand that controls the whip must be firm and implacable.

Although not generally viewed as such, the Olympic action was nevertheless fundamentally a military move. Having failed in four conventional wars to defeat the Israelis, the Arabs and Palestinians resorted to unconventional tactics—specifically, terrorism in the border zones and against Israeli installations in foreign lands. If the Arab leaders had not themselves been conventional, they might have utilized unconventional tactics much earlier—perhaps more successfully than their efforts to defeat the Israelis in "regular" warfare.

Basically, terrorism is a form of psychological warfare (frighten your enemy, publicize your cause). Seen within this context, the Olympic attack achieved its purpose. Kidnapping the Israeli athletes did not military harm to Israel. As a psychological blow, however, it probably boosted Palestinian morale and it certainly spotlighted world-wide the Palestinian cause. It encouraged future moves by Palestinian terrorists—the historical record attests to this. As a psychological blow, the Olympic attack demonstrated that wherever Israeli figures of prominence went abroad, whether they be diplomats or athletes or whatever, they were susceptible to terrorist attack.

War is armed conflict, and armed conflict is the province of the military. Terrorism is a form of armed conflict ; it is, therefore, within the military sphere. When diplomats fail, soldiers take over. When soldiers fail, terrorists take over. The political terrorist, however, is a soldier, too. He wears no uniform, he may have received little or no training, he may accept minimal discipline, his organization may be ephemeral—but he is a solider. He engaged in armed conflict in pursuit of a cause. His weapons are the gun and the explosive. His battlefield is the city street, and his targets are the vulnerable points of modern society.

Certainly not all terrorists are soliders, nor is all terrorism military. For our purposes, however, it is postulated that terrorism is military when :

1. It is utilized as a substitute for "regular" warfare, as in the case of the Palestinians against the Israelis.

2. It is used in conjunction with other military activities, as in the cases of Cuba (against Batista) and Vietnam (against the Saigon administrations).

3. It is used as the chosen weapon of conflict by a population segment against another segment and/or a foreign power, as in the case of Northern Ireland.

Terrorism is sometimes believed to be synonymous with urban guerrillas warfare. Urban guerrillas warfare, however, is a broader term : it encompasses urban terrorism but other actions as well, for example, street skirmishes, assaults on official installations, and other types of hit-and-run urban combat.

2502. Military might can never end terrorism. *Egyptian Gazette* 21 Apr 1986 ; 3.

2503. Sengupta, Prasun : Army's role in combating terrorism. *Daily* (Bombay) 4 Jun 1985 ; 10-11.

Multinationals

2504. Attali, J. *et.al.* : *Who's afraid of multinational—?* Brussels, 1978.

2505. Astapovich, A.Z. : *Strategy of transnational corporations.* Moscow. Progress, 1983. Pp. 287.

2506. Attar Chand : Develping countries and multinational corporations. *Industry and Economics.* (Bombay) February 1980 ; 49-52.

2507. Berger, Robert G. : Applying uniform margin requirements to foreign entities attempting to acquire U.S. Corporations. *Virginia Journal of International Law* 24(3) Spr 1984 ; 543-74.

2508. Bergsten. C. Fred *et. al.* : *American multinationals and American interests,* Washington, 1978.

2509. Bergsten, C. Fred : Coming investment wars ? *Foreign Affairs* 53(1) Oct 1974 ; 135-52.

2510. Bornschier, Volker : Multinational corporations in world system perspective. In *IAA* ; 241-46.

2511. Buckley, P. and M. Casson : *Future of the multinational enterprise* London, Macmillan, 1976.

2512. Cavanagh, John : Arms, multinational and foreign policy. *Economic and Political Weekly* 20(17) 27 April 1985 ; 753-55.

2513. Caves, R.E. : *Multinational enterprise and economic analysis* Cambridge, 1983.

2514. Chopra, V.D. : Penetration of US Capital. In *Pentagon Shadow Over India.* New Delhi, 1985 ; 16-32.

2515. Code for multinationals : *Amrita Bazar Patrika* (Calcutta) 21 June 1985 ; 6.

2516. Das, Madhuri : Dumping ground for multinationals. *Delhi Recorder* (New Delhi) June 1985 ; 74-77.

2517. Das, Nabagopal : Multinationals in India. *Amrita Bazar Patrika* (Calcutta) 9 Jan 1985 ; 6.

2518. Das, Tapan : American MNCs. Nazi Collusion. *Link* (New Delhi) 3 Feb 1985 ; 12.

2519. Datta, Pradip : Making MNCs acceptable in Third World. *Telegraph* (Calcutta) 9 Nov 1982 ; 9.

2520. Drucker, Peter F. : Multinationals and developing countries : Myths and realities. *Foreign Affairs* 53(1) Oct 1974 ; 121-34.

2521. Franko, L.G. : *European multinationals.* Stamford, Greylock Publishers, 1976.

2522. Franko, L.G. : Multinationals : The end of U.S. dominance. *Harvard Business Review* 56(2) Nov-Dec 1978.

2523. Franko, L.G. : *Threat of Japanese multinationals : How the West can respond.* New York, John Willey, 1983 Pp. 160.

2524. Freeman, O.L. : Testimonial for multinationals. *Mainstream* 20 March 1979.

2525. Girvan, N. : *Corporate imperialism : Conflict and expropriation.* New York, Monthly Review Press, 1976.

2526. Glynn, Leonard : *Multinationals in the world of nations.* New York, U.S. Council for International Business, 1983. Pp. 39.

2527. Gray, S.J. *et.al.* : *Information disclosure and the multinational corporation.* New York, Willey, 1984. Pp. 247.

2528. Hamilton, Geoffrey : International code of conduct for multinationals. *Multinational Business* (3) 1983 ; 1-10.

2529. Hanck, David etc. : *Two decades of debate the controversy over U.S. companies in South Africa.* Washington, 1983. Pp. 163.

2530. Harjinder Singh : TNCs exploit Namibia's resources. *Patriot* 27 May 1985 ; 4.

2531. Hodges, Michael : *Multinational corporations and national government.* Lexington. 1974. Pp. 307.

2532. Horowitz, Irving Louis : Transnational terrorism, civil liberties and social science. In *Terrorism* Ed. by Yonah Alexander and Seymour Maxwell Finger. New York, 1977 ; 283-97.

2533. Hutchinson, M.C. : Transnational terrorism and world politics. *Jerusalem Journal of International Relations* 1(2) Win 1975 ; 109-29.

2534. Kalia, Ravi : Multinational Corporations and the Third World. *India Quarterly* 38 (3-4) Jul-Dec 1982 ; 357-65.

2535. Kapoor, M.C. and Rajan Saxena : Taming the multinationals in India. *Journal of World Trade Law* 13, 1979 ; 170-78.

2536. Kaul, M.K. : Scientists (from India) worried over contract to multinationals. *Patriot* 29 Mar 1986 ; 1.

2537. Kindleberger, C.P. : *Multinational excursions.* Cambridge, MIT Press, 1984. Pp. 283.

2538. Lall, S. : *New Multinationals : The spread of Third World enterprises.* Chichester, John Willey, 1983. Pp. 278.

2539. Lall, Sanjaya and Sharif Mohammad : Multinationals in Indian big business. *Journal of Development Economics* (Holland) 13, 1983 ; 143-57.

2540. Lall, Sanjaya : Third World Multinationals : The Indian case. In South-South relations in a changing world. *Third World Quarterly* (Uppsala). 982.

2541. Levitt, Kari : *Silent surrender : The multinational Corporation in Canada* Toronto, 1970.

2542. Mann, Clarence J. : Personnel and property of transnational business operations. In *LAIT* ; 399-484.

While transnational business operations since World War II have contributed significantly to economic development in many parts of the world, they also have contributed to a growing conflict within host countries. In part, this conflict stems from the integrated global approach of transnational enterprises, whose priorities and mobility transcend national boundaries. Consequently, this impinges on the rising nationalism within many countries who fear that foreign investments threaten their sovereignty and enhance foreign dependence. "It is hard to overestimate," counsels Mira Wilkins, "how much less-developed countries desire economic and political independence from all great powers."

This conflict has been reinforced further by the fear among many host countries that the advanced management methods and technology of large foreign enterprises will subvert the traditional values and patterns of their cultures. They also may threaten governing elites by tending to undermine the privileged economic status of traditional groups and classes. This basic conflict and the fears behind it are amply reflected in the panoply of foreign investment regulations in many countries, the United Nations "Charter of Economic Rights and Duties of States," and the UNCTAD debate on a "Code of Conduct" for transnational enterprises.

The very economic success of the transnational enterprise in recent years has made it an attractive target for forces opposing the established order. This is true for at least four reasons. First, the assets of these enterprises are sizeable by comparison with national companies. Therefore the enterprise is a "deep pocket" that may be exploited for financing terrorist activities, and a symbol of wealth that may have propaganda value among the poorer segments of the population. A large company is hard pressed to plead that it has no resources to pay ransom.

Second, the long-term interest of the transnational enterprise normally lies with the established order and with political stability, as far as the latter safeguard a favourable business climate and fundamental human rights. Their investments normally are long-term decisions of 10 to 20 years, often involving very sizeable fixed assets. Once made, an enterprise cannot abandon its position with changes in the government or government philosophy or policy except at a heavy cost. Further, the successful operation of a major business entails a certain amount of interchange and cooperation with the government, whether or not management approves of the government's policies. For their own protection, transnational enterprises as a rule studiously avoid becoming embroiled in the politics of the host country. Terrorists, on the other hand, are seeking to overthrow or to change radically the established order. Undermining the position of the transnational enterprise can embarrass the existing regime and adversely affect the business climate for foreign investment as a whole.

Third, the transnational enterprise represents a foreign presence. Its name, which often copies the foreign parent name, may have been promoted vigorously in the host country. This permits the terrorist, through propaganda, to identify the economic power of the enterprise readily and to assert the presence of foreign domination and control. Finally, and largely as a result of the foregoing, the transnational enterprise possesses a relatively high profile in the host country. This presence may be highlighted by resident foreign executives and their families in the country and their patterns of conspicuous consumption.

2543. Mathias, Lina : Multinationals being encouraged in wrong areas : George Fernandes. *Free Press Journal* 17 May 1985 ; 3.

2544. Modeiski, O. : *Transnational Corporations and World Order*. San Francisco, W.H. Freeman, 1979.

2545. Living with MNCs. *Times of India* (New Delhi) 19 June 1985 ; 6.

2546. Mortinelli, Alberto : *Political and social impact of transnational corporations*. In *New International Economy*. Ed. by Harry Makler *et. al.* California, Sage, 1982 ; 79-116.

2547. Multinationals Vs. globals. *Economist* 5 May 1967.

2548. Nye, Joseph S. : Multinational Corporations in World Politics. *Foreign Affairs* 53(1) Oct 1974 ; 153-75.

2549. Power, Jonathan : In partial defense of the multinationals. *International Herald Tribuue* 15-16 Dec 1984 ; 8.

2550. Prais, S.J. : *Evolution of giant firms in Britain*. Cambridge, 1981.

2551. Research project : On Japanese transnational enterprises, draws to a close. *AMPO* 16(1-2) 1984 ; 26-27.

2552. Rugman, A.M. : *Inside the multinationals* London, Croom Helm, 1981.

2553. Rugman, A.M. *ed.* : *New Theories of the multinational enterprises*. London, Croom Helm, 1982.

2554. Stauffer, Robert S. : *U.S. TNCs in an area of global structural crisis*. University of Sydney, 1983. Pp. 64.

2555. Swamy, Dalip S. : *Multinational corporations and the Third world economy* New Delhi, Alps International, 1980. Pp. 256.

2556. Sweezy, P.M. : On the new global disorder. *Monthly Review* Apr 1979.

2557. Takeo, Tsuchiya : Japanese sphere of influence : Multinational investment in Asia. *AMPO* 16(1-2) 1984 ; 28-59.

2558. Tandon, Y. : *Role of transnational corporations and future trends in Southern Africa*. Dakar, IDEP, July 1678. Pp. 17.

2559. Taylor, M.J. and N.J. Thrift *eds.* : *Geography of multinationals* London, Croom Helm, 1982.

2560. Thomas, C.Y. : *Industrialization and the transformation in Africa, an alternative strategy to multinational companies expansion.* Dakar, IDEP, 1974.

2561. *Transnational Corporations.* New York, United Nations, 1976.

2562. Vernon, Raymond : *Storm over the multinationals : The real issues.* London, Macmillan, 1977.

2563. Wattenberg, Ben J. and Richard J. Whalen : *Wealth, weapon : US foreign policy and multinational Corporations.* New York, Transaction Books, 1980.

2564. Wells, L.T. : *Third World multinationals : The rise of foreign investment from developing countries.* Cambridge, 1983.

2565. Yoshihara, H. : Japanese multinational. *Long Range Planning* 18, 1977 ; 41-45.

Navy

2566. Adequacy of U.S. marine Corps security in Beirut. *Terrorism* 7(3) 1984 ; 341-45.

2567. Nyhart, J.D. and J. Christian Kassler : Ocean vessels and offshore structures. In *LAIT* ; 187-212.

The current jurisdictional limits of U.S. authority are clearly set out in international and domestic law. Excellent statements of U.S. geographical jurisdiction abound, and the statutes need be only briefly summarized. At the edges, the jurisdiction is fuzzy, so those parts will be examined here. The prospective limits of jurisdiction are also defined to a reasonable extent, assuming that the apparent consensus in the United Nations Third Law of the Sea Conference regarding new limits holds.

U.S. jurisdiction on the oceans may be delimited in a number of ways. Within its territorial sea, extending for 3 nautical miles from the baseline, the United States exercises sovereign power under the 1958 Convention on Territorial Sea and Contiguous Zone. In its contiguous zone—which extends out to 12 nautical miles—the United States may exercise control necessary to prevent and to punish infringements of regulations pertaining to sanitary, fiscal, immigration, and customs matters. On the high seas, which extend beyond the territorial sea, no nation may validly purport to exercise sovereignty, with the exceptions to the concept that are made by the contiguous zone and by the outer continental shelf concept.

Non-governmental Groups

2568. Islamic (Islamic Summit in Kuwait) leaders flay terrorism. *Hindustan Times* 31 Jan 1987 ; 23.

Kuwait, Jan. 30 (Reuter)—Islamic leaders on January 29, 1987 adopted a strongly worded resolution against terrorism and backed a Syrian-sponsored drive to call an international conference to define the term.

A communique issued at the end of the four-day summit of the 46-member Islamic Conference Organisation (ICO) "categorically condemned all acts of criminal international terrorism".

A Kuwait-sponsored resolution called for "total commitment by ICO members to refuse any assistance to terrorists and reject their demands," which it described as blackmail.

The meeting took place amid heavy security and threats by Islamic fundamentalist groups to disrupt the proceedings. Kuwait has been hit by a series of bombings in the past three years and an attempt on the life of the Emir, Sheikh Jaber Al-Ahmed Al-Sabah.

The summit also rejected "biased efforts by anti-Islam forces to link terrorism and its escalation to Muslims" in a move sponsored by Syria to counter Western accusation against it.

2569. Jenkins, Brian M. and Alfred P. Rubin : New vulnerabilities and the acquisition of new weapons by nongovernment groups. In *LAIT* ; 221-76.

The use of chemical or biological weapons is generally seen as the easiest and most available way to kill a large number of people. A crude nuclear explosive device, depending on its yield and where and when it was detonated, could cause casualties of greater magnitude. But the acquisition of the requisites material and fabrication of the device would require greater risks and technical skill on the part of perpetrators than would be involved in the case of either chemical or biological weapons. Dispersal of radioactive material rather than explosion of a nuclear device would involve fewer difficulties and to acquisition of the material, and the fabrication of a dispersal device is far easier than that of an explosive device, but the probable adverse effects of a dispersal of radioactive material are likely to be exceeded in magnitude by an effective dispersal of chemical toxins or biological agents.

When it comes to slaughter, terrorists actually have little need for such exotic or highly sophisticated weapons. They have already demonstrated their knowledge of explosives. Bombings are the principal form of terrorist activity. Detonated at places of assembly—railroad and subway stations, bus terminals, aircraft—conventional explosives can cause heavy casualties. But for all their bombings, terrorists thus far have rarely used explosives in ways calculated to kill great numbers of any civilian population. Nor have terrorists ordinarily used the primitive but potentially even more lethal weapons of fire against people. Moreover, some of the individual weapons now being developed for tomorrow's infantrymen—man-portable surface-to-air missiles, for example—seem potentially useful to terrorists and, used against certain categories of targets, are capable of causing heavy casualties.

Each of these possibilities—chemicals and biological weapons; nuclear explosive and dispersal devices; conventional explosives and incendiaries; manportable, precision-guided munitions; and other advanced infantry weapons—will be considered with regard to their characteristics and present or future uses. First we shall discuss the nature of the weapons, recent developments that make the particular means of violence more accessible or more attractive to terrorists, some of the possible applications terrorists might consider and the possible effects, and some of the technical problems involved as well as the political and moral arguments that could be mustered within a political extremist organization for or against use of a particular weapon or means of violence. We shall then examine the historical record for any direct evidence of terrorists using or seeking to use the particular weapon under discussion and try to estimate the likelihood of future use.

Terrorists or others entertaining schemes of mass murder using chemical or biological weapons will find plenty of inspiration in recent novels and screenplays, and in newspaper headlines describing such examples as the Central Intelligence Agency's reported use of shellfish toxin, Blackleaf-40 (a common insecticide), and other poisons in plots to assassinate foreign leaders; the mysterious "Legionnaire's Disease," which killed 24 conventioneers in Philadelphia and made 180 others ill, and which many suspected was an act of homicide, not an accident, until other cases were identified; and the recent revelations that the U.S. Army had actually used live bacteria on unsuspecting civilian populations in U.S. cities as part of its program of research on chemical and biological warfare. Ironically, among those calling attention to the possibilities of chemical and biological weapons are some of the proponents of nuclear power. Responding to warnings by opponents of nuclear energy that the widespread availability of fissionable material will enable terrorists and criminals to hold cities for ransom, they have pointed out that chemical and biological weapons offer easier and more readily available methods of mass murder than nuclear material.

Moved in the direction of chemical or biological weapons, terrorists will have no difficulty in locating a number of books written for the layman on the concepts of chemical and biological weapons. This literature provides as history of the development of chemical and biological weapons and of their use in warfare. It also identifies the chemical compounds and biological pathogens that have been examined as well as the technical problems of manufacture and delivery to the target, and it identifies sources of further information.

The reader is then directed to the techincal literature, which is extensive. To go beyond the point of imagining scenarios, some technical knowledge and material are needed as well as some basic laboratory facilities. Unfortunately, the level of requisite technical knowledge is not extremely high ; a colleged student in chemistry might be able to put together an extremely effective chemical weapon. The material is widely available ; in fact, it can often be easily purchased. And only primitive facilities are required to carry out some threats.

Chemical warfare dates back to the use of chlorine and mustard gas in World War I. Despite the Geneva Protocol of 1925 which prohibited chemical warfare, research aimed at developing new and more toxic chemical weapons continued during the 1920s and 1930s when major scientific advances were being made in the fields of physics and chemistry. The search for more toxic insecticides led to the discovery of organophosphorous anti-cholinesterases, a class of chemicals that disrupt the chemical toxins commonly known as the "nerve gases." Although chemical weapons were not used by either side in World War II, research continued during and after the war. Nerve gases of even greater toxicity were produced. Binary systems of delivery were developed ; these kept two non-lethal compounds separated until the moment of use, when they are combined into a deadly agent. Non-lethal incapacitants such as hallucinogens were developed and used in experiments.

Nuclear

2570. *Analysis of the terrorist threat to the commercial nuclear industry.* Washington, BDM Corporation Report submitted to the special

Special Safeguards Study, Nuclear Regulatory Commission, 1975.

2571. Ausland, John C. : Short of nuclear war : Facing more credible dangers. *International Herald Tribune* 7 Jan 1986 ; 4.

2572. Azeevn, Anwer : Nuclear terrorism : A balancing game. *Link* 8 Jun 1986 ; 29.

The first A-bomb over Hiroshima was no accident. Nor was the one that crippled Nagasaki. It was no accident when chemical weapons were used in Vietnam. The Texas City accident on April 16, 1947 involving 1400 tons of amonium at the Galveston Bay had left 576 dead and 2000 grievously injured.

Britain's Nypro chemical plant accident on June 1, 1974 levelled all buildings on the 60-acre site, killing 28 workers. Similarly, in Mexico City, a violent explosion killed 452 and injured 4248, not to speak of 1000 people who are described as "still missing".

The consequences are worse if for whatever reasons something goes wrong with a plant run on nuclear energy. This is what happened in Chernobyl. And this points to a much more dangerous situation created by the stockpiles of nuclear weaponry. If a nuclear power station, in a moment of accident, can prove so hazardous, one can imagine what will happen to this planet when an accident occurs at any site where n-arms are stockpiled. The nuclear abyss is but one step away.

The threat of universal death has rendered the whole question of being or not being so fundamentally universal that it cannot be dealt with ideological rhetoric or self-righteous demagogy.

2573. Barber, Benjamin R. : *Superman and commonmen : Freedom, anarchy and the revolution.* New York, Prayer, 1971.

2574. Barnaby, Frank and Geoffrey Thomas *eds.* : *Nuclear arms race : Control or Catastrophe* ? London, 1982.

2575. Beres, L.R. : International terrorism and world order : The nuclear threat. *Stanford Journal of Internationl Studies* 12 Spr 1977 ; 131-46.

2576. Beres, L.R. : Terrorism and the nuclear threat in the Middle East. *Current History* Jan 1976.

2577. Black, Edwin, F. : If terrorism goes nuclear. *Washington Report*, May 1976.

2578. Black, Hawld and Marin J Labes : Guerrilla Warfare. *American Journal of Orthopsychiatry* 37, Jul 1976 ; 666-70.

2579. Blau, Thomas : Plowshare, proliferation and the N+I country, In *ITWS* ; 118-30.

2580. Bocker, Eghert : Science and nuclear arms race. In *Nuclear arms race.* Control or catastrophe. Ed. by Frank Barnaby and Geoffrey Thomas, London, 1982 ; 95-110.

2581. Brown. Herbert H. : Nuclear facilities and materials. In *LAIT* ; 149-86.

Currently, there is no international legal regime for the physical protection of nuclear materials or facilities from terrorist or other malevolent acts. Rather, those physical protection systems in existence are imposed by each government and are applicable only to the limits of that government's jurisdiction. These physical protection systems are international only in the sense that they may be influenced through the exchange of technical information with other governments.

The reason for the national character of physical protection systems can be traced to the international legal principle of national sovereignty. Governments, to varying degrees, consider physical protection to be an intrinsically national responsibility tied to domestic police and security functions. Thus they claim not only the exclusive power to exercise such functions within their boundaries, but the inherent necessity to do so in the particular manner, reflective of their respective constitutional and legal systems. Accordingly, while governments may agree on the need for, the objectives of, and even the essential elements of a physical protection system, they do not agree on any concept or activity that would permit a state or an international organization to impose or enforce physical protection standards against another state.

Notwithstanding the strongly national character or present physical protection systems, governments are beginning to change their perspectives of the dimensions and implications of the issue. While national sovereignty prevails as an inviolate principle, various states are in fact beginning quietly to pursue several lines of internationll cooperation on physical protection. This movement is slow and subtle, and although still of modest consequence, it may be laying the groundwork for more systematic and meaningful international cooperation. There are several reasons for this change :

1. Governments fear that nuclear material stolen from one country could be used by terrorists against the interests of another country.

2. Governments fear that without a more common understanding of the problem and better knowledge of the most current techniques for physical protection, some states' systems may lag behind and become particularly attractive targets for terrorists.

3. Governments fear that the recent increase in public discussion of potential nuclear-related terrorism could feed this idea and actually encourage such terrorist attempts.

4. Governments fear that a serious breach of any state's physical protection system might permit a notorious incident that could bring into question the integrity of other states' systems, thus jeopardizing the public acceptance of these states' nuclear power programs.

The principal forum for international cooperation on nuclear energy has been the International Atomic Energy, a U.N. agency whose secretariat has historically acted on a strong consensus of its board of governors. The IAEA was established in 1957 "to accelerate and enlarge the contribution of atomic energy to peace, health and prosperity throughout the world." It was mandated to "ensure, so far as it is able, that assistance provided by it or at its request or under its supervision or control is not used in such a way as to further any military purpose. The agency's functions are basically two-fold : to assist member states in the safe application of nuclear technology and "to ensure" that governments subject to its jurisdiction do not divert nuclear materials from peaceful to military ends, i.e., the "safeguards" function.

IAEA safeguards are intended to "prevent the diversion of nuclear material by the risk of early detection while minimizing interference with a nation's peaceful nuclear programme." In practice, the IAEA administers safeguards by an accounting system for nuclear materials, supplemented by the imposition of containment locks, seals, and other devices that preclude the removal of nuclear materials from critical points of the fuel cycle, and by surveillance devices that monitor movements of nuclear materials within a facility.

These safeguards apply to :

1. Projects of the agency and projects of member states where the states request the agency's assistance in providing nuclear materials or technical expertise;
2. projects between member states, if so requested;
3. projects of a single member state, if so requested;
4. activities of states party to regional agreements calling for IAEA safeguards, of which the Treaty of Tlatelolco of 1970 is at present the only one (the IAEA function is to verify compliance with the treaty);
5. activities of states party to the Non-Proliferation Treaty (NPT) ;

2582. Buchanan, J.R. *ed.* : Safeguards against the theft or diversion of nuclear materials. *Nuclear Safety* 15, Sep-Oct 1974 ; 513-619.

2583. Dumas, L.J. : National security and the arms race. In *ITWS* ; 158-64.

2584. Feld, Bernard T. : Nuclear energy : Fact versus myth. In *ITWS* ; 131-38.

2585. Gsponer, Andre : Neutron bomb and the other new limited nuclear war weapons. *Strategic Digest* (New Delhi) 14 (8) Aug 1984.

2586. Gilinsky, Victor : Fuelling the Western World's reactors : Problems and issues. In *ITWS* ; 140-57.

2587. Glass, Andrew J. : Nuclear terrorism no fiction. *Amrita Bazar Patrika* 9 Apr 1986 ; 6.

2588. Jenkins, Brian : Consequences of nuclear terrorism. *Rand Corporation Paper* No. P-6373, Aug 1979.

2589. Kennan, George. *Nuclear delusion* New York, 1982.

2590. Krieger, D.M. : What happens if. . . . . . ? Terrorists, revolutionaries and nuclear weapons. *Annals* (USA) 430, Mar 1977.

2591. Larus, J. : *Nuclear Weapon safety and the common defense.* Columbus, Ohio State University Press, 1967.

2592. Leak Kills man at U.S. nuclear full plant. *International Herald Tribune* 6 Jan 1986 ; 1.

2593. Leventhal, Paul : Safeguards against nuclear terrorism. *International Herald Tribune* 22 Sep 1986 ; 4.

2594. Mengel, R. William : Impact of nuclear terrorism on the military's role in society. In *ITCW* ; 402-14.

From the foregoing discussion and evaluation of the consequences of nuclear terrorism for society, it is clear that the full range of nuclear malevolent actions has not in the past, nor would in the future, require military intervention. Although the specter of nuclear terrorism has been broadly represented as the most catastrophic event that could spoil society, in reality nuclear terrorism offers neither the greatest threat in terms of consequences nor the most probable with respect to the ability of the group to obtain necessary resources, personnel, and expertise. Much easier to initiate are acts using chemical and biological agents and their related technologies. In fact, several biological agents, such as anthrax, are potentially many times more potent than any use of nuclear material in terms of casualty-producing effects.

However, nuclear terrorism does offer the perpetrator the advantage of creating massive damage without inflicting large numbers of casualties. Other means of mass-destruction terrorism only provide a mechanism for creating tremendously large numbers of casualties. For this reason, as well as the fact that the nuclear industry and its potential dangers have been widely publicized, nuclear terrorism may be the first type of mass-destruction terrorism initiated on a scale that would have significant societal impact with respect to subjective and objective consequences.

Based on the previous analysis and extensive research on the threat to the commercial nuclear industry, lower-level malevolent actions of nuclear terrorism are more likely to occur than those of a higher order. Despite the probability of terrorists using nuclear material to perpetrate attacks, the constraints placed on the groups by resource and personnel requirements will limit activity to the lower end of the malevolent actions range. The societal consequences of these attacks will be negligible in terms of both objective and subjective criteria. Thus, threat (outside the context of theft and dispersal), harassment, and damage/disruption are not significant as the likelihood of military involvement appears minimal. Hostage situations, theft, dispersal, and fabrication of a bomb may create incidents where the consequences are such that the military is encouraged to intervene. The most probable application of nuclear terrorism is the occupation of a nuclear facility, establishing a hostage situation. Theft of a weapon or weapons-grade material is the next most probable occurrence, while dispersal and finally, fabrication of a bomb are the least. The basis for this determination is founded in the evaluation of a miniature of resources, motivations, and target vulnerabilities for each case.

2595. Mullen, Robert K. : *International Clandestine Nuclear THREAT, Senta Bonara.* California, Mission Research Corporation 1975.

2596. Namboodiri, P.K.S. : Nuclear terrorism. *Indian Express* 18 & 19 Sep 1985 ; 6.

2597. Namboodiri, P.K.S. : Nuclear terrorism. In *India and the nuclear challenge.* Ed. by K. Subrahmanyam. New Delhi, 1986 ; 123-40.

2598. Novick, S. : Basement H. Bombs. *Scientist and Citizen.* Dec 1968.

2599. Nuclear terrorism threat deemed trial. *Amrita Bazar Patrika* 19 Jul 1986 ; 10.

The threat of nuclear terrorism is real and increasing with the world "totally unprepared" to confront terrorists who have stolen or clandestinely manufactured nuclear weapons, a study says. An international task force which looked into the danger posed by a possible terrorist-nuclear weapons link, says that a nuclear attack by terrorists is as likely as the Challenger accident or the Chernobyl explosion.

One of the several measures that the group of 26 experts comprising the task force has suggested to counter the threat is installing a special coded electronic lock on every nuclear weapon to render stolen weapons useless, reports the US journal, 'Science'.

The lock can be opened only through the knowledge of a special code available only at a central command post. The lock also makes it impossible for soldiers to launch a nuclear attack without permission from a central higher authority.

The report highlights the need to protect nuclear weapons against theft and urges all nuclear weapon powers to strengthen physical barriers outside areas where nuclear materials are stored.

2600. Ponte, Lowell : Better do as we say : this is an Atom Bomb and we are not fooling. *Penthouse* Feb 1972,

2601. Pringle, Peter : If terrorists go nuclear. *Tribune* 5 Jul 1985 ; 4.

2602. Puri, Rakshat : Nuclear terrorists are coming. *Hindustan Times* 9 Jul 1985 ; 9.

2603. Sagan, Carl : Nuclear War and climate catastrophe : Some policy implications. *Foreign Affairs* 62 (2) Win 1983-84 ; 257-92.

2604. Schelling, Thomas C. : Can nuclear terrorism be neutralized ? In *ITCR* ; 146-54.

2605. Sharma, Madan Lal : Nuclear terrorism. In *Terrorism : American Style*. New Delhi, 1982 ; 100-132.

2606. Stonier, Tom : Unilateral disarmament re-examined. In *ITWS* ; 165-72.

2607. Subramanian, R.R. : Israel's nuclear terrorism in Iraq. *Patriot* 9 Jul 1981 ; 2.

2608. Taylor, Theodore B and D. Colligan : Nuclear terrorism—A threat of the future. *Science Digest* Aug 1974.

2609. Teller, Edwar : Spectre of nuclear terrorism. In *ITCR*, 141-45.

The real danger is proliferation of nuclear weapons. This is something we must stop, and furthermore, we should stop the next step : the possibility that a government, having made in secret a nuclear explosive, should then hand this nuclear explosive to selected agents, to selected terrorists.

What can be done to prevent proliferation ? A treaty has been signed, but not by all nations. It is unlikely to be more effective than the Kellog-Briand Pact which outlawed war a few years before Hitler started on his dreadful march. Paper is not the solution.

It has been suggested that tests of nuclear explosives should be forbidden. That too, runs into lots of difficulties. After so many years, after so much knowledge has become available, after so much thought has been given to the subject of atomic explosives, in a systematic manner or in fragmentary speculations, a government that makes a determined effort to make an atomic bomb, I believe—and I am only guessing—could make such an atomic bomb with considerable confidence that it actually will work. This is true particularly if the aims is to pass the bomb on to a terrorist group, and in case of failure the consequences could be limited. The risks they are taking will not be very great.

Otherwise, proliferation may turn out to be a somewhat lesser hazard because a country in possession of atomic weapons will be very reluctant to use them in open warfare, which would have unpredictable, and in all probability very dreadful, consequences to the very country that used the atomic weapons. This is the reason I am particularly afraid of the linkage between proliferation of atomic weapon and international terrorism.

The participants in this conference will not have any difficulty imagining occasions where a rich country and a radical country might make such weapons available to terrorists.

There is another proposal to stop proliferation ; in my opinion it is not hopeful. It has been suggested that the burned-up fuel elements from nuclear reactors which contain plutonium, a nuclear explosive, should not be reprocessed, thereby making plutonium less available. However, there are plenty of small nuclear reactors which are not under international inspection. The danger from reprocessing in the case of big reactors, where supervision already exists, is much less than the danger from the numerous small reactors. It may make good sense to bring all reactors under international supervision. If this is not done, an attached small reprocessing plant may well be built and operated in secrecy.

But even this is not a satisfactory solution. A nuclear explosive does not require plutonium ; the light isotope of uranium, uranium-235, can serve the purpose. Each year sees new and more practical methods on the separation of isotopes, and some of these methods can be, and in the course of time will be, applied to uranium. To stop nuclear explosions by trying to limit the availability of the explosive materials is something that should be tried, but it should be tried in the right way, and to eliminate reprocessing is not the practical approach.

2610. Udai Narain : *Reagan's nuclear terrorism.* New Delhi, Deep & Deep, 1984. Pp. 200.

2611. Wilson, George C. :New US strategy for nuclear war. *Washington Post* 20 Jul 1975.

2612. Willrich, Masson : *Global politics of nuclear energy.* New York, Prayer, 1971.

2613. Willrich, Masson and T.B. Taylor : *Nuclear theft : Risks and safeguards.* Cambridge, Ballinger 1977.

2614. York, Herbert F. : Outline history of nuclear proliferation. In *ITWS* ; 105-17.

Police

2615. Alesevich, Bugene : Police terrorism. In *ITCW* ; 269-75.

Police have come under fire for snooping into the lives of private citizens. Their spying has stirred criticism since it is not directed at suspected criminals, but at such individuals as bank presidents, civic leaders, politicians, and businessmen. Those attending various protest rallies or involved in civic action may find a dossier on them at police headquarters. Illegal wiretaps may have been used to gather the information. Homosexual arrest records, prostitution charges and wife-beating reporting reports become useful during political campaigns. This information is made available to other law enforcement agencies on a need-to-know or routine basis.

There is evidence uncovered by Maryland State Senator Edward T. Conroy that the Baltimore police regularly spy on meetings of community organizations, school boards, and utility rate-increase hearings; they take names of everyone in attendence and amass as much information about them as possible. One extreme abuse that was reported recently was the use of computerized criminal histories by city officials to check the names of signers of a recall petition against those same officials. Strict government guidelines prohibit such activity, but abuses are numerous. A 1974 lawsuit in Chicago has charged the police with infiltrating groups, harrassment, illegal wiretaps and break-ins, and physical assaults—all against individuals and groups not guilty of criminal activity as far as can be determined.

The Law Enforcement Assistance Administration has been aiding local police for years by funding the purchase of staggering amounts of "electronic surveillance equipment." A total of $ 160.8 million was designated to support 1,929 intelligence-related projects around the country. Approximately $ 2.5 million was earmarked directly for the purchase of electronic surveillance equipment. More than $ 1.3 million worth of bugging equipment went to states which either prohibited wiretaps or had no special laws on bugging. The state of California, which outlaws wiretapping except in unique circumstances, was given $ 98,565 for sophisticated surveillance. After receiving money from LEAA for such equipment, twenty-five states simply refused to provide LEAA with itemized breakdowns for the bugging equipment.

Recent Federal Bureau of Investigation "political abuses" uncovered by the Justice Department and the Senate Intelligence Committee have shocked government leaders and the American people. This agency's intelligence system had developed to such a degree that no one inside or outside it was willing or able to tell the difference between legitimate national security or law-enforcement and purely political intelligence gathering. Particularly interesting is that to date no physical violence or terror has been uncovered which would more closely compare this agency with Soviet-style police terror. This absence of physical methods of intimidation, technically removes the agency from a KGB-style organization.

Some examples cited by the report include the following :

1. Hitting at the credit ratings and job status of group members by notifying credit bureaus, creditors, employers, and prospective employers of illegal, immoral, or radical activities.

2. Obtaining tax returns of group members.

3. Interfering in "political or judicial processes" by such actions as revealing arrest records or group affiliations of candidates or defendants. Although there were "only 12 instances" of this type, the report said, they "are among the most troubling in all of the COINTELPRO efforts."

4. Staging an arrest by local police on a narcotics pretext, then using a police radio call to make one of the persons in custody think his comparion was a police informer.

5. Forging business and recruiting cards of groups and reproducing the signature stamp of a group leader.

6. Investigating the love life of one civil-rights leaders and leaking the information to the press.

7. Making anonymous telephone calls to the families and friends of group members, telling them of immoral or radical conduct.

8. Attempting to use religious and civil leaders to disrupt a group by putting pressure on local governments, landlords, and employers.

A December 1975 Gallup Poll illustrates all too clearly the plunging public esteem for the organization. A decade ago, 80 percent of the Americans surveyed gave the FBI a "highly favorable" rating. Today, only 37 percent do so.

Continual disclosures of FBI abuses and new financial wrongdoings within the bureau are reportedly causing "a fresh and devastating erosion of morale" among the more than 8,500 agents. Still more recently, Attorney General Levi has just ordered a new investigation into charges of corruption in the FBI's ranks—for the first time in the bureau's long and virtually corruption-free history.

2616. Beckley, Carol : Super-Cop Ray's (Kendall) beat covers 138 Countries. *Patriot* 4 Feb 1986 ; 8.

2617. Farah, S.A. : Terrorism and police. *Indian Nation* 25 Dec 1986 ; 4.

2618. Inderjit : Terrorism and the police. *Tribune* 13 Aug 1985 ; 4.

2619. Lewin, Walter : Justice cops out. *New Republic* 162(23) 6 Jun 1970.

2620. Mehra, Ajay K. : Collective violence and the police. *Mainstream* 12 Apr 1986 ; 26, 34.

2621. Pereira, Maxwell : Police cannot be omnipresent. *Delhi Recorder* Sep 1985 ; 33.

2622. Target now families of Sikh police informers : 11 Massacred in Punjab. *Daily* (Bombay) 10 Jan 1987 ; 1, 12.

2623. Terrorism and police. *Tribune* 7 Jan 1986 ; 4.

2624. Tewari, S.N. : Police and terrorists. *Hindustan Times* 20 Sep 1985 ; 9.

Why have the police failed to tackle the extremists ? The police system in our country is most weaponry of the police. Police constables usually carry the obsolescent bolt action 303 rifles or muskets and for every firing the bolt has to be pulled.

Rifles may be suitable for mob action to minimise casualties, but it is ludicrous to see police personnel guarding aircraft with such long rifles. Can ever a rifle be operated inside the aisle of plane ? Mr. Arjun Das, Metropolitan Councillor, was killed by a sten gun and 29 empty cartridges were found on the spot. Can a bodyguard with ordinary revolver or rifle deal with such terrorists ? It is high time rifles were withdrawn from the police and confined to long range operations and every constable on patrol duty is issued with a 9 m.m. pistol, as in European countries, and a hand wireless set.

At least every third police constable should be trained in handling and firing a sten gun when he is on security duty. If extremists strike with missiles and sten guns, it is ridiculous to think of challenging them with outdated weapons like rifles that the police possess. There is also need for a musketry course at least once a month as against the annual course.

The Police Station staff are not only inadequate but also overworked. No plant can run without a shift system but we expect policemen to work round the clock. Will this not jeopardise their efficiency ? Every Police Station, like a factory, should work in shifts of six hours. This means the strength of the police has to be raised fourfold. It is my experience that at night hardly one or two policemen are available at the Police Station. Can they ever deal with any organised gang or law and order situation ? Mere increase in police strength would also not help unless we give them adequate housing, medical and educational facilities. The housing problem is the most acute.

Prisoners of War

2625. Brutality against P.O.W.S. In *WTAZIT* ; 44-45.

2626. Iraqi POWs disclose maltreatment, torture. *Baghdad Observer* 14 Jan 1986 ; 1.

Iraqi disabled prisoners of war POWs returning from Iran recently disclosed today attempts made by the Khomeini regime to poison their food and using all kinds of physical and psychological torture against them.

In a press conference held in Baghdad and attended by foreign, Arab and local reporters a number of Iraqi prisoners of war said that they were subjected to barbaric and inhuman treatment in order to force them to dissociate themselves from their country, people and the Arab nation in violation of all international conventions relative to the treatment of prisoners of war.

The Iraqi POW said Anbar told reporters that many kinds of diseases are spread among Iraqi POWs because of malnutrition, lack of medical treatment and preventive measures against these diseases.

Munther Kadhim Abdulla another disabled Iraqi POW who returned from Iran said that the Iranian guards of the camps had killed an Iraqi Prisoner of War because he refused to give them his wedding ring after they chopped off his finger in order to get the ring out of it.

The Iraqi prisoner of war Muhssen Hanna Bahnam said that Iraqi POWs are confined in darkened camps deprived of sun and fresh air. He said that a number of Iraqi POWs were operated on without being given any aesthetic a matter which resulted in a number of death cases.

The returning Iraqi Prisoners of War vowed to continue fighting against the Iranian aggressors and expressed their readiness to join battlefront again.

2627. Segal, J. *et.al.* : Universal Consequences of captivity : stress reactions among diversent profulations of Prisoners of War and their families. *International Social Science Journal* 28(3) 1976,

Property

2628. Wanton destruction of civilian property. In *WTAZIT* ; 47.

Refugees

2629. Mass killings of civilians and refugees. In *WTAZIT* ; 38-39.

Research and Development

2630. Crelinstein, Ronald D. : International political terrorism : A challenge for comparative research. *Terrorism* 3(3-4) 1980;341-48.

2631. Salewski, Wolfgang D. : Latest theory recognized by sociological science research in terrorism and violence. *Terrorism* 3(3-4) 1980 ; 297-301.

Rural Society

2632. Broomfield, J.G. : *Elite conflict in a rural society.* Berkeley, 1968.

2633. Loomis, C. and J. Beegle : Spread of Nazism in rural areas. *American Sociological Review*; 11, 1946.

Sabotage

2634. Brown, Geoff : *Sabotage : A study of industrial conflict* Bristol, Spokesman Books, 1977.

2635. Chicago Eight : *Conspiracy.* New York, Dell Publishing, 1969.

2636. Chopra, V.D. : Forces of internal subversion and their global allies. In *Pentagon shadow over India.* New Delhi ; 1985 ; 175-203.

2637. *Note on subversive movement and organizations in India.* Simla, Government of India Press, 1933.

2638. Seeds of subversion. *International Herald Tribune* 16 Sep 1986 ; 4.

Scientific Aspects

2639. Baxi, Upendra : Aspects of scientific terrorism. *Tribune* 9 Dec 1985 ; 4.

Security

2640. Anable, David : Tackling the international problem. *Current History* (180) Feb 1976 ; 51-60.

2641. Anti-terror test, Part-II. *International Herald Tribune* 26 Jul 1985 ; 6.

2642. Anti-terrorism sovereignty. *International Herald Tribune* 19-20 Oct 1985 ; 6.

2643. Attar Chand : Asian security : New Challenges. *National Herald* 18 Apr 1986 ; 5.

2644. Bassiouni, M. Cherif : Prevention and Control of terrorism : International response. In *LAIT* ; 654-65.

2645. Blau, Thomas : Consultations in NATO during and after the October War. In *ITWS* ; 234-47.

2646. Bloomfield, M and Gerald F. Fitz Gerald : *Crimes against internationally protected persons : Prevention and punishment.* New York Prayer, 1975.

2647. Bowden, Tom : *Breakdown of public security.* London, Sage Publications, 1977.

2648. Chalfort, Lord : Terrorism and international security. *Terrorism* 5(4) 1982 ; 309-24.

2649. Claude, A Buss *ed.* : *National security interests in the Pacific Basin.* Stanford, 1985.

2650. Cole, Richard B. : *Executive security : A corporate guide to effective response to abduction and terrorism.* New York, 1980.

2651. Collin, Patrick : *Living in troubled lands : The complete guide to personal security abroad.* Boulder, Paladin Press 1981. Pp. 192.

2652. Crozier, Brian *ed.* : *New dimensions of security in Europe.* London, Institute for the Study of Conflict, 1973.

2653. Hassner, Pierre : Political aspects of European security. In *ITWS* ; 173-88.

2654. Healy, R.J. : *Design for security.* New York, Willy, 1968.

2655. Lineberry, William P. : *Struggle against terrorism.* Stanford, American Enterprises Institute, 1975.

2656. Pasti, Nino : Military balance between East and West in Europe. In *ITWS* ; 189-233.

2657. Shultz, Richard H and Stephen Sloan : *Responding to the terrorist threat : Security and crisis management*. New York, 1980.

2658. Willrich, Mason *ed.* : *Civil nuclear power and international security*. New York, Prayer, 1971.

2659. Zoppo, Ciro E. : Mediterranean and European security. In *ITWS* ; 248-76.

Social Change

2660. Falk, Richard A. : Terror, liberation movements and the process of social change. *American Journal of International Law* 63, 1969 ; 423-27.

2661. Johnson, Chalmers : *Revolution and the social system*. Stanford, Hoover Institution, 1964.

2662. Methvin, Eugene H. : *Riot markers* : *The technology of social demolition*. New York, Arlington House, 1970.

2663. Nearing, Scott. *ed.* : *Law of social revolution*. New York, Social Science Publishers, 1926. Pp. 262.

2664. Terrorism and society. *Nagpur Times* 17 Aug 1985 ; 4.

Star Wars

2665. Aldridge, Robert C. : Who will shoot first in space ? *Nation* 25 Mar 1978.

2666. Arceneanx, Joseph : Ringing off on SDI. *International Herald Tribune* 6 Feb 1987 ; 5.

2667. Attar Chand : SDI, terrorism and NAM. *National Herald* 28 Feb 1986 ; 5.

2668. Baker, David : *Shape of wars to come*. New York, 1982.

2669. Attar Chand : Star Wars and global economic security. *Clarity* (Bombay) 25 Jan 1987 ; 11, 14.

2670. Bailey, Martin : Britain's helping hand to Star Wars. *Times of India* 12 Feb 1987 ; 15.

2671. Ban on Satellite killers. *International Herald Tribune* 26 Dec 1985 ; 4.

2672. Bienen, Henry and Jeremiah P. Ostriker : For "Star Wars", only the narrowest of roles. *International Herald Tribune* 14 Jan 1985 ; 4.

2673. Bova, Ben : *Assured Survival : Putting the star wars defense in perspective.* Boston, 1984. p. 390.

2674. Broad, William J. : Fatal flow in the concept of space war. *Science* 215(4538) 12 Mar 1982.

2675. Broader, David S. : Star wars : New fangled boomerang. *International Herald Tribune* 22-22 Sep 1985 ; 4.

2676. Brown, William W : Balance of powers in outer space. Parameters *Journal of U.S. Army War College* 1977.

2677. Cannan, James : *War in Space.* New York, 1982.

2678. Cawault, Craig : Debate on space policy heats. *Aviation week and space technology* (New York) 5 Feb 1979.

2679. Challenger's tragic end. *Daily* (Bombay) 31 Jan 1986 ; 8.

2680. Cost of 'Star Wars' *International Herald Tribune* 19 May 1986 ; 6.

2681. Deudney, Daniel : Forging Missiles into spacerships. *World Policy Journal* 2(2) Spr 1985 ; 271-303.

2682. Deudney, Daniel : *Space : The high frontier in perspective.* Washington, 1982.

2683. Directed energy missile defense in space. *Background Paper* Apr 1984.

2684. Drozdiak, William : Kohl reports pact with U.S. on SDI study. *International Herald Tribune* 20 Mar 1986 ; 1-2.

2685. Favocett, J.E.S. : *Outer space : New challenges to law and policy.* Oxford, Clarendon Press, 1984. p. 175.

2686. Frieling, Thomas I. : Soviet space programme : Will experienceable to beautiful. *Technology Review* (New York) Oct 1981.

2687. Garwin, Richard L. : Are we on the verse of an arms race in space. *Bulletin of the Atomic Scientists* 37(5) May 1983.

2688. Gelb, Leslie H. : Progress in SDI research : the concept Vs. the reality. *International Herald Tribune* 18 Dec 1985 ; 1, 8.

2689. Geyelin, Philip : Star wars : Unattainable, harebrained, staggering. *International Herald Tribune* 5 Dec 1984 ; 4.

2690. Golden, Frederic : *Colonies in space : The next giant step.* New York, 1976.

2691. Gray, Colin S. : *American military space policy : Information systems, weapons systems and arms control.* Cambridge, Abt. Books, 1983. Pp. 138.

2692. Greenberg, Daniel S. : Lots of research, but too much of its military. *International Herald Tribune* 29-30 Mar 1986 ; 6.

2693. Greenberg, Daniel S. : U.S. ignores lessons of space junk. *International Herald Tribune* 30 Jan 1986 ; 4.

2694. Greenberg, Daniel S. : Without Science's stars no 'Star Wars'. *International Herald Tribune* 2 Aug 1985 ; 6.

2695. Growing danger of 'Star Wars' *China Daily* 22 Aug 1984 ; 4.

2696. Gupta, Rakesh : *Militarization of outer space : A case of US policy.* New Delhi, Patriot Publishers, 1985. p. 186.

2697. Hiatt, Fred : SDI revives U.S. effort on spacenuclear power. *International Herald Tribune* 17 Apr 1986 ; 3.

2698. Humble, Ronald D. : Space warfare in perspective. *Air University Review* Jul-Aug 1982.

2699. Jasani, Bhupendra M. : *Outer space : Battlefield of the future ?* London, 1978. Pp. 202.

2700. Jasani, Bhupendra *ed.* : *Outer space : A new dimension in arms race.* London, 1983.

2701. Jasani, Bhupendra *ed.*: *Space weapons : The arms control dilemma.* Philadelphia, Taylor and Francis, 1984. Pp. 270.

2702. Kamban, Major : Star Wars. *People's Comment* (New Delhi) 15 Feb 1987 ; 38-42.

2703. Kane, Francis X. : Anti-Satellite systems and US options. *Strategic Review* Win 1982.

2704. Karas, Thomas : *New high ground systems and weapons of space age war.* New York, 1983.

2705. Keller, Bill : Pentagon spending plan makes SDI largest weapons programme in Budget. *International Herald Tribune* 6 Feb 1986 ; 1, 3.

2706. Kleiman, Robert : Proper use for 'Star Wars' : Trade it for peace. *International Herald Tribune* 14-15 Sep 1985 ; 4.

2707. Kleiman, Robert : 'Star Wars' : A point of no return. *International Herald Tribune* 10 Dec 1984 ; 6.

2708. Kogut, John : Why US Scientist oppose SDI. *Secular Democracy* Apr 1986 ; 36-38.

2709. Kranthammer, Charles : How weapons in space promote arms control. *International Herald Tribune* 8 Jan 1985 ; 6.

2710. Levine, Arthur L. : *Future of the US space programme*. New York, 1975.

2711. Lewis, Flora : Star wars : Dreams and realities. *International Herald Tribune* 5 Feb 1986 ; 4.

2712. Lewis, Flora : Star wars. A political cover-up. *International Herald Tribune* 5 Dec 1985 ; 4.

2713. Logsdon, John M. : *Decision to go to the Moon : Project Apollo and the national interest* Mass, 1970.

2714. Lovenzini, Divo A. : Space power doctrine. *Air University Review* Jul-Aug 1982.

2715. Menshikov, S. : Space games of the military industrial complex. *New Wave* 14 Apr 1985 ; 9.

2716. Miles, Ian and Michail Schwarz : Alternative space future : The next quarter century. *Futures* 14(5) 1982 ; 461-83.

2717. Militarising space. *Patriot* 30 Jan 1985 ; 4.

2718. Monteiro, Vivek : Challenger, latest victim of star war. *Secular Democracy* Apr 1986 ; 38-41.

2719. Nations, Richard : Star-Wars dilemma : Tokyo considers formal participation in SDI. *Far Eastern Economic Review*. 13 Feb 1986 ; 32-33.

2720. Navy forms space command. *Defence Electronics* (California) Jul 1983.

2721. New space policy strong on defence. *Physics Today* (New York) Sep 1982.

2722. O'Toole, Thomas : Experts are still looking for cure to spacesickness. *International Herald Tribune* 16 Jan 1986 ; 9.

2723. Parmentola, John and Kosta Topis : Particle beam weapons. *Scientific American* 240(4) Apr 1979 ; 54-65.

2724. Peace wins space war ! *Blitz* (Bombay) 5 Apr 1986 ; 11.

2725. Pike, John : SDI contrasts : Will U.S. allies be sold short ? *International Herald Tribune* 16 Jan 1986 ; 7.

2726. Qizhi, He. : Treaties urged to restrain space arms race. *China Daily* 21 Nov 1984 ; 4.

2727. Raanan, Uri and Robert Pfaltzgruff : *International Security dimensions of space.* Hamden, Conn, Archon Books, 1984. Pp. 324.

2728. Resolving a space dilemma. *International Herald Tribune* 1-2 Feb 1986 ; 4.

2729. Sanger, David E. : Skepticism mounts on deploying SDI. *International Herald Tribune* 12 Feb 1987 ; 1, 6.

2730. Schaner, William H. : *Politics of space : A comparison of the Soviet and American space programs.* New York, 1976.

2731. Schuarz, Michael and Paul Stares : Perspectives on 25 years of space development. *Future* 14 (5) Oct 1982.

2732. Smith, Marcia S. : Anti-Satellite killers *CRS Issue Brief* No. IB 81123 9 Jul 1982.

2733. Smith, Marcia S. : First quarter century of space flight. *Future* 14 (5) Oct 1982.

2734. Smith, Marcia S. : Space policy and funding military uses of space. *CRS Issue Brief* No. 82117.

2735. Smith, R. Jeffrey : Anti-Satellite Weapon sets dangerous course. *Science* 222 (4620) 14 Oct 1983.

2736. Specialist risks in space. *International Herald Tribune* 8-9 Feb 1986 ; 4.

2737. Star Wars : *Democratic World* 30 Jun 1985 ; 4.

2738. Star Wars plan to cost $ 1000 B. 6 May 1986 ; 6.

2739. Star Wars Won't do-Deng. *Ta Kung Pao* 8 Aug 1985 ; 3.

2740. Starr, Joyce, R. : Star Wars and Israel : A celestial Attraction. *International Herald Tribune* 22-23 Mar 1986 ; 6.

2741. Stein, Jonathan B. : From H-Bomb to Star wars : The politics of strategic decision making. Mass, Lexington Books. 1984. Pp. 135.

2742. Steinberg, Gerald : Ultimate battle ground weapons in space. *Technology Review* (Mass) Oct 1981.

2743. Stop space arms race-Qian. *China Daily* 15 Nov 1984 ; 4.

2744. Thompson, E.P. *ed.* : *Star Wars*. London, Penguin Books, 1986 ; Pp. 165.

2745. Toth, Robert C : Debaters' confrontation over 'Star Wars' system ignored hard realities. *International Herald Tribune* 24 Oct 1984 ; 3.

2746. Trying to plug leaks in SDI. *International Herald Tribune* 9 Jan 1986 ; 1, 13.

2747. Tsipis, Kosta : Laser Weapons *Scientific American* 245 (6) Dec 1981 ; 35-41.

2748. Ulsamer, Edgar : Space : The fourth dimension. *Air Force Magazine* 1982.

2749. US to test anti-satellite weapon. *Ta Kung Pao* 22 Aug 1985 ; 12.

2750. Where does SDI originate ? *Moscow News* 8 Feb 1987 ; 5.

2751. Wilford, John Noble : After the loss of challenger : America reassesses its future in space. *International Herald Tribune* 19 Mar 1986 ; 6.

2752. Wilford, John Noble : Space and American vision. *Times* (New York) 3 Apr 1981.

2753. Yoder, Edwin, M. : Space is no longer a place too distant for tears. *International Herald Tribune* 3 Feb 1986 ; 4.

Technology

2754. Alexander, Yonah : Terrorism and high-technology weapons. In *POI* ; 225-40.

2755. Brown, Herbert H. : Transfer of nuclear technology : Dangers and safeguards. In *LAIT* ; 150-79.

2756. Clark, Richard Charles : *Technological Terrorism* Old Greenwich, 1980.

2757. Coll, Steve : Terror of technology. *Telegraph* (Calcutta) 17 Jan 1986 ; 9.

2758. Goldman, Maurice : Technology, Science and anarchism : The terrible flaw. Anarchy (25) Mar 1963 ; 70-74.

2759. Jenkins, Brian : *High technology terrorism and surrogate war : The impact of new technology on low-level violence.* Santa Monica Rand Corp. Nov. 1975.

2760. Jenkins, Brian M and Alfred P. Rubin : Technology to Combat terrorism. In *LAIT* ; 253-69.

2761. Mengel, R. : William *Terrorism and new technologies of destruction.* Vienna, the BDM Corporation, 1976.

2762. Ritter, Alan : *Technology and anarchism.* (Paper delivered at the 1974 annual meeting of the American Political Science Association, USA).

2763. Terrorism fallout. *Times of India* 25 Jan 1986 ; 8.

The increase in terrorist activities internationally has given a boost to U.S. businessmen selling counter-terrorism technology. There has been an explosive growth among U.S. companies selling barrier systems, closed-circuit TV cameras, entry-control devices, armoured cars and security gadgets. There has also been a remarkable growth in the number of security consultants, analysers and anti-terrorism training centres. Talking of the market fallout of terrorism. Warren H. Metzner, past chairman of the terrorist activity committee of the American Society for Industrial Security, recently for Industrial Security, recently told The Washington Post, "we have got so many exeperts on terrorism (that) it's nauseating... This is probably one of the most marketable commodities anybody's come up with in years. Hang the word terrorism on it and it's amazing how it causes people to respond. It might be shocking to go round and see how much is serving the purchaser ineffectively."

The size of the U.S. private security industry was estimated to be $ 22 billion in 1981, with an annual 12 to 15 percent growth rate, compared to $ 14 billion for all the tax-paid police, deputies, troopers and federal security organisations in the country. However, the share of the anti-terrorism related sector in the total figure is impossible to determine because nearly all the devices and services function primarily to halt ordinary crime : breaking and entering, employee theft and industrial espionage. The major purchaser of anti-terrorism expertise is the U.S. governments itself. Last year, the government approached the Congress for authorising a budget of $ 4.2 billion for a 10-year programme of anti-terrorism construction, training, organisation and electronic-security equipment for more than 300 U.S. facilities overseas. At least 75 per cent of this amount is likely to go to U.S. security contractors, manufacturers and transporters.

2764. Tsagolov, Georgi : *War is their business : the US military-industrial complex.* Moscow, Progress Publishers, 1985. Pp. 292.

Torture

2765. Arendt, Hannah : *Origins of totalitarianism.* New York, 1973.

2766. Alexander, Yonay and Kenneth A Myers. *Terrorism in Europe* New York, 1982.

2767. Alleg, Henri : *Question.* New York, 1958.

2768. *Annesty International Report on allegations of torture in Brazil.* London, 1977.

2769. Arendt, Hannah : *Crises of the Republic* New York, 1972.

2770. Arkoun, Mohammed : Death penality and torture in Islamic thought. In *Death penality and torture* Ed. by Bockle and Pohier.

2771. Bellamy, John : *Tudor law of treason.* Toronto, 1979.

2772. Berman, Harold J. : *Law and Revolution.* Cambridge, 1983.

2773. Berman, Harold J. and James W. Spindler *eds.* : *Soviet Criminal law and procedure : The RSFSR Codes.* Cambridge, 1972.

2774. Bernstein, Hilda : *South Africa : The terrorism of torture.* London, 1972.

2775. Bockle, Franz and Jacques Pohier *eds.* : *Death penality and torture.* Concilium : Religion in the seventies, Vol. 120 (New York, 1979).

2776. Brownlie, Ian. : *Basic documents on human rights.* Oxford, 1981.

2777. Brownlie, Ian. : *Basic documents in International law.* Oxford, 1983.

2778. Cain, Maureen and Alan Hunt : *Marx and Engels on the Law.* London, 1979.

2779. Cobb, Richard : *Police and the people : French popular protest. 1789-1820.* Oxford, 1970.

2780. Cutler, S. H. : *Law of treason and treason trials in later Medieval France.* Cambridge, 1982.

2781. Cygielman, Victor : Torture's Ugly head, *New Outlook* Apr-May 1976 ; 17-20.

2782. De Polnay, Peter : *Napoleon's police.* London, 1970.

2783. Edgerton, Samuel Y. : *Pictures and punishment : Art and Criminal prosecution during the Florentine Renaissance.* New York, 1984.

2784. Elton, G. R. : *Policy and police.* Cambridge, 1972.

2785. Esmein : *History of continental criminal procedure.*

2786. Fanon, Frantz : *Wretched of the earth.* New York, 1968.

2787. Finer, Herman : *Mussolini's Italy.* Hamden, 1964.

2788. Flynn, Peter : Brazil : A political analysis. London, 1978.

2789. Forsythe, David P. : *Human rights and world politics.* London, 1983.

2790. Foucault, Michel : *Discipline and punish : The birth of the prison.* New York, 1977.

2791. Frye, Willian R. : In *whitest Africa : the dynamics of opartheid.* Englewood Cliffs, 1968.

2792. Fuller, L. : Pashukanis and Vyshinsky. *Michigan Law Review* 47, 1949.

2793. Gage, Nicholas : *Eleni* New York, 1983.

2794. Garnsey, Peter : *Social status and legal privilege in the Roman empire.* Oxford, 1970.

2795. Gatrell, V.A.C. : Bruce Lenman and Geoffrey Panker. *eds. Crime and the law : The social history of crime in Western Europe since 1500.* London, 1980.

2796. Gerson, Lennard D. : *Secret police in Lenin's Russia.* Philadelphia, 1976.

2797. Goleman, Daniel : Torture's mind. *Nagpur Times* 26 May 1985.

2798. Gsovski, Vladimir and Kazimierz. *eds.*: *Government, law and courts in the Soviet Union and Eastern Europe. 2 Vols.* New York, 1960.

2799. Havelock, A. : *Greek concept of justice.* Cambridge, 1978.

2800. Heath, James : *Torture and English Law.* Westport, 1980.

2801. Heyd, Uriel : *Studies in old ottoman criminal law. Ed. by V.L. Manage.* Oxford, 1973.

2802. Hinghely, Ronald : *Russian secret police : Muscovite, imperial Russia and Soviet political security operations. 1565-1970.* London, 1970.

2803. Hopkins, E. J. : *Our lawless police* Washington, U.S. Govt. Printing Office, 1931.

2804. Horne, Alistair : *Sawage War of peace : Algeria, 1954-62.* New York. 1977.

2805. Ingraham, Barton L. : *Political crime in Europe : A comparative study of France, Germany and England.* California, 1979.

2806. Jardine, David : *Reading on the use of torture in the criminal law of England previously to the Common wealth.* London, 1837.

2807. Joyce, James Avery : *Human rights : International documents 3 Vols.* Alphen, 1978.

2808. Kaiser, Deniel H. : *Growth of the law in ruedieral Russia.* Princeton, 1980.

2809. Kirchheimer, Otto : *Political justice.* Princeton 1961.

2810. Kirchheimer, Otto : *Politics, law and social change. Ed. by E.S. Burin and Kurt L. Shell.* New York. *1969.*

2811. Kirchheimer, Otto and Georg Ruschl. *Punishment and social structure.* New York, 1939.

2812. Kostelianetz, Michael, and Ole Aalund : Torture : A challenge to medical science. *Interdisciplinary Science Review* 8 (1983).

2813. Kuttner, Stephan and Knut Norr. In *Renaissance and renewal in the twentieth century.* Ed. by Robert L. Benson and Ciles Constable. Cambridge, 1982.

2814. Langbein, John H. : *Prosecuting crime in the Reneissance.* Cambridge, 1974.

2815. Langbein, John H. : *Torture and the law of proof.* Chicago, 1977.

2816. Larson, Egon : *Flame in barbed wire : the story of Annesty International.* New York, 1979.

2817. Lapenna, Ivo. : *Soviet penal policy.* Toronto, 1968.

2818. Laqueur, Walter : *Terrorism.* Boston, 1977.

2819. Lavine, Emmanuel H. : *Third degree : American police methods.* Washington U. S. Govt. Printing Office, 1933.

2820. Lea, Henry Charles : *Materials for a history of witchcraft Ed. by Arthur Howland. Philadelphia, 1939.* (Represented New York, 1957).

2821. Lea, Henry Charles. : *Superstition and force.* Philadelphia, 1866.

2822. Ledesma, Luis : Stockholm clinic for torture victims. *Free Press Journal* 13 Feb 1986 ; 4.

Sweden's first clinic designed exclusively for the rehabilitation of political refugees who have been tortured recently opened here at Stockholm's Red Cross Hospital.

The first patients at the clinic—an experimental project that will operate until August 1987—are about 100 political refugees from different countries who now reside in Sweden. Treatment at the centre is aimed at healing the physical, psychological and emotional aftereffects of torture. The victim's family will also be brought into the programmes, according to Dr. Per Borgaa, the clinic's medical director.

Dr. Borgaa said that the staff includes 15 specialists with varied expertise—physicians, psychiatrists, physical therapists, social workers and nurses. "The work will be specially focused to provide a wholistic approach to the entire situation of people who have been torture victims," he said. "Continuity and comprehensiveness are key words in our task."

Special care has been taken to furnish the clinic with comfortable furniture, plants and pictures on the walls, he said, to provide a calm and secure atmosphere for the patients. Sterile rooms and white medical uniforms would only increase a torture victim's feeling of insecurity, he said.

Dr. Borgaa said the clinic team has three general goals : to decrease the patients' physical and psychological suffering ; strengthen their self-confidence and sense of personal identity ; and enable them and their families to lead normal lives.

Similar work at clinics in Belgium, Canada and Denmark has indicated that torture victims should not undergo any kind of physical treatment that causes them pain or upsets them, the medical director noted.

For this reason, Dr. Borgaa said, the main methods of physical therapy used here will be message, heat treatment and ultrasound. He stressed, however, that in most cases the physical results of torture are less severe than the psychological scars, and the medical treatment at the Stockholm centre is designed with this in mind.

2823. Leggett, George : *Cheka : Lenin's political police.* Oxford, 1981.

2824. Maestro, Marcello T. : *Voltaire and Beccaria as reformers of criminal law.* New York, 1942.

2825. Makepeace, R.W. : *Marxist ideology and Soviet criminal.* London, 1980.

2826. Melxack, Ronald and Patrick D. Wall. *Challenge of pain.* New York, 1983.

2827. Melzack, Ronald : *Puzzle of pain.* New York. 1973.

2828. Miller, Wilbur R. : *Cops and bobbies : Police authority in New York and London, 1830-1870.* Chicago, 1970.

2829. Monkonnen, Eric H. : *Police in urban America, 1860-1920.* Cambridge, 1981.

2830. Naipaul, *V. S.* : *Return of Eva Peron.* New York, 1981.

2831. Payne, Howard C. : *Police state of Louis Napoleon Bonaparte, 1851-1860.* Seattle, 1966.

2832. Peters, Edwards : *Heresy and authority in Medieval Europe.* Philadelphia, 1980.

2833. Peters, Edwards : *Torture.* Oxford, Basil Blackwell, 1985. Pp. 202.

2834. Philips, Paul : *Marx and Engels on law and Laws.* Oxford, 1979.

2835. Power, Jonathan. : *Annesty International the human rights story.* New York, 1981.

2836. Ramcharan, B. G. *ed.* : *Human rights : Thirty years after the Universal declaration.* The Hague, 1979.

2837. *Report of the Commissioner for the investigation of alleged cases of torture in the Madras Presidency*, Madras, 1855.

2838. Ruthven, Malise : *Torture : The grand conspiracy.* London, 1978.

2839. Sachs, Albie : *Justice in South Africa.* London, 1973.

2840. Salvemini, Gaetano : *Fascist dictatorship in fascist Italy.* New York, 1927.

2841. Sanford, Nevitt and Graig Gomstock. *et. al.* : *Sanctions for evil.* San Francisco, 1971.

2842. Seighart, Paul : *International law of human rights.* Oxford, 1983.

2843. Smith, Gertrude : *Administration of justice from Homer Aristotle. 2 Vols. 1930.* New York, 1970 (Reprinted).

2844. Harrison, A. R. W. : *Law of Athens.* 2 vols. Oxford, 1968.

2845. Solomon, Peter H. : *Soviet criminologists and criminal policy.* New York, 1978.

2846. Squire, P. S. : *Third Department.* Cambridge, 1968.

2847. Stiner, H. Arthur : *Government in Fascist Italy.* New York, 1938.

2848. Talmon, J. L. : *Myth of the nation and the vision of revolution* Berkeley, Berkeley, 1980.

2849. Talmon, J. L. : *Origins of totalitarian democracy.* New York, 1970.

2850. Talmon, J. L. : *Political messianism : The romantic phase.* New York, 1960.

2851. Taylor, Telford : *Nuremberg and Vietnam : An American tragedy.* New York, 1970.

2852. Tejada, A. M. Ruiz-Mateos Jiminez de. : Medical care of prisoners. In *Death penality and torture* ; 114-118.

2853. Thoma, Clemens : Death penality and torture in the Jewish tradition. In *Death penality and torture.* Ed. by Bockle and Pohier.

2854. Timerman, Jacopo : *Prisoner without a name, cell without a number.* New York, 1981.

2855. Timerman, Jacopo : Return to Argentina. *New York Times Magazine* 11 Mar 1984.

2856. Torture, execution of Peruvian prisoners. *Patriot* 10 Feb 1987 ; 7.

2857. *Torture : How to make the international convention effective.* Geneva, International Commission of Jurists and the Swiss Committee Against Torture, 1980.

2858. *Torture in Greece : The first torturer's trial 1975.* London, Annesty International, 195.

2859. *Torture in the eighties.* London. Annesty International, 1984.

2860. Torture widespread in Turkey. *Newstime* 14 Aug 1985 ; 8.

2861. Twining, W. L. and P. E. Bentham on torture. *Northern Ireland Legal Quarterly* 24, 1973 ; 305-56.

2862. Vidal-Naquet : *Torture : Cancer of democracy.* 1972.

2863. Walker, Samuel : *Popular justice.* New York, 1980.

2864. Walzer, Michael : Timerman and his enemies. *New York Review of Books* 24 Sep 1981.

2865. Watson, Alan : Roman Slave and Romanist ideology. *Phoenix* 37 (1978) ; 53-65.

2866. Welling, James C. : *Law of torture : A study in the evolution of law.* Washington, 1982.

2867. Whitfield, Stephen J. : *Into the dark : Hannah Arendt and totalitarianism.* Philadelphia, 1980.

2868. Wright, Gordon : *Between the guillotine and liberty* : *Two centuries of the crime problem in France*. New York, 1983.

TOTALITARIANISM

2869. Arendt, Hannah : *Origins of totalitarianism*. New York, Harcourt, Brace and World, 1966.

2870. Friedrich. Carl J. and Z.K. Brezenski : *Totalitarianism dictatorship and autocracy*. New York, Prayer, 1966.

2871. Hannah, Arendt : *Origins of totalitarianism*. London, 1967.

2872. Talmon, Jacob L. : *Origins of totalitarian democracy*. London, Mercury Books, 1961.

2873. Wilkinson, Paul : Resistance against totalitarianism. In *Political terrorism*. London, Macmillan, 1974 ; 107-9.

TOURISM

2874. Blumenthal, Ralph : Terrorism makes tourist shaky. *Amrita Bazar Patrika* 21 Jan 1986 ; 9.

Terrorist attacks on travellers have shaken the volatile travel industry and latered patterns of international tourism, according to industry and government representatives.

Around the nation, travel agents say, clients are calling to ask whether it is safe to take trips. Some fearful customers, they say, have cancelled overseas trips and others have shifted their destinations to places considered potentially less dangerous, choosing in some cases, the Soviet Union and other communist countries.

Immediately after the terrorist attacks on December 27 at the Rome and Vienna airports, for example, Trans-World Airlines lost about 4,000 bookings, according to a reliable airline source that TWA spokesmen did not dispute.

Travel agents are fielding many of the questions. "A year ago we would have said, go on a cruise," said Joseph Hallissey, President of the American Society of Travel Agents, who is head of his own agency in Dearboru, Mich the Achille Lauro blew us away.

The seizure of that Italian cruise ship on October 7 and the killing of an elderly American passenger followed an earlier terrorist assault, the hijacking of TWA flight 814 out of Athens.

After the ship hijacking, terrorists on November 23 hijacked an Egyptair flight from Athens to Malta. Egyptian commandos stormed the plane and 60 people died. The terrorist attacks, moreover, come during a record year of crashes and fatalities for commercial aviation.

2875. Blumenthal, Ralph : Terrorism, Weaker Dollar keeping American home. *International Herald Tribune* 3 Apr 1986 ; 1-5.

2876. Jamos, George : U.S. travellers more wary of Europe. *International Herald Tribune* 18 Apr 1986 ; 4.

2877. Nguyen, J.T. : Terrorism hurts Europe's tourist industry. *Egyptian Gazette* 27 Apr 1986 ; 5.

2878. Raju, R.K. : Tourism hit by terrorism. *Statesman* 12 Aug 1985 ; 1.

2879. Trucco, Terry : Europeans taking terrorism in stride. *International Herald Tribune* 22 Jan 1986 : 1-7.

2880. Viswam, S. : Terrorism guns down tourism. *Tribune* (Chandigarh) 4 Jun 1986 ; 5.

What do Kashmir, Britain, France, Switzerland, Spain, France, and Greece have in common? All of them are experiencing, in varying degrees, the adverse impact of international terrorism on tourism. Hotels in the tourist resorts in all these "tourist paradises" are faced with massive cancellation of bookings. And all of them are making desperate attempts to lure back international tourists, especially from the U.S.A. and Japan, with the dual objective of boosting their sagging revenues and proving that terrorism is not such a menace as has been made out.

Tourism has suffered for a variety of reasons in Kashmir but principally because of terrorism in Punjab, through which surface tourists have to pass to reach the valley. For the past three years, there has been a steady decline of domestic tourist influx into Kashmir, although a fair number of international tourists flying into Srinagar have been spending brief holidays at the height of the season. Since Kashmir's tourist revenues come mostly from domestic holiday-makers, there has been growing alarm in the valley over the unceasing terrorist activity in Punjab. One or two more years of terrorism in Punjab, and Kashmir may as well write off tourism as its principal "industry".

Transistor Bombs

2881. Chakravarty, Pratap : Transistor bomb suspect had international links. *Patriot* 26 May 1985 ; 1.

2882. Transistor bombs again : *Deccan Herald* 24 Sep 1985 ; 6.

2883. Transistor bomb : Deadly ploy. *India Today* 31 May 1985 ; 33.

2884. Viswam, S. : Recent transistor bomb blasts. Strategy and politics, of terrorism. *Deccan Herald* 17 May 1985 ; 8.

Urban Context

2885. Dynamiting of urban quarters and entire villages and mass expulsion of inhabitants. In *WTAZIT* ; 46-47.

2886. Grabosky, P.N. : Urban context of political terrorism. In *POT* ; 51-76.

Any discussion of urban terrorism must confront a set of fundamental questions. What, if my, is the relationship between the urban setting and the terrorist act ? Why is contemporary terrorist activity predominantly urban ? Is there anything specifically urban about the terrorism that occurs in cities ? Does terrorism "just happen" to occur in urban areas, or is there something in the structure of cities that produces or facilitates this form of political behaviour ? These questions are of special importance given the tendency of most commentators on urban terrorism to ignore them, or, at best, to deal with them superficially and implicitly.

What is it the, that characterizes cities ? What structural factors distinguish cities from other social systems ? The first hallmarks of the urban system are population size and density. Cities are inhabited by relatively large numbers of citizens living in relatively close proximity. Cities also tend to be heterogeneous, much more so that rural areas within the same society. Although racially or ethnically pluralistic societies may be characterized by regional concentrations of the various component groups, it is the urban places within these societies where these various social groups are likely to be found in closer proximity. Social heterogeneity is also likely to be a recognizable feature of an urban social structure ; social distances between rich and poor neighbourhoods tend to be greater than spatial distances. A corollary of these conditions is a characteristic familiar to most observers of urban society: anonymity. In the city, there are more strangers about ; any one individual is less conspicuous, particularly so in large dense, and socially differentiated populations. Although it may not be accurate to speak of the universal atomization of urban life, one can argue that in some cities, and to an increasing extent, people make a point of not knowing their neighbours' business.

Yet, at the same time, ironically, one of the more significant characteristics of urban societies is the interdependence of their members. Unlike more primitive social systems wherein individuals or families may be self-sufficient, urban living is marked by a differentiation of productive responsibilities. Complex economic, transportation, and communications systems, themselves interdependent, demand a certain level of cooperation uncalled for in simpler social settings. One other phenomenon merits mention here, for as one of the most significant trends in modern human civilization, its influence on social life and on terroristic activity is indisputable. The phenomenon is that of urbanization. Moreover, the pace at which this process has accelerated during the past decade alone is truly staggering. The growth rate of many Third World cities, attributable to urban drift as well as to natural population increase, can reach from 3 to 8 percent each year ; cities have doubled in size within a decade. It is estimated that by 1985, the population of the Mexico City metropolitan area will reach 17 million : Sao Paolo, 16 million ; Calcutta, 12 million ; and Buenos Aires, 11 million. By 1990, over 70 percent of the Brazilian and Mexican populations will inhabit metropolitan areas, and over 85 percent of the population of Argentina will be urbanized (Wilsher, 1975).

Thus, one explanation for the prevalence of terroristic activity in urban areas is the increasing salience of urbanization per se. And yet, it would be grossly simplistic to suggest that the link between cities and terrorism merely reflects the truism that there is a greater abundance of everything in cities. The pages that follow draw there is a greater abundance of everything in cities. The pages that follow draw from examples widely dispersed over time and space but do not pretend to present a systematic survey of urban terrorist activity. Rather, they are intended specifically to show how the structure of cities conditions various aspects of terrorist organization and practice, both repressive and insurrectionary.

The urban location bears upon the recruitment of prospective terrorists in a predictable manner, for it is the city that nurtures dissidence in general. Much has been said of the close juxtaposition of great wealth and abject poverty that may be seen in urban areas, and of the socially dislocative effects of urban migration (Moss, 1971, pp. 5-8). Those who find themselves toward the bottom of the socioeconomic ladder might be regarded as prospective participants in riots or unplanned collective disorders ; however, they tend not to engage in terrorist activity. Indeed, most contemporary terrorists, whether in Japan, Uruguay, the United States, or Germany, appear to have been drawn from the ranks of the middle classes.

It is the cities where universities provide for large concentrations of young members of the middle class. It is the city where these individuals tend to be exposed to fundamental principles of social justice and at the same time are confronted with the realities that so blatantly contradict those principles. And, of no little significance, it is the city where these individuals tend to be exposed to varieties of revolutionary theory (Hobsbawm, 1973, p. 221). Thus it is the young middle class, particularly the middle-class student population, from which most contemporary urban terrorists have been recruited.

2887. Mack, Andrew : *Non-strategy of urban guerillas warfare.* In *UG* ; 22-45.

Urban guerilla warfare enjoyed a brief vogue in the US in the late 1960s and the early 1970s. It was articulated by a number of militant black groups and by white militants like the Weathermen. It manifested itself in a wave of sabotage operations, arson attempts, bombings and shootouts. In 1970, there were over 4,000 bombings recorded—though it is not known how many of them were politically motivated. Like many other attempts at urban guerrilla warfare, the US model should be seen more as a reaction to the failure of previous programmes, most particularly the civil rights movement, than as a carefully thought-out strategy. In ideology the militants leant heavily on the work of Franz Fanon and were influenced to a degree by Marcuse. Tactics of disruption were spelled out in detail. In Chicago, for example, 'every fourth street is commercial, arsonists could set off fires in the principal white-owned businesses of each street, thereby occupying the fire and police departments, while saboteurs spread out over the city to derail trains (most of which run through the ghettoes), blow up power plants and despoil water systems.' The objective was clearly that of massive disruption—bringing the system to a standstill. But it was less clear what would be gained by this. It was a polarising strategy which made no sense. To polarise a conflict is strategically rational if as a consequence the enemy becomes isolated and the resulting alignment of forces favours the insurgents. Thus FLN terrorism against the French in Algeria had the effect of invoking savage counter-measures against the FLM which were—inevitably—indiscriminate. This politicised the mass of the Moslem population against the French along the lines of a pre-existing social and political cleavage. In other contests the opposite may be true. French partisan actions against the Germans in W.W. II led to savage and indiscriminate reprisals against the civil population for which the partisans were blamed as well as the Nazis. The French population was already divided into a majority of collaborators and a minority of resistance fithers. Terrorism polarised Frenchmen against Frenchmen rather than French against Germans. Nothing is easier than achieving polarisation. A group of fanatics only has to machine-gun children leaving school to polarise the entire community againt them. Such polarisation, needless to say, provides authorities with the necessary political backing for extreme measures of repression.

The real force of opposition to urban guerilla tactics in the US came not so much from the political elite which could afford to make concession—but rather from the so-called 'silent majority'. Initial tactical successes were possible for the militants because the repressive forces were not sufficiently geared up to cope with the bombings. The repressive forces were then increased, as was surveillance and infiltration. Increased repression did not result, however, in increased support for the militants but rather increased support for repression. Violence was the worst of all possible tactics in the American context since it meant confronting the enemy on his own terms. Force was met by infinitely superior force which by and large received popular backing.

The US provides a classic example of the futility of a revolutionary 'strategy' based on violent tactics employed by a minority whose status is ascriptive. Blacks cannot join the majority if the essence of black nationalism is the positive assertion of black culture in contradistinction to white culture. The ghetto provides a limited protection against moderate repression in a liberal society, but world provide no protection at all to policies of encirclement and massive repression if the escalation of violence swept away liberal constraints. (The clearest example of this is of course the Warsaw ghetto uprising). Thus if urban guerilla warfare were to be escalated as a conscious policy then the first requirement of strategy—that of not being defeated—would in all probability not be met. The separatist solution, as Martin Oppenheimer points out in his study Urban Guerilla, would—if it succeeded—simply lead to a policy of 'neo-colonialism' and reinforce existing tendencies of 'ghettoisation.' If we look at urban guerilla tactics in advanced industrial societies as tactics of reform rather than revolution—and under this rubric we could include non-violent disruptive tactics—then it is clear that liberal values such as 'justice', 'democracy' and 'fairness' are a useful resource. The espousal of such values may well be hypocritical—that is immaterial—the point is that they may be manipulated. The fact that governments frequently go to great lengths to deny that they contravene these values, show that they may provide a useful, though limited lever, for reform. By the same token liberal values may act—initially at least—as a brake on the repressive forces which will ultimately have to be released in order to crush a growing insurgency. The liberalism of the Pacheco government in Uruguay, for example, with the various constitutional guarantees of citizens rights which that liberalism entailed (albeit weakly), enabled the Tupamaros to flourish. By contrast, the abandonment of any pretence of liberal democratic rights by the succeeding Bordaberry regime has not only an external power with less than vital interests in continuing the struggle as were the NLF in Vietnam, the FLN in Algeria and the IRA in Ulster currently. They are confronting a power which does not see withdrawal as an option and which perceives the security of the state to be at stake. Such tactics against the Israelis do not significantly alter their military capability at all, have only a limited effect on their economic system, but increase their political capability to wage war by bridging over the conflicts which might in other circumstances undermine that capability. Jewish terrorist tactics employed by Irgun and the Stern Gang were not ineffectual in the struggle waged by the Jews in Palestine against the British. But the contemporary debate within Israel is not whether to fight the war (contrast the debate in the US over Vietnam) but how to fight it.

Urban guerilla warfare first came into prominence in Latin America during the 1960s, at the beginning of the decade, with the FLN activities in Venezuela. A widespread urban insurgency movement failed to galvanise the masses despite Communist Party support initially. The unpopularity of urban guerilla tactics was clearly indicated in the 1963 elections when, despite guerilla instructions to boycott the polls, the Betancourt government won an overwhelming mandate from the voters on a 90% turnout. The Venezuelan, experience had two important consequences. First, it gave urban guerilla warfare a bad name—it was bitterly attacked some years later by Regis Debray, the architect of the so-called guerrilla foco theory of revolution. Secondly, it created a bitter division between the orthodox Communist party and the more militant leftist groups which was to be the hallmark of the 1960s. The

Communists maintained that urban guerilla tactics were 'adventurist' and argued—with some logic—that such tactics tended to alienate masses who were not politicised. The success of the Castro rural guerilla movement, based on the 'foco' theory and the experience (more admired than emulated) of the Vietnamese revolutionaries were to become the models for the 1960s. Rural guerilla groups flourished throughout Latin America during the 1960s, but by the end of the decade, after some initial tactical successes, most of them had either been destroyed or heavily weakened. Richard Gott, in his authorative study of guerilla movements in Latin America, attributes this failure largely to the superiority of the American trained and sometimes American-led counter-insurgency operations. But this is simply another way of saying that the Latin American guerillas were considerably inferior to their Vietnamese counterparts, since the Vistnamese had withstood successfully an American counter-insurgency effort which dwarfed the relatively low intensity programmes carried out in Central and South America. The theoretical keystone of the rural guerilla campaigns was the so-called 'foco' theory which derived from the Cuban experience, and which was articulated by Debray in his Revolution in the Revolution. Crudely speaking, the foco theory broke with classical (Maoist) guerilla strategy by arguing that military action on its own could create the conditions for a revolution. However, the failure of the rural guerilla movements led to a re-evaluation of guerilla tactics. Critics of Debray argued that the increasing urbanisation of Latin America meant that the focus of action had to be the cities, and that rural guerilla warfare had an increasingly peripheral role to play in an overall revolutionary strategy. Since the Communist Party was seen as too timid and corrupted by its ties with an opportunistic Soviet Union, the guerilla 'foco' had to be transferred to the city. The strategy of urban guerilla warfare on the 'foco' model is not clearly and precisely articulated by Carlos Marighella in his Mini-Manual of Urban Guerilla Warfare. In essense, Marighella's strategy was both elitist and ruthless. 'It is necessary', wrote Marighella, 'to turn a political crisis into armed conflict by performing violent actions that will force those in power to transform the political situation of the country into a military situation. This will alienate the masses who, from then on, will revolt against the army and the police and thus blame them for this state of things.' In other words, the basic strategy is to catalyse repression by violent actions. It is remarkably similar in conception to that of Tom Hayden, one of the founder members of the SDS in the United States. 'The coming of repression will speed up time, making a revolutionary situation more likely—We are creating an America where it is necessary for the government to rule behind barbed wire, for the President to speak only at military bases and, finally where it will be necessary for the people to fight back'. Hayden argued, the key question is—do the masses blame the government for law and order measures or do they perceive these as a necessary inconvenience which has to be suffered in order to get rid of troublemakers. In the United States it would appear to be the later case. But even where the government is accorded little legitimacy and even actively despised, the situation presents an interesting example of the 'collective goods' problem. For the individual in such a situation, it can be argued that doing nothing presents minimal risks. This is true whichever side wins. Joining the guerrillas, on the other hand, presents very real and very obvious risks. One person's efforts will make no difference either way and, therefore, the best strategy is to lie low and do nothing. In doing nothing one risks nothing, while still standing to gain if the revolution succeeds.

2888. Mallin, Jay *ed.* : *Terror and urban guerillas.* Coral Gables, Univ. of Miami, 1971.

2889. Marighella, Carlos : *Minimanual of the urban Guerilla. New World Liberation Front*, 1970.

2890. Moss, Robert : *Urban Guerilla warfare* London, 1971.

2891. Niezing, John *ed.* : *Urban guerilla.* Rotterdam University Press, 1974.Pp. 149.

2892. *On organising urban guerilla units.* Afro-American Liberation Army, 1970.

2893. Teitler, G. : Urban guerilla, as a revolutionary phenomenon and as a recruiting problem. In *UG* ; 111-30.

Hearing or reading the term urban guerilla, one immediately thinks of the revolutionary action of left-wing youths in Latin-America. Characteristic of this action are the kidnapping of politicians, businessmen and diplomats (sometimes releasing them once a ransom has been paid), the robbing of banks in order to finance their organisational and propaganda work, and the liquidation of people who have made themselves particularly hateful in the eyes of the revolutionaries. Finally, with the term urban guerilla, one thinks of revolutionary action occurring only in large cities, that cannot therefore be regarded as an (more or less) important extension of rural revolutionary activities. However, if one is generally interested in the phenomenon of urban guerilla, one will naturally first have to abandon the geographical time bound limitation to the Latin-America of today, and have to concede that the direct association with left-wing youths does not hold water. In my opinion, the term guerilla denotes a certain violence technique, and the use of this is not reserved for the left wing of the political spectrum. During the French Revolution, peasants in the Vendee applied guerilla techniques in their resistance against the attacking revolutionary armies—successfully for a considerable time—whereas the use of the term guerilla probably originates in the resistance of the Spanish peasants against the Napoleonic regime. In both cases, the peasants found their leaders in the rural clergy and proved to be very attached to their old dynasties. Reason enough to assume that neither the guerilla nor the urban guerilla belong to the exclusive revolutionary set of instruments of left-wing political groups.

In other words he who wishes to pay attention to the phenomenon of the urban guerilla should, in my opinion, concentrate on the activities carried out in this, and not—at least not at first—to the political ideologies of the persons and groups promoting these activities. Where these ideologies can display an enormous diversity, that which is constant as regards the phenomenon of the urban guerilla continues to lie in the techniques used in this. It is on this aspect that one should focus.

What is most striking here is that those who start to wage an urban guerilla do not make life easy for themselves. Resisting the social status quo is a perilous affair. He who wishes to give form to this resistance with violent means, would at first be wise—weak as he will be in the beginning—to avoid direct confrontations with the defenders of the existing order. The guerilla is an attrition-techniques, in which the resistance takes a long time to prepare itself for the ultimate reckoning. Thus for the time being it will wisely keep a distance from the power centres of the ruling groups, which in the majority of cases will be found in the cities, Those now who carry the urban guerilla into effect, give up the advantages of a relatively undisturbed environment for their preparations, in order to venture directly into the lion's den : the cities, where the opposer can be regarded as being at his strongest. The initial handicap confronting the members of a resistance movement commencing their activities in the cities—compared to colleagues—able to start their resistance from—relatively quiet and safe rural areas—is clearly illustrated by the history of the Dutch underground during the Second World War.

The Dutch resistance organisations found their operational field in one of the most urbanized areas in the world. Here the adversary to be opposed—the German occupier—profited to the full by the fact, that (at least in modern times and at least in the West) urbanization always goes paired with a gradual extension and perfecting of population registration techniques.

The problems with which the Dutch resistance fighters were faced were so great, that those of the underground groups in less urbanized and 'durch-administrierte' areas were nothing in comparison. The French Maquis and the Yugoslavian and Russian partisans were in a very much better position as far as the problem of hiding were concerned, than the Dutch resistance groups. In my opinion, it is clear that the relatively small significance of the Dutch resistance—an otherwise impressionistic conclusion—was caused to a not unimportant extent by this factor.

It is not an exaggeration to suppose that hiding is one of the most important problems confronting a resistance group. Making propaganda, enlisting, recruiting, indoctrinating. training, testing, preparing, reflecting and the licking of wounds are activities which should preferably be carried out as undisturbly as possible. A good and safe hiding place is an essential help to this. Before a resistance group can start with its actual resistance activities (the direct and indirect harwing of the power of the adversary), it must, in other words, first have solved its main problem, i.e. that of the hiding-place. In this respect, the Dutch resistance was faced with enormous problems. In view of the environment in which it had to operate, it could expect little safety from physically going into hiding and had first to think of 'administrative' escapes. Members of the Dutch resistance had to sabotage the existing population-registration apparatus and to gain control of it. They acquitted themselves of this task ingeniously, using means such as false (legitimacy)—papers and coupons, while at the same time infiltrating, sabotaging and even destroying population-registration and distribution card centres. Only, when this task had been completed and members of the resistance had thus assured themselves of a 'hiding-place' within the administrative system, could they start with the actual resistance work. Attacks on Germans and collaborators, helping shot down allied aircraft crews, the protection of Jews and other persons sought by the occupier, the sabotaging of German war efforts, etc., etc., therefore depended in Holland on an administrative virtuousity, won with the greatest of difficulty. Where so much energy had to be invested in taking care of the first simple conditions of life for a resistance group, it need surprise no one that relatively little energy remained for fighting the adversary. Measured according to this 'resistance output', much more is thus to be expected of a guerilla (the prefix 'rural' is hardly necessary, a guerilla as a military technique is so clearly associated with the country as well as with the working environment, that this extra indication is usually left out) than of an urban guerilla. The escape to forests and mountains takes far less trouble than sabotaging a modern bureaucratic apparatus. In addition to this, the repression-measures of the ruling power present more problems to the recruiting work in an urbanized environment than in rural areas. We shall return to this point later.

From these remarks, rather gloomy for the urban guerilla, it may not be concluded however, that the defenders of the status quo are invulnerable in their cities. Such a conclusion would be too hasty. He however, who wishes to attain with some regularity satisfactory results in an urbanized area with resistance activities, should realize that, as experience has shown, techniques must be used which differ, to a fairly high degree. Recent Dutch history can once more provide us with an illustration of this statement. Undoubtedly, the highlights of the resistance against the German occupier were the February strike of 1942—a reaction to the escalating measures against the Jews in Amsterdam—and the Railway Strike of 1944—coinciding with the Battle of Arnhem. And how spontaneous the first strike was in comparison to the second proof of the increasing centralization and professionalization of the resistance —both strikes are valid examples of civil disobedience actions.

Violence

2894. Abraham, A.S. : Politics of violence, Varieties of terrorism. *Times of India* 18 May 1984 ; 6.

2895. Abu-Lughood, Ibrahim : Unconventional violence and international politics. *Proceedings. American Society of International Law* 67, 1973. *American Journal of Transnational Law* 13, 1974.

2896. Anable, David : Terrorism : Violence as theater. *Inter-Dependence* 3(1) Jan 1976 ; 1, 6.

2897. Anderson, W. : *Age of protest.* Pacific Palisades, California, Goodyear Publishing, 1969.

2898. Apter, David E. : Notes on the underground left : Violence and the national state. *Daedalus* Fall 1979 ; 155-72.

2899. Arendt, Hannah : Reflections on violence. *Journal of International Affairs* 23, 1969.

2900. Aron, Raymond. *History of the dialectic of violence.* Oxford, Baril Blackwell, 1975.

2901. Ben-Dak, Joseph D. *ed.* : *Future of collective violence : Societal and international perspectives.* New York, Humanities, 1974.

2902. Berkowitz, B.J. *et.al.* : *Super violence : The civil threat of mass destructive weapons.* Santa Barbara, ADCON Corp., 1972.

2903. Binen, Henry S. : and Mark Gersovitz : Consumer subsidy cuts, violence and political stability. *Comparative Politics* 19(1) Oct 1986 ; 25-44.

2904. Bingham, Jonathan B and Alfred M. Bingham : *Violence and democracy.* New York, 1971.

2905. Black, Cyril E. and Thomas P. Thornton *eds.* : *Communism and revolution : The strategic uses of political violence.* Princeton, 1964.

2906. Blumenthal, M.D. and R.L. Kahn : *Justifying violence-attitudes of American men.* Ann Arbor, University of Michigan, 1972.

2907. Bonante, Luigi. ed. : *Political violence in the contemporary world.* Nilan, 1979.

2908. Boudurant, John V and M.W. Fisher : *Conflict : Violence and non-violence.* Chicago, 1971.

2909. Boudurant, John V. : *Conquest of Violence.* Princeton, 1958.

2910. Calvert, P. : Diminishing returns of political violence. *New Middle East.* 56, May 1973 ; 25-27.

2911. Carlton, David : Future of political substate violence. In *TTP* ; 201-30.

2912. Chisholn, Henry J. : *Function of terror and violence in revolution.* George Town University, Master's Dissertation, 1948.

2913. *Civil Violence and the international system 2 Parts.* London, International Institute for Strategic Studies, 1971.

2914. Clutterbuck, Richard : *Britain in agony : The growth of political violence.* London, Faber and Faber, 1978. Pp. 335.

2915. Clutterbuck, Richard : Violence. In *Britain in agony.* London, Faber and Faber, 1978 ; 55-63.

2916. Conant, R. : *Prospects for revolution : A study of riots. Civil disobedience, and insurrection in contemporary America.* New York, Harper's Magazine Press, 1971.

2917. Connery, R.H. *ed.* : *Urban riots* : *Violence and social change*. New York, Random, 1969.

2918. Critchley, T.A. : *Conquest of Violence*. London, Constable, 1970.

2919. Daigan, Arthur. *Violence-USA*. New York, Bantam, 1975.

2920. Feierabend, IVO *et.al eds.* : *Anger, violence and politics*. N.J. Prentice Hall, 1972.

2921. Feldman, Arnold S. : Violence and voltility : The likelihood of revolution. In *Internal War*. Ed. by Harry EcKstein. London, 1964 ; 111-29.

2922. Fogeslson, R.M. : *Violence as protest* : *A study of riots and ghettos*. New York, Doubleday, 1971.

2923. Galtung, Johan. Violence, peace and peace research. *Journal of Peace Research* (3) 1969.

2924. Gross, Feliks. *Violence in politics* The Hague, Mouton, 1972.

2925. Gurr, T and C. Tuttenberg : *Conditions of civil violence*. Princeton, Center of International Studies, 1967.

2926. Hannah, Arendt : On violence. In *Crises of the Republic* Penguin, 1973 ; 83-103.

2927. Hudson, M.C. : *Conditions of political violence and instability*. 2 Vols. New York, Random House, 1970.

2928. Huntington, Samuel P. : *Civil violence and the process of development* London, IISS, 1971. (Adelphi Paper No. 83).

2929. Janos, Andrew C. : Authority and violence : The political framework of internal war. In *Internal War*. Ed. by Harry EcKstein. London, 1964 ; 130-41.

2930. Janowitz, M. : Patterns of collective racial violence. In *Violence in America* : *Historical and comparative perspectives*. Ed. by H.D. Graham and T.R. Gurr. New York, New American Library. 1969 ; 393-423.

2931. Kelman, Herbert C. : Violence without moral restraint. *Journal of Social Issues*. 29, 1974 ; 25-62.

2932. Kirkham, James F *et. al.* : *Assassination and political Violence*. New York, Times Books, 1970.

2933. Knopf, T.A. : Sniping—a new pattern of violence. In *Black experience* : *The transformation of activism*. Ed. by A. Meier. New Brusnswick, Transaction Books, 1970.

2934. Kourael, A Richard : Violence and the philosopher. *Journal of Value Inquiry* 8, Spr 1974 ; 37-45.

2935. Laqueur, Walter : Diversities of violence and the current world system. In *Adelphi Papers* (London) No 82, 1971 ; 9-16.

2936. Lee, Li, Ai. : Music with sex violence floods Third world. *Newstime* 14 Dec 1985 : 7.

2937. Leiden, Carl and Karl M. Schmitt : *Politics of violence : Revclution in the modern world.* Prentice-Hall, 1968.

2938. Lynn, L.F. : Combating violence with violence gets nowhere. *Ta Kung Pao* 10 Apr 1986 ; 12.

2939. MacFarlane, L. : *Violence and the State.* London, Nelson, 1974.

2940. Mahendra Kumar. : *Violence and non-violence in international relations.* Delhi, Thomson Press, 1975. Pp. 256.

2941. Mazrui, Ali A. : Contemporary case for violence. In *Adelphi Papers* (London) No. 82, 1971 ; 17-27.

2942. Mydans, Carl and Shelley : *Violent peace.* New York, Atheneum, 1968.

2943. Nardin, T. : *Violence and the state.* Beverly Hills, Calif, Sage, 1971.

2944. Nicburg, H.L. : *Political violence : The behavioural process,* New York, 1969.

2945. Popper, F.J. : Internal war as a stimulant of political development. *Comparative Political studies.* 3, Jan 1971.

2946. Powell, J. Bingham : *Contemporary democracies : Participation, stability and violence.* Cambridge, 1982.

2947. Pye, A. Kenneth and Cym H. Lowell : Criminal process during civil disorder. *Duke Law Journal* 3, Aug 1975 ; 581-690.

2948. Rivers, Charles R and Kanneth Switzer : *Violence.* New Jersey, Hayden, 1976.

2949. Rude, G. : *Crowd in history* 1730-1848. New York, Wiley, Willy, 1964.

2950. Sen, Mohit. : Violence, Non-violence and moral order. *Mainstream,* Republic Day 1987 ; 41-42.

In the discussions on violence, non-violence and the moral order, the general presumption seems to be that violence is immoral and non-violence is not immoral. At the highest level of abstraction this would be true. The taking of life and the compulsion of others on the basis of greater physical strength is against the canons and rules of human existence and civilisation. At the same time, violence and non-violence cannot be equated with the totality of morality nor with what is called the good or the bad.

The end of morality is the pursuit of such means as led to the coming into being by man and for man of the kingdom of freedom, based on the kingdom of necessity, to which both Marx and Engels drew our attention more than a century ago. Freedom was the recognition of necessity, according to Hegel and to them, but the freedom of man consisted in the "creation of his reality", on the basis of knowledge and the accomplishment of the making as the ruler of life, what were considered to be the norms of private behaviour.

Ends cannot be separated from means from both sides of the continuum. That is to say, "bad" means cannot lead to "good" ends, but it also is true that "good means" often lead to "bad" ends. We have seen that the use of violence and compulsion to achieve the goals of socialism does damage the ideal and the actuality of socialist society, though a lot of the fault cannot be laid at the door of those, who struggled for and built socialism in that manner.

There is, however, the other example, where the insistence on peaceful means in our country led to constraints on the mass movement, which finally erupted in the bloody partition of our country. It cast such a blight that Gandhiji cried out in anguish on August 14, 1947 that it was all "darkness within".

Ends and means are an organic or a dialectical unity, each not only reacting on the other, but representing a continuum. There is moreover, the indispensable element of historical conjuncture, the compulsions of the concrete situation. The struggle for socialism in India cannot and, indeed, must not be waged in the manner in which the battle against apartheid in South Africa can and must be fought. Both socialism and the abolition of apartheid are ethical and moral ends, but the means are anti-thetical and both are moral.

2951. Sharma, Udayan ed. : *Violence erupts*. New Delhi, Radha Krishna Prakashan, 1978. Pp. 148.

2952. Short, J.F. and M.E. Wolfgang eds. : *Why men rebel collective violence*. Chicago, Aldine Atherton, 1972.

2953. Sholmick, J.H. : *Politics of protest*. New York, Ballantine Books, 1969.

2954. Shorel, Georges : *Reflections on violence*. Glencoe, Free Press, 1950.

2955. Spitzer, Alan B. : *Old hatreds and young hopes*. Cambridge, HUP, 1971.

2956. Tolstoy, Leo : *Law of violence and the law of love*. New York, Bantam, 1971.

2957. Vohra, Gautam S.G. : Rising incidence of violence : Industrial unrest. *Times of India* 4 Dec 1973 ; 8.

2958. Walter, Eugene V. : Violence and the process of terror. *American Sociological Review* 29(2) Spr 1964 ; 248-57.

2959. Wilkinson, Paul : Social scientific : Theory and civil violence. In *TTP* ; 45-72.

2960. Wolff, R.P. : On violence. *Journal of Philosophy* 66(19) 1969 ; 601-16.

2961. Wolfgang, M and F. Ferracuti : *Subculture of violence*. London, Tavistock Press, 1964.

2962. Yablonsky, Leuis : *Violent gang*. New York, Macmillan, 1962.

2963. Zimring, Frank : Is gun control likely to reduce violent killings ? *University of Chicago Law Review* 35(4) Sum 1968 ; 721-37.

2964. Zinam, Oleg : Terrorism and violence in the light of a theory of discontent and frustration. In *ITCW* ; 240-68.

Violence and terror have existed since time immemorial. Yet those who believe in the perfectibility of human nature are puzzled by the observation that violence, organized crime, and terrorism are on the rise despite a remarkable improvement in human conditions. This experience seems to contradict the conventionally accepted notion that crime and violence are caused primarily by poverty and other kinds of human deprivations. Moreover, the increase in violence is proportionately greater in the most prosperous and technologically advanced countries.

The causes of this phenomenon are multifarious and extremely complex. But there is no doubt that it represents a serious and dangerous symptom of social disruption and malfunctioning. As Coser aptly stated, "human beings. . . will resort to violent action only under extremely frustrating, ego-damaging, and anxiety-producing conditions. It follows that if the incidence of violence increases rapidly. . . this can be taken as a signal of severe maladjustment."

Since the violence syndrome becomes more encompassing and menacing, it is necessary to analyze the historical conditions which have contributed to this problem. There are two major methods of studying social phenomena. One is to obtain the overall data on their incidence and relate them to values of other variables by using statistical methods in order to find some meaningful and useful generalizations. The other concentrates on a legitimate traditional question, "Why does individual A engage in deviating behaviour, when individual B does not ?" The causes of this type of behaviour have their deep roots in the overall social and cultural circumstances. Speaking of the relationship between the individual and international violence. McNeil comments that "without an increased understanding of the forces that shape the individual, we will forever fail to comprehend the direction that international violence may take."

In the late sixties a commission appointed to investigate the causes of violence found that one of the major obstacles in the way of understanding this social phenomenon was "the lack of a general theoretical framework with which to order our perceptions of the motives and attitudes that impel groups toward violence and the social conditions conductive to it."

The central purpose of this discussion is to analyze the impact of certain selected forces of modernization on the propensity for violence in contemporary society of the post-industrial type. The factors behind preference and focuses on the question of what causes a person to decide to act violently rather than within the limits of legitimacy and legality. An attempt is made to explain the rise in violence and terrorism in our modern age in terms of a theory of discontent and a theory of social change of the necessary and sufficient conditions type. The last part deals with an analysis of factors relevant to determining the legitimate use of force with some proposed long-range cultural changes which will eventually lead to a reduction in preference for violence.

One of the difficulties in conducting research in social sciences is the multiplicity of conflicting. Overlapping, and tautological definitions of terms. Though it has been stated that it is useless to argue about conflicting classifications, the use of terms and their definitions is not neutral. This is especially true if the term conveys a pejorative connotation, like violence. Therefore, this section is devoted to defining basic terms for the purpose of this study.

Power is defined here as "anything, the possession of which confers on the possessor the ability to proceed toward the desired goal despite resistance." This definition is akin to Max Weber's concept of power which he sees as "the probability that one actor within a social relationship will be in a position to carry out his own will despite resistance, regardless of the basis on which this probability rests". Nieburg, following Mumford and Walter, views power in terms of the social environment as "the ability to direct human energy (that is, attitudes and behavior) to express or realize certain values by the organization and use, modification and control of both physical and human (that is, behavior itself) materials".

While power conveys on its possessor the capability to use force, force can be defined as an actual application or exercise of power. It is power in action. Force is morally neutral like power, its source. It can be used for both good and bad ends. Violence is defined here as an illegitimate use of force. This distinction between force and violence is stressed by Holmes who described "the tacit assumption that force and violence are the same. While violence typically involves the use of force," he said, "and we often use 'force' and 'violence' interchangeably, the two cannot bo equated. We can use force. . . without in any way involving violence." Gray emphatically supports the distinction between force and violence." It is important," he wrote, "to keep the meaning of the word violence distinct from terms like power, force, strength and authority."

Women

2965. Akali Dal Women activist among 5 slaim in Punjab. *Hindustan Times* 25 Dec 1686 ; 1.

2966. Anand, Jo. : Should rapist be castrated ? Mid-Day New Delhi 16 Sep 1986 ; 7.

2967. Cohen, Geula : *Women of violence: Memories of a young terrorist, 1943-48.* Stanford University Press, 1966.

2968. George-Abeyle, Daniel E. : Women as terrorists. In *POT*; 71-84.

2969. Kelsen, Hans : Platonic love. *American Image* 3(1-2) Apr 1942.

2970. Khushwant Singh : Wife-beating. *Pioneer* 17 Aug 1986 ; 6.

2971. Lyall, Sarah : Call to police helps curb wife beating. *International Herald Tribune* 19 Aug 1986 ; 5.

2972. Panday, Mrinal : Wife abuse—A growing problem. *Times of India,* Sunday Review 8 Mar 1986 ; vii.

Physical violence against the wife becomes a form of socio-political control, ideologically supported for a variety of ways by the family and the state alike. Understandably women from the landless, agricultural wage labour families are more vulnerable to violence. Just as mass rapes are used by the landowners, to force the agitating landless labourers into submission, so also often one hears about cases, where the irate husband went to his estranged wife's parent's house (where she had sought refuge) and cut off her nose, or disfigure her in some way.

It must be reiterated here that Indian wives usually desert their husbands only when they become so violent, that they fear their lives. Mostly they go on acting as if nothing has happened. This is called 'covering up for the family honour', and is defined socially as the most dignified course for a woman to adopt. So when we hear of a wife living separately for fear of violence, we must assume it must be of the most awful degree.

The woman's owner inner censorship which is far more pronounced in the case of upper caste women is also a point worth mentioning. A lower caste woman may occasionally leave a violent husband and move in with another, while an upper caste woman, once married may never remarry, even if the husband is dead. Most upper caste families are reluctant to receive their daughters back at this point, because a woman living away from her husband, for whatever reason, is a stigma to her family. A Brahmin lady, summed up her dilemma thus :

"I am fifty years old now. My husband is impotent. We have no children but I could not speak of it to anyone. When I told my mother of this, she cried for me but sent me back to him. He drinks heavily and beats me up regularly. Two of my front teeth are broken, my body is full of bruises. When I talk to my sister, they say it was in your karama. Don't leave him. A husband is like a roof over your hand."

Conclusive statistics on wife-beating are not available in India. The Research Unit of SNDT Women's University, Bombay has done some work in this field. The Nari Kendra Prakashan of Bombay has published a small booklet on violence within the family which is available in Hindi and Marathi. The study was prepared in 1980 but the scene has not changed much since then. It is a small survey, but it has led to surprising and sometimes painful realisations. Prepared under the auspices of the Nari Atyachar Virodhi Manch (the protest forum for violence against women), it was based on personal interviews with 25 women from middle classes and 25 from the wage labourer class. The contact was established by close friends and acquaintances of women who were beaten regularly. The organisation realised that these women could not be contacted through counselling groups or remand houses. The findings of the group were published at the end of the survey, in various papers and magazines and the response from women all over the country, was truly astounding.

It is, therefore, not adequate only to demand and ensure equal wages and educational opportunities for women, though that too is necessary. What is more necessary is, one—that women's organisations also press demands for counselling and rehabilitation centres for battered wives; and a woman's share in the family property. And two—we must attempt to form women's committees in cities and villages which can take up cases like this and build social opinion, among men and women, against any kind of violence against women, and against any form of social sanction for assault on women.

2973. Paul, Seema : Agony of a girl sold for the sixth time. *Hindustan Times* 24 Sep 1985 ; 3.

2974. Singh, Onkar and Vinod Behl : On the threshold of terrorism. *Times of India* Sunday Review, 8 Mar 1986 ; 7.

However under-privileged or ignorant the average Indian women might be, her entry into male-dominated professions is not unheard of either because economic compulsions or other reasons we have Indian women entering into the dreaded world of terrorists.

The monster of terrorism that engulfed the border state of Punjab a few years ago is today rocking the entire nation. The onset of terrorism provided an entirely new dimension to the problem of women criminality as terrorism had taken women in its fold.

Though there may be only a handful of women who actually commit terrorist acts, there are many more whose indirect contribution to the cause is quite significant. They preach violence, store and smuggle arms, work as informers for terrorists, provide them with shelter and the much needed emotional support.

There are the familiar names of Bibi Amarjit Kaur, founder of the Akhand Kirtni Jatha, and Bibi Pritam Kaur, a close confident of Bhindranwale who could now be termed as veterans the terrorism scene in Punjab. Then there are the lesser-known names of women like Paramjit Kaur, an alleged arms smuggler, and Baljit Kaur who gunned down at aide of Bhindranwale.

Recently the names of Bimal Khalsa, the widow of Beant Singh, assassin of Indira Gandhi and Harjinder Kaur, a sikh woman from Delhi, have figured prominently. Harjinder Kaur was arrested by the Delhi police for allegedly harbouring a proclaimed terrorist and also for her involvement in a plot to kill several VIP's. Bimal Khalsa an active member of the militant splinter group of Akali Dal, headed by Bhindranwale's aged father Joginder Singh, has of late, been openly supporting the terrorists. Then there are a whole lot of unknown Sikh women who are engaged in spreading the gospel of violence.

The phenomenon of urban terrorism emerged in 1978 in India, after the bloody Akali-Nirankari clash in Amritsar. It also marked the onset of women's involvement in terrorism. It all started with Bibi Amarjit Kaur, Ravaged by the feeling of revenge, after her husband Fauja Singh, a right-hand man of Bhindranwale who was killed during the Akali-Nirankari clash, Amarjit Kaur decided to take a plunge into an alien world of terrorism. Her basic idea was to raise a strong army of militants and in order to do that she had to be trained herself in arms before she could impart training to her followers. Having trained herself she formed a group named Akhand Kirtni Jatha, with a handful of her followers. But within a short time she managed to mobilise a large number of youth. She organised several training camps for both men and women whom she successfully led into militancy. At that time she was even nick-named as 'teacher-in-terrorism' because before embracing militancy she was a school teacher.

Within a span of just two years, her dream turned into a reality when she successfully managed to raise a strong force of militants. One of the main acts of terrorism by her group was the murder of Baba Gurbachan Singh, head of the Nirankari Mission. This was a sweet revenge for her husband's killing. Amarjit Kaur's Akhand Kirtni Jatha was, however, overshadowed in the early 80's by Bhindranwale. So much so that most of her followers went over to his camp. During Operation Blue star she was arrested under the National Security Act.

Another woman whose name figures in the files of the Punjab Police and the intelligence agencies, for imparting armed training to Sikh youth is the 37-year-old wife of Surinder Singh Sodhi, a close associate of Bhindranwale, who fell victim to a group rivalry just a couple of months before Operation Blue Star. According to a senior intelligence officer, Sodhi's wife crossed over to Pakistan after Operation Blue Star. There, she is currently said to be training Sikh extremists in various camps in Pakistan close to the Indian border.

2975. Som Dev : Terrorism—delicate entry of women. *Indian Nation* (Patna) 20 Oct 1985 ; II.

Terrorism continues in Punjab due to the entry of women in it. The entry of women among the Sikh terrorists is a delicate and complicated problem on which the administration has not given its serious thought. The village women are giving shelter to under-ground and asconding terrorists. They supply eatables and other articles to the prisoners in jail. They collect funds for terrorists in urban areas. Some women tour the rural areas and are singing provocative songs regarding 'Operation Blue Star'. Some women in the urban areas are directly participating in terrorist activities by collecting money and arms for them. Some of them were apprehended while crossing over to Pakistan.

What are the root causes ? In fact the army action in Punjab was so cruel and shabby that it created an emotional upset among the Sikh women. The provocative rumours by so-called leaders added fuel to the fire. The indiscriminate arrest of women, children and innocent persons by army and para-military forces and the death of many suspects in police custody are the added reasons for their situation. 400 women were arrested in Golden Temple during 'Operation Blue Star'. Most of them had come with many Jathas and some of them were the relatives of the extremists. A mother of 5 children Zaida Khatun from Bangladesh had gone there to take free meal. One hundred women had sucking children in their laps. They were all arrested and released by the Supreme Court, after a petition was filed on their behalf.

2976. Torture of Muslim woman by Jamaat again. *Partiot* 2 Nov 1985 ; 1.

2977. Why terrorism attracts so many women, *Mid-Day* (New Delhi) 1 Jan 1987 ; 11.

Women are only responsible for between ten and 15 per cent of crime in West Germany, yet 14 of the country's 21 most wanted terrorists are women.

They plan the murders say terror authorities, and are brutal in putting the plans into action. Does terrorism have a particular attraction for German women ? Behavioural experts don't know.

In October, witness descriptions led in investigators to believe that Red Army Faction (RAF) terriorist Barbara Meyer was responsible for shooting dead diplomat Gerold von Braunmuhl at point-blank range.

In July, Meyer is thought to be the principal culprit for the remote-controlled bomb that blew up Professor Karl-Heinz Backurts, a Siemens executive, as he drove to work.

In the 1970s women were in leading positions in the RAF. In 1977 a third of top terrorists were women. Ulrike Meinhof decisively influenced the ideology of German terrorism in the bloody-years of politically-motivated violence.

The expression Baader-Meinhof gang is misleading, because Andreas Baader, as described by former colleagues, was a common criminal interested only in violence.

Gudrin Ensslin and Brigitte Mohnhaupt were later the group's ideologists,

The new generation of female terrorists are primarily pragmatists, more interested in murdering representatives of the state's military and economic establishment than on garnishing their crimes with "doctrines of salvation."

Dowry

2978. Adivasis fight dowry menace. *Blitz* 20 Oct 1984 ; 24.

2979. Alva, Margaret : Anti-dowry laws : How effective ? *Asiaweek* 23 Mar 1986 ; 66.

2980. Anklesaria, Shahnaz : Married for burning : No basic change in dowry law. *Statesman* 28 May 1984 ; 6.

2981. Bhattacharya, Mala : Evils of dowry, *Amrita Bazar Patrika.* 23 Aug 1983 ; 9.

2982. Bhattacharya, Rinki : "We have dowry deaths in Dhaka too". *Free Press Journal* 27 Apr 1986 ; III.

2983. Brelvi, Sahil : Women and dowry. *Pioneer* (Lucknow) 8 Mar 1986 ; 6.

2984. Chandra, Harish : Dowry prohibition. *Hindustan Times* 16 Oct 1985 ; 9.

2985. Chatterji, Shoma A. : Fighting the dowry syndrome. *Daily* (Bombay) 23 Feb 1986 ; 12-13.

2986. Chatterji, Shoma A. : Our toothless dowry laws. *Amrit Bazar Patrika* (Sunday) Magazine. 9 Mar 1986 ; I.

2987. Chowdhury, Neerja : Anti-dowry laws : How effective ? *Asiaweek* 23 Mar 1986 ; 66.

No, Laws have been amended, but their efficacy is another story. Dowry murders rarely end up in convictions, though in recent years there have been some exceptions. Often, the girl absolves the husband of responsibility in her dying declaration for the sake of her children, under pressure from her husband's people. And for money from the husband's family, the police hush up the case at the investigation stage. The legal process is so dilatory that circumstantial evidence gets lost. (Also), a large number of dowry deaths are suicides.

The government has enacted an amendment (against) acts of cruelty by the husband and in-laws. It's now for the accused to prove his innocence. (But the law) still allow gifts to the husband without a ceiling. Moreover, with both the giver and the taker liable for punishment it's hardly likely either will complain to the police. The redeeming feature is the right granted to women's organisations to file complaints on behalf of individuals.

2988. Das, Maya : Dowry : evil only when corrupted ? *Deccan Herald* 28 Oct 1984 ; 2.

2989. Dasgupta, S.P. : Dowry prohibition : The other view. *Amrita Bazar Patrika* 1 Jul 1985 ; 6.

2990. Deshpande, Anjali : Many dimensions of evil. *Mainstream* 20 Aug 1983 ; 32-34.

2991. Deshpande, Anjali : Survey on dowry system. *Mainstream* 21 May 1983 ; 10, 34.

2992. Diwan, Paras : Dowry law : All bark & no bite. *Tribune* 21 Mar 1986 ; 4.

Dowry is a widespread evil in India. While the practice, is rampant among the Hindus, is it not uncommon among the other communities. Cases of brides being tortured for not bringing in the promised or expected dowry are too many to be counted. The Dowry Prohibition Act of 1961 has not improved matters. A joint parliamentary committee was appointed to look into the working of the Act and it submitted its report in 1982. Accepting some of its recommendations, the Dowry Prohibition (Amendment) Act, 1984, was passed. It purports to give teeth to the dowry prohibition law.

Dowry is now defined as "any property or value security given or agreed to be given either directly or indirectly (a) by one party to the marriage to the other party to the marriage, or (b) by parents of their party to the marriage or by any other person to either party to the marriage or to any other person at or before person to either party to the marriage or to any other person at or before or after the marriage in connection with the marriage of the said parties........."

The words in the original Act were "as consideration for the marriage" This has been substituted with "in connection with the marriage". This certainly widens the definition of dowry, but it is hardly a definition, particularly when one notes that wedding presents, whatever be their value, are excluded from the purview of dowry. Seemingly, two safeguards against abuse are laid down ; (a) all presents made to the bride or the bridegroom at the time of the marriage (but not given before or after the marriage) are to be listed ; and (b) such presents are to be commensurate with the financial status of the giver. One can reasonably be sceptical about the efficacy of these provisions.

One brutal method of extracting dowry is to deny conjugal rights to the wife and to subject her to physical and mental torture, ultimately leading to such barbaric crimes as bride-burning or "dowry murderers". In such cases, the Committee suggested that the husband should be punished with imprisonment which may extend upto one year together with a maximum fine of Rs. 10,000. Parliament has rightly rejected this recommendation. It would virtually amount to restitution of conjugal rights through the arrest of the husband. No country in the world which recognises the matrimonial remedy of restitution of conjugal rights provides by arrest. In fact most countries have abolished the legal remedy of restitution of conjugal rights. This anachronism has been described as the worst form of slavery.

One reason for the failure of the dowry prohibition law has been the absence of any proper and effective enforcement machinery. The parliamentary committee suggested that State Governments should appoint dowry prohibition officers whose responsibility will be to take appropriate steps to enforce the provisions of the Act and prevent violations. In cases where a contravention of the Act has taken place, they should collect evidence for the effective prosecution of the offenders. These officers will also render all possible help and advice to persons subjected to the demand of dowry and to those who are tortured for bringing insufficient dowry. With such officers, the committee suggested, should be associated a non-official advisory body of five Government of India did not accept this suggestion of financial grounds.

If dowry cases are entrusted to family courts, the auxiliary services attached to it can look after these matters.

Dowry is an entrenched social evil in the country and cannot be eradicated through Act of Parliament. But legislation is necessary to promote public awareness of the evil and start a movement for the eradication of the menace. But then legislation must be such as to help deliver the goods and not be a half-hearted measure. Law imprisonment under the Act is still simple, considering that wedding presents are excluded from the definition of dowry and considering that enforcement machinery is week, this law does not have teeth strong enough to bite. Bark it may.

2993. Dowries still an irksome problem (in China). *China Daily* 9 Jul 1986 ; 4.

2994. Dowry deaths : *Deccan Chronicle* 30 Apr 1986 ; 6.

2995. Dowry deaths : A burning issue for the judiciary. *Delhi Recorder* Dec 1983 ; 26-27.

2996. Dowry death in A.P. : Plea for special cell. *Mainstream* 12 Apr 1986 ; 31-32.

2997. Dubey, Pratibha : Evil of dowry. *National Herald* 31 Mar 1985.

2998. Hattangadi, Rohini : Wage war against dowry and narcotic drugs. *Organiser* (New Delhi) 23 Feb 1986 ; 6.

2999. Imthiazuddin, Mohd : Why should marriage be a girl's only aim. *Newstime* 1 Dec 1984 ; 7.

3000. Joginder Singh : At war with dowry. *Illustrated Weekly of India* (Bombay) 24 Jun 1984 ; 20-23.

3001. Joshi, Uma : Putting teeth into dowry law. *Deccan Chronicle* 18 Feb 1984 ; 6.

3002. Joshi, Uma : Uprooting the dowry system. *Mainstream* 23 Oct 1982 ; 23-24.

3003. Khanna, A.K. : Dowry deaths. *Hindustan Times* 30 Sep 1983 ; 9.

3004. Mahadevan, S. : Growing menace dowry. *Deccan Chronicle* 22 Nov 1985 ; 6.

3005. Maheshwari, Sandra : Who needs dowry anyhow? *Newstime* Weekend 16 Mar 1986 ; 15.

3006. Mahipal : Fight against dowry exploitation, their main task. *Patriot* 7 Mar 1985 ; 5.

3007. Mitra, Sumit : Dowry law : Debating the delay. *India Today* 15 Apr 1984 ; 39.

There is a law against accepting or offering dowry in marriages. But the Dowry Prohibition Act, 1961, exonerates the givers and takers of marriage booty if they merely prove that the cash and goodies did not change hands "in consideration" of the marriage. The Government even set up a joint committee of both the houses of Parliament to make the act less of a farce (convictions in 23 years ; none). The committee submitted its report in July 1982. But last fortnight it became clear that not even a draft of the bill amending the 1961 act was ready. Fumed Pramila Dandavate, Janata MP and a vocal member of the committee ; "I see very little possibility of the new anti-dowry bill being legislated this year."

In a day dominated by women members of the Lok Sabha clamouring for the amendment to be presented before the house, a beleaguered Union Home Minister P.C. Sethi merely parrotted the Government's "will" to deter dowry deaths and abolish the "social evil". But the Law Ministry, entrusted with framing the amended legislation has not been able to make up its mind on whether it should make the act more stringent. Said Ram Dulari Sinha, minister of state for home : "The amendment calls for a good deal of cool thinking."

The joint committee which recorded evidence given by hundreds of witnesses suggested among other things that :

—Offences under the new act be made cognizable, instead of the present rule whereby the state's permission to prosecute the offender has to be sought ;

—punishment be given only to the taker, whereas it is applicable both to the giver and taker, of dowry now ;

– complainants are enable to lodge complaints within 10 years of marriage as against one year ;

—the clause, "in consideration", be removed from the act ; and,

—permissible wedding expenses be linked to the income of the bride's parents.

3008. Mukherji, Ena : Anti-dowry law still inadequate. *Amrita Bazar Patrika* 19 Jun 1984 ; 9.

3009. Mukherji, Ena : That evil called dowry. *Amrita Bazar Patrika* 10 Apr 1984 ; 9.

3010. Now giving or taking of dowry is not easy. Why ? *National Herald* 24 Jan 1986.

3011. Pandandikar, Surekha : Act of indifference. *Indian Express* 24 Jun 1984 ; 6.

3012. Pradeep Kumar : Dowry ; Root causes. *Mainstream* 20 Aug 1983 ; 31-32

3013. Ranade, Shobana : Traditional evils : Dowry, *Akashwani* (New Delhi) 16 Aug 1983 ; 7, 10.

3014. Rao, P.N.V. : Dowry evil. *Deccan Chronicle* 18 Jul 1984 : 5.

3015. Reddy, P.H. : Causes of dowry. *Indian Express* 1 Oct 1983 : 6.

3016. Saha, B.P. : Prevention of dowry deaths : Legislation is not enough. *Amrita Bazar Patrika* 27 Aug 1985 ; 6.

3017. Scindia, Madhavrao : Dowry—the continuing evil. *Hindustan Times* 29 Dec 1983 ; 9.

3018. Sharma, R.D. : Amending the dowry law. *Patriot* 11 May 1984 ; 4.

3019. Suresh, P. : Educate women against dowry. *Deccan Chronicle* 18 Jul 1984 ; 5.

2020. Verma. B.R. : Menace of dowry. *National Herald* 23 Feb 1986 ; 2.

3021. Wenliang, Xie. : Dowries grow with the times. *China Daily* 25 Mar 1986 ; 6.

"Today's young people are so lucky."

"Yes a truckful of new things. What Luxury".

Such are the typical reactions of older people when they see the dowry arrangements for a modern Chinese marriage.

The growth in size of dowries in recent years has brought remarkable change in matrimonial customs.

Only a few years ago, dowries were wrapped up in red cloth and carried by bicycle to the bridegroom's home by the bride's brothers and relatives. Bicycles can no longer do the job. TV sets, tape recorders, washing machines, refrigerators, and furniture have been added to the few cloth wrappers containing clothes and jewellery. No wonder young couples often complain their new homes are too small and too crowded for their possessions, one observer was heard to say while watching a recent procession of wedding gifts in Beijing.

Marriage customs have undergone rapid changes over the decades. The old custom of asking for betrothal gifts has widely disappeared, along with arranged marriages. Young people today choose their own partners ; they usually ask their parents' opinion but they make the decision themselves.

Couples of legal age need only go through the formalities of marriage registration, but many are not satisfied with only legal protection and recognition. They still want to hold a series of ceremonies to show the seriousness of the marriage. Many hold an engagement ceremony, too, where the bride's parents and close relatives are invited to the bridegroom's home for dinner. In the presence of the couple, parents are introduced, indicating their acknowledgement of the couple's love.

Then the two sides discuss the details of the wedding. In the old days, the bridegroom would present the bride with a large sum of money ; these days money is being replaced by expensive watches, gold rings and necklaces. This practice differs from the old marriage settlement in that these presents are not compensation for the future parents-in-law, but gifts for the bride.

When the wedding date is agreed upon, the bride will choose a suspicious day to deliver the dowries, already prepared, to the bridegrooms.

Though the government encourages a simple wedding, few couples have one. Most young people expect hired cars festooned with bunting for the guests.

However, there still remain some old customs. When the bride gets out of the car at the groom's home, firecrakers are set off. This adds to the festive atmosphere, but people also consider it as scaring away evil. Some brides throw away their shoes before entering the house because "throwing shoes" is homonymous in Chinese with "scaring away evil" (quxie). After the ceremony, the bride should be introduced to the bridegroom's relatives.

Recently wedding expenses have greatly increased. According to the Tianjin Statistical Department, in 1979 and 1980 young people in the city only spent 2,000 ($660) on their wedding. The average cost can now reach 5,000 yuan ($1,600) covering furniture, electrical facilities, banquet and travelling expenses.

Young people cannot afford the cost. Though most young couples are unwilling to live with their parents after marriage, they still rely on them to pick up the tab for the wedding. Asking for a large sum of money from one's parents for marriage is not considered untoward.

3022. William, Susheela : Death knell to dowry. *Akashvani* (New Delhi) 16-31 Aug 1984 ; 11-12.

3023. Woman's dowry rights. *Tribune* 21 Mar 1985 ; 4.

In yet another trail-blazing judgement the Supreme Court has dealt a powerful blow for the right of a woman to claim from her matrimonial home what she brought by way of "Istridan". Until now the judicial view tended to treat the husband as a joint owner of all items of dowry, gifts and even cash which a wife brings after her marriage, and hence the only remedy open to a harassed wife to get back "istridan" was to go to a civil court and wait for years to secure a decision—favourable or otherwise. After the latest judgement, the wife is entitled to file a criminal case of breach of trust and initiate a process that consumes much less time and also threatens the errant husband with severe punishment, including even a jain term. Interestingly, the Supreme Court delivered the judgement while upholding a revision petition filed by a women from this region after she lost her case before the Punjab and Haryana High Court in 1977. At that time the Chandigarh-based Court held that under the Hindu Marriages Act no criminal action lay in cases where the husband refuses to return any item which was presented to the wife, and that the Indian Penal Code did not have a role in solving disputes between a married couple. The highest court of the land has expressed astonishment at this attitude and has pointed out that as a result of the stand taken by the High Court the wife had been reduced to the status of "dumb-driven cattle", left with no alternative but dilatory tactics to seek justice. In a telling passage the three-Judge Bench has noted that "criminal law and matrimonial home were not strangers to each other, and crimes committed in the matrimonial home are as much punishable as anywhere else."

One immediate offshoot is to deter men who harass wives and ultimately drive them out of the home with the sole purpose of misappropriating "istridan". This is precisely that happened in the case which resulted in the latest judicial decision. Since a vast majority of cases of ill-treatment of young women have a direct bearing on the ownership of dowry they brought or did not bring, a clear-cut stand on this has tilted the balance of justice in favour of the long-oppressed half of the population. What is equally important is that a deserted wife does not automatically become a destitute, wholly dependent on her parents or brothers for sustenance. Now she can hope to regain at least the unspent part of "istridan" and thus feel a sense of economic independence. Financial insecurity has for long been the most important cause of the low status which middle class, educated women have come to occupy and accept in Indian society. Since it is this class that believes in demanding and giving sizeable "istridan", the Supreme Court judgement will have a favourable impact over a large area of social life.

A related question waits to be clarified. What is the legal status of the husband as owner of "istridan" in case a wife dies or is killed ? If the present attitude is stretched to its logical conclusion, a husband should not have any right over the gifts, and they should return to the parents of the bride. This may militate against the general view of gifts itself which is always given and never reclaimed. But this is a moral stand and should not normally, apply in cases where there is suspicion of a bride being done away with for the sole purpose of taking over her "istridan" and paving the way for receiving a second one. Such extraordinary cases need equally extraordinary legal solution. This is all the more so since the police and society at large have so far failed to evolve any method to ensure the safety of a woman in her matrimonial home. During its past few "activist" years the Supreme Court has chosen to interpret the law in favour of the underdog and has, in the process, set many breathtaking precedents. The judgement on the criminal liability of a husband in not returning "istridan" is the latest. This should be followed by a decision to legally bar greedy husbands and the in-laws to come to own a property which at present a crime makes it theirs.

Rape

3024. Abbas, K.A. : What is rape ? *Blitz* 31 Dec 1983 ; 24.

3025. Anklesaria, Shahnaz : Battle against rape. *Statesman* 1 Jul 1985 ; 5.

3026. Chakravarty, Meera : Seminar on rape bill. *Janata* (Bombay) 4 Dec 1983 ; 4.

3027. Chatterji, Shoma A. : Rape : Crime and punishment. *Amrita Bazar Patrika.* Sunday Magazine, 23 Dec 1984 ; I.

3028. Copsgang-rape adivasi woman. *Current* 8 Feb 1986 ; 17.

3029. Deshpande, Anjali : Rape Bill Constrictions. *Mainstream* 24 Dec 1983 ; 31-32.

3030. Dixit, D.K. : Crime against women : Sex sublime, violence despicable. *Daily* (Bombay) 15 Mar 1986 ; 10-11.

"To Rape is human," is the quotable quote of an ex-Chief Minister of Madhya Pradesh. "You can't thread a moving needle," asserts an advocate, of no mean standing.

Rape, categorised in the Indian Penal Code under "offences against the human body" is, in many senses, a crime in a class of its own. It is probably the least reported of all crimes. It is the only offence where resistance is often measured as proof of consent to the act. The victim of a robbery, for instance is hardly called upon to explain himself in court for not resisting the criminal. Rape is also the only crime where the "spoilt" victim is treated as a social outcast.

The recent survey on crime against women conducted by the Bureau of Police Research and Development stated that while the number of criminal cases in general rose by 33 per cent from 1971 to 1977, the number of rape cases in the same period rose by 63.2 per cent, the majority of victims being in the age-group of 16-30. The survey also revealed that the attitude of police personnel towards women, especially victims of atrocities, was no different from the general attitude of the public. The accused in rural areas were mostly those holding women in positions of economic subordination—businessmen in tribal belts, for example, or a large number of civil servants. These cases belong to 'power rape' in legal jargaon. The cases of Maya Tyagi of Baghpat in UP who was dragged in torn clothes through open streets to the police station for investigation and that of Rameeza Bee in Hyderabad who was gang raped by policemen while her husband was beaten to death are striking examples of 'power rape'.

Susan Brownmiller in her monumental work, "Against our will : men, women and rape", has defined rape thus : "If a woman chooses not to have intercourse with a specific man and the man chooses to proceed against her will, that is a criminal act of 'rape'." Admittedly, this definition from the woman's point of view transcends the legal limits.

The vexed issue of rape in all its ramifications bristles with many mind-boggling complexities and a plethora of semantic jugglery. Under the Indian Penal Code, Section 375, a man is said to commit rape when he has sexual intercourse with a woman (1) against her will, (2) without her consent, (3) with her consent when it has been obtained by putting her in fear of death or hurt, (4) with her consent when the man knows that he is not her husband and the woman believes that he is another man to whom she is, or believes to be lawfully married, and (5) with or without her consent when she is under 16 years. Section 376 of IPC deals with punishment for rape which can be life imprisonment/10 years fine.

To convict a rapist, the evidence required is : bruises on the body, torn bluses (marks of resistance) and a medical report proving physical penetration. Corroboration is equally essential for conviction. In the majority of cases, the accused get away with impunity which perhaps explains the increased incidence of rape and sexual violence in our society.

3031. Frankel, William : U.K. concern over spurt in rape cases. *Statesman* (New Delhi) 22 Mar 1986 ; 6.

3032. Gupta, Shubhra : Rape : The victim on trial. *Sunday Mail* (New Delhi) 9 Feb 1986 ; 9.

3033. Hui, C. Harry : Pornography and rape. *Asiaweek* 9 Mar. 1986 ; 66.

3034. Jabber Alam, M. : Adivasi women raped by forest guards. *New Age*. 8 Apr 1984 : 16.

3035. Kapoor, Coomi : Rape cases : Victims still suffer while culprits go scot-free. *Free Press Journal* 3 Aug 1985 ; 3.

3036. Kaur, Tarinder : Rape of the wife. *Tribune* 18 Dec 1983 ; 7.

3037. Law against rape. *National Herald* 21 Nov 1983 ; 5.

3038. Law of rape : *Daily* (Bombay) 11 Dec 1983 ; 12.

Say, what strange motive, goddess, could compel A Well-bred tord to assault a gentle belle ; O say, what stranger cause, yet unexplored, Could make a gentle belle reject a lord ?

Indian Society being still largely feudal, the lord of laire has ownership not only of the land and the produce thereof, but also of all those who work and weep thereon. An orthodox high caste Hindu, complete with holy thread and ashen stripes on his forehead, will consider a Harijan an untouchable, but if she be a village belle he must conquer her with threats or inducements. A bath in the village pond or the river nearby, will purify him of any contamination.

This is as much true of the south as of the north, where the honour of no wench is safe in the hands of poachers and paramours. The law does not reach these victims of lust nor do they get adequately compensated for satiating the appetites of the affluent. Laws, by and large, are meant only for the articulate and the literate who are conscious of their rights and have the audacity to assert them.

After long delays both Houses of Parliament have now amended existing laws as they deal with the crime of rape and more deterrent punishment has been provided for rape with the severest punishment falling on those who commit the crime while they are supposed to be the custodians either as police officers, jailors or hospital staff.

Laws pertaining to rape vary from State to State. In the United States, rape committed against a white woman by a black is punishable by death. If a black woman is the victim of the white man, the consequences are not really frightening as he may get away with two or three years.

In England lack of consent will be determined not by the protests of the woman, but by a more active form of unwillingness to be subjected to forced intercourse. And guild is established by the degree of penetration.

Though Indian laws make rape a serious offence, legal remedies are not always available. In the absence of a large woman police force, both to investigate crimes and conduct the prosecution's case, the enforcement of laws will continue to remain in the male domain.

As the amending bills were being discussed there were demands made for capital punishment ; others had suggested that a rapist must be castrated. The most heinous offenders are those who rape little girls and then put their lives to an end. Such sadists perhaps deserve even more drastic punishment than prescribed in the amended laws.

3039. Mitra, Anirudhya : I raped her out of curiosity. *Sunday Mail* (New Delhi) 9 Feb 1986 ; 9.

3040. Rape victim's quest for justice. *Hindustan Times* 20 Sep 1986 ; 3.

3041. Reddy, Rita : Pornography and rape. *Asiaweek* 9 Mar 1986 ; 66.

3042. Revenge on the rapists. *Newstime* 9 Jan 1985 ; 4.

3043. Rosen, Ellen Israel : New Bed ford rape trial. *Dissent* Spr 1985 ; 207-9.

3044. Sethi, Sunil : Rape : Controversial code. *India Today* 31 Dec 1983 ; 134-35.

3045. Singh, Atiya ; Loopholes in new anti-rape law, *Northern India Patrika* (Allahabad) 21 Feb 1984 ; 4.

3046. Sinha, Bharati : New rape law doesn't meet all of women's demands. *New Age* (New Delhi) 1 Jan 1984 ; 3.

3047. Sinha, Nagendra : Rape. *Statesman* 1 Jan 1986 ; 11.

3048. Sohaila : Rape still haunts me. *Sunday Mail* (New Delhi) 9 Feb 1986 ; 9.

3049. Three executed for gang-rape racket. *China Daily* 21 Feb 1986 ; 1.

3050. UP : Police rape Harijan woman. *New Age* 13 Nov 1983 ; 7.

3051. Why people rape ? *Nagpur Times* 9 Jun 1985.

3052. Seven year old girl raped. *Indian Express* 6 May 1986 ; 1, 7.

Youth

3053. Bander, Edward J. *ed.* : *Turmoil on the Campus*. New York, H.W. Wilson, 1970.

3054. Califano, Joseph : *Student revolutian*. New York, Norton, 1970.

3055. Cohn-Bendit, Daniel *et. al.* : *French student revolt*. New York, Hill and Wang, 1968.

3056. Hope, Marjorie : *Youth against the world*. Boston, Little Brown, 1970.

3057. Kampf, Herbert A. : On the appeals of extremism to the Youth of affluent, democratic societies. *Terrorism* 4(1-4) 1980 ; 161-94.

3058. Kim, B.S. : Student activism in Korea and Japan : A comparative analysis. *Asian Journal of Columbia University* 1(1) 1973 ; 3-13.

3059. Lipset, Seymour Martin and Sheldon Wolin *eds.*: Berkeley *Student revolt ; Facts and interpretations.* Garden City, N.Y., Doubleday, 1965.

3060. Lipset, Seymour Martin and Philip Altback *eds.* : Students in revolt. Boston, 1969.

3061. Mathur, S.S. : Youth terrorism in Punjab. *Deccan Chronicle* 4 Jan 1986 ; 6.

3062. Rooke, M.A. : *Anarchy and spathy* : *Student unrest, 1968-1970.* London, Hamilton, 1971.

3063. Roszak, Theodore : *Making of a counter-culture* : *Reflections on the technocratic society and its youthful opposition.* Garden city, N.Y. : Doubleday, 1969.

3064. Saksena, N.S. : Terrorism an attraction for section of idealistic youth. In *THF* ; 58-61.

3065. Shome, M.N. : Weaning away youth from terrorism. *Pioneer* 12 Aug 1986 ; 6.

3066. Unrest in China : (by the Youth). *Hindustan Times* 25 Dec 1986 ; 9.

Zionism

3067. Aines, Ronald C. : *Jewish underground against the British mandate in Palestine.* (Thesis) New York, Union College, Schenectady, 1973.

3068. Akehurst, Michael : Arab-Israeli conflict and international law. *New Zealand Universities Law Review* 5, 1973.

3069. Aronsfeld, C.C. : Soviet propaganda : Hitler and the zionists. *Midstream* Nov 1985 ; 13-16.

3070. Ashley, Mick, Zionism and apartheid are twin evils. *Baghdad Observer* 22 Jul 1986 ; 4.

3071. Avineri, Shlomo *ed.* : *Israel and the Palestinians* : *Reflections on the clash of two national movements.* New York, St. Martin's Press, 1971.

3072. Avishai, Bernard : New Zionism or Hebrew democracy ? *International Herald Tribune* 29 Jan 1986 ; 4.

3073. Avishai, Bernard : *Tragedy of Zionism.* New York, Farrar Straus and Giroux 1985. Pp. 373.

3074. Azeem, Anwer : Zionism on the rampage. *Link* 15 Dec 1985 ; 30-31.

3075. Bell, J. Bowyer : *Long War : Israel and the Arabs since 1946.* New York, 1969.

3076. Bell, J. Bowyer : *Terror out of Zion.* New York, St. Martin Press, 1977.

3077. Bialkin, Kenneth J. : Israel Foes' anti-Zionism is anti-Semitic racism. *International Herald Tribune* 12 Nov 1985 ; 6.

3078. Bober, Arie *ed.* : *Other Israel : The radical case against Zionism.* New York, Doubleday, 1972.

3079. Das, Tapan : Zionism : A view from Peking. *Patriot* 3 Jun 1981 ; 4.

3080. Davis, M. : *Jews fight tool.* New York, Jordan, 1945.

3081. Defeat of Zionism : *International Viewpoint* 3 Jun 1985 ; 27.

3082. Dinstein, Yorem : Terrorism and wars of liberation applied to the Arab-Israeli conflict : An Israeli perspective. *Israel Yearbook on Human Rights* 3, 1973.

3083. El-Erris, Tarik : Zionism continues to defy UN and world opinion. *Patriot* 4 Nov 1976 ; 2.

3084. Facts about racist Zionism. *Baghdad Observer* 23 Jul 1980 ; 3.

3085. Foley, Gerry : Historic defeat of Zionism—*International Viewpoint* 25 Mar 1985 ; 12-13.

3086. Garg, J.P. : *Israel and Zionism.* Ghaziabad, Vimal Prakashan, 1980. Pp. 150.

At a time when every Indian seems to be vying with every other to sing peans in praise of the Arabs a book purporting to set the record straight should be welcomed.

There are few subjects as fascinating as the chequered history of the Jews, and it might lend a balance to our perspective if we read it. Strangely Middle Ages till the last about 100 years the Jews produced scarcely any historical work. Today however, the vast community in North America—nearly half the Jewish population of the world—is engaged in a long "accounting of the soul" as the Hebrew phrase goes in reference to its past and its future.

The jews now have a new awareness of their basic problems. I started reading the book enthusiastically hoping that the author would make a challenging examination of the religious, ethnic and cultural development of the Chosen People from their emergence as recorded in the Bible to the present day, alas the attempt at explanation of the fundamental thesis, religion, nationalism and the Central Questions is far from satisfying.

The Central Ouestions are the Jewish uniqueness, Jewish monotheism, which imposed the pattern of faith and its religious tradition upon the Western World, the continuous stream of anti-Jewish feeling the survival of the Jew from the beginning of history and finally, the establishment of the State of Israel. The ancient or biblical period in its larger sense extended to the completion of the Talmud in the sixth century.

There is no attempt in this book either to draw the lesson of history for the present religious crisis in Israel and the relation of the Jewish State to the Diaspora or the polarity and tension between the religious and the ethnic loyalties. On the one hand, the Jews are a unique people, bound by a Covenant with God to be the carriers of an ethic for a universal society: on the other, they are a nation having a sense of a superiority (although a legitimate one) over their neighbours and attached to a particular land no less when they were dispersed in exile than when they were an independent nation.

In the biblical period the psychological machinery of tensions and poles, foci and oscillation externalism and internationalisation was so important that, when applied to the Hebrew patriarchs and to the story of the Children of Isreal it looks almost incongruous, making the simple obscure and turning spontaneous feeling into psychological mystery. The continuous struggle between the universal religion and isolated by its peculiar way of life is essential to the understanding of Jewish history after the Babylonian captivity.

The Jews in Egypt, the emergence of Pharisaism and the Jewish-Christian schism—no less essential to such an understanding—are dealt with here, if at all, very perfunctorily. Again, the medieval period, which extended over more than 1,000 years, revealed the strength and weakness of the Jewish people in the Christian society which was convinced that they must be allowed to live as "Witnesses of God" but must also be degraded and debased to bear the stigma of the divine curse. All this is unfortunately ignored here.

3087. Halbrook, Stephen P. : Left Hegelianism, Arab nationalism, and labor Zionism. *Journal of Libertarian Studies.* 6(2) Spr 1982 ; 181-99.

3088. Haqqi, S.A.H. : Zionism and the Arab-Israel Confrontation. *Radiance* (Delhi) 13-19 Nov 1983 ; 3-4.

3089. Jack, Homer : Is Zionism racism ? The 1975 debate in the United Nations. *Gandhi Marg* (New Delhi) Jan 1976 3,-12.

3090. Jaffar, Nouri : Zionism : Racist reactionary and aggressive trend. *Iraq Today* 1(12) 15 Mar 1976 ; 24-25.

3091. Jawad, Kadhim : Nazi-Zionist cooperation : *Iraq today* 1(10) 15 Feb 1976 ; 24-28, 32.

3092. Kohen, Martin : Zionist persecution of Jews, *Iraq Today* 1-15 Jun 1979, 15.

3093. Lahiri, Apla : Who backs Zionist-racist terror ? *Madhya Pradesh Chronicle* 30 Mar 1986 ; 6.

3094. Lilienthal, Alfred M. : Of Judaism and Zionism. *International Herald Tribune* 22 May 1986 ; 5.

3095. Litvinoff, Barnet : How Zionism became a dirty word. *Amrita Bazar Patrika* 3 Sep 1980 ; 6.

3096. Mathur, Girish : Zionists stalk US Arabs. *Blitz* 12 Apr 1986, 17.

3097. Mazrni, Ali. A. : Zionism and apartheid. *Alternatives* (Delhi) Dec 1982 ; 491-516.

3098. Method to the Zionist madness. (Israeli bombing of a PLO Camp near Tunis). *International Viewpoint.* 14 Oct 1985; 28.

3099. O'brien, Conor Cruise : What Zionism means for Israelis. *Times of India* 1 Jan 1983 ; 8.

3100. Sartre, J.P. : *Anti-Semite and Jew.* New York, 1965.

3101. Seale, Patrick : Zionism turns out the light. *Amrita Bazar Patrika* 18 Jun 1982 ; 6.

3102. Stein, Joshua B. : Josiah C. Wedgwood's Zionism. *Midstream* Nov 1985; 22-26.

3103. Sussholz, Mose Ben Yehudi : Zionist Crimes against humanity. *Iraq Today* 1-15 May 1978; 18-21.

3104. Tewary, K.K. : Zionist brutalities can't be condemned. *Blitz* 5 Feb 1983; 12-13.

3105. Weigert, Gideon : *Whose killeth a believer.* Jerusalem, Israeli Communications, 1971.

3106. *Who are the terrorists ? : Aspects of Zionist and Israeli terrorism.* Beirut, Institute for Palestine Studies, 1972. Pp. 74.

3107. Woolfson, Marion : Zionism—the unpalatable truth. *Iraq Today* 16-31 Oct 1979 ; 14.

When Simon Louvish arrived in London after having made a film in "Israel" in 1972, he seemed to be suffering from a complaint common to many Jewish Settlers in Palestine. Although he was aware of the injustice done to the Palestinian people, he appeared to be obsessed by the past sufferings of the Jews and he seemed incapable, then, of realising that one injustice is never righted by the imposition of another injustice. At the time, he was trying to find finance for his film. To Live in Freedom', which, as the months went by and as Simon Louvish became more politically aware, underwent many editing changes. Finally, the film emerged from the cutting-room with an emphatic message, for, it depicted clearly the suffering of Palestinians at the hands of the zionists, and it was obvious that Simon Louvish had changed too.

Now, Simon Louvish, who was born in Glasgow, Scotland in 1947 and was taken, by his parents, to "Israel" in 1949, has written a book called 'A Moment of Silence' which the publishers, Martin, Brian and O'Keeffee of London describe as "an autobiographical novel".

As the story, which is told in a somewhat confusing flashback style, unfolds, it becomes apparent that the author has been gradually learning the unpalatable truth hidden behind the glib lies of the zionist propaganda machine: it is obvious that the emotionalism which since obscured his vision has disappeared and he has become committed, like a number of other courageous Jews, to truth and justice.

Prevailing attitudes are described in a way which makes the reader realise that zionism is not just a colonialist settler movement but that it is also a gigantic confidence trick played upon a large section of the world's population by a group of people with truly sick minds.

In Chapter Eight, which is entitled "The Tale of Bir'am Village", one of the former inhabitants of the village from which the population was forcibly evacuated by the zionists in 1948 told of how the villagers received the zionist soldiers and "We shared with them our food and our beds, because we believed that with the "Israelis", or with the Jewish people, we can live better than with the Arabs, since we were (Christian) minorities in this country".

Nevertheless, the people of Bir'am were thrown out of their homes and the author has gone on to describe the struggle waged for twenty-five years by the villagers to return to their property and lands.

In citing a passage from the "Israeli" newspaper, Maariv, Simon Louvish has demonstrated the breathtaking effrontery of zionism. Mrs. Golda Meir, a former Prime Minister of "Israel" (who was born in Russia and educated in the United States) said that: "It is a lie to claim that zionism was built on evicition of Arabs", and she added : "No storms will suffice to blur the moral basis of the zionist project. There has never been in this area one war that we caused. Everything that happened has been contrary to our desires, and was not our fault" (pages 112-114). Yet, in 1937 at the Poale Zion conference in Zurich, when the zionist leaders plotted the seizure and colonisation of Palestine, Golda Meir (whose name was then Myerson, but she later "Hebraised" it) said: "I would agree that the Arabs leave the country and my conscience would be absolutely clear. But is there such a possibility? Let us go to the Jewish masses and ask them: "Are you ready to save one and a half million Jews within ten years, without any possibility to change the borders afterwards ? Only wars change borders. Maybe there will be a war in the near future; but how can we be sure that this war will change borders in our favour?"

Still dealing with the subject of Bir'am, Simon Louvish shows us the kind of emotional blackmail which is invariably used by zionists to stifle comment and suppress criticism. A member of the Knesset ("Israeli" parliament) said: "The sons of Israel are merciful, but to others, not to themselves! To ourselves we are crueller than cruel! Always we judge ourselves unfairly! Did we ask ourselves what was done by those who had the power when they put live people, Jews, into the ovens? The inhabitants of Ikrit (another Palestinian village which was also forcibly evacuated by zionist troops) and Bir'am are in better conditions than before, and that is called immoral ? And for what ? So that we too should live in this country ?"

The above passage is a typical one and it is always very effective for silencing the critics who never think of pointing out that the Jews were not the only victims of the Nazis, for, hundreds of thousands of non-Jewish political opponents of Hitler as well as gypsies and handicapped people also ended their lives in the gas chambers.

The tone of Simon Louvish's book is perhaps best illustrated by his thought-provoking final sentence. He has written: "But whatever happens in Washington and Cairo, Damascus or Amman, it is the Palestinian Arab in Gaza and Nablus, Jerusalem and Galilee and in the refugee camps with (in) and outside mandate Palestine, that the Israeli will still have to look in search of a true peace of mind."

3108. Yassine, Abdel Qader: Racist nature of Zionism. *Indian Observer* (New Delhi) 15 May 1980; 24.

On the 26th October 1966, the United Nations General Assembly adopted a resolution (2142) in which it proclaimed the 21st of March as International Day for Elimination of Racial Discrimination. On the 14th of December 1973, the General Assembly condemned *inter alia* the "unholy alliance between South African Racism and Zionism." At its thirtieth session the General Assembly considered and adopted its historic resolution in which it decided that "Zionism in a form of racism and racial discrimination."

The practices of Israel, as a Zionist racist state, against our Palestinian people are a clear violation of the United Nations resolutions and the Universal Declaration of Human Rights. In contravention of Articles 47 and 49 of the Fourth Geneva Convention, the Zionist authorities have established over 125 settlements in the occupied Arab territories with a total population of about 70,000 people excluding the Arab sector of Jerusalem since June 1967.

The Zionist Israeli authorities have expropriated an area equivalent to 27% of the best agricultural land of the West Bank and Gaza. Several thousand Palestinians have been prevented from returning to their homes and fields in the West Bank. To evaluate the scope of these violations, it is necessary to examine the manner in which Israeli laws and practices have operated to effectuate the result of de Palestinization of what was Palestine.

Israel "legalized" her tactics of de-Palestinization by the use of laws which legalized expropriation, arbitrary arrests and detentions and restricted freedom of movement in clear violation of international humanitarian law. Administrative regulations and police practices were designed so to effectuate expulsion, induce flight and prevent return. The military government exercised wide legislative, judicial, and executive powers and used them to that effect.

Of the 170 articles in the Defence Laws of 1945 (State of Emergency), Article 125 is the most frequently employed. It grants military governors the power to restrict liberty of movement by declaring "closed areas which no one can enter or leave without a written permit from the military governor." Articles 109 and 110 give the military governor the right to restrict possession, the choice of residence, and the right to leave a location. They further provide for control access to homes. Under Articles 111 and 112 the military government can detain anyone it chooses, for any reason whatsoever, for an unlimited period of time, without declaring the charge. It can expel a person from the country, banish him (or her) permanently, and forbid any person outside the country from returning. In addition, Article 124 confers the power to impose a total or partial curfew in any area. Among the most arbitrary powers are those regarding property. Article 119 grants the power "to confiscate or destroy a person's property if the military governor suspects that a shot has been fired or a bomb thrown from such property." Article 120 empowers the military government to confiscate an individual's property if the Minister of Defence is satisfied that this person has broken these laws or has committed an offence for which he is liable to be tried by military court.

Defence Laws of 1949 (Security Areas) impose the same restrictions on "security areas" as the State of Emergency Laws impose upon "closed areas." In addition, the Minister of Defence is granted the power to permanently evict persons from their residence in these areas. These two laws could thus be used to legitimatize arbitrary military actions by permitting denial of due process during arrest and by possibly summary executions. The massacre of Kufur Qassim is an example of the abuse possible under the sanction of these laws.

3109. Zionism—A cancer in Palestine *Iraq* 1 Jul 1981 ; 21-22.

3110. Zionism—A threat to place and international security. *New Times* (49) Dec 1984 ; 32.

3111. Zionism—Its origin and development. *Baghdad Observer* 9 Aug 1978 ; 3.

3112. Zlonism's failure : *Times of India* 21 Jan 1980 ; 8.

3113. Zionist pirates : *Patriot* 7 Feb 1986 ; 4.

There can hardly be any better illustration of why terrorism flourishes in the perfervid atmosphere of West Asia than the despicable Israeli hijacking of a Libyan aircraft carrying Syrians to Damascus. While there can be no defence of terrorism, it must be stated that Arab reaction to Zionist provocations in the face of the latter's acknowledgedly superior military strength (thanks to the US) can only be terrorism of an individual nature as that of Ms Leila Khaled or of groups fired by a legitimate desire to return to a homeland that had been wrested from them by an international conspiracy led by Britain and the US. The destruction of Palestine and the resurrection of the Zionist entity known as Israel in its place led to the displacement of Palestinians who have spent nearly 50 years either as second-class citizens in their own homeland or as refugees in other Arab lands, not always as welcome guests. Since then a combine of western governments have lent political and military support to Zionism in its terrorism against the Palestinians and such terrorist gangs as the Stern and the Irgun finally came to rule Israel. Little wonder, then, that Israel as a State indulges in terrorism as a matter of policy.

It is encouraged in its activities by the US who set a dubious precedent by hijacking the Egyptian aircraft after the Achille Lauro affairs, stooping, once again, to the very act it professes to be want to eradicate. Its misguided adventure against Libya for allegedly encouraging "international terrorism" has been exposed to be hoax of monumental proportions because it turns out that Col. Gaddafi was, indeed, not the one behind the hijacking of the Egyptian aircraft from Athens which was stormed so disastrously at Valletta, Malta, in November last. It became a handy excuse for Washington to try and get rid of Col. Gaddafi and settle scores for closing down the US military base in that country. Since then, the US Sixth Fleet in the Mediterranean led by two carrier task forces is indulging in daily provocations against Libya, and Israel thought it should get into the act by hijacking the Libyan aircraft from neutral skies and taking it to northern Israel. Tel Aviv's by-play is aimed more at Damascus than Libya and is the latest of a series of provocations beginning with the shooting down of Syrian jets before Syria moved in surface-to-air missiles into the Bekaa Valley of Lebanon to end further adventurism. The Israelis later cooperated with the Christian faction led by President Gemayal of Lebanon to quash a Syria-sponsored peace in that faction-torn nation by allowing South Lebanese militia to blow out the headquarters of the group that signed the accord.

The Government of India has done well not to mince words in condemning the State terrorism of Israel and in its reference to the "recent trend among certain States" has placed responsibility squarely where it belongs—at the doorstep of the US. Given the military might of the mentor and its protege there is little that anyone can do except exposing them for what they are : arch-terrorists.